PRINCIPLES OF
MICROECONOMICS
EDITION 3

FRED M. GOTTHEIL
UNIVERSITY OF ILLINOIS

SOUTH-WESTERN
THOMSON LEARNING

Australia · Canada · Mexico · Singapore · Spain · United Kingdom · United States

To my wife, Diane

To my children, Lisa and Joshua,
who grew up together, not just as
sister and brother, but as best friends.

Vice President/Publisher: Jack W. Calhoun
Acquisitions Editor: Michael Worls
Senior Marketing Manager: Lisa L. Lysne
Developmental Editor: Andrew J. McGuire
Production Editor: Elizabeth A. Shipp
Media Technology Editor: Vicky True
Media Developmental Editor: Peggy Buskey
Media Production Editor: John Barans
Manufacturing Coordinator: Sandee Milewski
Internal Design: Michael H. Stratton
Cover Design: Michael H. Stratton
Cover Images: © PhotoDisc, Inc.
Production House: Lachina Publishing Services, Inc.
Printer: QuebecorWorld-Taunton, MA

Printed in the United States of America
1 2 3 4 5 04 03 02 01

Library of Congress Cataloging-in-Publication Data

Gottheil, Fred M.
    Principles of microeconomics / Fred M. Gottheil.—3rd ed.
        p. cm.
    Includes index.
    ISBN 0-324-10678-5
    1. Microeconomics. I. Title.

HB172.G638 2002
338.5—dc21
2001020823

For more information contact South-Western, 5101 Madison Road, Cincinnati, Ohio, 45227 or find us on the Internet at http://www.swcollege.com

For permission to use material from this text or product, contact us by
• telephone: 1-800-730-2214
• fax: 1-800-730-2215
• web: http://www.thomsonrights.com

BRIEF CONTENTS

CONTENTS

PART 2 | INTRODUCTION TO MICROECONOMICS   73

ix

University of Illinois
at Urbana-Champaign

Department of Economics
Box 111
330 Commerce Building (West)
1206 South Sixth Street
Champaign, IL 61820

217-333-0120

Dear Student,

Economics is a part of your daily life, a part of how you make everyday decisions, a part of the way you think about and understand the world around you. Curious? If you are, this textbook is for you. There are no endless lists of facts here, no dry and obscure examples. Instead, you'll find stories, conversations, explanations, and powerful ideas. These are the tools and techniques that effectively teach economics.

Economics must be real, even personal. To truly understand economics—not just learn economic concepts and terminology, but understand the essence of economic thinking—you must relate on an emotional level to what you are learning. You must absorb the ideas in this book through your head, your heart, and your innards. Feel the ideas in your bones and relate them to what you know best—your life. Only then will you understand and remember economics, and only with this accomplishment will you enjoy your course in economics.

Over the next several weeks you will find that economics and economists have something important to say about how the world works. And with hard work, at the end of this journey you will be able to meaningfully join the conversation.

To help you along the way, I have included numerous learning aids in each chapter. Some features demonstrate the relevancy of what you are reading, some teach you how economic concepts apply to a variety of situations, some alert you to particularly important material, and some test your understanding of the principles presented in the chapter. In addition, you'll find that there are many additional print and technology resources available to enhance your learning experience. Look over the next few pages to become familiar with all of these aids. And enjoy! Economics is an exciting, inspiring, and relevant subject.

Fred Gottheil

FEATURES YOU'LL FIND IN EACH CHAPTER

PART OPENERS "Economics Chat" Part Openers capture real-life student conversations about economics. "Economics Chat" helps demonstrate why the chapters that follow are important to you.

LEARNING OBJECTIVES Each chapter opens with "Learning Objectives" that introduce the key principles raised in the chapter. "Learning Objectives" do not highlight everything in the chapter, only the most important principles.

CHECK YOUR UNDERSTANDING "Check Your Understanding" features raise questions at key junctures in the text, questions you should be able to answer if you understand the material. For help, arrows point to the portion of the text that contains the explanation.

INTERACTIVE EXAMPLES "Your Turn" features provide an example of a concept discussed in the text, and then ask you to go to the Gottheil Web site to create and post an example of your own, as well as to see what examples other students have come up with.

APPLICATIONS "Perspective" boxed features show you how the economic principles introduced in the chapter relate to real-world events in many different contexts. You'll find 5 types of "Perspectives" in the book: historical, global, interdisciplinary, applied (business and daily life examples), and theoretical. Most "Perspectives" include a question for further consideration and Internet addresses for further exploration.

KEY GRAPHS All exhibits illustrate key graphical concepts in a clear, efficient manner. "Key Graphs" icons highlight those exhibits that demonstrate crucial principles.

MARGIN DEFINITIONS Margin Definitions define important vocabulary introduced in the chapter.

ON THE NET "On the Net" margin notes show you where to find and how to use the best economic resources on the Internet. You'll be surprised what information lies at your fingertips.

The Bureau of Labor Statistics provides recent and historical data on labor productivity.
http://stats.bls.gov/eag.table.html

> **" I just wanted to comment on the structure and innovation that you have brought to learning. It has actually given me . . . a major reason to change my major to economics. This way of learning is the most interactive next to actually attending class. "**

Justin—Student, San Diego State University

END-OF-CHAPTER MATERIAL

ECONOMIC CONSULTANTS ACTIVITIES
"Economic Consultants" features place you in the role of the economist! "Economic Consultants" is a hypothetical economic research and analysis firm run by students for professionals. In your role, you need to prepare a report for a client that applies the fundamental economic issues you have learned in the chapter to his or her particular situation. Useful Internet addresses are included with these activities to help you with your research and analysis.

CHAPTER REVIEW & KEY TERMS Chapters end with a Chapter Review (a brief recounting of the principles covered in the chapter with explanation) and Key Terms (a list of the important vocabulary introduced in the chapter).

QUESTIONS & PRACTICE PROBLEMS Questions test your understanding of the qualitative concepts covered in the chapter. Practice Problems test your ability with quantitative and graphing techniques.

WHAT'S WRONG WITH THIS GRAPH? After the questions, a "What's Wrong with This Graph?" feature presents one of the chapter's key graphs with an error for you to correct. This activity tests your ability to read and understand graphs.

PRACTICE TEST To wrap up the chapter, a Practice Test presents 8–10 multiple choice problems, like those typically found on exams, addressing the key principles in the chapter. Answers are found in an appendix at the end of the textbook.

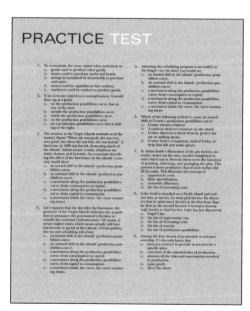

ADDITIONAL RESOURCES FOR STUDENTS

The following list of additional print, multimedia, and online resources available with this text is designed to help you in your economics class:

Print, Multimedia, and Online Ancillary Products:

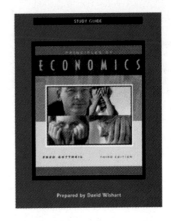

STUDY GUIDE: TOOLS FOR SUCCESS IN ECONOMICS

The Study Guide, available in a comprehensive version or in macroeconomics and microeconomics versions, explains, reviews, and tests the important principles introduced in every chapter. Featured sections include Chapter in a Nutshell, Concept Check, Am I on the Right Track?, Graphing Tutorials and Graphing Pitfalls, True/False Questions, Multiple Choice Questions, Fill-in-the-Blank Questions, and Discussion Questions.

A sample chapter of the Study Guide is available in the Learning Resources section of the Gottheil Web site http://gottheil.swcollege.com

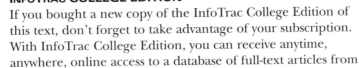

INFOTRAC COLLEGE EDITION

If you bought a new copy of the InfoTrac College Edition of this text, don't forget to take advantage of your subscription. With InfoTrac College Edition, you can receive anytime, anywhere, online access to a database of full-text articles from hundreds of scholarly and popular periodicals. You can use its fast and easy search tools to find what you're looking for among the tens of thousands of articles—updated daily and dating back as far as four years—all in this single Web site. It's a great way to locate resources for papers and projects without having to travel to the library.

To log on and get started, visit http://www.infotrac-college.com

THE WALL STREET JOURNAL EDITION

THE WALL STREET JOURNAL

If you bought a new copy of the special *Wall Street Journal* Edition of the Gottheil textbook, a 10-week subscription to both *The Wall Street Journal* Print and Interactive versions was included with your purchase. Be sure to take advantage of all *The Wall Street Journal* has to offer by activating your subscription to this authoritative publication that is synonymous with the latest word on business, economics, and public policy. It provides an excellent resource for you to observe economic concepts in action, in the real world, every day—and helps you prepare long-term for your successful economics/business career.

To activate your subscription, visit http://wsj.swcollege.com

PERSONAL WEBTUTOR

This Web-based study guide reviews critical text material chapter by chapter. Concepts are reinforced through extensive exercises, problems, cases, flashcards, self-tests, and other tools. If an access certificate for Personal WebTutor™ did not come bundled with your textbook, you can preview and purchase the product directly online for subscription periods of 1 month or 4 months.

For more details, visit http://pwt.swcollege.com

SMARTHINKING

Live online tutoring—get the help you need when you need it. Thomson Learning and Smarthinking have partnered to bring you the best academic assistance the Web has to offer. Purchasers of the Gottheil textbook are eligible for 1 free hour of online tutoring, as well as unlimited access to valuable online study resources. You can choose to get help in your subject, or in any subject Smarthinking covers: accounting, economics, mathematics, statistics, and psychology. Or get help with your writing through the online writing lab.

To sign up, visit http://www.smarthinking.com/thomsonfreehour.html

ECONOMICS ALIVE! CD-ROMS

These interactive multimedia study aids for economics are the high-tech, high-fun way to study economics. Through a combination of animated presentations, interactive graphing exercises, and simulations, the core principles of economics come to life and are driven home in an upbeat and entertaining way.

Macroeconomics Alive! CD-ROM
ISBN: 0-538-86850-3

Microeconomics Alive! CD-ROM
ISBN: 0-538-84650-X

For more details, visit the Economics Alive! Web site http://econalive.swcollege.com

TEXT-SUPPORTING WEB SITES:

SOUTH-WESTERN'S ECONOMICS RESOURCE CENTER

A unique, rich, and robust online resource for economics students, **http://economics.swcollege.com** provides customer service and product information, learning tips and tools, information about careers in economics, access to all of South-Western's text-supporting Web sites, and other cutting-edge educational resources, such as our highly regarded EconNews, EconDebate, EconData, and EconLinks online features.

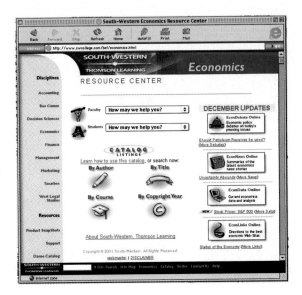

GOTTHEIL SUPPORT WEB SITE

The Gottheil Web site (**http://gottheil.swcollege.com**) provides you with open access to online study guide updates to the text, online quizzes with immediate student feedback, the opportunity to communicate with the author, direct links to all the Internet addresses and activities mentioned in the text, downloadable learning support tools, and much more.

> "The Internet access and the online quizzes are wonderful. It helps me to know what of the chapter I understood and what I need to re-read and study better. Thank you so much for this wonderful tool."
>
> Jamie—*Student*
> *Hope College*

GOTTHEIL XTRA! CD-ROM

Gottheil Xtra! CD-ROM, packaged with every new text, provides you with complimentary access to the robust set of additional online learning tools found at the site. If you don't have the CD, you can purchase access to the online version at **http://gottheil.swcollege.com**. Here is a tour through some of the study support features you will find there:

The Graphing Workshop

For most students, graphing is one of the most difficult aspects of the Principles course. The Graphing Workshop is your one-stop learning resource for help in mastering the language of graphs. You'll explore important economic concepts through a unique learning system made up of tutorials, interactive tools, and exercises that teach you how to interpret, reproduce, and explain graphs:

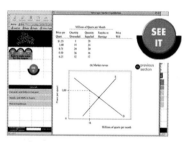

SEE IT! Animated graphing tutorials provide step-by-step graphical presentations and audio explanations.

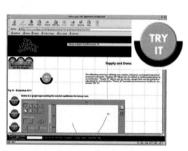

TRY IT! Interactive graphing exercises have you practice manipulating and interpreting graphs with GraphIt— a hands-on Java graphing tool. You can check your work online.

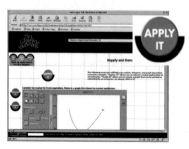

APPLY IT! Interactive graphing assignments challenge you to apply what you have learned by creating your own graph from scratch to analyze a specific scenario. You can print out and/or e-mail answers to your instructor for grading.

Video Lecture and Applications

Via streaming video, difficult concepts from each chapter are explained and illustrated by the text author. These video clips can be extremely helpful review and clarification tools if you had trouble understanding an in-class lecture or if you are more of a visual learner who sometimes has difficulty grasping concepts as they are presented in the text. In addition, CNN video segments bring the "real world" right to your desktop. The accompanying CNN video exercises help to illustrate how economics is an important part of your daily life.

Additional Self-Testing Opportunities

In addition to the open-access chapter-by-chapter quizzes found at the Gottheil Product Support Web site, Gottheil Xtra offers you an opportunity to practice for midterms and finals by taking online quizzes that span multiple chapters.

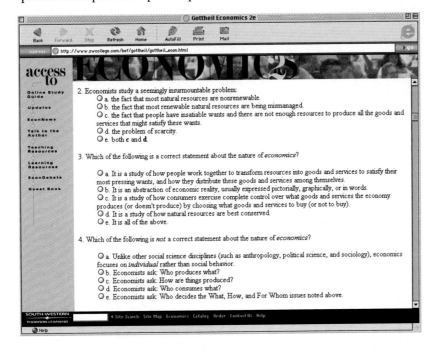

TO THE INSTRUCTOR

At the end of fall semester a few years ago, I told my class of 1,000 Economics 101 students that I wanted to see how much of the course they would be able to recall 4 months after the final exam. I asked them to take a post-final exam in early April, covering the same material. A few hundred showed up to take the April exam. The results were instructive, and perhaps not too surprising.

These were very bright students. The scholastic entrance requirements to the University of Illinois are quite high. During the semester, they were able to handle the math and graphs without difficulty. Yet, when it came to the April exam—only 4 months after the final—there was much confusion explaining, and even more graphing, market equilibrium, national income determination, and other basic ideas.

If I ever thought that the analysis offered in lectures and in the textbook is what students really ingest during the semester, that thought was very quickly dispelled.

Why is the half-life of what we teach so short? Are we trying to teach too much? Is our basic principles course getting away from being an analysis of basic principles? Have we forgotten that there is an opportunity cost every time we add material to a course or textbook? Are our textbooks more plumbers' manuals on technique than analyses of a social science subject? What do we want our students to know?

A Book Written for the Student

I wrote this textbook with the above questions in mind. It is written for the student, not for the professor. These are 2 very different readers. To my surprise, I found it difficult to keep the focus on the student who comes to the material without prior knowledge. It was much easier to write to the professor. Most of my rewriting had to do with correcting the focus. Much of the differences in style, content, and depth of analysis between my text and the others on the market reflect this focus. My preference was to sacrifice the number of topics for depth and to present the basics in as nonthreatening a style as possible. I tried always to keep the analysis within reach of students. Make it real, even personal. Allow them to enjoy the subject matter, not just to think about the coming exam.

We absorb ideas in many ways: through our heads, our hearts, and our innards. An idea that emotionally stirs you has staying power. If you can feel it in your bones, it becomes more than an intellectual exercise. I kept that in mind in every chapter and in every paragraph written. The style is intentionally conversational, but the discussion is always serious. If the story is really understood, it will be remembered. Economists have something to say. That's what my textbook is about.

• Cutting the Distance Between the Student and the Material

Think of it also as distance cutting, that is, cutting the distance between the professor, the textbook, and the student. Too often, the relationship between them turns out to be adversarial. The student sees the professor and the textbook as "endangering," as "obstacles that have to be overcome." How many times have you heard a student ask: "What chapters *do I have to* read for the exam?" Not: "What chapters will *help me understand* the material you covered in class?" Nothing subtle about the difference in character and tone, is there? And you've experienced the difference, haven't you?

So have I. And it's the reason for this textbook. *I try to put the professor, the textbook, and the student on the same side*. It's important to keep in mind that we're not just teaching economics, we're teaching students. Of course the subject matter is economics, but the focus of the economics must be the student.

This textbook makes the student the centerpiece of the analysis. It *talks* to the student. The economics is built on a foundation of stories and scenarios that makes sense to the student because the stories and scenarios are part of the student's life, or at least familiar to him or her. This personal identity and familiarity help internalize the economics for the student. As you know, one simple "ah ha" from a student reading a paragraph is worth a million paragraphs committed to memory. That's what I mean by distance cutting.

How do I achieve that? One way is to build the text's narrative on questions. There is hardly a page or paragraph in the text where a question concerning the analysis doesn't precede it. Why questions? Because I think the best way to understand an idea or a concept is to put the idea or concept in the form of a question and then answer it. That's built-in dialogue. That's conversational. That's learning. There is nothing passive about the student's involvement in this text. I make it virtually impossible for the student not to participate.

• The Focus Is on the Basics

I love the marvelous story about a young boy who goes to the library in search of material on penguins for a school essay. The librarian recommends a book. He takes it to the reading table but, after 10 minutes, returns it to the librarian. "What's wrong with the book?" she asks. "It tells me more about penguins than I really want to know," he replies.

Perhaps one reason students have trouble mastering the principles of economics at the introductory level is that we try to give them too much information. That's not what a principles course or text should be about. That's not what this text is about. A principles text should be about basic principles. The tough decision I had to make writing the textbook was not what to include but what to leave out. I chose to

sacrifice exciting new ideas and scores of recent research outcomes to keep the discussion basic. As you know, so much time can be spent on new developments that we end up with too little time on the fundamentals.

• An Interdisciplinary Emphasis

It is one thing to say that economics is part of the social sciences; it is quite another to make the text reflect that emphasis. This third edition strengthens the emphasis that was already a hallmark of the earlier editions. How is it done? I doubled the perspective boxes in each chapter (from 2 to 4) and differentiated them by focus. The perspectives are organized into 5 specific categories: *global perspectives* that take the student beyond our national borders; *interdisciplinary perspectives* that show how economics is rooted in or linked to our philosophical, psychological, cultural, social, political, and literary worlds; *historical perspectives* that provide historical economic thought content to the narrative; *applied perspectives* that offer real-world illustrations of a specific theoretical idea; and, finally, the *theoretical perspectives* that elaborate on new ways of thinking about economic problems. Many texts concentrate on the applied and theoretical, with some attention given to the historical. I think I do that well and better than most. But I honestly believe that no text can challenge mine in bringing philosophical, psychological, cultural, political, and literary content into the analysis. *It is another way of showing the students that economics matters in their lives.*

CONTENT INNOVATIONS

• Microeconomics Coverage

The importance of the profit maximization rule of $MR = MC$ cannot be overstated. In most texts, this paramount idea first appears in the context of price determination in perfect competition. It reappears again in each of the market structure chapters. I was never happy with this traditional approach. Why? It forces students to fight their way through to $P = MR = MC = ATC$ while simultaneously trying to grasp marginal revenue analysis and digest the significance of the $MR = MC$ rule. That may seem like a reasonable enough exercise to professors. However, to beginning students and nonmajors—who were probably warned through the grapevine that economics is difficult and boring—this presentation of the material may be ample confirmation. I think there is a better way to introduce one of the most important ideas we teach in microeconomic theory.

In this book, a complete chapter—Chapter 9, "Maximizing Profit"—is devoted to the idea. This chapter appears before we discuss the intricacies of market structures and price determination. Profit maximization is followed by Chapter 10, "Identifying Markets and Market Structures," which examines the outstanding characteristics of each market structure. This allows for an early comparison of market structures. The stage is then set for price determination in each market, which is done in one chapter.

With the $MR = MC$ rule already thoroughly developed and the various markets described, $MR = MC$ is both the organizing principle of the chapter and the universally applied rule. Price analysis focuses on this one central idea.

THE SUPPORT PACKAGE

For the Instructor

INSTRUCTOR'S MANUAL
The Instructor's Manual, written by the text author, provides ideas on how to approach each chapter, tips on how to present the chapter's material, and alternative illustrations that can be used to explain points of theory and policy. It also discusses how to turn student questions into teaching opportunities. In each chapter of the manual, the corresponding text chapter outline and its key terms are included for easy reference. The manual also provides detailed answers to the many questions that appear at the end of each chapter in the text.

TEST BANK
With the author's assistance, John Stoll of University of Wisconsin–Green Bay and Margaret Landman of Bridgewater State College have revised and rewritten the Test Bank. The Test Bank has been thoroughly edited, with numerous new questions added to each chapter.

EXAMVIEW TESTING SOFTWARE
ExamView—Computerized Testing Software contains all of the questions in the printed Test Bank. ExamView is an easy-to-use test creation software compatible with both Microsoft Windows and Macintosh. Instructors can add or edit questions, instructions, and answers and select questions by previewing them on the screen, selecting them randomly, or selecting them by number. Instructors can also create and administer quizzes online, whether over the Internet, a local-area network (LAN), or a wide-area network (WAN).

TRANSPARENCY ACETATES
A set of approximately 200 full-color transparency acetates has been created from the key graphs and diagrams in the text.

POWERPOINT SLIDES
A comprehensive set of PowerPoint slides is available to accompany each chapter in the text and includes most of the graphs and diagrams in the book as well as detailed lecture material.

CNN VIDEO
Professors can bring the real world into the classroom by using the *CNN Principles of Economics Video Updates.* This video provides current stories of economic interest. The video is produced by Turner Learning, Inc., using the resources of CNN, the world's first 24-hour, all-news network.

INSTRUCTOR'S RESOURCE CD-ROM
Get quick access to all instructor ancillaries from your desktop. This easy-to-use CD lets you review, edit, and copy exactly what you need in the format you want.

For the Student

STUDY GUIDE: TOOLS FOR SUCCESS IN ECONOMICS
The Study Guide, available in a comprehensive version or in macroeconomics and microeconomics versions, explains, reviews, and tests the important principles introduced in every chapter. Featured sections include Chapter in a Nutshell, Concept Check, Am I on the Right Track?, Graphing Tutorials and Graphing Pitfalls, True/False Questions, Multiple Choice Questions, Fill-in-the-Blank Questions, and Discussion Questions.

GOTTHEIL XTRA! CD-ROM
Gottheil Xtra! CD-ROM, packaged with every new text, provides you with complimentary access to the robust set of additional online learning tools found at the site. Some of the powerful study support features found on this CD include The Graphing Workshop, a unique learning system made up of tutorials, interactive tools, and exercises that teach students how to interpret, reproduce, and explain graphs; video lecture and application segments; and extensive self-testing opportunities. Students who do not buy a new text/CD package can purchase access to the site online.

THE WALL STREET JOURNAL

THE WALL STREET JOURNAL EDITION

The Wall Street Journal is synonymous with the latest word on business, economics, and public policy. *Principles of Economics* makes it easy for students to apply economic concepts to this authoritative publication, and for you to bring the most up-to-date, real-world events into your classroom. For a nominal additional cost, *Principles of Economics* can be packaged with a card entitling students to a 10-week subscription to both the print and interactive versions of *The Wall Street Journal*. Instructors who have at least seven students activate their subscriptions will automatically receive their own free subscription. Contact your South-Western/Thomson Learning sales representative for package pricing and ordering information.

INFOTRAC COLLEGE EDITION

With InfoTrac College Edition, your students can receive anytime, anywhere, online access to a database of full-text articles from hundreds of scholarly and popular periodicals such as *Newsweek, Fortune, American Economist,* and the *Quarterly Journal of Economics.* Students can use its fast and easy search tools to find what they're looking for among the tens of thousands of articles—updated daily and dating back as far as 4 years—all in this single Web site. It's a great way to expose students to online research techniques, while being secure in the knowledge that the content they find is academically based and reliable. An InfoTrac College Edition subscription card can be packaged free with new copies of the Gottheil text. Contact your South-Western/Thomson Learning sales representative for package pricing and ordering information, or, for more information on InfoTrac College Edition, visit **http://www.swcollege.com/infotrac/infotrac.html**

PERSONAL WEBTUTOR

This Web-based study guide reviews critical text material chapter by chapter. Concepts are reinforced through extensive exercises, problems, cases, flashcards, self-tests, and other tools. Access certificates for Personal WebTutor™ can be bundled with the textbook, or students can preview and purchase the product directly online (**http://pwt.swcollege.com**) for subscription periods of 1 month or 4 months.

SMARTHINKING

Live online tutoring—students can get the help they need when they need it. Thomson Learning and Smarthinking have partnered to bring students the best academic assistance the Web has to offer. Students purchasing the Gottheil textbook are eligible for one free hour of online tutoring, as well as unlimited access to valuable online study resources. They can choose to get help in their subject, or in any subject Smarthinking covers: accounting, economics, mathematics, statistics, and psychology. Or they can get help with their writing through the online writing lab.

For more information, visit http://www.smarthinking.com/thomsonfreehour.html

ECONOMICS ALIVE! CD-ROMS

These interactive multimedia study aids for economics are the high-tech, high-fun way to study economics. Through a combination of animated presentations, interactive graphing exercises, and simulations, the core principles of economics come to life and are driven home in an upbeat and entertaining way.

Macroeconomics Alive! CD-ROM, ISBN: 0-538-86850-3
Microeconomics Alive! CD-ROM, ISBN: 0-538-84650-X

Ask your Thomson Learning sales representative for more details, or visit the Economics Alive! Web site http://econalive.swcollege.com

THE NEW YORK TIMES GUIDE TO ECONOMICS

by Bernard F. Sigler, Cheryl Jennings, and Jamie Murphy
More than just a printed collection of articles, this Guide provides access, via password, to an online collection of the most current and relevant *New York Times* articles that are continually posted as news breaks. Also included are articles from *CyberTimes*, the online technology section of *The New York Times* on the Web. Correlation guides for many South-Western economics texts are available on the South-Western/*New York Times* Web site at **http://nytimes.swcollege.com**
ISBN: 0-324-04159-4

THE TOBACCO WARS

The Tobacco Wars, by Walter Adams (Michigan State University) and James W. Brock (Miami University of Ohio) presents the economic theory surrounding the tobacco litigation as a creative dialogue between many key players in the debate—including tobacco industry executives, consumers, attorneys, economists, health care professionals, historians, and political activists. Their fictional conversations illustrate the real-life issues, controversies, and points of view currently at play, giving readers a balanced and provocative framework to reach their own conclusions. The text provides a unique way to illustrate microeconomic principles, such as:
  • Consumer behavior
  • Industrial organization and public policy
  • Antitrust policy
  • Externalities, social costs, and market imperfections
ISBN: 0-324-01296-9

FOR STUDENTS AND INSTRUCTORS

GOTTHEIL ECONOMICS WEB SITE
(http://gottheil.swcollege.com)
The Gottheil Web site provides open access to an online study guide (with chapter review, quizzing, and more), updates to the text, the opportunity to communicate with the author, direct links to all the Internet addresses and activities mentioned in the text, and other teaching and learning resources.

SOUTH-WESTERN ECONOMICS RESOURCE CENTER

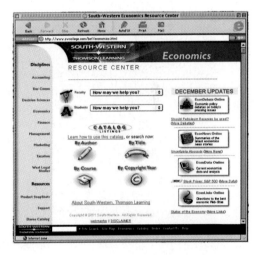

A unique, rich, and robust online resource for economics instructors and students, **http://economics.swcollege.com** provides customer service and product information, teaching and learning tips and tools, information about careers in economics, access to all of our text-supporting Web sites, and other cutting-edge educational resources such as our highly regarded EconNews, EconDebate, EconData, and EconLinks online features.

WEBTUTOR ON WEBCT AND ON BLACKBOARD
WebTutor™ on Web CT or *WebTutor on Blackboard* complements *Principles of Economics, 3e* by providing interactive reinforcement that helps students grasp complex concepts. WebTutor's online teaching and learning environment brings together content management, assessment, communication, and collaboration capabilities for enhancing in-class instruction or delivering distance learning. For more information and a demo of what WebTutor can do for your classes, visit **http://webtutor.swcollege.com**

PRINCIPLES OF MACROECONOMICS TELECOURSE
PRINCIPLES OF MICROECONOMICS TELECOURSE

Produced by MUCIA Global Education Network, this series of 56 one-half hour lectures by Fred Gottheil provides a complete introduction to the principles of economics. To learn more about this full distance learning package, contact MUCIA at **http://www.muciaglobal.edu**

FAREWELL

News-Gazette file photo

Friday, May 12, 1989
The Champaign-Urbana News-Gazette Weekend

"His eyes would light up and he'd talk fast and
you couldn't help being excited about the
band or record he'd discovered, too."

P. Gregory Springer

Part of being young is the feeling of being indestructible.
Josh Gottheil, who died last month after a two-year battle
against leukemia, probably understood that he wouldn't
live forever. But he never stopped working to bring the
music he loved to the world around him. Rock and roll
would carry on.

The punk movement—simultaneously cynical and realist
and suicidal and idealistic—tried in a frenzy to wipe out the
commercialism and mass media hallucination which blurred
life's realities, even unpleasant ones like death. There were
bands named Dead Kennedys, Dead Milkmen, the prototype
Dead Boys, and Gottheil's local band, Dead Relatives.

When he was only a sophomore in high school, Gottheil
became a drummer for the short-lived band, but he was no
angry punk. He heard the message in the music and he set
out, ambitious at a tender age, to deliver it to the community.

At 17, he already had promoted dozens of concerts for
teens in community centers and church foundations. He
was the least pushy music promoter I ever met, enticing
me to see at least one political rock and folk concert
through his complete, quiet reticence.

It was the music that spoke to and through him.

At one concert he arranged, I watched Billy Bragg and Michelle Shocked get their
introductions to the area. And I saw Josh, standing by the door at Mabel's, anxious
to see that the message and the feeling came across.

His bands rarely disappointed.

Among the many other national bands he brought to Champaign's clubs were
Living Colour, They Might Be Giants, Soul Asylum, Throwing Muses, Jane's Addiction, Dead Milkmen, Hüsker Dü, Let's Active, Timbuk 3, Ministry, and the Pixies.

"The scene wouldn't be what it was today without Josh," said Chris Corpora, an
area rock promoter of Trashcan Productions. "He didn't look the part and he
risked his own money. About four years ago he started teen nights when there was
a lull in the scene. I don't want to deify him, but he had an incredible will, poise,
and the wherewithal to get contracts signed and do things he probably shouldn't
have been able to do. When I was 15, I couldn't even read a contract."

Even in the hard-core punk scene, Josh maintained a romantic side, often bringing roses for the girls in his favorite bands, notably Throwing Muses and the Pixies.

"He was always in love with every girl in a band," said Katy Stack, one of many people who considered Josh a best friend.

"He made friends with the Pixies and we flew to California to see them play in San Francisco," Stack said. "They invited him on stage to sing."

For a couple of summers, he worked at the desk at Crystal Lake Pool, announcing the adult swim and checking in bags. After high school, he took some college classes in philosophy and math at Parkland and at the UI, where his father, Fred, is a professor of economics. When he got sick, "it didn't look like he needed to go to college," according to Stack. "He was real busy doing all the music and he always had a lot of money. He was the only 16-year-old that had $2,000 in his checking account."

Another friend, Shara Gingold, actually wrote a book about her crush on Josh.

"He was two years older. The book is called 'I Love You, Josh. Do You Even Know I Exist?'," said Gingold, who lives in Urbana. "I think that it was [the fact that] he was very understanding and caring. We'd meet to play tennis and then we'd just sit and hit the tennis ball against the wall and talk about everything."

Last year, his health started to improve. He gained weight. He was working at Record Swap, surrounding himself in music during the day for the concerts he promoted at night. He had teamed with Chicago promoter Tony Polous, established a limited partnership called Concert One Productions, rented an office in Chicago's Mercantile Building, and developed the financing for big arena shows.

"Josh was destined to be huge," said Polous from the Chicago office. "He was the most effective, easy-going person I ever met. It's not hard to master being pushy and strong. Josh mastered being effective in an unassuming way.

"When he had to go back to the hospital, he never let on how sick he was. Every day I'd call him and he'd ask about what this manager was doing or that agent and he'd make decisions. We never really talked about his health. I never thought he was going to die. I think about him every day."

Despite his illness, Josh moved to Chicago last fall to be immersed in the music business.

"It was a chance, a break, an exciting thing to do. The world was his to conquer," said Fred Gottheil from his UI office. "I remember going up to visit and spend the night. The wind was howling, but he was so proud of the apartment. He was designing tickets on his computer, telling me [about] all the bands he had booked, his new ideas, bubbling with enthusiasm for the possibilities. The move was exhilarating for him. He called home quite frequently, but [Chicago] was where he had to be."

Said former Champaign-Urbana DJ Charlie "The Quaker" Edwards, who shared the Chicago apartment, "He had a real vitality, youth, and infectiousness. His eyes would light up and he'd talk fast and you couldn't help being excited about the band or record he'd discovered, too. Even though there was almost 20 years age difference between us, we'd listen to albums and talk about the bands and share a mutual excitement.

"He was a really good, serious businessman. Much better than I could have been, always dealing with five shows at once. He really loved it, too. He just loved the music."

"Definitely, there are people who are into [punk] because it is a fad," Gottheil said three years ago. "But for the people who really believe in it, it won't die for them."

Josh Gottheil died April 4 at Barnes Hospital in St. Louis, three months short of his 20th birthday. There was a turn-away crowd for his funeral on April 7 at the Sinai Temple in Champaign. Because he did so much to bring a new attitude about music in this area, one of the bands he helped find national prominence, Throwing Muses, has donated its performance at a benefit concert this Sunday at Mabel's, with proceeds going to the Josh Gottheil Memorial Fund for Lymphoma Research.

AUTHOR

Fred M. Gottheil is a professor of economics at the University of Illinois in Urbana-Champaign. He came to Illinois in 1960, planning to spend one year before returning to his native Canada. But he fell in love with the campus, the community, and the Midwest, and he has been at Illinois ever since. He earned his undergraduate degree at McGill University in Montreal, Canada, and his Ph.D. at Duke University. His primary teaching is the principles of economics, and, on occasion, he has taught the history of economic thought, Marxian economics, and the economics of the Middle East. He is the author of *Marx's Economic Predictions* and numerous articles that have appeared in scholarly journals, among them the *American Economic Review,* the *Canadian Journal of Economics,* the *Journal of Post-Keynesian Economics,* and the *Middle East Review.* He has also contributed articles to several edited books on the Middle East. Although he enjoys research, his labor of love is teaching the principles course. His classes have been as large as 1,800 students. He has won the department's annual excellence-in-teaching award in economics 12 times during the past dozen years and, along with his college and university-wide teaching awards, holds the distinction of having won the most teaching awards on the Urbana campus. Aside from his research and publications as a professor of economics, Professor Gottheil is also on the university's medical faculty, co-teaching the College of Medicine's course on medicine and society. As well, he is director of the University of Illinois's Center for Economic Education. In this capacity, he organizes and team-teaches minicourses and workshops on the principles of economics. He was a White House consultant on the Middle East during the Carter administration and offered expert testimony to several congressional committees. Professor Gottheil was a visiting professor at Northwestern University and at the Hebrew University in Jerusalem, Israel. He has lectured at many universities in the United States, Canada, and abroad, including universities in Syria, Egypt, Israel, and Jordan.

I am grateful to many people for help and encouragement throughout the development of this textbook. Many came to the project in a strictly professional capacity; most ended up as good friends. I owe them more than they believe is their due. At the beginning, George Lobell was enthusiastic about the idea of the textbook and believed that it would make a difference in the profession. He read many chapters, stayed in close touch, and still does. I thank this textbook for introducing me to George. David Wishart was a dear friend before we started the project, and working together on this textbook added another dimension to our friendship. Jack Calhoun, South-Western's editor-in-chief, sold me on the idea of the team concept of publishing. It was Andy McGuire, the developmental editor at South-Western, who saw this third edition to completion. He also carefully managed and helped improve the comprehensive supplements package that accompanies this book. Lisa Lysne has contributed her insight and deftly handled the marketing campaign. Finally, Mike Stratton, Libby Shipp and the staff at Lachina Publishing Services played major roles in translating my word-processed drafts and rough sketches into the pleasing book you hold in your hands.

During this book's long gestation period, I have benefited from the comments and suggestions of many reviewers. My heartfelt thanks go to the following economists. This book is much improved because of their efforts.

Carl J. Austermiller, *Oakland Community College*

Michael Bodnar, *Stark Technical College*

John Booth, *Stetson University*

David Bunting, *Eastern Washington University*

Tom Cate, *Northern Kentucky University*

Robert Catlett, *Emporia State University*

Christopher Colburn, *Old Dominion University*

James Cover, *University of Alabama, Tuscaloosa*

Jerry Crawford, *Arkansas State*

Jane Crouch, *Pittsburgh State University*

Susan Davis, *SUNY College at Buffalo*

Daniel Fagan, *Daniel Webster College*

Abdollah Ferdowsi, *Ferris State University*

Eric Fisher, *Ohio State University*

Carol Hogan, *University of Michigan, Dearborn*

William Holmes, *Temple University*

Paul Huszer, *Colorado State University*

Bruce K. Johnson, *Centre College*

Patrick Kelso, *West Texas State University*

Alan Kessler, *Providence College*

Joseph Kotaska, *Monroe Community College*

Robert Litro, *Mattatuck Community College*

Lawrence Mack, *North Dakota State University*

Joseph Maddalena, *St. Thomas Aquinas College*

John Makrogianis, *Middlesex Community Collage*

Gabriel Manrique, *Winona State University*

John Marsh, *Montana State University*

G. H. Mattersdorff, *Lewis and Clark College*

John Merrifield,
University of Texas—San Antonio

James McBearty,
University of Arizona

Henry McCarl,
University of Alabama, Birmingham

James McLain,
University of New Orleans

Lon Mishler,
North Wisconsin Technical College

Norma Morgan,
Curry College

Allan Olsen,
Elgin Community College

Peter Pedroni,
Indiana University

Mitchell Redlo,
Monroe Community College

Terry Riddle,
Central Virginia Community College

Paul Rothstein,
University of Washington at St. Louis

Richard Schiming,
Mankato State University

Jerry Sidwell,
Eastern Illinois University

Phillip Smith,
DeKalb College

Philip Sprunger,
Lycoming College

William Stull,
Temple University

Tapan Thoy,
Eastern Connecticut State University

Doug Wakeman,
Meredith College

Jim Watson,
Jefferson College

Larry Wolfenbarger,
Georgia College

Finally, I want to thank Peter Schran, my colleague and close friend at Illinois, whose advice always made sense although it sometimes took me a while to appreciate it.

Fred Gottheil
University of Illinois

CHAT ECONOMICS

Tune into the conversation. It's about *your* course. Just change the names, and it's *your* campus, *your* classroom, *your* professor, *your* classmates, and *you.*

Picture the scene. Katy Stack, a freshman planning on majoring in economics, and Professor Gottheil are walking across campus after the first week of class. Katy introduces herself and immediately the conversation gets to the heart of her concerns.

GOTTHEIL: Well, good morning, Katy. How do you like the economics course so far?

KATY: Okay, I guess. I'm actually thinking about majoring in it.

GOTTHEIL: Good choice! I think you'll love economics. Not only do I find it intellectually exciting, but it tells us a lot about ourselves. It's about what we do and how we live.

KATY: Frankly, I'm a little uneasy about majoring in it. My friends tell me that economics is difficult.

GOTTHEIL: In what way?

KATY: I think it's just difficult to understand.

GOTTHEIL: Well, Katy, let me tell you an anecdote that addresses your concern. It's an honest-to-goodness story, by the way, told to me by my teaching assistant, Cliff Althoff, who was then working on his Ph.D. in economics here on campus.

KATY: What's he doing now?

GOTTHEIL: He's a professor of economics at Joliet Junior College. Well, here's his story. One day, a number of years ago, he was on his way to visit his then-fiancée, Maureen McGonagle, when, on the sidewalk close by her house, he ran into a small group of 10-year-old girls skipping rope, hopscotching, and playing ball and jacks.

KATY: They weren't economists!

GOTTHEIL: Not exactly, but that's part of the story. One of the girls who had been skipping rope blocked his path to the house and audaciously asked who he was and where he was going. Cliff politely told her who he was, that Maureen was his fiancée, and that he was going to visit her for the day. The girl, still very inquisitive, asked Cliff what he did for a living. Well, he told her he was an economics teacher at the University of Illinois. She then replied, "If you're a teacher of economics, can you teach me something about economics now?"

KATY: Right there on the sidewalk—to a 10-year-old?

GOTTHEIL: You have to know Cliff! He said, "Sure. You were busy hopscotching when I met you, right? But you could have been skipping rope. Now you know that you can't do both at the same time, can you? By choosing to hopscotch, you gave up the opportunity of skipping rope. Economists call that an opportunity cost. You see, the fun you have hopscotching—and it's fun, isn't it—cost you the fun you could have had skipping rope. Make sense? Opportunity cost is a really important economic idea, and now you know it. Well, I really enjoyed talking to you, but I must go."

KATY: That's sort of neat. Teaching opportunity cost to a 10-year-old. Do you think she really understood it?

GOTTHEIL: Well, listen to this: When Cliff walked past the children and was about to enter the house, he heard the girl call back to him, "Hey mister! The opportunity cost of going to see Maureen is not being able to stay here and talk to me. See, I understand economics."

KATY: Awesome!

GOTTHEIL: Not really. Much of what you will learn in economics is like that. It will not be too difficult to understand. Knowing how to use economic principles is another matter. But you'll get to know that as well. Katy, I think you'll enjoy the course, and I certainly will enjoy having you in class.

It is certainly normal to be concerned about how hard any course will be, and economics is no different. Yet, as Cliff showed, the basic concepts in economics are not difficult to understand. As you read through the next few chapters, consider Katy and your own assumptions about your economics course. Who knows, perhaps you will decide to major in economics as well!

1

INTRODUCTION

"In the beginning God created the heaven and the earth" is about as familiar a sentence as any written. The Bible tells us that in the five days that followed the creation of heaven and earth, God separated darkness from light and water from dry land, and brought forth a multiplicity of living plants and creatures to inhabit the newly created land, waters, and skies. And on the sixth day, God created people:

So God created man in his own image, in the image of God created he him; male and female created he them. And God blessed

them, and God said unto them, Be fruitful, and multiply, and replenish the earth, and subdue it: and have dominion over the fish of the sea, and over the fowl of the air, and over every living thing that moveth upon the earth.

And God said, Behold, I have given you every herb bearing seed, which is upon the face of all the earth, and every tree, in the which is the fruit of a tree yielding seed; to you it shall be for meat. And to every beast of the earth, and to every fowl of the air, and to every thing that creepeth upon the earth, wherein there is life, I have given every green herb for meat: and it was so.

THIS CHAPTER INTRODUCES YOU TO THE ECONOMIC PRINCIPLES ASSOCIATED WITH:

- THE EARTH'S RENEWABLE AND NONRENEWABLE RESOURCES
- THE CONCEPT OF INSATIABLE WANTS
- THE CONCEPTS OF SCARCITY AND CHOICE
- THE VALUE OF ECONOMIC MODEL BUILDING
- MICROECONOMIC AND MACROECONOMIC ANALYSIS
- POSITIVE AND NORMATIVE ECONOMICS

NO ONE EVER MADE AN OUNCE OF EARTH

What's the lesson we are supposed to draw from this creation narrative? To an economist, the first chapter of Genesis is both a powerful and humbling account of how our **natural resources** came into being. The message is clear. It doesn't even require particular religious conviction. After all, when you think about it, who ever made an ounce of earth? Who ever created a lump of coal or a nugget of gold? It seems that they have always been here for our use. Nobody ever added to nature's bounty.

Although the scientific interpretation of our resource availability differs dramatically from the biblical one, the message is similar. Natural resources have always been here. Physicists express this idea of prior existence and the continuance of matter in the first law of thermodynamics—the conservation principle—which asserts that energy can be neither created nor destroyed.

Economists, too, accept as fact that every resource on the face of this earth is a gift of nature. Resources were here before men and women arrived on the scene. Every ounce of iron, tungsten, nickel, petroleum, copper, zinc, asbestos, gypsum, and the many other metals, minerals, and energy sources, including those yet undiscovered, were here long before we learned how to make cement, gasoline, steel, plastics, and aspirin.

The nutrients attached to every grain of soil were already imbedded in the soil before people even began to think about working the land. The herds of goats, the schools of sea bass, the flocks of geese, the reindeer and rabbits, the forests and grasses, and all our other food resources were there for the taking.

And, of course, we took! We learned how to extract natural resources from the earth, how to fish them out of the waters, and how to harvest them from the lands. Most exciting of all, we learned the tricks of transforming resources from their original states into new ones. We transform iron ore into steel, crude petroleum into plastic, trees into furniture, rays of the sun into energy, coal into nylon, sand into glass, limestone into cement, bauxite into aluminum, and water flow into electricity. We are continually discovering newer techniques for transformation. And we have been doing this for a long, long time.

Are We Running Out of Natural Resources?

We live in a finite world. No matter how seemingly bountiful the quantity of our natural resources may be or how carefully we try to conserve them, if we keep using them, they eventually are going to run out. It just seems reasonable. Or does it?

Renewable and Nonrenewable Natural Resources

Many natural resources are renewable. Consider, for example, our supply of forests, sea and land animals, water, and grasses. Are not these resources self-renewing? But with rapidly growing human populations, overuse of productive lands can turn them into deserts, and overharvesting of fish and land animals can destroy these living resources. Properly managed conservation, on the other hand, can not only protect these natural resources but even increase their supply.

Admittedly, our metal and mineral resources are not self-renewing. Gold nuggets don't breed. Because the earth contains finite space, its mineral resources exist only in finite quantities. You do not have to be a rocket scientist to figure out that mining one ton of copper ore depletes that resource by one ton. In fact, we have been depleting our copper supply ever since King Solomon began mining copper in the Negev desert. However, before we work our way down to the last ton of copper, it

Natural resources
The lands, water, metals, minerals, animals, and other gifts of nature that are available for producing goods and services.

CHECK YOUR UNDERSTANDING

Can you describe the finite character of the earth's resources?

CHECK YOUR UNDERSTANDING

What distinguishes renewable from nonrenewable resources?

is very possible that we will have already abandoned it as a usable resource. In other words, even though copper may not be a renewable resource, we may be well advised to treat it as one.

Does this mean, then, that we will never run out of any natural resource? No such luck. It just means that our knowledge of a resource's relative scarcity, particularly when we consider its availability in the not-too-distant future, is less than exact.

Thousands of years ago, flint was a primary resource used in the production of tools and weapons. Do you know anyone today concerned about our flint supply? We still produce tools and weapons, but we have moved to other technologies that use very different resources. Is copper's future, then, mirrored in flint's past? If so, we may someday regret having conserved our copper supply. We might end up with mountains of unused, useless copper.

Should we conserve the world's oil supply or instead go full speed ahead, using up as much of it as we need to satisfy our current demands? After all, in a genera-

HISTORICAL PERSPECTIVE

COAL . . . THEN (1865) AND NOW (2000)

In 1865, the celebrated economist Stanley Jevons wrote a very sobering book, *The Coal Question.* Jevons set out to prove that England's economic progress and power were on the verge of collapse. The reason? The energy source that powered England's economic growth—coal—was being rapidly depleted. No alternative energy source seemed likely. Jevons estimated that England's commercially available coal supply would run out in one hundred years. He warned:

> . . . I must point out the painful fact that such a rate of [economic] growth will before long render our consumption of coal comparable with the total supply. In the increasing depth and difficulty of coal mining we shall meet that vague but inevitable boundary that will stop our progress. . . . A farm, however far pushed, will under proper cultivation continue to yield for ever a constant crop. But in a mine there is no reproduction, and the produce once pushed to the utmost will soon begin to sink to zero. (pp. 154–155)

Has England run out of coal? England's coal problem in 2000, ironically, seems to be too much coal! The *Economic Bulletin,* a bimonthly summary of the Nottinghamshire economy, reported in its March/April 2000 issue: "RJB Mining, Britain's biggest coal producer, announced a 130 million pound sterling pre tax loss for 1999. RJB said that without government aid it would be forced to close Ellington colliery [coal mine] in Northumbria and Clipstone in Nottinghamshire, with a loss of 450 jobs. Only 17 deep mines are left in the UK, 13 of them owned by RJB Mining, and nearly half are in trouble after a glut of coal on the world market sent prices plummeting."

It's not a new story. A decade earlier, the House of Commons energy committee published a report that outlined the bleak future facing the coal industry, despite the fact that productivity in the industry is relatively high. Britain, the committee report stated, still has three centuries' worth of coal at the present rate of consumption. Can you imagine Jevons reading the committee's report? He would be flabbergasted!

MORE ON THE NET

Learn more about Stanley Jevons (http://www.cpm. ll.ehime-u.ac.jp/AkamacHomePage/Akamac_ E-text_Links/Jevons.html). What problems does England face today with coal? Visit the United Kingdom Parliament (http://www.parliament.uk/).

tion or two our energy technologies may have already switched to solar and nuclear power, or to some yet unknown technology. What then do we do with oceans of unused, unwanted oil?

How Do You Satisfy Insatiable Wants?

Suppose we had an infinite supply of natural resources. We would still have an insurmountable economic problem. There simply are not enough hours in a day to allow us to transform those resources into all the goods and services we want. That is, the problem ultimately may not be the limited quantity of resources available to us, but rather our limitless, or insatiable, wants.

Let's go back to the biblical story to illustrate the point. Adam and Eve were happy in the Garden of Eden, not because the garden had so much but because they wanted so little. Their problem was eating the fruit from the Tree of Knowledge: One bite and they suddenly realized they had no clothes, no air

THEORETICAL PERSPECTIVE

IF NOT THE DEPLETION OF COAL, THEN PERHAPS OIL

In the 1970s, economists and government people looking at the soaring price of oil panicked. What did they see as the cause for rising oil prices? You guessed it! Listen to President Jimmy Carter:

> It is obvious to anyone that looks at it [the oil crisis] that we've got a problem that's serious now. It's going to get more serious in the future. We're going to have less oil. Those are the facts. They are unpleasant facts. (May 25, 1979)

Sound familiar? Perhaps President Carter should have read Stanley Jevons's 1865 book *The Coal Question*. He might have found some reason to be more optimistic about our future and less reason to assert his fears about oil supplies as "unpleasant facts."

In July 2000, the Energy Information Administration (EIA) of the U.S. Department of Energy

IT'S A LONG, LONG HAUL. BUT DON'T WORRY. THERE'S PLENTY OF OIL IN THE PIPELINE AND OCEANS MORE WHERE THAT CAME FROM.

reported that "data continues to confirm no shortage of crude oil in the open market." And that's no surprise. Why not? Because if we were really running out of oil, we would spend a great deal of time looking for it, wouldn't we? We would be drilling and drilling, using as many drilling rigs as we could employ. But look at the drilling rig data. In June 2000, the U.S. weekly rig count was 878. Since 1940, the highest weekly rig count was 4,530, recorded in December 1981. The lowest rig count was recorded in April 1999. The 878 rigs in operation tend to confirm the EIA report that nobody is really worried about crude oil supply.

MORE ON THE NET

Visit the U.S. Department of Energy (http://www.energy.gov/) and the White House (http://www.whitehouse.gov/). What about oil concerns the federal government?

conditioning, no videocassettes, no quartz watches, no phones, and no Buick. It was a quick trip from the state of ignorant bliss to paradise lost. Their wants became insatiable.

We inherited their genes. Our tastes for goods and services are virtually limitless. There is always something else we want. And once these wants are satisfied, our minds are just as capable of conceiving new wants as they are of conceiving ways of satisfying them. In this respect, we differ from lions and tigers who, after a kill, are prepared to rest until hungry again. Instead, we are perpetually in a state of hunger. Even if we had a never-ending supply of the natural resources required to satisfy our limitless wants, it would take more than 24 hours a day to transform them into all the goods and services we want.

Scarcity Forces Us to Make Choices

If we can't have everything we want today, what do we do? We are forced to make choices. We must choose to produce some goods and services and not others. Sometimes this kind of choosing can be visibly painful. Have you ever watched children in Toys "R" Us with a gift certificate in hand? It can take them all day before they make a choice. And instead of bubbling with excitement over the toy they bought, they usually appear frustrated over not being able to walk away with everything!

Life is like that. **Scarcity** governs us. Because we cannot have everything all at once, we are forever forced to make choices. We can use our resources to satisfy only some of our wants, leaving many others unsatisfied.

WHAT IS ECONOMICS?

What has **economics** to do with Genesis 1, Adam and Eve, the first law of thermodynamics, scarcities of resources, and infinite wants? Everything! *Economics is the study of how we work together to transform scarce resources into goods and services to satisfy the most pressing of our infinite wants, and how we distribute these goods and services among ourselves.*

The study of economics focuses on four central issues. Who produces what? How? Who consumes what? And who decides? Taken together, these issues form the analysis of how an economy works.

Economics Is Part of Social Science

It is sometimes difficult to separate the study of economics from the study of the other social sciences, such as sociology, anthropology, political science, and psychology. All the social science disciplines, including economics, examine individual and social behavior. While economics concentrates on those aspects of behavior that affect the way we, as individuals and as a society, produce and consume goods and services, our production and consumption are not done in a social vacuum.

What we consume, what we produce, how we produce, and how we go about exchanging resources and products among ourselves is determined, in part, by the character of our political system, by the customs and traditions of our society, and by the set of social institutions and ethical standards we have established.

Our political and economic rights and freedoms stem from the same root. Our right to vote at the ballot box, for example, is not unrelated to **consumer sovereignty** in the marketplace—that is, our freedom to buy or not buy the goods and services offered. This right to choose what we want dictates what producers will ultimately

CHECK YOUR UNDERSTANDING

Why does scarcity force people to make choices?

Scarcity
The perpetual state of insufficiency of resources to satisfy people's unlimited wants.

Economics
The study of how people work together to transform resources into goods and services to satisfy their most pressing wants, and how they distribute these goods and services among themselves.

Consumer sovereignty
The ability of consumers to exercise complete control over what goods and services the economy produces (or doesn't produce) by choosing what goods and services to buy (or not buy).

CHAPTER 1 | **7**

produce, just as our right to choose our political leaders dictates what kind of government policies we ultimately get.

We grow up in a society whose value system, sometimes described as the Protestant ethic, implants in us a belief in the importance of personal frugality, honest labor, and enterprise. To many of us, any alternative value system is considered deviant or antisocial. In this respect, our ethical standards establish the boundaries of permissible economic behavior. We are also taught from childhood to accept a broad set of social responsibilities, many requiring us to share part of our income, through taxes, with people who are less fortunate than us. These accepted social values and responsibilities contribute to the way we select and meet our economic goals and the role we expect our government to play in the economy.

The contributions that economics as a social science discipline makes to the other social sciences are also fundamental. For example, it is difficult to appreciate what federal, state, and local governments do without understanding the economic circumstances underlying their actions. After all, government budgets are economic documents. Taxes and government spending are economic tools used by the political system to meet economic as well as political and social objectives. Political debates on issues such as the national debt, budget deficits, and the welfare system require an understanding of economics.

It is difficult, as well, for sociologists to study the role of the family in society without at the same time studying how the family behaves as an economic unit. To some extent, even when and whom we marry, the number of children we have, and interpersonal relationships within the family are governed by economics.

Using Economic Models

Our real economic world is incredibly complex. Millions of people, making independent economic decisions every day, affect not only their own lives but the lives of everyone around them. In many cases, they influence even the lives of people great distances away. It is one thing to appreciate the fact that we are all mutually interrelating, but quite another to untangle these relationships to draw specific one-to-one, cause-and-effect economic correspondences. It's an imposing intellectual challenge, but economists have been working at it with at least modest success, and in some cases, quite remarkable results.

How do economists start? By abstracting from reality. The purpose of such abstraction is to reduce the complexity of the world we live in to more simplified, manageable dimensions. That is essentially what the economists' models do. The models capture the essence of an economic reality. They try to simplify it without distorting its truth.

In a way, when economists build economic models, they are like children playing house. In both cases, it is essentially reduction and imitation. In child's play, many of the household activities are ignored and many of the real problems are overlooked. However, the central figures are there, the accuracy of their behavior is uncanny, and the issues basic to most households are reflected in the children's mimicry of adult conversation.

Most **economic model** builders insist that while their models exclude many economic activities of the real world, overlook the complexities of how people really behave, and ignore many pressing issues that people confront every day, what they portray in their models is nevertheless the quintessence of how the real economy works.

Economic model
An abstraction of an economic reality. It can be expressed pictorially, graphically, algebraically, or in words.

And that's the point of economic analysis. Economists are not really interested in pure intellectual exercise. Their interest is not the economic model per se but the real world of economics. Their models are designed to serve only as vehicles to a fuller comprehension of what really goes on.

Ceteris Paribus

One of the most important aids economists use in model building is the assumption of **ceteris paribus,** which translated means "holding constant" or "controlling for the influence of other factors." Ceteris paribus allows economists to develop one-to-one, cause-and-effect relationships in isolation, that is, removed from other potentially influential factors. For example, when the price of filet mignon decreases, economists assert that the quantity of filet mignon demanded increases. But this one-to-one, cause-and-effect relationship between price and quantity demanded holds only if everything else going on in the economy is ignored. If the prices of other foods fall at the same time, then it is questionable whether more filet mignon would be demanded when its price falls. After all, people may be more attracted to the other price-reduced foods than they are to the lower-priced filet.

Or suppose people lost their jobs on the very day the filet prices were cut. Chances are fewer filets would be demanded. When you're out of work, filet mignon at any price is probably out of mind.

How then can economists make definitive statements about any economic relationship when so many economic events, all potentially influencing each other, may be occurring at the same time? They do so by assuming ceteris paribus. It focuses the analysis. That one-to-one, cause-and-effect relationship between price and quantity demanded, however limited by the exclusion of other considerations, is still highly insightful and turns out to be of critical importance to our understanding of price determination.

Ceteris paribus is not confined to economic analysis. When the surgeon general of the United States asserts that smoking causes lung cancer, isn't there a ceteris paribus assumption lurking in the background? After all, the smoking–cancer relationship ignores a host of other factors that may explain the cancer. Consider the science of meteorology. When the weather forecast is rain, isn't there a ceteris paribus assumption made as well? Weather fronts can and often do change direction.

The Circular Flow Model of Goods and Money

Let's look now at an honest-to-goodness economic model. Perhaps the simplest model illustrating how an economy works is the **circular flow model** of money, goods, and services shown in Exhibit 1.

In this model, people are both consumers and producers. They live in **households,** where they consume the goods and services they buy on the product market, and they supply their resources—land, labor, capital, and entrepreneurship—on the resource market to **firms** that use the resources to produce the goods and services that appear on the product market.

In the upper half, the purple arrow depicts the direction of the flow of goods and services from firms, through the product market, to households. Households pay for them with money earned in the resource market. The green arrow depicts the flow of money from households, through the product market, to the firms.

Let's look at households now in their capacity as money earners. They earn money—wages, interest, rent, and profit—by selling or leasing their resources—labor, capital, land, and entrepreneurship—to firms. The yellow arrow in the bot-

---

Ceteris paribus
The Latin phrase meaning "everything else being equal."

Circular flow model
A model of how the economy's resources, money, goods, and services flow between households and firms through resource and product markets.

Household
An economic unit of one or more persons, living under one roof, that has a source of income and uses it in whatever way it deems fit.

Firm
An economic unit that produces goods and services in the expectation of selling them to households, other firms, or government.

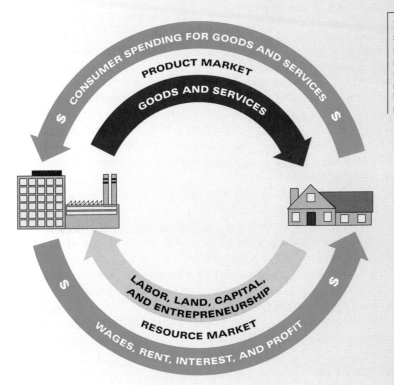

THE CIRCULAR FLOW MODEL

Households supply resources—land, labor, capital, and entrepreneurship—to firms through the resource market in return for money payments—rent, wages, interest, and profit. Firms use the resources to produce goods and services that they supply on the product market. There, households buy those goods and services with the incomes received from the resources they supplied.

tom half depicts the resource flow from households, through the resource market, to firms. Firms transform those resources into goods and services that eventually appear on the product market. The money firms earn selling goods and services pays for the resources they buy. The green arrow depicts the pay-for-resources flow of money from firms, through the resource market, to the households. As you see, for every flow of goods, services, and resources there is a counterflow of money.

How would *you* fit into the circular flow model of Exhibit 1? Suppose you have a summer job making cotton candy at a neighborhood water slide. The job pays $200 weekly. The yellow arrow represents your labor flow to the water slide firm, while the bottom-half green arrow represents the $200 you receive from the firm.

Now let's look at your activity in the upper half of the circular flow model. Using the $200 you earn at the slide—which is now your household income—you go to the product market to buy $200 of goods and services that firms have produced for sale on the market. (Among the goods available is cotton candy.) The purple arrow represents a $200 flow of goods and services to you, while the upper-half green arrow represents the flow of money from you to firms for the goods and services.

Is the circular flow model an accurate reflection of our economic reality? Not really. Where in Exhibit 1's portrayal of that circular flow are the banks? Where is government? Doesn't government, too, consume goods and services? Where are the unemployed? They consume some of the economy's goods and services, but if they are unemployed, they aren't providing resources. Where, then, do they get the money? How does the model account for retired people? They no longer work, but they continue to consume. Where in the model do we find the economy's exports and imports? Where are savings and investments?

Nowhere! The circular flow model of Exhibit 1 isn't designed as a complete picture of our economic reality. In fact, it ignores a host of major economic institutions and activities.

Can you think of any people or institutions in your life that do not fit into the circular flow model? Go to the Interactive Study Center at http://gottheil.swcollege.com and click on the "Your Turn" button to submit your example. Student submissions will be posted to the Web site, and perhaps we will use some in future additions of the book!

CHECK YOUR UNDERSTANDING

What are some advantages and limitations of the circular flow model?

But these omissions are far from being shortcomings of the model; in fact, they illustrate the model's strength. The model is designed to reflect one basic fact about how the economy works: It shows how money, goods, and services flow between households and firms through resource and product markets.

Most of the economic models analyzed in this text are no more complicated than this circular flow model. Some, like Exhibit 1, are portrayed pictorially, others graphically, and still others take the form of simple algebraic expressions. For example, economists build models of a firm to illustrate how market prices are determined. Other economic models are designed to show how unemployment and inflation arise. Models also illustrate why some nations grow faster than others and why some do not grow at all. Most of these models are expressed graphically. The one thing all of these models have in common is the use of abstraction—that is, the use economists make of simplifying assumptions to distill the essence out of the complicated economic realities they study.

Microeconomics and Macroeconomics

Economists who look at the real world and create simple models to illustrate what they see do not necessarily look at the same things, nor do they ask the same kinds of questions. **Microeconomics,** for example, looks at the behavior of individual households and firms. It asks, Why do firms produce what they do? How do they price their goods and services? How do markets work? What distinguishes competitive from noncompetitive markets? How are resource prices such as wage rates, interest rates, and rents determined? How do firms make profits? What determines people's demands for goods and services?

Microeconomics
A subarea of economics that analyzes individuals as consumers and producers, and specific firms and industries. It focuses especially on the market behavior of firms and households.

As these questions suggest, the focus of microeconomic analysis is on the individual. Microeconomists study individuals as consumers and producers. The economy is regarded as a composite of interacting individual economic units. To understand how the economy functions, then, requires an understanding of how each of these individual units behaves and interacts.

Read a copy of today's newspaper, such as *USA Today* (http://www.usatoday.com/). Can you find articles that address microeconomic and macroeconomic issues?

Macroeconomics, on the other hand, tries to explain a different set of facts about the economy. It focuses attention on the behavior of the economy as a whole. To macroeconomists, the economy is more than simply a collection of its individual parts. It has character. It has its own vitality and history. It has an identifiable substance. The macroeconomic unit of analysis, then, is the economy.

Macroeconomics
A subarea of economics that analyzes the behavior of the economy as a whole.

Invisible hand
Adam Smith's concept of the market, which, as if it were a hand, guides firms that seek only to satisfy their own self-interest to produce precisely those goods and services that consumers want.

The macroeconomic questions concern not the behavior and activities of individual households, firms, or markets, but the behavior and activity of the economy itself. They ask, for example, Why do national economies grow? Why do some grow faster than others? What determines a nation's savings, its investments, or its consumption? Why does it experience inflation? Why does it generate unacceptable

THEORETICAL PERSPECTIVE

THE LINK BETWEEN THE CIRCULAR FLOW MODEL AND ADAM SMITH'S VIEWS ON SELF-INTEREST, PUBLIC INTEREST, AND THE INVISIBLE HAND

In 1776, the Scottish moral philosopher and economist Adam Smith, in his *Wealth of Nations,* perhaps the most celebrated book ever written on economics, had this to say about why we end up having precisely the kinds of food we enjoy at our dinner table: "It is not from the benevolence of the butcher, the brewer, or the baker that we expect our dinner, but from their regard to their own self interest." That's a mighty statement! Smith assures us that there's no need to thank the butcher, the baker, nor anyone else who provides us with the goods we consume. These goods are provided only because producers hope to gain by providing them. Concern for your welfare? Don't be silly! But there's no reason to fret about self-centered motivation because working for their own self-interest works to your advantage. Smith explains: "Every individual generally neither intends to promote the public interest, nor knows how much he is promoting it. He intends only his own gain. And he is in this led by an **invisible hand** to promote an end, which was no part of his intention. By pursuing his own interest he frequently promotes that of society more effectually than when he really intends to promote it." In other words, greed can end up promoting munificence. The invisible hand Smith refers to is nothing more (or less) than the market. Anchored in consumer sovereignty, the product market guides producers to produce precisely those goods that consumers want and in this way transforms producers' private interest into our public interest.

How does invisible hand fit into the circular flow model? Unlike the ring on your finger that has no beginning or end, the circular flow of resources,

LOOK, IF THIS ISN'T FRESH, WOULD I SELL IT TO YOU AND RISK LOSING A GOOD CUSTOMER?

goods, and services begins somewhere. Its starting point is the household.

Why the household? Because that's where consumer sovereignty resides. What you choose to consume dictates what firms will ultimately produce. Feel the power? You really have it! If firms fail to produce precisely what you want, they simply won't be around very long. For example, if consumers want four-cylinder cars and General Motors ignores consumer preferences by manufacturing eight-cylinder cars, those eight-cylinder monsters will remain clogged in the product market of the circular flow model, never making it through the clockwise flow in Exhibit 1 from the product market to the households. And if those cars don't end up in households, the money that General Motors expects to receive from selling those cars—the counterclockwise flow of dollars from households to firms—never materializes.

But General Motors does produce four-cylinder cars precisely because your wishes are its command. For the same reason, other firms produce the tens of thousands of other goods and services we demand from the market daily. Firms produce these goods and services not to please us, but because they are interested in pleasing themselves. That is to say, we get the goods we want because firms pursue their own self-interest.

Even though no one actually tells firms in the circular flow model what to produce, the right goods get produced in the right quantities because firms keep their antennae fixed on the product market. That's where consumer sovereignty, originating in the households, is expressed.

Study the circular flow model again. You may not see it, but an invisible hand guides the firms to produce only those goods consumers want. This invisible hand is nothing more (or less) than the combination of consumer sovereignty and firms' self-interest operating on the product market.

unemployment? Why does it fluctuate from periods of economic prosperity to periods of economic recession?

Positive and Normative Economics

CHECK YOUR
UNDERSTANDING

What's the difference between positive and normative economics?

It is one thing for economists to explain why our economy grows at 2.6 percent per year and quite another to advocate that it ought to grow faster. It is one thing to explain why the price of corn is $2.10 per bushel and another to advocate that it ought to be higher. It is one thing to explain what happens when firms in certain industries merge and another to advocate that they ought to merge.

You see the differences, don't you? One is a statement of fact (the economy grows at 2.6 percent per year), while the other passes judgment (it ought to grow faster). Economists are typically very careful about differentiating between analysis of *what is* and *what ought to be.* These are not mutually exclusive, but they are different. Economists refer to *what is* analysis as **positive economics** and *what ought to be* analysis as **normative economics.**

Positive economics
A subset of economics that analyzes the way the economy actually operates.

Normative economics
A subset of economics founded on value judgments and leading to assertions of what ought to be.

There's nothing inherently wrong with advocacy, although these *oughts* are heavily laden with personal and social values. For example, should we have a minimum wage? Should we subsidize farmers? Should we protect our steel industry? Should we tax the rich more than the poor? Should we disallow mergers? Should we regulate bank loans? Should we monitor industrial pollution? Should we control population size?

These are serious economic issues. There is nothing improper about economists applying their own values to economic issues, as long as we know where their value judgments start and their economic analysis ends. It is sometimes difficult to separate the two. Economists, at times, unintentionally disguise advocacy in the language of positive economics. The simple cause-and-effect analysis of positive economics is sometimes taken one step further to advocate policy. For example, analyses of market structures are not always separated from the economists' general view that perfect competition is the most socially desirable market form. Most economists share that view, and some will even argue that their analysis of market structures leads inexorably to that view. Their *analysis* of markets may be positive economics, but their *judgment* that competitive markets are more desirable is normative.

WHAT DO ECONOMISTS KNOW?

Does it matter much what policies economists advocate? It matters very much. The White House, for example, has its own Council of Economic Advisers. Congress and the Federal Reserve System have their own cadres of economists. Many corporations, banks, and labor unions have economists on their payrolls. Economists are everywhere in the media, explaining and advising. Still, what do they know?

We listen attentively each morning to the weather forecast, although few of us fully trust what we hear. We know from experience that if the meteorologist predicts sunny skies, we take an umbrella along for insurance. Meteorologists seem to be forever explaining why yesterday's forecast turned out to be inaccurate. Sometimes we feel that they do not know much more about the weather than we do. But, in fact, they do.

The problem is not their forecast, but our reading of it. We expect too much. The forecast is sunny skies *if* the highs and lows behave properly. Remember ceteris paribus? The forecast depends on the fronts moving into our weather region as

The Council of Economic Advisers (http://www. whitehouse.gov/WH/EOP/ CEA/html/) and the Bank of America (http://www.bank ofamerica.com/) are two examples of organizations that hire economists to predict how the economy will behave.

expected. If they don't, all bets are off. How can meteorologists be held account-able for totally unpredictable changes?

In this respect, economic forecasting is similar to meteorological forecasting. Economic analysis is typically conditioned on the assumption of ceteris paribus, that is, that everything else remains unchanged, but it usually doesn't. The economists' world is one of uncertainty, and economists cannot take into account unforeseen future events that come to bear on their analyses. Explaining why previous economic forecasts were inaccurate doesn't build confidence. Instead, people think twice about whether economists really know more about the economy than anybody else. They do.

In the past fifty years, there has been a continuing, dramatic enrichment of our economic knowledge. New and more sophisticated models have been developed to represent our changing world. Also, the growth of economic data along with the ability to apply modern statistical methods to test models have created a branch of economics called **econometrics.** Econometricians are busy expanding these new and exciting areas of quantitative economic research.

In macroeconomics, for example, we now know more about what determines the levels of national income and employment than ever before. Knowing more doesn't necessarily resolve controversy, however. For example, there is no consensus among economists concerning the role government should play in our economy. Much of the debate is founded upon different readings of the same data.

In microeconomics, quantitative research on international trade, tax incidence, and market and investment behavior is adding more information to an already rich literature. New theories about uncertainty have given economists new insights into microeconomic questions.

Economists can rightfully claim to have covered an impressive intellectual distance in a very short period of time. Economists really do have something to say, but they realize that they must forever be on guard against claiming too much. As in medical research, the more we know, the more complex are the questions we can ask. Today, the task of the economist is no less difficult than fifty years ago, and the problems encountered no easier. The results of our economic research tell us just a little bit more about ourselves and are well worth the effort.

Econometrics
The use of statistics to quantify and test economic models.

Take a look at econometricians in practice. Visit the econometrics group at the University of Illinois (http://www.econ.uiuc.edu/) and the econometrics laboratory at the University of California, Berkeley (http://elsa.berkeley.edu/eml/).

CHAPTER REVIEW

1. Natural resources are gifts of nature. Our supplies of them are basically finite, fixed by what the earth makes available. Some natural resources are renewable, such as our forests and livestock. Others are nonrenewable, such as our supplies of copper and iron ore.

2. Our wants of goods and services seem to be unlimited and forever expanding. We are able to conjure up new wants just as readily as we have learned how to satisfy others.

3. The problem of economic scarcity is defined by these facts: Our natural resources are limited,

while our wants are unlimited. This universal scarcity forces us to make choices concerning which of our unlimited wants we will satisfy and which ones we will not.

4. Economics is the study of how we deal with scarcity. We define economics as the study of how we work together to transform resources into goods and services to satisfy our most pressing wants, and how we distribute these goods and services among ourselves.

5. Economics is an integral part of the social sciences discipline, which includes sociology,

political science, anthropology, and psychology. Each analyzes different aspects of individual and social behavior.

6. Economists use models to describe economic behavior. These models are abstractions of the real world, based on simplifying assumptions about that world, which allow us to focus on basic economic relationships in the model. By understanding cause-and-effect relationships in the model, economists believe they can better understand how the real world works.

7. Microeconomics explains economic relationships at the level of the individual consumer, firm, or industry, addressing such questions as what determines people's demand for goods,

why some prices increase while others decrease, and why some people earn higher incomes than others.

8. Macroeconomics considers the economic behavior of an entire economy, addressing such questions as what determines national economic growth and why unemployment and inflation occur.

9. Positive economic statements are statements of fact. For example, "When the price of popcorn increases, the quantity demanded of popcorn decreases." Normative economic statements are statements expressing value judgments. For example, "The price of popcorn is too high."

KEY TERMS

Natural resources
Scarcity
Economics
Consumer sovereignty
Economic model

Ceteris paribus
Circular flow model
Household
Firm
Invisible hand

Microeconomics
Macroeconomics
Positive economics
Normative economics
Econometrics

QUESTIONS

1. Does scarcity *always* require us to make choices? Why or why not?

2. Is the idea of insatiable wants unreasonable? Can you imagine a situation in which you have everything you want? What about everything you *need*?

3. What is the difference between renewable and nonrenewable resources?

4. Do you think we should be conserving our oil resources for future generations? After all, there is only so much oil on earth. List the main arguments you can make in favor of conservation. List arguments opposed to conservation.

5. What do you think would happen to our idea of the basic economic problem if we discovered a natural resource that could reproduce itself any number of times and could be transformed by labor into any good or service? Before answering, make sure you understand what the basic economic problem is.

6. What is economics? Why is economics considered one of the social sciences? What are some of the other social sciences? What do social scientists study?

7. What does *ceteris paribus* mean? Why is the concept useful to economists? Cite an example.

8. What defines an economic model? In what way is the circular flow model a simplification of reality? Why would economists want to simplify reality?

9. What is the difference between resource markets and product markets? Cite examples.

10. Consider these two statements: "Fifteen percent of our people live below the poverty line" and "Too many people live below the poverty line." Can you distinguish the positive economic statement from the normative economic statement? Compose two additional examples of each.

11. Suppose you look through the catalog of advanced economic courses and find two that particularly appeal to you: Economics 306, the study of the health care industry, and Economics 359, the study of why economies grow. Which would you take to satisfy the college's requirement for a microeconomics course?

12. Suppose your economics professor predicted that the rate of inflation would be 5 percent by the time you took the first economics exam. Instead, the inflation rate was twice the predicted rate. Would you categorically dismiss the professor as a poor predictor and, perhaps worse, an unknowledgeable economist? Why or why not?

13. Identify where each of the following belongs (upper or lower half, flowing in which direction) in the circular flow model in Exhibit 1: automobiles, automobile workers, your purchase of a new automobile, and a $100 rebate payment you receive from General Motors.

14. Consumer sovereignty is an integral part of a democratic society. Why?

PRACTICE PROBLEM

1. Construct a circular flow, and fill in the missing value.

CONSUMER SPENDING FOR GOODS AND SERVICES	$57
WAGES	
INTEREST	$ 6
RENT	$ 4
PROFIT	$ 7

ECONOMIC CONSULTANTS

ECONOMIC RESEARCH AND ANALYSIS BY STUDENTS FOR PROFESSIONALS

Computer Sell! is a retailer of computers and software. The owners of Computer Sell! are worried that they do not understand the economics of the computer industry or the economic events that affect this industry.

The owners of Computer Sell! have approached Economic Consultants for advice. Prepare a report for Computer Sell! that addresses the following issues:

1. In general, what resources are available?
2. What sources of economic news and analysis, if any, are available for the national economy? For the regional economy where you currently are?
3. What economic resources for the computer industry, if any, are available on the Internet?

You may find the following resources helpful as you prepare this report for Computer Sell!:

- **Yahoo!** (http://www.yahoo.com), **Excite** (http://www.excite.com/), and **Lycos** (http://www.lycos.com/)—These popular search engines and directories enable you to get a quick grasp of what is available on the Internet for certain topics, such as economics.
- **Resources for Economists on the Internet** (http://rfe.wustl.edu/EconFAQ.html) and **WebEc** (http://www.helsinki.fi/WebEc/WebEc.html)—Resources for Economists and WebEc are directories that focus exclusively on economic materials on the Internet.
- **ZDNet** (http://www.zdnet.com/) and **News.Com** (http://www.news.com/)—ZDNet and News.Com, sponsored by CNET, provide news coverage of the technology industry.

PRACTICE TEST

1. Which of the following is not microeconomic subject matter?
   a. The price of bananas
   b. The quantity of bananas produced for the banana market
   c. The cost of producing a fire truck for the fire department of Cincinnati
   d. The cost of producing a fire truck for the fire department of London, England
   e. The national economy's annual rate of growth

2. JULIE: My corn harvest this year is very poor.
   DANA: Don't worry. Price increases will compensate for the fall in quantity supplied.
   KIM: Climate affects crop yields. Some years are good, others are bad.
   LISA: The government ought to guarantee that our incomes will not fall.
   In this conversation, the normative statement is made by
   a. Julie.
   b. Dana.
   c. Kim.
   d. Lisa.
   e. There are no normative statements.

3. Consider the following and decide which, if any, economy is without scarcity.
   a. The pre–Civil War U.S. economy, where most people were farmers
   b. A mythical economy where everyone is a billionaire
   c. Any economy where there is full employment of resources
   d. Any economy where income is distributed equally among its people
   e. None of the above

4. In our economy, people have the freedom to buy or not buy the goods offered in the marketplace, and this freedom to choose what they want to buy dictates what producers will ultimately produce. The key term defining this condition is
   a. economic power of choice.
   b. consumer sovereignty.
   c. ultimate producer sovereignty.
   d. political economy.
   e. positive economics.

5. Economic models
   a. are designed to explain all aspects of the economy.
   b. never employ assumptions that cannot be tested.
   c. abstract from reality to reduce the complexity of the world we live in to more simplified, manageable dimensions.
   d. provide detailed statistical analysis of the economy.
   e. are more useful in macroeconomic applications than in microeconomic ones.

6. In the circular flow model,
   a. households supply resources to firms through the resource market.
   b. households buy goods and services in the product market.
   c. money flows from firms to households through the resource market.
   d. All of the above
   e. None of the above

7. Apply the idea of a nonrenewable resource to best describe one of the following as nonrenewable:
   a. Eggs used in baking a cake
   b. Corn used to feed hogs
   c. Copper tubing used in residential construction
   d. Hot water used in commercial laundries
   e. Lumber used in industrial construction

8. Which of the following is not one of the four central questions that the study of economics is supposed to answer?
   a. Who produces what?
   b. How are goods produced?
   c. Who consumes what?
   d. When are goods produced?
   e. Who decides what goods to produce?

9. Ceteris paribus is a tool used by economists to
   a. develop one-to-one, cause-and-effect economic relationships.
   b. link resources to goods and services.
   c. promote consumer sovereignty.
   d. distinguish microeconomics from macroeconomics.
   e. perform modern statistical testing of economic data.

10. Econometrics
    a. links positive to normative economics.
    b. applies modern statistical methods to test models.
    c. is an appropriate use of economic models.
    d. is real-world economics as distinguished from economic models.
    e. is the use of ceteris paribus in real-world situations.

APPENDIX

ON READING GRAPHS

THE ONLY THING WE HAVE TO FEAR IS FEAR ITSELF

It's happened a zillion times: Students buy their economics textbooks, flip through the pages, spot the dozens of equations and graphs, and fear, before they start, that it's going to be a losing battle. But it hardly ever is, and certainly not because of the graphs or mathematics. There simply isn't enough information in those graphs or equations to confuse or exasperate.

If you can shake the trauma of the graphic and mathematical form of expression, you will do just fine. As President Franklin D. Roosevelt said during his 1933 inaugural speech, "The only thing we have to fear is fear itself!"

A Graphic Language

Graphs and mathematics are simplified languages. Most of what appears in graphics or mathematics can be described in written form—in fact, most ideas are best expressed that way. In *some* circumstances, however, the written exposition becomes so convoluted that graphs and equations can present the idea more clearly.

Suppose, for example, that the simple arithmetic statement

$$(4)(6) + (8/2) - 12 = 16$$

were written as 12 subtracted from the product of 4 multiplied by 6 plus the quotient of 8 divided by 2 equals 16. You lose track of the calculations, don't you? The equation form is easier to read. Graphs are like that, too. They are pictorial representations of ideas that could be expressed otherwise, but not with the same degree of clarity.

Know Your Point of Reference

When you read a map, you typically measure out where you want to go from where you are. The where-you-are position is always your point of reference, putting everything else in place.

If you're sitting in St. Louis, Missouri, then Kansas City, Kansas, is 257 miles due west. If you're searching for Louisville, Kentucky, it's 256 miles due east. Kansas City and Louisville are west and east only because you're looking at them from St. Louis. People in Tallahassee, Florida, see Atlanta as due north, but viewed from St. Louis, Atlanta is southeast. In map reading, everything is measured from a point of reference.

Graphs are read the same way. If you can read a map, you can read a graph. Look at Exhibit A1.

The graph's point of reference is called the **origin.** Using our map example, the origin is the graph's St. Louis. Everything on the graph is measured from it. Points can be viewed as lying to the east of the origin, or to the west, or north, or south. More

Origin
A graph's point of reference.

THE FOUR QUADRANTS

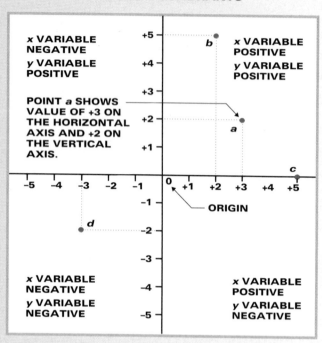

x VARIABLE NEGATIVE

y VARIABLE POSITIVE

POINT *a* SHOWS VALUE OF +3 ON THE HORIZONTAL AXIS AND +2 ON THE VERTICAL AXIS.

x VARIABLE POSITIVE

y VARIABLE POSITIVE

ORIGIN

x VARIABLE NEGATIVE

y VARIABLE NEGATIVE

x VARIABLE POSITIVE

y VARIABLE NEGATIVE

precise readings describe the points as "north by northwest" or "east by southeast." You can see them in your mind's eye.

Note that Exhibit A1 is divided into four quadrants (or parts). The vertical (*y*) axis—running north and south through the origin—and the horizontal (*x*) axis—running east and west through the origin—are its dividers.

Measuring Distances on Graphs

Have you ever seen a NASA space shot countdown? As you know, its point of reference is blastoff. Typically, NASA starts counting before ignition. If you're watching on TV, you'll see the digital readout register -10 seconds, then -9, then -8, counting down to 0. At 0, ignition occurs and the count continues from 0 to $+1$ seconds, then $+2$, and so on. The time scale is a continuum, with 0 separating the minuses from the pluses.

Graph scaling is also on a continuum. In Exhibit A1, the vertical scale north of the origin (which is 0) and the horizontal scale east of the origin (which is 0) measure positive values. For example, point *a,* located at $(+3, +2)$, reads $+3$ units away from the origin horizontally and $+2$ units away from the origin vertically. It marks the intersection of +3 and +2. Point *b,* located at $(+2, +5)$, reads $+2$ units away from the origin horizontally and $+5$ units away from the origin vertically. Look at point *c* $(+5, 0)$. It is $+5$ units away from the origin horizontally and at 0 on the vertical scale.

The vertical scale south of the origin and the horizontal scale west of the origin measure negative values. For example, point *d,* located at $(-3, -2)$, reads -3 units away from 0 horizontally and -2 units away from the origin vertically. As you see, every point in every quadrant has its own specific numerical bearings.

Graphing Relationships

It's generally true that the more you study, the higher your grade. Suppose somebody who is less convinced than you about the relationship between effort and reward insists on evidence. What can you do to make the point? If logic doesn't work, perhaps a test will. For example, you could experiment with Economics 101 and over the course of the semester, compare your exam scores with the number of hours spent studying for them.

The underlying assumption in such a relationship is that exam scores *depend* on the number of hours of study. By varying the hours studied, you vary the scores obtained. Hours studied is described as the **independent variable** in the relationship, exam scores as the **dependent variable.**

Typically, economists work with relationships that express dependence. For example, the quantity of fish people are willing to buy depends on the price of fish. The price of fish is the independent variable, and the quantity people are willing to buy is the dependent one. The amount of money people spend consuming goods and services depends on their income—again a link between a dependent variable and an independent one. Another such dependent relationship is the number of hours people are willing to work and the wage rate offered.

Suppose you find that with 0 hours of study, you fail miserably, scoring 20 out of a possible 100. With 2 hours per week of study, you score 50. With 5 hours per week, you raise your grade to 70. With 7 hours per week, your grade improves to 80. With 10 hours per week, you top the class with the highest score, 85.

If you experimented with Biology 101 exams, the effort-and-reward relationship would still be positive, but the specific payoffs might be different. For example, with 0 hours, you still fail, this time scoring only 12 out of a possible 100. With 2 hours per week, you score only 35. With 5 hours, you get considerably better, scoring 55; with 7 hours, you score 70; and with 10 hours a week studying biology, you score 75.

That's convincing evidence that increased hours of study produce higher grades, but the written presentation can get confusing, particularly when the number of exams and courses increases. The written form is not always the clearest way to express observations.

Perhaps a clearer presentation of the evidence could be made by converting the information into table form. Look, for example, at the table in Exhibit A2.

Is it any clearer? The information is the same; it's just displayed differently. It is easier to see that the more time spent on study, the higher the score, and comparisons between economics and biology are more readily observed.

Look how the same information is transcribed into graphic form. Exhibit A2, panel *a*, records the same information as the table.

As you see, in panel *a*, hours of study are measured along the horizontal axis. Exam scores are measured along the vertical axis. Both variables in our example are positive. Therefore, the corresponding points in the table—such as 5 hours of study and an exam score of 70 in economics—locate in the upper-right quadrant of the graph. Both graphs in Exhibit A2 show that quadrant.

Connecting Points to Form Curves

The table and graphs in panel *a*, Exhibit A2, are abbreviated

Independent variable
A variable whose value influences the value of another variable.

Dependent variable
A variable whose value depends on the value of another variable.

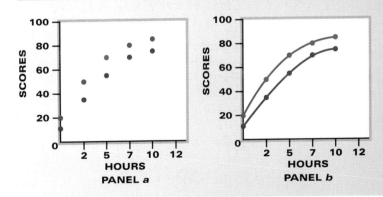

TEST SCORES FOR ECONOMICS 101 AND BIOLOGY 101

NUMBER OF HOURS SPENT STUDYING AND TEST SCORES FOR ECONOMICS 101 AND BIOLOGY 101

HOURS	ECONOMICS 101 SCORES	BIOLOGY 101 SCORES
0	20	12
2	50	35
5	70	55
7	80	70
10	85	75

displays of evidence. They record only ten pieces of data. The experiment could have been expanded to record an exam score for every hour of study, or even every minute instead of every five hours. That is, if the intervals between the points in panel *a* could be filled in to create a *continuous* series of data points connecting study hours and exam scores (unrealistic, of course, because nobody could take that many exams in one semester), such a completed series would trace a continuous curve on the graph, which is what we see in panel *b*.

But is it necessary to ascertain every point to create a curve? Suppose you want to graph the relationship between income and saving. And suppose the table accompanying Exhibit A3 presents the relevant data.

Note that the data set starts with $40,000 of income. If the graph were to plot *every* income value from $0 at the origin to, say, $43,000 in units of $1,000, 43 units would be marked off on the horizontal axis, but only the last 4 of the 43 units would bear any data. The graph becomes dominated then by empty, dataless space. And to keep the graph within the bounds of the page, it may even be necessary to make each income unit represent $2,000. By doing so, it becomes even more difficult to read on the vertical axis the increases in saving that are associated with the $1,000 increases in income.

Breaking the axes—as shown in Exhibit A3—cuts out the empty, dataless space. The break, introduced after the first units on both the vertical and horizontal axes, allows the graphmaker to magnify the data, making it easier for the reader to focus on the relevant part of the graph. The 40th unit of income follows the break on the horizontal axis, and the 80th unit of saving—each unit representing $1,000 of saving—follows the first unit on the vertical axis. The resulting graph maps out a clear picture of the saving curve.

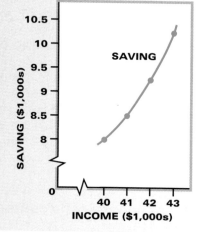

INCOME AND SAVING

INCOME	SAVING
$40,000	$ 8,000
41,000	8,500
42,000	9,250
43,000	10,250

THE SLOPE OF A CURVE

Consider the law of demand: As the price of a good falls, the quantity of the good demanded increases. The table and graph in panel *a*, Exhibit A4, depict such a relationship between the price of fish and quantity demanded. (The law of demand will be studied more closely in Chapter 3.)

Panel *a*, Exhibit A4, connects the discrete data given in the accompanying table to form a solid curve that, as you see, is in the form of a straight line.

The **slope of a curve** measures the ratio of change in the value on the vertical axis to the corresponding change in value on the horizontal axis between two points:

Slope of a curve
The ratio of the change in the variable measured on the vertical axis to the corresponding change in the variable measured on the horizontal axis, between two points.

$$\text{slope} = \frac{\text{rise}}{\text{run}} = \frac{\text{change in the value on vertical axis}}{\text{change in the value on horizontal axis}}$$

Downward-sloping curves—sloping from northwest to southeast—are considered *negatively sloped;* that is, a positive (negative) change in the independent variable is associated with a negative (positive) change in the dependent variable. Upward-sloping curves—sloping from southwest to northeast—are *positively sloped;* that is, a positive (negative) change in the independent variable is associated with a positive (negative) change in the dependent variable.

Look again at Exhibit A4, panel *a.* Every $1 change in price generates a 1-unit change in quantity demanded. For example, when price falls from $10 to $9 (−$1), the quantity demanded increases from 1 to 2 fish (+1). The slope of the curve, within the $10 to $9 price range, then, is

$$-1/+1 = -1$$

The slope is negative. Note that any other price change within any other price range in this example still generates a negative slope of −1. When price increases from $3 to $4 (+$1), the quantity demanded decreases from 7 fish to 6 (−1). The slope +1/−1 remains −1. *Any curve with a constant slope is a straight line.* That's precisely what we see in panel *a.*

Panel *b* represents a typical supply curve. It depicts the willingness of the fishing industry to supply varying quantities of fish at varying prices. The curve slopes upward, indicating that higher prices induce greater quantities supplied. Unlike the demand curve in panel *a,* the supply curve here is not a straight line. It is less steep at low price ranges than at higher ones. Let's calculate the slopes within different price ranges. When price increases from $2 to $3 (+$1), the quantity supplied increases from 3 to 5 fish (+2). The slope of the curve, within the $2 to $3 price range, then, is

$$+1/+2 = +0.5$$

But when the price rises from $3 to $4 (+$1), the quantity supplied increases only from 5 fish to 6 (+1). The slope of the curve within the $3 to $4 price range is

$$+1/+1 = +1$$

There's nothing peculiar or complicated about any curve on any graph or the measurement of its slope. The slope of the curve is only a

PRICE AND QUANTITIES DEMANDED AND SUPPLIED OF FISH

PRICE AND QUANTITY DEMANDED OF FISH

PRICE	QUANTITY DEMANDED
10	1
9	2
8	3
7	4
6	5
5	6
4	7
3	8
2	9
1	10

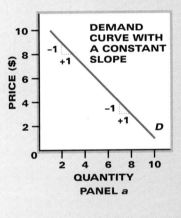

PANEL *a*

PRICE AND QUANTITY SUPPLIED OF FISH

PRICE	QUANTITY SUPPLIED
5	6.5
4	6
3	5
2	3
1	0

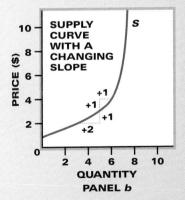

PANEL *b*

numerical way of expressing the curve's shape. The numerical value signals the strength of the relationship between changes in the variables measured on the vertical and horizontal axes.

U-Shaped and Hill-Shaped Curves

Some curves that are part of the economists' bag of tools contain both positive- and negative-sloping segments. Look, for example, at Exhibit A5, panels *a* and *b*.

The U-shaped curve in panel *a* shows the relationship between the average cost of producing a good and the quantity of goods produced. Typically, the average cost falls as more units are produced—that's the downward-sloping part of the curve. Beyond some point, however—100 units in panel *a*—average cost begins to increase with production, which is the upward-sloping part of the curve.

From 0 to 100 units, the slope of the curve, although changing, is always negative. Beyond 100 units, it becomes positive. There's nothing complicated about reading the graph if you consider each point on the curve, one at a time. *Every point on that U-shaped average cost curve represents a specific quantitative relationship between average cost and level of production.* Nothing more!

The hill-shaped curve in panel *b* is much the same. It shows the relationship between the total utility or benefit derived from consuming a good and the quantity of goods consumed. The basic idea is that for some goods—water, for instance—the more consumed, the greater the total enjoyment, but only up to a point. Beyond that point—100 units in panel *b*—the more water, the lower the total enjoyment. Who, for example, enjoys a flood? From 0 to 100 units, the slope of this curve is positive, but it becomes negative thereafter.

Vertical and Horizontal Curves

Economists also work with relationships that, when graphed, trace out as perfectly vertical or horizontal curves. These are represented in Exhibit A6, panels *a* and *b*.

Consider the circumstance where a fisherman returns home after a day's work with 100 fish. Suppose he is willing to supply those fish at whatever price the fish will fetch. After all, a day-old fish isn't something to prize. If the price is $10 per fish, he is willing to sell all 100. If the price is only $9, he is still willing to sell all of them. If the price is $100 per fish, he *still* will supply only 100 fish, because the day's work is done and there are no more fish available. The supply curve, shown in panel *a*, is a vertical line to denote a supply of 100 fish, whatever the price. Its slope is everywhere infinite. That is, when price changes from $10 to $9 (−$1), quantity doesn't change (0). The slope, then, is −1/0. That's infinity.

What about the perfectly horizontal curve? Suppose you are selling tomatoes in an outdoor market, competing against hundreds of other tomato growers. Suppose also that the price is $0.50 per

COST AND UTILITY CURVES

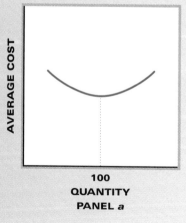

PANEL *a*

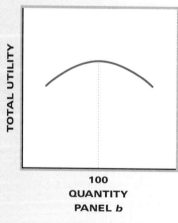

PANEL *b*

pound, and you can sell as much as you want at that price. If you were to raise your price by just one penny, or even less, you couldn't sell any tomatoes at all. What a difference a fraction of a penny makes! After all, why would anyone buy your tomatoes when they can buy all they want from your competitors at $0.50?

How would you graph the demand curve you face? It would be a straight horizontal curve, as shown in panel *b*. At $0.50 you could sell 10, 20, or 200 tomatoes. At just an infinitesimally small increase—approaching 0—in price, you sell 0 tomatoes. The slope, then, is 0 divided by any number, which is 0.

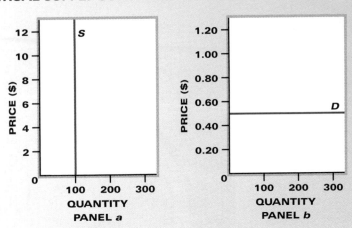

VERTICAL SUPPLY CURVE AND HORIZONTAL DEMAND CURVE

Measuring the Slope of a Point on a Curve

Look at the U-shaped curve of Exhibit A7.

To find the slope of any point on the curve, draw a **tangent**—a straight line just touching the curve—at the point where the slope is to be measured. The **slope of the tangent** is the same as the slope of the curve at the point of tangency. What is the slope of the tangent? Look at tangent *td* at point *a* on the curve. Its slope is *ac/cd*, or numerically,

$$-10/+15 = -2/3$$

Tangent
A straight line that touches a curve at only one point.

Slope of a tangent
The slope of a curve at its point of tangency.

The minus sign indicates that the point of tangency lies on the downward-sloping part of the curve.

What about the slope at point *b*? Draw the tangent, *et'*. Its slope is *bf/ef*, or numerically,

$$+10/+20 = +1/2$$

Its positive value indicates it is on the upward-sloping part of the U-shaped curve.

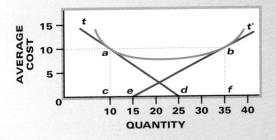

MEASURING THE SLOPE AT A POINT ON A CURVE

KEY TERMS

Origin
Independent variable

Dependent variable
Slope of a curve

Tangent
Slope of a tangent

EXHIBIT A6

EXHIBIT A7

2

PRODUCTION POSSIBILITIES AND OPPORTUNITY COSTS

Biologists talk about their field of study without worrying whether people will misunderstand the words they use. A monocotyledon is a monocotyledon— no one ever mistakes it for a screwdriver. Biologists have a language all their own.

Economists, too, have developed their own language, but the vocabulary they choose is rather commonplace. When economists talk about labor, most people feel right at home. People also know what capital, rent, profit, prices, competition, monopoly, money, income, and employment mean.

Unfortunately, what people understand these terms to mean is not always what economists understand them to mean. To understand how economists use these terms may sometimes require more effort to unlearn what we already know than to learn what the economists mean.

THIS CHAPTER INTRODUCES YOU TO THE ECONOMIC PRINCIPLES ASSOCIATED WITH:

- FACTORS OF PRODUCTION
- PRODUCTION POSSIBILITIES
- OPPORTUNITY COST
- THE LAW OF INCREASING COSTS
- TECHNOLOGICAL CHANGE AND ECONOMIC GROWTH
- DIVISION OF LABOR AND SPECIALIZATION
- ABSOLUTE AND COMPARATIVE ADVANTAGE

FACTORS OF PRODUCTION

Economists refer to the resources used in the production of goods and services as **factors of production.** The four factors are labor, capital, land, entrepreneurship.

The two human factors are labor and entrepreneurship. The other two, capital and land, are nonhuman factors.

Labor

Labor is the physical and mental exertion of people engaged in the production of goods and services. Labor willingly sells its skills in the resource market for agreed-upon prices. There is no coercion involved, and the agreements or contracts typically specify price per hour, per week, or per year.

The absence of coercion and the limitations specified in the contract are critical characteristics of the economists' definition of labor. No one sells his or her labor to a firm forever. To economists, slave labor is not regarded as a labor resource at all, since slaves never willingly offer their labor for a price. Bought and sold on slave markets, they are forced to work. Incredible as it may seem, slaves were regarded by slaveowners and the courts as personal property. What about prison labor today? Do inmates willingly offer their services? Who decides the price? If it's not labor, then what is it? You can see that the economists' concept of labor is narrowly defined and can be somewhat more complicated than first imagined. What about peasants who are harnessed to crude, wooden plows in Third World economies? In these economies people and animals are sometimes interchangeable, pulling plows across tough topsoils. Certainly a water buffalo isn't labor. What, then, is the peasant who substitutes for the water buffalo?

Capital

What identifies **capital?** Capital is a manufactured good used in the production and marketing of goods and services that households consume. Because capital is not directly consumed by households, it is sometimes referred to as an intermediate good. For example, shoemakers' tools and machinery used to produce shoes are not household items. The shoes, of course, are. The stocks of shoe inventory are capital goods. The shoes in inventory become household consumption goods only when they are actually consumed by the household. Obviously, the factory that houses the machinery and inventories is a capital good.

What about robots? Robots that do what labor does are still only pieces of machinery. Store window mannequins are also capital goods because they are used to convert the finished goods inventory into household consumption. In the same way, the thousands of compact discs in record shop inventories are regarded as capital goods because the inventories are as necessary as the disc-making machinery in providing CDs for household consumption. How could you buy a particular CD if the store didn't carry it? It becomes a consumption good only when it is purchased by the consumer.

What about Michael Chang's tennis racket? It is a capital good used to produce a service. The service is our enjoyment at Wimbledon. That same racket in your hand is not capital. After all, it is used only for your own pleasure. David Letterman's stylish wardrobe is a capital good. Yours isn't.

Can you think of other goods that would be capital to one person, but not to another? Go to the Interactive Study Center at http://gottheil. swcollege.com and click on the "Your Turn" button to submit your example. Student submissions will be posted to the Web site, and perhaps we will use some in future additions of the book!

Factor of production
Any resource used in a production process. Resources are grouped into labor, land, capital, and entrepreneurship.

Labor
The physical and intellectual effort of people engaged in producing goods and services.

Capital
Manufactured goods used to make and market other goods and services.

Sometimes, capital gets mixed in with labor, so we end up with a hybrid factor. For instance, would Linda Marshall, working as a chemical engineer for Dow Chemical, be considered labor? Perhaps the most significant difference between Linda's work and the work of an unskilled laborer is her four years of college education. That education is capital. What then is the engineer, capital or labor? Economists refer to special skills, acquired through education or training, as **human capital.**

As you see, what is obvious to some people is less than obvious to economists. Is intelligence capital? If so, what's left of labor? Confusing? As you may already sense, differentiations between labor and capital as factors of production are as much philosophical issues as they are economic.

Land

Land is a natural-state, nonhuman resource that is fixed in quantity. It includes both the real estate and the metals and minerals it contains. For example, an uncut diamond is land. A virgin forest is land. The oceans of oil underneath the North Sea are also land. To the economist, the Gobi Desert and the Pacific Ocean are land resources.

The problem with the economists' definition of land as a factor of production is that we seldom, if ever, see land in its natural state. A tree that is cut and used in production is no longer strictly a land resource. It becomes capital as well. It was cut down by labor and machines. Lumber, then, is a manufactured good. Irrigated land, too, is not strictly land. The irrigation system is capital. Any improved land is a combination of capital and land.

Entrepreneurship

No good or service is produced by spontaneous combustion. Resources just don't come together on their own. *Somebody* has to conceive of the essential idea of production, decide what factors to use, market the goods and services produced, and accept the uncertainty of making or losing money in the venture. This somebody is the *entrepreneur,* a word that comes from the French, "to undertake." Although **entrepreneurs** who own and operate businesses typically do all these things, economists define their entrepreneurial role only in terms of the uncertainties of business they assume.

After all, entrepreneurs can delegate the buying of land, labor, and capital and the overseeing of production to a hired managerial staff. That's precisely what most modern corporations do. Managerial activity is labor. When entrepreneurs manage the production process, they function as laborers. Entrepreneurs can delegate every other function of production to labor, except the function of assuming risk and uncertainty.

We have briefly surveyed the four factors of production. Now let's put them to work.

ROBINSON CRUSOE'S PRODUCTION POSSIBILITIES

Let's begin our analysis of production by imagining Robinson Crusoe, stranded and alone on an island. The resources at his disposal, while attractive, are limited. And being a person very much like you, he has unlimited wants. In other words, Crusoe, like all of us, faces the unshakable reality of economic scarcity. What can he do in this situation? Let's look at his options.

Human capital
The knowledge and skills acquired by labor, principally through education and training.

Land
A natural-state resource such as real estate, grasses and forests, and metals and minerals.

Entrepreneur
A person who alone assumes the risks and uncertainties of a business.

He can spend part of the day in leisure and part at work. He could pick mangoes right off the trees, or he can fish. He can plant and harvest crops. His principal factors of production are his own labor and the virgin land about him.

Let's suppose he decides to spend his waking hours gathering food for consumption. He climbs trees for mangoes and coconuts and spends the better part of the day trying to pick fish out of the lagoon. He ends each day with six units of consumption. It's enough to keep him going, but, of course, he wants more. How does he get it? Let's suppose he decides to make a fishing spear. That requires finding the right materials and fashioning a spear. He sets aside part of the day to find a young tree that will serve as the shank, a stone that can be sharpened to make a spearhead, and a length of vine to bind the two together.

This takes time. If he takes the time to produce the spear, he can gather only five units of consumption goods. Why then do it? Because with a fishing spear, he expects to catch more fish in the next round of production. It's a risk, of course. There's no guarantee he will catch more fish. Some expectations are never realized. But let's suppose he catches more. The spear is Robinson Crusoe's first unit of capital.

He decides to make a second spear as well to use as an extension tool so that he can reach the bigger, riper fruit at the top of the trees. He discovers that finding the right material for the second spear takes even more time than it did for the first. Why? He had already used the most available tree for the fishing spear's shank, the most available stone for the spearhead, and the most accessible length of vine to tie them together.

While he is producing both the fishing spear and the extension spear, he can manage to gather only three units of consumption goods. Why then do it? Because with both units of capital, he expects to produce considerably more consumption goods in the next round of production.

The Robinson Crusoe economy is simple, yet it contains all the elements of a modern, dynamic economy. It has capital goods production as well as consumption. Land, labor, capital, and entrepreneurship combine to create a set of goods and services.

The components of the set are variable. For example, these factors of production can be combined into any of the **production possibilities** shown in the table in Exhibit 1.

The first possibility is for Robinson Crusoe to allocate all his resources to producing consumption goods. If he does that, he ends up with six units of consumption. On the other hand, if he decides to produce a unit of capital, he ends up with only five units of consumption. As far as he's concerned, then, the unit of capital cost him one unit of consumption.

Opportunity Cost

What economists mean by cost is **opportunity cost**—that is, the quantity of other goods that must be given up to obtain a good. That's a powerful notion of cost. It applies universally. For example, the opportunity cost of watching the L.A. Lakers play the Boston Celtics the night before an exam is the five points that could have earned an A. The opportunity cost of renovating the high school auditorium is the new biology lab that the school had been thinking about. Opportunity cost applies even where you may least suspect. For example, for a married couple, the opportunity cost of marriage to each partner is the opportunities each gives up that would have been possible had they remained single.

CHECK YOUR UNDERSTANDING

Why do people produce capital goods?

Production possibilities
The various combinations of goods that can be produced in an economy when it uses its available resources and technology efficiently.

Opportunity cost
The quantity of other goods that must be given up to obtain a good.

EXHIBIT | 1

Robinson Crusoe's economy can produce six consumption goods and zero capital goods, shown at point *a*. Alternatively, it can produce five consumption goods and one capital good (point *b*) three consumption goods and two capital goods (point *c*) zero consumption goods and three capital goods (point *d*) or any other combination located on this curve. The law of increasing costs accounts for the balloon-like shape of the production possibilities curve.

PRODUCTION POSSIBILITIES FRONTIER

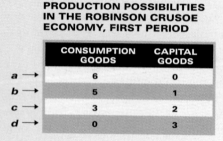

PRODUCTION POSSIBILITIES IN THE ROBINSON CRUSOE ECONOMY, FIRST PERIOD

	CONSUMPTION GOODS	CAPITAL GOODS
a →	6	0
b →	5	1
c →	3	2
d →	0	3

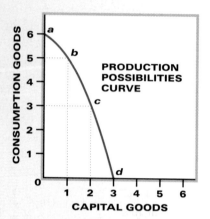

PRODUCTION POSSIBILITIES CURVE

You see the connection, don't you? The thought that goes through Crusoe's mind when contemplating production is the same kind of thinking that you do before studying for an exam. You both think about the opportunities given up. But you make choices. When Crusoe gives up a unit of consumption goods to produce that first unit of capital goods, it's probably because he values that first unit of capital goods more than the consumption good given up. If you spend the evening studying for the exam, it's probably because you value the expected higher grade more than you do the Celtics game.

You may have erred. The game was the season's best and the studying didn't make a difference in your exam score. In hindsight, you find that the studying wasn't worth the cost. But what could you have done otherwise? Opportunity costs are typically subjective. How could you possibly know with certainty what opportunity costs are? Even Robinson Crusoe, making simple choices on the island, must rely on calculating *expected* gains and opportunity costs of choices made.

The Law of Increasing Costs

If Robinson Crusoe decides to produce two units of capital, he ends up with only three units of consumption. Measured in terms of its opportunity cost, that second unit of capital costs Crusoe two units of consumption. That is more than he had to give up for the first unit of capital.

What happens if he decides to produce three units of capital? Look again at the table in Exhibit 1. Their production absorbs all the resources available. He ends up with nothing at all to consume! The opportunity cost of that third unit of capital is the remaining three units of consumption.

Law of increasing costs
The opportunity cost of producing a good increases as more of the good is produced. The law is based on the fact that not all resources are suited to the production of all goods and that the order of use of a resource in producing a good goes from the most productive resource unit to the least.

Do you notice what's happening? The opportunity cost of producing each additional unit of capital increases as more of the units are produced. Economists refer to this fact of economic life as the **law of increasing costs.** It applies no matter what goods are considered. For example, if Robinson Crusoe had started with three units of capital and began adding consumption, the amount of capital goods he

APPLIED PERSPECTIVE

DID YOU EVER FIND A PENNY ON A SIDEWALK?

How many times, strolling along a sidewalk, have you chanced upon a shiny new penny lying in your path? Picking it up is supposed to bring you good luck. But luck aside; it's fun to find it, isn't it? But what about nickels, dimes, and quarters, not to mention Susan B. Anthony dollar coins? When was the last time you saw one of those shiny silver coins lying on the sidewalk? If you're like most people, these silver coins are pretty scarce items on a sidewalk, at least compared to the copper coins we find.

Why? Is it because the supply of pennies is more plentiful than the supply of nickels, dimes, and quarters? It is more plentiful. The U.S. Mint produces about 10 billion pennies a year compared to the approximately 6 billion nickels, dimes, and quarters. But that really doesn't explain why we are more likely to see pennies on the sidewalk than silver coins.

SOME COINS YES, SOME COINS NO.

The answer has to do with opportunity cost. If you're walking home and spot a Susan B. Anthony dollar on the sidewalk, wouldn't you pick it up? You probably wouldn't turn your nose up at a quarter either. Even a dime or nickel is for many people worth the effort of bending down and picking up. A penny? Considerably less so.

The reason why you find so many pennies on the sidewalk relative to silver coins is because it takes time and energy to stop, bend down, and pick them up, and that time and energy are valued more than a penny. That's why pennies on the sidewalk are not an uncommon sight. We simply pass them up. The opportunity cost associated with picking them up is too high. The quarter? Most people place a higher value on a quarter they find than on the time and energy it takes to pick up, which explains why you find so few quarters on the street. They are quickly gobbled up. It's all a matter of opportunity cost.

would have to give up to produce each additional unit of consumption would also increase. The graph in Exhibit 1 illustrates the production possibilities of the table in graphic form.

Look at points *a, b, c,* and *d* in Exhibit 1. These are precisely the production possibilities shown in the table. Point *a*, for example, represents the choice of devoting all resources to the production of six units of consumption. The curve has a negative slope because any increase in capital goods production comes only at the cost of consumption goods production.

The bowed-out shape to the curve illustrates the law of increasing costs. When Crusoe decides to increase capital goods production from one unit to two, he is forced to use resources less suited to the production of capital goods than the

THEORETICAL PERSPECTIVE

GUNS AND BUTTER

Suppose Robinson Crusoe discovers that he is not alone on the island and that his new neighbors are somewhat less than friendly. Suppose they are downright threatening. It would be fool-hardy for Crusoe to continue producing only consumption and capital goods. After all, he may wake up one morning to find his uninvited neighbors helping themselves to his consumption and capital goods!

To protect life and property, Robinson Crusoe may have to devote some part of his working day to the production of defensive weapons. Instead of making a fishing spear, he may make several bows and arrows. Or, perhaps, remembering what the Chinese did, he might build a Great Wall to keep his neighbors out. But Robinson Crusoe knows that every bow, every arrow, and every stone in every defensive wall has an opportunity cost that reflects the quantity of nondefensive goods given up.

Crusoe's guns-versus-butter choices are the same kinds of choices every society has been forced to make from time immemorial. If an economy is operating on its production possibilities frontier, then guns can be produced only at the expense of butter. More guns means less butter.

What are choices in the Robinson Crusoe tale are also real choices for Americans. Dwight D. Eisenhower, the 34th U.S. president, was a five-star general during World War II and also the supreme commander of the Allied forces in Europe. The

THAT'S AN AWFUL LOT OF STEEL AND AN AWFUL LOT OF PEOPLE THAT COULD BE PUT TO OTHER USES.

1944 invasion of Nazi-occupied Europe under his command and the battles that followed led to Germany's unconditional surrender. But victory is always bittersweet. No one has expressed the costs of war better than President Eisenhower himself:

> Every gun that is made, every warship launched, every rocket fired signifies, in the final sense, a theft from those who hunger and are not fed, those who are cold and are not clothed. This world in arms is not spending money alone. It is spending the sweat of its laborers, the genius of its scientists, the hopes of its children. . . . This is not a way of life at all in any true sense. Under the cloud of threatening war, it is humanity hanging from a cross of iron. (Speech before the American Society of Newspaper Editors, April 16, 1953.)

CONSIDER

Can you imagine a situation in which two people, both agreeing on the opportunity costs of war preparedness, would disagree on whether to pursue a policy of preparedness? What other issues do you think they would consider? Do you think nations go to war—or stay out of war—strictly on the basis of economic calculation?

MORE ON THE NET

Visit a few pacifist organizations, such as the American Peace Network (http://www.apn.org/) and the Center for Economic Conversion (http://www.conversion.org/). What arguments do these organizations make for decreasing the size of the military? Do these arguments take into account the concept of opportunity cost?

resources employed in producing the first unit. After all, resources are not always of equal quality, and he obviously would use the best first. The result is a movement along the curve from point *b* to point *c* that, when plotted in Exhibit 1, traces out the bowing character of the curve. Suppose Crusoe decides on three units of consumption and two units of capital. He works busily, finishes production, eats the three consumption goods, and has available now what he had not had before—two new units of capital.

In the next period of production, he uses the two units of capital along with labor and land. The production possibilities now change. Look at the table in Exhibit 2.

Compare this table to the one in Exhibit 1. Working now with two units of capital, Robinson Crusoe can produce more. For example, ten units of consumption can now be produced when Crusoe, using the fishing spear and extension tool, devotes all his labor to consumption. Of course, he may again decide to produce more units of capital goods in order to be able to produce even more units of consumption in the following period. This can go on forever and does in most economies.

Suppose after deliberating over the production possibilities of the table in Exhibit 2, he selects seven units of consumption and two units of capital. This combination means that he not only adds two more units of capital to his resource base but also is still able to produce more consumption goods—seven—than he could have produced in the first period, even had he devoted all the resources exclusively to consumption goods production.

The graph in Exhibit 2 illustrates the change in the Crusoe economy over the two periods.

The production possibilities curve shifts outward to the right. The shift reflects the changing resource base available to Crusoe. In the second period, capital is added to the land and labor resource base of the first. The dashed curves represent later period production possibilities as long as Crusoe continues the strategy of adding units of capital to his resource base.

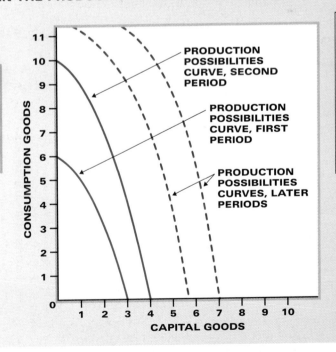

SHIFTS IN THE PRODUCTION POSSIBILITIES FRONTIER

PRODUCTION POSSIBILITIES IN THE ROBINSON CRUSOE ECONOMY, SECOND PERIOD

CONSUMPTION GOODS	CAPITAL GOODS
10	0
9	1
7	2
4	3
0	4

When more resources are available or when more productive technology is used, the quantity of goods and services an economy can produce increases. The increase is depicted by the outward shift to the right of the production possibilities curve.

Once Rich, It's Easy to Get Richer

This rather simple way of looking at an economy's production possibilities and growth potential is instructive. Imagine two economies, shown in panels *a* and *b* of Exhibit 3, whose initial production possibilities are described by the table in Exhibit 1. The different selections of consumption and capital these economies make along their identical first-period production possibilities curve trace out their productive growth—or lack of growth—over the course of several production periods.

In the first period, panel *a* people decide to produce three units of consumption and two units of capital (point *c*), while those in panel *b* choose six units of consumption and zero capital (point *a*). Comparing themselves to the people in panel *a*, those in panel *b* may think themselves lucky to have twice the consumption goods. But they won't feel that way in the following period.

The productive powers of the two economies are no longer the same. Panel *a*'s expanded resource base, now containing the two new capital goods, allows a new and more productive set of production possibilities. Panel *a*'s production possibilities curve shifts outward. Panel *b*, on the other hand, operating on its same resource base, remains locked on its initial production possibilities curve. In fact, the people in panel *a* now actually consume more than those in panel *b*, and they can still add to their capital stock.

Time is on their side. After several periods, the outward shifts in panel *a*'s production possibilities curve generate a widening gap between this curve and that of panel *b*. In time, the outward shifts in the panel *a* economy become even easier to obtain. Why? Because a solid consumption base is already in place, the opportunity cost of shifting resources to capital goods becomes less painful. Movements along the economy's production possibilities curve further into the *cd* range—more capital, less consumption—push the curve out even further in succeeding periods.

Once Poor, It's Easy to Stay Poor

Catching up is hard to do. If the panel *b* people decide to try, it may take some doing. Obviously, they must choose to move away from position *a* on their pro-

COMPARATIVE ECONOMIC GROWTH

Initially, the same quantities of resources and technology are available in the economies of panel *a* and panel *b*. Panel *a* chooses to produce three consumption goods and two capital goods, while panel *b* uses all its resources to produce six consumption goods. In succeeding years, the additional capital goods created in panel *a* are added to its resource base, shifting its production possibilities curve outward, while the production possibilities curve in panel *b* remains unchanged. The production gap between the two economies widens over time.

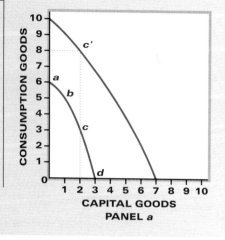

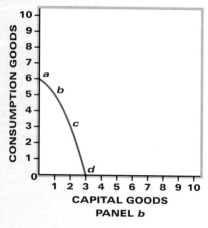

duction possibilities curve. The further away from *a*, the better. Movements along their curve into the *bc* range—much more capital, much less consumption—may force them to tighten their belts considerably. Where they position themselves along the curve depends upon how well they can tolerate low-level consumption and how quickly they want to catch up.

There are economies with resource bases so underdeveloped that they have little option but to devote all their meager resources to consumption. It is hard enough just to stay alive! Typically, these economies have high rates of population growth, so that it becomes a continuing, dispiriting struggle to feed their own people. The economies simply can't afford to produce the capital needed to shift their production possibilities curves outward. Economists refer to this condition as the vicious circle of poverty: The economies are so poor they can't produce capital; without capital, they remain poor. Poverty feeds on itself.

CHECK YOUR UNDERSTANDING

Why is it that focusing production on capital goods forces consumers to tighten their belts?

THE PRODUCTIVE POWER OF ADVANCED TECHNOLOGY

Ideas, more so than any factor of production, are the most revolutionizing force able to shift the production possibilities of any economy. Ideas can shift the curve out beyond imagination. Who would have thought just a century ago that we would be walking on the moon? Who would have expected commercial space satellites to beam images from the Superdome in New Orleans to an American air base in Turkey in a matter of seconds? Economists describe ideas that eventually take the form of new applied technology as **innovations.**

Even in the simple economy of Robinson Crusoe, innovation can be shown to cause dramatic leaps forward in the production possibilities available to an economy. The fishing spear Crusoe created was an idea fashioned into a unit of capital. Two fishing spears add more to an economy's productive potential than one, shifting the production possibilities curve out to the right, but the technology is still spears.

Suppose Crusoe hits on an altogether new and creative idea: the fishing net. He sketches out this completely new technology for catching fish that requires a different combination of land and labor. Crusoe uses more vine, less wood, no stone, and more labor. The results of this new technology are dramatic. Exhibit 4 compares the production possibilities of using spear and fishing net technologies.

The net technology yields 30 units of consumption goods compared to the 10 units produced with spears when all resources are devoted to the production of consumption goods. Production possibilities based on net technology make it easier to move down along the curve—producing even more capital goods—and, therefore, shifting the curve in succeeding periods out even further to the right.

Innovations creating even more advanced technology are possible. The exciting conclusion we reach, for the simple Robinson Crusoe economy and for our own,

Innovation
An idea that eventually takes the form of new, applied technology.

EXHIBIT 4

PRODUCTION POSSIBILITIES GENERATED BY SPEAR AND NET TECHNOLOGIES

CONSUMPTION	CAPITAL	CONSUMPTION	CAPITAL
10	0	30	0
9	1	26	1
7	2	18	2
4	3	10	3
0	4	0	4

is that there are no impassable limits to the growth potential of our economy. Resource limitations may impose a short-run constraint on what we are able to produce in any period of time, but given enough time and enough minds, new technology reduces the severity of scarcity. Our grandchildren will no doubt regard our technology as rather primitive, but their grandchildren will consider their technology as hardly more advanced.

The Indestructible Nature of Ideas

Capital goods can be destroyed, but ideas are far more durable. Wars can bring havoc to any economy's resource base. People's lives are disrupted. Many do not survive the war. Whole factories, complete with machinery, and roads, bridges, railway networks, electric grids, energy facilities, and any other form of the nation's capital stock can be reduced to rubble. But capital goods can also be replaced quickly. Look at Exhibit 5.

AD represents the economy's prewar production possibilities curve. The destructive effects of war, particularly on its people and capital stock, is shown as an inward shift to the left of the curve, to A'D'. Recovery, however, can be whole and swift because people, even with minimal capital stock, don't have to reinvent the wheel. Technological knowledge, once acquired, is virtually indestructible. In time, applying known and more advanced technology, the economy can shift its production possibilities curve back again to AD and even beyond to A''D''.

The physical devastation of Japan and Europe caused by World War II had some rather paradoxical consequences for these war-torn economies. Because so much of their capital stock in the form of factories and machinery was destroyed, these economies were forced to start over again. But they started over with the most advanced machinery and the most up-to-date factories. The result was an incredible increase in their economies' productivity. Ironically, economies that were spared the devastation of the war had their prewar technology still intact and grew less rapidly than those whose capital stocks were destroyed and replaced with the more modern technology.

EXHIBIT 5

INWARD AND OUTWARD SHIFTS OF THE PRODUCTION POSSIBILITIES CURVE

With resources destroyed, the economy's production possibilities decrease. The decrease is depicted by the shift to the left of the production possibilities curve, from AD to A'D'. In time, with the rebuilding of resources and the use of more advanced technology, the economy can recoup and even surpass the levels of production previously attained. This is shown in the shift to the right of the production possibilities curve, from A'D' to A''D''.

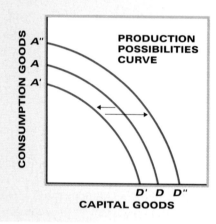

PRODUCTION POSSIBILITIES CURVE

CONSUMPTION GOODS

A''
A
A'

D' D D''

CAPITAL GOODS

POSSIBILITIES, IMPOSSIBILITIES, AND LESS THAN POSSIBILITIES

What an economy can produce depends upon the availability of resources and the level of technology applied. If the economy's resources are not fully employed, then obviously it cannot be producing as much as possible. For example, if the economy's labor force is not fully employed or if some of its land and capital resources remain idle, the combination of consumption goods and capital goods that it produces will be less than what is possible.

HISTORICAL PERSPECTIVE

THE DESTRUCTION AND RECONSTRUCTION OF ROTTERDAM

May 14, 1940, is an infamous date in the history of Holland's beautiful city of Rotterdam. It was on that day that Hitler's notorious air force (the Luftwaffe) bombed the city incessantly for 12 hours, until it lay in ashes.

Rotterdam became synonymous with disaster. German bombers, like tractors plowing a field, moved methodically back and forth until all that remained of the city was the shell of the ancient Saint Lawrence Church, the city hall, and a few buildings. Twenty-five thousand homes, 1,200 factories, 69 schools, and 13 hospitals were demolished. Overnight, 75,000 people became homeless and 900 were killed. The seaport, Rotterdam's economic lifeblood, was not spared. Thirty-five percent of the port was later gutted by the German army.

BEAUTIFUL, VIBRANT ROTTERDAM. A MARVELOUS PLACE TO VISIT AND AN IMPORTANT HISTORICAL REMINDER OF HOW CRUEL PEOPLE CAN BE AND YET HOW UNDAUNTED THE HUMAN SPIRIT IS.

But Rotterdam did not die. The city enjoys a geographical advantage by straddling the delta of the Rhine, which is the main artery of Europe's intricate network of inland waterways. Almost immediately after the war, rebuilding of the harbor began with the most up-to-date cranes, derricks, docks, and cargo-handling technology. By the end of reconstruction, ships were loading and unloading faster and at lower cost than anywhere else in the world. Rotterdam not only rebuilt but also strengthened its economic muscle, funneling a large part of the cargo trade between the prospering Common Market and the rest of the world.

MORE ON THE NET

What does Rotterdam look like today? Visit for yourself (http://www.euronet.nl/users/frankvw/rotterdamcon.html).

Such a condition is described by point *u* in the economy of Exhibit 6. At *u*, the economy is producing two consumption goods and two capital goods. Its production possibilities curve shows, however, that combination *b* or *c* is possible. In each case, more of one good can be produced without having to sacrifice any of the other. For example, it is possible to produce six units of consumption goods and two units of capital, or two units of consumption and six units of capital. Either combination is better than *u*.

Any point in the interior of the production possibilities curve, such as *u*, signals either the existence of unemployed or underemployed resources. What are **underemployed resources?** Some people working full time might appear to be fully employed, but in fact they still represent substantial unused resources. How come? They are producing much less than they are really capable of producing.

Imagine, for example, how much more our economy could have produced over the past 200 years if women, blacks, and other minorities had been allowed to

Underemployed resources
The less than full utilization of a resource's productive capabilities.

EXHIBIT 6

POSSIBLE, IMPOSSIBLE, AND LESS THAN POSSIBLE

Production combinations, located outside and to the right of the production possibilities curve, such as *e*, are unattainable with the resources and technology currently available. Combinations located within the curve, such as *u*, reflect less than full use of available resources and technology. All combinations that fall on the curve, such as *b* and *c*, represent maximum use, or the full employment of the resources and technology available.

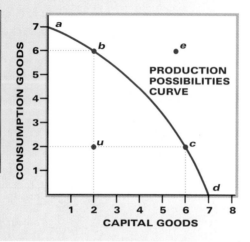

exercise their talents fully. How many entrepreneurs have we lost forever? How many innovations were allowed to go undiscovered? How many skilled craftspeople have wasted their talents? How much further out would our production possibilities curve be if racial, sexual, religious, and ethnic discrimination had been avoided? It staggers the imagination!

Who loses? The underemployed people and the economy. That is, the economy could be producing more, but it isn't. If these underemployed people were allowed to exercise their full productive potential, the economy's production would shift from a position inside the production possibilities curve to a position on it.

CHECK YOUR UNDERSTANDING

Why does discrimination create economic inefficiency?

Economic efficiency
The maximum possible production of goods and services generated by the fullest employment of the economy's resources.

Point *u* in Exhibit 6 describes an inefficiently producing economy. **Economic efficiency** refers to the condition in which all factors of production are used in their most productive capacity. In this sense, the only points of production that represent an efficiently run economy are those *on* the production possibilities curve. No one point on the curve is more efficient than any other, since all of them reflect the full employment and maximal use of the economy's available resources.

Any point lying outside the production possibilities curve in the economy of Exhibit 6, such as *e*, is an impossible production combination. After all, points on the curve, such as *a, b, c,* or *d,* represent production combinations that fully employ the economy's usable resources. How, then, can the economy produce beyond the curve? If the economy is growing, point *e*, impossible now, need not be an impossible dream.

PRODUCTION POSSIBILITIES AND ECONOMIC SPECIALIZATION

Labor specialization
The division of labor into specialized activities that allow individuals to be more productive.

The idea that labor productivity is a function of the degree of **labor specialization** goes as far back as 1776 and Adam Smith. In his *The Wealth of Nations,* Adam Smith tells about a visit to a pin factory:

> One man draws out the wire, another straightens it, a third cuts it, a fourth points it, a fifth grinds it at the top for receiving the head; to make the head requires two or three distinct operations; to put it on is a peculiar business, to whiten the pins is another; it is even a trade by itself to put them into the paper. . . .

The reason for such division of labor, he noted, is that these 10 people could make as many as 48,000 pins in a day. If they had each worked separately and independently, they could not have produced more than 200. That's an impressive point and certainly one that would not go unnoticed in the economy of Robinson Crusoe.

In Crusoe's economy, shown in the table in Exhibit 1, there is no division of labor. Alone, he is forced to produce everything—to fish, hunt, farm, and repair huts. He may be a talented carpenter, a mediocre farmer, and a terrible fisherman, but he is busy doing it all. The production possibilities shown in the table in Exhibit 1 reflect this circumstance.

Specialization on the Island

But suppose Robinson Crusoe was one of thousands stranded on the island. He probably would not have fished a day in his life. The fishing would have been done by people who were good at it. Crusoe would have become the island's carpenter, relieving those who seem only able to hammer their thumbs. Division of labor on that island allows all the castaways to do the specific things each does best.

Labor can be divided and divided again into specialized and even more specialized activities until people are incredibly proficient at doing incredibly minute activities. The result of such specialization and cooperative production can mean enormous production. The production possibility schedule of an economy with 1,000 people, for example, may be 100,000 times more productive than a single-person economy.

Of course, with everyone working at specialized jobs, the people will need to create an exchange system that allows them to exchange the goods produced under conditions of specialization. A shirtmaker, for example, producing 1,000 shirts, may keep only 1 and trade the remaining 999 shirts for goods she needs. After all, working at making shirts all day does not allow her to fish for the evening meal. But her neighbor, fishing all day, would probably want to exchange some of his fish for her shirts. In this way, it is possible for every islander who specializes in production to end up with more of everything.

International Specialization

If specialization among people on the island creates more goods for everyone, then imagine how much more could be produced if there were international specialization and exchange. Suppose contact was made with people on other islands, and the practice of exchanging goods with them became commonplace. Now, even more division of labor and specialization would occur. Instead of producing 1,000 shirts for the local island markets, a shirtmaker may produce 10,000 shirts for the larger islands' markets. More people would be engaged in producing shirts. But instead of every shirtworker making a complete shirt, each would specialize in a specific task in the shirt-making process, such as cutting material, sewing pieces, making buttonholes, and folding.

Perhaps four people working at specialized tasks can produce 10,000 shirts in the time it takes one shirtmaker performing all the tasks alone to produce 1,000 shirts. The more islands that are joined in international specialization and exchange, the greater are the opportunities for division of labor and specialization. Everyone produces more, exchanges more, and consumes more.

The Principle of Comparative Advantage

Let's take this idea of international division of labor and specialization one step further to demonstrate precisely how the advantages of such specialization prevail. Imagine two island economies—Crusoe Island and Yakamaya Island—that each produce fish and shirts. Their production possibilities are shown in Exhibit 7. Crusoe Islanders can produce 2 fish per day, while Yakamayans produce 8. (The

The Wealth of Nations in its entirety is available online (http://www.bibliomania. com/NonFiction/Smith/ Wealth/index.html).

EXHIBIT|7

PRODUCTION OF FISH AND SHIRTS PER EIGHT-HOUR DAY— ABSOLUTE ADVANTAGE

	PRODUCTION OF FISH	PRODUCTION OF SHIRTS
CRUSOE ISLAND	2	8
YAKAMAYA ISLAND	8	2

Absolute advantage
A country's ability to produce a good using fewer resources than the country it trades with.

Comparative advantage
A country's ability to produce a good at a lower opportunity cost than the country with which it trades.

EXHIBIT|8

PRODUCTION OF FISH AND SHIRTS PER EIGHT-HOUR DAY— COMPARATIVE ADVANTAGE

	PRODUCTION OF FISH	PRODUCTION OF SHIRTS
CRUSOE ISLAND	8	8
YAKAMAYA ISLAND	8	2

single-digit quantities are meant to keep the illustration simple.) On the other hand, Crusoe Islanders can produce 8 shirts a day, while Yakamayans struggle to produce 2.

In 2 days, then, if they each produce their own shirts and fish, total production on the 2 islands is 10 fish and 10 shirts. If, on the other hand, they agree to specialize—Crusoe Islanders producing only shirts and Yakamayans producing only fish—they can produce 16 fish and 16 shirts. As you see—and they experience—the gains from specialization are highly advantageous. Economists refer to such an advantage from specialization as **absolute advantage,** which occurs when each island can produce a good using fewer resources than the other island uses. Yakamayans have an absolute advantage in fish (1 hour of labor per fish versus 4 hours needed by Crusoe Islanders), while Crusoe Islanders have an absolute advantage in shirts (1 hour of labor per shirt versus 4 hours needed by Yakamayans).

But suppose their production possibilities look like those in Exhibit 8. Yakamaya Island now has no absolute advantage in fish. People there and on Crusoe Island produce 8 fish in an 8-hour day. On the other hand, Crusoe Islanders can still out-produce Yakamayans 4-to-1 in shirt production. Should the islands specialize? Without specialization, their total production is 16 fish and 10 shirts. With specialization, they produce 16 fish and 16 shirts. Specialization still makes them better off. But who produces what?

Look at their opportunity costs of producing fish. When Crusoe Islanders fish for a day, they catch 8 fish but give up the opportunity of producing 8 shirts. The opportunity cost, then, for each of the 8 fish they catch is 1 shirt. What about Yakamayans? When they fish for a day, catching 8 fish, they give up the opportunity of producing 2 shirts, so that the opportunity cost for each of the 8 fish they produce is ¼ of a shirt. That is, the opportunity cost associated with producing fish for Yakamayans is less than it is for Crusoe Islanders. Although Yakamayans do not have an absolute advantage in fish, they do have a **comparative advantage,** meaning that they have a lower opportunity cost producing fish than do Crusoe Islanders. The Yakamayans produce the fish.

Crusoe Islanders end up producing the shirts. Why? Look at the opportunity costs of producing shirts. When Crusoe Islanders produce 8 shirts in a day, they give up the opportunity of producing 8 fish, so that the opportunity cost associated with producing a shirt is 1 fish. What about Yakamayans? When they produce 2 shirts in a day, they give up the opportunity of producing 8 fish, so that the opportunity cost to them of producing a shirt is 4 fish. Crusoe Islanders hold a comparative advantage in shirts.

THE UNIVERSALITY OF THE PRODUCTION POSSIBILITIES MODEL

Resource limitations confronting insatiable wants are facts of life that apply to every economic system—large or small, rich or poor, east or west, north or south, capitalist or socialist.

The universality of the production possibilities model and the law of increasing costs create the same kinds of problems and decision making for all economies. Can the economy fully employ its resources? How much of the resources should be allocated to capital goods formation? Who gets what share of the consumption goods produced?

The same questions are asked about peace and war. Just as the production possibilities curve measures out the possibilities of consumption and capital goods production, it can measure out as well the production possibilities of butter and guns. Israeli as well as Egyptian economists knew firsthand the opportunity cost of desert warfare. In no small measure, that knowledge played its part in the countries' historic 1979 peace agreement.

Imagine a couple of Martian economists landing their UFOs undetected on Earth, say, one in Beijing, China, and the other in Dayton, Ohio. If their assignments were to detail how Earthlings behave, they would be struck, upon returning to Mars and comparing notes, not by the differences they observed, but instead by the incredible similarities of our experiences and behavior. They would probably be impressed as well by how similar our economic problems and economic choices are to their own!

CHAPTER REVIEW

1. The economy's resources—also referred to as factors of production—are labor, capital, land, and entrepreneurship. The two human resources are labor and entrepreneurship; the two nonhuman resources are capital and land. Labor is the physical and mental exertion of people willing to sell their skills for a specific period of time. Capital is a manufactured good used to produce other goods. Human capital represents the combination of labor and capital. For example, a medical education is capital, and the physician is the resulting human capital. Land, in its virgin form, is nature's gift. Entrepreneurs undertake the risks and uncertainties associated with business enterprise.

2. A production possibilities curve shows the combinations of goods that can be produced with a set of resources. The analysis of a two-goods economy in which consumption and capital goods are produced allows for fruitful discussion of issues associated with economic growth.

3. The opportunity cost of producing a unit of a good—say, a consumption good—is measured by the quantity of the other good—say, a capital good—that must be given up to produce the consumption good.

4. As more and more of a good—say, a consumption good—is produced, the quantity of the other good—say, a capital good—that must be given up to produce each additional

consumption good increases. This phenomenon is known as the law of increasing costs.

5. The production of capital goods in one year adds to an economy's resource base, ensuring that the quantities of goods that become possible to produce in subsequent years increase. Rich economies can more easily invest in capital goods production than can poor economies, so that, over years, greater and greater disparities among them may result.

6. New ideas that create innovations in the form of new technology enhance labor productivity and therefore economic growth. For example, when a few tractors replace many horse-driven plows, the production possibilities curve shifts out to the right.

7. An economy producing along its production possibilities curve is both at full employment and producing efficiently. If any factor is unemployed or if any factor is not being used to its fullest capacity (that is, it is underemployed), then the economy is not operating on its production possibilities curve, but somewhere inside it.

8. Division of labor and specialization increase labor productivity and therefore increase what an economy can produce. Absolute and comparative advantage show how nations gain when they specialize and trade among themselves.

KEY TERMS

Factor of production
Labor
Capital
Human capital
Land

Entrepreneur
Production possibilities
Opportunity cost
Law of increasing costs
Innovation

Underemployed resources
Economic efficiency
Labor specialization
Absolute advantage
Comparative advantage

QUESTIONS

1. What distinguishes entrepreneurship from the other factors of production?

2. Is a four-door 1998 Buick LeSabre taxi capital? Is a four-door 1998 Buick LeSabre parked in your garage capital?

3. Consider your economics lecture. From the point of view of your economics professor, is the lecture capital, labor, or neither? From your own point of view, is it capital, labor, or neither? What is your opportunity cost of that lecture?

4. Explain why the concepts of scarcity and opportunity cost are intricately related.

5. Explain the law of increasing (opportunity) costs. What causes costs to increase?

6. Everybody wants clean air. So why is the air polluted in so many of our cities? (*Hint:* Refer to the law of increasing costs in your answer.)

7. Why are most new technologies considered indestructible?

8. Suppose you were advising the government of Egypt. What policies would you recommend to achieve economic growth? Why should you expect some resistance to your policy suggestions?

9. Suppose government economists, on the request of the president, construct a production possibilities curve (for military and civilian goods) for the United States. Suppose also that two economics professors debate where the United States ought to be on that curve. Which set of economists is engaged in positive economics, and which in normative?

10. What factors or events could cause an inward shift of the production possibilities curve?

11. Why does the production possibilities curve bow out from the origin?

12. The Constitution guarantees the right to free speech. Does the *free* in *free speech* mean that there really is no opportunity cost to free speech? Explain.

13. Professor Kenneth Boulding once noted that Danish butter producers eat very little butter. They use margarine even though they produce some of the best butter in the world. Is this stupid behavior? Or is there a good reason for it?

14. What is meant by the term *vicious circle of poverty?* Draw a graph to illustrate the concept.

15. Immigration is a hot political issue these days. What arguments can an economist make to support a liberal policy of immigration? What arguments can he or she make to oppose immigration? (*Hint:* Think in terms of shifts in the production possibilities curve in the first case, and movements along the curve in the second.)

PRACTICE PROBLEMS

1. Fill in an appropriate number (there can be more than one) for the missing number of bushels of oranges in set C and graph the following sets of production possibilities.

SET	BUSHELS OF GRAPEFRUIT	BUSHELS OF ORANGES
A	200	0
B	150	19
C	100	
D	50	30
E	0	32

2. Graph the following sets of production possibilities and explain why the law of increasing costs is violated.

SET	BUSHELS OF GRAPEFRUIT	BUSHELS OF ORANGES
A	200	0
B	150	19
C	100	40
D	50	80
E	0	130

3. Production costs (in labor hours) of oranges and peaches in Florida and Georgia are shown in the following table.

If the states specialize, what should each produce? Why? (*Hint:* Think in terms of absolute and comparative advantage.)

	ORANGES	PEACHES
FLORIDA	5	5
GEORGIA	2	4

4. Imagine an economy with the following resource base for 2000: 100 units of labor (including entrepreneurs), 100 units of capital, and 100 acres of land. Draw a graph showing the economy's 2000 production possibilities from the following table:

2000	CONSUMPTION	CAPITAL
A	12	0
B	10	2
C	6	4
D	0	6

2001	CONSUMPTION	CAPITAL
A	16	0
B	14	2
C	10	4
D	4	6

On the same graph, draw the economy's production possibilities curve for 2001. Which possibilities in 2000 (among A, B, C, and D) can account for the 2001 curve, and how would such a production possibilities combination affect the economy's resource base for 2001?

WHAT'S WRONG WITH THIS GRAPH?

THE PRODUCTION POSSIBILITIES CURVE

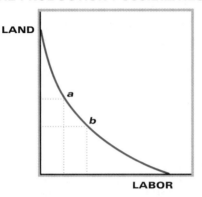

LAND

a

b

LABOR

ECONOMIC CONSULTANTS

ECONOMIC RESEARCH AND ANALYSIS BY STUDENTS FOR PROFESSIONALS

WaterUSA, located in Boise, Idaho, bottles and sells mineral water. This mineral water, drawn from underground springs, offers unparalleled taste and clarity. WaterUSA currently sells its water in the United States, but it is looking to expand its sales into the former Soviet Union, and into Russia in particular.

WaterUSA has approached Economic Consultants for advice on the firm's plans to expand its sales into European markets. Prepare a report for WaterUSA that addresses the following issues:

1. Are the conditions favorable in the former Soviet Union for selling mineral water? Are there businesses in Russia selling mineral water?
2. What issues does WaterUSA need to consider with regard to the principle of comparative advantage?

You may find the following resources helpful as you prepare this report for WaterUSA:

- **U.S. Department of Commerce, Business Information Service for the Newly Independent States (BISNIS)** (http://bisnis.doc.gov/bisnis/bisnis.html)—BISNIS provides economic information about Russia. In particular, BISNIS publishes market surveys and reports for common U.S. goods.
- **American Chamber of Commerce in Russia** (http://www.amcham.ru/)—The American Chamber of Commerce in Russia provides information for doing business in Russia.
- **Mineral Waters of the World** (http://www.mineralwaters.org/)—Mineral Waters of the World provides directories and ratings for various mineral waters around the globe.

PRACTICE TEST

1. To economists, the term *capital* refers exclusively to
   a. goods used to produce other goods.
   b. money used to purchase stocks and bonds.
   c. savings accumulated by households to purchase real estate.
   d. money used by capitalists to hire workers.
   e. machinery used by workers to produce goods.

2. If an economy experiences unemployment, it would show up as a point
   a. on the production possibilities curve, but on one of the axes.
   b. outside the production possibilities curve.
   c. inside the production possibilities curve.
   d. on the production possibilities curve.
   e. on a production possibilities curve that is shifting to the right.

3. The weather in the Virgin Islands reminds us of the nursery rhyme "When she was good, she was very, very good, but when she was bad, she was horrid." A hurricane in 1996 was horrid, destroying much of the islands' infrastructure (roads, telephone systems), homes, and factories. An economist describing the effect of the hurricane on the islands' economy would show
   a. an inward shift in the islands' production possibilities curve.
   b. an outward shift in the islands' production possibilities curve.
   c. a movement along the production possibilities curve, from consumption to capital.
   d. a movement along the production possibilities curve, from capital to consumption.
   e. a movement inside the curve, the curve remaining intact.

4. Let's suppose that the day after the hurricane, the governor of the Virgin Islands addresses the population to announce the government's decision to rebuild the economy's infrastructure. Of course, it means higher taxes, which means people will have less income to spend as they please. Ceteris paribus, the tax and rebuilding will create
   a. an inward shift in the islands' production possibilities curve.
   b. an outward shift in the islands' production possibilities curve.
   c. a movement along the production possibilities curve, from consumption to capital.
   d. a movement along the production possibilities curve, from capital to consumption.
   e. a movement inside the curve, the curve remaining intact.

5. Assuming the rebuilding program is successful, in the longer run (in time) you would see
   a. an inward shift in the islands' production possibilities curve.
   b. an outward shift in the islands' production possibilities curve.
   c. a movement along the production possibilities curve, from consumption to capital.
   d. a movement along the production possibilities curve, from capital to consumption.
   e. a movement inside the curve, the curve remaining intact.

6. Which of the following is likely to cause an inward shift in Crusoe's production possibilities curve?
   a. Crusoe invents a fishnet.
   b. A typhoon destroys resources on the island.
   c. Crusoe discovers a forest of trees, perfect for use in making spears.
   d. Crusoe finds a companion, named Friday, to help him fish and make spears.

7. In Adam Smith's illustration of the pin factory, one worker draws out the wire, another straightens it, and a third cuts it. Several others serve the functions of pointing, whitening, and packaging the pins. This process is more productive than if each worker did all the tasks. This illustrates the concept of
   a. opportunity costs.
   b. labor specialization.
   c. economic efficiency.
   d. the law of increasing costs.

8. Gabe Fried is stranded on a Pacific island and realizes that, to survive, he must pick berries. He discovers that he picks more berries in the first hour than he does in the second because it becomes increasingly harder to find berries. Gabe has just discovered
   a. Engel's law.
   b. the law of opportunity cost.
   c. the law of increasing costs.
   d. the law of scarcity.
   e. the law of production possibilities.

9. Among the four factors of production is entrepreneurship. It's the only factor that
   a. does not contract to provide its services for a specific price.
   b. conceives of the essential idea of production.
   c. assumes all the risks and uncertainties involved in production.
   d. earns profit.
   e. All of the above

3

DEMAND AND SUPPLY

One of the most exciting moments in Shakespearean drama—for economists, at any rate—has to be the final scene in *Richard III* where the king, tired and bloodied at the end of the battle, his horse slain, and standing helplessly alone upon the crest of a hill, sights the enemy about to charge at him. His sword drawn, Richard shouts in desperation: "A horse! A horse! My kingdom for a horse!"

To an economist, that's a dramatic moment, for never has so high a price been placed on a four-legged animal! Not before, and not since. Lassie and Flipper, themselves worth a small fortune, were still well within the reach of any millionaire. The legendary thoroughbred of the 1920s, Man O' War, won

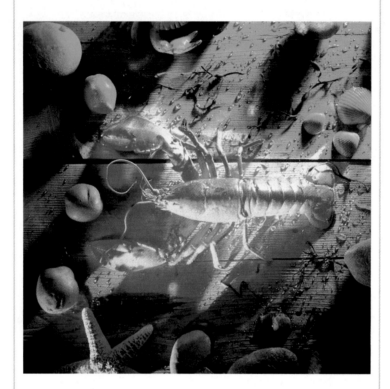

THIS CHAPTER INTRODUCES YOU TO THE ECONOMIC PRINCIPLES ASSOCIATED WITH:

- INDIVIDUAL AND MARKET DEMAND
- MARKET-DAY, SHORT-RUN, AND LONG-RUN SUPPLY
- THE DETERMINATION OF EQUILIBRIUM PRICE AND QUANTITY

every race he ran but one, but even he couldn't command *that* price. Shakespeare was not an economist by profession, yet he understood the market well. In all probability, he picked the right price.

This example raises a more general question about price formation: Why are prices what they are? Why, for example, do oranges sell for 30 cents each? Why not 25 cents? Or 34 cents? Is there something magical about a 30-cent orange? And what about cucumbers? Why are they 49 cents each? Why should they be more expensive than oranges? Why is butter $1.25 per pound? Why is a fresh fish $6?

We can go on identifying thousands of goods that make up our modern economy and ask the same question about each: Why that particular price? From aircraft carriers to salted peanuts, from sweetheart roses to Buick LeSabres, why are the prices what they are?

MEASURING CONSUMER WILLINGNESS

Price formation has to do with people's willingness to buy and sell. There is nothing mysterious about price. It has no life of its own. It has no will. Price simply reflects what people are willing to do.

Suppose that people on a small island are busily engaged each day in some productive activity that affords them a livelihood. The variety of their occupations fills up 40 Yellow Pages in their telephone directory. There are auto mechanics, dentists, farmers, plumbers, computer specialists, business consultants, and especially fishermen. After all, it's an island economy, and we should expect the community to take full advantage of its fishing grounds.

Of course, there's no sense in fishing unless some people like to eat fish. Chances are some prefer fish to filet mignon, although there must be others who wouldn't touch fish under any condition. As the Romans used to say: *De gustibus non est disputandum* (There's no disputing taste). But it would be the height of folly if fishermen went out on the water every day only to discover on returning to dock that nobody showed any interest in the fish they caught. Wouldn't you think that even the dullest of them would give up after a while? Fishermen go out every day because they know from long experience that there are always people willing to buy fish.

MEASURING CONSUMER DEMAND

Fishermen also know that when price falls, people's willingness to buy fish increases— it's so obvious and so sensible a response to price that fishermen regard it as natural. They know, for example, that if the price of fish is outrageously high, say $25 per fish, very few people would be willing to buy. On the other hand, if the price is $10, some people unwilling to buy at $25 now would be willing to buy fish.

If the price falls to $5, more people would be willing to buy even more fish. Some who bought a few at $10 would buy more at $5, and those who had not bought before would now get into the market.

When economists refer to **change in quantity demanded** for a particular good, they always mean people's willingness to buy specific quantities at specific prices. They define the inverse relationship between price and quantity demanded as the **law of demand.** Compare the two statements "I am willing to buy four fish at a price of $6 per fish" and "I am willing to buy fish." There is considerably more information in the first statement.

Measuring Individual Demand

Let's begin by measuring Claudia Preparata's and Chris Stefan's demand for fish. Claudia is the principal labor relations consultant on the island, and Chris is an actress. The tables in Exhibit 1 are **demand schedules** recording their willingness to buy fish at different prices.

You may not know much about these two women, but you do know that if the price of fish was $10, you wouldn't find Claudia Preparata at a fish market!

Chris Stefan, on the other hand, treats herself to a $10 poached salmon. If the price falls to $9, the quantity of fish demanded by both Claudia and Chris increases. Claudia buys one, and the quantity that Chris demands increases to three. If the price keeps falling, the quantity demanded keeps increasing.

The **demand curves** in Exhibit 1 represent Claudia's and Chris's demand for fish at different prices. They contain the same information offered in the tables. It is just a different, more visual way of looking at the information. The demand curves

CHECK YOUR UNDERSTANDING

How does price reflect what buyers are willing to do?

Change in quantity demanded
A change in the quantity demanded of a good that is caused solely by a change in the price of that good.

Law of demand
The inverse relationship between price and quantity demanded of a good or service, *ceteris paribus.*

Demand schedule
A schedule showing the specific quantity of a good or service that people are willing and able to buy at different prices.

Demand curve
A curve that depicts the relationship between price and quantity demanded.

EXHIBIT 1

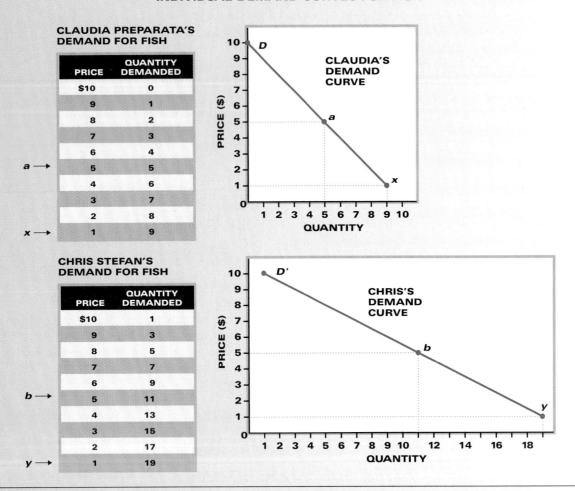

INDIVIDUAL DEMAND CURVES FOR FISH

CLAUDIA PREPARATA'S DEMAND FOR FISH

PRICE	QUANTITY DEMANDED
$10	0
9	1
8	2
7	3
6	4
5	5
4	6
3	7
2	8
1	9

a → (price 5), x → (price 1)

CHRIS STEFAN'S DEMAND FOR FISH

PRICE	QUANTITY DEMANDED
$10	1
9	3
8	5
7	7
6	9
5	11
4	13
3	15
2	17
1	19

b → (price 5), y → (price 1)

Ceteris paribus, the quantity of fish demanded depends on the price of fish. At a price of $5, the quantity of fish demanded by Claudia is 5—point *a* on demand curve *D*—and the quantity demanded by Chris is 11—point *b* on demand curve *D'*. At a price of $1, the quantity demanded by Claudia increases to 9—point *x*—and the quantity demanded by Chris increases to 19—point *y*.

are downward sloping because price and quantity demanded are inversely related. When price falls, the quantity demanded increases.

Measuring Market Demand

If we were able to record every person's willingness to buy fish at different prices, we would end up with complete information about the community's demand for fish. We can obtain such information only by observing and recording what quantities people actually buy in the market at different prices. Adding up all the individual demands for fish gives us the community demand, or **market demand.** The table and graph in Exhibit 2 represent the market demand for fish.

Market demand
The sum of all individual demands in a market.

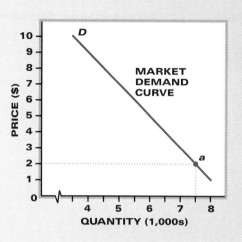

THE MARKET DEMAND CURVE

MARKET DEMAND FOR FISH

PRICE	QUANTITY DEMANDED
$10	3,500
9	4,000
8	4,500
7	5,000
6	5,500
5	6,000
4	6,500
3	7,000
a → 2	7,500
1	8,000

Individual demand curves, including Claudia's and Chris's, are added together to form the community, or market, demand curve. At a price of $2, the quantity of fish demanded by all demanders is 7,500—point *a*—which includes 8 demanded by Claudia and 17 demanded by Chris.

EXHIBIT | 2

MEASURING SUPPLY

On a beautiful April morning we see the fishermen going out in their boats. They live by the weather and by whatever daylight they can manage. At dawn, they head out to the fishing grounds while most people in the community are still asleep. Typically, they move from spot to spot, depending on the season, weather, and time of day. They search, locate, fish, and move on again.

Suppose they return home at the end of this fishing day with 6,000 fish. Imagine the scene: Fishermen unload their catch into their individual stalls, pack the fish in ice, and wash up. They sell them right on the docks. The last thing any fisherman wants to take home is a fish! They want dollars.

Market-Day Supply

Once the fish are in, there's really no decision making concerning what quantity to supply at what price. *Whatever the price,* fishermen are willing to dispose of all 6,000 fish. What else can they do with them? Have you ever handled a day-old fish?

Even if the price was $1 per fish, $P = \$1$, fishermen would be disappointed but still willing to sell all 6,000. Some would probably start thinking about other jobs. On the other hand, if $P = \$10$, the same fishermen would still supply the same 6,000 fish, but this time would be frustrated that they hadn't caught more. But they can't change the quantity supplied once the catch is in. Regardless of price, the quantity supplied is fixed for the market day.

The table and graph in Exhibit 3 represent the **supply schedule** and corresponding supply curve for the **market-day supply.**

Just as the demand curve graphs the relationship between price and quantity demanded, the **supply curve** graphs the relationship between price and quantity supplied. The supply curve for the market day shows that whatever the price, the quantity supplied remains unchanged.

Supply schedule
A schedule showing the specific quantity of a good or service that suppliers are willing and able to provide at different prices.

Market-day supply
A market situation in which the quantity of a good supplied is fixed, regardless of price.

Supply curve
A curve that depicts the relationship between price and quantity supplied.

EXHIBIT|3

The market-day supply curve is vertical, reflecting the fact that once the catch is in, fishermen cannot change the quantity they supply. At a price of $9, the quantity supplied is 6,000—point *a* on the supply curve. At a price of $5, the quantity supplied is still 6,000— point *b* on the supply curve.

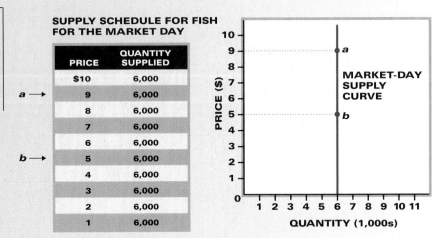

MARKET-DAY SUPPLY CURVE

SUPPLY SCHEDULE FOR FISH FOR THE MARKET DAY

PRICE	QUANTITY SUPPLIED
$10	6,000
9	6,000
8	6,000
7	6,000
6	6,000
5	6,000
4	6,000
3	6,000
2	6,000
1	6,000

DETERMINING EQUILIBRIUM PRICE

A fish market is a colorful and bustling sight. Demanders, suppliers, and flies swarm around the fish stalls, ready to strike deals. Suppliers busily encourage demanders to buy their fish, and demanders take their time looking for the best price. But fish are fish, and time is short.

Nobody knows what the other's preferences really are until they become expressed on the market through purchase and sale. But Claudia, Chris, and the many other demanders, as well as the fishermen who are the suppliers, know that 6,000 fish are on the docks for sale.

Suppose the Price Is $8

Let's suppose that the asking price, at least at the outset of the market process, is $8 per fish. This already spells trouble. Look at Exhibit 4.

At *P* = $8, the quantity of fish demanded is 4,500. Of this quantity, Claudia is willing to buy 2, Chris 5. But the fishermen are already nervous about the weakness they sense in the market. There is insufficient demand to absorb the entire 6,000 fish supplied. People are just not picking up fish as the fishermen had hoped. Look at the table in Exhibit 4. At *P* = $8, there is an **excess supply** of 1,500 fish that will not be sold. Every fisherman is afraid, in the end, of being left holding the bag. Sheila Reed, one of the many fishermen on the docks, knows that the only way to protect herself from this unpleasant eventuality is to cut price. She figures that since all fish are alike, if she is willing to cut her own price to $7, chances are that she will sell out.

Of course, Sheila isn't the only fisherman who thinks this way. Fishermen Lisa Muroga and Shari Zernich had already cut their prices to $7 for the same reason. They draw a crowd. Can you imagine what happens when word spreads among the demanders and suppliers that some fishermen are willing to sell at $7? They make it virtually impossible for other suppliers to maintain the price at $8.

Excess supply
The difference, at a particular price, between quantity supplied and quantity demanded, quantity supplied being the greater.

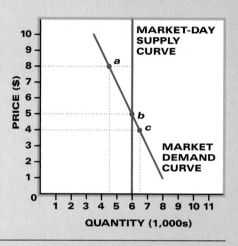

EXCESS DEMAND AND EXCESS SUPPLY

PRESSURES OF EXCESS DEMAND AND EXCESS SUPPLY WHEN MARKET SUPPLY IS 6,000

	PRICE	QUANTITY DEMANDED	QUANTITY SUPPLIED	EXCESS DEMAND	EXCESS SUPPLY
	$10	3,500	6,000		2,500
	9	4,000	6,000		2,000
a →	8	4,500	6,000		1,500
	7	5,000	6,000		1,000
	6	5,500	6,000		500
b →	5	6,000	6,000	0	0
c →	4	6,500	6,000	500	
	3	7,000	6,000	1,000	
	2	7,500	6,000	1,500	
	1	8,000	6,000	2,000	

At any price other than $5, point *b* on the supply and demand curves, excess demand or excess supply will force the price to $5. At $4, point *c* on the demand curve, an excess demand of 500 fish is created, driving up price. At $8, point *a* on the demand curve, an excess supply of 1,500 fish is created, forcing price downward.

Every supplier, then, has no alternative but to reduce the price to $7. Will that do the trick? Look again at the table in Exhibit 4. At P = $7, quantity demanded increases to 5,000 fish, but that still leaves an excess supply of 1,000. The pressure on suppliers persists.

As long as any excess supply exists on the market, there will always be an incentive for suppliers to cut price. The incentive is self-protection. They really don't enjoy cutting prices, but they enjoy even less the prospect of being caught at the end of the market day with unsold fish.

How much price cutting will they have to do? From the table in Exhibit 4 it's clear that suppliers will have to cut the price to $5. At P = $5, quantity demanded increases to absorb the entire 6,000 fish supplied. Excess supply is zero.

Suppose the Price Is $4

Suppose, at the beginning of the market process, price is not $8, but $4. What happens now? Market pressure is on the other side of the market. Claudia Preparata, Chris Stefan, and other demanders are the ones who become somewhat nervous.

For example, at P = $4, Claudia is willing to buy 6 and Chris is willing to buy 13 fish. The quantity demanded by the community is 6,500. Both demanders and suppliers now sense that there are insufficient fish to satisfy demand at $4. Fishermen seem less worried about being caught with unsold fish. Now demanders are worried about going home fishless.

As you see in the table in Exhibit 4, **excess demand** at P = $4 is 500 fish. What would you do if you were at the docks and really wanted fish? Afraid of getting caught looking at empty stalls, wouldn't you offer a little more? For example, if you announced that you were willing to pay $5, the chances are that you would draw suppliers' attention. Of course, you're not the only one with fish on your mind; many others are also willing to buy fish at $5.

CHECK YOUR UNDERSTANDING

What will suppliers do if there's an excess supply on the market?

Excess demand
The difference, at a particular price, between quantity demanded and quantity supplied, quantity demanded being the greater.

The $4 price, then, becomes untenable. Demanders, competing among themselves for the limited supply of 6,000 fish, will bid the price up. At $P = \$5$, some buyers drop out. The quantity demanded then falls to 6,000 and the excess demand disappears.

Price Always Tends Toward Equilibrium

In the fish market on this particular day, competition among suppliers to rid themselves of their supply will always force a price greater than $5 down to $5. In the same way, competition among demanders will always force a price lower than $5 up to $5. Price is stable only at $5. Economists refer to that price where quantity demanded equals quantity supplied as the **equilibrium price.** At $P = \$5$, the market clears. There is no excess demand or excess supply.

Exhibit 4 illustrates the forces driving price to equilibrium. At any price other than $P = \$5$, excess demand or supply results, triggering bargaining activity on the part of demanders and suppliers to overcome the market's inability to clear. They force price changes. Price simply reflects their behavior. It gravitates, without exception, toward equilibrium.

Equilibrium price
The price that equates quantity demanded to quantity supplied. If any disturbance from that price occurs, excess demand or excess supply emerges to drive price back to equilibrium.

MARKET-DAY, SHORT-RUN, AND LONG-RUN SUPPLY

But how realistic is this idea of a fixed supply? In Exhibit 4, the quantity supplied remains fixed at 6,000, regardless of price. Is it realistic to suppose that suppliers never think of adjusting the quantity they supply to changing prices? Do fishermen, for example, just keep fishing, day after day, bringing their catch to market without regard to the price their fish fetch on the market? Of course not. A fixed supply makes sense only for the market day. Once the catch is in, today's price cannot affect today's quantity supplied. What is done is done.

But what fishermen will do *tomorrow* depends very much on today's price. A high price today, say $10 per fish, makes fishermen happy and leaves them wishing they had more to supply. While they can't supply more today, they can prepare today to increase the quantity they supply tomorrow. A low price today, on the other hand, say $3 per fish, makes them less happy and less willing to supply fish. While they can't cut supply today—after all, the catch is in—they can prepare today to decrease the quantity they supply tomorrow. Unlike consumers, who can change their quantity demanded instantaneously when prices change, fishermen have to do something to adjust the quantity they supply to price. Doing something takes time.

Let's start with today. Suppose fishermen discover when they get to market that today's price is $10. Are they happy? They're ecstatic! The only regret they have is that their quantity supplied is only 6,000 fish. At that price they wish they had more fish to supply. But they can't undo what is done. What is done is their earlier decision to fish today with a certain amount of boats, crew, and equipment.

Well, what about tomorrow? With a $10 fish in mind, they would love to supply as many as 16,000 if they could. Look at the table in Exhibit 5, column 4.

But how can they possibly increase the quantity of fish supplied from 6,000 to 16,000 *by tomorrow?* They can't. But perhaps the first thing they can do is add more fishermen to their boats. Where would they find them? Well, suppose you are a potato farmer and not particularly happy about the money you are making in the potato business. You may be willing to try something else if that something else paid more; that is, if it met your opportunity cost. With fish now fetching $10, it may be just enough to make you switch from potato farming to fishing.

EXHIBIT|5

MARKET-DAY, SHORT-RUN, AND LONG-RUN SUPPLY

MARKET-DAY, SHORT-RUN, AND LONG-RUN SUPPLY

	PRICE	MARKET DAY	SHORT RUN	LONG RUN
a →	$10	6,000	8,500	16,000
b →	9	6,000	8,000	14,000
	8	6,000	7,500	12,000
	7	6,000	7,000	10,000
	6	6,000	6,500	8,000
	5	6,000	6,000	6,000
	4	6,000	5,500	4,000
c →	3	6,000	5,000	2,000
	2	6,000	4,500	0
	1	6,000	4,000	0

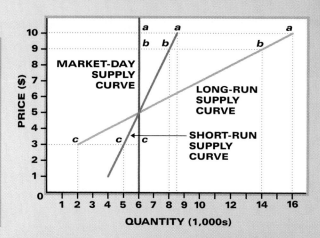

All three supply curves are upward sloping. At $P = \$10$, point a on the three supply curves, the quantity supplied on the market day is 6,000, the quantity supplied in the short run is 8,500, and the quantity supplied in the long run is 16,000. At $P = \$9$, point b on the three curves, the quantity supplied on the market day is 6,000, the quantity supplied in the short run is 8,000, and the quantity supplied in the long run is 14,000. At $P = \$3$, point c on the three curves, the quantity supplied on the market day is 6,000, the quantity supplied in the short run is 5,000, and the quantity supplied in the long run is 2,000.

But there are limits to how many people fishermen can add to their boats. If the boats are designed for crews of six, adding one or two more per boat may bring in more fish, but not the 16,000 fish that fishermen are willing to supply. Anyway, hiring more crew takes time, and the new crew may have very little experience.

What else can fishermen do to increase the quantity supplied? Another option is to stay out on the water for more hours. But staying out longer means consuming more fuel, more bait, and more ice packaging, all of which may be in short supply.

They do the best they can. Suppose their best effort, given the limitation of boat size, increases the quantity supplied from the market day's 6,000 to 8,500 fish. Look at column 3 in the table in Exhibit 5.

Now, 8,500 fish is more than 6,000 but still considerably less than the 16,000 that fishermen want to supply at $P = \$10$. But to reach 16,000 requires more boats (not just more crew or longer hours), and boat making, let's suppose, takes a full year. In other words, for tomorrow at least, they're stuck at 8,500. Until more or bigger boats are available, their only course of action is to produce as much as they can on the boats they already have. This time interval during which suppliers are able to change the quantity of some but not all the resources they use to produce goods and services is called the **short run.** The 8,500 fish, then, is the quantity supplied in the short run at $P = \$10$.

What about quantity supplied in the **long run?** What distinguishes the long from the short run? In the long run, suppliers have the time to change the quantity of *all* the resources they use to produce goods and services. In the fishing business, the long run is a year—the time it takes to acquire as many boats as fishermen wish. As we see in the table in Exhibit 5, fishermen end up in the long run acquiring enough boats to produce 16,000 fish.

Short run
The time interval during which suppliers are able to change the quantity of some but not all the resources they use to produce goods and services.

Long run
The time interval during which suppliers are able to change the quantity of all the resources they use to produce goods and services.

THEORETICAL PERSPECTIVE

HOW LONG DOES IT TAKE TO GET TO THE LONG RUN?

How long does it take to reach the long run? Well, it depends.

Focus on the time that elapses between the quantity supplied on a market day and the quantity the suppliers would have been willing to offer at that market-day price.

Consider the babysitting market of panel *a*. If the market-day price was $3 per hour on January 1, 2001, and on that day 100 hours had been supplied, babysitters would be less than ecstatic because $3 is a very unattractive price. How long will it take babysitters to find alternative employment? Not long, don't you think? Within a month or so, the quantity supplied of babysitters at $3 would fall from 100 to 30 hours, from point *a* to point *b* on the graph. On the other hand, if the market-day price was $20 per hour, then babysitters supplying those 100 hours would be delighted and it wouldn't take long—a month perhaps—for other people to switch from whatever else they were doing to babysitting. The quantity supplied would jump to 400 hours, from point *c* to point *d*.

Now think about Illinois farmers in the corn market of panel *b*. Suppose the price of corn was

YOU'RE A GRAPE NOW, BUT YOU'LL BE A DELICIOUS WINE IN 20 YEARS!

$20 per bushel and the market-day supply was 100 bushels. Farmers would be ecstatic, not having seen such a high price before! They would love to produce 400 bushels—but how do you supply more corn when the planting season was last spring? In order to increase the quantity supplied, they must wait for the next planting season to adjust their supply to the $20 price. That is, it takes them a full year to move from point *x* to point *y* on the graph.

How long do you suppose it takes California wine producers to increase their quantity supplied of 20-year wine from the market-day 100 bottles to the long-run 400 bottles—from point *r* to point *s* on the graph in panel *c*—when the market-day price is an attractive $20 per bottle? Think about it. How can you produce 20-year wine in less than 20 years? You see the picture, don't you? The length of time it takes to get from market-day supply to long-run supply depends on the character of the good. It takes little time for babysitting, and a much, much longer time for aged wine.

Why don't suppliers shift instantaneously to the long run when p[...]

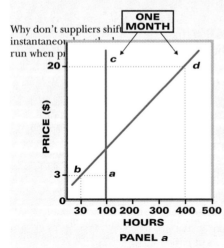

ONE MONTH

PANEL *a*

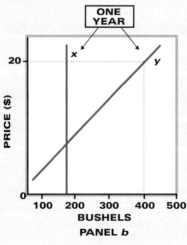

ONE YEAR

PANEL *b*

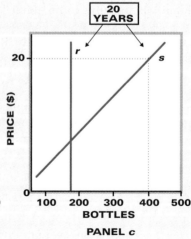

20 YEARS

PANEL *c*

The graph in Exhibit 5 translates the table into graphic form.

The higher the price of fish, the greater the incentive to produce more. As you see for the long run in the table, when the price is $9, fishermen are willing and able to supply 14,000, slightly less than the 16,000 they are willing and able to supply at a price of $10. Why do they supply less? Fishermen will tell you that a $9 fish is not as profitable as a $10 fish. As a result, they hire a smaller crew. As well, fewer potato farmers would be sufficiently motivated to leave potato farming for a $9 fish. Fewer boats are ordered. Still, $9 is a relatively good price for fish. Compare the 8,000 quantity they are willing to supply in the short run to the 14,000 they are willing to and do supply in the long run.

But look what happens at the relatively low $3 price. The market-day supply is fixed at 6,000. If fishermen have time to adjust supply, they will adjust downward. Some who have good options may quit fishing outright. (Some may end up on a potato farm!) Others may continue to fish but produce less with smaller crews.

It isn't easy to quit outright even if there are job opportunities for fishermen elsewhere. After all, many fishermen have an emotional investment in their business and little experience at other jobs. (Ask anybody going through job retraining today.) Moreover, they have boats and equipment that represent a substantial financial investment. It may pay them to continue fishing even if the prospects are not very attractive, at least until their boats need substantial overhauling. Then the decision to shut down or stay afloat is forced.

CHECK YOUR UNDERSTANDING

Why don't suppliers shift instantaneously to the long run when prices change?

As you see in the table in Exhibit 5, at $P = \$3$, fishermen cut back the quantity they supply in the short run to 5,000 and, given time, in the long run will trim back further to 2,000. At the much lower price of $1, very few fishermen go out on the water, cutting back further in the short run and supplying no fish at all in the long run.

All three supply curves are upward sloping, but the slope varies with the suppliers' ability to adjust to the different prices. The market-day supply curve is perfectly vertical, with no adjustment to price variations. The short-run supply curve shows moderate flexibility in adjusting quantity supplied to price, while the long-run supply curve has the most gradual slope, reflecting the fishermen's ability to adjust *fully* to price.

CHANGES IN DEMAND

Let's now look at the fish market of the table in Exhibit 6, whose short-run supply (column 2) is drawn from the table in Exhibit 5 and whose initial demand schedule (column 3) is drawn from the table in Exhibit 4. Now suppose that the demand for fish changes from the schedule shown in column 3 to the one shown in column 4.

Note what happens. At each price, 1,000 more fish are demanded. Prior to the **change in demand,** the quantity demanded at $P = \$10$ was 3,500 fish. It increases now to 4,500. It increases at $P = \$9$ from 4,000 to 5,000, and so on.

The graph in Exhibit 6 depicts the change in demand shown in the table. Demand curve D, graphing the initial demand schedule (column 3), shifts outward to the right to D', graphing the new demand schedule (column 4). Look at the impact on the equilibrium price of fish of the change in demand from D to D'. The old equilibrium price, $P = \$5$, is no longer tenable. Now, at that price, an excess demand of 1,000 fish emerges. The pressure of this excess demand forces the equilibrium price up to $P = \$6$, where the 6,500 quantity of fish demanded equals the 6,500 quantity supplied.

What could cause such a change in demand? There are a number of reasons why people change the quantity they demand at the same price. The principal reasons are changes in income, changes in taste, changes in other prices, changes in expectations about future prices, and changes in population size. Let's consider each.

Change in demand
A change in quantity demanded of a good that is caused by factors other than a change in the price of that good.

EXHIBIT 6

CHANGE IN DEMAND

FISH MARKET WITH CHANGE IN DEMAND

PRICE	QUANTITY SUPPLIED	INITIAL QUANTITY DEMANDED	INCREASE IN QUANTITY DEMANDED	DECREASE IN QUANTITY DEMANDED
$10	8,500	3,500	4,500	2,500
9	8,000	4,000	5,000	3,000
8	7,500	4,500	5,500	3,500
7	7,000	5,000	6,000	4,000
6	6,500	5,500	6,500	4,500
5	6,000	6,000	7,000	5,000
4	5,500	6,500	7,500	5,500
3	5,000	7,000	8,000	6,000
2	4,500	7,500	8,500	6,500
1	4,000	8,000	9,000	7,000

a → (row 6)
b → (row 4)

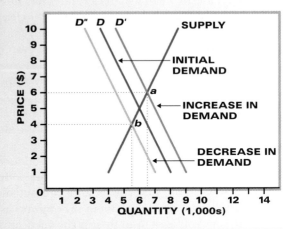

Ceteris paribus, an increase in demand from D to D' raises the equilibrium price from $5 to $6, point a on the graph. The quantity bought and sold increases from 6,000 to 6,500. A decrease in demand from D to D'' lowers the equilibrium price from $5 to $4, point b on the graph, and reduces the quantity bought and sold from 6,000 to 5,500.

Changes in Income

You don't suppose, do you, that when Madonna dines out in one of New York's finest restaurants, she checks the price of poached salmon to see whether she's willing to make the purchase? Wouldn't you be surprised if she orders the salmon at $P = $5 but passes at $P = $10?

The more income people have, the more they can afford to buy more of everything. If Claudia Preparata's income were to increase by 25 percent, she might be more willing to buy that first fish at $10. Before, she passed it up. It isn't surprising, then, that when people's incomes increase, the quantity demanded of fish at $P = $10 increases from 3,500 to 4,500. It increases as well at every other price level.

On the other hand, what do you suppose happens to the demand for fish when incomes fall? You would expect that the quantity demanded at $P = $10 would fall from 3,500 fish to something less and that the quantity demanded at $P = $9 would fall from 4,000 to something less, and so on. To economists, fish is a **normal good**— that is, a good whose demand increases (or decreases) when people's incomes increase (or decrease).

Normal good
A good whose demand increases or decreases when people's incomes increase or decrease.

Changes in Taste

Tastes seldom change overnight, but they do change. Suppose that the surgeon general reports that the consumption of red meat is detrimental to health. If enough people worry about the quantity of meat they consume and make a conscious effort to cut down, the demand for fish would increase.

Sometimes, tastes are learned or cultivated. Advertising has much to do with it. Suppose McDonald's came to the island and introduced its filet of fish. Wouldn't *some* people, tasting McDonald's fish for the first time, switch from meat to fish? Can you picture the McDonald's fish commercials? If a McDonald's

INTERDISCIPLINARY PERSPECTIVE

WHETHER IT'S LOVE OR WISDOM, THE ANSWER IS FISH

In the Broadway musical *Carousel*, Carrie Pipperidge confides to her good friend Julie Jourdan early in the first act that she's in love with Mr. Snow, a New England fisherman. She sings:

> The first time I saw him
> A whiff of his clothes
> Knocked me flat on the floor
> Of the room
> But now that I love him
> My heart's in my nose
> And fish is my favorite
>   perfume

That's one reason to be keen on fish, but certainly not the only one. You don't have to be love-struck to think of fish as a favorite.

JULIE, HOW ABOUT A FISH SANDWICH AFTER THE RIDE?

Just compare a swordfish dinner to any of the fast foods listed in the following table in terms of fat content—particularly saturated fat—and you will quickly understand that although we may enjoy those foods while we're busy eating, we eventually pay the "price." You don't have to be a rocket scientist to see why people's tastes are changing from beef and even chicken to fish. The result: The demand curve for fish keeps shifting to the right. Visualize the changing equilibrium price. Fish that used to be relatively inexpensive isn't any longer.

	WEIGHT (oz)	TOTAL FAT (g)	SATURATED FAT (g)	SODIUM (mg)	CALORIES
SWORDFISH	8	11	02.7	297	130
BIG MAC	8	31	10.0	880	560
WHOPPER	8	43	18.0	920	660
ARBY'S SANDWICH	8	28	11.0	1561	555
KFC CHICKEN PIECES	8	34	08.5	1530	540
HARDEE'S HAMBURGER	8	30	12.0	1030	530
WENDY'S HAMBURGER	8	20	07.0	920	420

commercial pushed fish, people on the island would probably end up buying more fish at each price. At $P = \$10$, for example, quantity demanded might increase from 3,500 to 4,500 fish.

Can you think of any other circumstances that could cause a change in taste? Go to the Interactive Study Center at http://gottheil.swcollege.com and click on the "Your Turn" button to submit your example. Student submissions will be posted to the Web site, and perhaps we will use some in future additions of the book!

Changes in the Prices of Other Goods

You don't have to be frightened by the surgeon general's report to substitute fish for beef. Prices alone can do it. For example, if the price of hamburger jumped suddenly from \$1.89 to \$2.45 per pound, that might be incentive enough for many people to switch from hamburger to fish. After all, fish and hamburger are **substitute goods.** When the price of one increases, the demand for the other increases.

Substitute goods
Goods that can replace each other. When the price of one increases, the demand for the other increases.

Suppose people on the island typically eat fish with fries. And suppose, as well, that the price of potatoes increases from $0.75 to $2.75 a pound. What happens to the demand for fish? It falls. People demand less fish at each price because the "fish 'n' fries" combo is more expensive. Fish and fries are **complementary goods.** When the price of one increases, the demand for the other decreases.

Can you think of other complementary goods? How about coffee and milk, milk and cookies, peanut butter and jelly, bagels and cream cheese? Coca-Cola once advertised that "Things go better with Coke." What happens to the demand for Coke when the prices of those "things" increase? It falls.

Changes in Expectations About Future Prices

The demand for fish may change just because people change their expectations about tomorrow's fish price. If you thought that the price of fish would increase tomorrow, you might be willing to buy more fish today; that alone could explain why, at $P = \$10$, the quantity demanded increases from 3,500 to 4,500 (and increases at every price level) in the table in Exhibit 6. Of course, if you had a notion that tomorrow's price would be lower, you might delay consumption by reducing the quantity demanded today. In such a case, the demand for fish decreases.

Changes in Population Size

Suppose an immigration wave increases the island's population by 10 percent. How does such an increase affect the demand for fish? With more mouths to feed, the quantity of fish demanded at each price increases. A baby boom on the island would have the same effect.

A Change in Demand or a Change in Quantity Demanded?

Changes in quantity demanded and changes in demand may seem to be two ways of expressing the same idea, but they are not. What's the difference?

Economists define *change in quantity demanded* to mean only the change in quantity demanded of a good that is brought about by a change in the price of that good. They define *change in demand* to mean a shift in the entire demand curve.

Look at demand curve *D* in Exhibit 7. When price falls from $P = \$10$ to $P = \$7$, the quantity demanded increases from 4,500 to 5,000. Economists describe this increase as "a change in quantity demanded." It traces out a movement *along the demand curve* from point *a* to point *b*.

When demand increases for other reasons, such as population growth, the entire demand curve shifts from *D* to *D'*. Economists call this shift "a

Complementary goods
Goods that are generally used together. When the price of one increases, the demand for the other decreases.

EXHIBIT|7

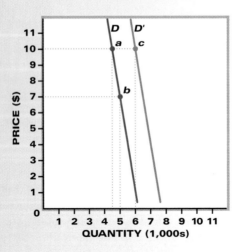

DISTINGUISHING CHANGES IN DEMAND FROM CHANGES IN QUANTITY DEMANDED

Movement along the demand curve *D* from a price of $10, at point *a*, to a price of $7, at point *b*, illustrates a *change in quantity demanded* from 4,500 to 5,000. A shift in the demand curve from *D* to *D'* illustrates a *change in demand*. At a price of $10, the quantity increases from 4,500 on demand curve *D* to 6,000 on demand curve *D'*.

change in demand." At the same price, $P = \$10$, the quantity demanded increases from 4,500 on D to 6,000 on D'. The shift in the demand curve from D to D'—point a to point c at $P = \$10$—occurs because of a determining factor such as a change in people's tastes or income. It is not a result of a change in the price of the good.

CHECK YOUR UNDERSTANDING

What's the difference between a change in demand and a change in quantity demanded?

CHANGES IN SUPPLY

Let us now consider what happens to price when changes in short-run supply occur. Let's suppose that the demand schedule is the same as the one in column 4 of the table in Exhibit 6. The change in short-run supply is 1,000 more fish added (at every price) to the supply schedule of Exhibit 6. The table in Exhibit 8 records this market condition.

The graph in Exhibit 8 depicts the **change in supply** shown in the table.

Supply curve S, graphing the initial supply schedule (column 3), shifts outward to the right to S', graphing the new supply schedule (column 4). Look at its impact on the equilibrium price of fish. The initial equilibrium, $P = \$6$, is no longer tenable. Now, at that price an excess supply of 1,000 fish emerges. The pressure of this excess supply drives the equilibrium price down from $P = \$6$ to $P = \$5$, and the quantities bought and sold up from 6,500 to 7,000 fish.

What could cause such a change in supply? There are a number of reasons why fishermen change the quantity they are willing to supply at every price. The principal reasons are changes in technology, changes in resource prices, changes in the prices of other goods, and changes in the number of suppliers. Let's consider each.

Change in supply
A change in quantity supplied of a good that is caused by factors other than a change in the price of that good.

Changes in Technology
Suppose Steve Scariano, an electronics tinkerer on the island, invents a sonar device that allows fishermen to detect the presence of fish at considerable depths. What a bonanza! Imagine JoAnn Weber, one of the island's fishermen, using the same boat and crew but installing Steve's sonar device on her boat. What do you

CHANGE IN SUPPLY

FISH MARKET WITH CHANGE IN SUPPLY

PRICE	QUANTITY DEMANDED	INITIAL QUANTITY SUPPLIED	INCREASE IN QUANTITY SUPPLIED	DECREASE IN QUANTITY SUPPLIED
$10	4,500	8,500	9,500	7,500
9	5,000	8,000	9,000	7,000
8	5,500	7,500	8,500	6,500
7	6,000	7,000	8,000	6,000
6	6,500	6,500	7,500	5,500
5	7,000	6,000	7,000	5,000
4	7,500	5,500	6,500	4,500
3	8,000	5,000	6,000	4,000
2	8,500	4,500	5,500	3,500
1	9,000	4,000	5,000	3,000

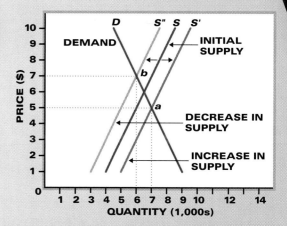

Ceteris paribus, an increase in supply from S to S', lowers the equilibrium price from $6 to $5, point a on the graph. The quantity bought and sold increases from 6,500 to 7,000. A decrease in supply from S to S'' raises the equilibrium price from $6 to $7, point b on the graph, and reduces the quantity bought and sold from 6,500 to 6,000.

EXHIBIT | 8

suppose happens to the quantity of fish she is now capable of bringing home? At every price the quantity supplied increases.

Why? New technology, such as Steve's sonar device, typically lowers the cost of producing a good. Each fish is now cheaper to produce. That means higher profit for fishermen. That higher profit makes fishing even more attractive and becomes an incentive for fishermen to supply more at every price.

Changes in Resource Prices

If lower costs raise profit and create incentive to supply more at every price, then any factor that contributes to lowering costs will increase supply. Consider what happens to the supply curve when resource prices associated with fishing fall. For example, suppose the price (wages) of hiring fishing crews falls. Instead of paying a boat pilot $300 a day, fishermen find that pilots are readily available at $200. Or suppose the prices of bait, fishing gear, fuel, and ice fall. These lower resource prices increase the spread between the market price a fisherman gets for a fish and the costs involved in producing it. That increased spread is greater profit per fish. In other words, lower resource prices increase the quantities of fish supplied at every price in the fish market.

Imagine what happens to the supply curve if resources associated with fish production become more expensive. The reverse occurs. More expensive resources decrease the quantities supplied at every price in the fish market. We see this in S'', a new supply curve to the left of S in Exhibit 8.

Changes in the Prices of Other Goods

Many boats, with minor alterations, can serve multiple purposes. For example, a sightseeing boat that transports tourists from island to island can be rigged to fish the same waters. Cargo boats can be scrubbed down and fitted for passengers. Fishing boats can haul cargo.

Suppose faltering island tourism causes the price of sightseeing boat tickets to fall. How long will it take before some of the sightseeing boat operators switch to fishing? And how will that switch affect the supply curve of fish? This change in price of other goods (sightseeing boat tickets) shifts the supply curve of fish out to the right.

Let's digress for a moment. Consider potato farmers. Their fields, too, can serve multiple purposes. If the price of corn skyrockets, many potato farmers may switch from potato to corn farming. How would the switch affect the supply schedule of potatoes? At every price in the potato market, the quantity of potatoes supplied falls. Graphed, it would show the supply curve of potatoes shifting to the left.

Changes in the Number of Suppliers

Perhaps the first thing that comes to mind when trying to explain what could cause the shift from S to S' is simply more suppliers. Somewhat akin to a change in demand occasioned by a change in taste, a change in supply caused by greater numbers of suppliers might reflect changes in people's occupational "taste." More people choosing to fish means more fish at every price.

WHY THE PRICE OF AN ORANGE IS 30 CENTS AT THE SUPERMARKET

The same factors governing the $6 equilibrium price of fish govern as well the 30-cent equilibrium price of oranges. The price of oranges depends upon the supply and demand conditions in the fruit and vegetable market.

If orange imports from Spain, Morocco, and Israel are added to our California and Florida orange supply, the supply curve in the orange market shifts out to the right, forcing the equilibrium price to fall.

Grapefruit and oranges are substitute goods. If the grapefruit harvest in both California and Florida is exceptionally large, resulting in a substantial fall in the price of grapefruit, the demand curve for oranges shifts to the left. The result? The price of oranges falls.

Suppose, on the other hand, that TV commercials sponsored by the orange-growers industry persuade people that orange juice is not only a breakfast drink but an excellent substitute for soft drinks, tea, coffee, or milk at any time of the day. What should the orange growers expect? The demand curve for their oranges shifts to the right, raising both price and quantity.

Exhibit 9 illustrates precisely how changes in demand and supply can generate changes in the equilibrium price and quantity of oranges.

Suppose both the demand for and the supply of oranges increase simultaneously. For example, health-conscious people switch from consuming soft drinks to consuming orange juice at the same time as orange growers switch to a new harvesting technology that lowers the cost of producing oranges. We see this in panels *a* and *b*, where demand shifts from *D* to *D'* and supply shifts from *S* to *S'*. But note the differences in the size of the shifts. In panel *a*, the demand shift is the more pronounced. In panel *b*, the supply shift dominates. How do these differences affect changes in the price and quantity of oranges?

Let's start with panel *a*. When either demand or supply increases, quantity increases. So when both demand and supply increase at the same time (more orange juice drinkers and newer technology), the combined result increases quantity from 100 to 200 oranges. What about price? Here, the outcome is less clear. An increase in demand, by itself, raises price. But an increase in supply, by itself, decreases price. The combined effect, then, depends on the relative size of the demand and supply increases. In panel *a*, the sizable increase in demand raises price from $0.30 to $0.50, or by $0.20. The less-than-sizable increase in supply lowers price from $0.30 to $0.20, or by $0.10. As you can see, the net effect is an

INCREASES IN DEMAND AND SUPPLY

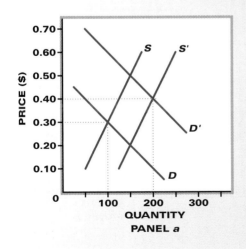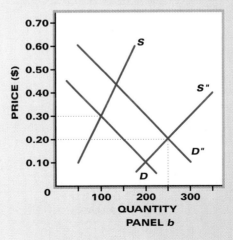

Increases in demand and supply increase the quantities demanded and supplied on the market. In panel *a*, quantity increases to 200 oranges; in panel *b*, to 250 oranges. But the effect of these increases on price depends on the relative size increases in demand and supply. When the demand increase is more sizable than the increase in supply, price rises, as we see in panel *a*, from $0.30 to $0.40. When the supply increase is more sizable than the increase in demand, price falls, as we see in panel *b*, from $0.30 to $0.20.

EXHIBIT 9

increase in equilibrium price to $0.40. This is because the effect of the change in demand dominates price.

Now look at panel *b*. Here the sizable increase occurs in supply. The increase in orange juice drinkers and new technology shifts the demand and supply curves to *D″* and *S″*, so that the combined effect raises quantity from 100 to 250 oranges. What about price? It falls to $0.20. This is because the effect of the change in supply dominates price.

Exhibit 10 depicts another version of supply and demand changes in the market for oranges. Now the changes move in opposite directions. More orange juice drinkers (increase in demand) combine with a late spring frost that destroys orange groves (decrease in supply). What happens to price under these circumstances? Since both an increase in demand and a decrease in supply raise price, their combined effect unequivocally increases price. This we see in panel *a*, where price increases from $0.30 to $0.50. What about quantity? Here, the combined effect is less clear. The increase in demand increases quantity, while the decrease in supply decreases quantity. Because the decrease in supply is more sizable in panel *a*, the combined effect is a decrease in quantity, from 100 to 75 oranges.

Finally, look at the panel *b* variation, where the increase in demand is more sizable than the decrease in supply. Now price ends up at $0.45 and quantity increases to 200 oranges.

POSTSCRIPT: PRICE AS A RATIONING MECHANISM

Consider again the fish market. The demand curve for fish, *D*, depicted in Exhibit 11, panel *a*, is not simply a line drawn on a graph. Each point on that curve represents somebody's willingness to buy fish at some price and, as well, that same person's unwillingness to buy at a higher one. For example, point *a* tells us that Faye Russo will pay $8 for a fish, but will not pay $9. Whether she eats fish or not depends strictly on its price. Point *b* tells us that Jackie Mathews is willing to buy a fish as long as price is no higher than $7. Kim Deal will go as high as $6, Wayne Coyne stops at $3, and Ian Rodier, who likes fish but can't put two pennies

EXHIBIT | 10

INCREASES IN DEMAND, DECREASES IN SUPPLY

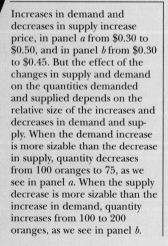

Increases in demand and decreases in supply increase price, in panel *a* from $0.30 to $0.50, and in panel *b* from $0.30 to $0.45. But the effect of the changes in supply and demand on the quantities demanded and supplied depends on the relative size of the increases and decreases in demand and supply. When the demand increase is more sizable than the decrease in supply, quantity decreases from 100 oranges to 75, as we see in panel *a*. When the supply decrease is more sizable than the increase in demand, quantity increases from 100 to 200 oranges, as we see in panel *b*.

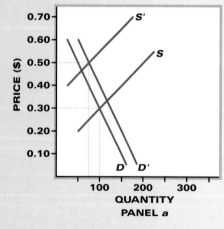

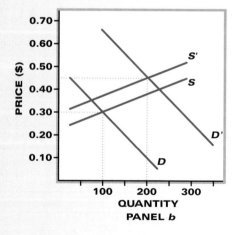

EXHIBIT|11

RATIONING FUNCTION OF PRICE

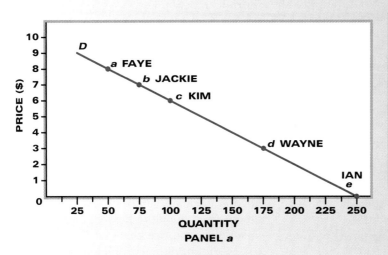

PANEL a

Panel *a* identifies specific people's willingness to buy fish at various prices. Altogether, 250 people express a willingness to buy fish. But who gets them? Panel *b* shows the market for fish and its equilibrium price. Only those willing to pay the market price get the fish. All others don't. The demand curve, *D,* and the supply curve, *S,* generate a market price of $6 and a quantity demanded and supplied of 100. It means 100 of the 250 end up with fish, among them Kim Deal. When the supply curve decreases to S', price rises to $7 and quantity falls to 75 fish. It means 75 people end up with fish, and 175 who want fish don't, among them Kim Deal. In this way, price services as a rationing mechanism.

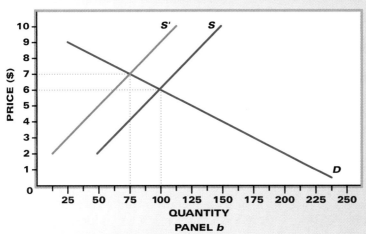

PANEL b

together, eats fish only when price is zero. Adding their demand for fish to everyone else's on demand curve *D* generates a total quantity demanded, albeit at different prices, of 250 fish.

Let's now introduce a supply curve, *S,* to the market. As we see in panel *b,* supply and demand create an equilibrium price of $6 and an equilibrium quantity of 100 fish bought and sold on the market.

Consider those 100 fish. How are they rationed among the 250 people who want fish? You already know the answer, don't you? Everybody positioned on the segment of the demand curve above $6 gets a fish; everyone positioned on the demand curve below $6 doesn't. *The $6 equilibrium price becomes the market's rationing mechanism.* Who are those 100 people? We know they include Faye, Jackie, and Kim. Who are the 150 people who end up without fish? We know they include Wayne and Ian.

If the supply curve shifts to the left to S′, the equilibrium price rises to $7 and the equilibrium quantity falls to 75. There are now fewer fish bought and sold. Faye and Jackie still get fish, but Kim, who would buy fish if price were $6, is shut out of the market at $7. She's disappointed. Her income hasn't changed, her taste for fish hasn't changed, but the price she confronts has. She knows, as you do, that price dictates who gets and who doesn't.

CHAPTER REVIEW

1. Consumer demand reflects people's willingness to buy a good. People supply goods on the presumption that there will be a demand for them.

2. The demand for a good represents people's willingness to purchase specific quantities at specific prices. The law of demand is the inverse relationship between price and the quantity demanded. As the price of a good decreases, the quantity demanded increases and vice versa.

3. Graphs translate tabular data for quantities demanded at different prices into individual demand curves. Demand curves have negative slopes because price and quantity demanded are inversely related.

4. Market demand curves represent the sum of individual quantities demanded at different prices.

5. Supply involves production activity over a period of time. The market day is a time period so short that the quantity supplied cannot be changed no matter what price is paid to the supplier. Therefore, quantity supplied is constant during the market day, regardless of price.

6. Market price is determined by the intersection of demand and supply. Because quantity demanded and quantity supplied are equal at the market price, it is also called equilibrium price. If price is above its equilibrium level, an excess supply results and creates competition among suppliers, which drives price down to equilibrium. If price is below its equilibrium level, an excess demand results and creates competition among demanders, which drives price up to equilibrium. There is no excess demand or excess supply in equilibrium. The market clears.

7. In a time period longer than the market day, suppliers can respond to changes in price.

The short run is a time period long enough to allow suppliers to make partial adjustments in production in response to price changes. The long run is a time period long enough to allow suppliers to completely adjust their production to changes in price. The longer the time period, the more flexible the response by suppliers to price changes. Thus, as time passes, the supply curve shifts from a vertical line to a flatter, positively sloped line.

8. Changes in demand cause changes in the equilibrium price. When demand increases (shifting the demand curve to the right), excess demand emerges at the original equilibrium, causing price to rise to a new and higher equilibrium where quantity supplied once again equals quantity demanded. When demand decreases (shifting the demand curve to the left), the excess supply at the original equilibrium causes price to fall to a new and lower equilibrium where quantity supplied once again equals quantity demanded.

9. Changes in demand are induced by changes in income, changes in taste, changes in the prices of other goods, changes in expectations about future prices, and changes in population size.

10. Complementary goods have inverse relationships such that an increase in the price of one results in a decrease in the demand for the others (for example, bread and butter). Substitute goods, on the other hand, have direct relationships among themselves such that an increase in the price of one results in an increase in the demand for the others (for example, bread and bagels).

11. Changes in supply cause changes in the equilibrium price. When supply increases (shifting the supply curve to the right), excess supply

emerges at the original equilibrium, causing price to fall to a new and lower equilibrium where quantity supplied once again equals quantity demanded. When supply increases (shifting the supply curve to the left), the excess demand at the original equilibrium causes price to rise to a new and higher equilibrium where quantity supplied once again equals quantity demanded.

12. Changes in supply are induced by changes in technology, changes in resource prices, changes in the prices of other goods, and changes in the number of suppliers.

13. Simultaneous shifts in demand and supply lead to changes in equilibrium price and quantity. Whether price increases or decreases, or whether quantity increases or decreases, depends on the direction and strength of these shifts.

14. Price serves as a rationing mechanism in our economy. As price increases, the available supply of a good is rationed to those who can still afford to buy it. A decrease in price makes a good available to a wider segment of the market because more people are able to buy it.

KEY TERMS

Change in quantity demanded
Law of demand
Demand schedule
Demand curve
Market demand
Supply schedule

Market-day supply
Supply curve
Excess supply
Excess demand
Equilibrium price
Short run

Long run
Change in demand
Normal good
Substitute goods
Complementary goods
Change in supply

QUESTIONS

1. Draw a demand curve representing King Richard's plea "A horse, a horse, my kingdom for a horse!"

2. Explain why the market-day supply curve for fish described in the chapter is drawn vertically.

3. Why are the slopes of the short-run supply curve and the long-run supply curve different?

4. "Prices always tend toward equilibrium." Discuss this statement by demonstrating why every other price is unsustainable.

5. Suppose NAFTA (the U.S. free trade agreement with Canada and Mexico) allows the neighboring economies to enter our slipper market. Draw a graph showing the probable effects of their entry on price and quantity of slippers demanded and supplied in the United States.

6. When the price of hamburger rises, the demand for fish rises. When the price of hamburger rises, the demand for hamburger buns falls. Why?

7. Hans Gienepp is frustrated every year. In March, the price of tomatoes is $1.75 per pound. That is sufficient incentive for him to plant tomatoes in his yard. But in August, when the crop is ready for picking, prices at the grocer have fallen to 25 cents per pound. "I always run into this bad luck," he laments. Why is his problem not a matter of luck?

8. Because there was a rumor in May that the price of compact disc players was going to increase in August, the demand for compact disc players went up in May. Explain.

9. How would each of the following events affect the international price of oil (in each case ceteris paribus): (a) the United States gives economic assistance to oil-rich Ukraine in the form of oil-drilling technology; (b) Iraq, in a war against Saudi Arabia, destroys 50 percent of Saudi oil wells; (c) a U.S. invention uses sea-water to fuel automobiles; (d) Western

European homes are heated solely by solar power; and (e) the world's population doubles.

10. How do you explain the fact that a single rose at the supermarket florist is $1.49 every day of the year except the week before and during Valentine's Day, when it increases to $3.50?

11. How do you explain the fact that years ago, cheese was considered the poor person's food, selling for less than a quarter of the price of beef? Today, beef and cheese are priced approximately the same.

12. Jeff Foxworthy is a very funny comedian. He always sells out. So how do you explain the fact that when ticket prices are $10, there are lines around the block a mile long for those tickets, and when the price is $40, he sells out, but there are no lines to be seen? Use a graph to aid your discussion.

13. Orange juice producers are dismayed and puzzled. An economist told them that the reason the demand for orange juice fell is that a new technology allows tomato producers to pick ripe tomatoes more quickly, with less damage and at lower cost. Can you make the connection?

14. Professor Carrie Meyer of George Mason University presents her students with the following scenario: "Suppose a frost destroys much of the coffee harvest in Colombia. Show why equilibrium price and quantity change. Suppose, during this period, many coffee drinkers learn to kick the coffee habit. What happens to price and quantity when coffee production returns to normal in the following year?" How would you answer her question?

PRACTICE PROBLEMS

1. Suppose the communities of Urbana, Champaign, Rantoul, and Danville make up the east-central Illinois market for eggplant. And suppose, at a price of $2, the quantity demanded in Champaign is 2,000, in Urbana 1,000, in Rantoul 400, and in Danville 600. When price falls to $1, the quantity demanded in Champaign becomes 3,000, in Urbana 1,500, in Rantoul 500, and in Danville 700. With these data, graph the east-central Illinois market for eggplant, connecting the points to form a demand curve.

2. Suppose people leave neighboring Indiana and Iowa to settle in east-central Illinois. Show on the graph of practice problem 1 what happens to the demand curve for eggplant in the east-central Illinois market.

3. Would such an influx of people to east-central Illinois change the demand curve for eggplant or the quantity demanded of eggplant?

4. Suppose the market for holiday candles was described by the following schedule:

PRICE	QUANTITY DEMANDED	QUANTITY SUPPLIED
$6	1,000	6,000
5	2,000	5,000
4	3,000	4,000
3	4,000	3,000
2	5,000	2,000
1	6,000	1,000

Draw the demand and supply curves and identify the equilibrium price. What effect would a 1,000-unit decrease in demand at every price level have on the demand curve, supply curve, and equilibrium price?

5. The following are the various demand and supply schedules for pizza. Let's start by assuming that the demand and supply on the pizza market are D_2 and S_2. (a) What is the equilibrium price and quantity of pizza? (b) Now suppose people's tastes switch to pizza. What happens to equilibrium price and quantity? (c) Let's add another change to the market. This time let's assume that, although with that change in taste, the price of pizza ingredients (cheese, onions, and so on) falls. What happens to equilibrium price and quantity? (d) Finally, let's suppose that a new health report reveals that pizza is bad for your health and people's demand for pizza falls dramatically, even below the original D_2 schedule. What happens to equilibrium price and quantity?

PRICE	D_1	D_2	D_3	S_1	S_2	S_3
$5	6	10	14	12	14	18
4	8	12	16	10	12	16
3	10	14	18	8	10	14
2	12	16	20	6	8	12
1	14	18	22	4	6	10

WHAT'S WRONG WITH THIS GRAPH?

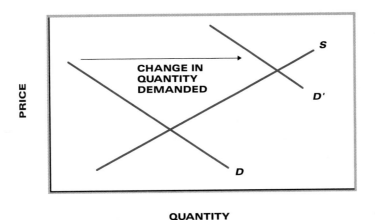

ECONOMIC CONSULTANTS

ECONOMIC RESEARCH AND ANALYSIS BY STUDENTS FOR PROFESSIONALS

Mort's Ostrich Farm produces high-protein, low-fat ostrich meat for restaurants and consumers. Mort's currently supplies a small number of customers, but the firm believes it can increase the quantity it produces and the price it charges with strategies to increase the demand for ostrich meat.

Mort's has approached Economic Consultants for advice on how to increase the demand. Prepare a report for Mort's that addresses the following issues:

1. What strategies can Mort's implement to increase the demand for ostrich meat?
2. Explain to Mort's the difference between changing the demand for ostrich meat versus changing the quantity demanded. Explain what

strategies will cause a change in demand versus a change in the quantity demanded.

You may find the following resources helpful as you prepare this report for Mort's:

● **Ostrich Central** (http://www. connect.net/ratites/), **Ostrich Growers Meat Company** (http:// www.ostrichgrowers.com), and **Warren Ostrich Foods** (http:// www.warrenfoods.com/)— These suppliers of ostrich meat offer distribution across the United States.
● **The Clio Awards** (http://www.clioawards. com)—The Clio Awards highlight the best advertising campaigns in print, radio, and television.

PRACTICE TEST

1. Dog food companies have developed a new technology that makes nutritious dog food out of garbage. We would expect, ceteris paribus, that the
   a. supply curve of dog food would shift to the left.
   b. supply curve of dog food would shift to the right.
   c. demand curve for dog food would shift to the left.
   d. demand curve for dog food would shift to the right.
   e. demand and supply curves would shift to the right.

2. We would also find that the price of dog food would
   a. fall because the supply curve shifted to the right.
   b. fall because the supply curve shifted to the left.
   c. fall because the demand curve shifted to the right.
   d. rise because the demand curve shifted to the right.
   e. rise because the demand curve shifted to the left.

3. When the demand curve for bicycles increases while the supply curve remains unchanged,
   a. the quantity demanded decreases.
   b. the equilibrium price increases and the equilibrium quantity decreases.
   c. the equilibrium price decreases and the equilibrium quantity increases.
   d. quantity supplied increases.
   e. quantity supplied decreases.

4. Which of the following will not shift the market short-run supply of corn?
   a. A change in the price of corn
   b. A change in the price of soybeans
   c. A change in the price of herbicides and pesticides
   d. A change in the storage of technology
   e. A change in the number of acres planted of corn

5. As long as an excess demand for fish exists on the market, there will always be an incentive
   a. for demanders to bid the price up.
   b. for demanders to buy fewer fish.
   c. for fishermen to produce and supply fish.
   d. for fishermen to lower the price of fish.
   e. for demanders and suppliers to seek the equilibrium price.

6. In March, if consumers expect the price of in-line skates to increase as the summer approaches,
   a. the market-day supply of in-line skates in March will shift to the right.
   b. the demand for in-line skates in March will shift to the right.
   c. the demand for in-line skates in March will shift to the left.

   d. the current price of in-line skates will fall.
   e. there will be a movement along the demand curve for in-line skates.

7. Ty manufactures Beanie Baby dolls. The market-day supply curve for Beanie Baby dolls is vertical because
   a. Ty is very responsive to price changes.
   b. the consumer demand curves are very responsive to even small price changes.
   c. the price will not change as the quantity supplied changes in the market.
   d. the equilibrium price dictates how many Beanie Babies will be sold each day.
   e. Ty cannot increase its supply during a given day in response to price changes.

SUPPLY AND DEMAND FOR BRIEFCASES

PRICE	QUANTITY SUPPLIED	QUANTITY DEMANDED
$50	100	600
60	200	500
70	300	400
80	350	350
90	400	300

8. The preceding table illustrates the supply and demand schedules for briefcases. The equilibrium price for briefcases in this market
   a. is $50.
   b. is $60.
   c. is $70.
   d. is $80.
   e. cannot be determined without more information.

9. The preceding table illustrates the supply and demand schedule for briefcases. If there is a reduction in the price of leather used to make briefcases, enabling manufacturers to supply 100 additional briefcases at each price, the new equilibrium price
   a. will be the same as the old equilibrium price.
   b. will cause a rightward shift in the market demand curve for briefcases.
   c. will cause a leftward shift in the market demand curve for briefcases.
   d. will be $90.
   e. will be $70.

10. If both the demand and supply curves in the market for oranges shift to the right,
   a. price falls and quantity increases.
   b. price rises and quantity decreases.
   c. price and quantity both decrease.
   d. price increases and it is unclear what happens to quantity.
   e. quantity increases and it is unclear what happens to price.

APPENDIX

ON READING GRAPHS

HOW MUCH IS THAT DOGGIE IN THE WINDOW?

The image of a young child's face pushed flush up against the window of a pet shop, watching puppies at play, is a sight that would warm the cockles of anyone's heart. Is it too great a leap from fish markets to the puppy market? Not really. After all, both fish and puppies are produced for and sold on markets. Supply and demand determine the price of puppies just as supply and demand determine the price of fish.

Look at Exhibit A1. In 1993, the supply, S, and demand, D, for Jack Russell terrier pups generated an equilibrium price of $600 and an equilibrium quantity of 1,000 pups. That was then. This is now. When the sitcom *Frasier* became a sensation on prime-time TV, the market for Jack Russell terriers changed dramatically. Why?

Because the sitcom included a Jack Russell terrier named Eddie who was the darling pet of Frasier's dad. The popularity of the TV sitcom increased the popularity of the Jack Russell terrier as a pet dog. As we see in Exhibit A1, the demand curve for Jack Russell terrier pups shifted from D to D', which caused the equilibrium price of the puppies to rise from $600 to $900 and quantity to increase from 1,000 to 1,400.

What about the child at the pet shop window? Try as he might—clutching 25 cents in his tiny fist—the Jack Russell terrier pup is far beyond his financial means. He may want that pup as badly as any child wants a puppy, but he confronts the rationing function of price and is just out of luck. The pup goes to someone who is willing and able to pay $900. It's as simple as that. It has nothing to do with love of animals, or love of children, or concern for the pup. It has all to do with willingness and ability to pay the price.

MARKET FOR JACK RUSSELL TERRIER PUPPIES

THE CASE OF THE GUIDE DOG

Let's look at a different dog market, this time for guide dogs, which as you know are indispensable to many blind people. Look at Exhibit A2. The supply curve, S, reflects the relatively high cost of training these animals; the demand curve, D,

MARKET FOR GUIDE DOGS

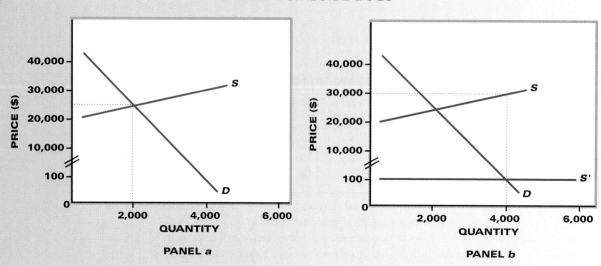

PANEL a

PANEL b

reflects the relatively high value sightless people place on having such a dog. Market equilibrium occurs at a price of $25,000 and a quantity of 2,000 dogs. It is pointless to dispute the market's $25,000 equilibrium price. Reasonable or not, it simply records the interaction of supply and demand on the market. Who gets these dogs depends solely on who can afford to pay $25,000.

But is that *really* the way we want to ration those dogs among demanders? Perhaps we can tolerate a child's longing for but not having a Jack Russell terrier puppy, but can we tolerate a sightless person longing for but not having a guide dog? If that's unacceptable, then how do we go about providing these people with guide dogs at affordable prices?

After all, the willingness and ability of suppliers to supply a good depends, as you know, on the opportunity cost of producing the good. Look at the supply curve in the guide dog market of Exhibit A2, panel *a*. What does it tell us? The willingness and ability of suppliers to supply those dogs depends on the opportunity cost of producing them. For example, suppliers' willingness and ability—measured by opportunity cost—to supply 100 dogs is $20,000. It takes $30,000 to create a quantity supplied of 4,000 dogs. How then can suppliers supply *any* quantity of guide dogs at affordable prices?

Look at Exhibit A2, panel *b*. The actual supply curve that functions in the market is the horizontal supply curve, *S'*, which shows that suppliers are willing and able to supply as many as 5,000 guide dogs at $100 each. But how can suppliers supply those dogs at $100 when the opportunity cost of producing them—reflected in supply curve *S*—is considerably higher than $100? The answer is that the suppliers are supported financially by people like yourself. These suppliers solicit donations—by direct mail, collection cans, and boxes at cashier counters—whose sums are sufficient to make up the $30,000 opportunity cost shown on supply curve *S* at the quantity of 4,000. (Have you ever slotted a quarter in their donation card?)

Why do these suppliers set their supply curve, S', at $100? It is an arbitrarily picked, very affordable price to indicate to their eventual owners that the dogs are not free goods. Can we create a similar donation-supported market for Jack Russell terriers? Of course. But why?

FROM DOGS TO HUMAN BEINGS

If it isn't a great analytical leap from the fish market to the dog market, is it any greater a leap from the pet puppy and guide dog markets to markets for human body parts? Not really. The powerful tools of supply and demand allow us to analyze the highly emotional and ethical issues associated with the buying and selling of human organs. How do we deal with these demands and supplies? Do we put these human body parts on the market as we do fish and puppies? Are their prices market-derived?

The Market for Organ Transplants

Perhaps the most emotionally charged and ethically engaged market we will ever encounter is the market for human organ transplants. At one time—not too many years ago—transplanting a human organ, such as a kidney or lung, from one person to another was strictly science fiction. Today it's a reality. Organ transplantation technology along with genetic engineering has allowed us to defy Mother Nature. How long will it be before we can order through the Internet an upgraded IQ, or a set of lungs, heart, and legs that would allow each of us to break the four-minute mile? Ludicrous? Don't bet on it.

THE MARKET FOR HUMAN KIDNEYS That's the good news. The bad news is depicted in Exhibit A3, panel a, the market for human kidneys. As you see, demand and supply generate an equilibrium price of $120,000, which is far beyond the financial reach of most who need a kidney. The demand curve, D_a, reflects the urgency and intensity of that demand; the supply curve, S_a, reflects the difficulty people have parting with a nonreplenishable organ of their own—a kidney, in this case—or even parting with one after death, or with that of a deceased relative.

Is there a problem with that $120,000 price? Theoretically, not any more so than the $900 price tag on a puppy. Price serves as the rationing function in both markets. People willing and able to pay the price get the kidneys and puppies. Others don't. The question is, Should price serve as the rationing function?

THE NATIONAL TRANSPLANT ORGAN ACT OF 1984 While people may hold strong opinions on this subject, this normative economic issue was resolved, at least legally, with the passage in Congress of the National Transplant Organ Act of 1984. This act disallowed the private sale of organs, making the only legal market for kidneys—and other human organs—the not-for-profit market of Exhibit A3, panel b.

Note the difference. Volunteer donors alone provide the entire supply of 25,000 kidneys, *and that supply has nothing to do with price*. The horizontal supply curve, S_b, reflects the willingness of suppliers—in this case, hospitals—to supply any quantity up to 25,000 kidneys at a price of $20,000, a price that simply covers the cost of harvesting the kidney procured from an unpaid donor.

What about demand? Before the advent of organ transplantation technology, people who suffered an organ failure simply didn't survive. Now, with transplant technology accessible, there is reason to hope—and this hope translates into the Exhibit A3, panel b, demand for kidneys, D_b.

CHECK YOUR UNDERSTANDING

Why is the supply curve horizontal at $20,000?

MARKET FOR HUMAN KIDNEYS

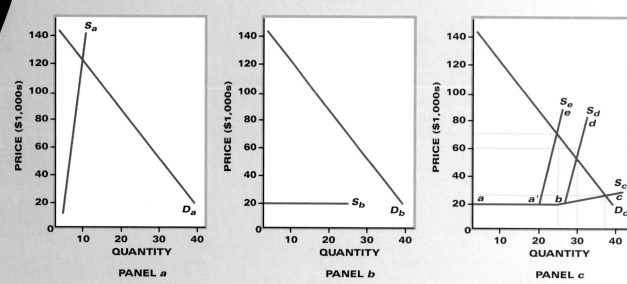

PANEL *a*

PANEL *b*

PANEL *c*

Suppliers (hospitals) supply the 25,000 kidneys at $20,000, but at that price, the quantity supplied falls considerably short of the 40,000 quantity demanded, creating a *chronic* excess demand of 15,000 kidneys.

How, then, are the kidneys allocated among demanders? The rationing function of price is not permitted to clear the market. Some other rationing function—such as age, urgency, or geography—must take its place. However reasonable and fair these rationing systems may appear to be, many who need a kidney transplant still end up without one. To these people, and to many others, the outcome generated by the strictly donor-supplied market is simply intolerable. Is there some way to improve the outcome?

WOULD ORGAN-FOR-A-PRICE SUPPLIERS HELP? Look at the horizontal supply curve, S_b, in Exhibit A3, panel *b*. It shows the willingness of hospitals to supply 25,000 unpaid-donor kidneys at a price of $20,000. This reliance on unpaid-donor kidneys acts as a formidable barrier to any increase in quantity supplied.

What incentive scheme motivated these unpaid donors to volunteer one of their two kidneys, or both upon death? For most donors, it is strictly a matter of altruism, touched perhaps by a history of some personal loss or otherwise moved by compassion and social responsibility.

It would be lovely (certainly for those needing kidney transplants) if more people volunteered an organ, extending the supply curve, S_b, to the right. But if that prospect were not immediately forthcoming, then perhaps another way of increasing supply would be to simply pay people for organs supplied.

Organ-for-a-price supply curves are depicted in Exhibit A3, panel *c*. If it takes just a modest payment to induce many people to supply one or more of their kidneys before or after death, then the supply curve of kidneys may very well look like S_c (line *abc*).

At $20,000, quantity supplied is 25,000 kidneys (line *ab*), reflecting the unpaid organ donors' supply. But thereafter, quantity supplied increases as payments kick in (line *bc*). For example, at a payment of $8,000, the equilibrium price for a kidney increases slightly—from $20,000 to $28,000, but the equilibrium quantity increases more than slightly, from $25,000 to $38,000. An attractive option, don't you think?

On the other hand, if the organ-for-a-price supply curve were S_d (line *abd*), it would take a significant payment to induce just a slight increase in quantity supplied. For example, a $40,000 payment to paid donors increases price from $20,000 to $60,000 and quantity supplied by only 3,000—from 25,000 to 28,000.

Consider yet a third organ-for-a-price supply curve possibility, S_e, (line *aa'e*). Here we see a rather perverse outcome. Suppose some unpaid donors are offended by what they consider to be a callous and coldhearted move toward the organ-for-a-price market and respond by reducing their unpaid organ supply by 5,000 so that quantity supplied at a $20,000 price falls from 25,000 to 20,000 kidneys (line *aa'*). If the organ-for-a-price supply curve is S_d-shaped, then S_e becomes the operative supply curve. Now a $50,000 payment for a kidney drives price to $70,000 and quantity supplied to 24,000. That's 1,000 short of the 25,000 kidneys that would have been supplied by unpaid donors in the absence of an organ-for-a-price market.

Which of these organ-for-a-price supply curves reflects the real world we live in? There is no strong consensus among economists on this vital question.

SCALPING TICKETS AT A YANKEE GAME

Let's end the discussion of supply and demand applications on a less somber note. Suppose you were thinking of going to a Yankee baseball game. Here's the picture. The stadium's capacity is 70,000 seats and when the Yankees are hot, many of their games are sold out. But a sellout doesn't mean you can't buy a ticket! It just means that you will probably have to buy your ticket from a scalper in a **scalper's market**. What does this market look like?

Scalper's market
A market in which a good is resold at a price higher than the original or officially published price.

Let's first look at the scalpers' supply curve. People with season tickets or who have bought tickets in advance may be willing to sell their tickets to a scalper instead of attending the game "if the price is right." If the Yankees are playing well, Yankee fans holding tickets may be reluctant to part with them unless they're paid handsomely for them. For example, a scalper could probably buy a few $35 tickets for $50 each. To get more tickets to resell, the scalper would probably have to pay even more than $50 because it would take a higher price to induce the more devoted fans to give them up. As a result, the supply curve for scalpers' tickets is upward sloping.

If the Yankees are having a rough season, losing many of their games, scores of fair-weather fans may be more than willing to sell their tickets for less than the original $35 price. A scalper may get a few $35 tickets for $20 each and more than a few if the supply price is raised to $30.

What about demand? As there are fair-weather suppliers, there are also fair-weather demanders. If the Yankees are doing well, people without tickets would be willing to pay more than $50 for a $35 ticket at a sold-out game. If the scalper lowers price, the quantity demanded increases. You see the outcome, don't you?

The equilibrium price on the scalper's market for a Yankee ticket depends upon supply and demand, as depicted in Exhibit A4; these supply and demand curves reflect the willingness of ticket holders to sell their tickets and the willingness of

CHECK YOUR UNDERSTANDING

What determines the scalper's price?

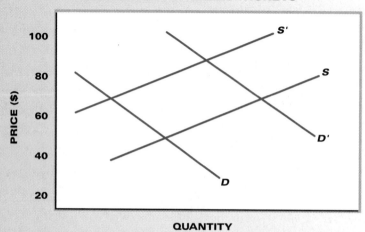

MARKET FOR YANKEES' TICKETS

ticket buyers to pay for those tickets. The scalper is the agent that makes these demands and supplies come to life. If the Yankees are pennant-bound, the demand curve may shift to the right, from *D* to *D'*, while the supply curve shifts to the left, from *S* to *S'*, driving the equilibrium price upward from $50 to $90. Is there anything wrong or unethical about a scalper's market? Not really. It actually represents an honest-to-goodness free market for baseball tickets.

QUESTIONS

1. Think about the market for drug-detecting police dogs and the market for pet dogs. Why would their equilibrium prices differ?

2. Make a case for allowing the market to determine the price and quantity of human body parts. Make the countercase that opposes such a pure market determination.

3. Why is the supply curve in the market for kidneys drawn horizontally when the kidneys obtained by the suppliers (hospitals, in this case) are provided by unpaid donors?

PRACTICE PROBLEMS

1. Let's get ready for the Super Bowl! Suppose the game is played in Chicago at Soldier Field, which has a capacity of 105,000 seats. Ticket prices are $75. The game is sold out, which brings the scalper's market to life. The willingness of ticket holders to sell their $75 tickets is shown in the Quantity Supplied column in the following table. The willingness of people to buy those tickets is shown in the Quantity Demanded column. If you were one of those suppliers, how much would you get for your $75 ticket?

PRICE	QUANTITY SUPPLIED	QUANTITY DEMANDED
$1,000	7,000	500
800	6,000	1,000
600	5,000	2,000
400	4,000	4,000
200	3,000	6,000

2. Now suppose the hype before the game was extraordinary and ticket holders were more reluctant to part with their $75 tickets. At each price level, 1,000 fewer tickets are offered. Fill in this quantity supplied in the following table. At the same time, more people were willing to pay a higher scalper's price. At each price level, 4,000 more tickets are demanded. Fill in this quantity demanded in the table. If you were still one of those suppliers, how much would you get for your $75 ticket?

PRICE	QUANTITY SUPPLIED	QUANTITY DEMANDED
$1,000		
800		
600		
400		
200		

PART 2

INTRODUCTION TO MICROECONOMICS

Tune into the conversation. It's about *your* course. Just change the names, and it's *your* campus, *your* classroom, *your* professor, *your* classmates, and *you*.

It's Friday morning, and Professor Gottheil is just concluding a review session to prepare his students for Monday's exam. The students seem to be questioned out, and Gottheil says, as he gathers his lecture notes, "Are there any more questions?" There's a momentary silence, and then Brad Fish, from the back of the room, calls out.

BRAD: Did you make up the exam yet?
GOTTHEIL: No, not yet. I plan to work on it over the weekend.
BRAD: Will the exam be like the last one: 50 multiple-choice questions?
GOTTHEIL: No, Brad, this time it will be strictly essay. You'll probably be asked to answer 10 essay questions. *(Class groans.)*
GOTTHEIL: What's the problem?
BRAD: Essay exams are a lot harder.
GOTTHEIL: No, they're not! Now I've heard that story countless times. It's just not so. And I ought to know, since I make up the exams.
BRAD: But we have to write them!
(Laughter.)
GOTTHEIL: Well, let me reassure you that test scores show no difference. There are about the same number of A's, B's, C's, D's, and F's. Listen, I'm willing to be democratic about this. I prefer essay exams, but I'm willing to put it to a vote. How many students prefer the multiple-choice exam? *(40 of the 50 students raise their hands.)*
GOTTHEIL: How many prefer an essay exam? *(10 of the 50 students raise their hands.)*
GOTTHEIL: Well, you chose multiple choice, and I'm prepared to go with it. But I'll tell you what I'm going to do. I'm willing to make the essay exam 10 percent less difficult than the multiple-choice exam I would write.
BRAD: How can you do that?

GOTTHEIL: I'll make the questions considerably more general. You'll just have to hit on the main points of the chapters. And you won't have to refer to as many graphs as you would on the multiple choice.
BRAD: Could we choose among the essay questions? Like write on 8 out of 10 questions?
GOTTHEIL: OK! I'll throw that in as well to guarantee a 10 percent less-difficult exam. Ready for a final vote. Remember, they're substitutes. Now, how many vote for the essay exam if I make it 10 percent less difficult? *(40 out of the 50 students raise their hands.)*
GOTTHEIL: That does it! It'll be an essay exam. By the way, note what happened here. A 10 percent reduction in the difficulty of the exam resulted in a 300 percent increase in the number of students voting for it. You weren't all that immovable on multiple choice, were you?
BRAD: Professor Gottheil, if you'll cut the difficulty by another 10 percent, I'll bet you can get the entire class to vote for it.
GOTTHEIL: Brad, don't stretch your luck!

Whether Brad realized it or not, he had just helped derive the elasticity of demand for a multiple-choice exam. As you read through the next chapter, keep this concept in mind. Consider how elasticity and the other concepts developed in the following chapters apply to your daily life. You will likely be surprised.

4

ELASTICITY

Billy Crystal is a very funny man. When he goes into the routine about his family dynamics, most people in the audience laugh hysterically. But Crystal's aware that some only chuckle, and a very few manage to just squeeze out a smile.

Comedians understand that. No two people respond the same way to the same humor. Our idea of what is funny is personal.

How we respond to humor is not unlike our responses to different foods, sporting events, cars, and the myriad of household goods that clutter our different homes. We are individuals, and our responses to acquiring more of these goods, or less of them, reflect our individuality. When we are confronted in the marketplace by changing prices for

THIS CHAPTER INTRODUCES YOU TO THE ECONOMIC PRINCIPLES ASSOCIATED WITH:

- DEMAND SENSITIVITY
- DETERMINANTS OF DEMAND SENSITIVITY TO PRICE CHANGES
- PRICE ELASTICITY OF DEMAND
- CROSS ELASTICITY
- SUBSTITUTE AND COMPLEMENTARY GOODS
- NORMAL AND INFERIOR GOODS
- SUPPLY ELASTICITY
- THE RELATIONSHIP BETWEEN PRICE ELASTICITY OF SUPPLY AND TAX REVENUES

goods, we typically respond by changing the quantities of the goods we demand. For each of us, however, *how much* we change the quantity we demand when the price of any good changes depends upon our own particular sensitivity to the price change.

For example, when the price of gasoline increases, most people buy fewer gallons of gasoline. But, experience shows, not that much less! On the other hand, if the ticket price of an R.E.M. concert were to fall, the quantity demanded of R.E.M. tickets would probably increase considerably. These different demand responses to changing prices not only strike us as reasonable but are confirmed by our everyday experience. For some goods, our response is moderate. For other goods, the response can be dramatic. That is, our sensitivity to price changes depends, in large measure, upon the character of the goods.

DEMAND SENSITIVITIES AND INSENSITIVITIES

Consider how you would react to a change in the price of chewing gum. If one morning you woke up to discover that the price of gum had risen 100 percent, from 5 to 10 cents a stick, the probability is very high that if you were a gum chewer, you would keep right on chewing. Anyone disagree? The 10-cent price tag would hardly deter you. The 100 percent price increase would generate a zero percent decrease in quantity demanded. That's about as demand-insensitive to a price change as one can get.

Suppose your doctor diagnoses pneumonia and prescribes a unit of penicillin. You rush to the pharmacy only to discover that the druggist just raised the price from $2 to $3 per unit. Would you walk away? Or suppose the pharmacy ran a two-for-$3 special. Would you demand more than the one unit prescribed? It seems reasonable, doesn't it, that your demand for penicillin would be completely insensitive to these price changes.

Gum and penicillin are just two of many goods whose demands are generally insensitive to price changes. The quantity demanded of light bulbs, cigarettes, aspirin, potatoes, shoelaces, nails, sugar, and spark plugs tends to be relatively insensitive to changes in price. If you think about it, you can probably name hundreds of other goods that fall into this category.

On the other hand, suppose movie prices rose 100 percent, from $6 to $12. How would you react? If you were like most people, you would cut down sharply on the number of times you go out to the movies. You would probably switch to video-cassettes or be satisfied with network television. That is, unlike gum chewing, the quantity demanded of movies tends to be relatively sensitive to price changes.

You can test your demand sensitivities to price changes for a variety of goods by asking yourself how you would respond to a specific percentage change in the price of each. Compare your own responses to those of your friends. You will probably find that for a wide range of goods you have much in common.

Expressing Demand Sensitivity Graphically

Exhibit 1 shows how Misty Coffman reacts to a $3 to $2 price cut on three goods: penicillin, spark plugs, and Coca-Cola.

Look at panel *a*. When the price of penicillin falls from $3 to $2, the quantity demanded by Misty remains unchanged. In fact, her quantity demanded is one unit for every price within the price range shown in panel *a*. Why would Misty want two units when only one is prescribed?

But what about spark plugs? Look at panel *b*. Misty is not totally insensitive to the $3 to $2 price change. The 33⅓ percent price decrease generates an increase in quantity demanded from eight to ten spark plugs, a rise of 25 percent.

Why? Perhaps Misty regards the price cut as temporary and takes immediate advantage of the lower price by buying plugs she otherwise would not buy. Or perhaps, with spark plugs at $2, she is inclined to change them more frequently.

Compare her demand for spark plugs to her demand for Coca-Cola, shown in panel *c*. Do you see the difference? When the supermarket cuts the price of a carton of Coke by 33⅓ percent, from $3 to $2, the quantity demanded by Misty increases from one to three cartons, or by 300 percent. As you see, her demand for Coke is quite sensitive to the price change.

CHECK YOUR UNDERSTANDING

How sensitive would you be to a price change in shoelaces?

EXHIBIT | 1

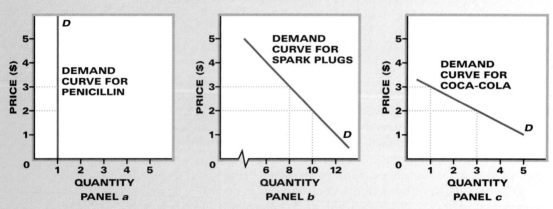

DEMAND RESPONSE TO PRICE CHANGE

Panels a, b, and c depict three different responses to a $3 to $2 price cut. In panel a, the response is zero for a price cut in penicillin. In panel b, price matters. The $3 to $2 cut in spark plugs generates an increase in quantity demanded from 8 to 10. The demand response to the same price cut in panel c is considerably greater. Quantity demanded of Coca-Cola increases from 1 to 3 cartons.

How do we explain that sensitivity? Although people's tastes for soft drinks are personal, most people still consider most soft drinks to be very good substitutes for each other. For example, many Pepsi-Cola drinkers don't really mind switching to Coke or 7-Up, or most any other brand if the price is right. Some are regarded as very close Pepsi substitutes, others as slightly less so. When Coke, then, cuts its price by 33⅓ percent, many people *almost* indifferent to brand would make the switch to Coke. How would you respond?

Are Our Demand Sensitivities Alike?

While people are not Xerox copies of each other, there is still a remarkable similarity in the way people respond to price changes across a wide variety of goods. Not everyone responds in the same way, but responses are typically more similar than dissimilar.

For example, Misty's response in Exhibit 1 to a change in the price of Coke describes most people's response to the price cut. Admittedly, some people are Dr Pepper fanatics and wouldn't switch even if Coke were given away, but there aren't too many of them around. Adding together people's highly sensitive individual responses to the Coke price cut produces in Exhibit 2, panel *a*, a highly sensitive market demand curve for Coke.

What about the market demand curve for spark plugs? It, too, reflects the simple aggregation of individual demand curves for spark plugs, including Misty's. As we see in Exhibit 2, panel *b*, the 33⅓ percent decrease in price creates an increase in the quantity of spark plugs demanded, but not by much.

How many people do you know who would buy aspirin because the price is right? Few indeed. There is good reason why most people exhibit roughly the same demand sensitivities to price changes.

EXHIBIT | 2

MARKET DEMAND FOR COCA-COLA AND SPARK PLUGS

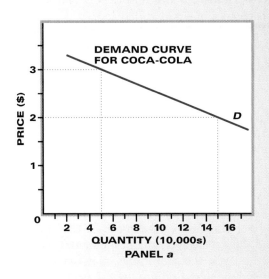

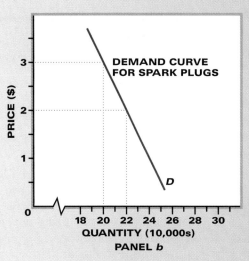

At a price of $3, the quantity of Coca-Cola demanded, shown in panel *a,* is 50,000 cartons, including Misty's demand for one carton. When price is cut to $2, Misty and all other buyers increase their willingness to buy Coke. Quantity demanded increases to 150,000 cartons.

The market for spark plugs is shown in panel *b.* Note the difference in the slopes of the demand curves in panels *a* and *b.* Buyers increase quantity demanded of spark plugs when price is cut from $3 to $2, but by a smaller percentage than in panel *a.*

WHAT FACTORS INFLUENCE DEMAND SENSITIVITY?

How do we explain why demand sensitivities are so commonly held? What influences our reactions to price changes?

Low-Priced Goods

If most people won't even bother to pick up a penny from a sidewalk, why would we expect them to be at all concerned about price changes on nickel-and-dime items? The fact is, we don't. That's why, in our chewing gum example, a price increase from 5 to 10 cents was anything but earthshaking. Even though it represents a 100 percent increase, the nickel increase goes virtually unnoticed.

Do you suppose a 100 percent price increase on a 25-cent comb would deter many from making the purchase? Would a 10-cent increase on a 10-cent parking meter turn people to public transportation? Because these prices are relatively low, they represent only a tiny fraction of our income. Any price change, therefore, even a 100 percent increase, on these low-priced goods has so little impact on our total spending that the quantities demanded of them tend to be almost independent of their prices.

Income Levels

What may be a little money to some people may be a lot of money to others. We must be careful, then, about making quick assertions concerning demand

CHECK YOUR UNDERSTANDING

Why does it have little effect on our quantity demanded for parking space when parking meter prices increase 100 percent?

sensitivities unless we know something about individual income levels. Rich people generally, it is safe to say, are less concerned about price changes than poor people. While a $75 to $200 price change on a graphite tennis racket might deter a university student whose income is $4,000 from making the purchase, the university's chancellor, earning $175,000, would make the purchase effortlessly. If you were to draw their demand curves for tennis rackets, how would they look?

What can we conclude? First, poor people are more sensitive to price changes than rich people, and second, as people's incomes increase, their demand sensitivities to these price changes become less intense.

Substitute Goods

Our sensitivity to price changes depends as well upon the alternatives available. After an eventful night, Rolaids, as the TV commercials tell us, spells relief. But so do Tums, Bromo-Seltzer, and Pepto-Bismol. Because they are all effective antacids, Rolaids has to be careful about raising its price. Why? Many who prefer Rolaids would switch to another brand if Rolaids raised its price.

Coke and Pepsi are close substitutes, and the demand for each is relatively elastic. What strategies do Coca-Cola (http://www.cocacola.com/) and Pepsi (http://www.pepsi.com/) use to make the demand for their products less elastic?

If Coca-Cola and Pepsi-Cola are *close* substitutes, and if Rolaids and Tums are *close* as well, what can we say about potatoes grown on two different potato farms in Idaho? An Idaho potato is an Idaho potato, yes? They are *perfect* substitutes. Can you imagine buying the more expensive potato when a cheaper, identical potato is available?

Because Idaho potato farmers produce perfect substitutes, they have no leverage over their prices. Were one of them, say, Steve Coombs, foolish enough to insist on charging a higher price than his competitors—even if the price increase were only a fraction of a penny—the quantity demanded of Steve's higher-priced potatoes would fall to zero. After all, why would anyone buy a single potato from him when a cheaper, perfect substitute is available?

It makes sense, doesn't it, to suppose that our demand sensitivity to price changes depends upon the availability and closeness of substitute goods.

Basic Goods

How many slices of bread could you eat at a sitting? You know without even trying that it wouldn't take much to reach your limit. Even at bargain prices, the quantity demanded by bread lovers could not really increase significantly.

What about price increases? Bread is a basic food in our diet. Were price to increase, even substantially, the quantity demanded would fall, but not by much. We demand bread for much the same reason that people in Southeast Asia demand rice. It is an important staple in our diet. What about our demand for milk and eggs? They, too, are staples in our diet. Would you expect the demand curve for these basic food goods to look most like the curve in panel *a, b,* or *c* of Exhibit 1?

Food items are not the only goods that represent basic needs in our society. Medicine, obviously, is another. We assumed, in our penicillin example, that the quantity demanded is totally insensitive to changes in price. Many other nonfood goods also have demand curves that look like Exhibit 1, panel *a*. There are considerably more whose demand curves take on the character shown in panel *b*. What about your textbooks? Or your demand for electricity?

CHECK YOUR UNDERSTANDING

Why are daytime telephone rates typically higher than evening rates?

Do you suppose businesspeople would be more careful about the number of long-distance calls they make and the time spent on each when the price of these calls increases? Their ability to cut calls is limited by the sheer necessity of business. Telephones are basic items needed to transact business. More calls might be made when prices fall, fewer when they increase, but probably not by much in either case.

Linked Goods

Some goods are coupled. Their particular linked or complementary relationship often determines our demand sensitivities to their price changes. For example, what do you suppose would happen to the quantity of shoelaces demanded if the price of shoelaces increased? Think about it. People can't go about their business with unlaced shoes! It would be silly to stop wearing a $75 pair of shoes because the price of shoelaces jumped from $1.25 to $1.50.

Perhaps a substantial price cut would prompt a few people to change their laces more often. Perhaps a price increase to $2.50 a pair might prompt some to tie a knot or two before buying another pair. But most people do not change their shoelace-buying behavior because of price changes.

Automobile dealers tell a story about a prospective buyer of a Rolls-Royce who asked the dealer how many miles per gallon the British import gets. The dealer coldly replied: "Sir, if you ask that question, you don't really want this car." The dealer knew something about linked goods and price insensitivity.

Time to Adjust

In the short run, we are typically less demand sensitive to price changes than in the long run. Given enough time, however, we might modify our tastes and broaden our range of would-be substitutes.

How did people initially respond to oil-producing countries' many-fold increase in oil prices? Paralysis! Prices rose from $2 per barrel in 1973 to $12 per barrel in 1974. What could we Americans have done? We were completely locked into our dependence on oil. We found it exceedingly difficult to make any demand adjustment even when oil prices soared to $34 a barrel in 1980.

But we *eventually* switched to smaller cars, lower speed limits, more efficient home insulation, and tolerance of a wider range of living room temperatures. The long-run response surprised oil producers as well as us! We discovered that, given time to adjust, we became rather demand sensitive to oil price changes.

FROM SENSITIVITY TO ELASTICITY

The observation that the quantities we demand of goods are sensitive to price changes, and that these sensitivities are different for different kinds of goods, is translated by economists into the concept of **elasticity.** That is, elasticity is nothing more than a term economists use to describe sensitivity. If you know how to derive simple percentages, you already know how to measure elasticity. It's a ratio of two percentages. **Price elasticity of demand** (e_d) is the percentage change in quantity demanded generated by a percentage change in price:

$$e_d = \frac{\text{percentage change in quantity demanded}}{\text{percentage change in price}}$$

The percentage change in quantity demanded is simply the change in quantity demanded divided by the original quantity. The percentage change in price is the change in price divided by the original price:

$$e_d = \frac{\text{change in quantity demanded}}{\text{quantity demanded}} \bigg/ \frac{\text{change in price}}{\text{price}}$$

Elasticity
A term economists use to describe sensitivity.

Price elasticity of demand
The ratio of the percentage change in quantity demanded to a percentage change in price. Its numerical value expresses the percentage change in quantity demanded generated by a 1 percent change in price.

For example, if Wendy's in Campustown cuts its grilled chicken deluxe sandwich from $3 to $2 to attract college students away from McDonald's and discovers that the quantity demanded of its deluxe sandwich increases from 1,000 to 2,000, we know that the price elasticity of demand for that sandwich is

$$\frac{2{,}000 - 1{,}000}{1{,}000} \bigg/ \frac{\$2 - \$3}{\$3} = -3$$

Simple enough? Perhaps too simple. Economists recognize a problem with such a formulation. Depending upon the direction of the change, different elasticities can be obtained from the same change in price and quantity. For example, a price cut from $3 to $2 represents a 33⅓ percent decrease in price. But if price rises from $2 to $3, the percentage change is 50 percent. What number, then, should economists use to represent any percentage change—direction unspecified—between $2 and $3?

Economists resolved the problem by averaging price and quantity over the range of the changes. The equation for price elasticity of demand, then, becomes

$$e_d = \frac{(Q_2 - Q_1)/[(Q_2 + Q_1)/2]}{(P_2 - P_1)/[(P_2 + P_1)/2]},$$

where Q_1 and Q_2 are the quantities before and after price change, and P_1 and P_2 are the original and new prices. Using this averaging equation, it makes no difference whether the price change measures an increase or a decrease in price, that is, whether the original price was $2 or $3. In both cases $P_2 - P_1 = 1$ and $(P_2 + P_1)/2 = 5/2 = 2.5$.

A price increase usually generates a decrease in the quantity demanded. Likewise, a price decrease generates an increase in the quantity demanded. Because the price–quantity relationship is inverse—when one rises, the other falls—demand elasticities are always negative. For example, if a 50 percent decrease in price generates a 75 percent increase in quantity demanded, then the elasticity is $+75/-50 = -1.5$. By convention, economists drop the negative sign, expressing elasticity only by its absolute value, 1.5. From now on, we will follow that convention.

CHECK YOUR UNDERSTANDING

Why are demand elasticities always negative?

DERIVING PRICE ELASTICITIES OF DEMAND

Let's calculate some more price elasticities of demand, displayed in Exhibit 3.

Demand curve D in panel a depicts the demand curve for high school football tickets on Friday nights. Remember those games? At a price of $4, the quantity demanded is 100. At a price of $3, quantity demanded increases to 300. At a price of $1, the 700-person-capacity stadium sells out.

Demand curve D' in panel b depicts the demand curve for milk. At $4 per gallon, Josh Gillespie, the proprietor of the grocery just down the street from the high school, sells 100 gallons. At $3, quantity demanded increases to 140 gallons. On sale at $1, the quantity demanded increases to 220 gallons.

Let's start with $4 tickets and milk. Suppose the high school cuts ticket prices from $4 to $3. Quantity demanded increases from 100 to 300 tickets, from point a to point b on demand curve D in panel a. Price elasticity of demand within this $4 to $3 price range is

$$\frac{(300 - 100)/[(100 + 300)/2]}{(\$3 - \$4)/[(\$3 + \$4)/2]} = \frac{200/200}{1/3.5} = \frac{1}{1/3.5} = 3.5$$

EXHIBIT|3

PRICE ELASTICITIES OF DEMAND FOR FOOTBALL TICKETS AND MILK

DEMAND FOR FOOTBALL TICKETS

	PRICE	QUANTITY	TOTAL REVENUE	PRICE ELASTICITY OF DEMAND
a →	$4	100	$ 400	3.50
b →	3	300	900	1.25
	2	500	1,000	0.50
	1	700	700	

DEMAND FOR MILK

	PRICE	QUANTITY	TOTAL REVENUE	PRICE ELASTICITY OF DEMAND
a →	$4	100	$ 400	1.17
b →	3	140	420	0.62
	2	180	360	0.30
	1	220	220	

Elasticity within the $4 to $3 price range is 3.5 for football tickets, shown in panel *a*, and 1.17 for milk, shown in panel *b*.

Within different price ranges—$3 to $2, and $2 to $1—elasticities differ. Note that elasticities are lower at the lower end of the price range. Those segments of the demand curve that reflect elasticities greater than 1.0 are *demand elastic*. Those that reflect elasticities less than 1.0 are *demand inelastic*.

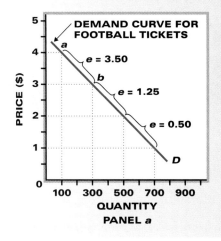

PANEL *a*

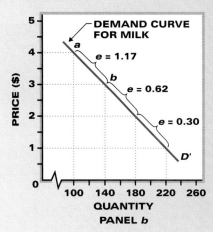

PANEL *b*

How do we interpret this elasticity of 3.5? It means that within the price range $4 and $3, a 1 percent change in price generates a 3.5 percent change in quantity demanded.

Suppose the high school cuts ticket prices again, this time from $3 to $2. Ticket sales jump to 500. What happens to price elasticity of demand in this price range?

$$\frac{(500 - 300)/[(500 + 300)/2]}{(\$2 - \$3)/[(\$2 + \$3)/2]} = 1.25$$

As you see, a 1 percent change in price now generates only a 1.25 percent change in quantity demanded. Note the change in the intensity of the fans' response to price changes. The $1 price change from $4 to $3 generated a 3.5 percent change in quantity demand, but the $1 cut from $3 to $2 generated a milder 1.25 percent change in quantity demanded.

INTERDISCIPLINARY PERSPECTIVE

PLANES, TRAINS, AND AUTOMOBILES

Film scene: Rush hour, downtown Manhattan. *(Characters played by Kevin Bacon and Steve Martin are on opposite sides of a crowded street when they spot,* two blocks ahead, what seems like an impossibility—an available taxi. They recognize that each has seen the taxi, and both purposefully make eye contact to indicate prior rights to it. They sprint after it like madmen, pushing people out of their way. Bacon wins, gets into the taxi, and triumphantly rides off. Panicky, Martin sees another man who is about to get into a taxi. Martin knows that any attempt to find another is futile. He needs to get to the airport so he can make it home to his family for Thanksgiving. Realizing it may be his last chance, Martin decides to go over and negotiate with this man for his taxi.)*

MARTIN: Sir, sir, excuse me. I know this is your cab, but I'm desperately late for a plane and I was wondering if I could appeal to your good nature and ask you to let me have it.

I MUST THINK OF IT THIS WAY: THE THANKSGIVING TURKEY MADE THE GREATER SACRIFICE.

THE MAN: I don't have a good nature, excuse me!

MARTIN: Could I offer you $10 for it. *(The man chuckles.)* . . . 20, I'll give you $20 for it.

THE MAN: Let's say 50.

MARTIN: *(Reluctantly, as he fishes in his wallet.)* All right, all right.

THE MAN: Anyone who would pay $50 for a cab would certainly pay 75.

MARTIN: Not necessarily! *(In a stern voice.)* . . . All right, 75. . . . *(Pause.)* You're a thief.

THE MAN: Close, I'm an attorney.

MARTIN: *(Sarcastically.)* Have a happy Thanksgiving. *(As Martin hands over the $75.)*

THE MAN: This will help.

CONSIDER

What does this Steve Martin movie scene have to do with the concept of price elasticity of demand? Draw a graph of Steve Martin's elasticity of demand for this taxi.

Look what happens when price is cut from $2 to $1. The price elasticity of demand falls to 0.50:

$$\frac{(700 - 500)/[(700 + 500)/2]}{(\$1 - \$2)/[(\$1 + \$2)/2]} = 0.50$$

The 1 percent change in price now generates only a 0.50 percent change in quantity demanded. Note that the price elasticities of demand for football tickets differ in different price ranges and fall—from 3.5 to 1.25 to 0.50—as we calculate them downward along the demand curve.

In panel *b*, the demand curve for milk reflects what Josh Gillespie knows from long experience: People are relatively insensitive to price changes in milk. For most, milk is a basic food. When Josh cuts the price from $4 to $3, the quantity of milk demanded increases from 100 to 140 gallons:

$$\frac{(140 - 100)/[(140 + 100)/2]}{(\$3 - \$4)/[(\$3 + \$4)/2]} = 1.17$$

A 1 percent change in price, within the $4 to $3 range, creates a 1.17 percent change in quantity demanded. Looking at the same price change, the price elasticity of demand for milk is less—1.17 compared to 3.50—than it is for football tickets. Does it make sense?

Compare the milk and football tickets elasticities in the $3 to $2 price range:

$$\frac{(180 - 140)/[(180 + 140)/2]}{(\$2 - \$3)/[(\$2 + \$3)/2]} = 0.62$$

Now a 1 percent change in the price of milk generates a 0.62 percent change in quantity demanded. When Josh puts the milk on sale at $1, the quantity demanded increases to 220 gallons. The elasticity of demand within this $1 to $2 range is 0.30:

$$\frac{(220 - 180)/[(220 + 180)/2]}{(\$1 - \$2)/[(\$1 + \$2)/2]} = 0.30$$

A 1 percent change in price now generates only a 0.30 percent change in quantity demanded.

ELASTICITY AND TOTAL REVENUE

When a 1 percent decrease in price generates a greater than 1 percent increase in quantity demanded—that is, when the price elasticity of demand is greater than 1.0—**total revenue** increases. When price elasticity of demand is less than 1.0, a 1 percent decrease in price decreases total revenue.

Look at the relationship between price elasticity of demand and revenues in Exhibit 3. In the case of football tickets, price cuts from $4 to $3 and from $3 to $2 produce elasticities of 3.50 and 1.25, both greater than 1.0. As you can see, with both cuts revenues increase—from $400 to $900 with the first cut and from $900 to $1,000 with the second. Were the high school to cut again, from $2 to $1, elasticity would fall to 0.50, which is less than 1.0. The high school's total revenue would fall from $1,000 to $700.

In the case of Josh Gillespie's milk sales, only the price cut from $4 to $3 has an elasticity greater than 1.0. The cut increases his revenue from $400 to $420. Price cuts from $3 to $2 and from $2 to $1 produce elasticities of 0.62 and 0.30, both less than 1.0. As you see, with both cuts revenues decrease from $420 to $360 and then from $360 to $220.

Economists define a price elasticity of 1.0 as being **unit elastic.** It is helpful to think of unit elasticity as the watershed value. Those parts of a demand curve with elasticities greater than 1.0 are described as **price elastic,** and those parts with elasticities less than 1.0 are said to be **price inelastic.**

Exhibit 4 shows how the relationship between price changes and revenue depends upon the elasticities.

Total revenue
The price of a good multiplied by the number of units sold.

Unit elastic
Price elasticity is equal to 1.0. In this range, price cuts or increases do not change total revenue.

Price elastic
Quality of the range of a demand curve where elasticities of demand are greater than 1.0.

Price inelastic
Quality of the range of a demand curve where elasticities of demand are less than 1.0.

EXHIBIT|4

ELASTICITIES, PRICE, AND REVENUE CHANGES

WHEN ELASTICITY IS	IF PRICE INCREASES	IF PRICE DECREASES
$e_d > 1.0$	REVENUE DECREASES	REVENUE INCREASES
$e_d < 1.0$	REVENUE INCREASES	REVENUE DECREASES
$e_d = 1.0$	REVENUE DOESN'T CHANGE	REVENUE DOESN'T CHANGE

ESTIMATES OF PRICE ELASTICITIES OF DEMAND

Price Elasticities for Selected Agricultural and Nonagricultural Goods

Compare the price elasticities in the left- and right-hand columns of Exhibit 5. Note the character of the goods in each of the two columns. On the left—milk, corn, wheat, barley, eggs, and potatoes—are representative agricultural goods, each with price elasticities less than 1.0, confirming the fact that for basic foods, demand is inelastic. The right-hand column, representing a set of nonagricultural goods, shows a mixed bag of goods with various price elasticities; the demand for some, such as women's hats and movies, is highly elastic, while the demand for others, such as cigarettes (doesn't 0.35 tell you something about the powers of addiction?) and legal services, is inelastic.

EXHIBIT|5

PRICE ELASTICITIES OF DEMAND FOR SELECTED GOODS

GOOD	PRICE ELASTICITY OF DEMAND	GOOD	PRICE ELASTICITY OF DEMAND
MILK	0.54	PEPSI	1.97
CORN	0.49	TIRES	1.20
WHEAT	0.08	CIGARETTES	0.35
BARLEY	0.39	LEGAL SERVICES	0.61
EGGS	0.26	MOVIES	3.70
POTATOES	0.31	WOMEN'S HATS	3.00

Source: Edward Mansfield, *Microeconomics* (New York: W. W. Norton, 1997); Robert Hall and Mark Lieberman, *Economics* (Cincinnati: South-Western College Publishing, 1998); Gary Brester and Michael Wohlgenant, "Estimating Interrelated Demands for Meat Using New Measures for Ground and Table Cut Beef," *American Journal of Agricultural Economics* (November 1991); and Heinz Kohler, *Intermediate Economics: Theory and Applications* (New York: Scott, Foresman, 1986).

GLOBAL PERSPECTIVE

GLOBAL ELASTICITIES OF DEMAND FOR LDC EXPORT GOODS

Imagine that you are an economic advisor to the government of Togo, a West African country located on the Atlantic Ocean. Suppose, after a hard day at the office, you relax by taking a leisurely walk along the beach and chance upon an Aladdin lamp look-alike. Remembering the childhood story, you rub it and behold! A genie appears, offering you a once-in-a-lifetime wish. Without a second thought, you say: "Genie, I wish for high price elasticities of demand for Togo's coffee and

IF THIS WORKS, WE'LL BE ROLLING IN REVENUE!

cocoa exports so that when their prices decrease, revenue will increase." Hearing your wish, the frightened genie jumps right back into the lamp. You hear his fading voice trail his departure: "My bad luck to run into an economist."

You see, even the awesome power of genies has its limits. The sad unalterable fact is that for the less-developed countries (LDC) of Asia, Africa, and Latin America, price elasticities of demand for their export goods are less than 1. When their exports increase and prices fall, they end up with *less* revenue. Look at the uncompromising data.

GLOBAL ELASTICITIES OF DEMAND FOR LDC EXPORT GOODS

COFFEE	0.27
COCOA	0.19
BANANAS	0.40
TEA	0.20
RUBBER	0.50
SUGAR	0.04
COTTON	0.18
PALM OIL	0.47
FERROUS METALS	0.65
TROPICAL TIMBER LOGS	0.16

Short-Run and Long-Run Elasticities

Time makes a difference. When consumers have more time, they are better able to find substitute goods. Exhibit 6 compares price elasticities of demand for the same goods and services over the short run and long run.

For most people, time is a critical factor in their ability to adjust demand to changing prices. Exhibit 6 shows precisely that. In every case, price elasticities in the long run are higher than those in the short run. Some are decidedly greater. Compare the short-run to long-run elasticities for air travel, hospital care, and toiletries.

CHECK YOUR UNDERSTANDING

How does time affect the price elasticity of demand?

EXHIBIT 6

PRICE ELASTICITIES OF DEMAND IN THE SHORT RUN AND LONG RUN

GOOD	PRICE ELASTICITY OF DEMAND— SHORT RUN	PRICE ELASTICITY OF DEMAND— LONG RUN
COMMUTER RAIL TRANSPORT	0.62	1.59
GASOLINE	0.10	1.50
AIR TRAVEL	0.05	2.36
JEWELRY AND WATCHES	0.43	0.72
TOILETRIES	0.76	3.13
CHINAWARE	1.16	1.31
HOSPITAL CARE	0.27	3.85

Source: H. S. Houthakker and Lester Taylor, *Consumer Demand in the United States, 1929–1970* (Cambridge, Mass.: Harvard University Press, 1970); Richard Voith, "The Long-Run Elasticity of Demand for Commuter Rail Transportation," *Journal of Urban Economics* (November 1991); and James Griffen and Henry Steele, *Energy Economics and Policy* (New York: Academic Press, 1980).

CROSS ELASTICITY

Cross elasticity of demand
The ratio of a percentage change in quantity demanded of one good to a percentage change in the price of another good.

Price elasticity of demand measures the percentage change in quantity demanded of a good generated by a percentage change in the price of that good. **Cross elasticity of demand** measures the percentage change in quantity demanded of one good generated by a percentage change in the price of another good.

Cross Elasticities Among Substitute Goods

When Rolaids raises its price, some people switch from Rolaids to Tums. When Coke raises prices, the quantity demanded for Pepsi increases. When *Time* magazine cuts its price, *Newsweek*'s sales fall. When taxi fares in New York increase, more New Yorkers take the bus. These are all pairs of *substitute goods*.

The more perfect the substitute, the more people replace one good with its substitute when the price of the first changes. Cross elasticity measures this cross relationship. For the Rolaids-to-Tums crossover, cross elasticity is written as

$$e_c = \frac{\text{percentage change in quantity demanded of Tums}}{\text{percentage change in price of Rolaids}}$$

The cross elasticity of Rolaids prices and Tums quantity is illustrated in Exhibit 7.

When the price of Rolaids increases from $1.50 to $2.25, shown in panel *a*, the demand curve *D* for Tums (panel *b*) shifts to *D'*. At $1.50, before Rolaids raised its price to $2.25, the quantity demanded of Tums was 1,000. After the Rolaids price increase, the quantity demanded of Tums increases to 1,500.

Why the shift in the Tums demand curve from *D* to *D'* in panel *b*? Because Rolaids is now more expensive, people will switch from Rolaids to the good substitute Tums. As long as Rolaids is more expensive than Tums at every price in Exhibit 7, then at every price the quantity demanded of Tums will increase.

CHECK YOUR UNDERSTANDING

Why is the cross elasticity positive for negative goods?

CROSS ELASTICITIES BETWEEN SUBSTITUTES

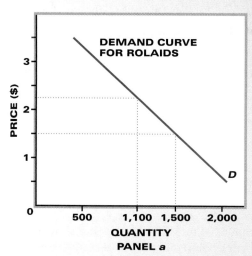

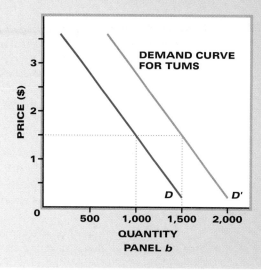

PANEL *a*

PANEL *b*

An increase in the price of Rolaids from $1.50 to $2.25 in panel *a* shifts the demand curve for Tums, in panel *b*, from *D* to *D'*. The quantity demanded of Tums at the price of $1.50 increases from 1,000 to 1,500. As with all substitute goods, an increase (or decrease) in the price of one good generates an increase (or decrease) in quantity demanded of the other.

Note that the cross elasticities for substitute goods in Exhibit 8 are positive. A decrease (or increase) in the price of one good generates a corresponding decrease (or a corresponding increase) in the quantity demanded of the other.

Look at the relationship between butter and margarine. When the price of butter falls, many people switch from margarine to butter. When the price of margarine falls, many people buy less butter. But their cross elasticities are not necessarily identical. When the price of butter increases, people are more likely to switch to margarine than they are likely to switch to butter when the price of margarine increases. As you can see, their cross elasticities differ, 0.81 and 0.67.

EXHIBIT | 8

CROSS ELASTICITIES OF DEMAND FOR SUBSTITUTE GOODS

CHANGE IN THE PRICE OF THE GOOD	CHANGE IN THE QUANTITY DEMANDED OF THE GOOD	CROSS ELASTICITY
COKE	PEPSI	0.80
PEPSI	COKE	0.61
TABLE CUT BEEF	GROUND BEEF	0.41
POULTRY	GROUND BEEF	0.24
NATURAL GAS	ELECTRICITY	0.20
BUTTER	MARGARINE	0.81
MARGARINE	BUTTER	0.67

Source: Edwin Mansfield, *Microeconomics* (New York: W. W. Norton, 1997); F. Gasmi, J. J. Laffont, and Q. Vuong, "Econometric Analysis of Collusive Behavior in a Soft Drink Market," *Journal of Economics and Management Strategy* (Summer 1992); and Gary Brester and Michael Wohlgenant, "Estimating Interrelated Demands for Meats Using New Measures for Ground and Table Cut Beef," *American Journal of Agricultural Economics* (November 1991).

Cross Elasticities Among Complementary Goods

What about cross elasticities among goods that are linked or complement each other? For example, think of hotels and air travel. Suppose airlines raise their fares by 15 percent. The quantity of airline tickets would fall, but so too would the quantity of hotel rooms demanded. Why? With fewer people traveling, fewer hotel rooms are needed. Have you noticed hotel advertisements at airports? Hotels and air travel are such obvious complements that travel agents typically book both.

What are some complementary goods in a college student's life? Go to the Interactive Study Center at http://gottheil.swcollege.com and click on the "Your Turn" button to submit your examples. Student submissions will be posted to the Web site, and perhaps we will use some in future editions of the book!

Among *complementary goods* such as air travel and hotels, the cross elasticities—airfares and hotel reservations, and hotel prices and air travel—are still not necessarily the same. Which do you think has the higher cross elasticity? What about VCRs and videocassettes?

Exhibit 9 illustrates the cross elasticity between plane flights and the decrease in demand for hotel rooms.

The increase in panel *a*'s airfare from $100 to $150 affects panel *b*'s market for hotel rooms. The demand curve in panel *b* shifts from *D* to *D'*, and the quantity demanded of $50-per-day hotel rooms decreases from 5,000 to 4,000. Unlike the cross elasticity between substitute goods, the cross elasticity between complements is *negative;* a percentage increase in the price of one generates a percentage decrease in the quantity demanded of the other.

INCOME ELASTICITY

Income elasticity
The ratio of the percentage change in quantity demanded to the percentage change in income.

The concept of elasticity is used to measure not only the relationship between changes in price and changes in quantity demanded, but also the relationship between changes in income and changes in quantity demanded. Economists define **income elasticity** as the percentage change in quantity demanded generated by a percentage change in income.

EXHIBIT | 9

CROSS ELASTICITIES BETWEEN COMPLEMENTS

An increase in the price of plane flights from $100 to $150 in panel *a* shifts the demand curve for hotel rooms in panel *b* from *D* to *D'*. The quantity demanded of $50 hotel rooms decreases from 5,000 to 4,000. As with all complementary goods, an increase (or decrease) in the price of one generates a decrease (or increase) in quantity demanded of the other.

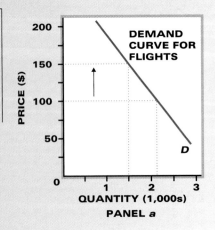

PANEL *a*

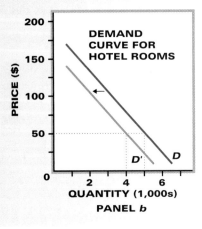

PANEL *b*

$$e_y = \frac{\text{percentage change in quantity demanded}}{\text{percentage change in income}}$$

Suppose that after a good season, Patrick Roy, the all-star goalie for the Colorado Avalanche, negotiated a 30 percent increase in salary. Would you not expect that with higher income, the quantities of goods and services demanded by the Roy family would also increase?

For some goods, the quantities demanded would increase by more than 30 percent. These would be **income elastic.** For goods that are **income inelastic,** the percent increase would be less than 1.0.

Suppose Mrs. Roy decides that with the increased family income, she and their children can afford to see Patrick play in more away games than they had the year before. Suppose their demand for airline tickets increases by 50 percent. The Roys' income elasticity for airline tickets, then, is 50/30 = 1.67. Compare this to the Roy family demand for bread. It is highly unlikely that the family would increase its demand for bread by as much as 30 percent.

Exhibit 10 illustrates the Roys' income elasticity for airline tickets.

The Roys' demand curve for airline tickets shifts from D_y to D'_y when the family income increases by 30 percent. Note that airfares don't change. The increase in the quantity demanded from 40 to 60 is for the unchanging $200 fares.

Income elastic
A 1 percent change in income generates a greater than 1 percent change in quantity demanded.

Income inelastic
A 1 percent change in income generates a less than 1 percent change in quantity demanded.

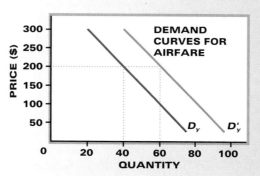

AIR TRAVEL

DEMAND CURVES FOR AIRFARE

An increase in a person's income typically results in that person increasing his or her quantity demanded of goods and services. Some increases are greater than others. For example, a 30 percent increase in income shifts the Roy family's demand curve for air travel to the right, from D_y to D'_y. At a constant $200 airfare, demand increases from 40 to 60 flights.

EXHIBIT | 10

What do we know about income elasticity? In 1857, Ernst Engel, a Prussian statistician, calculated the income elasticity of demand for food. His 0.70 estimate confirmed the idea that the relationship between income and the demand for food is inelastic. Recognizing his pioneering work, economists today refer to income inelasticities of food as obeying **Engel's law.**

Exhibit 11 provides a set of income elasticities of demand for both agricultural and nonagricultural goods. For each of the goods in the left-hand column—all food items—income elasticity of demand is less than 1.0. There's the clear imprint of Engel's law. Look at the non-food items in the right-hand column. Are we book readers? It seems so, doesn't it? A 1 percent increase in income generates a 1.44 percent increase in the sale of books. That is to say, our demand for books is income elastic.

Although Engel's law applies in every country, it appears

Engel's law
The observation that income elasticities of demand for food are less than 1.0.

EXHIBIT | 11

INCOME ELASTICITIES OF DEMAND

GOOD	INCOME ELASTICITY	GOOD	INCOME ELASTICITY
EGGS	0.37	FURNITURE	1.48
CHEESE	0.34	BOOKS	1.44
MILK	0.07	CIGARETTES	0.50
MEAT	0.35	ELECTRICITY	0.20

Source: Edwin Mansfield, *Microeconomics* (New York: W. W. Norton, 1997); and F. Chalemaker, "Rational Addictive Behavior and Cigarette Smoking," *Journal of Political Economy* (August 1991).

EXHIBIT | 12

COMPARISON OF INCOME ELASTICITIES OF DEMAND FOR FOOD, BY COUNTRY

COUNTRY	INCOME ELASTICITY	COUNTRY	INCOME ELASTICITY
UNITED STATES	0.14	INDIA	0.76
CANADA	0.15	NIGERIA	0.74
GERMANY	0.25	INDONESIA	0.72
FRANCE	0.27	BOLIVIA	0.68
UNITED KINGDOM	0.33	CHINA	0.67

Source: Ching-Fun and James Peale Jr., "Income and Price Elasticities," in *Advances in Econometrics Supplement,* ed. Henri Thell (Greenwich, Conn.: JAI Press, 1989); and Y. Wu, E. Li, and S. N. Samuel, "Food Consumption in Urban China: An Empirical Analysis," *Applied Economics* (June 1995).

that income elasticities of demand for food in the more industrialized countries are relatively lower. Look at Exhibit 12. Compare, for example, Canada's 0.15 to China's 0.67. But wouldn't you expect to find demand responses less sensitive to increases in income in the industrialized countries? After all, the rich already have their bellies filled!

Income Elasticity of Inferior Goods

Some goods, especially some food items, have peculiar income elasticities. When income increases, the quantities demanded of these goods actually decrease. Economists define such goods as **inferior goods.**

Inferior goods
Goods for which demand decreases when people's incomes increase.

Why inferior? People buy them because the more desirable substitutes are financially beyond their reach. Once richer, these people readily switch from the inferior goods to more attractive substitutes.

Cheap wine isn't just cheap wine, it's downright inferior! When incomes increase, people buy less of it and switch to higher-quality wines. Black-and-white television is an inferior good. As income increases, we switch from black-and-white to color. What about drugstore eyeglasses? What about vinyl luggage? Can you think of other examples of inferior goods?

SUPPLY ELASTICITY

Price elasticity of supply
The ratio of the percentage change in quantity supplied to the percentage change in price.

Price elasticity of supply is the percentage change in quantity supplied generated by a percentage change in price. The equation for measuring price elasticity of supply is

$$ e_s = \frac{(Q_2 - Q_1)/[(Q_2 + Q_1)/2]}{(P_2 - P_1)/[(P_2 + P_1)/2]}, $$

where Q_1 and Q_2 represent quantity before and after the price change, and P_1 and P_2 are the original and new prices. Supply curves are upward sloping, reflecting increases in quantity supplied generated by increases in price. As you see, price elasticities of supply are positive.

What could explain different supply elasticities? Look at the supply curves in Exhibit 13. These are market-day, short-run, and long-run supply curves for fish.

The sensitivity of supply to changing prices depends upon the time that suppliers have to adjust their supplies to new prices.

CHECK YOUR UNDERSTANDING

What may explain different supply elasticities?

Market-Day Supply Elasticity

In Exhibit 13, panel *a* represents the market-day supply curve for fish. It is vertical at 600 fish. The supply curve tells us that whatever the price, suppliers cannot change the quantity they are able to bring onto the market that day.

HISTORICAL PERSPECTIVE

CROSS ELASTICITIES IN THE SOUND BUSINESS

The music we listen to, and the sound equipment on which we listen to it, changed rather dramatically in the 1980s. In increasing numbers, we converted from stereos to tape decks, and then made the switch to compact disc players.

Of course, the shift in sound systems affected our choice of sound format. As the exhibit shows, we shifted from LPs to tapes, then from tapes to CDs.

Tapes and CDs, at least since the mid-1980s, appear to be good substitutes, while LPs, strong at

I WISH I COULD GIVE THIS CD TO MY GRANDFATHER FOR HIS BIRTHDAY, BUT HE STILL USES THAT OLD-FASHIONED RECORD PLAYER.

the beginning of the decade, became less and less attractive as a medium of recorded sound. By 1983, tape sales climbed to 500 million units, matching the sales volume of LPs. CDs were still in their infancy. But look what happened to sales after 1984! LP sales collapsed to under 200 million units by 1990, while CD sales soared to over 700 million units, matching the volume of the slower-growing tape sales. In 1996, CD sales were 780 million, the equivalent of three CDs for every person in the United States.

What does the future hold for CDs? The latest technology to capture the music industry's imagination is DVDs (variously referred to as "digital video disks" and "digital versatile disks"). DVDs hold up to seven times more information than CDs, but is this what customers want? Many industry experts are skeptical.

Finally, as ancient as they seem, LPs may have a resurgence thanks to a Stanford engineering student, Robert Stoddard, and a small Japanese company, ELP. Stoddard has created laser technology that can read LPs without wearing them down like a regular record player, and ELP has introduced a commercial player that makes use of this technology. Even scratched and warped records will sound fine with this technology. So don't throw out those old records yet!

CONSIDER

Think in terms of cross elasticities. Would the cross elasticities between LPs and CDs be high in the 1990s? What about cross elasticities between tapes and CDs?

**DIGITAL SOUND TRIUMPHS
(SALES IN UNITED STATES)**

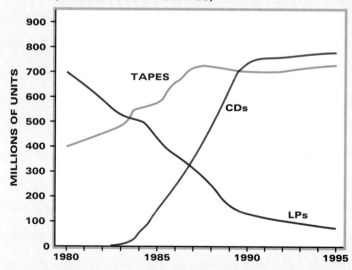

Source: "CD Markets Size 1996," Music Economy Basic Information Service (http://www.move.de/amm/CDMarket.htm); "Reviving LPs. Groovy," *The Economist,* September 9, 1997; and "Being Digital Is Not Enough," *The Economist,* September 28, 1996.

When boats return to the docks after a day out on the water, the supply is fixed. Fishermen cannot supply a single fish more than the 600, even if price rises from $4 to $5.

How do we translate this scenario into price elasticity of supply? If price increases from $4 to $5, the quantity supplied increases by 0. Price elasticity of supply on the market day, then, is 0:

$$\frac{(600 - 600)/[(600 + 600)/2]}{(\$5 - \$4)/[(\$5 + \$4)/2]} = 0$$

Short-Run Supply Elasticity

Consider the short-run supply elasticity for the same price change. In the short run of Exhibit 13, panel *b*, suppliers are able to put more crew on the same number of boats. The quantity supplied increases from 450 to 500 units:

$$\frac{(500 - 450)/[(500 + 450)/2]}{(\$5 - \$4)/[(\$5 + \$4)/2]} = 0.47$$

The short-run supply elasticity is 0.47. A 1 percent increase in price within the $4 to $5 range generates a 0.47 percent increase in quantity supplied. Suppliers may *wish* to supply more at $5, but can't because they are limited by their boats' capacities.

EXHIBIT | 13

KEY

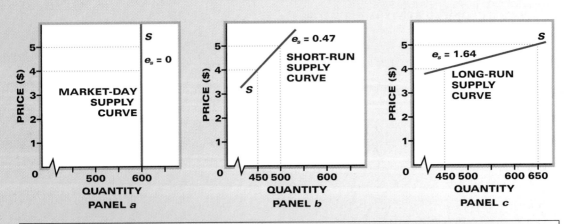

ELASTICITIES OF SUPPLY

Panels *a*, *b*, and *c* depict market-day, short-run, and long-run supply curves in a fish market. The market-day supply curve in panel *a* reflects suppliers' total inability to adjust supply to price.

In the long-run supply curve of panel *c*, suppliers encounter no obstacles adjusting quantity supplied to price. At a price of $4, suppliers are willing and able to supply 450. At $5, they are willing and able to supply 650.

Not so in the short-run supply curve of panel *b*. Here, at a price of $5, suppliers are willing but not able to supply 650. In the interim—that is, in the short run—suppliers increase production *with existing capacity* to 500.

These differences in ability to adjust supply to price are reflected in the different supply elasticities. Within the range $4 to $5, for the market day, the price elasticity of supply is 0. For the short run, it is 0.47, and for the long run, it is 1.64.

Long-Run Supply Elasticity

But suppose fishermen have more time to adjust their supply to price changes. Suppose they can have as many boats as they wish. The capacity of the fishing fleet, then, is no longer a limiting factor. Look at Exhibit 13, panel *c*. With time to build new boats, suppliers increase their quantity supplied from 450 to 650 fish:

$$\frac{(650 - 450)/[(650 + 450)/2]}{(\$5 - \$4)/[(\$5 + \$4)/2]} = 1.64$$

Long-run price elasticity of supply is 1.64. Now, a 1 percent increase in price within the same \$4 to \$5 price range generates a 1.64 percent increase in quantity supplied. As you see, price elasticity of supply increases when suppliers have more time to adjust price to quantities supplied.

How quickly suppliers adjust supply in response to changing prices depends essentially upon the time it takes to build capacity. And that varies from industry to industry. For example, wouldn't you think Domino's Pizza could produce 20 percent more pizza sooner than Boeing could increase its aircraft production by 20 percent?

If the price of 20-year-old French wine increases by 200 percent, shouldn't the French get busy producing 20-year-old wine? But how do you go about producing it in less than 20 years? On the other hand, you can probably increase the supply of moonshine by 300 percent overnight if price increases by only 20 percent.

ELASTICITIES AND TAXATION

We all understand perfectly well why we have to pay taxes. But understanding is one thing, and liking it is quite another. Many people spend a considerable amount of time trying to avoid paying taxes, and many government people spend just as much time devising means of preventing people from avoiding taxes. In truth, few escape.

Avoiding taxes on goods is possible if we can somehow avoid the goods that are taxed. A surefire way of escaping a tax on books, for example, is not to buy them. But if people can do without books, it would be silly for the government to tax them. To generate revenues, government typically taxes goods that are essential to households. Years ago, salt was one such good.

Before the advent of modern refrigeration, meat spoilage was commonplace. The primary way people preserved their supply of meat was by salting. Not surprisingly, people's demand for salt was both high and price inelastic. As a result, governments took to taxing salt like the proverbial duck to water. If governments today were looking for a good thing to tax, what would you suggest? How about cigarettes? Cigarettes are relatively demand inelastic, aren't they? It's hard to kick the smoking habit, which is one reason why cigarette taxes work as a steady source of revenue. Look at Exhibit 14.

Compare the economic consequences of a \$2 tax on panel *a*'s cigarettes and panel *b*'s lipstick. For convenience, the supply curves for cigarettes, *S*, and for lipstick, *S′*, are identical. But look at demand. The demand curve for cigarettes, *D,* is relatively inelastic. The demand curve for lipstick, *D′,* is relatively elastic.

Without taxes, the two equilibrium prices are \$4. Quantities demanded and supplied in both markets are 100.

EXHIBIT | 14

WHAT GETS TAXED?

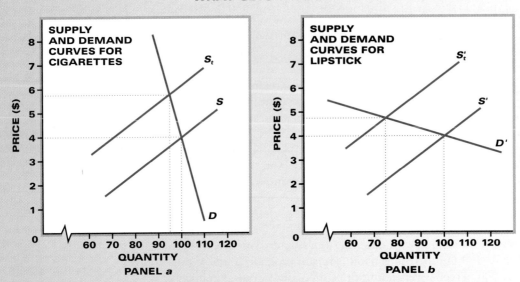

The markets for cigarettes and lipstick are distinguished by their demand elasticities. A $2 tax shifts the supply curves, S to S$_t$ in panel a, and S' to S'$_t$ in panel b. The equilibrium price in panel a moves from $4 to $5.75, and in panel b, from $4 to $4.75. The quantity of cigarettes demanded and supplied decreases from 100 to 95; the quantity of lipstick demanded and supplied decreases from 100 to 75.

The relatively low price elasticity of demand in the market for cigarettes results in higher tax revenues than in the market for lipstick, where the $2 tax results in a relatively large cut in quantity demanded.

Per-Unit Tax Shifts the Supply Curve

Suppose the government imposes a $2 per-unit tax in each market. How is this done? The government simply instructs the suppliers of cigarettes and lipstick to collect and forward to the government $2 for every pack of cigarettes and every lipstick sold. What happens?

Suppose you were one of the cigarette suppliers in Exhibit 14, panel a. Faced with the $2 cigarette tax, you would charge $6 instead of the $4 equilibrium price. If the equilibrium price had been $8, you would charge $10. That is, your supply curve, S$_t$, now including the tax, shifts upward by $2. The same shift in the supply curve, from S' to S'$_t$, is recorded in panel b's lipstick market.

Prior to the $2 tax, the equilibrium price was $4 and quantity sold was 100. The $2 tax raised price to $6, but at $6, an excess supply emerges, forcing price to a new equilibrium at $5.75. That is, the tax shifts the equilibrium price from $4 to $5.75. It also shifts the quantity demanded from 100 to 95. The price cigarette suppliers receive after paying the tax is $5.75 − $2 = $3.75. What about the government? It receives $2 × 95 = $190 in tax revenue.

The effect of the lipstick tax is somewhat different. Look at panel b. The demand for lipstick is relatively elastic. The tax shifts the equilibrium price upward from $4 to $4.75. The quantity demanded falls from 100 to 75 because many women would rather go without multiple shades of lipstick than pay the tax. The price lipstick suppliers receive after paying the tax is $4.75 − $2 = $2.75. What about the government? Because significantly fewer lipsticks are bought, the government receives only $2 × 75 = $150.

The Ultimate Per-Unit Tax?

To squeeze the maximum tax out of the French population, Jean-Baptiste Colbert, the 17th-century finance minister to King Louis XIV, suggested taxing the air people breathed! He reasoned that because the king was monarch over France's air as well as its land, the tax would be legitimate and absolutely unavoidable. Tyrannical? Perhaps, but he well understood the significance of demand elasticity!

CHAPTER REVIEW

1. The idea of demand sensitivity to price change is an integral part of demand analysis. It explains why demand curves look the way they do. The sensitivity issue is put thus: By how much (or how little) do you change your quantity demanded of a good when the price of that good changes? Your sensitivity (or lack of sensitivity) is reflected in the quantitative relationship between the change in price and the corresponding change in quantity demanded.

2. Economists refer to this sensitivity cause-and-effect relationship between a change in quantity demanded of a good and a change in the price of that good as the *price elasticity of demand for the good*. There is nothing esoteric about the concept of elasticity. It is simply another way of expressing sensitivity.

3. People's reaction to a price change is influenced by several factors, including whether the good is (a) a relatively low-priced item, (b) a necessity or a luxury, or (c) linked to other goods. Other factors include (d) people's income, (e) the number and closeness of substitutes in the market, and (f) the time people have to adjust to the price change.

4. Price elasticity of demand is the percentage change in quantity demanded that is generated by a percentage change in price. Because quantity demanded varies inversely with price, price elasticity of demand is negative. However, economists disregard the negative sign and refer only to its absolute value.

5. There is a unique elasticity associated with every price range along a demand curve. The elasticities are highest in the highest price range and become progressively lower as price descends into lower price ranges.

6. In price ranges where elasticities are greater than 1.0, a price cut increases total revenue. In price ranges where elasticities are less than 1.0, a price cut decreases total revenue.

7. Cross elasticity of demand measures the percentage change in quantity demanded of one good that is generated by a percentage change in the price of another. Cross elasticity is positive—an increase in price of one good leads to an increase in quantity demanded of the other—among substitute goods, and it is negative—an increase in price of one good leads to a decrease in quantity demanded of the other—among complementary goods.

8. Income elasticity measures the percentage change in demand that is generated by a percentage change in income. Normal goods have positive income elasticities, while inferior goods have negative income elasticities.

9. Supply elasticity measures the percentage change in quantity supplied that is generated by a percentage change in price. Supply elasticities become more elastic as suppliers have more time to adjust the quantities they supply to the price change. As a result, long-run supply elasticities are higher than short-run supply elasticities, which are higher than market-day supply elasticities.

10. The burden of taxation—how much of a tax is borne by consumers in the form of higher prices or how much of a tax is absorbed by the supplier in the form of higher costs— depends on the elasticity of demand. The greater the supply elasticity, the more the tax burden falls on the supplier.

KEY TERMS

Elasticity	Price inelastic	Income inelastic
Price elasticity of demand	Cross elasticity of demand	Engel's law
Total revenue	Income elasticity	Inferior goods
Unit elastic	Income elastic	Price elasticity of supply
Price elastic		

QUESTIONS

1. The purpose of advertising is to lower the price elasticity of demand for the advertised good. Explain why this is beneficial to a firm that advertises.

2. The 50,000-seat Duke Stadium in Durham, North Carolina, is the home of the Duke University Blue Devils. On Saturday afternoons of football, attendance is typically 40,000. By lowering price, the university could easily sell out Duke Stadium, but it chooses not to do so. Why? (*Hint:* Refer to price elasticities of demand and supply.)

3. When Exxon moved away from its location at the northeast corner of Wright and Green Streets, Shell, operating on the southwest corner of Wright and Green, promptly raised its prices. Is this a coincidence? Explain.

4. Suppose Wendy's cuts the price of its grilled chicken deluxe sandwich by 25 percent. What do you suppose would happen to the demand for (a) Wendy's hamburgers, (b) Wendy's Coca-Cola, (c) McDonald's Big Macs, (d) McDonald's fries, and (e) Nike shoes?

5. Suppose you were shown a demand curve for bananas and were asked to calculate price elasticity of demand. Applying the appropriate equation, you came up with 0.80. Your friend was asked to derive price elasticity of demand on the identical demand curve and came up with 0.50. Worried, you asked your professor which of the two answers was correct. The professor checked through both calculations and said both were! How can that be?

6. Suppose Jeff George, quarterback of the Washington Redskins, increased his annual income 20 percent by endorsing Selsun Blue shampoo. If his quantity demanded of Selsun Blue didn't change, what can we say about his income elasticity of demand for the product? Suppose he decides to upgrade his housing, moving from his $1 million home to a $1.5 million home. What can we say about his income elasticity of demand for housing?

7. Why are we relatively insensitive to price changes affecting low-priced goods such as bubble gum?

8. Why are price elasticities of demand typically higher for luxury goods such as 35-mm cameras than they are for essential goods such as bread?

9. Under what condition is the price elasticity of supply zero?

10. Why is long-run price elasticity of supply greater than short-run price elasticity of supply?

11. Suppose, at a party for economics majors, you win a choice among three mystery boxes. You don't know what each contains, but you know that each box has a pair of gifts. You know that one box has a CD and a pair of sunglasses, another has tickets to a Belly concert and a gift certificate to a close-by restaurant for dinner before the concert, and the other has two very similar textbooks on economics. The only clue given is the cross elasticities among the gifts in each box: for the red box, cross elasticity is +1.5, for the blue box, −1.5, and for the white box, 0. If you wanted the dinner and concert pair, which box would you pick?

12. Why do economists complicate the equation for elasticity by averaging prices and quantities?

13. Social psychologists note the noncontemplative, narrowly focused, and sometimes tena-

cious behavior that young children display when choosing or playing with toys. Economists, armed with these observations of children's temperaments, speculate that children would have relatively low price elasticities of demand for toys. Explain.

14. Government is advised to tax goods whose demand curves are inelastic if the goal is to raise tax revenues. If the goal is to discourage consumption, then it ought to tax goods whose demand curves are elastic. Explain.

PRACTICE PROBLEMS

1. The Gillette Company, manufacturer of razors and razor blades, used to sell its uniquely designed razor below cost. Why would it do so?

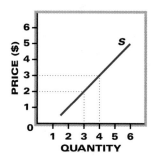

2. Calculate the price elasticity of supply for a price change from $2 to $3.

3. Calculate the price elasticities of demand for each one-dollar change in price.

PRICE	QUANTITY DEMANDED
$5	20
4	25
3	30
2	35
1	40

4. Calculate the income elasticities (at each income level) for boxes of Girl Scout cookies.

INCOME	QUANTITY DEMANDED
$1,000	5
2,000	15
3,000	40
4,000	50

5. Calculate the cross elasticities between the Snickers bar and M&Ms within the $2 and $1 range, and within the $1 and $0.50 range. What proof can you offer to show that these are substitute or complementary goods?

PRICE OF SNICKERS BAR	QUANTITY DEMANDED OF M&Ms
$2.00	20
1.00	10
0.50	5

6. Graph the demand and supply curves for gourmet, fat-free ice cream. Show how the burden of a $1 tax would be borne by the consumer and supplier.

PRICE	QUANTITY DEMANDED	QUANTITY SUPPLIED
$5	25	65
4	40	55
3	60	45
2	73	35
1	95	25

WHAT'S WRONG WITH THIS GRAPH?

PRICE ELASTICITY OF DEMAND

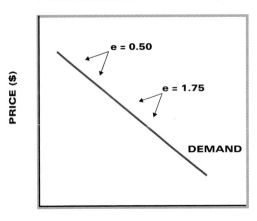

e = 0.50

e = 1.75

PRICE ($)

DEMAND

QUANTITY

ECONOMIC CONSULTANTS

ECONOMIC RESEARCH AND ANALYSIS BY STUDENTS FOR PROFESSIONALS

Pharmaceuticals, Inc., has developed Aspirnew, a new type of pain reliever. Aspirnew relieves pain longer than regular aspirin, and the drug does not cause stomach upset. Pharmaceuticals has been given permission to sell the drug without a prescription.

Before Pharmaceuticals introduces Aspirnew to the market, the creators have approached Economic Consultants to consider the economic implications of offering a new drug. Prepare a report for Pharmaceuticals that addresses the following issues:

1. How elastic is the demand for over-the-counter pain relievers?
2. What are the major competitors for Aspirnew? In relation to these competitors, what pricing strategy should Pharmaceuticals implement?
3. What issues regarding cross elasticities does Pharmaceuticals need to consider?

You may find the following resources helpful as you prepare this report for Pharmaceuticals:

- **Tylenol** (http://www.tylenol. com/)—Tylenol provides product information and advertising.
- **Pharmaceutical Research and Manufacturers of America (PhRMA)** (http://www.phrma. org/)—PhRMA represents approximately 100 U.S. companies committed to pharmaceutical research. Information includes drugs in development and industry statistics.
- **U.S. Food and Drug Administration (FDA)** (http://www.fda.gov/)—The FDA is the federal government's consumer protection agency for food and drugs.

PRACTICE TEST

1. If the quantity of gasoline demanded at a service station falls from 90 to 70 gallons per hour in response to an increase in gasoline prices from $1.50 to $1.70 per gallon, then we know that the price elasticity of demand for gasoline within the price range $1.50 to $1.70 is
   a. 0.25.
   b. 3.00.
   c. 2.25.
   d. 1.00.
   e. 2.00.

2. On Sundays, Fat City Saloon offers a $0.95 hamburger during the football season, $0.50 less than its regular price. Fat City discovers that its total revenue from hamburger sales increases. This reflects the fact that
   a. price elasticity of demand within the $0.95 to $1.45 price range is less than 1.0.
   b. price elasticity of demand within the $0.95 to $1.45 price range is greater than 1.0.
   c. price elasticity of demand within the $0.95 to $1.45 price range is equal to 1.0.
   d. Fat City should raise the price of its Sunday hamburgers to further increase its total revenue.
   e. the percentage change in quantity demanded of hamburgers had to be less than the percentage change in its price (from the $1.45 regular to the $0.95 special).

3. The staff economist for Barnaby's Boots estimates that if the firm increases the price of its boots by 10 percent, it would lead to a 6 percent reduction in the quantity of boots demanded. If the firm is interested in maximizing total revenue, it should
   a. increase price 10 percent.
   b. decrease price 6 percent.
   c. hold price constant.
   d. increase quantity demanded 10 percent.
   e. increase quantity demanded 6 percent.

4. Price elasticity of demand reflects
   a. the degree to which firms are willing to supply quantities of goods to match any change in the demand by consumers for the goods.
   b. the degree to which consumers are willing to demand goods to match any change in the quantities of the goods supplied by the firms.
   c. the sensitivity of consumer demand to changes in the price of goods.
   d. the sensitivity of prices to changes in consumer demand for the goods.
   e. the willingness of firms to change prices when they anticipate changes in consumer demand.

5. Consider the downward-sloping demand curves drawn in this chapter. In each,
   a. price elasticity of demand falls as price falls.
   b. price elasticity of demand rises as price falls.
   c. cross elasticity is zero because the demand curve is downward sloping.

   d. price elasticity of demand is zero because there is no cross elasticity.
   e. price elasticity of demand equals cross elasticity.

6. About those goods that have negative income elasticities: Economists refer to them as
   a. normal goods.
   b. inferior goods.
   c. superior goods.
   d. complementary goods.
   e. substitute goods.

7. According to Engel's law,
   a. the price elasticity of demand for food is inelastic.
   b. the income elasticity for food items is inelastic.
   c. the income elasticity for food items is elastic.
   d. inferior goods have lower price elasticities than normal goods.
   e. elasticities should be calculated at the midpoints of the respective quantities and prices.

8. Price elasticities of supply exhibit the following characteristic, within a specific price range, such as a $2 to $4 price range:
   a. Market-day supply elasticity is less than short-run supply elasticity, which is less than long-run supply elasticity.
   b. Market-day supply elasticity is greater than short-run supply elasticity, which is greater than long-run supply elasticity.
   c. Market-day supply elasticity is less than short-run supply elasticity but greater than long-run supply elasticity.
   d. Market-day supply elasticity is greater than short-run supply elasticity but less than long-run supply elasticity.
   e. Market-day, short-run, and long-run supply elasticities are the same as long as the price range affecting supply is the same.

9. If the cross elasticity between two goods is -0.50, we know that
   a. one of the two goods must be an inferior good.
   b. both goods are inferior goods.
   c. the goods are complements.
   d. the goods are substitutes.
   e. price elasticity for at least one good must be less than 1.0.

10. If the state of Georgia, hoping to generate the highest tax revenues, can tax only one good from among many, it would choose the good with
    a. inelastic demand and elastic supply.
    b. inelastic demand and inelastic supply.
    c. elastic demand and elastic supply.
    d. elastic demand and inelastic supply.
    e. unit elastic demand and unit elastic supply.

5

MARGINAL UTILITY AND CONSUMER CHOICE

Some things are so obvious that you don't think people need to mention them. For example, if you come in out of a sudden summer downpour, your friend might say to you, "Just look at you! You're soaking wet!" As if you didn't know it, standing there dripping all over the floor. Or, if you dart out onto a narrow street from between two parked cars and almost run smack into a moving car, an onlooker might say to you, "Gee, that was close!" As if you didn't already know it, your heart pounding like a jackhammer. Economists are sometimes inclined to do the same—point out what *seems* obvious—but they don't apologize for it. For they know that pursuing the obvious can sometimes lead to a more complete and even new understanding of the familiar.

THIS CHAPTER INTRODUCES YOU TO THE ECONOMIC PRINCIPLES ASSOCIATED WITH:

- TOTAL UTILITY AND MARGINAL UTILITY
- THE LAW OF DIMINISHING MARGINAL UTILITY
- THE RELATIONSHIP BETWEEN THE LAW OF DEMAND AND THE MARGINAL-UTILITY-TO-PRICE RATIO
- CONSUMER SURPLUS
- THE DIFFICULTIES ASSOCIATED WITH INTERPERSONAL COMPARISON OF UTILITY

For example, let's take the law of demand. The law states that as price falls, the quantity demanded of a normal good increases. Obvious? Seems so, but economists ask why. Why do we tend to demand more of a good when its price falls?

The reason, they discover, is that the good's marginal-utility-to-price ratio increases above the ratios of other goods. This higher ratio signals people to rearrange the kinds and quantities of goods they buy with their income—that is, they reduce their consumption of the other goods and increase their consumption of the good with the higher marginal utility ratio. Hence, its quantity demanded increases.

Confusing? Probably. After all, marginal utility and marginal-utility-to-price ratios are new concepts. But don't worry. They, too, will soon make good sense.

WHAT IS MARGINAL UTILITY?

When you were a child visiting family with your parents, you may have been asked by a doting uncle or aunt how much you liked them. They expected an enthusiastic response, and sensing that, you would oblige. Most likely, you would spread your hands apart as far as you could reach, indicating *that* much! They were always happy, weren't they? Imagine how they would have felt if you had paused, thought a while, and then held up your hands just three inches apart!

Economists ask the same kinds of questions. But they want to know how much you like tea, coffee, beer, milk, or ginger ale. Or any other set of goods. They don't expect you to indicate your particular likes by spreading your hands apart—although you could do that—but instead they expect you to reckon the **utils,** or the quantity of **utility,** you derive from consuming the goods. That's the hypothetical but very useful measure that economists use to gauge satisfaction. For example, after drinking a mug of beer, your satisfaction or sense of well-being increases by 26 utils. What about a mug of root beer? No more than 3 utils. A weekend on tour with the Breeders? Perhaps 4,000 utils!

Util
A hypothetical unit used to measure how much utility a person obtains from consuming a good.

Utility
The satisfaction or enjoyment a person obtains from consuming a good.

How the Law of Diminishing Marginal Utility Explains the Law of Demand

Most people would prefer having more of a normal good than less. For example, wouldn't you prefer having two boxes of chocolate to one per month? And wouldn't three boxes be preferable to two? But how much more preferable? *Can you quantify* preferences? That's what economists try to do. They measure preference, or satisfaction, or pleasure, or enjoyment, or—their term of choice—utility by creating the concept of the util, which is a hypothetical unit used to measure how much utility a person obtains from consuming a good. For example, after eating a box of chocolates, your utility increases by 10 utils. If you consume two boxes, your total utility increases to 15 utils. Apparently, the more the better! Let's keep going. If you consume three boxes, your enjoyment or total utility increases to 17 utils. That's more than the 15 utils you derive from consuming two. But look what's happening to the number of utils you derive from consuming more and more of them. Total utility increases, but by fewer and fewer utils.

That's what the marginal utility of boxes of chocolates measures. **Marginal utility** measures the change in **total utility** a person derives from consuming an additional unit of a good:

$$MU = \frac{\Delta TU}{\Delta Q}$$

where *MU* is marginal utility, *TU* is total utility, and *Q* is the quantity of the good. The Greek capital letter Δ, or delta, means "change in."

Marginal utility
The change in total utility a person derives from consuming an additional unit of a good.

Total utility
The total number of utils a person derives from consuming a specific quantity of a good.

The Law of Diminishing Marginal Utility

It's clear from Exhibit 1 that the more T-bones you consume during the month, the fewer utils you derive from each additional one. The first excites the taste buds, and the enjoyment is heightened by its uniqueness. The second is enjoyable and highly valued, but it lacks the oomph of the first. The third is appreciated, but familiar. The fourth becomes commonplace, almost a matter of habit. The fifth is just food, good calories, although a peanut butter sandwich would probably do as well.

EXHIBIT|1

TOTAL UTILITY AND MARGINAL UTILITY DERIVED FROM CONSUMING T-BONE STEAKS (UTILS)

NUMBER OF T-BONES	TOTAL UTILITY	MARGINAL UTILITY
0	0	—
1	35	35
2	60	25
3	75	15
4	80	5
5	80	0
6	78	-2

Of course, real steak lovers and NFL football players would attach a different set of utils to these T-bones and would probably derive considerable utility even from the twentieth one in a month. But other people would derive few utils after only a second, and vegetarians would derive zero utils from the first.

We are all very different people with very different tastes. But for everyone—you, your professor, the defensive tackle for the Indianapolis Colts, and the principal ballerina of the New York City Ballet—the utility derived from consuming additional steaks diminishes as more steaks are consumed.

This is true not only for steaks but for shakes, cakes, and rakes. In fact, it is true for every good. The more consumed of any good, the lower the good's marginal utility. Economists are so convinced of this that they formulate it into a law: the **law of diminishing marginal utility.**

Law of diminishing marginal utility
As more of a good is consumed, the utility a person derives from each additional unit diminishes.

Exhibit 2 maps out the total and marginal utility curves for the T-bones of Exhibit 1. Note what is measured on the vertical axes. In panel *a,* it is total utility. In panel *b,* it is *changes in* total utility, that is, marginal utility. Total utility reaches its maximum at 80 utils. Beyond five, total utility actually falls. Six steaks yield a total of only 78 utils, so the marginal utility of the sixth steak is −2.

Can you think of something that has a very high utility at first, but then after you consume the first unit, the utility drops immediately and dramatically? Go to the Interactive Study Center at http://gottheil.swcollege.com and click on the "Your Turn" button to submit your example. Student submissions will be posted to the Web site, and perhaps we will use some in future editions of the book!

Does negative marginal utility seem unreasonable? Think about it. You may pray for snow before a ski weekend, but how much utility would you derive from an additional 10-inch accumulation of snow just when you are trying to get out of your driveway? How much utility would you derive consuming a sixth hard-boiled egg at one sitting? How many utils do you suppose Noah derived from that fortieth day of rain?

Look at the correspondence between the upward-sloping total utility curve and the downward-sloping marginal utility curve in Exhibit 2. Total utility increases as more steak is consumed, but by smaller and smaller increments. The curve tends to flatten out. These increments are graphed in panel *b.* The curve starts high, at 35 utils, but the marginal utility of the fifth steak is zero. The curve then cuts the horizontal axis to reach −2 at the sixth steak. Obviously, consuming more than five T-bones is a real mis-steak!

The Water–Diamond Paradox

Some people find it hard to enjoy life because they simply have too much! Sad, isn't it? Can you imagine a rich teenager getting excited about a trip to Europe? You would probably hear the complaint: "What! Again?" The number of utils derived

Visit the Diamond Information Center (http://www.adiamondisforever.com/). What statement does this site make about the marginal utility of diamonds?

from such a trip may be very few. Why? For the teenager, a trip to Europe is about as routine as eating a slice of white bread. Perhaps that's an exaggeration, but not by much.

How much people value a good depends upon the utils they derive *from the last one consumed*. That explains the paradox between the values we place on water and diamonds.

Would you agree that the total utility we derive from consuming water is infinitely greater than the total utility we could possibly derive from any quantity of diamonds? And yet, look at the healthy disregard we show for the water we consume and the loving care we show for diamond earrings. Why? Don't our values seem misplaced?

Not really. They simply reflect the quantities available of these two goods. Even though we think nothing of taking leisurely daily showers or baths, or splashing about in our private swimming pools, or watering our lawns, or even washing our automobiles, the marginal utility of the first

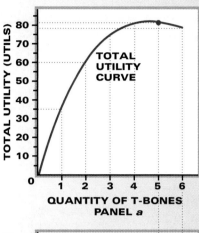

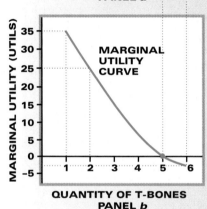

TOTAL AND MARGINAL UTILITY

In panel *a*, total utility increases until it reaches a maximum of 80 utils when five steaks are consumed. Additional steaks reduce total utility. In panel *b*, marginal utility falls with each additional steak consumed.

drop consumed is infinitely high. It's just that we're typically far removed from that first drop.

Other people are not quite so fortunate. Desert societies have precious little water available and conserve it diligently. The Israelis, for example, invented drip irrigation, a technology that feeds plants one drop of water at a time, with the timing fixed and monitored by a computer system. The scarcity of water in Israel causes the marginal utility of the last unit consumed to be very high.

But diamonds, satisfying neither thirst nor hunger, catering to our frivolous fancies, are regarded by many as being even more precious than water. Why? Because diamonds are more scarce. People who love diamonds still place infinite value on the first drop of water. But they have water gushing out of their faucets and only a few diamonds in their wall safes.

CHECK YOUR UNDERSTANDING

Why do Israelis value water differently than Americans do?

FRENCH CUISINE AND MARGINAL UTILITY

A good, solid American dinner consists of a bushel of salad, a 2-pound Idaho potato topped with a pint of sour cream and butter, and a healthy pound of rare

INTERDISCIPLINARY PERSPECTIVE

A PHILOSOPHICAL CRITIQUE ON THE MARGINAL UTILITY OF MONEY

No one has written a better critique of the assault that commerce makes on the quality of our lives than Thoreau provides in *Walden*. The cost of a thing, according to Thoreau, is not what the market will bear but what the individual must bear because of it: it is "the amount of what I will call life which is required to be exchanged for it, immediately or in the long run."

Many observers point out that as we work harder and consume more, we seem to enjoy our lives less. We are always in a rush. Idleness is suspect. Americans today spend less time with their families, neighbors, and friends than they did in the 1950s. Juliet B. Schor, an economist at Harvard University, argues that "Americans are literally working themselves to death." A fancy car, video equipment, or a complex computer program can exact a painful cost in the form of maintenance, upgrading, and repair. We are possessed by our possessions; they are often harder to get rid of than to acquire.

NO, THIS IS NOT MY IDEA OF A GOOD TIME. MY IDEA IS TO STAY HOME AND JUST PLAY WITH THE KIDS.

That money does not make us happier, once our basic needs are met, is a commonplace overwhelmingly confirmed by sociological evidence. Paul Wachtel, who teaches social psychology at the City University of New York, has concluded that bigger incomes "do not yield an increase in feelings of satisfaction or well-being, at least for populations who are above a poverty or subsistence level." This cannot be explained simply by the fact that people have to work harder to earn more money: even those who hit jackpots in lotteries often report that their lives are not substantially happier as a result. Well-being depends upon health, membership in a community in which one feels secure, friends, faith, family, love, and virtues that money cannot buy. Robert Lane, a political scientist at Yale University, using the concepts of economics, has written, *"If 'utility' has anything to do with happiness, above the poverty line the long-term marginal utility of money is almost zero."*

Source: Excerpted from Mark Sagoff, "A Philosophical Critique on the Marginal Utility of Money," *The Atlantic Monthly,* June 1977.

---

sirloin. Each ingredient is nutritious and delicious. But however marvelous the salad may be, plowing through a bushel of it must make the marginal utility of the last mouthful relatively low. The steak is, perhaps, a tastier cut than anything served in the restaurants of Paris, yet chewing our way through to the last mouthful must make its marginal utility relatively low. What about that giant potato? How many utils do you think you would derive consuming that last bite of Idaho?

The French do it differently. Just a touch of soup. Small enough so that the marginal utility of the last spoonful is still relatively high. Just a touch of salad. Small enough so that the marginal utility of the last mouthful is still high. Just a touch of goose liver appetizer. Just a touch of white asparagus. Just a touch of sautéed mushroom. Just a touch of snow peas. Just a touch of the entrée, coq au vin, with a modest serving of potato au gratin on the side. Just a touch of Camembert on baguette. Just a touch of Swiss chocolate. And voilà!

APPLIED PERSPECTIVE

THE FAT PRINCIPLES

The more everybody talks diets, and the more fat-free, sugar-free, low-cal foods available on supermarket shelves, the heavier we all seem to get.

According to the Institute of Medicine, fully one-third of adults today are obese, compared to only a quarter just a generation ago.

Are we missing something?

Probably so, but it's hard to say just what.

As far as scientists have looked, they've found no magic bullet in the diet wards. They've uncovered no secret peptide, no appetite suppressant, no fat-intake reactant that makes people turn up their noses at roast beef or chocolate cake and yearn for carrots.

We weren't exactly born to be fat, but we weren't born to live amid Coney Island–like constellations of fast-food emporia, either. Long ago, fat on the belly served a purpose—getting us through inevitable days of scarcity. Now it just sits there and balloons.

The stunning variety of available foods—15,000 in a modern supermarket—snares many of us. There's a phenomenon called sensory-specific satiety, which means that if you rate the first bite of spaghetti a 10, several bites later the same dish will fall to 9, and so on, explains Penn State University nutritionist Barbara Rolls.

But then if the host brings on a whole new course involving many different dishes, your tongue

HAVE ANOTHER! AND I'LL JOIN YOU.

may well register 10 again. This is why all-you-can-eat buffets are murder on the waistline.

It's not a hunger or a satiety issue, but an appetite issue, she stresses.

Variety is so much the spice of eating that if you serve a pasta dish using three different-shaped noodles instead of one, guests will eat about 15 percent more. Oddly, using different colors or flavors won't have this same effect.

Ditto with yogurt: You can give eaters varied colors and flavors and they won't consume more, but if you throw in little chunks of fruit, down the hatch will go an additional 20 percent.

Eat solo and you won't tend to take in as much. One study, notes Rolls, showed friends in groups of four eating 50 percent more per person than if dining alone or among strangers.

Footnote: Most of this increase was in dessert, as if the eaters were trying to prolong the good time they were having together.

MORE ON THE NET

How many different kinds and flavors of yogurt are there? Take a look at what Dannon (http://www.dannon.com/) has. Why so many flavors? How does this affect the marginal utility of each container of yogurt?

Source: Adapted from John McGervey and Bill Sones, "Those 50-50 Probabilities Under Biorhythm Theory Just Don't Prove Much," *News-Gazette etc.!*, October 31, 1997. Used with permission.

The secret of French cuisine, as you see, is in keeping the courses coming but the individual portions minute. The French understand well the law of diminishing marginal utility and play a strategy of never letting any portion's marginal utility get out of hand. We may end up with more total utils at an American table, but the feeling of satisfaction, the sense of well-being, expressed always by the marginal utility of the goods consumed, favors French cuisine.

CHECK YOUR UNDERSTANDING

What makes French cuisine so special?

INTERDISCIPLINARY PERSPECTIVE

NAPOLEON AND THE LAW OF DIMINISHING MARGINAL UTILITY

Is the law of diminishing marginal utility applicable to *everything?* Economists would probably insist that it is. What works for ice cream, they believe, should work as well for love and war. But does it really make sense to argue, for example, that adding more political power to an already powerful political base increases that political power by diminishing degrees? For instance, can you imagine Napoleon, fresh from his Austrian conquest, writing from Vienna to his beloved Josephine: "I have just conquered Austria. It's a mighty fine acquisition, but frankly, it doesn't generate quite the same utility as grabbing Italy. I'm off to conquer Spain, but I know the utility of that venture will be even less than Austria's."

PRICELESS!

Unlikely. In all probability, for Napoleon, as it was for Caesar and Alexander, each acquisition heightened the desire for the next so that the marginal utility increased as conquest followed conquest.

Perhaps the most challenging exception to the law of diminishing marginal utility is the family. Do you suppose the second child is less loved or appreciated than the first? Do you suppose the tenth child is shown less affection than the first? Think of friends. If you meet someone new, does it mean that the utility you derive from that friendship must be less than the utility you derive from your old friends? The law of diminishing marginal utility is a powerful idea. It explains much of our appreciations and behavior, but certainly not everything.

UNDERSTANDING THE LAW OF DEMAND

Let's take a closer look at that law of demand. When price falls, the quantity demanded of a normal good increases. This not only seems reasonable, but also is confirmed by our experience. But why?

Let's suppose you receive a number of birthday gifts from friends and relatives, some in the form of clothes, some in the form of amusement goods, and some cash.

Suppose Exhibit 3 records your marginal utility schedule for clothes and amusement goods.

If you were to pick your birthday gifts from a catalog of clothes and amusement goods in Exhibit 3, your first choice would be an amusement good. It gives you 23 utils. That's 5 more utils than you would get from the first unit of clothing.

With the first amusement good already in your possession, you look to the next best thing, which is still an amusement good. Although the marginal utility of the second amusement good is less than that of the first—21 utils compared to 23—it is still greater than the 18 utils of the first unit of clothes. Next, you would go to that first unit of clothes. The 18 utils is more than the 17 utils the third amusement good generates. You can trace through the rest.

Making Selections from a Given Budget

Suppose, instead of making choices from the catalog, your birthday gifts included $80 in cash—that's your budget—which you decide to spend on clothes and amusement goods. Suppose also, for simplicity's sake, that the price of a unit of clothes and a unit of amusement goods is $10 for either.

How would you spend the $80? You end up buying eight units in the sequence traced out in Exhibit 3. The first $10 is spent on the first amusement good because the marginal utility per dollar of the first amusement good is

$$\frac{MU}{P} = \frac{23}{10} = 2.3.$$

This is the most utils per dollar your first $10 could find. The next best buy would be the second amusement good, which gives you 2.1 utils to the dollar. And so on.

Exhibit 4 transforms Exhibit 3 into the marginal-utility-to-price ratios *(MU/P)* of the two goods.

It makes sense to keep choosing those goods that yield the highest marginal utility per dollar spent. The first $60 would be spent in the following sequence:

1st = 1st amusement good = 2.3 utils per dollar
2nd = 2nd amusement good = 2.1 utils per dollar
3rd = 1st unit clothes = 1.8 utils per dollar
4th = 3rd amusement good = 1.7 utils per dollar
5th = 2nd unit clothes = 1.6 utils per dollar
6th = 4th amusement good = 1.5 utils per dollar

MARGINAL UTILITIES OF CLOTHES AND AMUSEMENT GOODS (UTILS)

QUANTITY	CLOTHES	AMUSEMENT
1	18	23
2	16	21
3	14	17
4	12	15
5	11	14
6	9	13

EXHIBIT|3

MARGINAL-UTILITY-TO-PRICE RATIOS OF CLOTHES AND AMUSEMENT GOODS *(MU/P)*

CLOTHES

QUANTITY	UTILS	PRICE	MU/P
1	18	$10	1.8
2	16	10	1.6
3	14	10	1.4
4	12	10	1.2
5	11	10	1.1
6	9	10	0.9

AMUSEMENT

QUANTITY	UTILS	PRICE	MU/P
1	23	$10	2.3
2	21	10	2.1
3	17	10	1.7
4	15	10	1.5
5	14	10	1.4
6	13	10	1.3

EXHIBIT|4

With $20 of birthday cash left, you still have two more choices. What will the next purchase be? The marginal-utility-to-price ratio of the third unit of clothes is 1.4. But so, too, is the marginal-utility-to-price ratio of the fifth amusement good. At this point, you're indifferent. Either one gives you the most utility you can get for each dollar. Suppose you pick the third unit of clothes. The last $10, then, would be spent on the fifth amusement good, because its 1.4 utils per dollar is higher than the 1.2 utils per dollar generated by the fourth unit of clothes.

There you have it! Given market prices and the marginal utilities over the range of consumption goods shown in Exhibit 4, the quantity demanded of clothes, at a price of $10, is three units.

IF THE PRICE OF CLOTHES FALLS TO $8 Suppose that the clothing stores begin a 20-percent-off sale just as you are about to spend your $80 of birthday money on clothes and amusement goods. You would still check the *MU/P*s of each of the two goods and choose the highest, then on to the next highest *MU/P* good. Look at Exhibit 5.

Note the differences in the *MU/P* for clothes that the price change made. The first choice now will *still* be the first amusement good. It yields 2.3 utils per dollar, which is still the best buy. But choices change thereafter. The first $60 will be spent in this sequence:

1st = 1st amusement good = 2.30 utils per dollar
2nd = 1st unit clothes = 2.25 utils per dollar
3rd = 2nd amusement good = 2.10 utils per dollar
4th = 2nd unit clothes = 2.00 utils per dollar
5th = 3rd unit clothes = 1.75 utils per dollar
6th = 3rd amusement good = 1.70 utils per dollar

There are still two more choices remaining with the $20 of birthday cash. The marginal-utility-to-price ratio of both the fourth unit of clothes and fourth unit of amusement goods is 1.50. Again, you are indifferent. Either clothes or amusement will do for the seventh choice. If you pick clothes, then the eighth choice would be the fourth amusement good, because its 1.50 marginal-utility-to-price ratio is higher than the 1.38 ratio of the fifth unit of clothes.

With the $80 spent in maximizing utility and with the fall in the price of clothes from $10 to $8, the quantity of clothes demanded increased from three to four units.

EXHIBIT 5

COMPARING *MU/P*s AFTER A 20-PERCENT-OFF SALE ON CLOTHES

CLOTHES

QUANTITY	UTILS	PRICE	MU/P
1	18	$8	2.25
2	16	8	2.00
3	14	8	1.75
4	12	8	1.50
5	11	8	1.38
6	9	8	1.13

AMUSEMENT

QUANTITY	UTILS	PRICE	MU/P
1	23	$10	2.3
2	21	10	2.1
3	17	10	1.7
4	15	10	1.5
5	14	10	1.4
6	13	10	1.3

THEORETICAL PERSPECTIVE

ARE WHITE RATS RATIONAL CONSUMERS?

Have you ever said to yourself, while looking over the dessert menu at an upscale restaurant, "Tonight's the night I splurge! I'm going to treat myself to that $12.50 baked Alaska.

I've eaten their $4 apple pie before and it's mighty good, but tonight that baked Alaska, even at that price, is just too good to pass up!"

What you were really saying to yourself, of course, was, "Let's see now. The ratio of marginal utility to price of the baked Alaska is higher than the ratio of marginal utility to price of the apple pie. And since I'm a rational consumer, I'll pick baked Alaska."

Well, rats behave—and perhaps even think—the way people do. Consider this experiment. Economists J. H. Kagel and R. C. Battalio put two white rats in separate cages and provided them with "free" food and water. In addition, each cage was rigged with two levers that operated two dipper cups, one cup containing root beer, the other nonalcoholic Collins mix. The rats could get to these drinks by pressing the levers. The "price" of each drink was set by controlling the number of presses required per measured drink. Kagel and Battalio also fixed the total number of presses the two rats were allowed.

What happened? In the initial two-week run, the rats were given 300 presses per day—their "income"— and both drinks were priced at 20 presses. Root beer was clearly their favorite. The first rat ended up consuming 11 units of root beer and 4 units of Collins mix per day. The second rat was really a root beer junkie, averaging less than a unit of Collins mix per day.

Kagel and Battalio then changed the prices and incomes. The price of root beer was doubled to 40 presses, while the price of Collins mix was cut in half, to 10 presses. The rats' incomes—the total number of presses they were given—were adjusted to provide each rat the opportunity to make the same choices they had made earlier.

Did they make the same choices, or anywhere near the same choices? Not at all. The first rat now chose 8 units of root beer and 17 units of Collins mix per day. The second switched to 9 root beers and 25 Collins mixes per day! They probably still preferred root beer to Collins mix, but what guided their choices were the ratios of marginal utility to price.

MORE ON THE NET

For information about other economic experiments, visit Al Roth's Game Theory and Experimental Economics Page (http://www.economics.harvard.edu/~aroth/alroth.html).

Source: Adapted from J. H. Kagel and R. C. Battalio, "Experimental Studies of Consumer Behavior," *Economic Inquiry*, March 1975.

IF THE PRICE OF CLOTHES FALLS TO $5 If the price of clothes were to fall again, from $8 to $5, the marginal-utility-to-price ratios for clothes would change again, as shown in Exhibit 6.

Now the utility-maximizing strategy for the $80 of birthday cash buys six units of clothes (assuming MU/P for the seventh is 1.0). That is, when the price of clothes falls from $8 to $5, the quantity demanded increases from four to six units.

The MU/P Equalization Principle

The law of demand rests on this ***MU/P* equalization principle** of consumer behavior. Consumers will always arrange their sequence of choices among goods starting with the highest MU/P and running down to exhaust the expenditure budget. In the end, the MU/P ratio for each good consumed will be equal:

$$\frac{MU}{P} \text{ (clothes)} = \frac{MU}{P} \text{ (amusement)} = \frac{MU}{P} \text{ (any other good)}$$

MU/P equalization principle
The idea that a person's total utility is maximized when the ratios of marginal utility to price for each of the goods consumed are equal.

EXHIBIT|6

COMPARING *MU/Ps* AFTER A 50-PERCENT-OFF SALE ON CLOTHES

CLOTHES

QUANTITY	UTILS	PRICE	MU/P
1	18	$5	3.6
2	16	5	3.2
3	14	5	2.8
4	12	5	2.4
5	11	5	2.2
6	9	5	1.8

AMUSEMENT

QUANTITY	UTILS	PRICE	MU/P
1	23	$10	2.3
2	21	10	2.1
3	17	10	1.7
4	15	10	1.5
5	14	10	1.4
6	13	10	1.3

It makes sense because the rational consumer will always shift a dollar from a good whose *MU/P* is lower to one whose *MU/P* is higher. Since consuming one less of a good increases its *MU/P*, and consuming one more of the other good lowers its *MU/P*, the rearranging of goods consumed will drive their *MU/P*s to equalization.

The *MU/P* Equalization Principle and the Law of Demand

While it may be obvious to everybody that when price falls the quantity demanded increases, economists dig deep into the behavior of individual consumers—who are always trying to maximize utility from a given expenditure budget—to explain why the obvious is indeed so.

The demand curve of Exhibit 7 provides a graphic view of the data offered in Exhibits 4–6.

The three points *a, b,* and *c* on the demand curve correspond to the quantities of clothes demanded at prices of $10, $8, and $5 when the consumer has an $80 expenditure budget and the set of marginal-utility-to-price ratios shown in Exhibits 4–6. The three points outline what the demand curve for clothes would look like if other prices for the clothes were considered. This derivation of the demand curve for clothes is simply a more complete explanation of demand determination than that presented in Chapter 3.

Changes in the marginal-utility-to-price ratios of any good—caused either by a change in the marginal utility of the good or in its price—change the quantities demanded. We can summarize here as we did in Chapter 3:

1. *If the price of clothes changes, the quantity demanded of clothes changes.* For example, when the price of

EXHIBIT|7

THE DEMAND CURVE FOR CLOTHES

When the price of clothes falls, ceteris paribus, the *MU/P* for clothes increases, increasing the attractiveness of clothes as a consumer good. As a result, the quantity of clothes demanded increases.

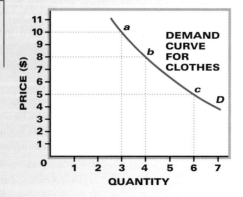

clothes falls from $10 to $8 (compare Exhibit 4 and Exhibit 5), the quantity of clothes demanded increases from three to four.

2. *If the price of clothes changes, the demand for other goods changes as well.* For example, when the price of clothes falls from $10 to $8 (look again at Exhibit 4 and 5), the demand for amusement goods at the price of $10 falls from five to four.

3. *If consumer taste for clothes changes—reflected in changing marginal utilities for clothes—the demand for clothes changes.* For example, if the marginal utility of clothes doubles—it's now more fashionable to own a more extensive wardrobe—the marginal-utility-to-price ratio of clothes also doubles, which would prompt consumers to shift some of their dollars out of buying other goods and into buying more clothes.

4. *If consumer income changes, the demand for clothes changes.* For example, if the birthday cash were $120 instead of $80, more of each good would be demanded.

THE *MU/P* GUIDE TO AUCTION BIDDING

Suppose you arrive at an auction with all your birthday cash just when the auctioneer is about to ask for bids on an amusement good, say a windup Elvis doll. You're interested. Suppose the bidding starts at $3, and before you can get into the game, the price runs up to $15. What do you do?

Probably nothing. After all, the marginal utility of that first amusement good for you (check Exhibit 6) is 23 utils. Its *MU/P*, then, at that stage in the bidding had already dropped to 23/$15 = 1.53—too low to get excited. You would do better putting the $15 into the purchase of some other good whose *MU/P* is greater than 1.53.

But what if the bidding is weak? For example, suppose the bidding stalls at $4. If you raise the bid to $5, the doll's *MU/P* is 23/$5 = 4.6. That's mighty attractive! Where else can you get that many utils for your dollar?

When you saw the amusement good sitting on the auctioneer's table, didn't you mentally fix a maximum price that represented how high you would bid? That's what most people do. Considering that you could get 3.6 utils per dollar by buying the first unit of clothes (check Exhibit 6 again), your top bid for the auctioned amusement good would be $6.40. A $6.40 bid would equal the *MU/P* of clothes; that is, 23/$6.40 = 3.6 utils per dollar. But suppose, to your surprise and delight, the bidding stays at $4, and when the auctioneer is about to slam the gavel down to signal the sale, you raise the bid to $5. Nobody tops you. It's yours! You end up paying $5, although you would have been willing to go as high as $6.40.

CREATING CONSUMER SURPLUS

Economists call the difference between what you pay for a good and what you would have been willing to pay for it **consumer surplus.** Most consumers walk away from every market with some degree of consumer surplus. For example, suppose Exhibit 8 represents the market for horseback riding.

The hourly market price for horseback riding is $6. The demand curve in Exhibit 8 represents an aggregate of all the individual demand curves of people who make up the market. At $6 an hour, 720 hours are demanded by them.

Exhibit 9 represents three individual demand curves that are part of the Exhibit 8 market. They show how many hours of riding Kim Deal, Tony Poulos, and Randy Seals would demand at varying prices.

Consumer surplus
The difference between the maximum amount a person would be willing to pay for a good or service and the amount the person actually pays.

EXHIBIT | 8

THE MARKET FOR HORSEBACK RIDING

The demand curve reflects the willing-ness—at each price—of consumers, such as Tony, Randy, and Kim, to buy hours of horseback riding. At a price of $6, the quantity demanded for horse-back riding is 720 hours. Total con-sumer surplus is *abe*. When price falls to $4, total consumer surplus is *ab'e'*.

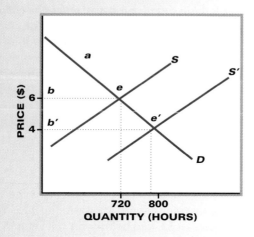

In panel *a,* at the $6 equi-librium price established on the Exhibit 8 market, Kim ends up demanding four hours of riding. Although she pays $6 for each hour, she would have been willing to pay $15 for that first hour (point *a*). The con-sumer surplus she gains, then, from that first hour is $15 − $6 = $9. She would have been willing to pay $12 for the sec-ond hour (point *b*), but pays only $6. The consumer surplus she receives from the second hour of riding, then, is $12 − $6 = $6. What about the third hour? She pays $6, but would have been willing to pay $9 (point *c*). She draws a con-sumer surplus on this third hour of $9 − $6 = $3. Since she was willing to pay only $6 for that fourth hour (point *d*), she buys that hour, but it yields no consumer surplus.

The total utility, expressed in dollars, that Kim gains from the four hours of riding is $15 + $12 + $9 + $6 = $42. She pays only $6 × 4 = $24. She ends up, then, with a total consumer surplus of $42 − $24 = $18.

Tony's interest in riding is, as you see in panel *b,* less intense than Kim's. At a price of $6 an hour, he ends up riding three hours, drawing a total consumer sur-plus of ($10 + $8 + $6) − ($6 × 3) = $6. Panel *c* shows that Randy takes only two hours of riding and draws a total consumer surplus of ($9 + $6) − ($6 × 2) = $3.

The consumer surplus for the entire market—for everyone who buys hours of horseback riding, including Kim, Tony, and Randy—is depicted in Exhibit 8 by the

EXHIBIT | 9

CONSUMER SURPLUS ON THE HORSEBACK-RIDING MARKET

At the $6-per-hour price for horseback riding, Kim derives a con-sumer surplus of $42, Tony derives a consumer surplus of $6, and Randy ends up with a consumer surplus of $3.

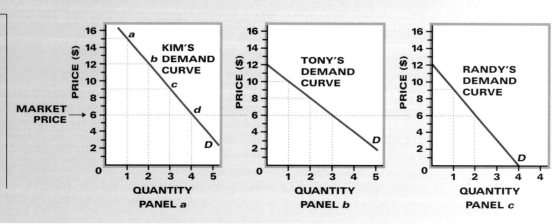

triangle *abe,* the difference between price and what people would have been willing to pay for each hour bought and sold. Note that if, for some reason, the supply curve shifts to the right from *S* to *S'*, the equilibrium price falls from $6 to $4 and consumer surplus for the market as a whole increases from *abe* to *ab'e'*. Consider Kim Deal's case. Whether price is $6 or $4, she still derives utility valued at $15 for that first hour of horseback riding. After all, her enjoyment is derived from riding, not from the price she pays. But if price falls to $4, her consumer surplus on that first hour becomes $15 − $4 = $11, which is more consumer surplus for that hour than she received before.

Can you imagine the consumer surplus people gain from consuming water at market prices? Can you imagine how much consumer surplus we derive from everyday consumption of food?

CHECK YOUR UNDERSTANDING

What happens to consumer surplus when price falls?

A number of commercial firms, such as USADATA (http://www.usadata.com/), conduct research on consumer choices and preferences.

INTERPERSONAL COMPARISONS OF UTILITY

Economists argue that the law of diminishing marginal utility applies not only to goods but to money as well. After all, money represents the power to buy goods. If the marginal utility of the goods that money buys falls as more goods are consumed, then it makes sense to argue that the marginal utility of money falls as well.

The concept of diminishing marginal utility of money implies that your hundredth dollar yields you less utility than your first. It implies also that Bill Gates's millionth dollar yields him less utility than his hundredth. But does it imply that Bill Gates's millionth dollar yields him less utility than the utility you derive from your hundredth dollar? That is, does the law of diminishing marginal utility of money apply as well to **interpersonal comparisons of utility?**

Bill Gates would probably insist that his millionth dollar generates a utility for him greater than the utility you derive from your hundredth. He would insist that he derives greater satisfaction from spending his millionth dollar on a racehorse than you derive from spending your hundredth dollar on a meal. How can you prove him wrong? How can we compare the satisfaction or utility that different people derive from their money? The answer is, we can't.

Our inability to compare interpersonal utilities of money has sobering implications on tax and social welfare policy. After all, if Bill Gates were right about deriving greater utility from his millionth dollar than you do from your hundredth, then were government to tax that dollar away from him and give it to you, his loss would be greater than your gain. Total utility generated in the economy would fall. If we can't calculate interpersonal utilities of money, how can we justify higher income taxes for the wealthy? How can we justify subsidized housing? Or even aid to dependent children?

However impossible it may be to calculate interpersonal comparisons of utility, many economists nonetheless rely on the *reasonableness* of the idea. Since the marginal utility of money diminishes for each individual, it just seems reasonable to suppose that the utility a Bill Gates derives from his marginal dollar is less than the utility you derive from yours.

Allowing interpersonal comparisons of utility to be made on such reasonable grounds provides the justification, then, for the kinds of tax and social welfare programs that government has enacted. These kinds of interpersonal comparisons of utility are at the core of the government policy favoring a more equitable distribution of society's income.

Interpersonal comparison of utility
A comparison of the marginal utilities that different people derive from a good or a dollar.

CHAPTER REVIEW

1. Utility is the concept economists use to represent the satisfaction or enjoyment people derive from consuming a good. Typically, the more of the good consumed, the higher the total utility derived. For example, the total utility you derive consuming three chocolate bars is greater than the total utility you derive consuming two.

2. Marginal utility measures the increase in total utility that you derive from consuming one more unit of a good.

3. The law of diminishing marginal utility states that as more of the good is consumed, the utility derived from each additional unit diminishes. For example, the marginal utility of the second chocolate bar is less than the marginal utility of the first.

4. When graphing the relationship between total and marginal utility, the total utility curve is hill-shaped, sloping upward to a maximum, then sloping downward. The marginal utility curve is downward sloping. When the total utility curve is at its maximum, marginal utility is zero.

5. The conceptual differences between total and marginal utility explain the water–diamond paradox. The paradox is, Why do we value a diamond more than a glass of water, when water is clearly more important to our well-being than diamonds? The answer has to do with the law of diminishing marginal utility and the comparative availability of water and diamonds. Because our water supply is abundant, the marginal utility of the last unit of water consumed—which measures the value people place on water—is relatively low. And because there are so few diamonds, the marginal utility of a diamond is relatively high. On the other hand, the total utility people derive from water—the sum of the utilities gained from consuming the very first to the last drop—is considerably higher than the total utility derived from diamonds.

6. Drawing from among a set of goods, a consumer will always choose to consume the good that has the highest marginal-utility-to-price ratio (MU/P). This ratio reflects how much enjoyment the consumer gains per dollar spent. The MU/P of a good increases either by a fall in the price of the good or by an increase in its marginal utility. That's why a sale or cut in price raises the good's MU/P and leads to an increase in the quantity demanded for the good. The consumer maximizes enjoyment when the MU/P ratio is the same for all goods.

7. Consumer surplus is the difference between the most a consumer is willing to pay for a good and the actual price of the good. For example, if the price of a chocolate bar is $0.50 and the marginal utility of the first bar consumed is valued at $2.10, then the consumer surplus garnered by the consumer on that first bar is $1.60.

8. The law of diminishing marginal utility applies as well to money. The marginal utility you derive from your 10,000th dollar is less than the marginal utility you derive from your 1,000th dollar. But the law does not apply to interpersonal comparisons of utility. It does not allege, for instance, that the marginal utility of your 10,000th dollar is less than the marginal utility of your neighbor's 1,000th dollar. People have different tastes and different intensities of appreciation for money. You may derive more enjoyment from that 10,000th dollar than your neighbor does from the 1,000th dollar.

KEY TERMS

Util
Utility
Marginal utility

Total utility
Law of diminishing marginal utility
MU/P equalization principle

Consumer surplus
Interpersonal comparison of utility

QUESTIONS

1. Suppose, at a student–faculty party, you over-hear four economics professors make the following comments:

   a. "Did you see the painting George bought? He paid $450 for it! I wouldn't have paid a nickel."

   b. "It's still snowing! That makes 10 inches since last night. I'd gladly offer a student $20 to clear my driveway."

   c. "It's funny, I can recall everything about my first romance but I can't remember the names of those who followed."

   d. "Do I give charity to the poor? Of course!"

   Apply utility analysis to each of these comments.

2. Suppose that after drinking four cups of coffee late at night, your close friend, who is studying economics with you, tells you that the total util-ity of the coffee she consumed is positive, but the marginal utility of the last cup is decidedly negative. Does the comment make sense to you? Explain.

3. An auto mechanic says to you, "I know you like your car and derive great satisfaction driving it. But if I were you, I wouldn't put another penny into it." Explain his reasoning in terms of util-ity analysis.

4. How can proponents of a more equitable distri-bution of income use the law of diminishing marginal utility of money to justify their position?

5. What arguments can their opponents use to undermine that position?

6. Stephanie Howard likes mystery novels. Her marginal-utility-to-price ratio for those novels is 60/$10. If the price of the novels falls from $10 to $5, the number of novels Stephanie demands increases. Explain.

7. Mezzanine tickets to hockey games at the St. Louis Arena are $20. When the Montreal Canadiens come to St. Louis, the game usually sells out. Scalpers get as much as $50 a ticket. Most people at the game, including many who paid scalper prices, end up with consumer sur-plus. Explain.

8. The more people show up at an auction and the greater their participation in the bidding, the less consumer surplus is realized by the buyers. Explain.

9. Picture that great scene in Shakespeare's *Richard III*. King Richard, alone on the crest of a hill, his horse lost, his sword drawn, fac-ing the oncoming enemy, shouts: "A horse, a horse, my kingdom for a horse!" Translate and explain his desperate cry in terms of marginal utility analysis. What do you suppose the marginal utility of a second horse would be to Richard?

10. Suppose you went to a pet shop to buy a puppy. You saw one you liked, and it cost as much as the highest price you would pay. You take it home and immediately fall in love with it. The next day, your friend offers you twice the price for the puppy, but you refuse. Explain your behavior in terms of marginal utility analysis. What can you say about your consumer surplus, yesterday's and today's?

PRACTICE PROBLEMS

1. Suppose the following exhibit expresses your demand schedule for flowers:

PRICE	QUANTITY DEMANDED
$5	1
4	2
3	3
2	4
1	5

   How much consumer surplus would you derive if price were $2? Using marginal utility analysis, explain what is meant by consumer surplus.

2. The following table gives your marginal utili-ties for three desserts: pie, ice cream, and cus-tard. Each dessert is priced at $1.

Suppose you had $10 to spend on desserts. How much of each dessert would you buy? Now suppose there's a custard special that reduces its price to $0.50. What would be your new quantity demanded of custard?

PIE	ICE CREAM	CUSTARD
21	20	13
18	17	10
15	14	7
12	11	4
9	8	1

3. The water–diamond paradox explains why we place a relatively low value on a unit of water. Look at the following table and show what value we place on water, assuming we consume all ten units, and how that value compares to the total utility we derive from consuming water.

QUANTITY	MARGINAL UTILITY	QUANTITY	MARGINAL UTILITY
1	100,000	6	250
2	10,000	7	100
3	1,000	8	40
4	750	9	15
5	400	10	3

4. Choosing any set of numbers to represent utils, draw a total utility curve that shows your increasing enjoyment—then decreasing enjoyment—as you consume more and more chocolate-covered donuts. Draw the corresponding marginal utility curve.

5. Suppose you are already at the point of maximizing utility in your consumption of four goods—T-shirts, movies, CDs, and books—and the following table represents this maximization. Fill in the missing numbers for prices and marginal utilities to make the maximization work.

	T-SHIRTS	MOVIES	CDs	BOOKS
MARGINAL UTILITY	45		15	
PRICE	$10	$5		$20

WHAT'S WRONG WITH THIS GRAPH?

DERIVING CONSUMER SURPLUS

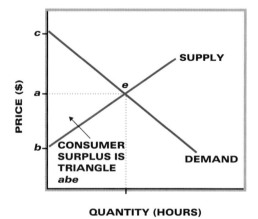

ECONOMIC CONSULTANTS

ECONOMIC RESEARCH AND ANALYSIS BY STUDENTS FOR PROFESSIONALS

Recently, a group of scientists have developed a method for producing nearly flawless diamonds from coal at very little cost. These artificial diamonds are indistinguishable from real diamonds to the naked eye. A few of the scientists have formed the Diamond Institute to explore strategies to profit from this process.

The Diamond Institute has approached Economic Consultants for advice about how to best profit from this new procedure. Prepare a report for the Diamond Institute that addresses the following issues:

1. What issues regarding the law of demand and the marginal-utility-to-price ratio does the Diamond Institute need to consider?
2. What issues regarding consumer surplus does the Diamond Institute need to consider?

You may find the following resources helpful as you prepare this report for the Diamond Institute:

- **Diamond Information Center** (http://www.adiamondisforever. com/)—The Diamond Information Center offers tips and guidelines for purchasing diamonds. The center is sponsored by De Beers, which controls 80 percent of the world's diamond trade.
- **Independent Gemmological Services (IGS)** (http://web. idirect.com/~igs/)—IGS provides buying and appraisal information for diamonds.
- **Diamontrigue** (http://www.diamontrigue. com/) and Rostar (http://www.rostar.com/ RostarSD/)—Diamontrigue and Rostar manufacture and sell simulated diamonds.
- **USDiamond Exchange** (http://www. usdiamond.com/)—USDiamond Exchange is an electronic exchange for trading polished diamonds.

PRACTICE TEST

1. Suppose you just purchased a violin and realized you ended up with a consumer surplus. You tell your friend about it and explain that the consumer surplus arose because
   a. the price you were willing to pay was less than the market price.
   b. the price you were willing to pay was more than the market price.
   c. the price you were willing to pay was the equilibrium price.
   d. you were willing to pay the market price, but the equilibrium price was lower.
   e. the price you were willing to pay was equal to both the violin's market price and equilibrium price.

2. The law of diminishing marginal utility refers to the fact that
   a. the total utility curve for a good is its demand curve, which, being always downward sloping, causes the good's marginal utility to diminish.
   b. when total utility of a good falls, and since marginal utility is the change in total utility divided by the change in quantity, the good's marginal utility, too, falls.
   c. as more of a good is consumed, the total utility a person derives from each additional unit diminishes.
   d. as more of a good is consumed, it diminishes, which causes the good's marginal utility to diminish.
   e. the total utility of a good eventually decreases, which eventually causes the good's marginal utility to diminish.

3. Lisa plans to brighten up her street-level co-op in New York with house plants and framed prints. The total utility she derives from plants and prints is as follows:

NUMBER OF PLANTS	TOTAL UTILITY OF PLANTS	NUMBER OF PRINTS	TOTAL UTILITY OF PRINTS
1	120	1	20
2	200	2	36
3	264	3	50
4	304	4	60
5	334	5	68
6	360	6	74

Suppose the price of plants is $40 and the price of prints is $20. The marginal utility per dollar spent on the fourth print is
   a. $6.00.
   b. $10.00.
   c. $1.00.
   d. $0.80.
   e. $0.50.

4. Suppose there is a sale on prints, reducing price from $20 to $10. If Lisa had $140 to spend on plants and prints, how many of each would she buy to maximize total utility?
   a. three plants, two prints
   b. four plants, three prints
   c. six plants, two prints
   d. two plants, two prints
   e. six plants, zero prints

5. Suppose Lisa, who is a freelance publicist for several alternative rock labels, earns $50,000 annually. To maximize her total utility, she will spend the income in such a way that
   a. the marginal utility she derives from every good she buys is zero.
   b. the marginal-utility-to-price ratio for each of the goods she buys is zero.
   c. the marginal-utility-to-price ratio for each of the goods she buys is at its maximum.
   d. the marginal-utility-to-price ratio for each of the goods she buys is at its minimum.
   e. the marginal-utility-to-price ratio for each of the goods she buys is equal.

6. The problem associated with interpersonal comparisons of utilities stems from
   a. inequality of income, leading to inequality of utility people derive from income.
   b. the likelihood that calculating people's utilities will be error-free.
   c. the impossibility of comparing the utility any two people derive from money.
   d. the unwillingness of people to declare the utility they derive from money.
   e. the unwillingness of people to share income to derive maximum social utility.

7. Think of Lisa, chocolate pudding, and pumpkin pie. An indifference curve, with regard to these two goods, represents for Lisa
   a. the maximum utility she derives consuming these goods.
   b. combinations of the two goods that yield the same total utility for her.
   c. the quantities of the two goods she will buy if their prices are identical.
   d. the quantities of the two goods she will buy at different levels of income.
   e. her indifference to both goods if they cannot be purchased individually.

APPENDIX

THE INDIFFERENCE CURVE
APPROACH TO DEMAND CURVES

Although the idea of mooring the law of demand to the law of diminishing marginal utility makes perfectly good sense, the measure of utility developed in this chapter—units of utils—is still somewhat troubling to economists. It just seems so highly unrealistic. After all, who really keeps count of utils? And even if we wanted to, how could we measure 25 utils? What kind of yardstick would we use?

Util counting is admittedly indefinite and far-fetched. Aware of this credibility problem, economists have devised a rather ingenious alternative method for tracing demand to its utility roots. How does it work? Instead of counting utils, the new method simply records consumers' preferences between sets of goods offered. The utilities of the goods, then, are not actually measured; they're just rated as greater than, less than, or equal to the utilities of other sets of goods.

For example, given a choice between chocolate ice cream and vanilla, either you prefer chocolate to vanilla or vanilla to chocolate, or you are indifferent between the two. If you prefer chocolate, then it seems obvious that a pint of chocolate yields greater utility to you than does a pint of vanilla. If you prefer each equally, then it seems equally obvious that their utilities are the same.

IDENTIFYING EQUALLY PREFERRED SETS OF GOODS

Using the example in this chapter, let's suppose you were offered a choice between combinations of clothes and amusement goods. Among most sets of choices, it doesn't take long to decide which to choose. But there are times when the given choices yield the same total utility; you simply can't make up your mind. That is, you sometimes end up completely indifferent between the two choices offered. Look at Exhibit A1.

Exhibit A1 shows combinations of clothes and amusement goods that yield identical utility for you. These equally preferred combinations are determined simply by asking you to compare choices. If you're presented with the 2 units of amusement goods and 16 units of clothes, *you* decide which other combinations of clothes and amusement goods are equally preferred.

Compare combination *a* to combinations *b, c,* and *d.* Declaring complete indifference means that the 2 units of amusement goods and 16 units of clothes generate the same utility as the 4 and 8, or the 6 and 6, or the 8 and 5 combinations.

CHECK YOUR UNDERSTANDING

If a person is indifferent among various combinations of different goods, then what is true about the total utility of these combinations?

EXHIBIT A1

COMBINATIONS OF AMUSEMENT GOODS AND CLOTHES YIELDING IDENTICAL UTILITY (UNITS OF GOODS)

COMBINATION	AMUSEMENT	CLOTHES
a	2	16
b	4	8
c	6	6
d	8	5

INDIFFERENCE CURVE

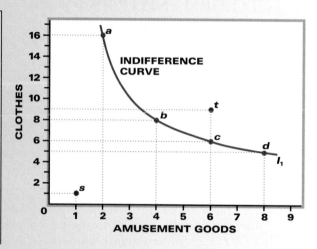

The indifference curve I_1 records combinations of amusement goods and clothes, such as *a, b, c,* and *d.* When choosing among these combinations, the consumer is absolutely indifferent. Any combination on the curve is preferred to combinations that fall below the curve, while any combination above the curve, such as *t,* is preferred to combinations on the curve. The shape of the curve reflects the declining marginal rate of substitution between the two goods.

Exhibit A2 graphs these equally preferred combinations into the indifference curve I_1.

Points *a, b, c,* and *d* mark the combinations shown in Exhibit A2. But look at *t*—6 units of amusement goods and 9 units of clothes—lying off the curve to the right. What about it? It represents a combination of clothes and amusement goods preferred to any combination lying on the curve. Compare, for example, *t* to *c,* the 6 and 6 combination.

Obviously, 6 units of amusement goods and 9 of clothes are preferred to 6 amusement goods and 6 clothes. And since *c* is as preferred as any other point on the indifference curve, *t* is preferred to every combination on the curve. Make sense? Any combination located outside the curve is preferred to any point on it.

The same logic shows that any combination located on the curve is preferred to any point inside it. Compare, for example, *s*—1 amusement good and 1 unit of clothing—to the combination at *c.*

Marginal Rate of Substitution

Why is the indifference curve downward sloping and convex to the origin? Because it reflects the diminishing marginal utility of goods. As more of a good is consumed, the utility derived from consuming additional units diminishes. Look at Exhibit A3, which just rearranges the information in Exhibit A1.

Each time you move from *a* to *d* through *b* and *c,* you are willing to give up less and less clothes for each additional amusement good, all the while maintaining the same level of utility. For example, in going from *a* to *b* along indifference curve I_1, 2 units of amusement goods are substituted for 8 units of clothes. That is, because you value the *a* and *b* combinations equally, the 2 units of amusement goods gained are worth the equivalent value of 8 units of clothes given up.

But when you move from *b* to *c,* you're now willing to give up only 2 units of clothes to get the 2 additional units of amusement goods. The additional 2 units of amusement

MARGINAL RATE OF SUBSTITUTION BETWEEN CLOTHES AND AMUSEMENT GOODS

RATE GOING FROM	CHANGE IN UNITS OF CLOTHES	CHANGE IN UNITS OF AMUSEMENTS	MARGINAL RATE OF SUBSTITUTION
a TO *b*	8 – 16 = –8	4 – 2 = +2	–8/+2 = –4
b TO *c*	6 – 8 = –2	6 – 4 = +2	–2/+2 = –1
c TO *d*	5 – 6 = –1	8 – 6 = +2	$-1/+2 = -\frac{1}{2}$

goods are now worth to you the equivalent of only 2 units of clothes. In other words, the amusement goods' utility, expressed in units of clothes, drops from 8 to 2. This is a reflection of the law of diminishing marginal utility. Going from *c* to *d,* the utility of the 2 additional units drops even further. They're now worth only 1 unit of clothes.

Economists refer to this decline as the *declining marginal rate of substitution.* This term is a record of the rate at which consumers are willing to substitute one good for another while maintaining the same level of utility.

Constructing Indifference Maps

Look again at combination *t.* Although it is preferred to every combination along the indifference curve I_1 in Exhibit A2, it is neither preferred to nor not preferred to—that is, indifferent among—the combinations *x, y,* and *z* shown in Exhibit A4. They all lie on the same indifference curve.

Compare Exhibit A2 to Exhibit A4. Since *t* is preferred to *c,* every combination in Exhibit A4 is preferred to every combination in Exhibit A1. Exhibit A5 maps both tables.

In Exhibit A5, look at point *k,* a 7 and 11 combination. It lies outside indifference curve I_2 and is preferred to any point on it for the same reason *t* is preferred to any point on I_1. The indifference curve I_3 traces out the combinations of clothes and amusement goods that are neither preferred to nor not preferred to—that is, indifferent among—*k.*

Curves I_1, I_2, and I_3 form a series of ascending indifference curves, with the curve farthest from the origin representing the combinations of highest utility. Such a set of indifference curves is called an indifference map. Obviously, if you were given the choice, you would prefer a combination of clothes and amusement goods on the curve I_3, since it is farthest from the origin.

COMBINATIONS OF CLOTHES AND AMUSEMENT GOODS YIELDING IDENTICAL UTILITY (UNITS OF GOODS)

COMBINATION	AMUSEMENT	CLOTHES
x	4	16
y	5	11
t	6	9
z	7	8

THE BUDGET CONSTRAINT

But what choices do you *really* have? Typically, we have to pay for things we consume. Our choices, then, are always limited by our income. Somebody flat broke may have a well-developed set of indifference curves but still end up without any clothes or amusement goods.

What about you? In this chapter, we assumed that your consumption budget was $80, so you were able to choose $80 worth of clothes and amusement goods. Let's also suppose—as in Exhibit 6 in the chapter—that clothes are priced at $5 and amusement goods at $10. Exhibit A6 then describes your *ability* to buy combinations of clothes and amusement goods.

With a budget of $80, you have a variety of choices. For example, you can pick *e*—16 units of clothes and 0 amusement goods. That adds up to (16 × $5) + (0 × $10) = $80. Alternatively, you can spend the $80 entirely on 8 units of

AN INDIFFERENCE MAP

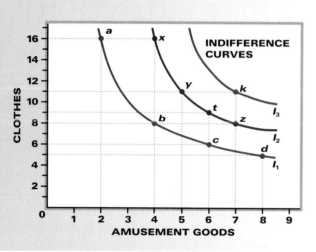

Any point in Exhibit A5 falls on an indifference curve. For example, points x, y, and z combine with point t to form the indifference curve I_2. All combinations located on I_2 are preferred to any combination on I_1. Point k's combination falls along the indifference curve I_3 and is preferred to any point on I_2.

Economists refer to the budget line as a budget constraint.

Price Changes Shift the Budget Constraint

But suppose prices change. For example, suppose all prices increase by 100 percent. You know the consequences, don't you? Your $80 now just won't buy what it did before. Your new options now shrink from the earlier budget constraint B to budget constraint B' in panel a, Exhibit A7.

amusement goods. That puts you at point f. Of course, these aren't your only options. The $80 budget allows you to consume g, 4 units of amusement goods and 8 units of clothes, or any other combination along the line.

What you can't do is consume 8 units of amusement goods and 8 units of clothes, point h in Exhibit A6. After all, that costs $(8 \times \$5) + (8 \times \$10) = \$120$, or $40 more than your $80 budget. That is, given an income of $80 and prices of $5 and $10 for clothes and amusement goods, the budget line defines the limits of your consumption of clothes and amusement goods.

THE BUDGET LINE

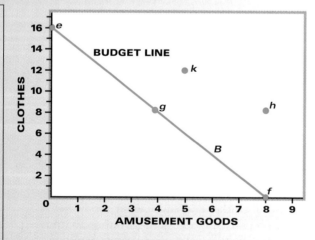

The slope of the budget line B depends on the relative prices of clothes and amusement goods. Given these prices, the budget line's polar points, e and f, are determined by the size of the budget. At a $5 price of clothes and $80 budget, the consumer can buy 16 units of clothes. At a $10 price of amusement goods, 8 units can be bought. Point g represents the possible purchase of 8 units of clothes and 4 amusement goods. What the consumer cannot buy is any combination of clothes and amusement goods that lies above the line. For example, the cost of 8 units of clothes and 8 amusement goods—point h—exceeds the $80 budget.

With amusement goods now $20 each, your $80 affords you a maximum of four units. Your position shifts from point f on budget line B to f' on budget line B' in Exhibit A7. On the other hand, if you choose to buy only clothes, you end up at e' on budget line B', with eight units of clothes.

But suppose only the price of amusement goods changes. Suppose it alone increases 100 percent to $20. The price of clothes remains at $5. What happens to the budget line?

Look at panel b, Exhibit A7, where the budget line shifts from B to B''. The change in relative prices— the ratio of one price to another—changes its slope. You now have the choice of

EFFECT OF PRICE CHANGES ON THE BUDGET LINE

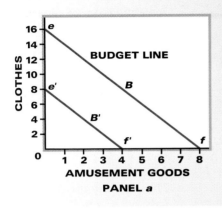

PANEL a

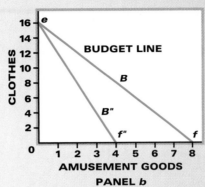

PANEL b

Panel *a*'s budget line *B'*, reflecting the doubling in prices of clothes and amusement goods, lies closer to the origin than budget line *B*, even though the budget remains at $80. Its end points, *e'* and *f'*, are 8 and 4 units, respectively.

Budget line *B"* in panel *b* depicts the same $80 budget, but now only the price of amusement goods doubles, from $10 to $20.

consuming 4 units of amusement goods, *f"*, or 16 units of clothes, *e*, or, of course, any other combination along *B"*.

Income Changes, Too, Shift the Budget Constraint

There's just so much you can buy with $80. If your income goes up enough to increase the consumption budget from $80 to $160—prices remaining unchanged—your consumption possibilities increase as well. For example, instead of being able to consume a maximum of 8 amusement goods at $10 each, the $160 budget now affords 16. If income increases even more to raise your consumption budget to $240, then 24 amusement goods become possible.

DERIVING THE DEMAND CURVE FOR AMUSEMENT GOODS

Everything is in place now to derive the demand curve for amusement goods without having to measure utils. The determinants are your indifference map and budget constraint. Look at Exhibit A8. Here, the indifference map of Exhibit A5 and the budget constraint of Exhibit A6 are brought together to create the demand for amusement goods.

Clothes are priced at $5, amusement goods at $10. With $80 available to spend, you really have no choice but to limit your buying of clothes and amusement goods to those combinations along the budget constraint *B*. What would you end up buying?

Examine the opportunities offered by *p, b,* and *f* along the budget constraint. These are all affordable combinations, each summing to $80. But which provides the greatest utility for your budget dollar?

Compare, for example, *p* and *m* (*m* is nonaffordable). Since *p* lies inside I_1 while *m* lies on it, *m* is clearly preferred to *p*. Since *b* also lies on I_1, it, too, is preferred to *p*. As far as best choice, then, *p* is out.

But how do you choose between *m* and *b*? Although you are indifferent between them, one is more expensive than the other. Point *m*, lying off to the right of the budget constraint, costs ($5 × 14) + ($10 × 2) = $90. That's $10 more than the ($5 × 8) + ($10 × 4) = $80 cost of *b* on the constraint. In terms of utility per budget dollar, then, *b* is the best choice. By this same logic, *b* is preferred to *f*.

DERIVING A POINT ON THE DEMAND CURVE

Facing the budget line, the consumer selects a combination of clothes and amusement goods that is preferred to any other affordable combination. Combination *m*, on the same indifference curve as *b*, is nonaffordable. Combination *p*, on the same budget line as *b*, lies below indifference curve I_1, and is less preferred.

The combination that forms tangency *b* represents the most satisfying combination, given the consumer's budget and the set of prices. Point *b* on I_1 records that 4 units of amusement goods are demanded at a price of $10. That information locates one point on the consumer's demand curve for amusement goods.

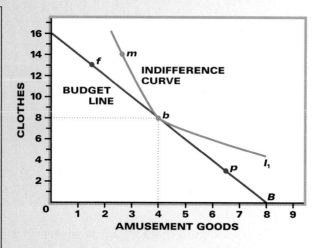

Think of it this way. Imagine yourself in Exhibit A8 stepping up to higher indifference curves, one at a time, away from the origin, but still remaining on or within the budget line. How far could you go? You could go only as far as *the indifference curve that is tangent to the budget line.* The point of tangency, then, is your best choice. That's *b*.

Let's transfer this best choice position onto a demand curve. Point *b* tells us that when the price of amusement goods is $10—your income, preferences, and other prices given—the quantity demanded of amusement goods is 4 units. (*Note:* Point *b* in Exhibit A8 signals that 4 units of amusement goods are demanded and 8 units of clothes.) This is the first derived price–quantity relationship that makes up the demand curve for amusement goods.

Relating Quantity Demanded to Price

Suppose the price of amusement goods falls from $10 to $5.72. With everything else remaining unchanged, the $80 budget line rotates out from *B* to *B**. Look at Exhibit A9.

Point *b* in panel *a* is now an interior point to *B**. Given budget line *B**, *b* is no longer your best choice. But what is? The highest utility-yielding indifference curve that still touches the budget constraint *B** is *I**, forming a tangent at *r*. Your high-

DERIVING THE DEMAND CURVE

In panel *a*, with the price of a unit of clothes remaining unchanged, different prices of amusement goods—$10, $5.72, and $4—generate differently sloped budget lines—B, B*, and B**. The consumer will select points of tangency b, r, and w to maximize satisfaction. These points trace out the demand curve for amusement goods shown in panel b.

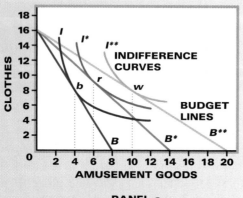

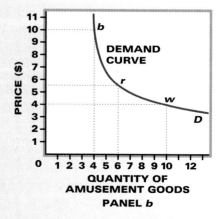

PANEL *a*

PANEL *b*

est possible utility-yielding combination now is *r*—6 units of amusement goods and 9 units of clothes. In other words, when price falls from $10 to $5.72, quantity demanded of amusement goods increases from 4 to 6 units.

If price falls to $4, the budget line rotates to *B*** and the combination chosen is *w*, the new point of tangency between the higher indifference curve *I*** and *B***. The quantity demanded of amusement goods now increases to 10 units.

Panel *b* in Exhibit A9 transposes these combinations of price and quantity demanded into a demand curve for amusement goods. As you see, with income, preferences, and other prices remaining unchanged, *the quantity demanded increases as price falls*.

Mission accomplished. Demand curves can be generated for any good and for any person by selecting tangency points between indifference curves and budget lines. The need to count utils has been eliminated.

APPENDIX REVIEW

1. The concepts of marginal utility and the counting of utils seem somewhat far-fetched. To sidestep the unrealistic character of these concepts, economists have developed another approach to demand derivation based solely on recording consumers' preferences among different sets of goods. Consumers are said to be indifferent among sets of equally preferred goods. Such sets comprise indifference curves.

2. By graphing indifference curves, it is clear that to compensate a consumer for the loss of one good, increasing amounts of the second good must be furnished. This is the law of diminishing marginal rate of substitution.

3. An indifference map displays a number of indifference curves. Curves located closer to the origin are associated with less-preferred combinations of goods than are curves located farther away from the origin.

4. A budget constraint represents the choices that are actually available to a consumer. Along a budget constraint, the sum of the prices of goods to be purchased times the quantities of the goods is equal to the income.

5. In a graph of a budget constraint, an increase in income will allow a consumer to purchase more of both types of goods. The budget constraint undergoes a parallel shift to the right, given an increase in income.

6. A demand curve can be derived for a good by using the indifference curve–budget constraint apparatus. A point on the demand curve is represented by the tangency of the highest indifference curve to the budget constraint. As price is allowed to fall, the intercept of the budget constraint for the good whose price has fallen shifts outward. A consumer can now choose a larger quantity of the good represented by the tangency of another indifference curve to the new budget constraint. Price falls and the quantity demanded increases. The law of demand is supported once again.

QUESTIONS

1. Why are indifference curves called indifference curves?

2. What is an indifference map? Why would consumers prefer any combination of two goods on an indifference curve that is farther from the origin to any other combination of those goods on indifference curves closer to the origin?

3. What is the marginal rate of substitution?

4. Explain why indifference curves are convex to the origin.

5. Explain the significance of the point of tangency between the budget line and an indifference curve.

6. Explain how points of tangency between budget lines and indifference curves create a demand curve.

Have you ever spent a relaxed moment just gazing at the summer midnight sky? If you have (of course you have!), then you've seen that awesome array of hundreds of thousands of brilliant stars suspended in a vast expanse of darkness. If you were particularly lucky, you may even have glimpsed a shooting star cutting across the sky. It's a rare and exciting event. Most nights, the stars just seem to hang there in glittering patterns.

What has all this to do with prices? Each day, hundreds of thousands of prices appear in our markets, each seemingly fixed about an equilibrium point. At any one time, these prices create relative positionings that, like star constellations, appear to be stable. But they really are not. If you were to keep your eyes focused on these prices long enough,

chances are you would see some of them shifting out of position.

In fact, the equilibrium prices of most goods continually shift their positions because the demand and supply conditions for those goods are themselves continually shifting. Typically, these price shifts are quite moderate. But there are times when price changes can be sudden and dramatic. Like falling stars, they sometimes seem to shoot right out of the sky.

We cannot control the movement of stars, but our ability and willingness to control prices is quite another matter. In fact, price control—although always an exception to a general rule of allowing markets to determine price—has always played an important role in the functioning of our economic system. This chapter identifies some of the occasions when government has intervened in the market to control prices and examines the economic consequences of such intervention.

**THIS CHAPTER INTRODUCES YOU TO THE
ECONOMIC PRINCIPLES ASSOCIATED WITH:**

- GOVERNMENT INTERVENTION IN MARKETS
- PRICE CEILINGS
- PRICE FLOORS
- PARITY PRICING
- TARGET PRICES
- CROP LIMITATION PROGRAMS

THE FISHING ECONOMY, ONCE AGAIN

Consider again our fishing economy in Chapter 3. Recall that every day, weather permitting, fishermen take to their boats, spend the better part of the daylight hours fishing the coastline, and in late afternoon return home to sell their catch.

Some days are good, others less so. Luck and experience have much to do with success. The quantities of fish brought back to market change each day, creating different market-day prices.

This model economy is meant to represent a typical, peaceful community of people going about their honest business, working diligently, earning income, saving some, and spending most on a variety of goods and services, including fish. We probably behave much like these model people.

And like any other group of people living in a productive, peaceful community, they don't really spend too much time thinking about national security issues. After all, why should they? They have been good neighbors, and their neighbors have reciprocated. The fishermen have fished in those waters unmolested for generations. No one has ever contested their right to do so.

Now, a National Security Crisis

But let's change that. Suppose their rights to fish the waters are challenged. A neighboring economy decides that those fish-laden waters belong to it. It not only insists on exercising its property rights but also threatens the peaceful fishing economy with military force. Out of the blue, there's a national security problem.

How would you expect our fishing economy to respond? Sooner or later it will have to make some hard choices about national security. What can it do? It can mobilize, redirecting some of its resources away from the production of civilian goods to national defense. Such a response to the perceived threat is illustrated in Exhibit 1.

As shown in Exhibit 1, the fishing community chooses more defense and fewer civilian goods. The economy shifts from position *a* to position *b* along its production possibilities curve. How does it make the shift? One quick way is by drafting people out of civilian occupations, including fishing, into the armed forces.

Mobilizing Fishermen

How would such an armed forces mobilization affect the fishing industry? Fishermen, like everyone else in the economy, would be subject to the draft. One day they're busy fishing, the next day they're on a bus headed for boot camp. Obviously, fewer fishing boats would be out on the water. And, consequently, fewer fish would be supplied.

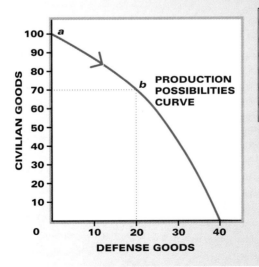

PRODUCTION POSSIBILITIES CURVE FOR CIVILIAN AND DEFENSE GOODS

The community shifts resources out of civilian production into the production of defense goods. The change is recorded along the curve from *a* (100 civilian goods and 0 defense goods) to *b* (70 civilian goods and 20 defense goods). The opportunity cost of the new 20 defense goods is the 30 civilian goods given up.

EXHIBIT 1

Panels *a* and *b* in Exhibit 2 compare the predraft and postdraft conditions in the fish market.

Would the draft affect the economy's demand for fish? Not really. After all, people's tastes for fish don't change just because there's a national security problem. Think about your own demand schedules. Note that the demand curves in panels *a* and *b* are drawn identically.

But what about supply? With fewer boats on the water, the supply curve naturally would shift to the left. That's exactly what we see in panel *b*. We also see that the shift in the supply curve drives the equilibrium price from $4 to $10. And look what happens to the quantity bought and sold. It falls from 10,000 to 7,000 fish. That's a very large impact.

Who Can Afford a $10 Fish?

Obviously, fewer people will be eating fish. A $10 fish, by anyone's count, is an expensive meal. Those with low incomes cannot afford fish at all. They may have had a few fish meals in the predraft days, but at $10 a fish, it becomes unthinkable. The richer people in the economy are still in the market, buying perhaps fewer fish at $10 than they would have in the predraft days. The very rich, on the other hand, if they bought fish before, would buy them still.

In other words, the threat to the economy's security is felt differently by different people. The mobilization of the fishermen into the military means the community has to sacrifice some civilian goods to attend properly to its security needs. But not all citizens sacrifice to the same degree. The poor go fishless. The rich hardly notice the difference.

Is this fair? Should the burden fall disproportionately upon the poor? Suppose some people in the fishing economy find the unequally shared burden both unfair and unacceptable. What can they do about it? The answer is that there is nothing sacred about equilibrium prices. There is no reason in the world why the community has to live with a $10 fish. There are, as we saw in Chapter 3, compelling economic reasons why equilibrium prices are desirable, but there may be compelling *noneconomic* reasons to reject them as well.

EXHIBIT 2

THE FISH MARKET BEFORE AND AFTER THE DRAFT

In the predraft fish market of panel *a*, demand and supply curves intersect at an equilibrium price of $4 and a quantity demanded and supplied of 10,000. In the postdraft market of panel *b*, the supply curve decreases from S to S', raising the equilibrium price from $4 to $10 and lowering the quantity demanded and supplied from 10,000 to 7,000.

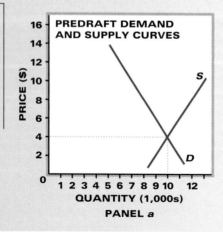

PANEL *a*

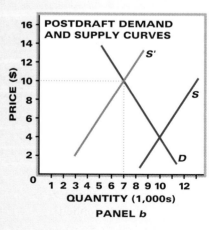

PANEL *b*

SETTING A CEILING ON PRICE

Suppose the community decides to impose a ceiling on the price of fish, by setting a maximum permissible price for fish. The community will allow the market to determine price only as long as the price the market derives is below or equal to the community's permissible maximum. That is, the community fixes a **price ceiling.** Let's suppose it decides to set such a ceiling at the predraft equilibrium level of $4.

What happens to the fish market now? Look at Exhibit 3.

The $10 equilibrium price is no longer allowed. Fishermen, who could sell 7,000 fish at $10 when the free market was allowed to function, can no longer get $10 per fish. The highest price allowed now is $4.

How many fish are fishermen willing to supply at $4? Look at the supply curve. Only 4,000. But see how many fish consumers demand at that price—10,000. Obviously, there's a problem. Perhaps consumers were initially happy to learn that the price was limited to $4, but what's the good of a $4 fish if there aren't many available? As you see, there's an unsatisfied, excess demand of 6,000 fish.

Let's not lose sight of why there are too few fish. The problem was created by drafting fishermen off their boats. Fewer fishermen mean fewer fish. Allowing price to rise to $10 doesn't create more fish. Nor are more fish created by imposing a price ceiling at the old equilibrium price. In fact, the price ceiling merely transforms the problem from living with an intolerable $10 equilibrium price to living with chronic excess demand at $4 per fish.

Can you think of other rationing criteria? Go to the Interactive Study Center at http://gottheil. swcollege.com and click on the "Your Turn" button to submit your examples. Student submissions will be posted to the Web site, and perhaps we will use some in future editions of the book!

Living with Chronic Excess Demand

How would you go about rationing the 4,000 fish supplied at the $4 price ceiling when the quantity demanded at that price is 10,000? One practical way is for the community to print up 4,000 **ration coupons,** each one entitling the coupon holder to buy a $4 fish. The quantity of coupons printed matches the quantity of fish supplied.

But who gets the coupons? What criteria should be used? First come, first served? Imagine consumers' reactions! The 4,000 fish would be gobbled up by the few enterprising early risers. But are they the most deserving? What about distributing the 4,000 coupons by lottery? Chance dictates who gets the coupons. But why leave distribution to chance? Perhaps priority should be given to the elderly. If equity were a criterion, perhaps the distribution should be made among households according to family size. Or to households according to how many

Price ceiling
A maximum price set by government below the market-generated equilibrium price.

CHECK YOUR UNDERSTANDING

What could justify a price ceiling?

Ration coupon
A coupon issued by the government, entitling the holder to purchase a specific quantity of a good at or below the price ceiling.

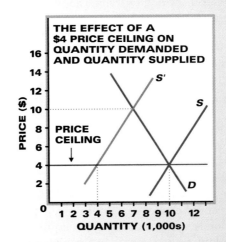

SETTING A $4 PRICE CEILING IN THE FISH MARKET

THE EFFECT OF A $4 PRICE CEILING ON QUANTITY DEMANDED AND QUANTITY SUPPLIED

The postdraft supply curve, *S'*, and the demand curve generate a $10 equilibrium price, and 7,000 fish are demanded and supplied. Allowing a price ceiling of $4 to substitute for the $10 equilibrium price, the quantity demanded is 10,000 fish, but the quantity supplied falls to 4,000, creating an excess demand in the market for 6,000 fish.

EXHIBIT 3

people in the households serve in the military. There is no end to rationing schemes. The only one excluded is the scheme that rations fish to those willing to pay the highest price.

Price Ceilings and Ration Coupons During World War II

The fish story is not too far-fetched. The idea of society opting for price ceilings and ration coupons instead of market pricing during periods of national crisis is part of our economic history. In August 1941, President Franklin D. Roosevelt established the Office of Price Administration (OPA), which was given the power to control prices. Why? At that time, when war seemed inevitable, Congress and the administration believed that some form of control over strategic raw materials was essential.

The economy had already mobilized for the war effort. Men, women, and materials were shifted out of civilian pursuits and redirected to military preparedness. Steel, rubber, and petroleum were desperately needed for the production and deployment of aircraft, tanks, and ships. Fats and oils were critical raw materials used in the manufacture of munitions. It was obvious that the new and considerable demands for such raw materials would play havoc with their market prices and, as a result, play havoc with the distribution of these goods among consumers.

What did the government do? On January 5, 1942, within a month after our entry into the war, OPA introduced the rationing system. It was first applied to rubber tires. Shortly after, in May, gasoline was rationed on the East Coast, and by the year's end the rationing was extended across the nation. Fuel oil rationing began in the fall of 1942 on the East Coast and became nationwide by the end of 1943.

Other consumer goods also came under OPA price control. The first of the basic foods to come under control were sugar and coffee. Our traditional sugar suppliers—Philippines, Hawaii, and Cuba—were unable to provide adequate quantities because of the increased difficulty of ocean transportation. In May 1942, to avoid the expected soaring of sugar prices, OPA imposed a price ceiling and issued sugar ration coupons to consumers.

By March 1, 1943, prices on foodstuffs such as canned, bottled, frozen, and dried vegetables, fruits, juices, and soups were under OPA control. In fact, by June 1, 1943, price ceilings and rationing affected 95 percent of our nation's food supply. It was a complicated set of price controls. Over 1,000 price ceilings had been placed on grocery items in over 200 cities.

Price ceilings were applied as well to manufactured goods. Back in February 1942, 35 percent of wholesale prices on these items were formally brought under OPA supervision. By mid-October, the system was extended to cover 90 percent of wholesale prices. Because of the almost complete halt in residential housing construction during the war, OPA froze rents in over 450 designated areas. By the war's end, most of our agriculture, manufacturing, and housing markets were under some form of price control.

Did the Price Control System Work?

Wouldn't you think that implementing such a widespread price control system in such a short period of time under such supply-related pressure would create problems? At best, the task was exceedingly difficult. In some instances, it was next to impossible. As price ceilings were extended throughout the economy, the pressures of excess demand built up dramatically.

How do economists, looking back at the war years, assess OPA's price control policy? As you would expect, reactions range from highly supportive to highly critical. Many economists critical of the effort argue that OPA's price ceiling and rationing cure turned out to be worse than the high equilibrium price disease.

To make their point, critics cite the distortions created in the housing market. Intentions aside, **rent control,** they argue, was counterproductive. Price ceilings on rent dampened landlords' incentives to properly maintain their existing rental units and discouraged many from investing in new construction. In other words, rent ceilings actually made the housing shortages worse. They decreased the supply of housing in both the short run and the long run.

Critics of rent ceilings would have handled the housing shortage by allowing the market to determine rent and by compensating the low-income renters with rent subsidies. At least such a policy, they insist, avoids the distortions of resource allocation that rent controls generate.

But price ceiling advocates are also persuasive. They argue that market-determined rents coupled with rent subsidies *still* create distortions. After all, the rent subsidies would have had to be financed by some form of taxes, and raising taxes to pay for these subsidies would alter, in some way, what people consume and produce.

Moreover, the kinds of bureaucratic problems involved in deciding who should and who shouldn't receive rent subsidies or whose taxes should be raised might be as distorting as the kinds of problems associated with the administration of rent control.

In retrospect, the decision to create OPA and accept price ceilings and rationing as a policy response to the unavoidable shift from civilian to military production during the war years was, at least, understandable. If the objective was survival, we survived. We muddled through the war with chronic excess demand. However uneven our compliance was and however many abuses were created, the population generally accepted the difficulty, the necessity, and the effort involved in putting aside, temporarily, market-determined equilibrium prices for most goods.

> **Rent control**
> Government-set price ceilings on rent.

THERE'S ALSO REASON FOR PRICE FLOORS

Price ceilings are imposed as alternatives to equilibrium prices shooting sky-high. But equilibrium prices, for other reasons, can just as well drop through the floor. And just as unusually high prices are thought to be unacceptable, so too are some unusually low prices. Too-low prices are prevented by setting a *minimum* permissible level. That is, the equilibrium market price is allowed only as long as it is above or equal to an established **price floor.**

Imagine again our fishing economy. But this time, rather than a military threat problem, the issue is too much of a good thing. Let's suppose our fishermen are riding a wave of good luck. The weather cooperates, and a new technology is adopted by all the fishermen, producing for each a sizable increase in catch.

The result? The supply curve shifts dramatically outward. Look at Exhibit 4.

The equilibrium price falls to $2 and the quantity demanded and supplied increases to 12,000 fish. Fishermen aren't too happy. Look what happens to their revenues. In the old days before the new technology was used, 10,000 fish were sold at an equilibrium price of $4. The fisherman took home $40,000. Now, with their supply curve shifting from *S* to *S′*, their new revenue is $2 × 12,000 = $24,000. For the fishermen, it's economic disaster. Consumers, on the other hand, are not at all disturbed by the course of events. They pay less and consume more.

> **Price floor**
> A minimum price set by government above the market-generated equilibrium price.

Setting a Floor on Price
Fishermen have worked themselves into an uncomfortable position. They can't undo the new technology. There's no retreating to the old way of doing things. They are stuck with the demand and supply conditions of Exhibit 4. But they can modify its consequences. How?

CHECK YOUR UNDERSTANDING

What could justify a price floor?

EFFECT OF NEW TECHNOLOGY ON THE FISH MARKET

The adoption of new technology shifts the supply curve in the fish market from *S* to *S'*. The equilibrium price falls from $4 to $2 and the quantity demanded and supplied increases to 12,000.

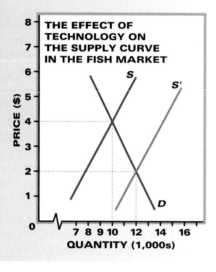

One way they can overcome the misfortune of being so productive is to abandon equilibrium prices. Just as price ceilings were introduced before as an alternative to the $10 fish, so the community can now introduce some minimum limit to how far prices will be permitted to fall.

Suppose it is set at $4. What happens now? Look at Exhibit 5. At the $4 price floor, fishermen are willing to supply 15,000 fish. But look at the demand curve. The quantity demanded is only 10,000. Now an *excess supply* of 5,000 fish emerges.

What do you do with 5,000 extra fish? Someone has to absorb this excess supply, or fishermen get stuck again. Let's suppose government buys up the 5,000 extra fish. That would do the trick.

CHECK YOUR UNDERSTANDING

Who ultimately pays for the price-floor-generated surplus?

Living with Chronic Excess Supply

Why government? Because it's essentially a societal matter. Either the community, represented by government, agrees to support the economic well-being of the fishermen or it doesn't. If it does, government buys the extra fish. That is, the taxpayers lose what the fishermen gain. If the decision is to allow the market alone to dictate price, the taxpayers enjoy lower prices at the expense of fishermen.

SETTING A $4 PRICE FLOOR IN THE FISH MARKET

The posttechnological supply curve, *S'*, and the demand curve intersect at a $2 equilibrium price. Twelve thousand fish are demanded and supplied. Substituting a price floor of $4 for the $2 equilibrium price, the quantity demanded is 10,000 and the quantity supplied is 15,000, creating an excess supply on the market of 5,000 fish.

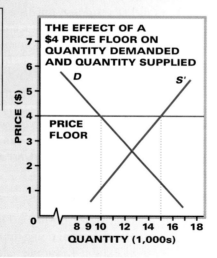

Suppose the government decides to protect the fishermen. What could it do with the 5,000 excess fish? One option would be to freeze and store them. Perhaps tomorrow's supply curve will shift to the left, driving future equilibrium prices above the price floor. The government then could release the surplus fish—sell the supply back to the market—to keep future prices from rising much above the $4 target.

A less-complicated option would be to simply dump the excess supply back into the water. Or, it can always be ground up and used as fertilizer. Or, the government can ship it overseas as economic aid. Maybe a new technology can convert the excess fish into an energy source! Actually, there's no want of ideas. You could probably think of a few yourself.

AGRICULTURE'S TECHNOLOGICAL REVOLUTION

We don't have to look too far into our economic history to reproduce the fishing scenario. Agriculture, at least during the last half of the 20th century, has produced a record of overwhelming productive success. The source of its success is traced out in Exhibit 6.

Note the dramatic takeoff after World War I and the distinct shifts in technologies that accompany the years since then. The conversion from human and animal power to mechanical and scientific power separates most of the past century from the earlier 150 years of American agriculture.

But, as with our troubled fishermen and their new technology, the advent of modern agriculture was both good and bad news for the farmer. Productivity soared, but farmers' incomes collapsed. The story is worth telling, partly because it provides us with another example of price controls substituting for free market equilibrium prices. But it's also a very human story of our ingenuity in creating a system that provides more and more food for an ever increasing population—but creating, at the same time, the demise of that system.

American farmers always have been receptive to new technologies. Around 1920 they began to substitute tractors for the horse and mule, and by 1960, 40 years after the substitution took off in earnest, the transition was virtually complete.

By 1960, horses and mules had all but disappeared. Twenty-five million worked our farms in 1917, but there were less than 5 million by 1960. Their departure

The science and practice of agriculture today is high tech. For example, visit the Biotechnology Information Resource (http://www.nal.usda.gov/bic/) and the Technology Transfer Information Center (http://www.nal.usda.gov/ttic/), both part of the U.S. Department of Agriculture.

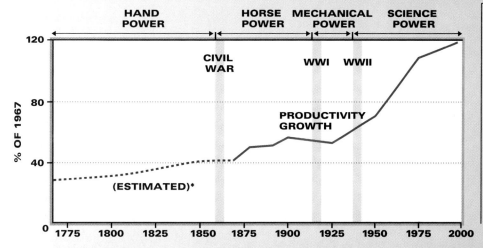

GROWTH OF U.S. AGRICULTURAL PRODUCTIVITY THROUGHOUT U.S. HISTORY

Changes in the dominant energy source technology used on farms, from hand power to horsepower to mechanical power and finally to science power, have generated notable increases in agricultural productivity. The major upward thrust came with the advent of mechanical power during the interwar period (1919–39), and even more so with the application of new fertilizers, pesticides, and other scientific advances after World War II. These factors more than doubled the growth rate of agricultural productivity from the 1940s to the 1980s.

*Precise data are not available.
Source: James Zelner and R. M. Lamm, "Agriculture's Vital Role for Us All," *Food—From Farm to Table, 1982 Yearbook of Agriculture,* Department of Agriculture, Washington, D.C., p. 3.

EXHIBIT 6

Review *A History of American Agriculture 1776–1990* (http://www.usda.gov/history2/front.htm), provided by the U.S. Department of Agriculture.

signaled more than a technological shift. With the horse and mule displaced from agriculture, the acreage required to feed them also diminished.

Mechanization, however, was more broad-based than just tractor substitution. Between 1910 and 1960, motor trucks more than doubled, grain combines increased fivefold, corn pickers increased by a factor of seven, and the number of farms using milking machines increased almost fourfold. Farmers now had to be mechanics as well as crop specialists.

Rural electrification accompanied mechanization. It, too, had a profound impact on agricultural productivity. Less than a quarter million farms were linked to central-station electricity in 1925, but only a decade later, almost 2 million had such access.

The image of Grant Wood's painting *American Gothic,* which had faded considerably through the decades of farm mechanization and electrification, virtually disappeared in the petroleum age after World War II.

New chemical insecticides, soil fumigants, weed killers, fertilizers, plant and animal disease inhibitors, defoliants, crop ripeners, and food preservatives—all petrochemical-based—were mass-produced and mass-marketed to further increase farm productivity.

Modern chemistry developed nitrogen, phosphorus, and potassium fertilizers. The use of chemical fertilizers, for example, doubled between 1910 and 1940, doubled again between 1940 and 1950, and doubled once more between 1950 and 1970. The quantities applied per acre increased fivefold from 1950 to 1980.

To take full advantage of these farm technologies, farmers increased the size of their farms. They expanded farm acreage by buying out neighbors or by negotiating leases with them. Farms were becoming bigger, and they were becoming fewer. The dramatic shift in farm size and number of farms is shown in Exhibit 7.

EXHIBIT|7

NUMBER AND SIZE OF U.S. FARMS: 1945–95

The decline in the number of farms continued virtually uninterrupted from 6.81 million in 1935 to 2.0 million by 1995. During this period, the average size of the surviving farms grew from 155 to 496 acres.

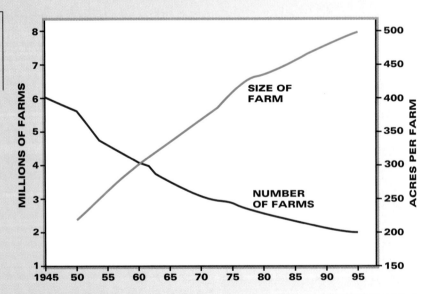

Source: *Public Policy and the Changing Structure of American Agriculture,* Congressional Budget Office, The Congress of the United States, Washington, D.C., September 1978, p. 2; *Agricultural Statistics, 1995–1996,* United States Department of Agriculture, Washington, D.C., 1996.

The number of farms peaked at 6.8 million in 1935. A decade later, it had fallen to 5.9 million. As Exhibit 7 shows, the decline continued virtually uninterrupted to 2.0 million farms by 1995. On the other hand, the size of the surviving farms grew steadily. Average size in 1935 was 155 acres. A decade later, it rose to 195 acres, and by 1995 it had reached 496 acres.

THE EFFECT OF TECHNOLOGICAL CHANGE ON AGRICULTURAL SUPPLY

The radical conversion of the farm to mechanization and chemistry made the agricultural sector one of the most productive in the 20th century. Exhibit 8 records the changes in output.

Total farm output, including crops and livestock products, almost tripled between 1940 and 1996.

Exhibit 9 translates the effect of long-run technological improvement into the familiar shift to the right of the economy's supply curve of farm goods. As you see, the supply curve keeps shifting farther and farther to the right, representing the ability and willingness of farmers to supply much greater quantities at every price.

Unfortunately for farmers, the increase in demand for their output simply couldn't keep pace with the expanding supply. The long-run impact on equilibrium price became abundantly clear and distressing.

But what could farmers do? Go back to horses and mules? Discard chemistry? Forget mechanization? Revert to smaller farms? Even if they wanted to, they couldn't. American agriculture seemed to be forever stuck with its incredible productive capacity. Too many farmers were still producing too many farm goods to generate tolerable incomes for themselves.

INDEXES OF TOTAL FARM OUTPUT: 1940–96 (1982 = 100)

YEAR	TOTAL FARM OUTPUT
1996	123
1980	92
1970	73
1960	66
1950	53
1940	44

Source: *Historical Statistics of the United States: Colonial Times to 1970: Part 1,* Bicentennial Edition, Bureau of the Census, U.S. Department of Commerce, Series K, Washington, D.C., pp. 414–29, 498–99; *Economic Report of the President, 2000,* Washington, D.C., p. 416.

EXHIBIT|8

EXHIBIT|9

EFFECT OF NEW TECHNOLOGY IN FARMING

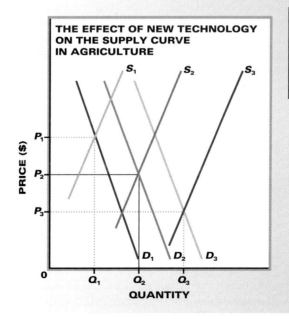

THE EFFECT OF NEW TECHNOLOGY ON THE SUPPLY CURVE IN AGRICULTURE

Shifts in the supply of farm goods, from S_1 to S_2 through to S_3, reflecting the new technologies in energy source and modern chemistry, create price movements from P_1 to P_3. Quantities demanded and supplied increase from Q_1 to Q_3.

TO INTERVENE OR NOT TO INTERVENE: THAT IS THE QUESTION

The issue was clear enough in the 1930s. Either permit the free market and its harsh consequences to prevail, or rely upon nonmarket strategies to solve the problem of low farm incomes. In 1933, the choice was made to intervene.

Many considerations persuaded people in private and public life to support intervention. The combination of high productivity yields and low price and income elasticities of demand for farm goods guaranteed the continuing depression of farm incomes.

Had agriculture not been as significant an industry as it was, affecting so many people directly, the choice might have been different. After all, technological change always involves some unpleasant consequences for some people. If government intervened to redress every economic injury, equilibrium pricing would be an endangered species.

But farming drives the economic life of whole regions of the country, and even more so back in 1933. And the damage could spread. If the forces of changing supply and demand continued to depress prices in the farm economy, that price slide, it was thought, could undermine the vitality of the nonfarm industries as well.

That is to say, farming has never been regarded as just another industry in our economy. Its economic health has always been thought to have very important noneconomic dimensions. Senator Joseph O'Mahoney of Wyoming, for example, in an address to the U.S. Senate on January 5, 1942, put the case to an already convinced audience:

> Agriculture and the farmers today represent practically the only barrier between this country and totalitarianism. If we wish to save democracy, if we want to save the institutions of private property, if we desire to maintain the basis of free individual life, we must prevent the further decline of agriculture.

This kind of politically charged reasoning prevailed in Congress even among representatives from nonfarm regions. To a large extent, it reflected as well the feelings held by many in the larger population.

Once the decision to intervene in the agricultural market was made, the actual task of selecting an intervening strategy became incidental. Techniques of monitoring supply, setting price floors, and handling the excess supply were, as we saw in the fishing case, after the fact.

The farm policy objective was clearly mandated by Congress in 1933. It was to buttress farm incomes above what the market would have provided. But to what level?

PARITY PRICING AS A PRICE FLOOR

There are a number of ways to buttress farm incomes. One quick way is simply to give farmers income subsidies. For example, if the goal is to assure farmers that their annual income will not fall below $25,000, then for those who sell their farm goods at equilibrium prices and earn less than $25,000, the government just makes up the difference. If equilibrium prices fall, then income subsidies rise. If we choose to raise the minimum acceptable income level higher than $25,000, subsidies will be greater.

Another way to buttress farm income is by substituting price floors for market-determined equilibrium prices; in this way, farm incomes can be anything we choose.

The Invention of Parity Pricing

But how do we go about picking a specific price floor? What criteria make sense? Many ideas floated about, but the one that stuck in 1933 when Congress passed the Agricultural Adjustment Act was parity pricing. This means simply that farmers deserve to get for their bushel of wheat the same value that their parents and grandparents got for theirs. It's really quite simple.

Parity pricing asks for a parity, or equality, between the prices farmers have to pay for the goods they buy and the prices they get for the goods they sell. Because farm prices have fallen rather dramatically relative to nonfarm prices, farmers buying nonfarm goods with a bushel of wheat find that as time goes by, they can buy fewer and fewer nonfarm goods with that bushel. The idea of parity pricing, then, was to restore for farmers a parity between farm and nonfarm prices.

The period selected as the benchmark for parity pricing was 1910–14 because farmers believed that this period represented a set of farm and nonfarm prices that traded equal value for equal value. It seemed to reflect for them an ideal exchange standard. For example, if the market price of corn was $2 per bushel in 1910–14 and the price of a pair of shoes was also $2, then farmers could buy a pair of shoes with their bushel of corn. That exchange seemed reasonable. But see what happens in the hypothetical case of Exhibit 10.

CHECK YOUR UNDERSTANDING

What is the value of parity pricing to farmers?

EXHIBIT | 10

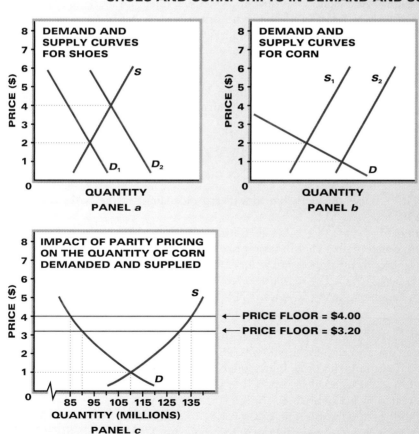

SHOES AND CORN: SHIFTS IN DEMAND AND SUPPLY: 1914–64

DEMAND AND SUPPLY CURVES FOR SHOES

PANEL a

DEMAND AND SUPPLY CURVES FOR CORN

PANEL b

IMPACT OF PARITY PRICING ON THE QUANTITY OF CORN DEMANDED AND SUPPLIED

← PRICE FLOOR = $4.00
← PRICE FLOOR = $3.20

PANEL c

In both the 1914 shoe and corn markets, the supply and demand curves—S and D_1 in panel a and D and S_1 in panel b—generate a $2 equilibrium price for both shoes and corn. Fifty years later, the demand for shoes increases from D_1 to D_2 in panel a, raising price from $2 to $4. During the same period, technological change in the farm industry shifts the supply curve of corn from S_1 to S_2 in panel b, reducing the price of corn from $2 to $1. The demand and supply curves in panel c generate a $1 equilibrium price, and quantity is 110 million bushels. The government-designed price floor of $4 for corn restores the exchange parity between shoes and corn, but creates an excess supply of 50 million bushels. With 80 percent parity, the price floor drops to $4 × 0.8 = $3.20. Excess supply becomes 40 million bushels.

The 1910–14 supply and demand curves for shoes and corn generate for both an equilibrium price of $2. But look what happens 50 years later. In the shoe market, the demand for shoes shifts from D_1 to D_2, raising the price from $2 to $4. On the other hand, in the corn market the shift in the supply curve from S_1 to S_2 lowers the price of corn from $2 to $1. Left to the dictates of the market, the farmer in 1964 now finds that he or she needs to exchange four bushels to buy what his or her grandparent bought with one. The farmer's lot seemed better in 1910–14.

To restore parity, the government would intervene in the corn market by setting a price floor for corn at $4. Panel *c* illustrates the economic consequences.

The forces of supply and demand in the corn market generate 110 million bushels demanded and supplied at an equilibrium price of $1. If a $4 price floor is imposed on the market, the quantity supplied by farmers increases from 110 million bushels to 135 million. Consumers, facing the $4 floor price, now take only 85 million off the market. Farmers soon discover that they are left with an excess supply of 50 million bushels. How can they dispose of it? The government buys it up.

Of course, the government may decide not to provide *complete* parity. It could, instead, design a price floor that offers farmers, say, 80 percent of parity. In this case, the price floor is established at $3.20, not $4. At that price, farmers supply 130 million bushels and consumers buy 90 million bushels. The excess supply is thus reduced to only 40 million bushels. Of course, the farmer, then, gets only 80 percent of the pair of shoes his or her grandparent got with the bushel of corn.

If the government fixed parity at 50 percent, the price floor would fall to $2. But excess supply would again be reduced. As you see, once the market price is abandoned and a price floor established, the price farmers get is subject to political determination—unless, of course, the market price is above the price floor.

Deriving Parity Price Ratios

Farmers buy more than just pairs of shoes. The parity price, then, should express the ratio between an index of the prices farmers receive for their goods and the index of prices of goods that farmers buy:

$$\text{parity price ratio} = \frac{\text{prices received by farmers}}{\text{prices paid by farmers}}$$

Parity price ratio
The relationship between prices received by farmers and prices paid by farmers.

Exhibit 11 traces the persistent downward movement of the **parity price ratio** since 1910.

It isn't hard to spot the good years. Between 1910 and 1920, the parity price ratio was approximately 100. That is, farm prices were about as firm as nonfarm prices. Note how severely the depression years of the 1930s hit the farmers. The decade of the 1940s—World War II—saw farm prices climb back to 100 percent parity, but it has been an almost steady downward slide since.

Living Under Parity

How does the government intervene? The Agricultural Adjustment Act of 1933 established not only the price floor system but also the Commodity Credit Corporation (CCC), the agency set up by the government to absorb the excess farm supply created by parity pricing.

How did the CCC work? The CCC provided farmers with loans based on their expected sales. If the farmers did not sell all their supply at government-established parity prices—and, of course, they typically didn't—they paid off their loans to the

EXHIBIT | 11

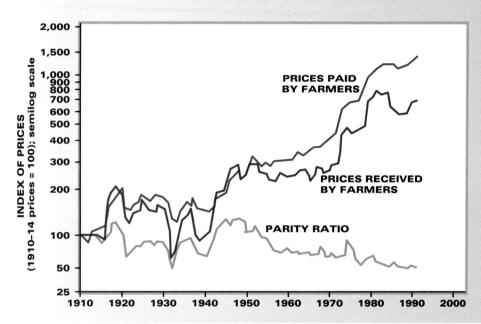

PARITY PRICE RATIOS OF PRICES RECEIVED AND PAID BY FARMERS: 1910–96

Except for war years, 1914–18 and 1940–45, prices paid by farmers for nonfarm goods exceeded the prices they received for farm output. From 1950 to 1980, the parity price ratio declined; by 1980 it was approximately 50 percent of its 1910–14 ratio. From 1980 to 1996, the drop was even more dramatic.

CCC with the unsold supply. In this way, farmers ended up with government subsidies, and government with the excess farm supply.

What do you think the CCC did with all its excess supply? Some goods were actually resold on U.S. markets during years of relatively buoyant prices. But there weren't very many of these years. The CCC, operating through federal, state, and private agencies, also donated substantial quantities of farm goods for child nutrition programs and for needy persons. Some of CCC's stockpiled grains were sold at much-reduced prices to American livestock farmers. That is to say, the CCC was in the business of virtually giving farm goods away.

And giving it away was precisely what the CCC did through Public Law 480, also referred to as Food for Peace, a piece of legislation enacted by Congress in 1954 that authorized the agency to "sell" its food stocks overseas to Third World countries under terms highly favorable to the buyers. In emergency situations, outright donations were made. The recipient countries paid for our surplus farm goods not with dollars, but with their own currencies. As a result, during the 1950s and 1960s our government stockpiled foreign currencies along with farm goods!

Even though PL 480 was principally designed to help our own farmers, its impact on the Third World countries cannot be ignored. In India, Bangladesh, Pakistan, Egypt, and other countries, our PL 480 farm goods were, at times, the difference between survival and national disaster.

Target Prices and Deficiency Payments

In 1973, Congress tackled the problem of overhauling the 40-year-old parity system. The Agricultural and Consumer Protection Act, as its name implies, brought the consumers' interests into the picture. What changes did the act make? Instead of

CHECK YOUR UNDERSTANDING

Who benefits from our farm-goods economic aid?

INTERDISCIPLINARY PERSPECTIVE

POLITICS AT WORK: WHO GETS THE FARM SUBSIDIES?

Farmers get them, of course. But which farmers? It may surprise you, but the distribution of farm subsidies, *by design*, highly favors the relatively well-to-do farmers, while the rest end up with relatively thinner slices of the government's farm subsidy pie. The imprint of politics is unmistakable. Look at the following table:

GOVERNMENT PAYMENTS TO FARMS, ACCORDING TO FARM RECEIPTS: 1997

FARM SIZE (IN TERMS OF TOTAL RECEIPTS)	NUMBER OF FARMS	VALUE OF GOVERNMENT SUBSIDIES	PERCENTAGE OF TOTAL FARMS	PERCENTAGE OF GOVERNMENT SUBSIDIES
$1–$4,999	416,152	$ 734,417	60.8	14.5
$5,000–$9,999	118,057	$ 831,652	17.2	16.5
$10,000–$24,999	105,699	$1,627,749	15.4	32.2
$25,000–$49,999	37,003	$1,254,523	5.4	24.8
$50,000 OR MORE	8,118	$ 606,132	1.2	12.0
TOTAL	685,029	$5,054,473	100.0	100.0

Source: *Census of Agriculture, 1997,* Volume 1, Part 51, U.S. Department of Commerce, Economics and Statistics Administration, Bureau of the Census, Washington, D.C., October 1999, p. 17.

The last two columns tell the story. Farms with receipts of $50,000 or more amount to no more than 1.2 percent of all farms, yet they take home as much as 12 percent of the total government payments to farms. Put differently, their share of the subsidy pie is 10 times their numbers. But look at the top end of the table. Farms with receipts of less than $5,000 make up more than 60 percent of all farms, yet they receive only 14.5 percent of government payments. In other words, the less-well-off farms, representing almost 60 times the number of the most-well-off farms, get about the same farm subsidies that the most-well-off farms get.

Is that a mistake? Did the government really intend to give a higher than proportional share of the farm subsidies to the richest farms? What kind of a "welfare" program is that? Well, it's not really a welfare program for the less-well-off. What the government subsidizes is not people, but output. The more you produce, the more you get. The less you produce, the less you get. If the government really intended to subsidize the poor, struggling farmers, it would have focused on income, not output. Make sense?

MORE ON THE NET

For statistics about agriculture, visit the U.S. Department of Agriculture at http://www.usda.gov/. Also visit the Bureau of the Census (http://www.census.gov/econ/www/agrimenu.html) and the National Agricultural Statistics Service (http://www.usda.gov/nass/).

Target price
A minimum price level for specific farm goods that the government sets and guarantees.

consumers paying a parity-determined price floor, they faced a considerably lower, market-determined price that resulted from a government-designed **target price** that farmers received.

The differences between the old parity price system and the new target price system are illustrated in panels *a* and *b* of Exhibit 12.

In panel *a*, consumers buy 85 million bushels at $4 per bushel. Because farmers are willing to produce 135 million bushels at $4, the government is obliged to sop up the remaining 50 million bushels, paying farmers $200 million.

COMPARING THE OUTCOMES OF PARITY AND TARGET PRICING

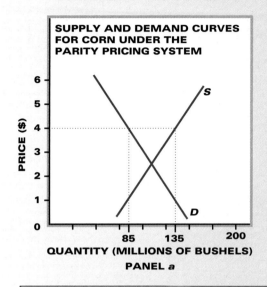

SUPPLY AND DEMAND CURVES FOR CORN UNDER THE PARITY PRICING SYSTEM

PANEL *a*

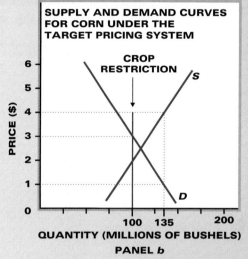

SUPPLY AND DEMAND CURVES FOR CORN UNDER THE TARGET PRICING SYSTEM

PANEL *b*

Under the parity pricing system of panel *a*, consumers pay $4 per bushel of corn and receive 85 million bushels. The government absorbs the excess supply of 50 million bushels, paying out a farm subsidy of $200 million. Under the target pricing system of panel *b*, the government guarantees $4 bushels, prompting farmers to supply 135 million bushels. Consumers pay the market equilibrium price of $1 per bushel. Government ends up making deficiency payments of $405 million. Adding a crop restriction program to target pricing reduces supply to 100 million bushels, which creates a market equilibrium price of $3 per bushel, which is what consumers pay. Now government ends up making deficiency payments of $100 million.

In panel *b*, the government guarantees a target price of $4, inducing farmers to supply 135 million bushels. With that supply determined, and given the demand curve, *D*, the equilibrium price is $1. Consumers, now paying only $1 per bushel, are clearly better off under this new target pricing system. What about farmers? How do they fare? Because they are guaranteed $4 per bushel, farmers receive from the government a **deficiency payment** of ($4 − $1) × 135 million bushels = $405 million. That's an awful lot of deficiency payments!

To moderate the size of these payments, the government added two qualifiers to the program. First, deficiency payments to any individual farmer cannot exceed $20,000. Second, to be eligible for these payments, farmers must agree to reduce their acreage under cultivation. The Farm Act of 1990 decreased by 15 percent the acreage covered by target prices.

It wasn't the first time the government played with acreage restriction (sometimes referred to as soil bank) programs. The most ambitious was the Conservation Reserve Program (Food Security Act of 1985), which paid for retiring highly erodible cropland. The idea behind this and other acreage restriction programs was to induce farmers to cut back supply so that farm prices would rise along with the parity price ratio. The problem was that farmers who signed on to these programs understandably took their poorest lands out of cultivation so that, although their supply of farm goods did fall, it fell proportionately less than their acreage.

Deficiency payment
Government payment to farmers based on the difference between the target price set by government and the market price.

CHECK YOUR UNDERSTANDING

What's the economic motive underlying acreage restriction?

GLOBAL PERSPECTIVE

FARM SUBSIDIES AROUND THE WORLD

There's an old Chinese saying: "Be careful what you wish for because you may end up getting it." You would hardly expect rice farmers in Japan to wish for a market free from government intervention. After all, as much as 65 percent of farmers' annual incomes in Japan are in the form of government subsidies. Their situation is not unique. In the countries of the European Community, close to 50 percent of farmers' incomes come by way of govern-

THE MESSAGE IS CLEAR:
NE TOUCHE PAS LES
SUBSIDIES!

ment subsidies. In France, farmers are downright belligerent when it comes to protecting their government protection. If the French government merely whispers that it may review the issue of farm subsidies, farmers abandon their fields and head straight to Paris on tractors and trucks, bringing the already congested capital to a virtual standstill. Compared to their global cousins, U.S. farmers, receiving 30 percent of their incomes as government subsidies, are almost runts of the litter! Look at the exhibit.

GOVERNMENT SUBSIDIES AS A PERCENTAGE OF FARMERS' INCOME

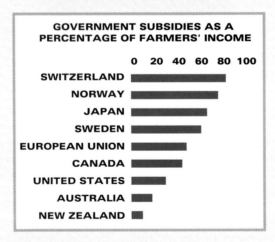

Source: Organization for Economic Cooperation and Development.

How do these acreage limitations play out in panel *b*'s illustration? The agreed-upon acreage reduction cuts output by approximately 25 percent, to 100 million bushels. Now the equilibrium price that consumers pay is $3 per bushel, but still below the old $4 parity price. The government's deficiency payments are cut to ($4 − $3) × 100 million bushels = $100 million. And note: The government no longer ends up holding vast surpluses of corn.

INTERDISCIPLINARY PERSPECTIVE

"CROP" LIMITATIONS OF ANOTHER KIND

Just as the Federal Government for many years paid corn farmers to let fields lie fallow, 41 of New York State's teaching hospitals will be paid $400 million to not cultivate so many new doctors, their main cash crop.

The plan's main purpose is to stem a growing surplus of doctors in parts of the nation and to save Government money. But the payments are manna to New York's cash-starved hospitals, which are struggling to trim the size of their staffs and adapt to the world of managed care.

Health care experts across the country were stunned by the plan, which is officially titled the Medicare Graduate Medical Education Demonstration Project. It was approved by the Health Care Finance Administration, which is part of the Department of Health and Human Services.

"It's an amazing treatment of health care as a commodity—like grain or milk or meat," said Dr. Alan Hillman, a professor of health policy at the University of Pennsylvania. "I've never heard anything like this before. But I really can't find any fault with it. Maybe this is one of the first rational collaborations between the hospitals and the Government." . . .

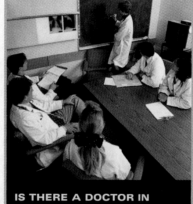

IS THERE A DOCTOR IN THE HOUSE? YOU BETTER BELIEVE IT!

Under the new program, 41 hospitals in the state have agreed to reduce the number of residents they train by 20 to 25 percent over the next six years, resulting in 2,000 fewer residents in the state. In exchange, Medicare will initially continue to pay participating hospitals as if those young doctors were still there, slowly phasing out the payments over the next six years. . . .

. . . Bruce Vladeck, the administrator of the Health Care Financing Administration, who announced the program, . . . said that while the Federal Government would pay out about $400 million to the hospitals, that is $300 million less than what it would spend if the current system were continued.

MORE ON THE NET

Visit the Health Care Financing Administration (http://www.hcfa.gov/) to learn more about the Medicare graduate medical education demonstration program.

Source: Excerpted from Elisabeth Rosenthal, "U.S. to Pay New York Hospitals Not to Train Doctors, Easing Glut," *New York Times*, February 18, 1997. Copyright © 1997 by The New York Times Company. Reprinted by permission.

The Freedom to Farm Act of 1996

Perhaps target pricing and deficiency payments seemed a better way of dealing with the farm problem than the old parity pricing and surplus acquiring system, but it still involved the heavy hand of government in farm decision making. And as far as the government was concerned—with most farmers concurring—it was time to cut the government out of the farm economy entirely. The best farm program for both farmers and government was no farm program at all. That's what the **Freedom to Farm Act of 1996 (FFA)** took as its core value.

FFA was based on the idea that the farm economy had to become strictly market-oriented. Farmers alone should determine what crops to produce and what

Freedom to Farm Act of 1996
Legislation enacted by Congress that phases in, over a seven-year transitional period, the complete dismantling of the government's farm price support and crop restriction systems.

CHECK YOUR UNDERSTANDING

How does FFA differ from all other farm bills?

quantities to produce, and rely on the market to determine farm prices. If the price of one crop falls, then farmers should be free and enterprising enough to switch to other crops. If all crop prices fall, then farmers should be free to decide whether to stay on the farm or not. That's the kind of decision making other producers in other industries engage in and it seemed reasonable to believe—certainly in the prosperity of the 1990s—that farmers should be no exception. The FFA was not really turning the clock back to the pre-1930s days as much as it was making the clock tell the correct time for the 21st century. The message was clear: Production incentives should come from the marketplace and not from government programs.

But how do you wean farmers off government subsidies and get the government off the farmers' backs? Cold turkey? Or in stages? The FFA used the staged approach to free markets.

The stages were marked by calendar year, 1996 through 2002. During each of these transitional years, farmers were guaranteed fixed dollar payments whether farm prices rose or fell. These payments, based on what farmers received before the enactment of the FFA, diminished gradually to zero. The idea behind the staged declining payments was to moderate the shock of "government withdrawal." By 2002, the FFA projected that the farmer's income will have become solely dependent on what he or she earns on the market.

Whether FFA will be successful in keeping government out of the farm economy is yet to be tested. Political pressures—by some farmers, by farm-related industries (such as farm implement–producing companies), by politicians too eager to please—may in the end keep the subsidy payments flow alive. As well, it is not entirely clear whether the family farmers and the large agribusinesses, who both profess to want government out of their hair, will really be happy in the free marketplace.

A LONG TRADITION OF PRICE CEILINGS AND PRICE FLOORS

The use of price ceilings and price floors to undo pure market outcomes is certainly not an invention of the modern world. In fact, ever since markets first came into being, societies have been busy tailoring market prices to conform more closely to their social, political, and religious values.

In ancient economies, for example, the market price of borrowing money—the interest rate—was capped by a price ceiling. Usury laws, fixing the maximum price of borrowing money, are at least as old as biblical literature. Such laws are also found in the Islamic Koran and in the descriptions of the ideal society envisaged by Greek and Roman philosophers, for much the same reasons. Interest taking, particularly at market rates, was universally regarded as exploitative, socially disruptive, and morally corrupting.

That view, along with usury laws, survives today. State governments have the constitutional right to enact usury laws and many still do in a variety of consumer lending markets.

Some moneylenders, whose only crime in life is charging what the market allows—just as butchers, bakers, and candlestick makers do—are nonetheless still singled out and regarded as unsavory, exploitative loan sharks. Their negative image collides with our belief in the virtues of the market system and serves to accent the sometimes contradictory sets of social and economic values we hold.

Although price ceilings and price floors have always played an important role in our economy, they have always represented exceptions to the rule. In most markets, market-

determined prices prevail. They do so because we allow them to. Only unusual circumstances prompt their abandonment. A national security crisis or dramatic changes in the fortunes of critical industries in our economy have, at times, allowed noneconomic considerations to dominate over pure market outcomes.

CHAPTER REVIEW

1. Sometimes, market-determined prices move out of line with their historical levels, and society decides to control the price rather than to accept the market outcome. A national security crisis is an example of such a situation.

2. Establishment of a price ceiling below the equilibrium market price results in excess demand. An economy might cope with chronic excess demand through a rationing system.

3. Price ceilings and ration coupons were used extensively in the U.S. economy during World War II to mobilize resources for war production. Resources had to be shifted from civilian production, which resulted in decreased supply in civilian markets and would have caused skyrocketing prices had not price ceilings been imposed.

4. Price floors can be implemented when society decides that a price has fallen too low relative to its historical levels. Setting a price floor above the equilibrium price results in chronic excess supply. Disposing of the excess supply presents a new problem for society.

5. Because agriculture is such a significant industry in the United States, the decision was made in the early 1930s to intervene in farm markets. The Agricultural Adjustment Act of 1933 set parity prices for farmers' products. Parity pricing was intended to restore parity—equality— between farm and nonfarm prices.

6. Between 1933 and 1973, farmers lived with parity pricing, which established price floors for farm products. Excess farm supply was absorbed by the Commodity Credit Corporation. The CCC made loans to farmers, which they could repay with unsold crops.

7. The 1973 Agricultural and Consumer Protection Act created the target price alternative to parity pricing. The government guarantees a target price, which determines how much farmers supply. Consumers pay the market price, which is established by that supply and consumer demand. Farmers receive, from the government, a deficiency payment, which is the difference between the target and the market price times the quantity of goods bought and sold.

   In 1996, Congress legislated the Freedom to Farm Act, which phases in, over a seven-year transitional period, the complete dismantling of the government farm price support and crop restriction systems.

8. Another example of a price ceiling is usury laws, which have been imposed worldwide since ancient times.

KEY TERMS

Price ceiling
Ration coupon
Rent control

Price floor
Parity price ratio
Target price

Deficiency payment
Freedom to Farm Act of 1996

QUESTIONS

1. Some people argue that people are homeless because rents are too high. If the government is willing to impose a price ceiling on rent, the problem of the homeless would disappear. Do you agree? Why or why not?

2. Why are price ceilings a more practical intervention than price floors in times of war?

3. The reason farmers have not done as well as nonfarm people is because of the following:
   a. The government has interfered in the agricultural market.
   b. The government has not interfered sufficiently.
   c. The character of demand and supply in the farm goods market works against the farmer; government interference is not the problem.
   Discuss the merit or lack of merit in each argument.

4. Paradoxically, farmers' remarkable success as producers undermines their ability to achieve financial success. Discuss.

5. If the government decides not to interfere in the farm economy, who gains? Who loses?

6. What is parity pricing? How does it work? What is the rationale for using such a mechanism in the agricultural market?

7. How do you view minimum wage laws? (A wage is the "price" of workers.) Do they represent price floors or price ceilings? Can you make a case for them? A case against them?

8. What are usury laws? Why do you think they have been so universally applied?

9. If a price ceiling were imposed in a fish market whose equilibrium price was substantially above the ceiling, what effect would the price ceiling on fish have on the demand for meat and fowl?

10. Why are ration coupons typically coupled with price ceilings?

PRACTICE PROBLEMS

1. Given the demand and supply schedule shown in the following table, what would happen to (1) the price students pay for textbooks, (2) the quantity they demand, and (3) the quantity textbook producers supply if (a) the government imposed a $20 price ceiling or (b) a $10 price floor on textbooks?

PRICE	QUANTITY DEMANDED	QUANTITY SUPPLIED
$50	250	650
40	350	550
30	450	450
20	550	350
10	650	250

2. Determine the parity price ratio for the following years and comment on how it would most likely affect the volume of the Commodity Credit Corporation's loans.

YEAR	PRICES RECEIVED BY FARMERS	PRICES PAID BY FARMERS
1990	100	100
1991	105	125
1992	110	160
1993	115	190

3. Graph the parity ratio for 1990 to 1993.

4. Look at the following graph, representing target price policy:

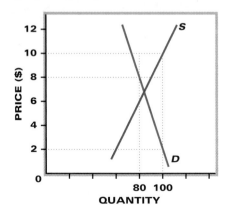

Suppose the government guarantees a $10 target price for cotton. How many bales of cotton will farmers produce? What price do consumers pay per bale? Calculate the deficiency payments government makes to cotton farmers. Now suppose the target pricing is coupled with an acreage restriction program that cuts supply to 80 bales. What happens to the price consumers pay? What happens to deficiency payments?

WHAT'S WRONG WITH THIS GRAPH?

A PRICE FLOOR

ECONOMIC CONSULTANTS

ECONOMIC RESEARCH AND ANALYSIS BY STUDENTS FOR PROFESSIONALS

A group of Illinois farmers has formed Farmer's Cooperative to market and sell its crops. These farmers primarily produce grain. While these farmers understand how to grow and harvest crops, they are unfamiliar with the economics of the agriculture industry.

Farmer's Cooperative has approached Economic Consultants to offer advice on how to make its venture successful. Prepare a report for Farmer's Cooperative that addresses the following issues:

1. What are the conditions of the market for grain? What organizations are available to assist Farmer's Cooperative?
2. What types of government policies affect these farmers?
3. What does Farmer's Cooperative need to understand about farm subsidies?

You may find the following resources helpful as you prepare this report for Farmer's:

- **U.S. Department of Agriculture (USDA)** (http://www.usda.gov/)—the USDA provides data and information about U.S. agriculture.
- **American Farm Bureau** (http://www.fb.com/)—The American Farm Bureau Federation is the nation's largest general farm organization.
- ***Progressive Farmer*** (http://www.ProgressiveFarmer.com)—*Progressive Farmer* is a journal about agriculture and rural living.
- **AgriBiz** (http://www.agribiz.com/)—AgriBiz, a free information resource, organizes agricultural resources on the Internet.
- **Agri-America NetCenter** (http://www.vrms.com/agri/)—Agri-America provides links to national, state, and local agricultural resources.

PRACTICE TEST

1. Why would the government impose a price ceiling in the sugar market? Because
   a. the market price of sugar is above the equilibrium price.
   b. the market price of sugar is below the equilibrium price.
   c. it considers the market price to be too high.
   d. it considers the market price to be too low.
   e. excess demand for sugar at the market price creates shortages.

2. The need for price floors in the markets for farm goods arose in part due to
   a. pressure from consumer groups that were angry over paying high prices.
   b. inefficiencies in markets for farm goods.
   c. persisting rightward shifts in the market supply curves for farm goods, due to technological improvements in agriculture.
   d. excessive government regulation.
   e. persisting rightward shifts in the market demand curves for farm goods, due to higher incomes of consumers.

3. Some economists have criticized rent control programs because they
   a. are applied in situations where there is already an excess supply of housing.
   b. lead to a higher quantity of housing on the market than would exist otherwise.
   c. increase the price of rental housing.
   d. increase landlords' profits.
   e. reduce the incentive for landlords to maintain and expand rental housing.

4. Ration coupons issued by the government during World War II were intended to
   a. subsidize producers affected by price floors.
   b. subsidize producers affected by price ceilings.
   c. deal with the problem of excess demand created by price ceilings.
   d. deal with the problem of excess demand created by price floors.
   e. deal with the problem of excess supply created by price ceilings.

5. When a price ceiling is imposed on a market (assuming the price ceiling is below the equilibrium price),
   a. the quantity of the good will fall.
   b. the quantity of the good will rise.
   c. the demand curve for the good will shift to the left.
   d. the demand curve for the good will shift to the right.
   e. decisions must be made concerning the sale of excess supply.

6. Price floors are usually designed to help _____, while price ceilings are intended to help _____.
   a. producers/consumers.
   b. consumers/producers.
   c. the relatively poor/the relatively rich.
   d. those burdened with deficiency payments/those receiving deficiency payments.
   e. those receiving deficiency payments/those burdened with deficiency payments.

7. Parity pricing
   a. leads to an excess demand for a good.
   b. is another name for target pricing.
   c. is a means of subsidizing producers.
   d. provides incentives for producers to adopt new technologies.
   e. leads to a rightward shift in the demand curve.

8. One criticism of the parity pricing system is that it
   a. promotes higher market prices.
   b. provides incentives for producers to increase the quantity they supply, thus reducing market prices.
   c. leads to a leftward shift in the market supply curve.
   d. leads to a leftward shift in the market demand curve.
   e. pays producers for not producing goods.

9. One problem that the Commodity Credit Corporation had to address with regard to the parity pricing system was
   a. how to raise market prices of farm goods to their equilibrium levels.
   b. what to do with the excess supplies of goods the parity pricing system creates.
   c. how to induce farmers to adopt new agricultural technologies.
   d. how to protect consumers from higher farm and farm-related prices.
   e. whether to subsidize farmers who have no credit in their parity price system accounts.

10. When the government sets a price ceiling below the equilibrium price in the market for gasoline
    a. an excess supply of gasoline emerges in the market.
    b. the equilibrium price of gasoline will fall to the price ceiling level.
    c. not everyone who is willing and able to consume gasoline at the ceiling price will be able to do so.
    d. the supply curve for gasoline will shift to the right.
    e. the demand curve for gasoline will shift to the right.

A fishing business can conjure up all kinds of images. For example, picture running a seafood empire—as many Fortune 500 corporations are run—from a plush executive suite at corporate headquarters on the 50th floor of the World Trade Center in New York. That's considerably different, isn't it, from a small fleet of shrimp boats run from a fish-scented, uncarpeted, undersized, cluttered office located just off the fishing pier?

Yet both images are true. These different types of business coexist in the fishing industry, as they do in most other industries. And for good reason. Both offer clear advantages. Some people running businesses prefer the relatively small-scale, one-person or two-person operation—

BUSINESS OWNERSHIP AND ORGANIZATION: PROPRIETORSHIPS, PARTNERSHIPS, AND CORPORATIONS

THIS CHAPTER INTRODUCES YOU TO THE ECONOMIC PRINCIPLES ASSOCIATED WITH:

- SOLE PROPRIETORSHIPS
- PARTNERSHIPS
- CORPORATIONS
- UNLIMITED AND LIMITED LIABILITY
- STOCKHOLDERS (SHAREHOLDERS)
- STOCKS AND BONDS
- INTERNATIONAL AND MULTINATIONAL CORPORATIONS

in the form of either a *proprietorship* or a *partnership*. These people are willing to forgo the benefits of a *corporate* form of business in favor of a proprietorship or partnership.

Yet, for other people, operating perhaps at a different level of production, the advantages gained from the corporate form of enterprise outweigh the advantages derived from either proprietorship or partnership.

Why? What issues decide which business form to adopt? What are the specific advantages and disadvantages that businesspeople associate with these different forms of business organization?

SOLE PROPRIETORSHIP

Sole proprietorship
A firm owned by one person who alone bears the responsibilities and unlimited liabilities of the firm.

Let's start with **sole proprietorship.** Imagine yourself being the sole proprietor of a fishing enterprise. The business is yours alone. You own the boat, hire the crew, and operate near productive capacity. All decision making belongs to you. You decide whether to go out on a fishing run, whether to add crew (or perhaps reduce crew size), whether to purchase new equipment, and whether to add still another boat to your operations.

Of course, much of the day-to-day decision making is routine. But there are times when the decisions you make can substantially change the character of the business. They can even determine whether you stay in business. As sole proprietor, you must assume complete responsibility. That can be downright unnerving. But ask proprietors and they are likely to tell you that the responsibility also gives them a sense of personal pride and control over their working life. It's not surprising, then, that many people who own and run businesses choose to be sole proprietors.

What does it take to set up a proprietorship? Owners typically rely on their own financial means to purchase, rent, or hire such elements as a physical plant, raw materials, and labor. They hire principally, but not exclusively, family labor. Most produce for local markets.

What do they look like? Proprietorships are typically run as family businesses. If there's a shoe repair shop in your neighborhood, it's probably a proprietorship. So, too, are florist shops, restaurants, travel agencies, taxi services, cattle ranches, and chicken farms. Portrait photographers and scrap metal firms are typically proprietorships. So, too, are many fishing firms. The variety is endless. Just scan the Yellow Pages of your telephone directory.

In many cases, sole proprietorship is the ideal form of business organization. The personal independence it provides the proprietor, its focus on local markets, its lack of bureaucratic structure, and its access to familiar and even family labor gives it advantages that, say, corporations do not typically have.

CHECK YOUR UNDERSTANDING

What are the disadvantages of sole proprietorships?

But there are disadvantages, too, and these can become overriding concerns, particularly when proprietors contemplate expanding their production capacities. *In proprietorships, the proprietor and the firm are legally inseparable.* This legal indivisibility of proprietor and firm could result in *personal* losses for the proprietor far beyond the proprietor's own financial commitment to the business.

For example, suppose you set up a fishing business with an initial investment of $100,000. After a few rough years, the firm succeeds only in accumulating debt. By the end of the third year, you discover that your firm owes its creditors $500,000 but has only $75,000 of firm assets to cover the debt. Reluctantly, you decide enough's enough. What happens?

If you liquidate those assets to pay off the debt, you still fall $425,000 short. What do you do? You can't simply walk away from your unpaid obligations. You are personally liable. With the firm's assets depleted, your creditors can make claim to your personal assets. They can, for example, compel you to liquidate personal belongings such as your automobile, stocks, bonds, and even home furnishings. In other words, *the proprietorship form of business organization puts in jeopardy the proprietor's entire personal net worth.*

Unlimited liability
Personal responsibility of the owners for all debts incurred by sole proprietorships or partnerships. The owners' personal wealth is subject to appropriation to pay off the firm's debt.

You can see, then, why some proprietors would be reluctant to expand their production capacity much beyond its current level, even when the prospects for a successful expansion of business activity seem particularly attractive. The specter of business misjudgments that might trigger **unlimited liability** serves to cramp ambition.

PARTNERSHIP

How, then, can firms run by proprietors expand, without at the same time endangering the species? One option is for sole proprietors to find one or more partners willing to buy into the business. In this way, liability is shared and the firm acquires greater access to capital resources.

Think, again, about your fishing enterprise. Suppose, as sole proprietor, you encounter an excellent expansion opportunity that is simply beyond your own personal means. Suppose you persuade two people, less experienced in the business, to join you in **partnership.** You sell your $40,000 boat and put that sum, coupled with your partners' finances, toward a $400,000 purchase of two larger boats. Your productive capacity increases twentyfold, from 3,000 to 60,000 fish per run. This kind of business expansion would not be possible under a sole proprietorship.

But partnership also affects decision making, because business decisions are now made jointly. And although partnerships are founded upon trust, that trust may quickly erode when decisions—made either by you or by your partners—are challenged by the other partners.

There are other problems as well. Although the firm's liability is now shared, partnership makes each partner personally liable for all debts incurred by the business. It is one thing to be held liable for your own mistakes, and quite another to be held liable for the other partners' mistakes as well. Some partners, who may have only a minimal share in the business, may end up absorbing considerably more than a minimal share of its losses. Liability is always regarded as 100 percent by each partner. Imagine what would happen if the firm goes bankrupt and your partners claim no personal net worth. The burden of unlimited liability falls solely on you. You can see why people with substantial personal wealth would be reluctant to join partnerships.

> **Partnership**
> A firm owned by two or more people who each bear the responsibilities and unlimited liabilities of the firm.

CHECK YOUR UNDERSTANDING

What are the disadvantages of partnerships?

CORPORATION

Is there any way of facilitating substantial expansion of the firm and, at the same time, protecting yourself against the possible onslaught of unlimited liability? The corporate form of business organization is designed to do precisely that. It's as simple an idea as it is revolutionary. How does it work?

The Security of Limited Liability

The **corporation,** unlike the sole proprietorship and the partnership, is created as a separate legal being, *independent of its owners.* That's the key to limited liability. As a legally created being, it has its own legal rights. It can borrow funds, hire and fire people, produce goods and services, make a profit, and plow that profit back into the business or spend it. Sole proprietorships and partnerships can do these things, too, but if a corporation suffers strings of losses instead of making a profit, it alone—not its owners—is liable for its debts.

Of course, if the corporation goes bankrupt, its investors may end up losing their entire investment. But that is all they can lose. Their own personal wealth is not in jeopardy, because the owners are not the corporation. And only the corporation is liable. In this way, the separation of the corporation from its owners protects the owners from unlimited liability.

> **Corporation**
> A firm whose legal identity is separate from the people who own shares of its stock. The liability of each stockowner is limited only to what he or she has invested in the firm.

Setting Up the Corporation

Suppose you decide to set up your fishing enterprise as a corporation. The first thing would be to obtain a charter from your state government. The charter is the legal document that recognizes the corporation as an independent person, separate from you. Like any other legal person, it is subject to the laws of the state, has the right to organize for business, and can sue and be sued.

OWNERSHIP The corporation is owned by individuals who buy shares of its **stock.** If the corporation decides to issue 1,000 shares at $100 per share, and if you buy all 1,000 shares, then you are the only stockholder. **Stockholders (shareholders)** elect the corporation's board of directors, and the board appoints the corporation's management. By owning 100 percent of the shares, you have complete control over who runs the business. (To maintain unchallengeable control of the business, all you really need is one share more than 50 percent.)

You now make yourself the corporation's chief executive officer (CEO). And the corporation, with its $100,000, buys a boat and equipment and hires a crew. If the firm makes a profit, it can distribute the profit to its stockholders (in this case, just you) in the form of dividends. Or it can use some or all of that profit to buy more equipment, hire more crew, or even buy a second boat. The stockholders decide.

If stockholders continually decide to allow the corporation to reinvest its profit, then the value of the corporation's stock, reflecting the corporation's growing assets, would become somewhat greater than its original $100,000. Each of the 1,000 shares you own, then, would be worth more than its original $100.

Many small corporations are actually owned and run this way. Many sole proprietors, for example, to protect themselves against unlimited liability, convert from proprietorship to the corporate form of business organization.

STOCK ISSUES Suppose, as CEO, you encounter an excellent opportunity to expand your fishing operations a hundredfold, but it requires an investment of $900,000. Although the corporation is profitable and enterprising, this is not a sum that can be generated internally out of profit. What can it do?

One solution is to issue another 9,000 shares at, say, $100 per share. Suppose the issue is successfully subscribed. People read the corporation's prospectus and like what they read. The fishing firm's performance record is impressive and the idea for expansion exciting. Many people buy varying quantities of the new issue, and within a week the corporation has at its disposal the necessary $900,000.

The total outstanding stock now rises to 10,000 shares. Your 1,000 shares represent, then, only 10 percent of the total, but when there are many stockholders, 10 percent typically is sufficient to keep control of management. Anyway, there's no reason to suppose that the new stockholders would want to change management. After all, their interest in the corporation is primarily to receive as high a **dividend** as possible. As long as the corporation performs well, why would they even contemplate changing management?

Corporations have the option of varying the kinds of stock they issue. For example, the $1 million of outstanding stock in your fishing enterprise—entitling each stockholder to a vote that is proportional to his or her share of total outstanding stock—is defined as common stock. Stockholders receive dividends in proportion to the quantity of stock they own, assuming, of course, that the corporation makes a profit and decides to distribute it as dividends.

In addition to common stock, corporations can issue preferred stock. This type of stock differs from common stock in three respects: (1) it does not carry voting privileges, which to most stockholders is only a minor consideration; (2) the divi-

Stock
Ownership in a corporation, represented by shares that are claims on the firm's assets and earnings.

Stockholder (shareholder)
A person owning stock in a corporation, that is, a share of a corporation.

Dividend
That part of a corporation's net income that is paid out to its stockholders.

dend yield is fixed; and (3) it has prior claim on dividends; that is, owners of preferred stock receive their dividends before any dividends are distributed to common stock owners. Of course, if the corporation doesn't make enough profit to fully cover the fixed dividends on preferred stock, preferred stockholders end up receiving something less. As you can see, holding preferred stock also involves risk. But compared to common stock, whose dividend returns are not fixed—that is, holders of common stock are more willing to chance greater or lesser gain—the preferred stock option appeals to the more conservative stockholder. It's a matter of preference.

A third type of stock provides the stockholder further choice. Like preferred stock, convertible stock carries no voting privileges and yields a fixed dividend. But it differs from preferred stock in two respects: (1) convertible stock has prior claim on dividends over both common and preferred, and (2) it gives stockholders the privilege of converting their stock into common stock. Convertibles, then, offer people yet another way to buy into corporate ownership.

CORPORATE BONDS A completely different source of corporate funding is the **corporate bond.** Instead of issuing a new $100 share of corporate stock to a stockholder, the corporation can issue a $100 bond. The person who buys the $100 corporate bond holds the corporation's promise—which is its bond—to pay a specified return on the bond and to repay the principal at a specified time.

The advantage of holding bonds, as opposed to stocks, is that bondholders have first claim on the corporation's profit. Before any stockholder receives one penny in dividends, bondholders must be fully paid. Bonds, then, represent the safest form of participating in corporate business.

But this safety comes at a cost. If the corporation's profit increases year after year, stockholders can expect their returns to increase as well. After all, they are the owners. Bondholders do not enjoy this benefit. They are lenders, not owners. It's a question, once more, of people's preferences. Some prefer the security of prior claim on corporate profit and a fixed return, while others are more willing to wager their returns on the performance of the corporation.

> **Corporate bond**
> A corporate IOU. The corporation borrows capital for a specified period of time in exchange for this promise to repay the loan along with an agreed-upon rate of interest.

The Sky's the Limit in Stock Issues

What about your fishing business? If its performance record is strong enough, there is no reason why you couldn't take advantage of the full range of stock and bond issues to build the corporation into a nationwide enterprise.

It's hard to imagine United Airlines, Exxon, or any of the Fortune 500 companies being run as sole proprietorships. It would be close to impossible to raise the enormous sums of capital required. The value of United Airlines's plant and equipment, for example, is over $8 billion. You couldn't begin to raise that sum as a sole proprietor.

Consider your own case. How could you raise large sums of capital without issuing stocks and bonds? Perhaps a few very wealthy people would come along, see the long run potential in your fishing operation, and each invest $10 million. But counting on that possibility must rank among the most unreliable ways of planning a business venture.

One of the beauties of the corporate form of business organization is that it allows people of even modest means to become participants in enterprise ownership. The size of your business organization and its rate of growth aren't intractably tied to the whims of a few people. The corporation is open to hundreds of thousands of people who can afford, say, five shares of a $100 stock. It's your track record that counts. The sky's the limit!

THEORETICAL PERSPECTIVE

WANT TO MINIMIZE RISK? TRY A MUTUAL FUND

STUDENT: Professor Gottheil, I have a problem and I think you can advise me.

GOTTHEIL: I hope I can. What's the problem?

STUDENT: My grandmother gave me a $1,000 high school graduation gift. I don't want to just put it in a bank to earn relatively low interest. I was thinking about buying a stock because almost every night on network news, economic commentators report on how well the stock market is doing. I have an IBM computer and really like it, so I was considering using the $1,000 gift to purchase some shares of IBM stock. What do you think?

GOTTHEIL: Not a bad idea. But why invest your gift in one stock? That can be risky.

STUDENT: What do you mean?

GOTTHEIL: Well, admittedly, IBM is a relatively high-performing company with an excellent reputation for quality products. But the truth of the matter is that there is now a lot of competition in the computer industry. That may affect IBM's future sales. If it loses sales to competitors, the loss may affect the value of its stock. Instead of IBM's stock value increasing as it has in the past, it may decrease, and there goes part of your $1,000. Why not diversify? Spread your investment dollars among a number of companies.

STUDENT: Oh, I think I know what you mean. You're saying that investing in just one stock is like putting all of your eggs into one basket.

GOTTHEIL: Exactly! And you know what will happen to those eggs if that basket weakens.

STUDENT: Suppose I put $500 in IBM stock and $500 in Chrysler stock?

GOTTHEIL: Well, you're on the right track. Now you've created an investment portfolio of two stocks, IBM and Chrysler. You've spread the risk. If the value of IBM stock goes down, the value of Chrysler stock may go up, neutralizing IBM's decline. Owning two different stocks is much less risky than owning one, but still riskier than owning

LET'S SEE . . . WHAT IF I JUST THREW DARTS AT THIS STOCK MARKET PAGE?

three. Perhaps you should think of diversifying even further by increasing the number of different stocks in your investment portfolio.

STUDENT: Oops! Now I'm getting nervous. I don't know that many companies. How do I pick three or five from among the thousands, and isn't there a minimum amount of money I can invest in one stock? After all, I can't pick one thousand companies and invest $1 in each, can I?

GOTTHEIL: Well, yes and no. You can't by yourself, but you can if you buy into a mutual fund.

STUDENT: What's that? I always hear people talking about mutual funds, but I don't know exactly what they are.

GOTTHEIL: A mutual fund is a company whose assets are simply the stocks and bonds of other companies. Typically, many, many other companies. The mutual fund produces nothing itself. It just owns stocks and bonds of companies that do, like IBM. Now, if the stocks and bonds of the companies it owns increase in value, the mutual fund does well.

STUDENT: What does that have to do with me?

GOTTHEIL: Well, you can invest your money in a mutual fund. If ten thousand people like you each invest $1,000 in a mutual fund, then that mutual fund has $10 million and can invest it in hundreds of different stocks. In other words, by owning stock in a mutual fund, you, in effect, end up owning fractions of stocks in hundreds of companies.

STUDENT: Great! Who picks the stocks for the mutual fund?

GOTTHEIL: Each mutual fund, and there are a lot of them out there—T. Rowe Price, for example—has a team of managers who are responsible for choosing which stocks to put into the mutual fund's investment portfolio. It is their job to determine which companies' stocks will increase most in value. They make money on your money, and you pay them for their service. But think about it: The mutual fund allows you to diversify your $1,000 among hundreds of companies, something you couldn't have done on your own. And that's really minimizing risk.

STUDENT: So, I don't have to worry about what stocks to choose, then?

GOTTHEIL: That's right. You just buy shares of a mutual fund, sit back, and relax. Well, maybe not completely relax. After all, some mutual funds have done poorly. Their stock selections have been chronic losers. You see, you can never guarantee success in this game. But because you're well diversified, you reduce the probability of such a disaster.

STUDENT: Thanks for your help. I think I'll look into this mutual fund option. It sounds like that's the route I ought to take. I like to minimize risk.

You know, when I'm at the race track, I always bet on the favorite. I guess my personality is suited for a mutual fund portfolio.

MORE ON THE NET

Morningstar.com (http://www.morningstar.com/) provides news and commentary about mutual funds, and E*Trade Securities (http://www.etrade.com/) enables you to invest in mutual funds. Perhaps you haven't any money to spend on mutual funds. Try your hand at the E*Trade investment game (http://game.etrade.com/)—it won't cost you a dime.

BUT THERE'S A DOWNSIDE, TOO!   Why, then, would anyone choose sole proprietorship when they can just as easily incorporate? Even if you decide to remain a small business, why not form a corporation and own all its stock? This way, you avoid unlimited liability.

In many cases, the decisive negative to the corporate form of business organization is that both the owners and the corporation itself pay taxes on the same corporate income. That spells *double taxation*. The corporation, chartered as an independent, legal entity, must pay a tax on corporate profits (also called corporate income tax). But when the corporation's after-tax profit is distributed to its stockholders in the form of dividends, those dividends are taxed as well. This double taxation is enough to discourage many from taking the corporate route.

From the stockholders' point of view, another negative to corporate ownership is that stockholders exercise corporate control only theoretically. In practice, management is in a much stronger position to control the corporation than are the corporation's stockholders. Typically, a stockholder or even a large group of stockholders hold only a minute fraction of the total outstanding stock. It is difficult for them to draw together the necessary 50 percent plus one share to vote out management. It does sometimes happen, but these are rare and notable events.

THE THREAT OF TAKEOVER   Corporate management has its own problem with stockholders. While individual stockholders or groups of stockholders may themselves not have the ability to gather the necessary voting stock to change management, an outsider—typically, another corporation—may decide on a takeover. By aggressively buying up enough of the target corporation's common stock, it can eventually come to own the corporation outright. It's an old rule of the sea. Big fish eat little fish.

How can management defend itself against a hostile takeover attempt? It may resort to an array of antitakeover, or "shark-repellant," activities. One strategy may be to do precisely what the aggressor corporation does: It can buy up its own corporate stock. That is, instead of providing its stockholders with dividends, the threatened management uses the corporation's profits to buy its own stock until the corporation virtually owns itself, making it impossible for a hostile takeover attempt to work.

CHECK YOUR UNDERSTANDING

What are the major disadvantages of corporations?

Management can sometimes avoid a takeover by making the corporation less attractive to the potential acquirer. How? It can purposely accumulate considerable debt by borrowing on the value of the corporation's assets and using the proceeds to pay a one-time cash dividend to its own stockholders. This newly acquired corporate debt may make the targeted corporation less appetizing.

Management could also pursue a "lesser of two evils" strategy, encouraging a friendly corporation, a "white knight," to make a competitive takeover bid. Under friendly new ownership, the threatened management stands a better chance of surviving.

You can see why small yet successful corporations are attractive targets for corporate takeover. Many of them, with impressive track records, simply cannot withstand a determined, financially well-heeled corporate aggressor.

The Issue of Corporate Governance

Supreme Court Justice Louis Brandeis (for whom Brandeis University is named) once wrote about corporate enterprise: "There is no such thing as an innocent stockholder. He accepts the benefits of the [corporate] system. It is his business and his obligation to see that those who represent him carry out a policy which is consistent with the public welfare." While Justice Brandeis was clear about where corporate responsibility lies, he was much less clear about how stockholders can put into effect their rights to **corporate governance.**

In theory, stockholders own the corporation. They hire management to run it and appoint a board of directors to oversee management's activities. The relationship between the board and the owners is based, fundamentally, on trust. Owners entrust the board with the task of ensuring that management works loyally and effectively to promote the owners' best interests. *In practice,* boards of directors may do little of that. Instead, they tend to function more as management's rubber stamp. Management frequently pursues goals that it sets for the corporation—and particularly for itself—and too often with incomplete accountability to the board of directors. The board, whose job it is to ensure accountability, is either ill-equipped to do so or, even worse, reluctant to demand it. That is, too often, corporate governance is stood on its head. It may not be a matter of stockholders' innocence—or lack of it, as Justice Brandeis thought—as much as a matter of stockholders' corporate powerlessness.

How did this inversion of corporate governance come about, and what are its consequences? In part, the fault lies with the way boards of directors are chosen.

The CEO—chief executive officer of corporate management—often plays a major role in the board's selection process and, understandably, the CEO favors board members with whom he or she would be most comfortable working. In turn, the CEO-picked board members end up accommodating CEO executive decisions. Who's left out of this arrangement? Owners.

It seems reasonable, doesn't it, that if boards of directors

Corporate governance
Corporate governance is concerned with the rules governing the structure of the corporation and the exercise of power and control of the corporation by shareholders, directors, and management.

EXHIBIT | 1

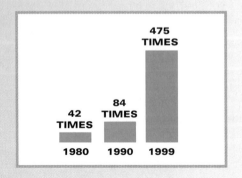

U.S. CEO-TO-WORKER PAY RATIO

475 TIMES — 1999
84 TIMES — 1990
42 TIMES — 1980

pursued the owners' interests, they would reward successful management according to the degree of success and replace unsuccessful ones. It seems no less reasonable that under management-picked boards, regardless of managements' performance, their rewards end up being abnormally high and replacements rare. That precisely what you see in the graphic of Exhibit 1.

Look at the ratio of CEO pay to the average earnings of blue-collar workers. In 1980, CEOs earned 42 times the blue-collar average. Setting aside the issues of whether that ratio is deserved or whether owners had a say in determining it, the ratio of CEO pay to blue collar-earnings doubled to 84 by 1990 and climbed again—sixfold in nine years—to 475 times by 1999. Accountability? Owners seem to be totally out of the picture. They can either accept it or sell their ownership. They typically have no other *practical* recourse.

HOW U.S. BUSINESS IS ORGANIZED

One of the marvelous features of U.S. business is its diversity. Like a fully dressed pizza, where every slice contains every ingredient, you can find on almost every square inch of the U.S. economic landscape almost every form of business organization.

For example, just outside Peoria, Illinois, family farm proprietorships coexist alongside corporate agrobusinesses. In Peoria itself, a hamburger place, Steak N Shake, sits in the shadow of one of the world's largest multinational corporations, Caterpillar. Steak N Shake is a corporation, too. It's a five-minute walk from Caterpillar to Moira's tavern, run by partners Adam Baird and Moira Knight. Next door to Moira's is Brad's Tools. Brad Fish, proprietor and master toolmaker, provides custom-made tools and bolts for Caterpillar. Well over 100 proprietorships, partnerships, and corporations are located within a quarter mile of Moira's. Peoria is a microcosm of the U.S. business world. Look at Exhibit 2.

As you can see, proprietorships are alive and well in the United States. There were more than 16 million in 1996, representing 73 percent of the total number of operating businesses. Proprietorships not only are far more numerous than other business concerns, but also constitute an increasing share of the total. In 1970, for example, proprietorships were 69 percent of the total.

The number of firms, however, is a much different matter than the volume of business handled. In 1996, proprietors transacted $843 billion worth of business. That volume represented 5 percent of the U.S. total. It's like the pennies in a cookie jar, visible from every angle but still adding up to small change.

Clearly, corporations dominate business activity. The 4.6 million corporations in 1996, representing 19 percent of the total number of operating

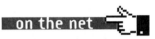

The Small Business Advancement National Center (http://www.sbaer.uca.edu/), the Small Business Advisor (http://www.isquare.com/), and the U.S. Small Business Administration (http://www.sba.gov/) provide educational materials addressing business ownership and organization.

EXHIBIT 2

PROPRIETORSHIPS, PARTNERSHIPS, AND CORPORATIONS: 1970–96 (000s AND $BILLIONS)

	1970	1980	1996
PROPRIETORSHIPS			
NUMBER	5,770	11,932	16,955
RECEIPTS ($)	199	411	843
PARTNERSHIPS			
NUMBER	936	1,380	1,654
RECEIPTS ($)	93	292	1,042
CORPORATIONS			
NUMBER	1,665	2,711	4,631
RECEIPTS ($)	1,751	6,361	14,890
TOTAL NUMBER	8,371	16,023	23,240
TOTAL RECEIPTS ($)	2,043	7,064	16,775

Source: *Bulletin, Statistics of Income,* Summer 1992, Internal Revenue Service, Washington, D.C., pp. 161–163; *Statistical Abstract of the United States, 1999,* Department of Commerce, Washington, D.C., p. 545.

GLOBAL PERSPECTIVE

GLOBAL CEO EARNINGS: UP, UP, AND AWAY (FOR SOME)

The battle for global markets has created exciting competition among producers everywhere in the world. Goods produced in every continent compete globally, services produced in every continent compete globally, and even factors of production, such as capital and labor, everywhere end up competing against each other in global markets. This global competition has had profound leveling effects on the prices of goods in every market as well as on the rewards (earnings) to factors of production in every market, *with one notable exception:* CEO earnings in the United States. The ratio of CEO earnings to employee earnings in the U.S. differs radically from ratios in other countries. According to Towers Per-

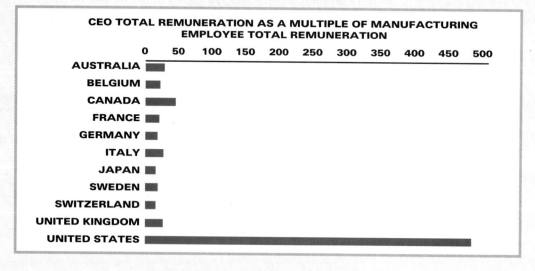

ALL THOSE IN FAVOR OF GIVING OURSELVES A WHOPPING SALARY INCREASE, RAISE YOUR HANDS!

rin's *1999 Worldwide Total Remuneration* report (see exhibit), Japanese CEOs make 11 times what the average manufacturing worker in Japan makes. That's pretty much in line with the German experience (13 times), the Italian (20 times), the French (15 times), and the Swiss (11 times). Canadian CEOs fare relatively better, with earnings 49 times the Canadian worker average. But these multiples pale in comparison to U.S. data. American CEOs earn 475 times what the average American worker makes. What explains this extraordinarily high American outlier? Perhaps the issue of corporate governance has something to do with it.

Exhibit from Towers Perrin's 1999 *Worldwide Total Remuneration Report.* Reprinted with permission. Copyright © 1999 Towers Perrin.

CEO TOTAL REMUNERATION AS A MULTIPLE OF MANUFACTURING EMPLOYEE TOTAL REMUNERATION

	0	50	100	150	200	250	300	350	400	450	500
AUSTRALIA											
BELGIUM											
CANADA											
FRANCE											
GERMANY											
ITALY											
JAPAN											
SWEDEN											
SWITZERLAND											
UNITED KINGDOM											
UNITED STATES											

businesses, accounted for fully 88.7 percent of 1996 receipts. This same disparity between number of businesses and receipts shows up even within the corporate ranks. Look at Exhibit 3.

The 3.79 million corporations with receipts under $1 million made up 81.8 percent of all corporations. But they accounted for only 5.2 percent of total receipts.

EXHIBIT | 3

**SIZE OF CORPORATION AND CORPORATE RECEIPTS,
1996 (000s AND $BILLIONS)**

SIZE	NUMBER	%	RECEIPTS	%
	4,631	100.0	14,890	100.0
UNDER $1 MILLION	3,791	81.8	783	5.2
$1–4.9 MILLION	626	13.5	1,326	8.9
$5–9.9 MILLION	101	2.1	705	4.7
$10–49.9 MILLION	91	1.9	1,856	12.5
$50 MILLION OR MORE	22	0.3	10,220	68.6

Source: *Statistical Abstract of the United States, 1999,* Department of Commerce, Washington, D. C., 1999,
p. 545.

Big cannons make big noises. Look at the $50-million-or-more class. These 22,000 corporations alone accounted for 68.6 percent of total corporate receipts. Clearly, these corporations are like a few silver dollars in the corporate cookie jar.

PROFILE OF STOCKHOLDERS

Who owns the corporations? How many people actually buy stock? What do they look like? Exhibit 4 gives us some idea about who they are.

Stockholders are certainly not rare animals. In the 1990s, more than 50 million stockholders made up more than 25 percent of the adult population, 18 years and older. In other words, approximately one out of every four adults held some form of corporate ownership. They have been that visible for a long time. Back in 1970, 30 million stockholders made up 23 percent of the population.

Look at their characteristics. It's no surprise that income and education count. Seventy percent of stockholders had some college experience, and 55.6 percent earned more than $50,000 per year. They weren't all bald-headed, potbellied old fogies, either. About 50 percent of them were 44 years old or younger. Still, most stockholders cannot even begin to live off their dividends. Look at Exhibit 5.

The distribution is highly skewed. More than 80 percent of all the shares owned were owned by only 17 percent of the shareholders. Look at the other end of the distribution. Almost 60 percent of the shareholders—those with portfolios of less than $25,000—owned less than 5 percent of total shares.

Indirect Stock Ownership

Although people buy into corporate ownership by purchasing stock directly through stockbrokers or through employee stock-purchase plans, there are many more people who come to corporate ownership indirectly. Exhibit 4 describes only those people who themselves own stock. It does not include those who own stock indirectly through pension plans, life insurance policies, and other financial intermediaries.

For example, in 2000 the pension fund for state employees in California, administered by CALpers, owned $100 billion in corporate stock. That is to say, perhaps as many as hundreds of thousands of state employees in California who have never seen a corporate stock certificate are in fact owners of corporations. If account is made for these people and for the tens of million others who, in the United States,

EXHIBIT|4

NUMBERS AND CHARACTERISTICS OF STOCKHOLDERS: (000s)

	NUMBER OF SHAREHOLDERS	PERCENTAGE OF SHAREHOLDERS	PERCENTAGE OF SHARES OWNED
EDUCATION			
1–3 YEARS HIGH SCHOOL	2.8	5.4	3.0
HIGH SCHOOL COMPLETION	12.7	24.8	15.6
1–3 YEARS COLLEGE	12.7	24.8	24.1
4 YEARS OF COLLEGE	12.9	25.2	27.6
POSTGRADUATE WORK	10.2	19.9	29.7
INCOME			
0–$14,999	2.7	5.3	2.9
$15,000–$24,999	4.9	9.5	2.6
$25,000–$49,999	15.2	29.6	15.6
$50,000–$74,999	13.2	25.6	18.2
$75,000–$99,999	6.1	11.9	12.0
$100,000 AND OVER	9.3	18.1	48.7
AGE			
21–34	11.1	21.7	5.1
35–44	13.8	27.0	17.8
45–64	18.9	36.9	47.3
65 YEARS OR MORE	7.4	14.4	29.8

Source: *Shareownership 1997,* New York Stock Exchange, 1998, p. 59. Data are for 1992.

EXHIBIT|5

SIZE DISTRIBUTION OF STOCK PORTFOLIOS

SIZE OF PORTFOLIO	NUMBER OF SHAREHOLDERS	PERCENTAGE OF SHAREHOLDERS	PERCENTAGE OF SHARES OWNED
0–$4,999	16.5	32.2	0.6
$5,000–$9,999	5.7	11.2	0.8
$10,000–$24,999	8.0	15.7	2.8
$25,000–$49,999	6.3	12.3	4.7
$50,000–$99,999	6.0	11.7	9.3
$100,000 AND OVER	8.7	17.0	81.7

Source: *Shareownership 1997,* New York Stock Exchange, 1998, p. 59. Data are for 1992.

GLOBAL PERSPECTIVE

MULTINATIONALS ARE BECOMING MORE AND MORE MULTI

The 20th century has been a century on wheels, at least in North America and Europe. There is no reason to believe that the 21st century will not just keep rolling along. At least that's the way it appears when you consider what the giant multinationals in the automobile industry—General Motors, Ford, Chrysler, Toyota, Honda—are doing. These automakers are busy at work building huge new assembly lines and factories all over the world, including in once-ignored Southeast Asia and China.

DID YOU KNOW MOST AMERICANS THINK THAT FORDS ARE STRICTLY AMERICAN-MADE CARS?

Consider, for example, Ford's new 1997 truck plant in Vietnam. It represents Ford's resolve to get into what it perceives to be a very promising market. "Our feeling," says Tim Dunne, a consultant with Automotive Resources Asia (ARA) in Bangkok, "is that the longer you wait, the more difficult it will be to get into Vietnam." The Vietnamese have already licensed 14 foreign automakers to manufacture and assemble cars and trucks there. ARA's forecast for new-and-used-vehicle demand in Vietnam is optimistic. It anticipates that demand will climb from 20,000 in 1997 to 50,000 by 2001.

continued on next page

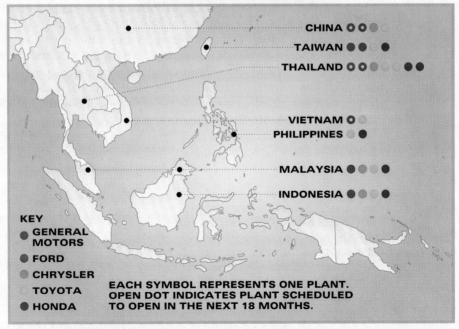

KEY
- GENERAL MOTORS
- FORD
- CHRYSLER
- TOYOTA
- HONDA

EACH SYMBOL REPRESENTS ONE PLANT. OPEN DOT INDICATES PLANT SCHEDULED TO OPEN IN THE NEXT 18 MONTHS.

Source: "Unafraid in Asia," *New York Times*, November 9, 1997. Copyright © 1997 by The New York Times Company. Reprinted with permission.

Ford is starting very modestly in Vietnam with a production target of 350 trucks. "They could build that in a couple of hours at a Ford plant in the United States, but it's still an important toehold in the market," Dunne explains.

As the exhibit shows, Ford is also busy building automotive production facilities in Thailand, Malaysia, China, and Taiwan. And as you see, it is not the only auto multinational in the region. Some have opened full-scale factories, while others, not quite there, have relied on smaller assembly operations. But one thing is clear: The auto multination-als are intent on extending considerably the geographic boundaries of their multi character.

MORE ON THE NET

Auto multinationals worldwide demonstrate their multinational character through their Web sites. For examples, visit the DaimlerChrysler Global Gateway (http://www.international.chrysler.com/), Ford Motor Company (http://www.ford.com/global/), and Volkswagen Asia-Pacific (http://www.vw.com/worldwide).

---

are covered by such pension funds, it is reasonable to argue that corporate stocks are held by or on behalf of a vast majority of the U.S. population.

INTERNATIONAL AND MULTINATIONAL CORPORATIONS

Although there's nothing to prevent proprietorships from operating in international markets, and many do, we generally think of corporations when we think of businesses with interests overseas. And we're generally right. Most of our economic relations with other countries—imports and exports—are essentially corporate relations.

Many of these corporate links to overseas markets simply reflect a geographic extension of what these corporations market domestically. For example, the Kellogg plant in Battle Creek, Michigan, produces the same cornflakes for markets in France, Belgium, Australia, and Egypt as it does for its domestic East and West Coast markets. Its sales on the West Coast are regarded as purely domestic trade. But sales in France or Egypt are considered international trade. The cornflakes are all the same, but if Kellogg's exports overshadow its domestic trade, it is viewed as an American-based international corporation.

But exporting its Battle Creek cornflakes to Egypt is not the only way Kellogg can sell cornflakes there. *It can also build a Kellogg cornflakes plant in Cairo.* Why should Kellogg bother? Because a Kellogg Cairo subsidiary can take advantage of Egypt's lower labor costs, avoid overseas transportation costs, and circumvent tariffs that Egypt may place on imported foods. That may be enough reason for Kellogg to opt for an Egyptian branch instead of shipping its cornflakes from Battle Creek.

Corporations that rely on overseas production to handle their overseas markets are described as **multinationals.** The difference, then, between an international corporation and a multinational is the presence of overseas production branches.

Imagine your own corporation as a U.S.-based multinational, with a number of fishing subsidiaries overseas. Suppose you own a large fleet and cannery operation

Have you recently consumed any good made by a foreign multinational? Go to the Interactive Study Center at http://gottheil.swcollege.com and click on the "Your Turn" button to submit your example. Student submissions will be posted to the Web site, and perhaps we will use some in future editions of the book!

Multinational corporation
A corporation whose production facilities are located in two or more countries. Typically, multinational corporate sales are also international.

EXHIBIT|6

FOREIGN REVENUES AS A PERCENTAGE OF TOTAL REVENUES AND FOREIGN ASSETS AS A PERCENTAGE OF TOTAL ASSETS FOR THE TEN LARGEST U.S. MULTINATIONALS: 1985 AND 1999

	1985			1999	
	REVENUES	ASSETS		REVENUES	ASSETS
EXXON	69.4	43.0	EXXON/MOBIL	71.8	63.9
MOBIL	55.9	41.2	IBM	57.5	43.7
TEXACO	50.1	30.1	FORD	30.8	44.2
CHEVRON	38.9	31.2	GENERAL MOTORS	26.3	38.0
IBM	40.4	36.1	GENERAL ELECTRIC	31.7	47.4
PHIBRO SALOMON	59.8	9.1	TEXACO	77.1	45.2
FORD	29.7	47.4	CITIGROUP	35.1	41.0
GENERAL MOTORS	17.3	21.3	HEWLETT-PACKARD	55.2	51.5
DUPONT	32.0	29.0	WAL-MART	13.8	36.0
CITICORP	49.8	53.7	CITICORP	55.0	28.2

Source: *Forbes,* July 29, 1985, and July 24, 2000. Reprinted by permission of Forbes Magazine © 2000. Forbes, 1985 and 2000.

in Alexandria, Egypt, that is charged with handling the African markets. You own another fleet and cannery branch, located in Singapore, that handles the Asian markets. Not quite the same business, is it, as a sole proprietorship selling in a local market? Even if you owned a dozen such subsidiaries, you probably still wouldn't rank among the top 100 multinationals based in the United States. Most multinationals are corporations with over $1 billion in foreign revenues.

What is their profile? Exhibit 6 describes some of the financial attributes of the top ten U.S. multinationals for 1985 and 1999.

Exxon/Mobil's foreign revenues in 1999, which accounted for 72 percent of its total revenues, rank it top among the U.S. multinationals. Its foreign assets—representing the asset value of its subsidiaries—are as much as 64 percent of its total assets.

Living among the giants is no guarantee that you'll stay there. For example, TWA was ranked 64th in 1985 but failed to make the top 100 list in 1999. Somebody had to make room for young, dynamic newcomers like Wal-Mart, ranked 9th, in 1999. Perhaps, someday, even a fishing multinational.

on the net

Exxon (http://www.exxon.com/), General Motors (http://www.gm.com/), Mobil (http://www.mobil.com/), Ford (http://www.ford.com/), and IBM (http://www.ibm.com/) are among the largest U.S. multinational corporations.

CHAPTER REVIEW

1. A sole proprietorship is a business that is owned and operated by one person. The single most important advantage of proprietorship is the independence it affords its owner, but the disadvantages are unlimited liability and the difficulties in acquiring capital for expansion.

2. To overcome the difficulties in acquiring capital for expansion, a sole proprietor can take on a partner to form a partnership. Business decisions are now jointly made by both owners, and liability, still unlimited, is shared, so that each partner can be held liable for the business's entire debt.

3. Corporations exist as legal entities independent of their owners. In this way, a corporate owner's—or shareholder's—liability is limited to the value of his or her shares.

4. Different kinds of stocks—such as common, preferred, and convertible—are sold to people who join the corporation's list of shareholders. The money realized through this stock expansion provides the corporation with capital for expansion.

5. A corporation can acquire capital for its expansion by selling corporate bonds. These bonds represent the corporation's obligation to pay the bondholder a specified rate of return. Because bondholders have first claim to the corporation's profit, bonds are a less risky form of investment than corporate stocks.

6. The corporation's profit can be distributed to its owners as dividends or can be retained by the corporation and reinvested in capital expansion.

7. Corporate dividends are taxed twice. First, they are taxed at their source—the corporation—through a tax on corporate income. The corporation's after-tax income is then distributed to its shareholders as dividends, which are taxed once more through a tax on each shareholder's personal income.

8. A corporate takeover involves the aggressive purchase of common stock by another corporation until it owns a sufficient percentage of the targeted corporation's stock to control it. A targeted corporation, under threat of takeover, can counter by buying up its own stock, so that the corporation literally owns itself, or it can seek to be bought by a "white knight" to avoid a hostile takeover.

9. The issue of corporate governance concerns the inability of corporate owners to exercise, through its board of directors, the power and control of the corporation. Rather than monitor management's performance, the board of directors too often rubber-stamps management's decision making.

10. In 1996, 73 percent of U.S. businesses were proprietorships, but they accounted for 5 percent of total business receipts. Corporations, on the other hand, made up only 19 percent of U.S. businesses, but their receipts accounted for 89 percent of the total.

11. More than one in four adults in 1992 owned stock. About 70 percent of them had some college education, and about 50 percent earned more than $50,000. If indirect stock ownership, such as stock held in pension funds and life insurance policies, is also counted, then nearly all adults in the United States are stockholders.

12. Although a significant part of the sales of both international corporations and multinationals are exports, only multinationals have production facilities located in more than one country.

KEY TERMS

Sole proprietorship
Unlimited liability
Partnership
Corporation

Stock
Stockholder (shareholder)
Dividend

Corporate bond
Corporate governance
Multinational corporation

QUESTIONS

1. Suppose you were thinking about going into the business of custom-imprinted balloons for birthdays, graduations, weddings, and other special events. Why would you want to own and run the business as a sole proprietor? What disadvantages would you face in choosing that form of business organization?

2. Under what conditions would you think about switching from a sole proprietorship to a partnership? What disadvantages would you now face?

3. Under what conditions would you think about switching from a partnership to a corporation? What disadvantages, compared to the other business forms, face you now?

4. Who are the stockholders? Why would anyone choose to become a stockholder?

5. Why would anyone choose to become a bondholder instead of a stockholder in your balloon corporation?

6. Under what circumstances would your balloon corporation be considered an international corporation?

7. Suppose *Fortune* magazine decides to publish a feature story on the evolution of your balloon business. The story's title is "From Sole Proprietorship to Multinational." Why multinational?

8. Suppose the CEO of Exxon, one of the world's largest and richest multinationals, reads the *Fortune* story and, impressed with your business, decides to take it over. How could Exxon do this? How could you prevent it from happening?

9. In theory, stockholders own the corporation and exercise, through the corporation's board of directors, power and control over its life. In actuality, stockholders are often powerless with respect to corporate decision making. How come?

ECONOMIC CONSULTANTS

ECONOMIC RESEARCH AND ANALYSIS BY STUDENTS FOR PROFESSIONALS

Geoff Merritt owns Software for Sale, a computer software store in Urbana, Illinois. Geoff's sales have doubled in the past year, and more than quadrupled over the past three years. Based on this success, Geoff wishes to expand his business to other areas around campus. Currently, Geoff operates Software for Sale as a proprietorship. However, he is concerned that this is not the optimal form of business organization. Also, Geoff is worried that he doesn't have enough money to fund his new stores.

Geoff has approached Economic Consultants for advice about how to organize his business. Prepare a report for Geoff that addresses the following issues:

1. What are the benefits and drawbacks to the different forms of business ownership?
2. What steps might Geoff take to fund the expansion of his business?

You may find the following resources helpful as you prepare this report for Geoff:

- **U.S. Small Business Administration** (http://www.sba.gov/)— The U.S. Small Business Administration provides information on starting, financing, and expanding a business.
- **Inc. Online** (http://www.inc.com/)—Inc. magazine provides news and information for growing businesses.
- **U.S. Internal Revenue Service (IRS)** (http://www.irs.ustreas.gov/prod/bus_info/index.html)—The irs provides tax information for businesses.
- **The Small Business Advancement National Center** (http://www.sbaer.uca.edu/)—The Small Business Advancement National Center provides information and assistance for small business owners.
- **The Small Business Advisor** (http://www.isquare.com/)—(This site offers online information for the entrepreneur and new business owner.

PRACTICE TEST

1. The most common form of business organization is the
   a. sole proprietorship.
   b. partnership.
   c. corporation.
   d. multinational.

2. The business organization that generates the largest annual receipts is the
   a. sole proprietorship.
   b. partnership.
   c. corporation.
   d. multinational.

3. One of the principal advantages the sole proprietorship affords its owner is
   a. independence of decision making.
   b. complete control over its stockholders.
   c. its dividends are not taxed.
   d. it cannot go bankrupt.
   e. relatively easy access to capital for business expansion.

4. Suppose your business is organized as a corporation. Let's also suppose that your own personal assets are $150,000, of which $50,000 is in the form of shares you own in the corporation. If the corporation goes bankrupt with corporate assets of $300,000 and corporate liabilities of $420,000, you stand to lose
   a. $420,000.
   b. $270,000.
   c. $120,000.
   d. $100,000.
   e. $50,000.

5. Suppose your business is organized as a sole proprietorship. Let's also suppose that your own personal assets are $150,000, of which $50,000 is invested in the business. If the business goes bankrupt with assets of $300,000 and liabilities of $420,000, you stand to lose
   a. $420,000
   b. $270,000.
   c. $120,000.
   d. $100,000.
   e. $50,000.

6. Suppose your business is organized as a partnership. Let's also suppose that your own personal assets are $150,000, of which $50,000 is invested in the partnership. If the partnership goes bankrupt with assets of $300,000 and liabilities of $420,000, you may still stand to lose
   a. $420,000.
   b. $270,000.

   c. $120,000.
   d. $100,000.
   e. $50,000.

7. Which of the following is true?
   a. Preferred stock is a riskier form of stock ownership than common stock.
   b. Owners of common stock receive fixed dividends.
   c. Owners of preferred stock receive fixed dividends.
   d. Multinationals are subject to unlimited liability.
   e. Bondholders can convert their bonds to convertible stock.

8. The principal difference between bondholders and stockholders is
   a. stockholders own a share of the business; bondholders do not.
   b. bondholders own a share of the business; stockholders do not.
   c. stockholders have limited liability; bondholders do not.
   d. bondholders have limited liability; stockholders do not.
   e. stockholders receive interest; bondholders receive dividends.

9. Which of the following is true?
   a. Corporate income is taxed; dividends are not.
   b. Dividends are taxed; corporate income is not.
   c. Both corporate income and dividends are taxed.
   d. Neither corporate income nor dividends are taxed.

10. Multinationals are distinguished from all other business organizations in that they
    a. produce goods in one country and sell in another.
    b. produce more than one kind of good.
    c. have corporate production facilities in more than one country.
    d. have limited liability in their home country but are subject to unlimited liability elsewhere.
    e. are subject to unlimited liability in their home country but have limited liability elsewhere.

PART 3

THE MICROECONOMICS OF PRODUCT MARKETS

CHAT ECONOMICS

Tune into the conversation. It's about *your* course. Just change the names, and it's *your* campus, *your* classroom, *your* professor, *your* classmates, and *you*.

The bell rings to end the class period. Most of the students head for the rear exits of the lecture hall, but Amar Bazzaz hangs back, waiting for Professor Gottheil to finish answering a fellow student's query about a point in the lecture just given. Gottheil spots Amar and signals him to join him in his office, only two doors away. And that's where the conversation begins.

AMAR: Thanks for the tutoring job. It's fun to explain things to other students, and I find that tutoring is also the best way of learning. You think you know the material until you try to explain it to others. Then you realize, it's not as clear to you as you thought.

GOTTHEIL: I find that true even today. I always learn when I teach. So what's up?

AMAR: Well, I plan to review the differences between the market structures of perfect competition, monopoly, monopolistic competition, and oligopoly in this afternoon's tutorial. I want to make the point—which you make in class—that it's not just that the number of firms in the industry distinguishes market structures, but that the different number of firms in the industry also affects the way the firms behave.

GOTTHEIL: Excellent idea! Stress that essential point. Get them to see the connection between numbers and behavior. Stay with that one idea. Don't try to do too much in one tutorial. If you can, use examples that students can appreciate. I mean examples that relate to their own lives.

AMAR: That's why I'm here. Got any suggestions? I need an example, preferably not an economic one, to illustrate that essential idea.

GOTTHEIL: I always use a dating situation to make the point. For example, start with one fellow dating a woman on campus. Suppose they date each other exclusively. Let's give them names—Joel and Reesa—and let's observe how Joel behaves. He's somewhat relaxed. After all, he faces no competition. A typical weekend date is a party at a friend's apartment, soft drinks, and pretzels.

On occasion, dinner at McDonald's. He feels no need to impress her, because she's dating no one else.

AMAR: Being the only date she has, he essentially monopolizes her time. That's the analogy to a firm having a monopoly position in a market.

GOTTHEIL: Right. But suppose she meets Balty and Steve in class, and both express interest. She decides to go out with them. That's bad news for Joel. He is now only one of a few on her list. Joel now has to pay more attention not only to her, but also to what Balty and Steve do. For example, if Balty takes her to a Tanya Donelly concert and candlelight dinner, Joel better forget about the old pretzel days. And Balty, of course, is aware of Joel and Steve, and he, too, reacts to what they do. They know what each must do: try to outdo each other for her affections. That can become expensive.

AMAR: Can't Joel, Balty, and Steve collude by getting together and agreeing not to try to outdo each other?

GOTTHEIL: Absolutely, but can they trust each other? After all, they see each other as rivals and know that everything goes in love and war.

AMAR: And in economics! At least in this market structure of oligopoly, where only a few firms compete. They are mutually interdependent and behave that way.

GOTTHEIL: Right again! Now switch to a scenario where Reesa dates at least 15 men on campus. Joel is now one of many. Do numbers matter? Ask Joel! He can't react to everybody and certainly can't outdo them all.

AMAR: So what's his best strategy?

continued on next page

CHAT ECONOMICS

GOTTHEIL: To differentiate himself from the pack somehow—convince her he's not just one of the guys—in the hope that she will regard them all as poor substitutes. It may take some creative thinking and clever persuasion.

AMAR: Persuasion? That's a euphemism for self-advertising, isn't it?

GOTTHEIL: Advertising himself, yes. But if he's successful at it, you can count on someone else copying what it is he does, with perhaps a slightly different twist. In other words, it's just going to be very hard, if not impossible, for Joel to capture a large share of her time.

AMAR: I see the connection. Joel's behavior is comparable to what firms do in the monopolistically competitive market, isn't it?

GOTTHEIL: That's the point. Now let's pursue the analogy to perfect competition. Suppose Reesa really doesn't see very much difference among her suitors, who are now countless. To her, they are all excellent, if not perfect, substitutes. As much as Joel would like to distinguish himself from others, it just doesn't work. Reesa sees them alike in every respect. Enjoyable, but it's the same personalities, movies, concerts, and dinners. Joel ends up occupying an insignificant part of her time. And if he retreats to pretzels, he's plumb out of luck and out of the competition as well.

AMAR: The moral: In love, war, and economics, numbers dictate behaviors and their outcomes. Joel knows.

Every concept in economics finds an application in your daily life, even product markets. Who would think that dating would have economic implications? But it does. Keep this in mind as you read through the next few chapters, and try to think of other applications.

Have you read John Steinbeck's *Cannery Row?* The fishing industry, circa 1920s Monterey, California, comes alive in his wonderful pages. He captures the pulse, smells, and sounds of those canneries and the fishing people who made their living in and around them. But today, his Cannery Row beats with a different pulse. That celebrated row has been converted into a modern shopping mall, catering to the tourist traffic.

Still, the fishing industry along the California coast is alive and well. Modern technology may have changed its character from Steinbeck's day, but there are still honest-to-goodness canneries operating in close proximity to Cannery Row. For example, look beyond the restaurants and gift shops on San Francisco's Fisherman's Wharf, and you'll see commercial fishing boats returning to dock every morning. You'll see tired fishermen unloading their catch, packing their fish in crates of

COSTS OF PRODUCTION

8

THIS CHAPTER INTRODUCES YOU TO THE ECONOMIC PRINCIPLES ASSOCIATED WITH:

- THE CHARACTER OF ENTREPRENEURSHIP
- TOTAL COST, TOTAL FIXED COST, AND TOTAL VARIABLE COST
- THE LAW OF DIMINISHING RETURNS
- AVERAGE TOTAL COST, AVERAGE VARIABLE COST, AVERAGE FIXED COST, AND MARGINAL COST
- ECONOMIES OF SCALE, CONSTANT RETURNS TO SCALE, AND DISECONOMIES OF SCALE
- THE RELATIONSHIP BETWEEN SHORT-RUN AVERAGE TOTAL COST AND LONG-RUN AVERAGE TOTAL COST
- DOWNSIZING

crushed ice, ready for market.

The fishing industry thrives in the gulf towns of Texas, Louisiana, and Florida; along the New England coast; in the Chesapeake Bay; along the Mississippi River; and in the states of Washington, Oregon, Alaska, and Hawaii. Fishing is a major industry in Canada, Japan, Mexico, Peru, Chile, Iceland, Norway, Italy, France, Spain, Denmark, Finland, Egypt, Greece, China, and Russia. Even Saudia Arabia has a fishing industry. People now eat more fish, and more people everywhere are earning their livelihoods fishing.

Imagine that you were born and raised in the fishing community of Chapter 3. The water, the fishing stories, the canneries, the people working the docks, would be all second nature to you.

CHAPTER

169

GETTING INTO THE FISHING BUSINESS

Now let's suppose you just graduated from the island's college. You could take the first ferry to the mainland and expand your job opportunities at least tenfold. Many people on the island have already done this. But suppose you decide, instead, to make your life's work right there on the island.

What could you do? Fishing is one thing you would probably consider. You have had some summer experience working on the boats and rather enjoyed it. Moreover, it is one thing you really know something about. But how do you convert a familiar and comfortable activity into an occupation?

Any fisherman will tell you that the art of fishing is quite distinct from the art of making money. If you fish commercially, your success indicators are profits and losses, not the beautiful yellowfin tunas that can fight you for the better part of a day. Fishermen—both men and women—like other entrepreneurs, must confront a world of uncertainty, making decisions about prices, costs, and production. These decisions are critical to survival.

Fishing is a particularly risky business. The size of the catch is a matter of hard-earned experience and downright luck, and the price of fish can be highly volatile. Good fishermen have gone to ruin making inaccurate guesses.

It pays to take a long, hard look at the fishing business before jumping in. It may not be a bad idea to work a year on someone else's boat before committing yourself and your money to setting up on your own. If you keep your eyes and ears open, you can pick up a lot of information about the technical and financial aspects of the business. Of course, time spent working on somebody else's boat is time lost on your own. But, as you already know, most choices involve some opportunity cost.

Let's push the scenario further. Some of your friends have also made up their minds to stay on the island. To no one's surprise, their choices are varied. Some join established crews, intending to remain on permanently. A much smaller number set up their own firms.

Entrepreneurship is not everybody's forte. For many, an honest day's labor for an honest dollar seems right. As working people, they choose to avoid the risk that entrepreneurship entails. Of course, they miss out on the possibilities of profit. Many have no choice. After all, it takes money to start up a business, and some talented people who would like to start their own businesses just don't have access to money.

But that's not your situation. After much soul searching and long hours of discussion with people in the industry, you decide to set up your own fishing business. Where do you start?

TOTAL FIXED COSTS

Committing to Fixed Costs

Buying a boat is your first and most expensive single purchase. What kind of boat do you buy? There's more than one kind available. Let's simplify your options. The least expensive, the miniboat, built for a crew of 3, costs $40,000. A more expensive model, the midiboat, built for a crew of 5, costs $70,000. The flagship of the industry, the maxiboat, built for a crew of 12, costs $200,000.

How would you decide which boat to buy? Why, for example, would you consider spending $200,000 when a $40,000 boat is available? Obviously, the more expensive boat must have features that, for some people, make the additional cost worthwhile. One advantage would be its greater capacity to catch fish.

Now, *if* the weather is cooperative, *if* the fishing grounds are rich, and *if* the price of fish is about as high as it has been in years, you could do well harvesting a lot of fish. But that's a lot of *ifs*! Suppose the price of fish turns out to be lower than anticipated, or the quantity of fish not as plentiful. You may regret committing yourself to a $200,000 boat.

Why not go with the $40,000 boat? Because the maximum number of fish you can harvest per fishing run is only 2,000. That's not a lot of fish. Of course, if you go into business expecting to produce within a range of 1,000 to 2,000 fish per monthly run anyway, it's probably the more sensible choice. You simply don't think of a 5,000- or 25,000-fish run with a miniboat.

Calculating Fixed Costs

How do you go about buying a $200,000 boat? Most often, the same way you would go about buying a $200,000 home. You take out a $200,000 loan, paying a fixed monthly cost (mortgage) of, say, $2,000 over a period of 15 years. (That's probably what you will be doing someday soon, as a homeowner.) If you were in the auto body repair business and wanted to buy a $200,000 garage, you'd most likely end up doing the same thing: taking out a $200,000 loan on the purchase of a garage, and paying a fixed monthly mortgage payment.

It's no surprise, then, that the most reasonable and commonplace way of financing the purchase of your $200,000 boat is to take out a $200,000 loan and pay a fixed monthly mortgage of, say, $2,000.

Now, here's the point: Just as buying the home commits you to the fixed monthly payment whether you live in it alone, with spouse and teeming with children, or not at all, the fixed monthly payment on your boat is a fixed cost obligation whether you use it to catch 1,000 fish, 10,000 fish, or no fish at all.

That's why **fixed cost** is sometimes referred to as a sunk cost or historical cost—*sunk* meaning once made, it's a fait accompli and there's no changing your mind about it; *historical* meaning once made, there's no more discussion. It's history!

The table in Exhibit 1 records these fixed-cost monthly mortgage payments for the three boats across the output range of 0 to 15,000 fish.

The miniboat has a maximum capacity of 2,000 fish per monthly run. It simply can't handle more fish. (Try loading four cubic feet of topsoil into a wheelbarrow whose capacity is three cubic feet. Can't be done, can it?) That is why the miniboat column in the table in Exhibit 1 is blank after 2,000 fish. Look at the maximum capacity of the midiboat. It is 4,000 fish per run. The maxiboat's capacity is 15,000 fish per run. Fishing anywhere along the output range shown in the table—0 to 15,000 fish per run—can be accommodated by the maxiboat alone. The total fixed cost of producing either 1,500 or 15,000 fish on a maxiboat is $2,000.

Let's suppose you decide to buy the $200,000 maxiboat that has a 15,000-fish capacity. The graph in Exhibit 1 translates the table into graphic form.

Fixed cost
Cost to the firm that does not vary with the quantity of goods produced. The cost is incurred even when the firm does not produce.

CHECK YOUR UNDERSTANDING

Why are fixed costs sometimes referred to as historical?

TOTAL VARIABLE COSTS

A boat is not the only thing you need to run your fishing business. A fishing boat without a fishing crew yields no fish. You also need an arsenal of fishing equipment. Your supply of nets, hooks, lines, and sinkers can quickly diminish in foul weather and at some fishing grounds. You need bait and a stock of crushed ice to keep the fish fresh

EXHIBIT | 1

TOTAL FIXED COST FOR THE MAXIBOAT

The straight-line, horizontal curve portrays the total fixed costs for the maxiboat, with 15,000-fish capacity. It can accommodate any level of production in the table. The total fixed-cost curve is horizontal at $2,000 per run across the entire output range.

FIXED COSTS PER BOAT PER MONTHLY FISHING RUN

QUANTITY OF FISH (1000s)	$40,000 MINIBOAT WITH 2,000-FISH CAPACITY	$70,000 MIDIBOAT WITH 4,000-FISH CAPACITY	$200,000 MAXIBOAT WITH 15,000-FISH CAPACITY
0	$400	$700	$2,000
1	400	700	2,000
2	400	700	2,000
3		700	2,000
4		700	2,000
5		700	2,000
6		700	2,000
7			2,000
8			2,000
9			2,000
10			2,000
11			2,000
12			2,000
13			2,000
14			2,000
15			2,000

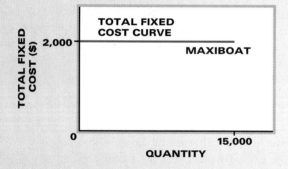

Variable cost
Cost that varies with the quantity of goods produced. Variable costs include such items as wages and raw materials.

during a run. Your boat needs fuel to move from fishing ground to fishing ground. These items, and many more, make up the **variable costs** of a fishing business.

Why are these cost items described as variable? Because, unlike the cost of a boat, which is fixed regardless of the quantity of fish produced, the costs of labor, equipment, fuel, and ice vary with the quantity of fish produced.

If the boat stays in dock, it still costs $2,000. But at dock, no labor, fuel, equipment, or ice is needed. Variable costs for the fishing firm at an output of 0 are $0. Producing 15,000 fish per run, on the other hand, is not costless. Fishermen must venture out to new fishing grounds that are scattered some distance beyond the more accessible ones. It takes time to get there. Time and distance mean higher crew and fuel costs. Moreover, catching 15,000 fish requires large quantities of bait and crushed ice.

Obviously, if you operate within a more modest output range, say 8,000 fish, the more accessible fishing grounds would do. Less labor time, less fuel, less bait, and less ice are required. In other words, *the costs of labor, fuel, and bait vary with the size of the catch.* This variation in costs is shown in Exhibit 2.

The total variable cost of producing 15,000 fish is $11,500, which represents a $9,405 cost of labor, a $1,345 cost of fuel, and a $750 cost of equipment, including bait. Look carefully at how the particular items of variable cost increase as production levels increase. Look at labor costs over the production range of 0 to 15,000 fish.

The Cost of Labor

Clearly, if you don't fish, you don't need fishermen. But to get 1,000 fish into the boat requires a crew. The labor cost for a 1,000-fish run is $240. The cost increases with the quantity of fish produced. For example, the labor cost for a 2,000-fish run is $430, and it increases to $575 for a 3,000-fish run.

Do you see what happens to labor costs as greater numbers of fish are added to production? The labor cost per 1,000 fish increases, but by lesser amounts for each additional 1,000 fish until *output reaches 4,000 fish.* Then it begins increasing by increasing amounts. For example, the cost of labor increases by $1,365 − $1,050 = $315 when output increases from 6,000 to 7,000 fish, and it increases even more, by $1,825 − $1,365 = $460, when output increases from 7,000 to 8,000 fish. Why?

Why does the cost of labor increase at a decreasing rate at low levels of output and, at a higher level, begin to increase at an increasing rate? Three factors explain its behavior: changes in labor productivity, changes in the quality of labor, and changes in the price of labor.

LABOR PRODUCTIVITY **Labor productivity** measures the output per laborer per hour. In the case of the fishing boat, the fishing crew's productivity depends on the relationship between the size of the crew and the size of the boat. The maxiboat

Labor productivity
The output per laborer per hour.

EXHIBIT | 2

TOTAL VARIABLE COSTS PER FISHING RUN

QUANTITY OF FISH (1,000s)	LABOR	FUEL	BAIT, ICE, AND EQUIPMENT	TOTAL
0	$ 0	$ 0	$ 0	$ 0
1	240	50	50	340
2	430	110	100	640
3	575	175	150	900
4	695	245	200	1,140
5	830	320	250	1,400
6	1,050	400	300	1,750
7	1,365	485	350	2,200
8	1,825	575	400	2,800
9	2,380	670	450	3,500
10	3,180	770	500	4,450
11	4,075	875	550	5,500
12	5,115	985	600	6,700
13	6,350	1,100	650	8,100
14	7,780	1,220	700	9,700
15	9,405	1,345	750	11,500

THEORETICAL PERSPECTIVE

THE LAW OF DIMINISHING RETURNS

Let's examine the concept of labor productivity a little more closely. If you discover that by adding a second fisherman to your boat, you can more than double the number of fish produced, shouldn't you expect—by extending that observation—that by adding ten more fishermen, your output will increase tenfold? Whether you should or shouldn't expect it, the fact is it doesn't. Why not? The answer has much to do with the *law of diminishing returns*. This law states that after reaching some output level in production, each time you add another laborer to production, total output increases, but each time by smaller and smaller amounts. Economists formalize the law as follows: When at least one factor of production is fixed, increases in a variable factor beyond some point lead to increasingly smaller additions to output. Let's suppose, using our fishing scenario as illustration, that the variable factor is labor and that all other factors are fixed, in place, and unchanging. That is, the boat's at the dock, fully loaded with bait, ice, and equipment. All that's missing are the fishermen.

THAT'S WHAT I CALL A GREAT DAY'S CATCH! YOU KNOW, WHEN I WORKED ALONE, I NEVER SAW THIS MANY IN A WEEK OF FISHING!

Under these conditions, how many fish could you produce? The answer is given in row 1, columns 1 and 2 of the following table. With 0 laborers, total product is 0.

Consider the rest of the table. Suppose you hire one fisherman. Total product increases from 0 to 4 fish (row 2, column 2). Economists define this 4-fish increase in total product as the *marginal product* of the first laborer. This is shown in row 2, column 3. Because the boat, equipment, bait, and ice were already given and unchanging, economists attribute this marginal product of the 4-fish increase to the only new event that occurred: the addition of the first laborer.

Let's now add a second laborer. With two laborers working, total product increases to 10 fish, so that the marginal product of the second laborer is 6 fish (row 3, column 3). Note that you doubled your labor (from 1 to 2) and more than doubled your total product (from 4 to 10). Why is this so? Because the two laborers, working together, created opportunities for division of labor and specialization that were absent when one laborer was on the boat.

Let's add more laborers and create more division of labor and specialization. Can you keep doubling your labor and keep more than doubling your total

LABORERS	TOTAL PRODUCT	MARGINAL PRODUCT	LABOR COST PER FISH
0	0		
1	4	4	$1.20
2	10	6	0.83
3	25	15	0.33
4	35	10	0.50
5	40	5	1.00
6	42	2	2.50

product? Only up to a point. Beyond that, doubling your labor yields less than a doubling of total product. Economists describe this outcome as diminishing returns. Look again at the table. The marginal product diminishes when the fourth, fifth, and sixth laborers are added to the boat. What explains these diminishing returns?

Consider this: The boat size is unchangeable. The equipment on board, along with the quantity of bait and ice, are fixed. As more laborers crowd into the boat, each eventually runs out of needed physical space to work efficiently. As well, each has less access to the equipment and bait. In other words, the relationship between the fixed and variable factors of production become less than a perfect match. Adding more laborers to the fixed factors of production may increase total product (we see this in column 2), but it does so in diminishing amounts (column 3). So universal is this phenomenon that economists describe it as a law.

How is the law of diminishing returns related to the shapes of the total and average variable cost curves? Assuming labor is of uniform quality—an unrealistic assumption made to simplify the argument—and the price of labor is $5, adding the third laborer to the boat adds 15 fish to production, so that the labor cost associated with each of these 15 fish is $5/15, or $0.33 (row 3, column 4). The marginal product of the fourth laborer is 10, so that the labor cost for each of these 10 fish is $5/10, or $0.50, and so on. Look at column 4. It shows, beyond three laborers, that the average labor cost per fish rises as more laborers are put to work producing more fish. Graphing column 4 generates the U-shaped average variable cost curve.

was built for a crew of 12. But the boat can accommodate more. It can also work with fewer.

How many fewer? Well, you couldn't manage it alone. But suppose you had a crew of 4. Such a skeleton crew would have to double up on chores. For example, the tasks of navigating, charting, and operating the sonar fish-locating equipment would most likely be combined into one. And instead of assigning 1 person to bait nets, 3 to cast them and monitor their positions, another 2 to help haul in the catch, and another to pack the fish in ice, these assignments would be handled by 2 people. However, because few people can master more than one task, the productivity of each crew member would suffer.

Adding a 5th or 6th crew member creates a more workable environment for everybody. As crew size approaches 12, the greater division of labor allows for a more productive use of each person's talent. Crew and boat become a perfect match.

The boat could take on still more crew. But pushing crew size beyond 12 would, again, adversely affect each person's productivity. In an overcrowded situation, the mix of labor and equipment becomes less than optimal, damaging labor's performance.

A crew of 16 fishermen would probably bring in more fish than a crew of 12, but the contribution of those 4 fishermen to output would be somewhat less than any other 4 on the boat. It's simply more difficult to exercise the full measure of talent under overcrowded conditions.

CHECK YOUR UNDERSTANDING

Why does labor productivity fall as more crew are added to the boat?

QUALITY OF LABOR   Not all labor is alike. Ability and experience stamp labor with very different qualities. This fact *alone* may explain why, as more fish are harvested, the labor cost associated with the fish harvest increases at an increasing rate.

If you were doing the hiring, who would be the first hired? Obviously, the best fisherman available—someone who can bring more fish into the boat in one hour than anybody else. Who would be second? The second best. And so on. The importance of quality differences in labor depends on the kind of work performed and the availability of the qualified labor. If people exhibit considerable differences in ability and experience, then whom you hire and how many you hire very much affects the rate at which labor costs increase.

PRICE OF LABOR You need more fishermen to catch more fish. But it may be difficult to recruit increasing numbers without raising the wage rate. How much more needs to be offered depends on the availability of labor at varying wage rates. At some level of production, it may require bumping up the wage rate to bid workers away from other boats and even from other occupations.

Moreover, fishermen, like other people, are not eager to work beyond regular working periods. Pushing production to 12,000 or 15,000 fish per run requires staying out longer and working through more than one shift per day. To get fishermen to do that, you may have to offer double the usual wages for the extra hours. Those last few thousand fish, then, come at expensive labor costs.

The Cost of Fuel

Producing 1,000 fish requires a fuel cost of $50. To expand production to 2,000 fish increases this cost to $110. That is, doubling production more than doubles the fuel bill. Every additional 1,000 fish produced requires even larger increases in fuel costs.

Why? At relatively low output levels, the nearby fishing grounds would do. But continually raising the scale of operation involves not only going greater distances from port but also moving more frequently from one fishing ground to another to locate the most productive fishing area.

Look at fuel cost as output increases from 3,000 to 4,000 fish. It increases from $175 to $245, or by $70. Increasing output to 5,000 increases fuel cost by $320 − $245 = $75. The fact that fuel costs keep increasing by greater amounts as output increases reflects the increasing difficulty of finding fish.

The Costs of Bait, Ice, and Equipment

The costs of bait, equipment, and ice vary proportionately with the quantity of fish produced. For example, it requires $50 of bait, ice, and equipment to produce 1,000 fish, $100 to produce 2,000 fish, $150 to produce 3,000, and so on. Fishermen require twice as much ice to handle twice as many fish. The unit cost of these items neither increases nor decreases costs in relation to the scale of production.

Adding Up the Variable Costs

Total variable cost (TVC) sums these specific variable costs in the firm's cost structure. Because labor appears as the most important of the variable cost items, the character of the total variable cost reflects, in large measure, the cost of labor. This is what you see in Exhibit 2. It isn't that surprising, is it? For many industries, labor is the single most important variable factor of production. Exhibit 3 maps out the total variable cost curve.

Compare the slopes of the two segments of the total variable cost curve. Between zero

EXHIBIT | 3

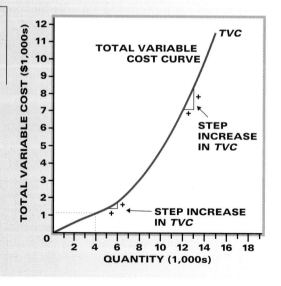

TOTAL VARIABLE COST

The *TVC* curve starts at the origin—zero variable cost at zero output. It increases at a decreasing rate to an output level of 4,000 fish. Above 4,000, it increases at an increasing rate.

TOTAL VARIABLE COST ($1,000s)

TOTAL VARIABLE COST CURVE

TVC

STEP INCREASE IN *TVC*

STEP INCREASE IN *TVC*

QUANTITY (1,000s)

output and 4,000 fish, *TVC* increases, but at an ever- decreasing rate. Look at how the steps become less steep as output increases to 4,000. But note what happens after 4,000. Total variable cost now increases at an increasing rate. Notice how much steeper the steps have become.

TOTAL COST

Total cost (TC) is simply the sum of the total fixed and total variable costs of production:

$$TC = TFC + TVC$$

The table in Exhibit 4 records total cost across the 0-to-15,000-fish production range.

As you see, the *TC* curve is the vertical sum of the *TFC* and *TVC* curves, its shape determined principally by the shape of the *TVC* curve. Compare Exhibit 3 with the graph in Exhibit 4. Note that the only difference between them is the addition in Exhibit 4 of the *TFC* curve, the horizontal line at $2,000.

The fishing firm's total cost when $Q = 0$ is $2,000. Why? Because even though no fish are being produced, the firm is still obligated to meet its fixed-cost commitment. What about *TVC* at $Q = 0$? It's $0. After all, if no fish are being produced, there are no labor, fuel, ice, or equipment costs to be met.

Note also that at production levels ranging from 0 to 7,000 fish, *TFC* is the dominating factor explaining *TC*. But beyond 7,000, it's clearly *TVC*.

WHAT'S THE AVERAGE COST OF PRODUCING FISH?

We can easily reorganize the data in Exhibit 4 to derive the average cost of producing fish. It's a piece of information fishermen would want to know. After all, suppose the price of a fish was $0.70. Wouldn't it be useful to know whether the average total cost of producing that fish was greater or less than its price? Obviously, if the fish costs more to produce than it fetches on the market, then it would be silly to fish. No one is in business to lose money. On the other hand, if price is greater than the cost to produce the fish, fishermen make money.

How do you go about calculating the average cost of producing fish? **Average total cost (ATC)** is simply total cost divided by quantity:

$$ATC = \frac{TC}{Q}$$

It can't be simpler, can it? What about **average fixed cost (AFC)**? *AFC* is total fixed cost divided by quantity:

$$AFC = \frac{TFC}{Q}$$

Average variable cost (AVC) is total variable cost divided by quantity:

$$AVC = \frac{TVC}{Q}$$

Average fixed, average variable, and average total costs are recorded in Exhibit 5.

Total cost (TC)
Cost to the firm that includes both fixed and variable costs.

CHECK YOUR UNDERSTANDING
What determines the shape of the total cost curve?

Average total cost (ATC)
Total cost divided by the quantity of goods produced. *ATC* declines, reaches a minimum, then increases as more of a good is produced.

Average fixed cost (AFC)
Total fixed cost divided by the quantity of goods produced. *AFC* steadily declines as more of a good is produced.

Average variable cost (AVC)
Total variable cost divided by the quantity of goods produced. *AVC* declines, reaches a minimum, then increases as more of a good is produced.

EXHIBIT | 4

The firm's total fixed cost is $2,000 across the entire output range. The *TC* curve is the vertical sum of the *TFC* and *TVC* curves at every quantity of fish produced. Because *TVC* = 0 at zero output, *TC* = *TFC* = $2,000. Beyond zero output, the *TC* curve assumes the shape of the *TVC* curve. This is because at every output level, the only difference between the *TC* curve and the *TVC* curve is the *TFC* curve.

TOTAL COST CURVE

TOTAL COST PER FISHING RUN

QUANTITY OF FISH (1,000s)	TOTAL FIXED COST (TFC)	+	TOTAL VARIABLE COST (TVC)	=	TOTAL COST (TC)
0	$2,000		$ 0		$ 2,000
1	2,000		340		2,340
2	2,000		640		2,640
3	2,000		900		2,900
4	2,000		1,140		3,140
5	2,000		1,400		3,400
6	2,000		1,750		3,750
7	2,000		2,200		4,200
8	2,000		2,800		4,800
9	2,000		3,550		5,550
10	2,000		4,450		6,450
11	2,000		5,500		7,500
12	2,000		6,700		8,700
13	2,000		8,100		10,100
14	2,000		9,700		11,700
15	2,000		11,500		13,500

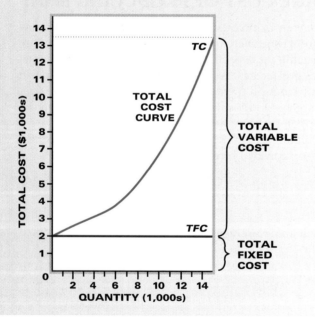

EXHIBIT|5

AVERAGE FIXED COST, AVERAGE VARIABLE COST, AND AVERAGE TOTAL COST CURVES

AVERAGE COST PER FISHING RUN

QUANTITY (1000s)	AVERAGE FIXED COST (AFC)	+	AVERAGE VARIABLE COST (AVC)	=	AVERAGE TOTAL COST (ATC)
0					
1	$2.00		$0.34		$2.34
2	1.00		0.32		1.32
3	0.67		0.30		0.97
4	0.50		0.29		0.79
5	0.40		0.28		0.68
6	0.33		0.29		0.63
7	0.29		0.31		0.60
8	0.25		0.35		0.60
9	0.22		0.39		0.62
10	0.20		0.45		0.65
11	0.18		0.50		0.68
12	0.17		0.56		0.73
13	0.15		0.62		0.78
14	0.14		0.69		0.84
15	0.13		0.77		0.90

The *AVC* and *ATC* curves are U-shaped. The *AFC* curve is downward sloping. The difference between the *ATC* and *AVC* curves is *AFC*. As output increases, *AFC* approaches 0, so that the gap between the *ATC* and *AVC* curves narrows.

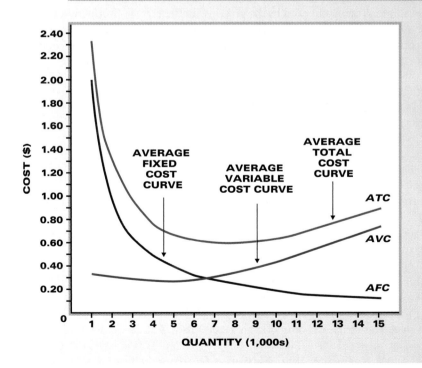

Average Fixed and Average Variable Costs

Note what happens to the averages over the output range as output increases from 0 to 15,000.

CHECK YOUR UNDERSTANDING

Can the average fixed cost for producing fish equal 0?

AFC continuously declines as production increases. Why? The $2,000 fixed cost is simply spread out over increasing quantities. When $Q = 1,000$, the $2,000 total fixed cost is divided among 1,000 fish. $AFC = \$2,000/1,000 = \$2$. When $Q = 2,000$, $AFC = \$2,000/2,000 = \$1$. When output is 15,000, $AFC = \$2,000/15,000 = \$0.13$.

The *AFC* curve is downward sloping, approaching but never reaching 0.

What about the average variable cost of producing a fish? *AVC* decreases from $0.34 per fish at $Q = 1,000$ to a minimum of $0.28 at $Q = 5,000$. It rises to $0.77 at $Q = 15,000$. Mapped into Exhibit 5, *AVC* traces out a U-shaped curve.

Average Total Cost

The *ATC* curve combines the *AFC* and *AVC* curves:

$$ATC = AFC + AVC$$

The influence of *AFC* and *AVC* on *ATC* depends on how many fish are being produced. For example, at an output of 1,000, *AFC* dominates *ATC*, accounting for a whopping $2.00 share of the $2.34 average total cost. But at an output of 15,000, *AVC* dominates. Only $0.13 of the $0.90 average total cost is accounted for by average fixed cost.

In Exhibit 5, *ATC* is a U-shaped curve. It falls rapidly as output increases from 0. Why? Two factors influence its rate of decline: The rapidly decreasing *AFC* combines with the falling *AVC*, reflecting the firm's increasing efficiency.

But as production approaches 6,000 fish, the influence of the falling *AFC* on *ATC* is considerably less, being checked by the growing inefficiency of production reflected now in the rising *AVC*. Average total cost rises slightly. As production reaches 15,000 fish, the continuing, but now weak, effect of *AFC* on *ATC* is completely overshadowed by the rise in average variable costs. As a result, *ATC* increases more rapidly.

TO PRODUCE OR NOT TO PRODUCE, THAT IS THE QUESTION

It's quite clear from just a cursory glance at *ATC* in Exhibit 5 that if the price of fish were $0.50, there is no possible way fishing could be profitable. There is no output level along the 0 to 15,000 production range that can produce a fish for less than $0.60.

Even producing 8,000 fish, where *ATC* is $0.60 and is at its minimum, you still lose $0.10 on each fish. Multiplying this by 8,000 fish gives you an $800 loss. Producing more than 8,000 is even more disastrous. For example, at 15,000 fish, *ATC* = $0.90, so that the loss increases to $15,000 \times \$0.40 = \$6,000$.

However, if the price was $1.00, money-making possibilities abound! Suppose you produce 11,000 fish. At $Q = 11,000$, *ATC* = $0.68, so that for every one of the 11,000 fish sold, you make $1.00 - \$0.68 = \$0.32$ profit. Multiplying this by 11,000 gives you $3,520 profit.

If you were to increase production to 12,000 fish, *ATC* increases to $0.73, and profit now becomes $(\$1.00 - \$0.73)(12,000) = \$3,240$. Was it worth the extra cost to catch 12,000? Not really. Although you produce and sell more, your *ATC* also increases. The net result is less profit. It's a matter of simple arithmetic.

THEORETICAL PERSPECTIVE

EXPLICIT AND IMPLICIT COSTS

For years now, Elaine Rodier had been thinking about going into business. She is an excellent cook, and her preparation of appetizers such as hummus and eggplant salad are outstanding. Everyone who tried them assured her that she could make a fortune if she went into the business of producing gourmet appetizers.

With that kind of encouragement, she plunged into the business world. She asked her good friend, Kim Neis, to work with her. She withdrew $20,000 from her savings account, borrowed $30,000 from her neighborhood bank, signed a $5,000-per-year lease for rather limited space in a shopping mall, bought the ingredients and utensils, and waited for business.

She didn't have to wait long. People stopped by to place orders almost immediately after she opened her doors. After the first few months of business, she realized that the space she had rented was much too small but decided against moving. Instead, she used her own garage as a warehouse for her supplies and her guest room as an office. She also hired Lars Gustafsson as her accountant. He told her to keep account of costs—every monetary payment she made—and record every item of sale.

After one year in business, Lars gave her the good news. He categorized her cost, revenue, and profit:

Cost of ingredients	$ 25,000
Cost of labor	22,000
Cost of depreciation of equipment	7,500
Cost of borrowing $30,000	3,000
Cost of rent, insurance, and advertising	9,500
Total cost	67,000
Total revenue	115,000
Total profit	$ 48,000

THIS RECIPE I PUT TOGETHER LAST NIGHT IS A GEM. LET'S START WITH 25 POUNDS AND SEE HOW IT SELLS.

Elaine was pleased to learn that she had made a $48,000 profit. But her friend Mark Neuman, an economist, examined her accounts and told her that the record of her costs was incomplete. The cost items recorded by Lars, he explained, were explicit costs only, that is, costs in the form of actual monetary payments. But these were not her only costs.

For example, her own labor was a cost, but because it did not take the form of a monetary payment she made to herself, it does not appear in the table of costs Lars used. Nor was account taken for the use of her garage, her guest room, or her $20,000 savings. These, he advised her, were all *implicit costs,* that is, the opportunity costs of using her own resources. He itemized them for her:

Cost of own labor	$23,000
Cost of the use of her $20,000 savings	1,400
Cost of the use of her garage	3,600
Cost of the use of her guest room	3,000
Total implicit cost	31,000

Elaine had given up a job as a nursery school teacher that paid $23,000. The $23,000 represented the opportunity cost she incurred working for herself. She had also withdrawn $20,000 from her savings account at the bank. Since it would have earned her $1,400 (the lending rate was 7 percent), her use of her own savings represented a $1,400 opportunity cost. Garage rental was estimated at $3,600, and her guest room could have been rented for $250 per month.

Mark sketched a U-shaped ATC curve on the back of an envelope for Elaine and pointed out that even though we normally think of production costs as being explicit—monetary payments in exchange for the use of resources—economists see that ATC curve as a composite of both explicit and implicit costs.

In either case, you make profit. But what you really want is to make the most profit possible. Look at the cost curves in Exhibit 5. Can you tell where the most profitable position is on the 0-to-15,000-fish production scale when price is $1.00? Don't bother trying.

MARGINAL COST

Marginal cost (MC)
The change in total cost generated by a change in the quantity of a good produced. Typically, *MC* is used to measure the additional cost incurred by adding one more unit of output to production.

A lot of guesswork or pencil calculations can be avoided by consulting the firm's **marginal cost (MC)**. Marginal cost helps you determine precisely where profit can be maximized. Understandably then, marginal cost is one of the most important pieces of information you would want to consult before deciding production levels.

Marginal cost, like average total cost, is just another way of rearranging the total cost data of the table in Exhibit 4. Marginal cost measures the change in total cost resulting from a change in the quantity produced:

$$MC = \frac{\Delta TC}{\Delta Q}$$

The table in Exhibit 6 records the fishing firm's marginal cost over the production range of 0 to 15,000 fish.

How should you read marginal cost in Exhibit 6? Keep this in mind: You always want to know what happens to your total cost when you add another unit to production. For example, when output increases from 0 to 1,000 fish—that is, when the first 1,000 fish are added to production—total cost increases from $2,000 to $2,340. The marginal cost of each of the first 1,000 fish, then, is the change in total cost divided by the change in quantity, or ($2,340 − $2,000)/(1,000 − 0) = $0.34.

That's not the same as saying that the average cost of each of the first 1,000 fish is $0.34. *ATC* at 1,000 is $2.34. What marginal cost tells us is how much total cost increases when output increases. Since sitting in dock costs fishermen $2,000 anyway—they're committed to pay the monthly mortgage—producing the first 1,000 fish adds only $2,340 − $2,000 = $340 to total cost, or $0.34 for each of the first 1,000 fish. This *add-on* is what marginal cost measures.

Suppose output increases from 1,000 to 2,000. What happens to marginal cost? The total cost of producing 2,000 fish is $2,640, or $300 more than the total cost of producing 1,000 fish. For each of the second 1,000 fish, *MC* = ($2,640 − $2,340)/(2,000 − 1,000) = $0.30.

Look how marginal cost changes across the 0-to-15,000-fish production range. The marginal cost of adding fish to production decreases to a minimum of $0.24 at 4,000 fish and increases thereafter, $0.26 to $0.35 to $0.45 and so on. At 15,000 fish, *MC* = $1.80.

Exhibit 6 shows the relationship between marginal cost and the average total cost of Exhibit 5.

Note the relationship between the *MC* and *ATC* curves. When *MC* < *ATC*, *MC* causes *ATC* to fall. Look at any output level within the production range 0 to 8,000. For example, at 3,000 fish, *MC* is $0.26 and *ATC* is $0.94. And look at the *ATC* curve at that level of production. It's falling. Note also that at production levels greater than 8,000 fish, *MC* > *ATC*, causing *ATC* to rise. Why this causation?

Suppose a class of 100 students takes an exam, and the average grade is 75. Suppose a new student, the 101st—the marginal student—takes the exam and

EXHIBIT 6

MARGINAL COST AND AVERAGE TOTAL COST CURVES

THE MARGINAL COST OF PRODUCING FISH

QUANTITY	CHANGE IN QUANTITY	TOTAL COST (TC)	CHANGE IN TOTAL COST	MARGINAL COST (MC)
0		$ 2,000		
1,000	1,000	2,340	$ 340	$0.34
2,000	1,000	2,640	300	0.30
3,000	1,000	2,900	260	0.26
4,000	1,000	3,140	240	0.24
5,000	1,000	3,400	260	0.26
6,000	1,000	3,750	350	0.35
7,000	1,000	4,200	450	0.45
8,000	1,000	4,800	600	0.60
9,000	1,000	5,550	750	0.75
10,000	1,000	6,450	900	0.90
11,000	1,000	7,500	1,050	1.05
12,000	1,000	8,700	1,200	1.20
13,000	1,000	10,100	1,400	1.40
14,000	1,000	11,700	1,600	1.60
15,000	1,000	13,500	1,800	1.80

Like the *ATC* curve, the *MC* curve is U-shaped. Within the output range 0 to 8,000, *MC* is below *ATC*, causing *ATC* to fall. Beyond 8,000, *MC* is above *ATC*, causing *ATC* to increase. At 8,000, *MC* = *ATC*. At that point, *ATC* is at its minimum. The *MC* curve always cuts the *ATC* curve from below at the *ATC* curve's minimum.

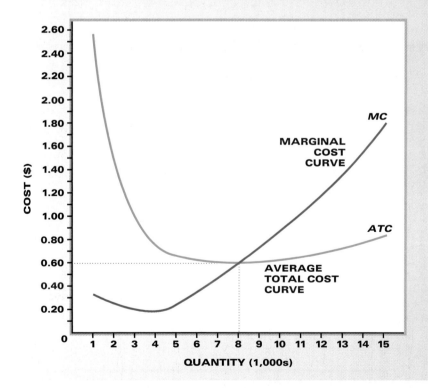

CHECK YOUR UNDERSTANDING

Why does $MC = ATC$ at minimum ATC?

scores 60. Doesn't the class average fall? Intuitively, we know that when the marginal grade is lower than the average, it pulls the average down.

If the new student's grade is 90, it raises the average. That's essentially what we see in Exhibit 6. When $MC > ATC$, everywhere along the output range beyond 8,000 average total cost is increasing because it is being drawn up by the higher MC.

Look at MC and ATC at $Q = 8,000$. Here, $MC = ATC = \$0.60$. Because MC is neither greater nor less than ATC, it neither lowers nor raises ATC. ATC is at its minimum point; it is neither rising nor falling.

ECONOMIES AND DISECONOMIES OF SCALE

People in the fishing business, of course, do not all use the same size boat, employ the same size crew, fish the same waters, or combine their fixed and variable cost items in the same way. Instead, a rich variety of cost structures exists in the industry. The tables in Exhibits 5 and 6, which show *your ATC, AVC,* and *MC* across the production range of 0 to 15,000, represent only one cost structure of many.

Exhibit 7 depicts two fishing firms with different cost structures. Suppose Phil Strang owns a small boat, and his neighbor, Lisa Burnett, owns a larger one.

If you spoke to a member of Lisa Burnett's fishing crew and asked how many fish Lisa's boat produces on a typical fishing run, what would you expect to hear? 2,000? 14,000? Look at Exhibit 7 carefully. If all Lisa had on her mind when she headed out on her boat to the fishing grounds was 2,000 fish, she was on the wrong boat! She should have been fishing on a boat similar to Phil Strang's. There's a mighty big difference between the fixed costs of the two boats. Look how the fixed cost difference affects their ATC curves. Look at Strang's ATC when producing

EXHIBIT 7

AVERAGE TOTAL COST CURVES FOR TWO FISHING FIRMS WITH DIFFERENT FIXED COSTS

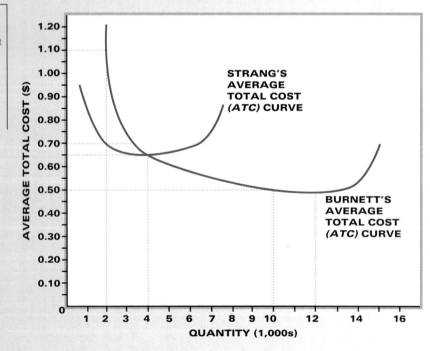

Strang's ATC curve and Burnett's ATC curve reflect the different fixed costs associated with the different-capacity boats that Strang and Burnett use. For outputs less than 4,000 fish, Strang's operation is more efficient. His ATC is less than Burnett's at every output level. But when output exceeds 4,000 fish, Burnett becomes the more efficient. At output levels beyond 4,000, her ATC is lower than Strang's.

2,000. It's $0.70. Compare that $0.70 to Burnett's $1.10 *ATC* when producing the same 2,000 fish on her larger, more expensive boat. It makes no sense for Burnett to use that boat, does it? Not if she produces 2,000 or any other output within the 0 to 4,000 production range. *But she never intends to produce within that range.* That's why she bought the bigger boat.

As you see in Exhibit 7, her more expensive boat makes economic sense once production increases beyond 4,000. For example, at an output level of 10,000 fish, Burnett's *ATC* falls to $0.50, which is $0.10 lower than Strang's minimum *ATC* ($0.65).

Strang's production range is limited to 7,000 fish. *But he never intends to produce beyond that range.* In fact, if he produces more than 4,000 fish, he's at a cost disadvantage. Burnett's *ATC* falls below Strang's after 4,000.

Burnett's *ATC* reaches its minimum at *Q* = 12,000, well beyond the range that Strang would consider workable. Beyond 12,000 fish, her *ATC* curve is upward sloping. What set of cost structures is the most appropriate, then, depends on the firm's planned scale of operations.

Let's relax our unrealistic assumption that only three sizes of boats exist. There are, in fact, many sizes. Some boats are actually floating fishing factories, capable of harvesting and dressing hundreds of thousands of fish. For them, production ranges can extend beyond a million fish per run.

What happens to a firm's *ATC* curve when the size of the boats keeps increasing? Do the minimum points on the *ATC* curves keep falling? Not forever. Increases in the scale of operations, that is, moving to larger and larger boats producing more and more fish, can shift a firm's *ATC* curve so that its minimum *ATC* keeps falling, *but only to a certain point.* Beyond that, further increases in the firm's scale of production will eventually cause its *ATC* curve, and the minimum point on the *ATC* curve, to rise again. This effect is illustrated in Exhibit 8.

CHECK YOUR UNDERSTANDING

Why doesn't Lisa, like Phil, buy the less expensive boat?

CHECK YOUR UNDERSTANDING

What determined which set of cost structures is most appropriate?

EXHIBIT | 8

ECONOMIES OF SCALE, DISECONOMIES OF SCALE, AND CONSTANT RETURNS TO SCALE

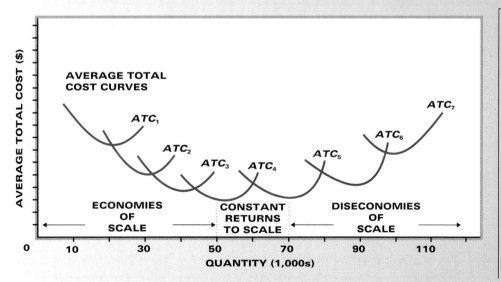

Seven *ATC* curves—*ATC₁* to *ATC₇*—represent costs associated with different-size firms. Economies of scale occur within the output range 0 to 50,000. Here, increases in firm size from *ATC₁* to *ATC₄* result in decreases in *ATC* minimums. Constant returns to scale occur within the output range 50,000 to 70,000. Here, firm size increases from *ATC₄* to *ATC₅*. Within that range, the firm's *ATC* minimums are the same. Diseconomies of scale occur beyond 70,000. Here, firm size increases from *ATC₅* to *ATC₇*. As the firm produces more, its *ATC* minimums increase.

APPLIED PERSPECTIVE

BIG, BIGGER, BIGGEST

When do economies of scale end? When do diseconomies of scale set in? Look at the size of the *Alaska Ocean,* which operates out of Anacortes, Washington. Not anything like our 15,000-fish-capacity maxiboat, is it? This 376-foot trawler can process more than 600 *tons* of fish a day! It is one of the largest fishing boats in the world—virtually a self-contained floating factory. Its 125-person crew affords it considerable divisions of labor and specialization, which probably makes the average total cost of producing a fish on the *Alaska Ocean* much less than the average total cost associated with fishing on smaller boats. But that's only if hundreds of tons are produced daily. Considering its fixed costs, imagine how high its average total cost would be if it produces only what our maxiboat produces!

Division of labor can be extensive with a fully engaged 125-person crew. Some crew members haul in the boat's half-mile-long net (1); others load the fish into bins (2) at the same time as others handle the net's respooling (3). Crew members also specialize in weighing the fish (4), gutting and cleaning them (5), and converting and storing fish waste products into fish meal (6 and 7). The resulting fish fillets are treated with additives by still other crew members (8) and squeezed into surimi paste (9). The fish are then quick-frozen (10) and finally stored in refrigerated compartments (11). A far cry from a small fishing craft, isn't it? How do you think this affects the average total cost of producing a fish?

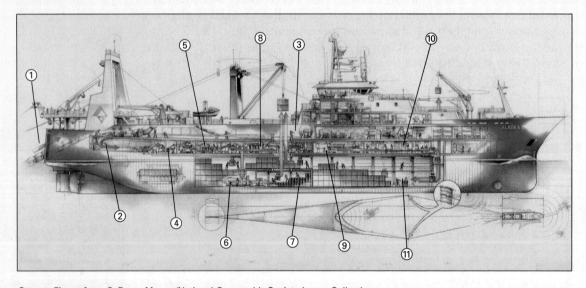

Source: Figure from C. Bruce Morser/National Geographic Society Image Collection.

Economies of scale
Decreases in the firm's average total cost brought about by increased specialization and efficiencies in production realized through increases in the scale of the firm's operations.

Shifting from smaller to larger boats generates a series of *ATC* curves—ATC_1 to ATC_2 to ATC_3—whose minimums, at first, are decreasing. In Exhibit 8, this phenomenon occurs within the output range of 0 to 50,000 fish per run. Economists refer to this range as having **economies of scale.** Fishing companies producing at $Q = 50,000$, compared to those producing at $Q = 25,000$, can take advantage of greater labor specialization, more productive equipment, price discounts through large-quantity purchases, and more cost-efficient methods of marketing.

By doubling its scale of operations within this output range, a firm's total cost will increase, but not double—that is, by doubling scale, average total cost falls.

But look what happens to the firm's *ATC* minimums within the production range of 50,000 to 70,000. The minimums remain unchanged. Economists refer to this range as having **constant returns to scale.** Increasing the scale of operations within this range just increases the firm's total cost proportionately. The advantages of bigness, seen in the 0-to-50,000-fish output range, have dissipated.

Look at the range of production beyond 70,000 fish. There, increasing scale from ATC_5 to ATC_6 to ATC_7 generates *ATC* minimums that actually increase. By doubling the scale of operations in this range, the firm's total cost more than doubles. Economists refer to the range beyond 70,000 as having **diseconomies of scale.** Why? Why has bigness now turned into a disadvantage?

Because a firm can get too big for its own good! Problems of management, organization, and information flow emerge.

On small boats, say with 10 crew members working under one person, bureaucracy is virtually nonexistent. Information about production flows easily and freely from management to crew, from crew to management, and from one crew member to another. Production adjustments are typically made on the spot. Communication is direct and informal.

Consider now a larger boat with two levels of management and a working crew of 35. The new line of management is created to facilitate communication and execute top-level decisions. The information flow from crew to top management or from top management to crew now gets filtered through a layer of middle managers. Information among the 35 crew members, separated by more specific function, becomes somewhat delayed and sometimes misunderstood. A fledgling bureaucracy emerges.

Imagine yourself on a much larger boat that supports a crew of 100. Lines of communications between the crew and management become extended as several new layers of management are added. As a result, standard procedures replace on-the-spot decision making. Problems occur, but if unrelated to specific tasks, remain unattended. Information is highly filtered, often misunderstood, and sometimes purposely modified by middle managers who pursue their own agendas. Crew efficiency suffers. In many cases, the gains expected from economies of scale are checked by the bureaucratic inefficiencies inherent in bigness.

Constant returns to scale
Costs per unit of production are the same for any level of production. Changes in plant size do not affect the firm's average total cost.

Diseconomies of scale
Increases in the firm's average total cost brought about by the disadvantages associated with bureaucracy and the inefficiencies that eventually emerge with increases in the firm's operations.

LONG-RUN AND SHORT-RUN AVERAGE TOTAL COST CURVES

How do fishing firms view the *ATC* structures available to them? Can they pick and choose among them? As we have already noted, once the purchase of a boat is made, the firm is committed, for some period of time, to a **short-run** average total cost (*SRATC*) curve. It loses the freedom to move easily from one *SRATC* curve to another and regains that freedom only when the firm is released from (typically, by paying off) the contractual obligations associated with the purchase of the boat. At that point, the firm can either buy another just like it, move to a smaller version, or upgrade to a larger one.

Exhibit 9 is a simplified version of Exhibit 8. Look at the relationship between the *SRATC* curve and the **long-run** average total cost (*LRATC*) curve. The *SRATC* curve reflects the degree of inflexibility firms face in expanding production. They are able to change the quantity of some but not all the resources they use. For the fishing firm, the unchangeable resource is the boat. Remember, the firm can still

Short run
The time interval during which producers are able to change the quantity of some but not all the resources they use to produce goods and services.

Long run
The time interval during which producers are able to change the quantity of all the resources they use to produce goods and services. In the long run, all costs are variable.

EXHIBIT 9

SHORT- AND LONG-RUN COST CURVES FOR A FISHING FIRM

Each of the *ATC* curves represents the firm's short-run cost choices. Once one is selected, the firm is committed to it until the fixed cost items associated with the chosen *ATC* depreciate. The firm's long-run cost curve is the envelope curve formed by drawing a line enclosing the short-run cost curves. It represents the cost options open to the firm before any specific commitment to boat size is made.

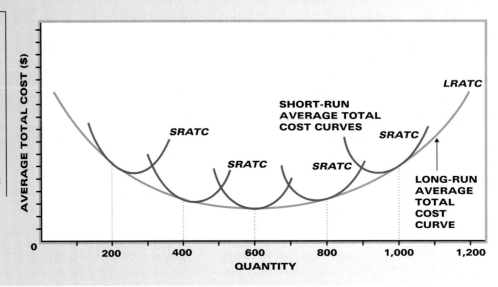

increase or decrease its other resource items, such as its crew size, bait, fuel, and ice. But its range of possible output is limited by the boat's capacity.

The *LRATC* curve reflects the complete flexibility the firm has in choosing its output range. In other words, when the firm is in its long-run position, it is able to *change each and every one of the resources it uses in production,* including the boat. It can replace it with another just like it, buy a larger one, or cut back to a smaller one. But once the choice and purchase are made, the firm is back to a *SRATC* curve. The firm's *LRATC* curve in Exhibit 9—called the envelope curve—is tangent to the *SRATC* curves.

Rightsizing or Downsizing Along the Long-Run Average Total Cost Curve

Rightsizing—a firm's attempt at getting its plant size just right—suggests that the firm's plant size is either too big or too small to handle the volume of output the firm is currently producing or expects to produce. **Downsizing** indicates the direction of the firm's rightsizing, that is, reducing its productive capacity.

How does a firm get itself in a predicament where downsizing becomes necessary? Perhaps an overzealous or highly optimistic management builds excess productive capacity in anticipation of increasing sales that fail to materialize, or perhaps a short-run excess demand that fails to sustain itself into the long run justifies a plant expansion that soon appears inappropriate. In many instances, plant expansion is both rapid and wholesale, pushing firms into diseconomies of scale. Rightsizing becomes a corrective activity.

The 1990s were a decade of considerable plant rightsizing. Firms in the 1960s, 1970s, and 1980s opted to "go east" (sometimes, too far east) along their *LRATC* curves by extending their scale of production, but in the 1990s many reversed

CHECK YOUR UNDERSTANDING

Why can't a firm always be in the long run?

Rightsizing
Implementing a firm's decision to adjust its plant size to produce in the most efficient manner its current volume of output.

Downsizing
Implementing a firm's decision to decrease its plant size to produce in the most efficient manner its current volume of output.

Few business practices have caused more controversy than downsizing. For different viewpoints, visit Michael Moore's *Downsize This!* (http://www.dogeatdogfilms.com/ds.html) and Paula Becker's Personal Coaching for Business Success page (http://www.visioncoach.com/).

GLOBAL PERSPECTIVE

GOOD-BYE "MADE IN THE USA," HELLO "MADE IN THE WORLD"

Chances are that if you bought a "I ♥ Houston" hat in a souvenir shop at the Houston International airport, that hat—like most others—would have been made in either China, Bangladesh, or Sri Lanka. Check the labels on the hats you own. But if you were to walk just 100 yards down the airport concourse to an electronics store and check out their computers, chances are that you would be hard-pressed to identify its production source *even if the company's name was identified on the computer.* That's because most electronic goods you buy are an assemblage of pieces, each of which is produced independently and typically in a number of different countries. The final good you see in the store is about as international in production as the United Nations. The buzzword is outsourcing.

Outsourcing is not just confined to the parts and components of a good but involves as well a variety of support services, such as product customization, product design, and production technology. Compaq, for example, ostensibly an American company, outsources everything associated with the manufacture and sale of its computers, except its marketing. Its design and development, as well as its manufacturing, transport, and after-sales services, are outsourced to different facilities located in a host of countries, among them Taiwan, China, Britain, and Australia.

Is a Compaq computer, then, really an American-made good? What's American about it? No one country can lay claim to its production. Made in where? Actually, the world.

There's nothing unique about Compaq or computers. Although Nike is a registered U.S. corporation, not one of the 40 million pairs of shoes that Nike produces annually is made in the United States. Nike's management has found ways to connect the different geographies of its shoe production, from the lowest-paid, unskilled activities to the highest-paid research and development (R&D). The physical production of the Nike shoe is outsourced to firms in Taiwan and South Korea, who in turn outsource its manufacturing to production facilities in China, Thailand, Indonesia, and Malaysia. The shoe you wear is as global as migrating birds!

Why would Compaq or Nike (or Boeing, or Ford, or even producers of the garden vegetables on supermarket shelves) outsource? For two good reasons: (1) Producers can choose among the lowest-cost suppliers in the world. Geography is no longer an issue. (2) Because global specialization has been so carefully nurtured in this way, greater economies of scale can be realized in every branch of production. In the end, successful outsourcing can shift the firm's cost structures significantly downward. But "made in where?" is getting to be more and more of a mystery.

JUST DO IT! JUST DO IT!
THAT'S ALL THE BOSS SAYS.

direction, downsizing their scale of production. In many cases, they did so to unburden themselves from the unanticipated diseconomies of scale that accompanied their eastward movements. For many in the 1990s, scale retrenchments became a matter of firm survival. In the short run, rightsizing firms have been limited to downsizing their labor force and other variable costs, but in the long run, they have been able to downsize their physical plants as well.

EXHIBIT | 10

WHAT IS TRUE FOR THE FISHING INDUSTRY IS TRUE FOR ALL INDUSTRIES

The *ATCs* and *MCs* for all firms in all industries—fishing, boatmaking, farming, legal services, steel, public relations, plastic tubing—reflect in each the rich variety of short-run and long-run cost combinations. No two Texas farms are exactly alike. Nor should we expect their *ATC* structures to be alike.

J. Patrick Madden of the U.S. Department of Agriculture estimated the average cost curves for different kinds of irrigated cotton farms in the Texas High Plains. His results are shown in Exhibit 10.

Each of the six cost curves has the familiar U-shape. They also illustrate economies of scale. Differences in farm size affect the *ATC* of producing Texas cotton. For example, shifting along the curve from a one-person farm to a four-person farm generates progressively lower *ATC* minimums.

There's essentially no difference in the general character of cost structures among fishing firms, cotton farms, and automobile firms. In your fishing business, you make decisions concerning the size of the boat, the size of the crew, the types of fishing equipment, the level of production, and so on. On Texas cotton farms, the same kinds of decisions are made.

At General Motors, the board of directors and the research, engineering, finance, and marketing departments do what you do. They too decide on the size of their plants, the number of assembly lines, the size of their labor force, the level of output, and so on. General Motors derives its *ATC* and *MC* in precisely the same

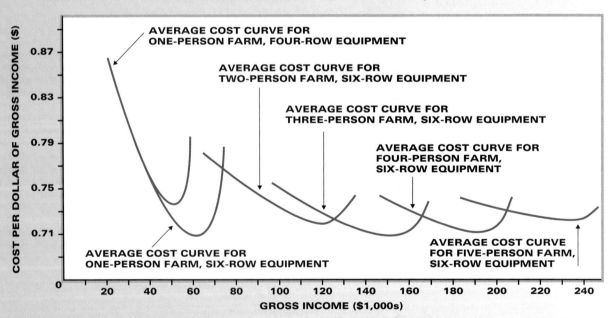

AVERAGE COST CURVES FOR IRRIGATED COTTON FARMS, TEXAS HIGH PLAINS

Source: J. Patrick Madden, *Economies of Size in Farming,* U.S. Department of Agriculture, AER No. 107, Washington, D.C., February 1967, p. 44.

Economies of scale are depicted as technologies, and scales of production vary from a one-person farm with four-row equipment to a five-person farm with six-row equipment.

manner you do. It, too, confronts economies and diseconomies of scale. If the price of automobiles cannot cover its *ATC,* it closes assembly lines, just as you would put the fishing nets away if the price of fish didn't cover your *ATC.* The only difference between the *ATC* curves of your fishing firm and General Motors is size. General Motors counts in billions, you count in thousands.

WHAT BUSINESSPEOPLE THINK ABOUT THE CHARACTER OF THEIR AVERAGE TOTAL COSTS

Some years ago two economists, Wilford Eiteman and Glenn Guthrie, decided to ask businesspeople what they thought their own cost curves looked like. Were they decreasing, increasing, or constant over their production range?

Each businessperson was asked to identify, from a set of diagrams offered, the one that best represented his or her situation. The 8 diagrams shown in Exhibit 11 were the choices offered. The results of the canvass are shown in Exhibit 12.

Of the 1,082 products produced by the firms surveyed, 636 products, or 58.7 percent of the total, were described as having been produced under conditions portrayed by panel *g*—that is, continuous downward sloping until production reaches physical capacity.

For 35.2 percent of the total, panel *f* was identified as representing the character of *ATC.* For these products, *ATC* was essentially downward sloping, but it increased slightly as the firms neared production capacity. Panels *d* and *e*, representing only 5.1 percent of the products produced, were also chosen.

One businessperson wrote: "The amazing thing is that any sane economist could consider [panels *c, d,* and *e*] as representing business behavior." A manufacturer of road-building equipment said: "Even with the low efficiency and premium pay of overtime work, our unit costs would still decline with increased production, since the absorption of fixed expenses would more than offset the added direct expenses incurred."

Were these views rational, or more closely akin to wishful thinking? Several cost structure studies lend support to their views, although the specific shape of *ATC* curves can vary tremendously from one industry to another.

Does anyone you know run a business? If so, which of the 8 panels reflects the average total cost of their firm? Go to the Interactive Study Center at http://gottheil.swcollege.com and click on the "Your Turn" button to submit your example. Student submissions will be posted to the Web site, and perhaps we will use some in future editions of the book!

EXHIBIT | 11

ALTERNATIVE SHAPES OF AVERAGE TOTAL COST (ATC) CURVES

Panels *a* to *h* show alternative shapes of the *ATC* curve. Panels *a* and *b* depict the *ATC* increasing to capacity, panels *c* to *f* depict U-shaped *ATC* curves reaching minimum points at different output levels, panel *g* shows the *ATC* curve sloping downward throughout the output range, and panel *h* shows *ATC* as sloping downward and then becoming constant for most of the output range.

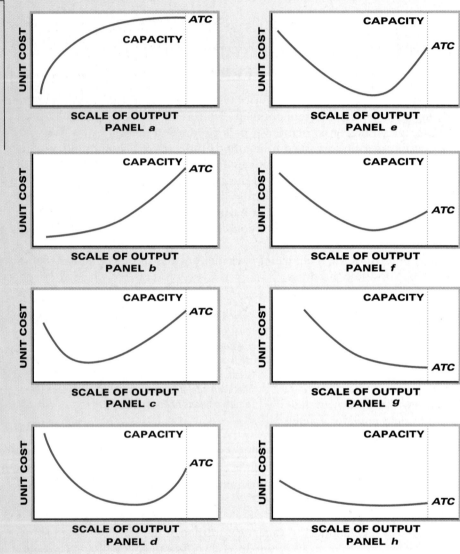

Source: Wilford J. Eiteman and Glenn E. Guthrie, "The Shape of the Average Cost Curve," *American Economic Review* 42, no. 5 (December 1952), pp. 832–838.

EXHIBIT | 12

THE AVERAGE TOTAL COST *(ATC)* CURVES IDENTIFIED BY BUSINESSPEOPLE AS REPRESENTING THEIR PRODUCTS' COST STRUCTURE

PANEL FROM EXHIBIT 11	NUMBER OF PRODUCTS PRODUCED	PERCENTAGE OF TOTAL PRODUCTS PRODUCED
a	0	—
b	1	—
c	5	—
d	15	1.3
e	42	3.8
f	381	35.2
g	636	58.7
h	2	—
TOTAL	**1,082**	**100.0**

Source: Wilford J. Eiteman and Glenn E. Guthrie, "The Shape of the Average Cost Curve," *American Economic Review* 42, no. 5 (December 1952), pp. 832–838.

CHAPTER REVIEW

1. Becoming an entrepreneur requires careful consideration. An entrepreneur usually has considerable knowledge of a business before entering it, as well as the willingness to assume business risks and sufficient access to money to start up a firm.

2. Fixed-cost items are costs to the firm that do not vary with the firm's level of output. The cost is incurred even when the firm chooses not to produce.

3. Variable-cost items are those that vary with the level of production. For example, to catch more fish, more labor must be hired.

4. Labor costs increase at a decreasing rate and then increase at an increasing rate as production is expanded. Three factors contribute to this labor cost behavior: changes in labor productivity, changes in the quality of labor, and changes in the price of labor.

5. Average total cost is computed by dividing total cost by the quantity of output. Similarly, average variable cost is total variable cost divided by the quantity of output. Average fixed cost is total fixed cost divided by the quantity of output.

6. Marginal cost is the change in total cost divided by the change in the quantity of output produced. Thus, marginal cost is the addition to total cost when producing one more unit of output.

7. A firm experiences economies of scale when, by increasing its scale of operations to afford greater specialization and efficiencies in production, its average total cost falls. Constant returns to scale occur when an increase in the scale of production (say, a doubling of output) leads to a proportionate increase (doubling) in total cost, so that the firm's average total cost remains unchanged. Diseconomies of scale occur when an increase in the scale of operations leads to increases in the firm's average total cost. These diseconomies are explained by problems associated with bigness, such as managerial attitudes and behavior.

8. A firm's short-run average total cost curve is distinguished by the firm's inability to change

its physical plant, although it can increase or decrease the other resources it uses. In this respect alone, it differs from the firm's long-run average total cost curve, which reflects the firm's complete freedom to change all its resources, including physical plant.

9. A variety of industries exhibit the U-shaped average total cost curves. However, most firms believe they operate on the downward-sloping portion of their U-shaped average total cost curves.

KEY TERMS

Fixed cost
Variable cost
Labor productivity
Total cost (TC)
Average total cost (ATC)

Average fixed cost (AFC)
Average variable cost (AVC)
Marginal cost (MC)
Economies of scale
Constant returns to scale

Diseconomies of scale
Short run
Long run
Rightsizing
Downsizing

QUESTIONS

1. If you're a would-be entrepreneur thinking of starting up a short-haul trucking business, what would be the first, and perhaps most expensive, purchasing decision you would have to make?

2. What would be some of the variable-cost items? Explain why you consider them variable.

3. Explain the law of diminishing returns. What assumptions do we make about the abilities of each laborer?

4. What would be TWA's marginal cost of adding a passenger to its Boeing 747 flight from Minneapolis to Seattle, assuming seats are available?

5. Why would you expect the long run to be different for different firms?

6. The average fixed-cost curve is downward sloping, approaching zero. Why?

7. Explain why economies of scale, constant returns to scale, and diseconomies of scale occur.

8. Why is the long-run average total cost curve described as an envelope curve? What is it enveloping?

9. What do economists mean by downsizing?

10. At relatively low levels of output, the firm's average fixed cost dominates its average total

cost, but at relatively high levels of output, the firm's average variable cost dominates. Why?

11. Why would a firm switch from one short-run average total cost structure to another?

12. Look at the atypical total cost curve. What can you say about this firm's total fixed cost?

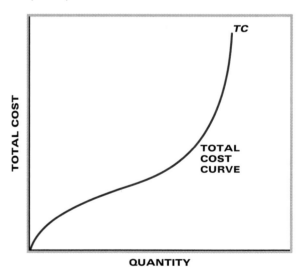

13. Suppose at output 100, average total cost is $50 and marginal cost is $20. Is the firm producing at an output level at which average total cost is increasing or decreasing?

14. Although labor is considered a variable cost item in most industries, it is perhaps more accurate to consider the labor employed in the major league baseball industry (i.e., baseball players) as fixed-cost items. Explain.

15. Describe the major fixed-costs and variable costs associated with each of the following:

a. grass cutting
b. making pizza
c. bus transportation
d. babysitting
e. making automobiles
f. heart transplants
g. hotel accommodations

PRACTICE PROBLEMS

1. Complete the following table, then plot the *TC* curve on a graph.

OUTPUT	TOTAL FIXED COST (TFC)	TOTAL VARIABLE COST (TVC)	TOTAL COST (TC)
0	$120	$ 0	
1		60	
2		80	
3		90	
4		105	
5		140	
6		210	

2. Plot *TFC* and *TVC* and compare the graphs to the *TC* curve. What relationship do you see?

3. Compose another table that shows *AFC, AVC, ATC,* and *MC* drawn from the data in practice problem 1, then graph each.

4. Suppose a watch firm faces the short-run average total cost curves and the long-run average total cost curve that envelops them, shown here. Which short-run average total cost structure would it choose if it plans to produce 100 watches? 400 watches?

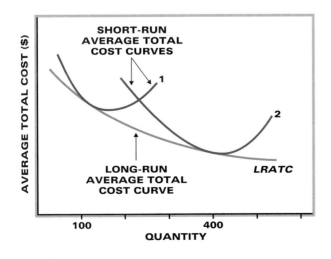

5. Complete the table.

OUTPUT	TOTAL COST	MARGINAL COST	AVERAGE TOTAL COST
0	$100		
1	150		
2	184		
3	208		
4	227		
5	250		
6	280		
7	318		

6. Complete the table.

OUTPUT	TOTAL FIXED COST	AVERAGE FIXED COST
0	$1,000	
1		
2		
3		
4		
5		

7. Complete the table. Can you cite an example of a good whose cost structure approximates the characteristics of this table?

OUTPUT	TOTAL FIXED COST	TOTAL VARIABLE COST	TOTAL COST	MARGINAL COST
0	$10,000	0		
1,000		0		
2,000		0		
3,000		0		
4,000		0		
5,000		0		

WHAT'S WRONG WITH THIS GRAPH?

MARGINAL COST AND AVERAGE TOTAL COST CURVES

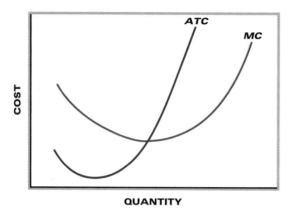

ECONOMIC CONSULTANTS

ECONOMIC RESEARCH AND ANALYSIS BY STUDENTS FOR PROFESSIONALS

Burgermania, a fast-food restaurant corporation, has grown tremendously over the past few years and has restaurants in 50 cities in the United States and Canada. Burgermania, however, recently has been experiencing growing pains.

The owners of Burgermania have hired Economic Consultants to suggest how the firm can improve its productivity and decrease its costs. In particular, Burgermania would like to know how its primary competitor—McDonald's Corporation—has maintained cost efficiency while sustaining rapid growth.

Prepare a report for Burgermania that addresses the following questions:

1. Approximately how many restaurants does McDonald's have, and how quickly are new restaurants being added? Has McDonald's taken any steps to reduce fixed costs associated with these restaurants?

2. The fast-food industry requires a large and diverse workforce. How many people does McDonald's employ? Has McDonald's taken any steps to reduce the cost of labor through initiatives to (1) increase efficiency, (2) improve quality, and/or (3) decrease price?

3. Review any information you can find addressing other variable costs, such as equipment, raw

materials, and energy. Has McDonald's taken any steps to reduce these variable costs?

4. Large restaurant corporations enjoy economies of scale and face diseconomies of scale in their operations. Has McDonald's taken any steps to take advantage of economies of scale or minimize diseconomies of scale?

You may find the following resources helpful as you prepare this report for Burgermania:

● **McDonald's Corporation** (http://www.mcdonalds. com/)—McDonald's provides information about its operations and financials. In particular, McDonald's maintains its annual report.
● **Hoover's Online Company Capsules** (http:// www.hoovers.com/)—Hoover's Online provides for more than eleven thousand companies a description, address, the names of officers, sales and employment figures, and hyperlinks to more information, such as financial reports, stock quotes, Securities and Exchange Commission filings, and news searches.
● **CNNfn** (http://www.cnnfn.com/)—CNNFN, the financial news component of CNN, provides current news stories on corporations.

PRACTICE TEST

1. Picture a four-chair shoe shine business at the Miami International Airport. The total fixed cost associated with the business is
   a. the cost of the chairs.
   b. the cost of labor.
   c. the cost of the shoe polish.
   d. the cost of leasing space at the airport.
   e. the cost of leasing space and the cost of the chairs.

2. Economists make a distinction between the short and the long run. The difference is that in the long run, as opposed to the short run,
   a. all factors of production are fixed.
   b. all factors of production are variable.
   c. only constant returns to scale are possible.
   d. labor productivity is maximized.
   e. the law of diminishing returns takes effect.

3. Which of the following cannot explain the eventual rise in average variable cost as output increases?
   a. Poorer quality of labor employed
   b. Higher wage rates paid
   c. Greater labor specialization
   d. Lower labor productivity
   e. Higher prices paid for raw materials

4. By increasing its plant size, Nike was able to double its output. But the change resulted in a more than doubling of its total costs. Economists would say that by moving to the larger plant, Nike was experiencing
   a. the effects of the law of diminishing returns.
   b. the effects of the law of increasing costs.
   c. economies of scale.
   d. diseconomies of scale.
   e. constant returns to scale.

5. Without knowing the specifics about the costs associated with airline travel, it is safe to assume that when American Airlines adds a last-minute passenger to its Chicago–San Francisco flight, all of the following are true except
   a. average fixed cost falls.
   b. average variable cost falls.
   c. average total cost falls.
   d. marginal cost is greater than average total cost.
   e. marginal cost is less than average variable cost.

6. The textbook relates an interesting story concerning how businesspeople view their cost structures. When asked to identify the shape of their average total cost curve from among eight choices offered, the majority chose the curve that is
   a. U-shaped.
   b. downward sloping at the outset but quickly becomes upward sloping.
   c. upward sloping at the outset but quickly becomes downward sloping.
   d. continuously upward sloping until production reaches capacity.
   e. continuously downward sloping until production reaches capacity.

7. Picture the production of American flags. If average total cost increases within the production range of 1,000 to 3,000, we know that within that range
   a. marginal cost is greater than average total cost.
   b. marginal cost is less than average variable cost.
   c. marginal cost is greater than average fixed cost.
   d. average total cost is less than average fixed cost.
   e. average total cost is less than average variable cost.

8. A firm's long-run average total cost curve is formed by
   a. points of tangency with its short-run average total cost curves.
   b. points of tangency with its short-run marginal cost curves.
   c. linking the intersections of its short-run marginal cost curves and its short-run average variable cost curves.
   d. linking its short-run average fixed cost curves.
   e. linking the minimum points of its short-run marginal cost curves.

9. What best explains diseconomies of scale?
   a. Greater specialization
   b. Increasing bureaucracy
   c. Not producing at minimum average total cost
   d. Not producing at minimum marginal cost
   e. Not producing at the intersection of the marginal and average total cost curves

10. What best explains economies of scale?
    a. Greater specialization
    b. Increasing bureaucracy
    c. Producing a minimum average total cost
    d. Producing a minimum marginal cost
    e. Producing at the intersection of the marginal and average total cost curves

MAXIMIZING PROFIT

There's a story told about a 25th high school reunion. Those attending were shocked to discover that the most unlikely of their classmates, Jeff Stevens, who had had trouble passing chemistry, literature, history, biology, mathematics, and even gym, turned out to be the only multimillionaire! How had he done it? What was his magic? They gathered around their one outstanding success story to learn his secret. "It's simple," he told them. "Buy at $10, sell at $20, and be satisfied with your 25 percent profit."

The point of this silly story is that you don't necessarily

have to be a Nobel laureate to be successful in the business world. Most entrepreneurs rely on instinct, on their wits, on taking chances, on a great deal of luck, and on extraordinary effort. Perhaps the most important weapon in their profit-making arsenal is *personal drive*.

Vince Lombardi, the legendary coach of the Green Bay Packers, once philosophized about football: "Winning isn't everything. It's the *only* thing." Entrepreneurs understand Lombardi. He wasn't satisfied with just a winning season. It was always a losing season for him if the Packers didn't win the championship. Entrepreneurs are like that. They are never satisfied with just making profit. They want to **maximize profit.**

THIS CHAPTER INTRODUCES YOU TO THE ECONOMIC PRINCIPLES ASSOCIATED WITH:

- ENTREPRENEURIAL BEHAVIOR
- TOTAL REVENUE, AVERAGE REVENUE, AND MARGINAL REVENUE
- PROFIT MAXIMIZATION
- LOSS MINIMIZATION
- THE APPLICATION OF THE *MR* = *MC* RULE
- CORPORATE EMPIRE BUILDING

ENTREPRENEURS AND PROFIT MAKING

Entrepreneurs live in two very different spheres of economic life at the same time. Their survival in each requires them to master very different kinds of knowledge, decision making, and uncertainties. In the sphere of production, entrepreneurs must commit themselves to cost obligations even before production starts. They must make decisions about the kinds of products they will produce and about leasing or buying their physical plant. They need to know what machinery and raw materials to purchase. They must decide on managerial staff before production workers get on the production line. For many firms, the costs of establishing the business are financed by banks, committing the entrepreneur to interest payments on loans as well. All these cost obligations take place before the first unit of goods rolls off the production line.

Entrepreneurs must therefore make production decisions that require some degree of expertise in both the mechanics of production and in accounting. What kinds of technologies are appropriate? What kinds of labor should they hire? How can they arrange these factors of production in the most efficient way? Although costs are committed before production starts, there is no assurance that all the effort and expense will end up generating sufficient revenues to cover costs, let alone provide for profit.

In the other sphere of economic life that entrepreneurs operate in—the world of markets—the problems confronted and the decision making required are very different. The trick here is to *anticipate* what prices will be.

There's obviously no way of knowing. Entrepreneurs rely on their best judgment, sometimes on a sixth sense. Whatever their source of knowledge, it is still basically guesswork. If they guess correctly, if prices turn out to be what they anticipated, or perhaps even higher, they may make a **profit.** On the other hand, if prices fall short of expectation, they may lose. If they are too far off the mark, they may lose everything. Many novice entrepreneurs do lose everything.

The issues they confront daily concern not only the uncertainties of their own market, but also the uncertainties associated with the state of the economy. After all, even if they know their own market well, they cannot possibly know how the economy will fare in six months. Will there be prosperity or recession?

What happens to prices if the economy slumps? Typically, national employment, income, and consumption fall. Markets weaken and prices drift downward. But many entrepreneurs have already undertaken cost obligations. Profits, under these conditions, can disappear rather quickly.

On the other hand, if the national economy swings into full employment, demand typically increases and prices bounce upward. The difference now between already committed costs and increasing price widens, creating more attractive profit margins.

PROFIT-MAXIMIZING FISHERMEN

Picture fishermen as entrepreneurs. The average total cost of producing a fish depends on the number of fish caught. Exhibit 1 summarizes the average and marginal cost data from the tables in Exhibits 5 and 6 in the previous chapter.

Profit Depends on Price and Costs

Suppose the fishermen return from a fishing run with 11,000 fish. We see in Exhibit 1 that the average cost of producing each of these 11,000 fish is $0.68.

Profit maximization
The primary goal of a firm: To achieve the most profit possible from its production and sale of goods or services.

Entrepreneur magazine (http://www.entrepreneur mag.com/) provides professional information for entrepreneurs and small-business owners.

Profit
Income earned by entrepreneurs.

Was it worth the effort? It depends on the price of fish. Suppose the price is $0.75. How much do the fishermen make on a $0.75 fish? The calculation is simple. The profit per fish is $P - ATC$. At a production run of 11,000 fish, profit per fish is $0.75 - $0.68 = $0.07.

What about the fishermen's total profit? Total profit is simply $(P - ATC) \times Q$. With a production run of 11,000 fish, total profit is ($0.75 - $0.68) × 11,000 = $770. What could be any more simple than that?

Suppose price increased from $0.75 to $0.80. The fishermen may have been on the water when the price rose, creating a rather pleasant surprise when they return to the docks. Their total profit increases. They still bring in the same 11,000 fish, and ATC is still $0.68. But with a price of $0.80, total profit increases from $770 to ($0.80 - $0.68) × 11,000 = $1,320.

Should Fishermen Produce More Fish?

Suppose the $1,320 profit encourages fishermen to increase production. They hire more crew and stay out longer, increasing their catch from 11,000 to 12,000 fish per run. This higher production level means, of course, more $0.80 fish. *But it also means that average total cost changes as well.*

Look at Exhibit 1. The average total cost of producing a fish at a 12,000 production run is $0.73. That is, ATC increases $0.05, from $0.68 to $0.73. The fishermen now get only $0.80 - $0.73 = $0.07 profit per fish. Look what happens to total profit. It decreases from $1,320 to ($0.80 - $0.73) × 12,000 = $840. Did it pay the fishermen to run production up to 12,000?

Obviously not. The increase in total revenue generated by the additional 1,000 fish was not enough to overcome the increase in the total cost of catching those 12,000 fish. Of course, it's not the end of the world. The fishermen are still making $840 profit.

But making profit is not exactly the same as making the most profit possible. Fishermen, like all other entrepreneurs, are in business to *maximize* profit. If their production choices were only 11,000 or 12,000 fish, there's no question where they would choose to produce. But why only two options? Their production capacity, fixed by the size of their boats, allows them to choose *any* output level along the production range of 0 to 15,000 fish per run. How do fishermen figure out where that profit-maximizing output is?

EXHIBIT 1

AVERAGE TOTAL COST AND MARGINAL COST OF PRODUCING FISH PER FISHING RUN ($ PER FISH)

QUANTITY	AVERAGE COST (AC)	MARGINAL COST (MC)
0		
1,000	$2.34	$0.34
2,000	1.32	0.30
3,000	0.97	0.26
4,000	0.79	0.24
5,000	0.68	0.26
6,000	0.63	0.35
7,000	0.60	0.45
8,000	0.60	0.60
9,000	0.62	0.75
10,000	0.65	0.90
11,000	0.68	1.05
12,000	0.73	1.20
13,000	0.78	1.40
14,000	0.84	1.60
15,000	0.77	1.80

INTERDISCIPLINARY PERSPECTIVE

ON THE ORIGINS OF ENTREPRENEURSHIP

Reuven Brenner, in his interesting book *Rivalry,* raises the question about the origins of entrepreneurship. Why do people become entrepreneurs? Is there anything particularly different about these folks? Brenner cites several studies on the subject whose findings may surprise you. For many entrepreneurs, overcoming adversity starts at an early age. For example, troubled family backgrounds pop up as a possible explanatory factor. A disproportionate number of entrepreneurs experience, as a child, the loss of a parent by death, divorce, or estrangement. In one survey, more than 25 percent reported a very unsatisfactory relationship with absent or bullying fathers.

Psychologist Albert Shapero found that the simplest route to entrepreneurship is falling on hard times. Many entrepreneurs were displaced persons who had been dislodged from comfortable and familiar niches. No shock then that immigrants and minorities rank high among their numbers.

Joshua Ronen discovered that one of the main factors that pushed people into entrepreneurship is the relative unattractiveness of alternative employments. Being fired from a job is a good start to entrepreneurship! Another study focusing on job insecurity shows that almost a third of the entrepreneurs sampled had been fired before taking the entrepreneurial route.

What about scholastic performance? Are entrepreneurs "the best and the brightest"? Not necessarily so. A 1985 study shows corporate managers outscoring their entrepreneurial counterparts, 83 percent to 59 percent, on achieving above-average academic distinction. As well, these corporate managers attended the more prestigious schools, and fully 94 percent of them completed college compared to only 76 percent of entrepreneurs.

Is entrepreneurship a genetic trait? The evidence points in the other direction. According to Ronen, success frequently diminishes the entrepreneurial drive. Why? Because having achieved success (and with it, social position), entrepreneurs typically become reluctant to change their way of doing things, or to experiment with new designs or technologies, or even to entertain new ideas. In other words, they lose that very quality that had been the essence of their entrepreneurship.

THE $MR = MC$ RULE

One laborious way of discovering the most profitable level of production is to calculate total profit for each and every output across the 0-to-15,000-fish production range and choose the one that yields the most profit. That's 15,000 calculations! A simpler way of arriving at maximum profit is by *looking only at the last unit produced* and calculating whether it adds to or subtracts from total profit.

Thinking on the Margin

Economists define the one unit as the marginal unit. Think of it this way. Imagine yourself playing chess. Your game is always ahead of you, isn't it? The lay of the board is what you face. There's nothing you can do about past moves. It's the one coming up that counts. Whatever decision you make concerns the very next move. That's how entrepreneurs approach choices on production. If a fisherman is already producing 11,000 fish, that is a fait accompli. The focus of consideration switches to the next fish, the 11,001st. The 11,001st fish is the marginal fish. Should

THEORETICAL PERSPECTIVE

DRAWING THE MARGINAL REVENUE CURVE

There's no secret to it. It's a straight-forward mathematical relationship.

The downward-sloping marginal revenue curve lies below the downward-sloping demand curve and falls at twice the demand curve's rate of decline. To sketch the relationship between the two curves, start at any point (price and quantity) on the upper left part of the graph. Draw the downward-sloping demand curve to intersect the horizontal axis. Note the quantity on the horizontal axis at the point of intersection. To create a corresponding marginal revenue curve, start at the initial point on that demand curve and draw a curve that intersects the horizontal axis at exactly one-half the distance to demand. In every case, this relationship traces out a marginal revenue curve falling at twice the rate of the demand curve.

But what if the demand curve isn't downward sloping? What if it's horizontal? Well, think about it. If the demand curve's rate of decline is zero, then twice zero is still zero! In this unique circumstance, the marginal revenue curve starts at the initial point on the demand curve and, like the demand curve, is horizontal. That is to say, because the rate of decline of both the demand and the marginal revenue curves is zero, both are horizontal, coinciding with each other.

The three demand schedules and curves shown in the accompanying table and graph illustrate the demand and marginal revenue relationship under conditions of different price elasticities of demand.

Look at the table. In demand schedule *a*, a 10 percent change in price—$10 to $9—generates a 100 percent change in quantity demanded—1 to 2 units. In schedule *b*, that same 10 percent change in price generates a 500 percent change in quantity demanded—1 to 5 units. That is to say, demand in schedule *b* is more elastic than demand in schedule *a*. In schedule *c*, price is unchanging along the entire range of quantity. Its elasticity is infinity.

These schedules are graphed into the three demand curves shown in panel *a*. As you see, the curve flattens with rising elasticity and becomes horizontal when elasticity is infinite. What about the corresponding marginal revenue curves? Look at panel *b*. If you were to extend the marginal revenue curves to reach the horizontal axis at half the distance to their respective demand curves, then, the more elastic the demand, the closer lies the marginal revenue curve to the demand curve. When demand elasticity is infinite, the gap between the demand curve and marginal revenue curve completely disappears.

SCHEDULE *a*				SCHEDULE *b*				SCHEDULE *c*			
Q	PRICE	TR	MR	Q	PRICE	TR	MR	Q	PRICE	TR	MR
0				0				0			
1	$10.00	$10.00	$10.00	1	$10.00	$10.00	$10.00	1	$10.00	$10.00	$10.00
2	9.00	18.00	8.00	2	9.75	19.50	9.50	2	10.00	20.00	10.00
3	8.00	24.00	6.00	3	9.50	28.50	8.50	3	10.00	30.00	10.00
4	7.00	28.00	4.00	4	9.25	37.00	7.50	4	10.00	40.00	10.00
5	6.00	30.00	2.00	5	9.00	45.00	7.00	5	10.00	50.00	10.00
6	5.00	30.00	0	6	8.75	52.50	6.50	6	10.00	60.00	10.00
7	4.00	28.00	-2.00	7	8.50	59.50	6.00	7	10.00	70.00	10.00

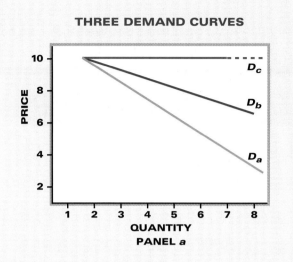

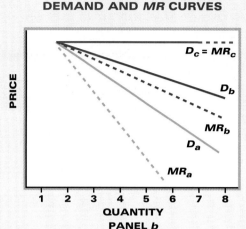

that fish be produced? It depends on whether the sale of that 11,001st fish adds more to total revenue than its production adds to total cost.

Total, Average, and Marginal Revenue

Let's assume that the price for fish is $0.90. The table in Exhibit 2 records the fishermen's total, average, and marginal revenue for production ranging from 0 to 15,000 fish.

TOTAL REVENUE **Total revenue (TR)** is simply market price multiplied by the quantity of fish sold:

$$TR = PQ$$

Total revenue increases by $900 every time fishermen sell an additional 1,000 fish. At 0 fish, $TR = \$0.90 \times 0 = 0$. At 11,000 fish, $TR = \$0.90 \times 11,000 = \$9,900$. At 12,000 fish, $TR = \$0.90 \times 12,000 = \$10,800$. Panel a maps the total revenue curve over the range 0 to 15,000 fish at $P = \$0.90$. As you see, the TR curve is a straight line drawn from the origin, its slope determined by price. If the price falls to $0.50, the TR curve becomes TR' in panel a.

AVERAGE REVENUE **Average revenue (AR)** is simply another way of describing price. Every fish sold puts the price it fetches on the market into the fishermen's pockets. That's another $0.90. With 1,000 fish sold, the fishermen end up with $900. Just keep adding $0.90—the price of the fish—every time another fish is sold. If 2,000 are sold, the fishermen end up with $1,800 total revenue. Average revenue or price is calculated as

$$AR = \frac{TR}{Q} = \frac{P \times Q}{Q} = P$$

MARGINAL REVENUE Just as marginal cost measures the change in total cost generated by a change in quantity produced, **marginal revenue (MR)**

Total revenue (TR)
The price of a good multiplied by the number of units sold.

Average revenue (AR)
Total revenue divided by the quantity of goods or services sold.

Marginal revenue (MR)
The change in total revenue generated by the sale of one additional unit of goods or services.

EXHIBIT | 2

TOTAL AND MARGINAL REVENUE CURVES DERIVED FROM SELLING FISH WHEN *P* = $0.90

When *P* = $0.90 and remains unchanged no matter what quantity the firm produces and sells, the total revenue curve, *TR*, takes the form of an upward-sloping straight line from the origin (panel *a*). If price changes to *P* = $0.50, the total revenue curve is *TR'*.

The revenue from each additional unit of production is $0.90. The marginal revenue curve takes the form of a horizontal straight line at *P* = $0.90 (panel *b*). The marginal revenue curve coincides with the price (and average revenue) curve at *MR* = *AR* = *P*.

TOTAL AND MARGINAL REVENUE DERIVED FROM SELLING FISH WHEN *P* = $0.90

QUANTITY	PRICE PER FISH	TOTAL REVENUE (TR)	MARGINAL REVENUE (MR) PER 1,000 FISH	MARGINAL REVENUE (MR) PER FISH
1,000	$0.90	$ 900	$900	$0.90
2,000	0.90	1,800	900	0.90
3,000	0.90	2,700	900	0.90
4,000	0.90	3,600	900	0.90
5,000	0.90	4,500	900	0.90
6,000	0.90	5,400	900	0.90
7,000	0.90	6,300	900	0.90
8,000	0.90	7,200	900	0.90
9,000	0.90	8,400	900	0.90
10,000	0.90	9,000	900	0.90
11,000	0.90	9,900	900	0.90
12,000	0.90	10,800	900	0.90
13,000	0.90	11,700	900	0.90
14,000	0.90	12,600	900	0.90
15,000	0.90	13,500	900	0.90

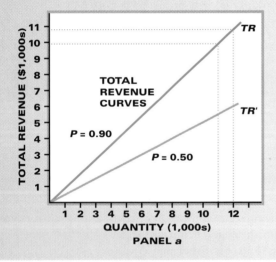

PANEL *a*

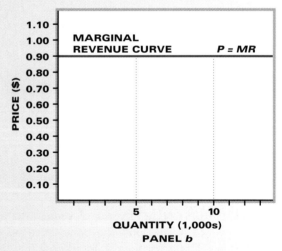

PANEL *b*

measures the change in total revenue generated by a change in quantity sold. It is written as

$$MR = \frac{\Delta TR}{\Delta Q}$$

Look at the table in Exhibit 2, column 4. Every time a unit of 1,000 fish is added, total revenue increases by $0.90 × 1,000 = $900. For example, if production increases from 11,000 to 12,000 fish, total revenue increases by $10,800 − $9,900 = $900. If production decreases from 11,000 to 10,000 fish, total revenue decreases by $9,900 − $9,000 = $900. For *each* of these 1,000 additions or subtractions of fish, the *MR* per fish is $900/1,000 = $0.90. That's what we see in the table in Exhibit 2, column 5.

The *MR* curve corresponding to column 5 is shown in panel *b*.

It's almost impossible not to note from the table in Exhibit 2 that price and marginal revenue per fish are identical. It's not surprising. After all, adding another fish to sales raises total revenue precisely by the price of the fish. *That is why the MR curve of panel* b *coincides with the price curve:*

$$P = MR$$

at any production level. As we shall see in the chapter on price determination in perfectly competitive markets, the *P = MR* identity is characteristic of the perfectly competitive firm's price and marginal revenue curves.

APPLYING THE *MR = MC* RULE

Exhibit 3 brings together the five most important pieces of data that a fishing company needs to determine its most profitable level of production. It also tells the fishermen whether to stay in business.

The marginal cost and marginal revenue data alone provide all the information necessary for the fishermen to determine where maximum profit can be made. The price and average cost data determine how much profit—if there's any profit at all—the maximum represents.

CHECK YOUR UNDERSTANDING

What guideline does a firm use to decide when to add to or cut back production?

EXHIBIT | 3

KEY DATA ON PROFIT MAXIMIZATION

QUANTITY	PRICE	AVERAGE VARIABLE COST (AVC)	AVERAGE TOTAL COST (ATC)	MARGINAL COST (MC)	MARGINAL REVENUE (MR)
0	$0.90				
1,000	0.90	$0.34	$2.34	$0.34	$0.90
2,000	0.90	0.32	1.32	0.30	0.90
3,000	0.90	0.30	0.97	0.26	0.90
4,000	0.90	0.29	0.79	0.24	0.90
5,000	0.90	0.28	0.68	0.26	0.90
6,000	0.90	0.29	0.63	0.35	0.90
7,000	0.90	0.31	0.60	0.45	0.90
8,000	0.90	0.35	0.60	0.60	0.90
9,000	0.90	0.39	0.62	0.75	0.90
10,000	0.90	0.45	0.65	0.90	0.90
11,000	0.90	0.50	0.68	1.05	0.90
12,000	0.90	0.56	0.73	1.20	0.90
13,000	0.90	0.62	0.78	1.40	0.90
14,000	0.90	0.69	0.84	1.60	0.90
15,000	0.90	0.77	0.90	1.80	0.90

The profit maximization guideline is incredibly simple. The rule is to keep adding to production as long as the marginal revenue gained from adding production is greater than the marginal cost incurred from adding it. That is, keep producing more as long as $MR > MC$. It stands to reason then that if the marginal revenue gained from any unit produced is less than the marginal cost involved in producing it, you simply don't produce it. Take it out of production and keep subtracting from production as long as $MC > MR$.

Exercising the maxim of adding when $MR > MC$ and subtracting when $MC > MR$ leads inexorably to the powerful **$MR = MC$ rule** of profit maximization. Exhibit 4 illustrates how the profit-maximizing $MR = MC$ rule is applied.

Suppose the price of fish was $0.90 and quantity was 6,000 fish. Is the firm maximizing profit at 6,000? Should it produce more or cut back? Look at the marginal cost and marginal revenue of the 6,000th fish. $MC = \$0.35$ and $MR = \$0.90$. The 6,000th fish generates a profit of $0.90 − $0.35 = $0.55. The guideline states, If $MR > MC$, keep producing more.

How much more? Look at the 7,000th fish. Compare its MC to its MR. $MC = \$0.45$ and $MR = \$0.90$. Does it pay to produce that 7,000th fish? Of course. The fishermen *add* $0.90 − $0.45 = $0.45 to profit. That is to say, profit is increasing.

But why stop there? Look at the next 1,000 fish. MC increases to $0.60. Should the fishermen produce that 8,000th fish? Of course. As long as $MR > MC$, producing it *adds* to total profit. The $0.90 − $0.60 = $0.30 generated by the 8,000th fish may not add as much to total profit as the 7,000th did, but still, $0.30 represents $0.30 more total profit. Even if $MR > MC$ on the next fish yielded only a penny, wouldn't it pay to produce it? It *adds* a penny more to total profit. Why not take the penny?

To take a different example, suppose a friend plays a money game with you, tossing coins in your lap. You get to keep whatever you collect. The only rule is that your friend must keep tossing until you tell her to stop. Suppose she starts by tossing quarters. After a while, she switches to dimes. Soon she's down to nickels, and finally pennies. Would you tell her to stop because the last toss was a penny? After all, didn't that last penny still add to your total money?

Suppose the game now costs you a nickel a toss. Wouldn't you keep the game going as long as the coins tossed were quarters or dimes? You could stop when nickels appear, because you break even with each nickel toss. You've maximized your money when the first nickel appears. If your friend tries to continue the game with penny tosses, you would lose four cents on every additional toss.

That's how fishermen play the fishing game. As long as $MR > MC$ on the next unit of production, they produce that unit. In Exhibit 4, MC increases to $0.90 when the 10,000th fish is added to production. At the 10,000th fish, $MR = MC$. The fishermen stop.

The profit on the 10,000th fish is $0.90 − $0.90 = $0.00. On the 11,000th fish, $MC > MR$. The *loss* on that 11,000th fish is $1.05 − $0.90 = $0.15. The fishermen will not produce it. The rule is simple and compelling: Keep on producing until $MR = MC$. At that point, profit is maximized.

MR = MC rule
The guideline used by a firm to achieve profit maximization.

Can you think of an illustration similar to the coin toss that makes the same point? Go to the Interactive Study Center at http://gottheil.swcollege.com and click on the "Your Turn" button to submit your example. Student submissions will be posted to the Web site, and perhaps we will use some in future editions of the book!

EXHIBIT|4

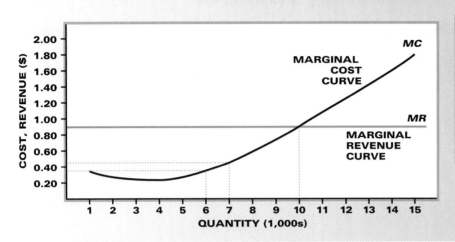

APPLYING THE *MR* = *MC* RULE

The firm's marginal cost is *MC*, and its marginal revenue curve is *MR*. At a production level of 6,000 fish, *MC* = $0.35 and *MR* = $0.90. When *MR* > *MC*, the rule is to produce more. When 7,000 fish are produced, *MC* = $0.45 and *MR* = $0.90. *MR* still exceeds *MC*. The firm continues to increase production. At a production level of 10,000 fish, *MC* = *MR* = $0.90. When *MR* = *MC*, production is at a profit-maximizing level.

HOW MUCH PROFIT IS MAXIMUM PROFIT?

The *MR* = *MC* rule gets us to profit maximization, but it doesn't tell us how much that maximum profit is. We know that maximum profit is the total of the differences between marginal revenue and marginal cost for each of the 11,000 fish. But that's like knowing when you've reached the top of Mount Everest. It's a great achievement, but, standing on top, how do you know the height of the mountain?

That's where price, average variable cost (*AVC*), and average total cost (*ATC*) come into play. Since we already know that profit is maximized at 10,000 fish and, from the table in Exhibit 4 in the previous chapter, that *ATC* = $0.645 (rounded to $0.65) and P = $0.90, then maximum profit is

$$(\$0.90 - \$0.645) \times 10,000 = \$2,550$$

It's as simple as that. No other production level yields a profit as large as the $2,550 generated at 10,000.

Exhibit 5 provides a graphic illustration of profit maximization.

Since we know from the *MR* = *MC* rule that maximum profit is obtained at 10,000 fish, then the shaded rectangle showing the difference between price and average total cost at 10,000, $0.90 − $0.645, multiplied by 10,000 fish, generates the $2,550.

MAXIMIZING PROFIT AND MINIMIZING LOSS

Let's now consider some tough problems. In business it's always pleasant searching for maximum profit outputs. It's much less pleasant when the climate of business turns and the problem is deciding whether to stay in business. Entrepreneurs, including fishermen, know that the possibility of incurring losses is always part of business life. And however successful entrepreneurs may be in controlling costs, the one thing most cannot control is price.

EXHIBIT | 5

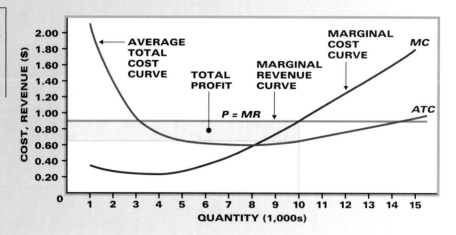

MEASURING PROFIT MAXIMIZATION

The firm calculates the difference between its *ATC* at 10,000 and its price, multiplying this difference by the quantity produced and sold. At 10,000, total profit is ($0.90 − $0.645) (10,000) = $2,550, the shaded rectangle.

Fishermen may *expect* price to remain at $0.90, but that may be wishful thinking. Price responds to market pressures. If these pressures are strong enough, they can drive any price anywhere. Suppose the price of fish drops dramatically to $0.45. What would fishermen do? Look at Exhibit 6.

Following the *MR* = *MC* rule, production should be at 7,000 fish. But there's a problem. At 7,000 fish, *ATC* = $0.60, and with *P* = $0.45, total profit is

$$(\$0.45 - \$0.60) \times 7{,}000 = -\$1{,}050$$

Fishermen end up *losing* $1,050! That's not what they had in mind when they went into business. But they never counted on a $0.45 fish. What can they do? Producing less than 7,000 or producing more than 7,000 *or not producing at all* yields even greater losses. For example, if fishermen were to keep the boats in dock—no fishing at *P* = $0.45—they still have costs. *Not producing is not costless.* After all, that $2,000 fixed cost for the boat has to be paid whether they fish or not. Aren't they better off producing the 7,000 fish and losing $1,050 than producing 0 and losing $2,000?

The *MR* = *MC* rule, then, is both a profit-maximization and **loss-minimization** guide to production. And that, in turn, leads us to another rule: If you can't cover *average variable cost in the short run, shut down!*

Loss minimization
Faced with the certainty of incurring losses, the firm's goal is to incur the lowest loss possible from its production and sale of goods and services.

Since the fixed cost of the boat is already committed, the guiding rule on whether to fish, at least in the short run, is determined by whether price covers average variable cost. That is, does the cost of hiring crew and using bait, ice, and fuel per fish add up to more than $0.45? Is *P* > *AVC*?

Look again at Exhibit 6. At 7,000 fish, although *ATC* = $0.60, *AVC* = $0.31428 (rounded out in the table to $0.31). Ignoring the $2,000 fixed cost, fishermen clear

$$(\$0.45 - \$0.31428) \times 7{,}000 = \$950$$

This $950 profit means that producing 7,000 fish is more profitable than not producing at all. After all, producing or not producing, the fishermen are obliged to absorb the $2,000 cost of the boat.

But suppose price falls to $0.26. Given the data in the table in Exhibit 6 in the previous chapter, the *MR = MC* rule guides the fishermen to produce 5,000 fish. At that quantity, *AVC* = $0.28. Does it pay to produce? No, because now *P < AVC*. Producing 5,000 fish creates

$$(\$0.26 - \$0.28) \times 5{,}000 = -\$100$$

a loss of $100. The $0.26 price does not cover the cost of hiring crew and using bait, ice, and fuel. Why not **shutdown** the business and accept the $2,000 loss on fixed costs rather than incur that $2,000 cost *plus* the $100 loss on the variable costs when producing at 5,000? When *P* = $0.26, it pays to shut down.

Shutting down or not shutting down in the short run depends on whether the market price covers average variable costs. Look again at the table in Exhibit 5 in the previous chapter. The critical watershed quantity is 5,000 fish, where *AVC* = $0.28. If price falls below $0.28, don't produce at all. If it's above $0.28, produce where *MR = MC* to minimize the loss.

What about the long run? After all, losing money is not why fishermen fish. They may stay in business to minimize their losses in the short run because they are locked into the $2,000-per-run fixed cost of the boat. In a loss situation, then, the fishermen stay in business until these fixed-cost obligations are ended, allowing them the freedom to decide whether to buy another boat. Shutting down or not shutting down in the long run depends on whether the market price covers average total cost. Obviously, no one will renegotiate another $2,000 fixed-cost commitment if the firm continues to lose money. In this unpleasant circumstance, the fishermen close shop permanently.

Shutdown
The cessation of the firm's activity. The firm's loss minimization occurs at zero output.

CHECK YOUR UNDERSTANDING

Why would a firm stay in business if it's losing money?

DO FIRMS REALLY BEHAVE THIS WAY?

Some years back, a short-lived, but rather exciting, controversy arose among economists over this issue of firms' profit-maximizing behavior. Do entrepreneurs *really* think on the margin? Do they really ask themselves whether they should produce the next unit of production? Do they really focus on marginal cost and revenue

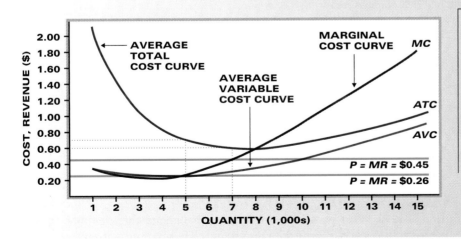

MINIMIZING LOSS

The *P* = *MR* = $0.45 curve is lower than the firm's *ATC* at every level of output. The firm must incur losses no matter where it produces. The firm's least undesirable level of output—although not desirable—is where losses are minimized. The *MR* = *MC* rule still applies. At 7,000 fish, *P* = *MR* = $0.45. The loss is ($0.45 − $0.60) × 7,000 = −$1,050. No other output level generates as low a loss as 7,000 fish. Producing zero would still involve fixed costs of $2,000.

EXHIBIT|6

GLOBAL PERSPECTIVE

MAXIMIZING PROFIT ON ISRAEL'S KIBBUTZIM

An Israeli kibbutz can claim to be the most collectivized form of political, social, and economic organization in the world. Kibbutzim (plural of *kibbutz*) are productive communities—engaged in both agricultural and manufacturing activity—in which every kibbutz member contributes to the kibbutz according to his or her ability and receives from the kibbutz according to his or her needs. That is, no link exists between an individual's effort and reward.

How is a kibbutz run? All decision making on the kibbutz, including that associated with managing the kibbutz economy, is rotated among its members. The kibbutz trademark is universal equality.

If you think that people who opt to live and work under such conditions would place less value on acquiring material things than we do, you would be basically right. If you also think that these people would be adverse to profit-maximizing behavior, you would be wrong!

According to Professors David Levhari and Haim Barkai, who are experts on the economics of the kibbutz, the kibbutz behaves as if it were a profit-maximizing firm. Kibbutz members know what marginal cost and marginal revenue are, and they know as well the usefulness of the *MR = MC* guideline. After all, why wouldn't they keep producing oranges (if that's what they're producing) so long as the marginal revenue is greater than the marginal cost of producing them? If producing until *MR = MC* makes sense to you, why shouldn't

I THINK THIS CROP WILL FETCH SOME MIGHTY FINE SHEKELS!

it make sense to members of a kibbutz? What they do with the maximum profit they make is another matter.

When the kibbutz decides what crops to produce, price is an important consideration. If cotton prices increase, it may signal the kibbutz to switch from bananas to cotton. If competition from Spain, Morocco, and other orange-producing economies drives the price of oranges down, it may also drive orange-producing kibbutzim out of producing oranges.

Many kibbutzim shifted their productive focus out of agriculture into manufacturing in the 1960s when the prices of farm goods weakened. Why? Manufacturing, and particularly high-tech manufacturing, pays more than farming. The guideline was *MR = MC*. Kibbutz members see no conflict in maximizing profit and living modestly in an environment of equality.

CONSIDER

How would you make your case if you were a kibbutz member opposing profit maximization? What kind of an argument could a fellow kibbutz member make to counter your argument? (*Hint:* What the kibbutz does with its profit is another matter.)

MORE ON THE NET

The United Kibbutz Movement (http://kibbutz.org.il/) provides information about kibbutzim and their activities.

---

in making production decisions? In other words, are they actually guided by the *MR = MC* rule?

The Lester-Machlup Controversy

In the mid-1940s, Princeton's Richard Lester challenged the idea that entrepreneurs look to the margin for production signals. He surveyed entrepreneurs in 58 firms, asking them to explain how they chose their production levels. Their response indicated that they did *not* think in terms of marginal units. Lester considered his findings nonsurprising, since he believed that insuperable problems are involved in applying marginal analysis to the modern multiproduct firm.

Lester's conclusions, however, did not go unchallenged. Among the defenders of marginal analysis was Professor Fritz Machlup of The Johns Hopkins University. He dismissed Lester's findings on the grounds that the $MR = MC$ theory of profit maximizing doesn't depend on what entrepreneurs *think* they do, but rather on observing what they *actually* do. Entrepreneurs should be seen, not heard!

Milton Friedman's *The Methodology of Positive Economics*, published just a few years later, commented on the Lester-Machlup controversy. To Friedman, the critical issue was whether there was "conformity to experience of the implications of the marginal analysis." And for him, the "experience" was as unmistakable as the "implications" of marginal analysis. In other words, marginal analysis was alive and well.

Most economists share Friedman's view. They accept the idea that no matter how entrepreneurs may describe their own behavior, the $MR = MC$ rule is still the most satisfactory explanation of how they really behave.

Empire Building

Another perspective on this issue of profit maximization argues that the firm's decision makers are not as one-dimensional as marginalists suggest. According to this view, the idea that a firm goes about squeezing every last bit of profit out of its production run, as the $MR = MC$ rule implies, simply flies in the face of reality.

The advent of the modern corporation changed the character of the firm. The corporation separates owners—stockholders—from decision makers. They are different people with different ideas about what the firm ought to be doing.

Stockholders typically want the firm to maximize profit. The firm's managers, on the other hand, have quite a different view of appropriate goals. To them, the firm is more than an economic machine grinding out profit for stockholders. It also has social, political, and historical dimensions that are important to them. The firm is the playing field on which they advance their careers. The firm's status in the industry, not necessarily the profit it produces, is a matter of much consideration.

For example, the owner of a taxi business who, herself, is not involved in running the business, may not care if the taxis are old or new. If more profit can be generated using old taxis, then as far as she's concerned, the old are better. But her salaried managers, who run the business, may think differently about the taxis they use. They may prefer new taxis because this will enhance their own self-image and generate fewer complaints from drivers and passengers. In other words, the managers' interests in the business may not be entirely profit motivated.

Such a sociological account of a modern corporate economy was first set out by Adolf Berle and Gardiner Means in *The Modern Corporation and Private Property* and later by James Burnham in *The Managerial Revolution*.

More recently, William Baumol's *Business Behavior and Economic Growth* put a new twist on the old argument. To Baumol, the firm that is run by nonowning managers generally chooses to maximize sales, not profit. Success is measured by the size of the production range. But why sales? In Baumol's view, a much-sought-after managerial goal is empire building. John K. Galbraith's *New Industrial State* continued the attack on the traditional $MR = MC$ description of firm behavior. He concludes that the managerial bureaucracy controls the corporation and dictates its goals.

How does this come about? In Galbraith's view, the primary goal is the survival of the corporation and, in particular, the survival of its managerial bureaucracy. It aims, then, to reduce the risks and uncertainties that the market tends to generate. Managers are not the only ones who have a stake in the survival of the corporation.

CHECK YOUR UNDERSTANDING

Are stockholder and corporate manager goals always identical?

HISTORICAL PERSPECTIVE

WHY PROFIT MAXIMIZATION? OF THE ORIGIN OF AMBITION, AND OF THE DISTINCTION OF RANKS

For to what purpose is all the toil and bustle of this world? What is the end of avarice and ambition, of the pursuit of wealth, of power, and pre-eminence? Is it to supply the necessities of nature? The wages of the meanest labourer can supply them. We see that they afford him food and clothing, the comfort of a house, and of a family. If we examine his economy with rigour, we should find that he spends a great part of them upon conveniences, which may be regarded as super-fluities, and that, upon extraordinary occasions, he can give something even to vanity and distinction. What then is the cause of our aversion to his situation, and why should those who have been educated in the higher ranks of life, regard it as worse than death, to be reduced to live, even without labour, upon the same simple fare with him, to dwell under the same lowly roof, and to be clothed in the same humble attire? Do they imagine that their stomach is better, or their sleep sounder, in a palace than in a cottage? The contrary has been so often observed, and, indeed, is so very obvious, though it had never been observed, that there is nobody ignorant of it. From whence, then, arises that emulation which runs through all the different ranks of men, and what are the advantages which we propose by that great purpose of human life which we call bettering our condition? To be observed, to be attended to, to be taken notice of with sympathy, complacency, and approbation, are all the advantages which we can propose to derive from it. It is the vanity, not the ease, or the pleasure, which interests us. But vanity is always founded upon the belief of our being the object of attention and approbation. The rich man glories in his riches, because he feels that they naturally draw upon him the attention of the world, and that mankind are disposed to go along with him in all those agreeable emotions with which the advantages of his situation so readily inspire him. At the thought of this his heart seems to swell and dilate itself within him, and he is fonder of his wealth, upon this account, than for all the other advantages it procures him.

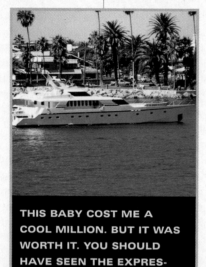

THIS BABY COST ME A COOL MILLION. BUT IT WAS WORTH IT. YOU SHOULD HAVE SEEN THE EXPRESSION ON R. J.'S FACE WHEN HE SAW IT!

CONSIDER

Do you think Adam Smith, the author of the excerpt, has a point? Why else would anyone want five Rolls-Royces, for example, in his or her garage? What other explanations make sense to you?

MORE ON THE NET

Review Adam Smith's *The Theory of Moral Sentiments* (http://melbecon.unimelb.edu.au/het/smith/moral.1), from which this excerpt is taken, in its entirely.

Source: Adam Smith, *The Theory of Moral Sentiments*, 1759.

Stakeholder
Someone who has a personal and consequential interest in the viability of the firm.

Corporate employees, too, concerned about job security, have a personal long-run stake in the corporation and in its continuity. After all, that's where they earn their daily bread. In this respect, corporate managers and their employees may be said to represent a class of corporate **stakeholders** who view the corporation quite differently than profit-maximizing corporate stockholders.

The $MR = MC$ rule of firm behavior has been largely overshadowed by these new theories. Corporate stability displaces profit maximization. Industrial planning and cooperative arrangements with government are preferred to the unfettered activity implied in the $MR = MC$ rule.

Lester Thurow of MIT raises the same doubts and criticisms of the $MR = MC$ rule:

American government may be bureaucratic and inefficient, but American industry is just as bureaucratic and inefficient. Who works for a firm that has not added some new layers of management in the last ten years? Who works for a firm that does not generate huge amounts of paper reports—most of which do not get read, much less acted upon? Who works for a firm that has fired secretaries and insisted that managers do their own typing since the introduction of word processors? What firm does not now have a bigger legal staff? What private managers are trying to improve decision making so that they can fire managers?

Where does squeezing the last dollar of profit out of production come into Galbraith's or Thurow's account of business activity? It doesn't. In their view, the preservation of the managerial class, even at the expense of profit, is what managers seek. His and Galbraith's conclusion is inescapable. The modern corporation, owned by a set of stockholders, is run by managers, for managers. The $MR = MC$ rule serves fewer and fewer decision makers. To them, the $MR = MC$ rule seems to be obsolete.

WHAT SURVIVES OF MARGINALISM?

What survives of the $MR = MC$ thinking? In a word, *everything!* For most economists, these broadside attacks on the $MR = MC$ profit-maximizing theory are parenthetical notes, interesting and perhaps even useful in explaining *some* aspects of corporate behavior. But they offer insufficient evidence to seriously undermine the basic postulate of the marginalist economists: Firms must be guided by the $MR = MC$ rule to maximize profit.

Defenders of the $MR = MC$ profit-maximization doctrine argue that our modern economy is still represented by the overwhelming number of firms that look more like our fishing firm than like the corporate giant. For these firms and for most corporations as well, the drive to maximize profit dominates.

Of course, even the strongest advocates of the marginalist view agree that firms are not really as one-dimensional as the profit-maximizing rule suggests. But, to them, profit maximizing is only a *first approximation to reality.* They accept the view that other interests, many identified by the critics of the $MR = MC$ rule of behavior, are included in the firm's set of goals. Still, they insist that as a first approximation, the $MR = MC$ approach to profit maximizing is not only logical, but empirically verifiable.

CHAPTER REVIEW

1. Entrepreneurs engage in two distinct activities. First, they oversee the production process, deciding on what goods to produce, what technologies to employ, and how to go about financing the enterprise. These decision-making activities require some degree of technical expertise. Second, entrepreneurs assume the risks and uncertainties associated with cost obligations and anticipated prices. The firm's profit depends on the spread between costs and prices.

2. Entrepreneurs don't just want to make profit, they want to maximize profit.
3. Marginal revenue is the change in total revenue generated by the change in the level of output.
4. Average revenue and price are identical. Each is total revenue divided by quantity.
5. Firms maximize profit by producing at that output where $MR = MC$. Production at any other output level may generate profit, but not the most profit. The maximum profit output level is the difference between price and average total cost multiplied by output, that is, $(P - ATC) \times Q$.
6. The $MR = MC$ rule applies as well to loss minimization. Because the firm's fixed cost is already committed in the short run, a loss-incurring firm should produce as long as price is greater than average variable cost at the $MR = MC$ output level. This loss will be less than the loss at a zero output level.

7. Richard Lester analyzed business surveys indicating that firms do not think in terms of marginal units. Fritz Machlup's response to Lester was that firms don't necessarily do what they say they do (or don't do). Milton Friedman shares Machlup's view that the $MR = MC$ rule to profit maximization is still the best way to explain firm behavior.
8. Other economists challenge the idea that firms seek to maximize profit. Alternative explanations address the sociological character of the modern corporation. These explanations offer the view that managers, as stakeholders in the corporation, may be more interested in empire building or maximizing sales, or simply safeguarding the viability of the corporation, than in maximizing profit.
9. Despite the variety of challenges to the $MR = MC$ rule of profit maximization, most economists still accept it as the dominant characteristic of modern businesses.

KEY TERMS

Profit maximization
Profit
Total revenue (TR)

Average revenue (AR)
Marginal revenue (MR)
$MR = MC$ rule

Loss minimization
Shutdown
Stakeholders

QUESTIONS

1. What talents would you expect to find in successful entrepreneurs? How would a college education benefit an entrepreneur? In what areas of entrepreneurial activity does a college education cease to be of much value to the entrepreneur?
2. Consider your own experiences. Do you think in terms of marginal revenue (or gain) and marginal cost when you decide to do or not do things? Cite examples.
3. How does total revenue differ from total profit?
4. What is the relationship between average revenue and price?
5. According to the $MR = MC$ rule, when the firm is producing at an output level where $MR > MC$, the firm should produce more. Explain.

6. Explain how the Boston Celtics of the NBA can use the $MR = MC$ rule to decide whether to sign a college superstar to a first-year $1 million contract.
7. How does the $MR = MC$ rule apply to loss minimization?
8. What rule should the firm use in deciding when to shut down production in the short run? In the long run?
9. What is the Lester–Machlup controversy about?
10. Some economists believe that firm behavior expressed by the $MR = MC$ rule of profit maximization is an oversimplification of reality. What views do they offer as alternative explanations of firm behavior?

PRACTICE PROBLEMS

OUTPUT	P	AR	MR	MC	AVC	ATC
0	$40.00			—	—	—
1	40.00			$31.00	$31.00	$54.00
2	40.00			28.00	29.50	41.00
3	40.00			31.00	30.00	37.67
4	40.00			34.00	31.00	36.75
5	40.00			37.00	32.20	36.80
6	40.00			40.00	33.50	37.33
7	40.00			43.00	34.86	38.14
8	40.00			46.00	36.25	39.13
9	40.00			49.00	37.67	40.22
10	40.00			52.00	39.10	41.40

1. Using the preceding table, calculate the firm's marginal revenue at each output level.
2. Calculate average revenue at each output level.
3. At what output level is profit maximized?
4. What is the firm's total profit?
5. Suppose price falls to $34. Where should the firm produce, if at all? Does the firm maximize profit or minimize loss at that output level? How much?
6. Suppose the demand curve is downward sloping, as shown in the following table. Calculate marginal revenue at each output level.

OUTPUT	P	AR	MR	MC	AVC	ATC
0				—	—	—
1	$140.00			$31.00	$31.00	$54.00
2	130.00			28.00	29.50	41.00
3	120.00			31.00	30.00	37.67
4	110.00			34.00	31.00	36.75
5	100.00			37.00	32.20	36.80
6	90.00			40.00	33.50	37.33
7	80.00			43.00	34.86	38.14
8	70.00			46.00	36.25	39.13
9	60.00			49.00	37.67	40.22
10	50.00			52.00	39.10	41.40

7. At what output level is profit maximized (or loss minimized)?
8. What is total profit (or total loss)?
9. Four firms produce four different goods. Determine which firms should shut down in the short run and/or in the long run, given the following data for each.

	PRICE	TC	AFC	AVC
CRAYON	$1.00	$80		
PENCIL	0.50			$0.65
PEN	2.00	700		1.40
HIGHLIGHTER	2.50		1.00	2.00

	QUANTITY MC = MR	SHUT DOWN IN THE SHORT RUN?	SHUT DOWN IN THE LONG RUN?
CRAYON	100		
PENCIL	200		
PEN	300		
HIGHLIGHTER	400		

WHAT'S WRONG WITH THIS GRAPH?

APPLYING THE *MR* = *MC* RULE

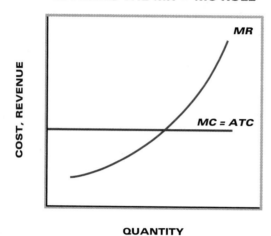

ECONOMIC CONSULTANTS

ECONOMIC RESEARCH AND ANALYSIS BY STUDENTS FOR PROFESSIONALS

The dream of many college students is to start a business, to be an entrepreneur. Professor Kim Deal always has a number of these students in her principles of economics class, and the questions are familiar. What does it take to start a business? Will the business succeed? Is it worth the risk?

Professor Deal has asked you to speak to her Principles of Economics class about entrepreneurship (after all, Economic Consultants was founded by entrepreneurs). Prepare a presentation for Professor Deal's class that addresses the following issues:

1. What economic factors do entrepreneurs need to consider when starting their own businesses?
2. How can entrepreneurs maximize the profit generated by their business ventures?
3. What resources are available for entrepreneurs and small businesses?

You may find the following resources helpful as you prepare this presentation for Professor Deal's class:

- *Entrepreneur* **Magazine** (http://www.entrepreneurmag.com/)—*Entrepreneur* provides professional information for entrepreneurs and small business owners.
- **A Virtual Solution** (http://www.avirtualsolution.com)— A Virtual Solution is an organization of entrepreneurs who assist businesses and professionals with day-to-day administrative tasks.
- **Be Your Own Boss** (http://www.be-your-own-boss.com/)—The Be Your Own Boss site contains information about how to start and operate a home-based business.
- **Entrepreneurs' Help Page** (http://www.tannedfeet.com/)—The Entrepreneurs' Help Page is created by a group of corporate attorneys, financial industry professionals, business owners, and consultants who are all in their twenties.

PRACTICE TEST

1. Marginal revenue is defined as
   a. a change in quantity demanded generated by a change in price.
   b. a change in price generated by a change in quantity demanded.
   c. a change in total revenue generated by a change in quantity.
   d. total revenue divided by quantity.
   e. quantity divided by total revenue.

2. Cost of producing bicycles:

QUANTITY (Q)	TOTAL COST (TC)	FIXED COST (FC)	VARIABLE COST (VC)
0	$ 50	$50	—
1	100	50	$ 50
2	140	50	90
3	150	50	100
4	180	50	130
5	230	50	180
6	300	50	250

   If the price of bicycles is $50, the profit-maximizing firm will produce
   a. 1.   d. 4.
   b. 2.   e. 5.
   c. 3.

3. The firm's total profit (or loss) will be
   a. a $20 loss.   d. a $60 profit.
   b. a $20 profit.   e. a $100 profit.
   c. a $60 loss.

4. Suppose the price fell to $30; the firm's total profit (or loss) now is
   a. a $50 loss.   d. a $60 profit.
   b. a $50 profit.   e. a $100 profit.
   c. a $60 loss.

5. If the firm suffers a loss at its loss-minimizing output, it has to decide whether to produce or shut down. The deciding factor is:
   a. If average total cost is higher than price, then shut down.
   b. If average variable cost is less than price, then shut down.
   c. If average variable cost is less than price, then continue to produce.
   d. If marginal revenue equals marginal cost, then continue to produce.
   e. If marginal cost is less than average variable cost, then continue to produce.

6. Now consider the long run. If the firm is at its loss-minimizing output, should it produce or shut down? The deciding factor is:
   a. If average total cost is higher than price, then shut down.

   b. If average variable cost is less than price, then shut down.
   c. If average variable cost is less than price, then continue to produce.
   d. If marginal revenue equals marginal cost, then continue to produce.
   e. If marginal cost is less than average variable cost, then continue to produce.

7. The profit-maximization rule is:
   a. Produce at the output level where marginal cost equals marginal revenue.
   b. Produce at the output level where the difference between marginal revenue and marginal cost is greatest.
   c. Produce at the output level where the difference between price and average total cost is the greatest.
   d. Produce at the output level where price is equal to average total cost.
   e. Produce at the output level where marginal cost, price, and average total cost are the same.

8. To determine how much profit is maximum profit, calculate
   a. marginal revenue times quantity, $MR \times Q$.
   b. marginal revenue minus average variable cost times quantity, $(MR - AVC) \times Q$.
   c. price minus average total cost times quantity, $(P - ATC) \times Q$.
   d. average total cost times quantity, $ATC \times Q$.
   e. price times quantity, $P \times Q$.

9. Suppose a firm maximizes profit by producing an output of 500. If its total fixed cost increases—say its rent goes up—profit will fall. How would the firm react? To continue to maximize profit under this higher cost condition, it will
   a. produce more than 500.
   b. produce less than 500.
   c. continue to produce 500.
   d. reduce its total variable cost—for example, hire fewer workers.
   e. reduce its marginal cost—for example, hire fewer workers.

10. The idea of profit maximization has come under attack from many quarters. Many economists believe that firms don't behave that way. They offer competing views of firm behavior, among them all of the following except
    a. survival of the managerial bureaucracy.
    b. empire building.
    c. maximizing sales.
    d. believing that stockholders, who would choose to maximize profit, do not determine firm behavior.
    e. believing that stockholders have become more sensitive to the noneconomic concerns of the firm.

10

IDENTIFYING MARKETS AND MARKET STRUCTURES

To market,
　to market
To buy a fat pig
Home again,
　home again
Jiggety-jig

Is the nursery rhyme familiar? Think back! Even as a little child, you were already acquainted with markets. And the nursery rhyme makes it very clear that markets are where you buy fat pigs. What the nursery rhyme does not tell you, however, is the price you pay for fat pigs. It doesn't tell

you whether goods are available to substitute for fat pigs, or whether the market's structure is a monopoly or an oligopoly, whether there is perfect or monopolistic competition. Perhaps that is asking too much.

This chapter and the two following go beyond the nursery rhyme. In this chapter we discuss how we go about identifying which goods belong to which markets and how to distinguish among the market structures. The next two chapters analyze how prices are determined in monopoly and oligopoly, and in perfectly competitive and monopolistically competitive markets.

THIS CHAPTER INTRODUCES YOU TO THE ECONOMIC PRINCIPLES ASSOCIATED WITH:

- THE USE OF CROSS ELASTICITY TO DEFINE MARKETS
- THE RELATIONSHIP BETWEEN FIRMS, INDUSTRIES, AND MARKETS
- MARKET STRUCTURES
- THE CHARACTERISTICS OF MONOPOLY
- THE CHARACTERISTICS OF MONOPOLISTIC COMPETITION
- THE CHARACTERISTICS OF PERFECT COMPETITION
- THE ROLE OF ADVERTISING

DEFINING THE RELEVANT MARKET

Rose Is a Rose Is a Rose Is a Rose?

When Gertrude Stein wrote her celebrated line "Rose is a rose is a rose is a rose," she was not making a botanical statement, nor was she implying that an American Beauty rose and a Peace rose are identical. That idea probably never occurred to her. In all likelihood, she knew the difference but figured it simply wasn't worth noting. Florists, certainly, and perhaps many other people, view roses very differently.

What is true for roses is also true for fish. To some people, and possibly to Gertrude Stein, "A fish is a fish is a fish" and "A fish market is a fish market is a fish market." But to fishermen, and to many others, differences among fish are worth noting.

After all, fish come in many varieties. Fish are sold in a market, *but what kinds of fish in what markets?* For example, how do you describe the market that sells only cod? Is it a fish market or a cod market? It makes a difference.

Suppose David Holtgrave switches from cod to halibut fishing. When he brings his catch to market, does he become the only fisherman in an exclusive halibut market, or is he still just one of the many fishermen selling fish in a fish market? In other words, are cod and halibut just two different kinds of the same good, or are they two very different goods?

If consumers are completely indifferent about cod and halibut—if they regard these fish as perfect substitutes—then what relevance does a halibut market have? Rather than being the only seller in a halibut market, David Holtgrave quickly discovers that he is actively engaged along with a hundred others in a more inclusive fish market.

Are fishermen in competition only with each other? Not at all. Imagine yourself at a restaurant looking through the menu. Each item competes with every other. You can choose grilled red snapper, broiled cod, fried catfish, or baked halibut. But you can also choose fried clams, tiger shrimp, or lobster tails. What, then, should fishermen regard as their **relevant market?** Is it strictly the fish market or the broader seafood market?

Yet there's more on the menu. There are cold sandwiches, hearty soups, salads, hamburgers, hot dogs, and pizza. Many who consider seafood as a possible meal can also consider these choices. The fishermen's relevant market may be not only fish or seafood but rather the larger set of goods associated with home-cooked or restaurant meals. In such an inclusive market, David Holtgrave finds himself competing with *thousands* of producers.

Relevant market
The set of goods whose cross elasticities with others in the set are relatively high and whose cross elasticities with goods outside the set are relatively low.

Movies and Entertainment

Consider a more commonplace example. Don't you sometimes relax after a long day of classes by going to an evening movie? Suppose four independent theaters are close to campus. Do you think the theater owners regard themselves as competing only with each other for your movie dollar?

Most likely not. They know that home videos offer a viable option. You can also relax at the video arcade, or at the bowling alley in the student union. That is, it may make more sense to describe the good you want as *entertainment*. In the entertainment market, the theater owners are only one group among many competitors.

Automobiles and Transportation

Does the automobile industry make up a relevant market, or are automobiles an integral part of the much larger transportation market that includes taxis, buses,

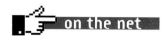

Is the U.S. Postal Service (http://www.usps.gov/) a monopoly?

railways, and airlines? After all, for most people, the primary purpose of the automobile is transportation.

Do videos compete with stereos, compact discs, television, and books in the home entertainment market? Do chocolate bars, peanuts, licorice, and popcorn compete in the snack food market? Ask interior decorators what they consider competing goods in their market. It's not only wall hangings, but paintings, lithographs, prints, and photographs as well. If Saudi Arabia were the only producer of crude oil, would it still be alone in its market? Probably not. In reality, Saudi Arabia's relevant market is not oil but energy. It competes with countries that produce hydroelectric power, coal, wood, solar power, and nuclear energy.

What about the U.S. Postal Service? It's often regarded as a monopoly even though it competes with Federal Express, Emery, United Parcel Service, Airborne Express, and Purolator, and with the telephone, the telegram, e-mail, and the fax in the communications market. This can hardly be called a monopoly.

COURTS AND MARKETS

How do you decide what constitutes *the* market? Deciding what goods make up what market is more than just an academic exercise. Unless we understand what makes a market, how can we decide whether a market is competitive? And if we decide to encourage competition, how do we know when we have succeeded? These are real issues.

In many cases, courts decide what constitutes the relevant market. In 1953, the government filed suit against DuPont, charging that it illegally monopolized the cellophane market. It argued that DuPont produced more than 80 percent of all cellophane and thus undermined the competitive character of the cellophane market.

In defending itself in court, DuPont did not contest its dominant position in cellophane. Instead, it argued that its relevant market was not cellophane but the much broader market of flexible packaging materials. Because DuPont controlled less than 20 percent of production in this market, the market's competitive character had not been damaged by DuPont's cellophane. Impressed by the argument, the court decided in favor of DuPont. The government appealed the verdict, but the Supreme Court upheld the lower court's decision.

In a similar case a few years earlier, a circuit court of appeals overturned a trial court's verdict on the same issue. The trial court denied the government's charge that Alcoa monopolized the aluminum market, accepting Alcoa's argument that the aluminum market consists of scrap aluminum as well as primary aluminum production. In this broader definition of the aluminum market, Alcoa had only a 33 percent share. In reversing the trial court's decision, the circuit court of appeals redefined the market to exclude scrap aluminum. In this narrower interpretation of the market, Alcoa had a 90 percent market share.

Do the courts possess some inner wisdom that allows them special privilege to decide on matters of market definition? Of course not. The decisions the courts hand down cannot be taken as revealed truth but rather as impartial judgments concerning the issue of what constitutes a relevant market.

How do the courts decide on relevant markets? Historically, the court system has borrowed heavily from economic theory. One of the conceptual tools it uses to identify the relevant market is *cross elasticity of demand,* a concept already analyzed in the chapter on elasticity of demand and supply. How are cross elasticities used?

INTERDISCIPLINARY PERSPECTIVE

THE DIAMOND NECKLACE

Here is a brief synopsis of Guy de Maupassant's short story *The Diamond Necklace:* Mme. Loisel is an unhappy Parisian housewife, frustrated because she married into a lifestyle considerably below the one to which she aspired. Her husband, an ill-paid, insignificant government bureaucrat, comes home one day with an unexpected invitation to the Commissioner's ball. Mme. Loisel reminds him that they cannot go because she has nothing appropriate to wear. To please her, he spends the modest inheritance he received from his father on a gown and persuades her to borrow jewelry from her very rich friend, Mme. Forestier.

Choosing a beautiful necklace, Mme. Loisel is ready. The evening at the ball was divine and the couple, happy for the moment, comes home late only to discover that the borrowed necklace is lost. Panic-stricken and finding no alternative but to replace it quickly, they find its replica at an expensive jeweler and borrow heavily at an exorbitant rate of interest to buy it. Forced to trim down their already scanty lifestyle, he works evenings and weekends while she launders clothes and prepare meals for boarders who now live with them. After 10 years of this unrelenting burden, the loan is repaid. Shortly thereafter, during a Sunday walk, Mme. Loisel encounters Mme. Forestier, who fails to recognize her old friend. Guy de Maupassant ends the story with their conversation:

"But Madam—I do not know—you must be mistaken—."

"No, I am Matilda Loisel."

Her friend uttered a cry of astonishment. "Oh, my poor Matilda! How you have changed—."

"Yes, I have had some hard days since I saw you; and some miserable ones—and all because of you—."

"Because of me? How is that?"

"Recall the diamond necklace that you loaned me to wear at the Commissioner's ball?"

"Yes, very well."

"Well, I lost it."

"How is that, since you returned it to me?"

"I returned another to you exactly like it. And it has taken us ten years to pay for it. You can understand that it was not easy for us who have nothing. But it is finished and I am decently content."

Madame Forestier stopped short. She said: "You say you bought a diamond necklace to replace mine?"

"Yes. You did not perceive it then. They were just alike."

And she smiled with a proud and simple joy. Madame Forestier was touched and took both her hands and replied:

"Oh! My poor Matilda. Mine were false. They were not worth over five hundred francs!"

To an economist, it's not just a heartbreaking story of misplaced pride, but a question of market identification. Why isn't the cross elasticity between a fake and diamond necklace high? After all, if people really can't tell them apart—Mme. Loisel and Mme. Forestier couldn't—aren't they perfect substitutes? Shouldn't they belong in the same market? What about excellent forgeries of great paintings? Often, museum curators are duped. Why shouldn't they be considered close substitutes, belonging to one market? Or is it strictly snob appeal—not the beauty of the good that matters, but the high price it commands—that accounts for the difference in markets?

CROSS ELASTICITY DEFINES THE MARKET

Let's go back to Gertrude Stein's celebrated "Rose is a rose is a rose is a rose." Exhibit 1 shows a spectrum of cross elasticities among a set of goods, enabling us to decide—as the court system does—what makes up a relevant market. For example, *if we choose* to define the relevant market as a set of goods whose cross elasticities within the set are infinite and are zero with all goods outside the set, then the market is limited to zone A.

Zone A describes a market whose goods are exclusively Peace roses. Every Peace rose in the market is a perfect substitute for every other, and each is perfectly non-substitutable with every other good. Imagine going to a florist on Mother's Day and buying a dozen American Beauty roses only to have them tossed into the trash when you get home because they're not Peace roses! It's as if you had brought home a dozen kangaroos!

If that's how people really feel about Peace roses, then Peace roses make up an exclusive market. If people react the same way about the American Beauty rose or the Madam del Bard rose or the Koba rose, then each belongs to a unique market. Each variety of rose is a very different good. Does it make sense, then, to refer to a market for roses?

Cross Elasticities in the Flower Market

But we don't really think about roses that way, do we? Even for those who can differentiate among roses and prefer the Peace rose to any other, a bouquet of American Beauty roses still is fine. For most people, they are excellent substitutes. An appropriate definition of a relevant market is this: a set of goods whose cross elasticities among any two goods in the set are *relatively high* and whose cross elasticities with goods outside the set are *relatively low*. This definition allows the relevant market in Exhibit 1 to include goods in zone B as well as zone A. That is to say, a rose market now makes sense.

What about tulips, carnations, and lilies? You don't have to be Dutch to tell the difference between a tulip and a rose. The cross elasticity of demand between roses and tulips is lower than the cross elasticities among the varieties of roses, but probably still relatively high. For many people, flowers are substitutable. Many people partial to roses will switch from a bouquet of roses to a bouquet of tulips if tulip prices fall. In this circumstance, the relevant market expands from zones A and B to include zone C. Zones A, B, and C describe a flower market.

CHECK YOUR UNDERSTANDING

Why do we speak of a flower market instead of specific markets for specific flowers?

EXHIBIT | 1

Zone A defines the Peace rose market; zones A and B define the rose market; zones A, B, and C define the flower market. Zone D lies outside these markets.

DELINEATING THE MARKET

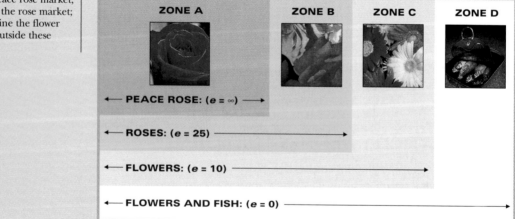

ZONE A   ZONE B   ZONE C   ZONE D

←—— PEACE ROSE: ($e = \infty$) ——→

←—— ROSES: ($e = 25$) ——————→

←—— FLOWERS: ($e = 10$) ——————————→

←—— FLOWERS AND FISH: ($e = 0$) ——————————————→

APPLIED PERSPECTIVE

NIKE: FROM SHOES TO SWOOSH

Is Nike a shoe company? If so, what's its market? Is it high-performance running shoes? That's precisely what the company thought it was when it started out. Phil Knight and three of his close friends who ran track at the University of Oregon saw a need for a better running shoe and sat down to design and produce one. The result was the sturdy "classic Nike" that revolutionized the small-niche running shoe market. How would you define that market? Think cross elasticity.

But Nike is more than a high-performance running shoe company. What happened? Why did Nike change? And how did the change affect its market? The catalyst that forced Nike out of its exclusive high-performance running shoe market was Reebok. How? In the early 1980s, Reebok launched its highly successful, attractively colored, soft-leather shoe designed for the growing aerobics market, particularly targeting women. It invaded Nike's market. Nike's market share in its own high-performance running shoe market began to weaken, forcing it to rethink who it was. Could Nike survive as a producer of high-performance running shoes when Reebok was capturing the

RAN BILLIONS AND BILLIONS OF MILES.

broader athletic shoe market? Nike saw only one option. It responded with a cross-training shoe of its own, a multiple-use shoe designed for the tennis, basketball, football, racquetball, and aerobics market. To get its "cross" message across, Nike signed superstar athletes to promote the shoe, among them the superstar of superstars, Michael Jordan. Very quickly, Nike realized it was selling Michael Jordan, not shoes. But Michael Jordan *was* the Nike shoe. And it worked!

What was left of the elite company that produced elite shoes for elite runners in an elite market? Gone! Reebok pushed less-than-reluctant Nike into a very different market, and Nike's successful response changed the character of the company for-

ever. The magic of Michael Jordan and his close identity with Nike propelled the company into possibilities that could not have been imagined when Nike was born. The company not only expanded out of its core market into athletic shoes but exploded from that into the almost limitless sports apparel and accessories market. It signed Tiger Woods and acquired the second-largest hockey equipment company to stretch its market boundary even further. It created Nike Town stores, which combined the likenesses of the Smithsonian, Disney World, and Ralph Lauren. Its Chicago store has a two-story photo mural of Michael Jordan and a mini–basketball court, and it has become the city's busiest tourist attraction, drawing more tourists than either Chicago's world-renowned Museum of Science and Industry or the Sears Tower. What's Nike now? Once again, think cross elasticity.

Nike understood that it was no longer a production company marketing shoes, but a marketing company whose principal asset was the *swoosh* logo. That *swoosh* could be put on virtually *anything*, transforming that *anything* into a Nike product. It was Nike's business to make those products *swoosh*-worthy.

Promoting the *swoosh* was all Nike had to do to promote its products. It found ingenious ways of getting the *swoosh* in your face, signing, for example, agreements with universities who, for multimillion-dollar grants from Nike, would display the *swoosh* on their football and basketball uniforms (provided as well by Nike). Televised college sporting events became, in effect, Nike events.

What business is Nike in? When you consider where the *swoosh* has taken it, it is entertainment. Its market is entertainment. But its horizons are not yet reached. Nike sees itself entering the vast mind-space market, where its competitors include Disney, Microsoft, and Sony. What's its market now? Think cross elasticity!

Although people may substitute varieties of flowers, it is highly unlikely that they think of substituting fish for flowers. The cross elasticity of demand between these two goods is zero. Even when the price of fish falls 99 percent, few people stick a fish in a vase. In Exhibit 1, fish belong in zone D.

How High Is a High Cross Elasticity?

But how high is a high cross elasticity? Economist F. M. Scherer suggests that when any two goods have a cross elasticity greater than or equal to 3.0, they can be regarded as belonging to the same market. In Exhibit 1, zone B includes a variety of roses whose cross elasticities, although less than infinity, are much higher than 3.0. These varieties qualify as belonging to the same market. But to what market? If the cross elasticities among roses, tulips, and carnations are all greater than 3.0, then according to Scherer's 3.0 criterion, the relevant market is the flower market.

Why 3.0? There's nothing magical about a 3.0 cross elasticity; it is simply an arbitrary benchmark along a spectrum of cross elasticities used to divide sets of goods into specific markets. In fact, most economists are reluctant to identify a specific benchmark cross elasticity, leaving the question of how high is high "up in the air."

CHECK YOUR UNDERSTANDING

Why is a cross elasticity of 3.0 chosen as high enough for goods to belong in the same market?

MARKETS AND MARKET STRUCTURES

Let's look at fish and fishermen again. Suppose the cross elasticities among a variety of fish are relatively high and the cross elasticities among fish and other goods are relatively low, so that fishermen see themselves as operating in a fish market. If you are a fisherman, it probably makes a big difference whether you are the only producer in that market or just one of several hundred. That is because the control an individual fisherman can exercise over the market depends primarily on how many fishermen there are. The number of producers influences how producers respond to decisions consumers make, to decisions other producers in their market make, and to the market prices they face.

The most direct way to determine how many fishermen make up the market is simply to count them. **Market structure** is defined by the count. With only one fisherman, the market structure is defined as a monopoly. On the other hand, if considerable numbers, perhaps thousands of fishermen, are bringing their catch to market, then the market structure is defined as perfectly competitive. With few producers, the market is defined as an oligopoly. With more than a few producers, but still less than considerable numbers, the market structure is considered monopolistic competition.

As you see, the most important characteristic that distinguishes one market structure from another is *the number of producers selling in the market*. Exhibit 2 plots these structures along a spectrum that records numbers of producers in a market—from one to considerable numbers—marking out the ranges on the spectrum that identify specific market structures.

Each market structure is defined by the number of firms, the ease or difficulty with which new firms can enter the market, and the quantity and closeness of substitute goods produced by the firms in the market. Monopoly and perfect competition occupy polar points on the spectrum. A monopoly consists of only one firm that produces goods that have no substitutes; no other firm can enter the market. The perfectly competitive market structure on the far right in Exhibit 2 consists of a considerable number of firms producing goods that are perfect substitutes for each other. New firms can easily enter these markets.

Market structure
A set of market characteristics such as number of firms, ease of firm entry, and substitutability of goods.

CHECK YOUR UNDERSTANDING

What defines a market structure?

EXHIBIT|2

THE MARKET STRUCTURE SPECTRUM

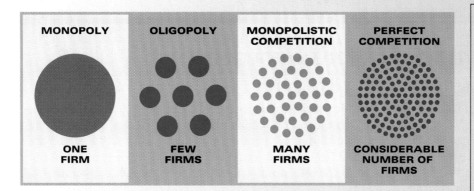

MONOPOLY — ONE FIRM

OLIGOPOLY — FEW FIRMS

MONOPOLISTIC COMPETITION — MANY FIRMS

PERFECT COMPETITION — CONSIDERABLE NUMBER OF FIRMS

The market structure spectrum consists of a continuum of markets characterized by the numbers of firms in them, the ease or difficulty that firms have in entering them, and the quantity and closeness of substitute goods. At the polar points on the spectrum are monopoly and perfect competition. The monopoly structure consists of only one firm producing goods that have no substitutes. No other firm can enter.

The perfectly competitive market structure consists of a considerable number of firms producing goods that are perfect substitutes for each other. Firms can enter easily into these markets.

The oligopolistic market structure consists of few firms. Entry into an oligopoly is relatively difficult.

The monopolistic competition market structure consists of greater than a few, but fewer than considerable numbers of firms. Firms can enter this market, but typically without the ease allowed in perfectly competitive markets.

Few honest-to-goodness examples of either pure monopoly or perfectly competitive markets exist. *The real world is essentially a world of oligopoly and monopolistic competition,* covering a rich variety of markets, some more monopolistic than competitive, others more competitive than monopolistic.

Oligopoly (*olig-* means "few") describes a market with only a few producers. Entry into an oligopoly is relatively difficult. As important a market structure as oligopoly is in our economy—most Fortune 500 firms are oligopolies—economists are less than exact in quantifying "fewness." In fact, fewness is identified not only by the number of producers in the market (typically more than 2, but less than 20), but also by firm behavior, that is, the way firms in oligopoly take into consideration what others will do when they do something. For example, an oligopolistic firm is keenly aware that whatever it does—say, change its price or change its output—it is being closely watched by other firms in the oligopoly, who, being directly affected by the change, will counteract by changing their own price or output levels. Anticipating this kind of reaction may inhibit the oligopolistic firm from initiating any change in the first place. Its behavior may reflect the wise prescription: "Don't do unto others what you don't want them to do unto you." In oligopoly, the fewness of firms creates **mutual interdependence** among the firms.

Mutual interdependence
Any price change made by one firm in the oligopoly affects the pricing behavior of all other firms in the oligopoly.

To the right of oligopoly in Exhibit 2 is monopolistic competition. This market structure consists of more than a few but fewer than a considerable number of firms. New firms can enter monopolistically competitive markets more easily than they can enter an oligopoly, but less easily than they can enter a perfectly competitive market. The market structure tends to become more competitive the greater the number of firms.

THE WORLD OF MONOPOLY

Size Is Not Important

We usually think of bigness and monopoly as synonymous, and for good reason. Typically, the firms closest to dominating any market are large, highly financed, large-volume producers and major employers of labor. *But it isn't the firm's size that makes it a monopoly.* If a fisherman doesn't produce 100,000 or even 1,000 but just 100 fish per run, yet is the only producer and seller in the fish market, that fisherman is a monopolist. It's the "oneness" in the market that defines the **monopoly.**

Monopoly
A market structure consisting of one firm producing a good that has no close substitutes. Firm entry is impossible.

Industry
A collection of firms producing the same good.

The Firm Is the Industry

An **industry** is a collection of firms producing the same good. If only one firm produces the good, then *the firm is the industry.*

Suppose only one fisherman produces and sells fish in the market. Panel *a* in Exhibit 3 portrays the market demand curve for fish, and panel *b* portrays the demand curve that the fish monopolist faces. As you see, they are identical.

Look at panel *a*. At a price of $1, the quantity demanded by the community is 20,000 fish. When price falls to $0.80, quantity demanded increases to 21,000. Look at panel *b*. *The monopoly rightly regards the community's demand curve for fish as its own.* If the community is willing to buy 20,000 fish at $1, the monopoly correctly identifies that willingness as its own ability to sell 20,000 fish. The monopoly also knows that if it lowers the price to $0.80, it can increase sales to 21,000.

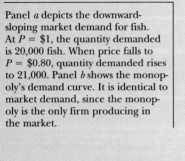

EXHIBIT | 3

A MONOPOLY'S DEMAND CURVE

Panel *a* depicts the downward-sloping market demand for fish. At *P* = $1, the quantity demanded is 20,000 fish. When price falls to *P* = $0.80, quantity demanded rises to 21,000. Panel *b* shows the monopoly's demand curve. It is identical to market demand, since the monopoly is the only firm producing in the market.

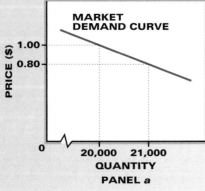

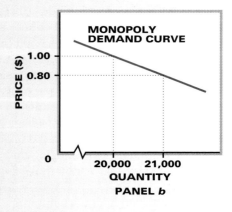

PANEL *a*

PANEL *b*

No Entry into the Industry

One reason some monopolies stay monopolies is that would-be competition finds entering the industry impossible. Several factors contribute to a monopoly's staying power.

THE NATURAL MONOPOLY Some markets simply cannot support more than one firm. The fixed cost involved in setting up production for some goods is so high that the firm must have access to a large market to bring its average total cost down to reasonable ranges.

Consider, for example, the potential market and the costs involved in bringing another baseball team to Cincinnati. Suppose a new team, the Cincinnati Blues, becomes the next expansion team in the American League. Before the first ball is pitched, it must build a superdome stadium with parking for 20,000 cars. That's an awful lot of building and real estate. The team needs ballplayers, too. A superstar earns $5 million per year whether the ballpark is filled or only 2,000 diehard fans show up at the game. These are examples of fixed costs.

The problem for the Blues is that the Cincinnati Reds at Cinergy Field—a monopolist in Cincinnati until the Blues arrived—have equal access to Cincinnati's baseball market. The bad news is illustrated in Exhibit 4. The demand curve, *D*, depicts the demand for baseball in Cincinnati. Before the Blues enter the market, the Reds maximize profit by charging $7 and drawing 40,000 to their ballpark. At 40,000, *ATC* = $5. The Reds' profit is $80,000.

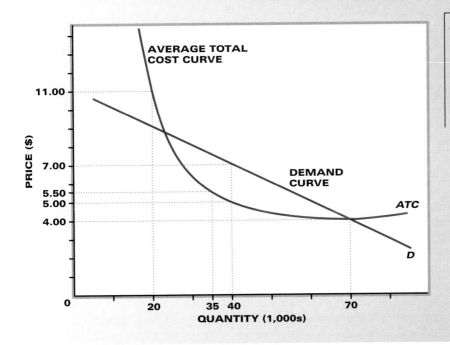

THE NATURAL MONOPOLY

As a monopolist, the Reds maximize profit at *P* = $7, *ATC* = $5, and attendance at 40,000. When the Blues enter the market at *P* = $7, each team's *ATC* = $11, and attendance is split at 20,000. Both incur losses. If they compete, price falls to $4, total attendance increases to 70,000, and each *ATC* = $5.50. Both incur losses. Only one can survive.

EXHIBIT | 4

Why can't two baseball teams succeed in a city like Cincinnati while both the New York Yankees (http://www.yankees.com/) and the New York Mets (http://www.mets.com/) can succeed in New York City?

Natural monopoly
The result of a combination of market demand and firm's costs such that only one firm is able to produce profitably in a market.

CHECK YOUR UNDERSTANDING

What's the key characteristic of a natural monopoly?

Now suppose the Blues enter the market and can wrestle half of the Reds' fans away to their superdome. Success? Not by a long shot! With 20,000 attendance each for Reds and Blues games, the *ATC* for both climbs to $11. Each now loses ($7 − $11) × 20,000 = $80,000.

If they price tickets down to $4 and succeed in driving total attendance up to 70,000, they each draw 35,000 fans, but they have *ATC*s of $5.50. And they still incur losses.

After all, total fixed cost remains the same regardless of market size. The stadiums don't change. The parking lots are still the same size. The ballplayers still earn their attractive salaries. But now, neither the Reds nor the Blues can stay in business at the higher average total cost shown in Exhibit 4. One team must fold. The survivor becomes a **natural monopoly,** so called because market splitting in the industry comes only at the expense of driving up the firms' average total cost to prohibitive levels.

Like baseball teams, city bus companies are natural monopolies. They require heavy fixed-cost expenditures on large garages, staff, and buses. A sizable market for passenger usage is necessary to bring the average total cost per passenger mile within reach of reasonable bus fares. If two bus companies compete in the same community, each with its own garages, staff, and buses, neither can survive by servicing one-half the community's market demand. One must fold. The other survives as a natural monopoly.

That's why we typically find only one water company, only one electric power company, and only one cable television company in the community market. Public utilities are typically natural monopolies.

EXCLUSIVE ACCESS TO RESOURCES   Some firms, by chance or design, acquire exclusive access to a nonreproducible good, such as a mineral resource. For example, if a firm acquires all the diamond mines in the world, it becomes a monopoly. After all, how can any other firm enter the diamond market unless it has access to diamonds? In the same way, any firm acquiring all the oil wells in the world becomes a monopoly.

Just as easily as acquiring exclusive access to resources creates monopolies, new discoveries of these resources by other firms can undo the monopolies. Prior to World War II, the world's entire known supply of helium was located in the Texas panhandle and New Mexico. Because of helium's strategic role in military preparedness, the U.S. government exercised monopoly control. The result of this monopoly control was dramatically played out in 1937 when Germany, unable to obtain helium, was forced to use highly combustible hydrogen to lift its celebrated zeppelin, the *Hindenburg*. While attempting to land in Lakehurst, New Jersey, the zeppelin exploded and within seconds was engulfed in flames. Instantly, the world learned about helium and monopoly.

Helium is still a strategic military resource. It not only is an inert lighter-than-air gas, but also has an exceptionally low boiling point. Therefore, aerospace programs use it to chill rocket engines before launch and to pressurize fuels into the rocket engines. But the monopoly has been broken. Since the 1950s, helium has been found in Algeria, South Africa, Canada, and Russia.

Resource monopolies are also destroyed when new technologies create viable alternatives to the resource. Coal made wood an obsolete energy resource. Nuclear and solar energies are now reducing our dependence on coal and oil. Exclusive access to a resource that becomes increasingly substitutable makes the industry increasingly competitive as well.

HISTORICAL PERSPECTIVE

PURITY LAWS AND BARRIERS TO ENTRY

Beer is central to German diet and culture. Germans consume more than 3 billion liters of beer annually, or more than 300 liters per capita, the highest in the world.

You would think, then, wouldn't you, that the German market would be a magnet for foreign brewers? Not so. Barriers to entry are formidable. Foreign brewers confront the German beer purity law—based upon Bavarian custom—enacted in 1516, which permitted only four ingredients in the beverage: water, hops, barley, and yeast.

Many non-German brewers substitute rice, maize, sorghum, and other cost-effective raw cereal for barley in the initial stages of brewing. The German beer purity law allows no such substitutes. Germans brewers claim that the purity law serves the public interest, promoting public health by safeguarding beer drinkers from the possible harmful additives used by foreign brewers. Competitors don't buy that argument at all. They see the purity law as a pure and simple ploy to shut them out of the German market. After complaining for decades about the unfairness of the law, they brought their case to the European Economic Community. In 1987, the European Court of Justice repealed this ancient law, arguing that the purity law created intra-European trade barriers that were in direct violation of the Rome Treaty (Article 30) banning protectionism. The repeal led to a spirited German consumer outcry that lower-standard foreign products would invade their prized beer market. Although officially repealed, the purity law's *tradition* is intact. The German beer market remains a difficult one for foreign competitors to enter, and even those who want to sell German-style beer still cannot substitute ingredients.

On the other hand, German brewers enjoy competing in foreign markets. They have established thriving industries in the United States, Mexico, China, and elsewhere. They compete with brewers worldwide who produce countless types of beer based on formulas similar to the Bavarian one, but many add different cereals, fruit juices, or chemicals to enhance the flavor and foaming ability. More recently, the market for German beer has expanded to include microbrewers worldwide, especially in North America. Smartly, many microbrewers adapted the more traditional slow- and pure-brewing techniques to emulate the German process and to compete with German beer in both North America and Europe, often adjusting the taste of their beers to the likes and dislikes of specific nations, regions, and ethnic groups.

Are purity laws unique to Germany or to the beer industry? Certainly not. Europeans have been fighting the entry of American meat products into their markets on grounds that American meat contains unsafe hormones used in cattle feed, even though the U.S. Department of Agriculture has approved their use.

But not all purity laws are designed as barriers to entry. Objection to genetically manipulated or so-called Frankenstein foods reflects scientifically based health care concerns. For example, the French blocked imports of Canadian genetically modified canola into the European Union because they feared it was unsafe. Canadian Prime Minister Jean Chrétien conceded that the industry has not come up with the kind of indisputable proof that the French are looking for. Can you blame the French?

THE PATENT SYSTEM Monopolies are sometimes government-promoted. To encourage firms to develop new technologies and even new goods, the government grants **patents**—monopoly rights—on innovations for 20 years. By law, others are prohibited from producing patented technologies and goods. In this way, the patent holder is assured that imitators will not undermine the profit expected from introducing the new technology or good into the market. Patent holders can, however, license their monopoly rights to others.

Patent
A monopoly right on the use of a specific new technology or on the production of a new good. The monopoly right is awarded to and safeguarded by the government to the firm who introduces the new technology or good.

The U.S. Patent and Trademark Office (http://www. uspto.gov/) issues patents in the United States.

Monopolistic competition
A market structure consisting of many firms producing goods that are close substitutes. Firm entry is possible but is less open and easy than in perfect competition.

Oligopoly
A market structure consisting of only a few firms producing goods that are close substitutes.

Polaroid's instant-film camera was introduced under the patent system. Xerox's breakthrough in photocopier technology was secured by patent. Most of the miracle drugs, from penicillin to AZT, have been patent protected. More than 5 million major and minor technological changes have been introduced into our economy under the protection of the patent. The familiar and convenient stay-on tabs on beer and soft drink cans were patent protected.

Even patent-bred monopolies, however, are constantly eroded by the creation of newer and technically more advanced close substitutes. Innovations replace innovations. New patents make older ones obsolete. In most cases, the useful monopoly life of a patent seldom reaches its full 20 years.

ACQUISITION, ACQUISITION, AND MORE ACQUISITION Andrew Carnegie, the first U.S. steel mogul, built his empire by consuming, or buying out, his competition. He devoted his time and energy to organization and financial manipulation. "Pioneering," he philosophized, "don't pay."

Carnegie bought control of his first steel firm in 1873, and by the close of the century owned a fair slice of his competition. When he left the steel business, Carnegie was producing more steel than the combined steel output of Great Britain. He sold out to his equally aggressive rival J. P. Morgan. By 1901 Morgan had combined 11 large firms, including Carnegie's, to form a new colossus, U.S. Steel.

The strategy that produced the Carnegie and Morgan empires was not unusual during the years of America's greatest industrial growth. Many Fortune 500 giants owe their creation to the simple technique of firm expansion by firm acquisition.

THE WORLD OF MONOPOLISTIC COMPETITION AND OLIGOPOLY

What about monopolistic competition? As the term suggests, **monopolistic competition** is a market structure that has elements of both monopoly and competition. **Oligopoly,** too, has elements of competition and monopoly, but oligopolistic firms have more market power than firms in monopolistic competition.

Perhaps the best way to view these hybrid market structures is to consider them as sets of firms struggling unsuccessfully to achieve monopoly positions. Their lack of success in achieving monopoly status results from their inability to shut out competition. Other firms actually break into their markets.

No Easy Entry, but Entry Nonetheless

Entry of new firms into monopolistically competitive and oligopoly markets, particularly those markets characterized by firms with substantial fixed costs, isn't easy. Not everybody can compete with USX (formerly U.S. Steel). Imagine how much money it takes to get that first ton of steel rolling off the production line.

Still, as difficult as it is to put together the financial resources required to compete successfully with USX, some firms managed to do it. USX is not the sole provider of steel. The steel industry, which is composed of not one but a *few* firms, might be described as an oligopoly.

In reality, however, steel is no longer an oligopoly. The few steel firms in the United States compete not only among themselves but with steel companies in Japan, India, Nigeria, Brazil, Canada, and the European Economic Community. After all, steel produced in Germany or Nigeria can substitute perfectly well for steel produced in Gary, Indiana.

Adding up all the steel-producing companies in the world that have access to the U.S. market means that USX, far from being a firm in oligopoly, operates in a world of sizable competition. But USX's market is even more competitive than the number of firms competing in the steel industry would suggest.

Firms Producing Close Substitutes

Steel competes with steel in the steel industry and with aluminum and fiberglass, both close substitutes for steel, in the automobile market. It also must compete with aluminum and reinforced concrete, both close substitutes for steel, in the construction market. The real extent of competition in an oligopolistic market—in this case the automobile and construction markets—therefore must be measured by the *number of firms in all the industries producing close substitutes.*

This relationship between firms, industries, and markets is illustrated in Exhibit 5.

The firms that compose an industry in Exhibit 5 are spaced horizontally. For example, the 5 steel firms shown in the top row make up the steel industry. The second row shows the 5 firms producing reinforced concrete; they make up the reinforced concrete industry. The third row shows the firms that make up the aluminum industry.

These 15 firms, representing three industries, make up the construction market, which is spaced vertically in boxes in the last column of Exhibit 5.

As much as USX would like to be a monopoly in the construction market, it has to compete not only with other steel firms within its industry but also with firms in other industries that produce close substitutes.

We can find close substitutes everywhere. Fire extinguishers, dishwashing detergents, 35-mm cameras, sunglasses, stereo receivers, spaghetti, nursing home insurance, garbage bags, blenders, razors, paint, vacuum cleaners, facial tissues, popcorn poppers, microwave ovens, air conditioners, hair dyes, canned tomatoes, clock radios, lawn mowers, clothes dryers, sewing machines, fast foods, VCRs, personal

How do Pepsi (http://www. pepsi.com/) and Coca-Cola (http://www.cocacola.com/) use their Web sites to differentiate their numerous colas?

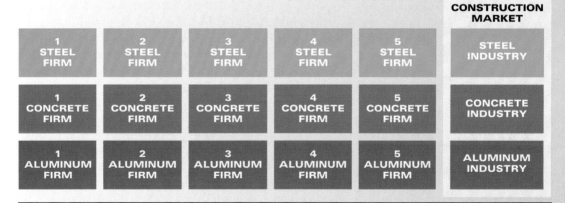

RELATIONSHIP BETWEEN FIRMS, INDUSTRIES, AND MARKETS

Industries consist of firms producing the same good. Markets consist of sets of industries producing close substitute goods. The steel industry's five firms compete with the aluminum industry's five firms and the reinforced concrete industry's five firms in the construction market.

Product differentia-tion
The physical or perceived differences among goods in a market that make them close, but not perfect, substitutes for each other.

computers, and software are just a few of the familiar goods you own or will own some day.

Each good is produced by many firms that offer some degree of **product differentiation.** For example, *Consumer Reports* once rated 18 different washing machines sold by 18 different firms in the washing machine industry. No two are exactly alike, although all are considered close substitutes. Of the top 4 recommended—Sears, Whirlpool, KitchenAid, and Maytag—3 were actually produced by Whirlpool. How close can close substitutes be?

Consider the soft drink industry. Can you really tell the difference between Coca-Cola and Pepsi-Cola? Don't be too sure. Blind tests show that many people cannot even distinguish between Coca-Cola and 7-Up once their taste buds have been washed by any carbonated drink. But people still have favorites and pay a higher price for their choice. You probably know people who buy Coke even when Pepsi is on sale at the supermarket.

Holiday Inn offers accommodations that, for most people, are close substitutes for accommodations offered at Sheraton, Ramada, Radisson, Best Western, Howard Johnson, Marriott, Hilton, Hyatt, and Hampton Inn. They are not identical, but all seem to serve the same purpose.

And if you get a headache trying to choose among hotels, you can always take MacNeil Labs's Tylenol. But Tylenol is a close substitute for American Home's Anacin, Sterling's Aspirin, Bristol-Myers's Bufferin and Excedrin, Rorer's Ascriptin, Burroughs Wellcome's Empirin, and DuPont's Percogesic.

As More Firms Enter the Market, Firm Demand Curves Become More Elastic

Let's trace the impact of entry on a firm's demand curve in a monopolistically competitive market. Consider the demand for Coca-Cola, the most recognized product in the world. An Atlanta pharmacist, John Pemberton, who made his living concocting homespun snake-oil remedies, invented Coca-Cola in 1886. In the beginning, Coca-Cola was just another of his medicinal potions. Already in poor health, Pemberton quickly sold two-thirds of his interest in the product for $1,200, and in 1888, just before he died, he sold the remaining third for $500. Ingenious marketing subsequently converted Coca-Cola from a questionable medicine to a popular soft drink.

Coke remains an original. As you know, dozens of close substitutes are now on the market, but only Coca-Cola can claim to be the real thing. It is 99.8 percent water and sugar, but it's the remaining 0.2 percent that counts! Coca-Cola's transition from a monopoly to one of many firms in monopolistic competition is traced out in Exhibit 6.

Let's look at Coca-Cola in the soft drink market before any substitutes appear. As a monopoly, its demand curve is the demand curve for the entire market, shown as D_1 in Exhibit 6. If monopolist Coke raises the price of its two-liter bottle from $1 to $1.25, the quantity demanded of Coke falls from 1,000 to 900. Smart move for Coke? Probably. After all, price elasticity of demand within the $1 to $1.25 price range is 0.47, so that Coke's total revenue increases.

Now suppose five firms enter the soft drink market. What happens? Coke is now one of six firms in monopolistic competition. While market demand remains at D_1, Coke's own demand curve shifts inward, from D_1 to D_2. Although no longer a monopoly, it still has a dominant position in the market, selling 500 at the $1 price. That's a 50 percent market share.

EXHIBIT|6

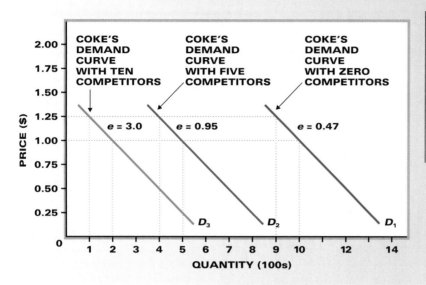

THE DEMAND CURVE FOR COCA-COLA: BEFORE AND AFTER SUBSTITUTES APPEAR ON THE MARKET

Before substitute goods appear on the market, Coca-Cola has a monopoly position. Its demand curve is identical to the market demand curve, D_1. When five new firms enter the market, Coca-Cola's market share falls. Its demand curve, D_2, shifts to the left. Market demand, D_1, remains unchanged. When five more firms enter the market, Coca-Cola's market share falls even further. Its demand curve, D_3, shifts further to the left, while market demand, D_1, remains unchanged.

Note that Coke's demand curve is still downward sloping. Coke could still raise its price to $1.25 and sell Coke, but if it does, the quantity demanded of Coke falls from 500 to 400. Consumers respond to Coke's price increases in one of three ways: Some stay with Coke, even with five substitutes available at $1. That's **brand loyalty!** Some decide to switch to any of the five substitutes, and some switch out of soft drinks altogether. Still a smart move for Coke? Probably so. Price elasticity of demand within the $1 to $1.25 range on Coke's demand curve, D_2, is 0.95, so that its total revenue still increases.

But suppose more firms enter the market, raising the number of firms competing with Coke to ten. The monopolistically competitive market for soft drinks is getting more crowded. Coke's demand curve shifts inward again, from D_2 to D_3. Although no longer dominating the market, Coke is still a major seller. Look at D_3. At a price of $1, Coke sells 200, which represents 20 percent of market share. But now Coke may be reluctant to raise its price to $1.25. Why? With ten other soft drinks to choose from, consumers are more likely to find a close substitute. Some consumers still remain loyal to Coke, but these loyalists become fewer and fewer. If Coke raises its price to $1.25, it sells 100. Smart move? Probably not. Why? Because price elasticity of demand within the $1 to $1.25 range on demand curve D_3 is 3.0, so that Coke's total revenue now falls.

Brand loyalty
The willingness of consumers to continue buying a good at a price higher than the price of its close substitutes.

CHECK YOUR UNDERSTANDING

Why does Coke become increasingly reluctant to raise its price when more firms enter the market?

The Role of Advertising

Firms in monopolistic competition, like Coca-Cola, and firms in oligopoly have a strong incentive to advertise. They expect advertising to undo the effects of increasing competition.

INTERDISCIPLINARY PERSPECTIVE

WHO CAN BE LOYAL TO A TRASH BAG?

Loyalty is a highly valued quality in our society. Friendships and family thrive on it. Loyalty often explains why sports fans endure with love and affection the agony of chronic defeat. Dogs are devotedly loyal to their owners, and grateful dog lovers, in turn, are loyal to their pets. But how far does loyalty reach? For example, does loyalty to a particular brand of canned soup make sense? Can you really be loyal to a trash bag? The answers may surprise you.

When generic products were coming on strong a few years ago, J. Walter Thompson, the New York–based ad agency, measured consumers' loyalty to brands in 80 product categories. It found that the leader in market share was not necessarily the brand-loyalty leader. At that time, Bayer aspirin was the market share leader among headache remedies, but Tylenol had the most loyal following.

Thompson measured the degree of loyalty by asking people whether they'd switch for a 50 percent discount. Cigarette smokers most often said no, making them the most brand-loyal consumers (see table). Film is the only one of

HMM, THE INGREDIENTS ARE IDENTICAL, AND IT'S CHEAPER. . . . OH HECK, I'LL STAY WITH MY BRAND.

the top five products that consumers don't put in their mouths—so why such loyalty? According to Edith Gilson, Thompson's senior vice president of research, 35-mm film is used by photography buffs, who are not your average snapshooter: "It's for long-lasting, emotionally valued pictures, taken by someone who has invested a lot of money in his camera." Plenty of shoppers will try a different cola for 50 percent off, and most consumers think one plastic garbage bag or facial tissue is much like another.

CONSIDER

Test yourself. Suppose prices of your favorite brands rose by 25 percent. How loyal would you be to the brands you prefer in the table?

MORE ON THE NET

Facial tissues, according to J. Walter Thompson, are a product with low consumer loyalty. What is Kimberly-Clark (http://www.kimberly-clark.com/), makers of Kleenex, doing to increase product differentiation and brand loyalty?

Source: Adapted from *Fortune,* August 5, 1985. Copyright © 1985 by FORTUNE. Reprinted with permission.

HIGH-LOYALTY PRODUCTS	MEDIUM-LOYALTY PRODUCTS	LOW-LOYALTY PRODUCTS
CIGARETTES	COLA DRINKS	PAPER TOWELS
LAXATIVES	MARGARINE	CRACKERS
COLD REMEDIES	SHAMPOO	SCOURING POWDER
35-MM FILM	HAND LOTION	PLASTIC TRASH BAGS
TOOTHPASTE	FURNITURE POLISH	FACIAL TISSUES

Exhibit 7 compares the before-advertising and the after-advertising position of a monopolistically competitive firm, such as Coca-Cola. The goal of advertising is to increase the firm's **market share** while reducing consumer sensitivity to price changes.

Market share
The percentage of total market sales produced by a particular firm in a market.

INCREASING MARKET SHARE Lowering price is one way to persuade consumers already in the market to switch brands, but advertising may engineer that switch without lowering price. It provides consumers with selective information—sometimes misinformation—that may be the only information available to many in the market. It often suggests associations between the advertised good and such highly valued activities, events, or institutions as sex, sports, and family. It is typically highly repetitious, to create consumer familiarity and confidence.

Not all advertising is slick or sleazy; much is genuinely informative. If Chrysler offers a 7-year or 70,000-mile warranty, that's important information for the consumer. Consumers may have difficulty finding the lowest-priced goods without those double-page newspaper advertisements published by supermarkets. And how would you know what movie is playing where and at what time if theaters didn't advertise?

MAKING DEMAND MORE INELASTIC Advertising's response to the growing flood of substitutes in a monopolistically competitive market is to deny quite aggressively that any substitutes exist! How can advertising perform such magic? By simply insisting. In almost all cases, the advertising message is identical: *There are no substitutes. Our product is different.* Over and over again, in these efforts at product differentiation, we are told that Coke is the real thing, that others—notably Pepsi-Cola—are unsatisfying imitations. If its advertised message is successful, a firm can raise its price without much decrease in quantity demanded.

Exhibit 7 shows that successful advertising can shift a firm's demand curve outward to the right. For example, at $1, the quantity demanded of advertised Coca-Cola increases from 200 to 400 cases, a sizable 100 percent change. Successful advertising lowers the firm's price elasticity of demand. Before advertising, an increase in price from $1 to $1.25 cut quantity demanded from 200 cases to 100, or by 50 percent. After advertising, the same price increase cuts quantity demanded from 400 to 350 cases, or only by 12.5 percent. Price elasticity of demand within the $1 to $1.25 price range falls dramatically from a before-advertising level of 3.00 to 0.60 after advertising.

on the net

How does Chrysler (http://www.chrysler.com/) use the Internet to advertise its products? Is Chrysler different from General Motors (http://www.gm.com/) or Ford (http://www.ford.com/)?

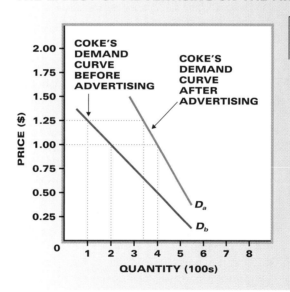

THE EFFECT OF ADVERTISING ON THE FIRM'S DEMAND CURVE

After advertising, Coke's demand curve shifts to the right and becomes more inelastic.

EXHIBIT|7

THE WORLD OF PERFECT COMPETITION

If in monopolistic competition the goods that firms produce are close substitutes, in **perfect competition** they are absolutely *perfect* substitutes.

If in monopolistic competition there are many firms in the industry, each with an accountable market share, in perfect competition there are many, many firms in the industry, each with an insignificant share of the market.

If in monopolistic competition it is not too difficult for new firms to enter the industry, in perfect competition there are no barriers whatsoever to firm entry.

Perfect competition
A market structure consisting of a large number of firms producing goods that are perfect substitutes. Firm entry is open and easy.

If in monopolistic competition product differentiation allows each firm choice in raising or lowering price, in perfect competition firms producing perfect substitutes have no influence whatsoever on price.

Let's examine each of these characteristics of firms operating in perfectly competitive markets.

Perfectly Competitive Firms Produce Perfect Substitutes

Can you really distinguish between Ben & Jerry's and Baskin-Robbins ice cream? Perhaps if you tasted each from its own designer container, you could (or think you could). But even then, they taste alike, don't they? To most people, Ben & Jerry's and Baskin-Robbins are very, very close substitutes. To some people, they are not just very, very close substitutes, but *perfect* substitutes. These people are simply incapable of distinguishing between them.

Some goods are like that. They are *characteristically* perfect substitutes. For example, salt. Each ounce of salt is identical to every other ounce. If your life depended on it, you couldn't distinguish a local supermarket's brand from a national one.

Potato farmers in Idaho produce identical goods. Each Idaho potato looks exactly like an Idaho potato, they taste exactly alike, they *are* exactly alike. Each potato is a perfect substitute for any other. What about fish? On the grill, one freshly caught one-pound red snapper is exactly like any other freshly caught one-pound red snapper. They are perfect substitutes as well. Chances are you could name dozens of other goods that are perfect substitutes. Milk? If dairy cows are dairy cows, then milk from one dairy is a perfect substitute for milk from any other dairy.

Create your own illustration or example of a perfect substitute. Go to the Interactive Study Center at http://gottheil.swcollege.com and click on the "Your Turn" button to submit your example. Student submissions will be posted to the Web site, and perhaps we will use some in future editions of the book!

Perfectly Competitive Firms Have Insignificant Market Share

Imagine a tornado slicing through Kim Deal's 200-acre potato farm. Bad news for Kim? Of course. Bad news for potato eaters? Not really. After all, Kim's farm is just one of 50,000 farms producing in the national market, so that without Kim, the potato market loses only 1/50,000 of its total output. Who really notices? Kim's market share is so close to zero that it becomes virtually impossible to detect the dent in the market. It's equivalent to pouring a bucket of water into the Pacific Ocean and expecting to notice a change in the ocean's depth.

Suppose Kim, instead of suffering the tornado, doubles her output. That represents a mighty significant increase for her, doesn't it? But what about its impact on the market? Again, zero. The fact is that Kim, *no matter what she does,* is an insignificant producer. Whether she doubles her potato output or drops out completely, it makes absolutely no difference to the market.

The Kim Deal scenario is illustrative of all firms producing in perfectly competitive markets. They are all, as the saying goes, just small potatoes. You don't have to be 1 of as many as 50,000 firms. Competing in a market with just 100 firms may well produce the same results. Consider, for example, the bed and breakfast market in Stratford, Ontario, Canada, home of the Shakespearean Festival. Because Stratford is a relatively small town and the festival runs only during the summer months, there are few hotels, so festival enthusiasts are accommodated by approximately 1,000 resident bed and breakfasts. With few exceptions, these are perfect substitutes. People don't typically go about differentiating. An overnight stay is an overnight stay. Because there are as many as 1,000, if any 1 should drop out, it would hardly be noticed. For the same reason, if any bed and breakfast doubles its output—making two bedrooms available instead of one—that too would go by undetected in the market. Each bed and breakfast has an insignificant share of the market.

Perfectly Competitive Firms Have Free Entry

In monopolistic competition, barriers to entry are less than formidable, and in many cases they are easily overcome. For example, it may be somewhat difficult to break into the catalog mail-order business to compete with Victoria's Secret or L.L. Bean, but it is far less difficult to enter the microbrewery industry and easier still to enter the garment industry—dresses, suits, blouses, shirts, coats—where a pair of scissors and a sewing machine might do (although most garment firms operate with more extensive use of machinery and labor).

In perfect competition, firm entry is everywhere free and open. If you want to join Kim in the potato market, she can't keep you out. If you're thinking about entering the grass-cutting business, get yourself a mower and start cutting. If you want to make T-shirts, no one can stop you. If you've always dreamed of opening a florist shop, you can. If you want to get into the egg business, start with a few laying hens, and you're on your way. There are simply no restrictions to firm entry.

Perfectly Competitive Firms Cannot Influence Price

Let's put these features of perfect competition together—perfect substitutes, so many firms that each has an insignificant market share, and free entry—to show how they undermine the perfectly competitive firm's ability to influence price. Consider again Kim Deal's potato farm.

CHECK YOUR UNDERSTANDING
What happens if a firm in perfect competition raises price?

If Kim raises her price by so much as a penny, consumers will switch to any one of her many competitors because, to potato farmers and to consumers, all Idaho potatoes are perfect substitutes. Why would anyone choose to buy a higher-priced potato from her when an identical potato is available at a lower price? What happens to Kim's firm if she insists on raising price? The quantity demanded for its potatoes falls immediately to zero.

Exhibit 8 illustrates the perfectly competitive firm's inability to influence price and the resulting shape of the demand curve for the firm's goods.

Panel *a* represents the market demand curve for potatoes. It's downward sloping. At a price of $0.65 per pound, quantity demanded is 44 billion pounds. It really makes no difference to consumers whether 500, 5,000, or 50,000 firms produce them. It's strictly price that determines how many pounds are demanded.

What about the individual potato-growing firm? How does it view its market? Suppose each of 50,000 firms produce 800,000 pounds. As far as any one of them is concerned, it can probably increase its own output by 10 percent—to 880,000 pounds—without straining capacity. It hires more labor and applies more chemical technology to increase yield per acre. On the other hand, the firm may find it difficult doubling output and close to impossible increasing output tenfold.

In other words, no matter what any of the 50,000 potato-growing firms do or want to do, the quantity that any one of them can produce is always insignificant compared to the market's total output. After all, the 800,000 pounds produced by any one firm represents only 1/500 of 1 percent of the 44 billion pounds that reach the market! Even if a firm adds another 800,000 pounds to production, wouldn't that doubling be virtually lost in a market of 44 billion pounds? That's precisely

EXHIBIT | 8

MARKET DEMAND CURVE AND THE DEMAND CURVE FACING A FIRM IN PERFECT COMPETITION

Panel *a* depicts the market demand curve for potatoes, D_1, in a perfectly competitive market. The market demand curve is downward sloping. When $P = \$0.65$, quantity demanded is 44 billion pounds. Panel *b* shows the demand curve facing a firm in the potato market. As far as the firm is concerned, it can sell any quantity it chooses—800,000 pounds or 1.5 million pounds—at $P = \$0.65$. The horizontal shape of the firm's demand curve reflects its ability to sell any quantity it chooses at $P = \$0.65$.

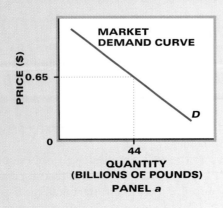

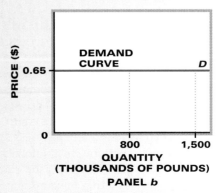

why each firm in perfect competition never needs to consider the effect of its own production on price.

Look again at Exhibit 8, this time at panel *b*. The firm knows that it can sell all the potatoes it is capable of producing. It can sell its 800,000 pounds or even push output up to 1.5 million pounds and still sell every pound at the market's price of $0.65.

If the firm can sell all it wants at $0.65, what incentive does it have to lower price below $0.65? None at all. On the other hand, because it produces goods that have perfect substitutes, it can't raise its price above $0.65 without inviting disaster. At $0.66, quantity demanded falls to zero. For these reasons, the perfectly competitive firm sees the demand curve for its own potatoes as horizontal.

CHECK YOUR UNDERSTANDING

Why is the demand curve for a perfectly competitive firm horizontal?

PUTTING TOGETHER A SCORECARD ON MARKET STRUCTURES

Producers typically know their markets well. They know what kind of competition they face as well as something about the relative ease or difficulty other firms experience in entering their markets. They even have a good idea about the price elasticity of demand for the goods they produce. They know whether it pays to advertise. They can probably locate themselves easily on the scorecard in Exhibit 9.

Let's review. A monopoly faces no competition, and it has the added security of knowing that no new entry into the market is possible. It views the market as its own. The demand curve it faces is downward sloping. The incentive to advertise is relatively weak since it need not fight for market share, although it may still choose to advertise in order to shift its market demand curve out farther to the right.

A firm in perfect competition operates in a very different world. It is overwhelmed with competitors and faces the prospect of even more competition, since entry into its market is open and easy. It produces a good that is identical to those produced by its competition, and it recognizes its own insignificance as a member of its market. The demand curve it faces is horizontal. Under these conditions, advertising is of no use to the firm.

EXHIBIT|9

SUMMARY SKETCH OF MARKET STRUCTURES

TYPE OF MARKET	NUMBER OF FIRMS	TYPE OF PRODUCTS	ENTRY	INFLUENCE OVER PRICE?	DOES THE FIRM WORRY ABOUT RESPONSES OF ITS COMPETITION?
PERFECT COMPETITION	MANY, MANY	IDENTICAL	FULL	NO	NO
MONOPOLISTIC COMPETITION	MANY	DIFFERENTIATED	DIFFICULT/EASY	YES	NO
OLIGOPOLY	FEW	USUALLY DIFFERENTIATED	DIFFICULT	YES	YES
MONOPOLY	ONE	—	IMPOSSIBLE	YES	NO

In the monopolistically competitive and oligopolistic market structures, entry into the market is possible but not always easy. Firms produce goods that are close but not perfect substitutes, and each firm therefore faces a downward-sloping demand curve for its good. A firm in monopolistic competition can raise its price without having the quantity demanded of its good fall to zero, but the presence of close substitutes raises the price elasticities of demand for its goods. For this reason, firms in monopolistic competition find that it pays to advertise. They advertise to capture a larger piece of the market and to reduce price elasticity of demand.

CHAPTER REVIEW

1. Cross elasticity of demand is an important tool used to associate specific goods to specific markets. A market consists of a set of goods whose cross elasticities among goods within the set are relatively high and whose cross elasticities among goods outside the set are relatively low.

2. Market structures can be scaled along a spectrum, with monopoly at one extreme and perfect competition at the other. Oligopoly, with a few producers, lies close to monopoly. Between oligopoly and perfect competition is monopolistic competition.

3. Monopoly has only one seller. The firm is the industry. Monopoly is maintained through barriers to entry. These may take several forms, including natural monopoly, exclusive access to resources, patents, and acquisition.

4. Monopolistic competition and oligopoly are marked by the potential entry of firms, although entry may be difficult. Firms in these markets produce close substitutes. The more substitutable products in these markets become, the more elastic are the demand curves facing individual firms. Entry into these industries reduces each firm's market share.

5. Advertising plays a significant role in monopolistic competition and oligopoly. Firms advertise to increase market share and to make their demand curves more inelastic.

6. Perfect competition consists of many, many firms producing goods that are perfect substitutes. Entry is easy in perfect competition. The demand curve facing a firm is horizontal. The firm's market share is insignificant, so the decision by the firm to sell more or less has no impact on price.

KEY TERMS

Relevant market

Market structure

Mutual interdependence

Monopoly

Industry

Natural monopoly

Patent

Monopolistic competition

Oligopoly

Product differentiation

Brand loyalty

Market share

Perfect competition

QUESTIONS

1. Why would a monopolist choose to advertise? Why wouldn't a firm in perfect competition choose to advertise?

2. What advantages would a firm in monopolistic competition gain from advertising?

3. What is the relationship between cross elasticities of demand and the identification of specific goods to specific markets?

4. What is meant by market structure?

5. What is a natural monopoly? Give specific examples of monopolies you consider natural.

6. Why does the government issue patents?

7. Describe the major factors distinguishing market structures.

8. Explain why an economist and a zoologist, looking at horses, cows, and automobiles, would not choose the same two out of three as having something in common.

9. Why is the size of the firm not a very reliable criterion in identifying monopoly?

10. There is hardly any good that does not have substitutes. Discuss.

11. What is the relationship between firms, industries, and markets?

12. What distinguishes oligopoly from monopolistic competition?

13. Why is the demand curve for a firm in monopolistic competition downward sloping?

PRACTICE PROBLEMS

1. Given the following price and average total cost data, pick the natural monopoly and explain your choice.

FIRM A

QUANTITY	PRICE	AVERAGE TOTAL COST (*ATC*)
1	$9.00	$6.00
2	8.00	5.00
3	7.00	4.00
4	6.00	3.50
5	4.50	3.00
6	3.50	2.50
7	2.00	2.00
8	1.00	1.75

FIRM B

QUANTITY	PRICE	AVERAGE TOTAL COST (*ATC*)
1	$9.00	$6.00
2	8.00	4.00
3	7.00	3.35
4	6.00	3.25
5	4.50	3.50
6	3.50	4.50
7	2.00	5.50
8	1.00	7.00

2. The following demand schedules are given for Todd Fletcher's T-Shirt Company. What market structures is Todd Fletcher *not* in?

Calculate the firm's market share at $9 and at $6 with 0, 10, and 20 competitors.

PRICE	QUANTITY, WITH ZERO COMPETITORS	QUANTITY, WITH TEN COMPETITORS	QUANTITY, WITH TWENTY COMPETITORS
$10	10,000	5,000	1,000
9	11,000	6,000	2,000
8	12,000	7,000	3,000
7	13,000	8,000	4,000
6	14,000	9,000	5,000

3. Identify the market structures associated with Firm A, Firm B, and Firm C.

PRICE	MARKET DEMAND	FIRM A DEMAND	FIRM B DEMAND	FIRM C DEMAND
$5	200	200	50	0
4	400	400	100	0
3	600	600	150	3
2	800	800	200	3
1	1,000	1,000	250	3

4. Complete the table for a Taco Bell burrito special, using any numbers you wish, to illustrate (1) Taco Bell's most effective advertising and (2) its more moderately effective advertising, relative to the demand schedule for the burrito special with no advertising. Explain your choices.

PRICE	QUANTITY DEMANDED WITH NO ADVERTISING	QUANTITY DEMANDED WITH MOST EFFECTIVE ADVERTISING	QUANTITY DEMANDED WITH MODERATELY EFFECTIVE ADVERTISING
$4.50	100		
$4.00	150		
$3.50	200		
$3.00	250		
$2.50	300		
$2.00	350		

5. Complete the table for a Taco Bell burrito special, using any numbers you wish, to illustrate the impact on Taco Bell of (1) Wendy's most effective advertising and (2) its more moderate effective advertising. Explain your choices.

PRICE	QUANTITY DEMANDED WITH NO WENDY'S ADVERTISING	QUANTITY DEMANDED WITH MOST EFFECTIVE WENDY'S ADVERTISING	QUANTITY DEMANDED WITH MODERATELY EFFECTIVE WENDY'S ADVERTISING
$4.50	100		
$4.00	150		
$3.50	200		
$3.00	250		
$2.50	300		
$2.00	350		

WHAT'S WRONG WITH THIS GRAPH?

THE EFFECT OF ADVERTISING ON THE FIRM'S DEMAND CURVE

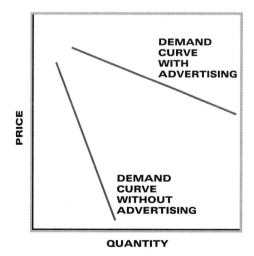

DEMAND CURVE WITH ADVERTISING

DEMAND CURVE WITHOUT ADVERTISING

PRICE

QUANTITY

ECONOMIC CONSULTANTS

ECONOMIC RESEARCH AND ANALYSIS BY STUDENTS FOR PROFESSIONALS

Misty Coffman is an engineer who, in her spare time, invents gadgets for around the home. One of Misty's inventions is a mailbox with a light attached to the top. When mail is delivered, the light automatically turns on to alert the recipients that their mail has arrived. Misty has never considered profiting from her inventions, but a mail-order catalog company has expressed interest in selling her mailbox.

Misty has approached Economic Consultants for advice about how to protect the rights to her mailbox invention, yet still profit from it. Prepare a report for Misty that addresses the following issues:

1. Where can inventors look to ensure that their inventions are original?

2. If these inventions are original, what do inventors need to do to obtain a patent?

3. Once a patent is obtained, what economic concepts does an inventor need to consider to maximize the profit earned from the invention?

You may find the following resources helpful as you prepare this report for Misty:

- **U.S. Patent and Trademark Office (PTO)** (http://www.uspto.gov/)—The pto provides general information about patents. Visitors may also search for patents (http://patents.uspto.gov/).

- **Patents Pending** (http://www.patentspending.com/home.html)—The Office of Patents Pending home page discusses the processes and procedures involved in the issuance of a patent.

- **NameProtect.com** (http://www.nameprotect.com/)—NameProtect.com offers patent, copyright, and trademark services for the inventor, entrepreneur, company, and attorney.

- **Delphion Intellectual Property Network** (http://delphion.com/)—The Delphion Intellectual Property Network provides access to more than 26 years of PTO patent descriptions.

- **The National Association of Patent Practitioners (NAPP)** (http://www.napp.org/)—NAPP, a nonprofit organization, supports patent practitioners in matters relating to patent law, its practice, and technological advances.

- **Patent Cafe** (http://www.patentcafe.com/)—The Patent Cafe contains directories and resources for inventors.

- **National Patent Association (NPA)** (http://www.nationalpatent.com/)—The NPA provides legal and political information about patents.

PRACTICE TEST

1. Economists classify all markets into _____ different market structures.
   a. 4
   b. 6
   c. 8
   d. 10
   e. 12

2. The concept used by economists to determine whether goods belong to the same market is
   a. product differentiation.
   b. market share.
   c. cross elasticity.
   d. brand loyalty.
   e. barriers to entry.

3. What can you say about monopoly?
   a. The firm is the industry.
   b. Because a monopoly faces no competition, its demand curve is not downward sloping.
   c. The firm is larger than any other one in the industry.
   d. The good it produces has low cross elasticities with all other goods in the industry.
   e. The good it produces has high cross elasticities with all other goods in the industry.

4. A natural monopoly results from
   a. the ownership of patent rights.
   b. a combination of market demand and high fixed costs such that only one firm can operate profitably.
   c. acquisition of other firms by a firm through the natural process of competition.
   d. exclusive access to natural resources.
   e. the natural inclination of oligopolistic firms in the same industry to coordinate output and price policy.

5. Should firms in perfect competition advertise? No. It makes no sense because they
   a. produce agricultural goods, and these goods are not suitable for advertising.
   b. know that if they all advertise, they cancel each other out, so that no one can gain from advertising.
   c. have no control over price and can sell as much as they want at the prevailing price anyway.
   d. each face a horizontal demand curve, so that advertising will only distort demand by creating a perfectly competitive downward-sloping curve.
   e. are perfectly competitive, so they do not view each other as real competitors.

6. One difference between oligopoly and monopolistic competition is that
   a. the monopolistically competitive industry has fewer firms.
   b. goods are differentiated in oligopoly, not in monopolistic competition.
   c. both have barriers to firm entry, but barriers in oligopoly are impossible to overcome.
   d. fewer firms compete in oligopoly than in monopolistic competition.
   e. goods in oligopoly have higher cross elasticities among themselves than goods produced in monopolistically competitive industries.

7. Consider the monopolistically competitive industry alone. You know that
   a. it has insurmountable barriers to firm entry.
   b. it has differentiated products.
   c. some of its firms are monopolies, while others are competitive.
   d. it has a small number of very large firms, and each faces a horizontal demand curve.
   e. because it is monopolistic as well as competitive, firms produce goods that are poor substitutes.

8. Brand loyalty is associated with
   a. monopoly, because having no alternatives, consumers eventually become loyal to the goods the monopolist produces.
   b. monopolistic competition, because monopolistically competitive firms advertise to create a stronger loyalty to their goods.
   c. monopolistic competition, because not producing differentiated products, monopolistically competitive firms must find a way to create a loyalty to their goods.
   d. perfect competition, because perfectly competitive firms cannot influence price, so they compete by creating brand loyalty.
   e. monopoly, oligopoly, monopolistic competition, and perfect competition, because all firms want to increase their market share, so each engages in creating brand loyalty.

9. As more firms enter a monopolistically competitive industry, each firm's demand curve
   a. shifts to the left and becomes more elastic.
   b. shifts to the right and becomes more elastic.
   c. shifts to the right and becomes more inelastic.
   d. shifts to the left and becomes more inelastic.
   e. does not shift but becomes more inelastic.

10. If you were thinking about starting up your own new firm, the industry you would find easiest to enter would be
    a. monopoly, because there is only one firm in the industry.
    b. oligopoly, because firms have considerable market power and therefore are less concerned about you entering.
    c. monopolistic competition, because firms have differentiated products, which means you can enter to compete with a product of your own.
    d. perfect competition, because there is free entry.
    e. unclear, because all have barriers to entry that you can overcome, so it really depends on the circumstances particular to the good you intend to produce.

11

PRICE AND OUTPUT IN MONOPOLY, MONOPOLISTIC COMPETITION, AND PERFECT COMPETITION

Suppose, after graduation, you land a job as an economist on the White House staff. And suppose, on the Friday evening of your first week, just when you are about to leave the executive wing of 1600 Pennsylvania Avenue, the president drops by to chat. In the course of conversation, he tells you that he is concerned about the degree of monopoly in our economy and wonders if there is anything he should do about it. He asks you: "What is it that monopolists *really* want?" What would you say?

Wouldn't you want to emphasize that monopolists, like everybody else in business, simply want to maximize profit? That's it. Nothing more. Yet, were you to take the president's question to the man and woman on the street, or even to members of Congress, or to network news broadcasters, chances are that their overwhelming response would be: "Monopolists

THIS CHAPTER INTRODUCES YOU TO THE ECONOMIC PRINCIPLES ASSOCIATED WITH:

- PRICE, OUTPUT, AND ECONOMIC PROFIT UNDER CONDITIONS OF MONOPOLY
- PRICE, OUTPUT, AND ECONOMIC PROFIT FOR THE FIRM IN MONOPOLISTIC COMPETITION
- NORMAL PROFIT
- PRICE, OUTPUT, AND ECONOMIC PROFIT FOR THE FIRM IN PERFECT COMPETITION
- THE PERFECTLY COMPETITIVE FIRM'S SUPPLY CURVE
- MARKET SUPPLY IN PERFECT COMPETITION
- THE SCHUMPETERIAN ILLUSTRATION OF LOW PRICE AND HIGH EFFICIENCY UNDER CONDITIONS OF MONOPOLY

want to raise prices." For those unschooled in the principles of economics, raising prices is synonymous with raising profits.

Perhaps that's why George Stigler, 1982 Nobel laureate in economics, wrote in the very first sentence of the chapter on monopoly in his *Theory of Price:* "A monopolist is no less desirous of profits than a competitive firm and is in a somewhat better position to achieve them."

Stigler wanted to make the point, early and with clarity, that it is the monopoly's *market position,* not motivation, not morality, not strategy, and not objective, that distinguishes the monopolist from any other entrepreneur. If a monopolist firm discovers that it could increase profit by lowering price, don't you think it would? In fact, many do precisely that. There are even situations where the price chosen by the monopolist is lower than the price that would be obtained if the market were competitive. How do profit-maximizing monopolists go about determining what price to charge and how much to produce?

PRICE AND OUTPUT UNDER MONOPOLY

Let's look again at our fishing economy, except this time let's analyze the ice manufacturing industry that caters to the fishermen. Suppose only one firm on the island, the Nick Rudd Ice Company, manufactures ice. Nick Rudd is a monopoly. Fishermen have no alternative but to buy their ice from Rudd.

Suppose Exhibit 1 represents the market demand that the Nick Rudd Ice Company faces. It is a **price-maker.** It can charge any price it wishes, but it knows that at higher prices, fewer tons will be demanded.

Although it cannot dictate how much ice people should demand at different prices, it can select price and quantity combinations from Exhibit 1. For example, it can choose $275 per ton and count on people demanding 50 tons, or it can lower price to $125 per ton and sell 350 tons.

How does Rudd go about finding the profit-maximizing price and quantity combination? As we saw in Chapter 9, the profit-maximizing rule is simple: Keep producing as long as $MR > MC$. When $MC > MR$, cut back. Profit maximization occurs at $MR = MC$.

The $MR = MC$ Rule Applied

Let's look at how Nick Rudd Ice Company derives its marginal revenue schedule. The data are shown in Exhibit 2.

Total revenue, TR, is price multiplied by quantity:

$$TR = PQ$$

Marginal revenue, MR, measures the change in TR generated by a change in Q:

$$MR = \frac{\Delta TR}{\Delta Q}$$

For example, increasing production from 200 to 250 tons, that is, adding 50 tons to production, increases revenue by $43,750 - $40,000 = $3,750. The marginal revenue for each of these 50 additional tons of ice, then, is $3,750/50 = $75.

Does it pay Rudd to produce the 250th ton of ice? It depends on the marginal cost of that 250th ton. Rudd consults its cost schedule, shown in Exhibit 3.

Columns 3, 5, and 7 record total cost, average total cost, and marginal cost across the production range of 0 to 600 tons. Recall that marginal cost is the increase in total cost when an additional unit of output is added to production.

Columns 4 and 8 record the total and marginal revenues

MARKET DEMAND FOR ICE

PRICE	QUANTITY (TONS)
$300	0
275	50
250	100
225	150
200	200
175	250
150	300
125	350
100	400
75	450
50	500
25	550

EXHIBIT | 1

EXHIBIT 2

PRICE AND REVENUE SCHEDULE FOR THE NICK RUDD ICE COMPANY

QUANTITY (TONS)	PRICE	TOTAL REVENUE	MARGINAL REVENUE
0	$300	$ 0	$ 0
50	275	13,750	275
100	250	25,000	225
150	225	33,750	175
200	200	40,000	125
250	175	43,750	75
300	150	45,000	25
350	125	43,750	−25
400	100	40,000	−75
450	75	33,750	−125
500	50	25,000	−175
550	25	13,750	−225

Economic profit
A firm's total revenue minus its total explicit and implicit costs.

derived from Exhibit 2. Column 9 subtracts the total cost of column 3 from the total revenue of column 4; this is the monopoly's **economic profit.**

When production is zero, Rudd's total cost is $4,000 because it is still obligated to pay its fixed costs. No revenue is earned at zero production.

Now look what happens when Rudd increases production to 50 tons. Total cost increases from $4,000 to $8,500. Total revenue is $13,750, generating an economic profit for Rudd of $13,750 − $8,500 = $5,250. Is Rudd satisfied? Is 50 tons Rudd's profit-maximizing output? Not by a long shot.

Look at the marginals of columns 7 and 8. At the 50th ton, $MR = \$275$ and $MC = \$90$. The profit-maximizing rule counsels Rudd to increase production. As long as $MR > MC$, every additional ton of ice produced adds to the company's profit. As Exhibit 3 records, $MR > MC$ at every output level up to the 300th ton. At the 300th, $MR = MC = \$25$.

EXHIBIT 3

COST AND REVENUE SCHEDULES FOR THE NICK RUDD ICE COMPANY

QUANTITY (TONS)	PRICE (P)	TOTAL COST (TC)	TOTAL REVENUE (TR)	AVERAGE TOTAL COST (ATC)	AVERAGE VARIABLE COST (AVC)	MARGINAL COST (MC)	MARGINAL REVENUE (MR)	PROFIT
(1)	(2)	(3)	(4)	(5)	(6)	(7)	(8)	(9)
0	300	$ 4,000	$ 0					$ −4,000
50	275	8,500	13,750	$170	$90	$ 90	$ 275	5,250
100	250	11,000	25,000	110	70	50	225	14,000
150	225	12,250	33,750	82	55	25	175	21,500
200	200	13,250	40,000	66	46	20	125	26,750
250	175	14,350	43,750	57	41	22	75	29,400
300	150	15,600	45,000	52	39	25	25	29,400
350	125	17,100	43,750	49	37	30	−25	26,650
400	100	18,950	40,000	47	37	37	−75	21,050
450	75	21,300	33,750	47	38	47	−125	12,450
500	50	24,300	25,000	49	41	60	−175	700
550	25	28,200	13,750	51	44	78	−225	−14,450
600		33,200	0	55	49	100	−275	−33,200

Note: Figures are rounded to the nearest dollar.

Rudd's profit-maximizing output, then, is 300 tons, generating a monopoly profit of $29,400. *Although the monopoly can charge any price it wishes, the price that yields the highest profit is $150.* If Rudd raises price to $200—it can, of course—it would sell only 200 tons and make a profit of $26,750. But why would Rudd choose $26,750 profit instead of $29,400?

CHECK YOUR UNDERSTANDING

If a monopolist faces no competition, why doesn't it charge the highest price possible?

Maximum Profit, but Less Than Maximum Efficiency

Look at Rudd's average total cost in column 5. At 300 tons, $ATC = \$52$. It is not the most efficient level of output, is it? By expanding output to 450 tons, Rudd could cut its ATC to $47. Shouldn't the monopoly want to produce at its lowest average cost? No! That's not why Nick Rudd is in the ice-making business. If producing at the lowest point on its ATC curve—maximum efficiency—results in the monopoly generating less than maximum profit, why do it? Rudd is interested in maximizing profit, not maximizing efficiency.

Exhibit 4 translates Exhibit 3 into graphic form.

The ATC and MC curves are U-shaped. The monopoly's demand curve, identical to the market demand curve for ice, is downward sloping. The downward MR curve cuts the rising MC curve at 300 tons. At that output, price is $150 and the average total cost is $52. The shaded rectangle represents the monopoly's profit.

As long as market demand and Rudd's cost structures remain unchanged, the monopoly will have no inclination to move from producing 300 tons at a price of $150. As far as Rudd is concerned, it is willing to stay at that price and output forever.

PRICE AND OUTPUT DETERMINATION IN MONOPOLY

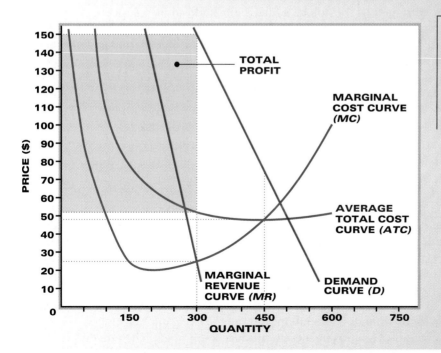

The monopoly, like all other firms, maximizes profit where $MR = MC$. The MC curve meets the MR curve at an output of 300 tons. At $Q = 300$, the price—read off the demand curve—is $150, and the average total cost—read off the ATC curve—is $52. The shaded rectangle represents ($150 − $52) × 300 = $29,400, which is the monopoly's profit.

EXHIBIT|4

PRICE AND OUTPUT IN MONOPOLISTIC COMPETITION

Monopolies, however, don't last forever. And certainly not in this ice-making business. Let's suppose a number of high school graduates decide not to follow their families' fishing tradition but instead go into ice making. It isn't an altogether crazy idea. The ice business looks profitable. The patent on ice-making technology that has protected Rudd's monopoly position in the market has expired.

With a little imagination, a lot of energy, and a big enough loan from the bank, a number of new ice manufacturers appear on the market. Wayne Coyne, for example, adds a new twist to ice making: color. Fishermen can now buy blue ice, green ice, red ice, and yellow ice, as well as Rudd's clear.

Product Differentiation in Monopolistic Competition

To many people, ice is ice is ice. But to many others, and perhaps to most, product design, color, packaging, and particular taste add to quality. People really do have strong preferences for product differentiations, even though they may agree that the products are functionally equivalent.

Holding such preferences or product loyalties is not necessarily unreasonable. If people are satisfied with the product's performance, they are usually reluctant to experiment with substitutes, even when the price of substitutes is slightly lower. Why tamper with success? That's why newcomers to the industry typically face an uphill struggle for a share of the market.

If new firms are going to break into the market, they must provide something that isn't already offered. The trick is to *differentiate* the product sufficiently to claim uniqueness, and yet keep it close enough to existing competition. In this way, consumers may be coaxed to experiment, knowing that even if they switch, they get pretty much what they got before, and maybe more.

Let's suppose new firms enter the market to manufacture colored ice. A few fishermen, intrigued by the colors, switch from Rudd to its competitors. Their products are new, different, and yet still keep fish fresh. Some fishermen use red ice for red snapper, yellow ice for yellow perch, blue ice for blue marlin, and several colors for rainbow trout. But not everybody is impressed with color. Some fishermen, those with more traditional tastes, stay with Rudd. Yet all the competing kinds of ice are regarded by consumers as close substitutes.

Rudd's Short-Run Equilibrium Position in a Monopolistically Competitive Market

The new entries into the ice business must be upsetting to Rudd, now an ex-monopoly. But there's nothing it can do. It has no control over entry. With several competing ice firms now in the market, Rudd's market share dwindles. Look at Exhibit 5.

Rudd's demand curve shifts to the left, from D to D'—the size of the shift depending upon the number and success of Rudd's competitors—and becomes more elastic. If Rudd raises price above its competitors' price, it must now expect some of its customers to switch to its competitors. Before, as a monopolist, Rudd never had to worry about competition.

What about Rudd's cost curves? They remain unchanged. Picture its ice factory. With or without competition, the same ice-making machines are used. The same quantity of labor is needed to produce a ton of ice. The same insurance pol-

CHECK YOUR UNDERSTANDING ▶

Why do demand curves for an existing firm become more elastic as entry occurs?

icy applies. The same trucks make deliveries. In other words, Rudd's cost curves don't change. The firm may end up producing at *different points on the cost curves,* but the curves themselves remain unchanged.

Under monopolistic competition in Exhibit 6, Rudd does exactly what it did in the monopoly market of Exhibit 4. It produces where $MR = MC$.

In Exhibit 6, $MR' = MC$ at 200 tons. That's where Rudd produces. Its short-run equilibrium price is $90 and its ATC is $66. Rudd's economic profit is ($90 − $66) × 200 = $4,800. As you see, losing its monopoly position in the market cuts deeply into Rudd's profit.

What about consumers? They are better off. Compared to the old monopoly market, the price they pay is lower and the quantities they buy are greater.

Rudd's Long-Run Equilibrium Position in a Monopolistically Competitive Market

But the game isn't over. As long as *any* economic profit can be made producing ice, other firms, with product differentiations of their own, enter the market. With each new entry, Rudd's demand curve shifts further to the left, reducing Rudd's market share. How far to the left will it shift? Exhibit 7 depicts Rudd's price, output, and profit position when its demand curve, because of increasing competition, becomes D''; that is, tangent to its ATC curve.

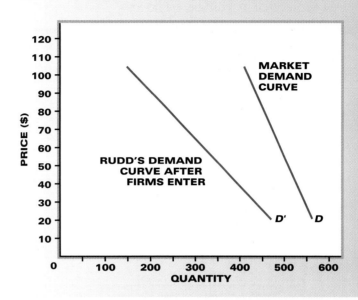

RUDD'S DEMAND CURVE AS NEW FIRMS ENTER THE MARKET

When new firms enter the market, the market demand curve remains unchanged at *D*, but the competition from the new firms forces Rudd, now an ex-monopoly, to share market demand. Its demand curve shifts from *D* to *D'*, the extent of the shift depending on the strength of competition in the market. Because of the presence of close substitute goods, *D'* is more elastic than *D*.

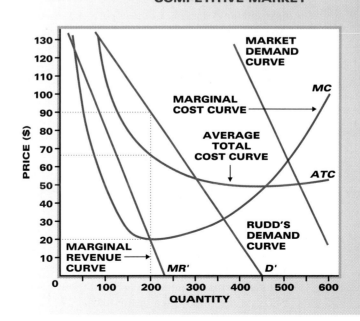

RUDD'S PRICE AND OUTPUT IN A MONOPOLISTICALLY COMPETITIVE MARKET

As it did in monopoly, the firm in monopolistic competition produces where $MR' = MC$. This occurs at $Q = 200$ tons. Price is $90 and ATC is $66, generating an economic profit of $4,800.

EXHIBIT|7

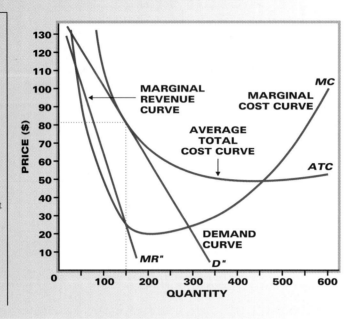

RUDD'S LONG-RUN EQUILIBRIUM PRICE AND OUTPUT IN MONOPOLISTIC COMPETITION

As more firms enter the industry, each firm's demand curve shifts further to the left and becomes more elastic. Rudd produces where $MR'' = MC$, but output falls to 150 tons. Note the uniqueness of this output level. The demand curve D'' is tangent to the ATC curve. $P = ATC$. The economic profit rectangle shrinks completely away. Because firms no longer make an economic profit, no new firms are attracted into the market.

Rudd produces 150 tons, where $MR'' = MC$. At that output, price *and* average total costs are \$82. Rudd's economic profit is (\$82 − \$82) × 150 = \$0. Rudd's competitors, too, face the same zero economic profit situation.

If Rudd makes no economic profit at $Q = 150$, shouldn't it be producing at some other output? No. The $MR = MC$ rule always signals the firm's most profitable output level, even if profit is zero. It simply means that every other output level generates less than zero profit, that is, a loss. Zero economic profit, then, is Rudd's maximum profit.

Gone are the days when Rudd was a monopoly making profit. Now, in monopolistic competition because of easy firm entry into the market, it finds itself in long-run equilibrium earning zero profit. Consumers, of course, are happy. They get more ice from the competing firms, and at lower prices.

Making Normal Profit

With economic profit at zero, no new firms enter the market. But why would any firm making zero economic profit stay in the ice-making business? Consider the Nick Rudd Ice Company. Although the firm's economic profit disappears in long-run equilibrium, Nick Rudd, as entrepreneur, still draws a **normal profit,** that is, a wage—accounted for in the firm's ATC—which is at least as much as he can earn elsewhere. That is to say, he does as well or better staying in business than he would do elsewhere.

Normal profit
The entrepreneur's opportunity cost. It is equal to or greater than the income an entrepreneur could receive employing his or her resources elsewhere. Normal profit is included in the firm's costs.

PRICE AND OUTPUT IN PERFECT COMPETITION

Let's change the story slightly. We saw that as more and more firms enter a monopolistically competitive market, the individual firm's market share shrinks. Although the goods these firms produce are very close substitutes, each firm still produces a unique good. Each firm faces its own downward-sloping demand curve. Each can raise price above its competitor's price without losing its entire market to its competitors. But as more firms crowd into a monopolistically competitive market, differences among the goods become less marked. They become more easily substitutable for each other. For example, Coca-Cola and 7-Up differ in taste and color. Still, many consumers regard them as fairly close substitutes. But with Sprite, Slice, Squirt, and Fresca in the market, 7-Up faces an even greater number of even

APPLIED PERSPECTIVE

SUBSTITUTE GOODS: CLOSE, CLOSER, AND EVEN CLOSER

The in-laws are coming for brunch. You start cooking the omelettes and realize you are out of Swiss cheese. You zoom to the nearest grocery store, run down the aisle to the dairy case, and there you stare, sweating and panting, at eight brands of Swiss cheese, all priced about the same, all made from the same ingredients, all aged 60 days.

You want to yell, "WHAT'S THE DIFFERENCE?!!" You want to maybe nuke the entire Swiss cheese industry.

Sometimes, having so many choices is bad. But not always, say experts—not if the choices make sense.

No question consumers are getting deluged with new product choices—new brands, new sizes, new styles. Look down the cereal aisle, where 123 products were unveiled in one year alone. Look at the car ads. You can choose from more than 300 models. Open a directory of mutual funds and try to sort through all 2,718. *Progressive Grocer* says the average grocery store carries more than 18,000 items, up from 7,800 in 1970.

"In most cases, the more choices the better," says Michael Johnson, a University of Michigan marketing professor who studies how consumers decide to buy certain products. A greater variety means shoppers can find exactly what they want. Now you can choose from eight different kinds of Coke: Coca-Cola, Coca-Cola Classic, Caffeine Free Coca-Cola, Caffeine Free Coca-Cola Classic, Diet Coke, Caffeine Free Diet Coke, Cherry Coke, and Diet Cherry Coke. Twenty years ago, there was just one, regular Coca-Cola.

AT ONE TIME COKE HAD ONLY ONE STYLE OF BOTTLE, IN ONE SIZE, AT ONE PRICE. REALLY? HOW PRIMITIVE!

"It takes a little reading to know what drugs to buy," says John Walden of the Nonprescription Drug Manufacturers Association. There are, he says, about 200,000 brands, varieties, and sizes of over-the-counter drugs available. Phil Lempert, publisher of *The Lempert Report* newsletter, writes: "Gone are the days of unique products. Instead it's all 'me-too's'"—like all the products with "oat bran," "fat-free," or "no cholesterol" labels. The differences become so small that most consumers don't want to take the time to figure out which is the best to buy. So if none are on sale, they grab the brand name their parents used, Lempert says. "That's the safety valve."

Or as Mick Jagger put it: "You can't always get what you want/ but if you try sometimes/you just might find/you get what you need."

It even applies to paper towels.

CONSIDER

In your opinion, are there too many brands—of most everything—on the market? Or is it "the more, the merrier"? Do you think there is such a thing as "too much choice"?

MORE ON THE NET

Is there too much choice for what to visit on the Web? As you consider this question, take a look at What's New at Yahoo! (http://www.yahoo.com/new/) for today and the past few days.

Source: Adapted from "No Shortage of Selection: Consumers Face Flood of Products," *USA Today,* July, 12, 1991. Copyright 1991, USA TODAY. Reprinted with permission.

closer substitutes. In every monopolistically competitive situation, as more firms enter, product differentiation narrows, and at the same time, *each firm's demand curve shifts to the left and becomes more elastic.*

There's No Product Differentiation in Perfectly Competitive Markets

Why might Morton International produce over a dozen different types of table salt (http://www.mortonsalt.com/prod/prflprod.htm)?

How far to the left can the demand curve shift? How elastic can it become? Well, let's now suppose there is no product differentiation in the ice-making business. Ice is ice, just as a tomato is a tomato and salt is salt. People can switch from one firm's ice to another's without having to sacrifice preference. That is, the goods produced are identical.

The Firm in Perfect Competition

Let's also suppose that entry into the market is free and open and that ice can be manufactured with relatively low-fixed-cost technology. Then the market conditions that the Nick Rudd Ice Company faces as a firm in perfect competition are quite different from those it enjoyed in its salad days as a monopolist.

Can you think of a non-agricultural good produced by a number of competing firms that is essentially identical? Go to the Interactive Study Center at http://gottheil.swcollege.com and click on the "Your Turn" button to submit your example. Student submissions will be posted to the Web site, and perhaps we will use some in future editions of the book!

SMALL-SCALE PRODUCTION Typically, firms operating in perfectly competitive markets are modest in size. Exhibit 8 describes the cost structure for the perfect competitor Nick Rudd.

The fixed cost associated with this scaled-down version of the Nick Rudd Ice Company monopoly of Exhibit 3 is only 1 percent—$40 versus $4,000—of what it was when the firm was a monopoly. The graph in Exhibit 8 converts the *ATC* of the table into graphic form.

As you see, minimum *ATC* for the competitive firm is $47, which occurs at production levels of 4.5 tons. If the firm increases production to 6 tons, its *ATC* climbs to $55.

FACING A HORIZONTAL DEMAND CURVE As one of a considerable number of ice manufacturers, Rudd has no control whatsoever over market price. Before, as a monopoly, Rudd could pick a price and quantity combination that maximized its profit. It was a price-maker.

As a perfect competitor, it has no freedom to select price. The competitive firm is a **price-taker.** It must take as its own whatever price the market generates. Suppose panel *a* in Exhibit 9 portrays the market for ice.

The market demand curve, *D*, is downward sloping. It is the same demand curve that Rudd once faced as a monopolist. The market's short-run supply curve, *S,* is upward sloping, reflecting the suppliers' willingness to produce more ice at higher prices. The equilibrium price established in the market shown in Exhibit 9 is $78. The equilibrium quantity demanded and supplied is 440 tons.

Look at panel *b,* representing the demand curve Rudd itself faces. The demand curve is horizontal across all the quantities—0 to 6 tons—that Rudd can produce. *Rudd sees the same market demand curve that you see in panel* a. However, since Rudd is only a very minor contributor to market supply—producing within the 0-to-6-ton range, out of a market supply of 440 tons—it cannot influence price. For example,

Price-taker
A firm that views market price as a given and considers any activity on its own part as having no influence on that price.

EXHIBIT|8

THE COMPETITIVE FIRM'S COST STRUCTURE

RUDD'S COST STRUCTURE IN PERFECT COMPETITION

This perfectly competitive firm's minimum *ATC* is $47, which occurs at a quantity of 4.5 tons.

QUANTITY (TONS)	TOTAL COST (TC)	AVERAGE TOTAL COST (ATC)	MARGINAL COST (MC)
0	$ 40.0		
0.5	85.0	$170	$ 90
1.0	110.0	110	50
1.5	122.5	82	25
2.0	132.5	66	20
2.5	143.5	57	22
3.0	156.0	52	25
3.5	171.0	49	30
4.0	189.5	47	37
4.5	213.0	47	47
5.0	243.0	48	60
5.5	282.0	51	78
6.0	332.0	55	100

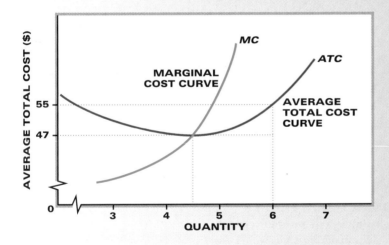

if Rudd reduced its own output significantly, that reduction would not be enough to raise price. If Rudd increased its own output significantly, it would not be enough to depress price. Increasing output from, say, 3 tons to 6 tons may represent a 100 percent increase for Rudd, but only a minuscule 0.7 percent increase in market supply.

Since the good it produces is identical to all the others on the market, it would be foolhardy for Rudd to raise its own price by so much as a penny. If it did, it wouldn't be able to sell a single ice chip. Why would anyone buy ice from Rudd at $78.01 when it could buy ice from other firms at $78? Nor would Rudd cut price by a penny. After all, why should Rudd sell ice at $77.99 when it can sell all it wants at $78? Rudd has no choice but to accept the equilibrium price at $78.

CHECK YOUR UNDERSTANDING

Why is each firm's demand curve horizontal?

EXHIBIT|9

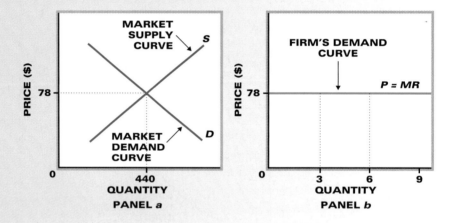

DEMAND AND SUPPLY FOR ICE IN A PERFECTLY COMPETITIVE MARKET

In panel *a*, market demand, *D*, and market supply, *S*, produce an equilibrium price of $78 and a quantity demanded and supplied of 440 tons. Once market demand and supply establishes $78 as the price, the competitive firm, a price-taker, takes $78 as its price. The firm, in panel *b*, faces a horizontal demand curve at *P* = $78.

PRICE AND REVENUE SCHEDULE FOR RUDD IN PERFECT COMPETITION

QUANTITY (TONS)	PRICE (P)	TOTAL REVENUE (TR)	MARGINAL REVENUE (MR)
0	$78	$ 0	$ 0
1	78	78	78
2	78	156	78
3	78	234	78
4	78	312	78
5	78	390	78
6	78	468	78

FOR THE COMPETITIVE FIRM, *P* = *MR* Because Rudd faces a horizontal demand curve, its marginal revenue curve coincides with the demand curve it faces. *This P = MR condition applies to all firms in perfect competition.* The table in Exhibit 9 displays this situation.

When Rudd increases production from 0 to 6 tons, it increases its total revenue by $78 × 6 = $468. Every ton added to production adds another $78 to total revenue. The added revenue—the marginal revenue—is simply the price the firm gets for selling the additional ton.

SHORT-RUN EQUILIBRIUM PRICE AND OUTPUT FOR THE FIRM IN PERFECT COMPETITION

We have seen that panel *a*, Exhibit 9, represents the market condition in which the Nick Rudd Ice Company operates. What should it do? As a price-taker, it knows *P* = $78. But how much ice should it produce?

INTERDISCIPLINARY PERSPECTIVE

FROM THOMAS HARDY'S *THE MAYOR OF CASTERBRIDGE*

It was the eve of harvest. Prices being low Farfrae was buying. As was usual, after reckoning too surely on famine weather the local farmers had flown to the other extreme, and (in Farfrae's opinion) were selling off too recklessly—calculating with just a trifle too much certainty upon an abundant yield. So he went on buying old corn at its comparatively ridiculous price: for the produce of the previous year, though not large, had been of excellent quality.

When Henchard had squared his affairs in a disastrous way, and got rid of his burdensome purchases at a monstrous loss, the harvest began. There were three days of excellent weather, and then—"What if that curst conjuror should be right after all!" said Henchard.

The fact was, that no sooner had the sickles begun to play that the atmosphere suddenly felt as if cress would grow in it without other nourishment. It rubbed people's cheeks like damp flannel when they walked abroad. There was a gusty, high, warm wind; isolated raindrops starred the window-panes at remote distances: the sunlight would flap out like a quickly opened fan, through the pattern of the window upon the floor of the room in a milky, colorless shine, and withdraw as suddenly as it had appeared.

From that day and hour it was clear that there was not to be so successful an ingathering after all. If Henchard had only waited long enough he might at least have avoided loss though he had not made a profit. But the momentum of his character knew no patience. At this turn of the scales he remained silent. The movements of his mind seemed to tend to the thought that some power was working against him.

"I wonder," he asked himself with eerie misgiving; "I wonder if it can be that somebody has been roasting a waxen image of me, or stirring an unholy brew to confound me! I don't believe in such power; and yet—what if they should ha' been doing it!" Even he could not admit that the perpetrator, if any, might be Farfrae. These isolated hours of superstition came to Henchard in times of moody depression, when all his practical largeness of view had oozed out of him.

Meanwhile Donald Farfrae prospered. He had purchased in so depressed a market that the present moderate stiffness of prices was sufficient to pile for him a large heap of gold where a little one had been.

ONE OF A HARVEST—THE HARVEST DETERMINES THE PRICE.

CONSIDER

Thomas Hardy draws a striking picture of Casterbridge's competitive corn market. Henchard is a corn supplier and price taker. Anticipating an abundant harvest and falling prices, he decides to act quickly, selling his stocks of corn to avoid what he expects to be even lower prices tomorrow. But he guesses wrong. The harvest is less than he expected and the competitive price ends up being higher. He loses. Farfrae, on the other hand, is a buyer. As sellers deplete their corn stocks, he accumulates. But he's a price taker as well. His guess about the eventual size of the harvest and the price of corn turns out to be right and he reaps windfall profit. The point of this illustration: When uncertainty enters a market process—as it does in Casterbridge's competitive corn market—the calculation of MR in the $MC = MR$ guide to profit maximization includes not only prices given, but also prices expected.

The table in Exhibit 10 combines the firm's price and revenue schedule from the table in Exhibit 9 with its cost structure from the table in Exhibit 8.

There's little question what Rudd should do under the circumstances of the table in Exhibit 10. $MR = MC = \$78$ at 5.5 tons, and that is the quantity the firm chooses to produce. Its economic profit at 5.5 tons is $\$429 - \$282 = \$147$, which is more profit than could be generated at any other output level.

EXHIBIT | 10

THE PERFECTLY COMPETITIVE FIRM IN THE SHORT RUN

To maximize profit, the firm produces where *MR = MC*. The firm's *MC* curve cuts the *P = MR* curve at 5.5 tons. *ATC* = $51, generating an economic profit—the shaded rectangle—of $147.

DEMAND SCHEDULE AND COST STRUCTURE FOR RUDD IN A PERFECTLY COMPETITIVE MARKET

QUANTITY (TONS)	AVERAGE TOTAL COST (ATC)	MARGINAL COST (MC)	MARGINAL REVENUE (MR)
0			
0.5	170	$ 90	$78
1.0	110	50	78
1.5	82	25	78
2.0	66	20	78
2.5	57	22	78
3.0	52	25	78
3.5	49	30	78
4.0	47	37	78
4.5	47	47	78
5.0	49	60	78
5.5	51	78	78
6.0	55	100	78

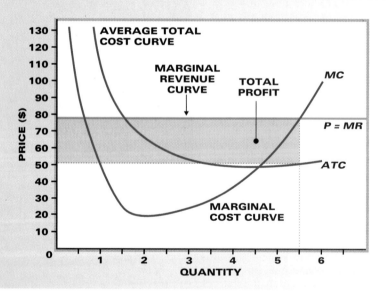

CHECK YOUR UNDERSTANDING

Why is economic profit in perfect competition short-lived?

The graph in Exhibit 10 translates the table into graphic form. The *P = MR* curve facing the competitive firm is horizontal at $78. The *MC* curve cuts the *MR* curve at 5.5 tons, where *ATC* = $51. The shaded rectangle, which represents *(P − ATC) × Q*, measures Rudd's economic profit at 5.5 tons.

Rudd makes $147 economic profit but discovers rather quickly that this profit is short-lived. The profit attracts new firms into the competitive market. Since entry is free and open, these firms add to the market's supply. Look at Exhibit 11.

Panel *a* of Exhibit 11 shows what happens to the short-run equilibrium price as more firms join the market. Initially, the market supply curve shifts to the right from S_1 to S_2. The increased competition among the larger number of firms forces price to fall from $78 to $60.

Rudd, under these changing circumstances, is forced to reexamine its production decision. Look at panel *b*. Being a price-taker, it now accepts $P = \$60$ and establishes a new level of output at 5 tons, where $P = MR = MC = \$60$. Its profit now is maximized at $(\$60 - \$49) \times 5 = \$55$.

This $55 profit is sufficient to attract even more firms to the market. The supply curve in panel *a* shifts to the right again, from S_2 to S_3, and market price is once more forced downward, this time to $P = \$47$.

Back to panel *b*. Rudd has no choice but to accept $P = \$47$, and once more it reexamines its production decision. It produces now at 4.5 tons, where $P = MR = MC = \$47$. But at 4.5 tons, the firm's *ATC* is also $47. That is, at 4.5 tons, $P = ATC$. The firm's profit becomes $(\$47 - \$47) \times 4.5 = \$0$.

LONG-RUN EQUILIBRIUM PRICE AND OUTPUT FOR THE FIRM IN PERFECT COMPETITION

Rudd sees its economic profit dwindle from $147 to $55 and finally to $0, and it can do nothing to prevent it. The character of the perfectly competitive market guarantees this outcome. As long as any economic profit is made, firms will enter the market, shifting market supply to the right. This in turn drives down price and, in the end, economic profit as well. This process comes to rest only when economic profit is $0. At this point, the lure of profit disappears. No new firms appear.

Long-run equilibrium in perfect competition is shown in Exhibit 12.

In panel *a*, the firm's no-profit position is $Q = 4.5$ tons, where $P = ATC$. Since the firm is a profit maximizer, it produces where $MR = MC$. And since $P = MR$ for a firm in perfect competition, its long-run equilibrium position is identified by

$$P = MR = MC = ATC.$$

CHECK YOUR UNDERSTANDING

If the entry is free in perfect competition, why do firms stop entering?

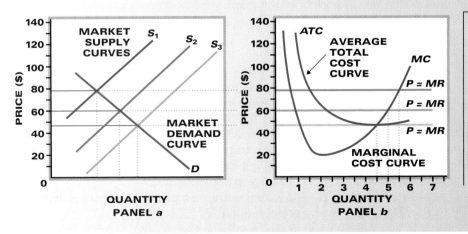

EFFECTS OF A SHIFT IN MARKET SUPPLY

As more firms enter the market of panel *a*, the supply curve shifts from S_1 to S_2, causing the short-run equilibrium price to fall from $78 to $60. The firm in panel *b* produces where $MC = MR = \$60$, which is at 5 tons. Its economic profit is $55. Firms continue to enter, shifting the supply curve to S_3. Price falls to $47. At $MC = MR = \$47$, $Q = 4.5$ tons and $ATC = \$47$. Economic profit disappears, and no new firms are attracted to the market.

EXHIBIT|11

EXHIBIT | 12

THE MARKET AND FIRM IN LONG-RUN EQUILIBRIUM

In panel *b*, market demand, *D*, and market supply, S_3, establish market equilibrium at *P* = $47 and *Q* = 504 tons. For the firm in panel *a*, equilibrium—*P* = *MR* = *MC* = *ATC*—occurs at $47 and at *Q* = 4.5 tons.

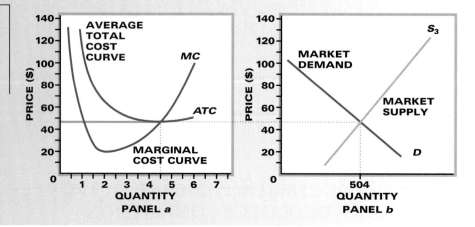

Not necessarily by intent, but by the circumstance of the competitive market, a firm in perfect competition ends up producing at the lowest point on its *ATC* curve. In Exhibit 12, this point is $47. This position is defined as maximum efficiency.

Now look at panel *b*, representing the entire market for ice. Market demand, *D*, intersects market supply, S_3, at *P* = $47 and at *Q* = 504 tons. If every firm in the market looks like Rudd—each producing 4.5 tons—then 112 firms would supply the market with 504 tons.

Lowest Prices and Greatest Output

Compared to monopoly and monopolistic competition, the perfectly competitive market structure produces the greatest output at the lowest prices. Remember the monopoly outcome. Monopoly price was $150 and the monopoly produced 300 tons. But when firms gained entry into the market, changing its character from monopoly to monopolistic competition, the market's long-run equilibrium price and output changed as well. Price fell to $82 and total output increased to 440 tons. Under conditions of perfect competition, the long-run equilibrium price falls to $47 and market supply reaches 504 tons.

The Firm's Supply Curve

Intuitively, it seems reasonable to suppose that producers would increase the quantities they supply in response to higher prices. It seems reasonable to suppose too that they would be less willing to supply the market when prices fall.

The economic argument underlying the firm's upward-sloping supply curve is related to the *MR* = *MC* rule. After all, the quantity firms produce is always determined at the *MR* = *MC* output level. In perfect competition, *P* = *MR*, so that the firm's long-run supply curve—relating price to quantity supplied—simply traces out the segment of its *MC* curve that lies above its *ATC*.

At every price above *P* = *ATC*, the quantity supplied by the firm is determined at its *P* = *MC* output level. Look at Exhibit 13.

EXHIBIT | 13

ANATOMY OF THE FIRM'S LONG-RUN SUPPLY CURVE

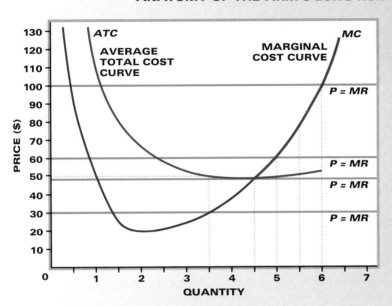

The firm is a price-taker. Whatever the price, the firm will produce where $MR = MC$. Since $P = MR$, when $P = \$100$ the firm is willing to supply 6 tons. At $P = \$78$, it is willing to supply 5.5 tons. At $P = \$60$, it is willing to supply 5 tons. At $P = \$30$, it is unwilling to supply any because it will incur a loss, since $ATC > P$. The firm's supply curve is its MC curve above the $MC = ATC$ point.

When $P = \$100$, $MR = MC$ at $Q = 6$ tons. When $P = \$78$, $MR = MC$ at $Q = 5.5$. When $P = \$60$, $MR = MC$ at $Q = 5$. And when $P = \$47$, $MR = MC$ at $Q = 4.5$. These price and quantity combinations trace out the firm's marginal cost curve. At prices below $47, the firm will shut down. Why?

Look at the firm's ATC when $P = \$30$. At that price, $MR = MC$ at $Q = 3.5$. At 3.5 tons, the firm's $ATC = \$49$. That is, the firm's most attractive output level when $P = \$30$ is 3.5 tons, but it still generates a ($\$30 - \$49$) × 3.5 = \$66.50 loss. Why stay in business? That is why the firm's supply curve—what it is *willing to* supply— starts at the $MC = ATC$ point on its marginal cost curve.

The Market's Supply Curve

What explains the firm's supply curve, explains as well the market's supply curve. The quantity supplied on the market at a given price is the horizontal sum of the quantities each firm supplies. Each firm's supply coincides with that part of its MC curve lying above its $MC = ATC$ point. Market supply, then, represents the results of summing all firms' MC curves above their $ATCs$.

Exhibit 14 portrays the summing process. Suppose the cost curves of the competitive firms are similar to those of Rudd. Panel *a* depicts their individual supply curves, and panel *b*, depicting the market, aggregates or sums the supply curves of panel *a*.

When $P = \$100$, the firms of panel *a* are each willing to supply 6 tons, so that, together, the 150 firms in the market of panel *b* are willing to supply 900 tons. When $P = \$78$, each firm is willing to supply 5.5 tons, so that market supply in panel *b* for 130 firms is 715 tons. When $P = \$60$, each firm is willing to supply 5 tons, so that the 120 firms in the market are willing to supply 600 tons. When $P =$

CHECK YOUR UNDERSTANDING

What is the relationship between an individual firm's marginal cost curves and market supply?

EXHIBIT|14

ANATOMY OF THE MARKET SUPPLY CURVE

The market supply curve is the aggregation of the long-run MC curves of the firms in the market. Panel a shows the Nick Rudd Ice Company—one among the 150 producing on the panel b market. When $P = \$100$, Rudd and the 149 other firms produce a total of 900 tons. When price falls, fewer firms remain in the market, and each remaining firm produces less tonnage. The aggregation of their outputs at different prices makes up the supply curve of panel b.

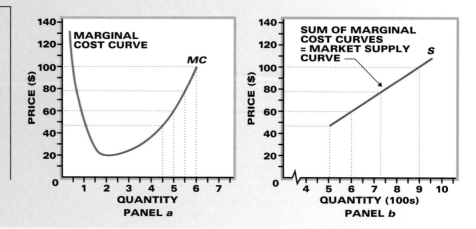

PANEL a

PANEL b

$47, each firm is willing to supply 4.5 tons, and the 111 firms in the market are willing to supply 500 tons. At $P = \$30$, market supply is 0, reflecting each firm's decision to shut down at that price.

INNOVATORS AND IMITATORS IN THE PERFECTLY COMPETITIVE MARKET

Suppose one of the firms, struggling along with zero economic profit at $P = \$47$, hits upon a new idea. Adopting a technology that substitutes computers for labor, the firm is able to significantly reduce its costs of producing ice. Exhibit 15, panel a, depicts the cost structure of Paola Flygare Ice Works Company, the innovator firm.

EXHIBIT|15

THE INNOVATOR FIRM IN PERFECT COMPETITION

The innovator firm in panel a introduces new technology that lowers its cost structure from ATC_1 to ATC_2 and from MC_1 to MC_2. As a competitive firm, it faces $P = \$47$, produces where $MC_2 = \$47$, and makes an economic profit of $55. Firms in the market adopt the new technology. Other firms, attracted by the prospect of profit, join the market. The market supply curve of panel b shifts from S_1 to S_2, driving price down to $37. In panel a, the firms' new long-run equilibrium is established at $P = MR = MC_2 = ATC_2 = \$37$.

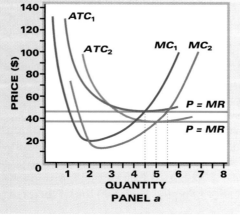

PANEL a

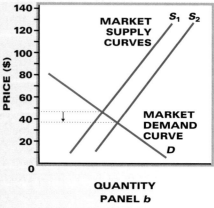

PANEL b

HISTORICAL PERSPECTIVE

PERFECT COMPETITION IN THE 17TH-CENTURY GLASS ENGRAVING INDUSTRY

There's a treat in store for you if you haven't already visited the Corning Glass Museum in Corning, New York. Allow yourself a full day. The displays of glassware and glassware technology date back to antiquity. When you reach the mid-17th century, you will read in showcase #58 a letter dated 1686, written by Friedrich Winter, a glass engraver, to Count von Schaffgotsch lamenting the plight of glass engravers. To students of economics, this letter is exciting. It describes a perfectly competitive glass engraving industry and the consequences to glass engravers of working in such a competitive environment. Winter writes: ". . . glass engravers and also cutters are so numerous that the one spoils it for the other and hardly anyone can earn a proper living, and each should teach two or three young-

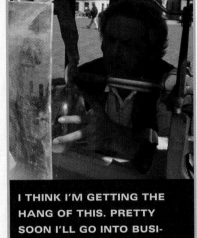

I THINK I'M GETTING THE HANG OF THIS. PRETTY SOON I'LL GO INTO BUSINESS ON MY OWN.

sters, but when they have brought it so far as to be able to do a bit of scratching, they run away from the masters and set up their own tools, and bungle away, each one for himself."

Can't you feel Winter's frustration? After all, he's describing life in long-run perfect competition. It's not necessarily a rosy picture, is it? Entry into the glass engraving industry is obviously free and easy. No barriers to entry at all. The goods they produce are easily reproduced (once you know how) and there are many, many producers and it seems more are entering the industry every day. Every worker turns out to be a future competitor! The result? Winter states it clearly: ". . . hardly anyone can earn a proper living." If we translate that 1686 comment into the language of modern economics, it reads: "In the long run, economic profit is zero."

Flygare Ice Works faces the same $47 equilibrium price that its competitors face. It knows that it cannot raise price, nor need it reduce price to sell any quantity it chooses to sell. It chooses to produce, of course, where its $MR = MC$. This originally occurred at $Q = 4.5$ tons, where $MC_1 = MR = P = ATC_1$. After introducing the new technology, however, Flygare's cost structure changes to MC_2 and ATC_2, and production increases to 5.5 tons, where $MR = MC_2$. At $Q = 5.5$ tons, $ATC = 37. As you see, the Paola Flygare Ice Works Company now makes an economic profit of ($47 - $37) \times 5.5 = 55.

In perfect competition, innovations cannot remain anybody's secret for long. The other firms in the industry become imitators—they mimic the innovator. They, too, adopt the new technology to resemble panel *a*. Still other firms, attracted by the prospects of profit, enter the market. Everybody's cost structure is now represented by MC_2 and ATC_2.

Now look at panel *b*. These additional firms in the market shift the market supply curve to the right, forcing the market price to fall from $47 to $37. Flygare's economic profit, which emerged through innovation, gets wiped out by imitation.

All firms now use Paola Flygare technology. They face a $37 market price and produce at $Q = 5$ tons, where $MR = MC_2$. There, the new zero-profit equilibrium for firms in perfect competition is established.

DOES COMPETITION ALWAYS GENERATE LOWEST PRICES AND HIGHEST OUTPUT?

Do monopolies always end up charging the highest prices and producing the lowest quantities? Do monopolistically competitive firms always end up producing more than monopoly, but still less than firms in perfect competition, and charge a price higher than the competitive price? And does perfect competition generate innovative firms that force others to imitate, driving prices even lower and production even higher?

The Schumpeter Hypothesis

According to economist Joseph Schumpeter, "It ain't necessarily so!" The idea that monopoly is ipso facto bad flies in the face of economic reality. Monopolies don't always end up producing at higher prices. He argues that modern technology creates enormous economies of scale that are typically enjoyed by larger firms, many of which are monopolies. Therefore, a more realistic comparison of cost structures is not the constant return to scale depicted in Exhibit 16, panel *a*, for competitive firms, but the economies of scale depicted in panel *b*, for monopolies. Although Schumpeter acknowledges that monopolies are defined by their oneness, not their bigness, in reality, bigness and oneness are often linked.

If we accept Schumpeter's linkage, the economies of scale may allow monopolies to maximize profit at market prices lower than those that would obtain under more competitive market conditions. Look at Exhibit 17.

Panel *a* depicts a competitive book-binding firm in equilibrium, producing 20 bindings at a price of $25 per binding. If there were 200 competitive firms in the market, the quantity supplied to the market would be 4,000 bindings.

The demand curve facing the monopoly in panel *b* is the market demand. Look at the monopoly's cost structure. It reflects the advantages of large-scale production. At very low levels of output, ATC is exceptionally high. For example, at $Q = 1,000$, $ATC = \$60$. But ATC keeps decreasing until it reaches its minimum at $Q = 12,000$.

EXHIBIT | 16

CONSTANT AND INCREASING RETURNS TO SCALE

Panel *a* illustrates constant returns to scale. It shows cost structures of small and large firms whose minimum ATCs are the same. This reflects the assumption that increasing firm size increases total output and total cost proportionately. Panel *b* illustrates a different relationship between output, cost, and firm size. Increasing returns to scale means that increasing firm size increases total output and total cost disproportionately. Average total cost falls as firm size and output increase.

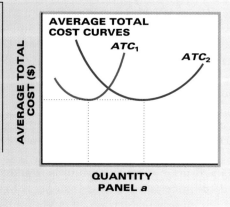

AVERAGE TOTAL COST CURVES

ATC₁   ATC₂

QUANTITY
PANEL *a*

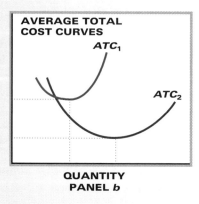

AVERAGE TOTAL COST CURVES

ATC₁   ATC₂

QUANTITY
PANEL *b*

EXHIBIT|17

PRICE AND PRODUCTION IN MONOPOLY AND PERFECT COMPETITION: SCHUMPETER'S VIEW

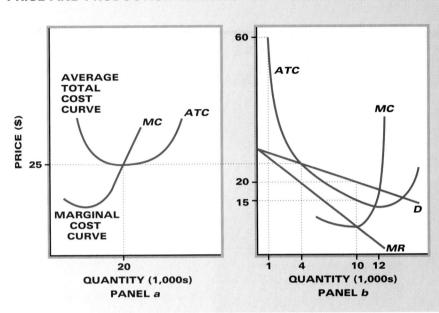

Panel *a* shows a competitive firm in long-run equilibrium. $P = ATC = MR = MC = \$25$. Output is 20 units. With 200 firms in the market, total quantity supplied is 4,000 units. The monopoly in panel *b* supplies 10,000 units; at $Q = 10,000$, $P = \$20$ and $ATC = \$15$. The firm's monopoly profit is \$50,000. Note that the monopoly price is less than the competitive price—\$20 versus \$25—and the quantity supplied by the monopoly is greater than the quantity supplied by the competitive firms on the market—10,000 versus 4,000 units.

The monopoly, applying the $MR = MC$ rule, produces 10,000 bindings. At that output level, $P = \$20$ and $ATC = \$15$. The monopoly ends up making ($\$20 - \$15$) × 10,000 = \$50,000 profit. The economies of scale in the industry are so pronounced that even with monopoly profit of \$50,000, its price of \$20 is lower than the competitive firm's price of \$25, and its quantity supplied, 10,000, is greater than the competitive firms' 4,000. That's Schumpeter's point.

To Schumpeter, the economies of scale and the steady flows of technological innovations that occur with monopoly—not with perfect competition—don't happen by accident. The monopoly, using its profit to experiment with new technologies, ultimately creates the new cost structures that promote greater efficiency in production. The monopoly, like firms in other market structures, is self-serving. It strives to maximize profit. But intent is not the issue. Price and quantity supplied are.

Why can't competitive firms innovate? Because competition undermines profit, which is the source of innovation and experimentation. In long-run equilibrium, competitive firms earn zero economic profit. Even if a competitive firm had the innovation, why should it go through the innovating effort when it knows that competition will quickly wipe out its rewards? Still another compelling reason why competitive firms shy away from experimenting with cost-saving technology is the possibility of failure. Not every experiment works. If a zero-profit competitive firm in long-run equilibrium tries to innovate and fails, the loss would drive it out of the market. For the competitive firm, then, there's little to gain by innovating, and everything to lose.

The monopoly, on the other hand, can afford to make mistakes without having to pay with its life. If a cost-saving technology flops, the monopoly loses a fraction of its profit. That's all. It can try again and again.

THEORETICAL PERSPECTIVE

HOW MONOPOLY SEIZES CONSUMER SURPLUS AND CREATES A DEADWEIGHT LOSS FOR SOCIETY

Ever play the board game Monopoly? If you did, you know that if you end up owning Park Place and Boardwalk, you're a winner. But who manufacturers the board game? And why does it sell at the price it does? Let's suppose—we must suppose because it's untrue—that anyone can produce the game. There are absolutely no barriers to entry. The industry is perfectly competitive; panel *a* in the accompanying figure depicts the long-run position of each firm. The market is depicted in panel *b*. The long-run average total cost is assumed to be constant across the entire production range so that the *ATC* curve is horizontal and everywhere *ATC* = *MC*. Market price is $15 and the quantity bought and sold is 100,000 units. Consumer surplus generated for consumers in this perfectly competitive market is area *A* (triangle *acb*).

Now let's suppose that the market structure changes from perfect competition to monopoly. That is, there's a monopoly on the manufacture of the Monopoly board game. (There really is!) Let's assume that the monopoly's demand curve and *ATC* curve are the same as those depicted in perfect competition, which is what we see in panel *c*.

LEAVE NOTHING TO CHANCE: OWN THE BOARD AND GET ALL THE MONEY!

The monopolist, producing where *MR* = *MC*, charges a monopoly price of $25 and produces a quantity of 50,000 units. What happens to the consumer surplus going to consumers? It falls from area *A* (triangle *acb*) to area *C* (triangle *xyz*). That is, they lose areas *D* and *E*. To whom?

Some of the lost consumer surplus ends up as revenue for the monopoly. That's area *D*. The monopoly's revenue is $25 (price) times 50,000 (quantity), or $1,250,000. Part of that, $25 − $15 (the difference between the monopoly and competitive price) times 50,000 units (the quantity the monopoly sells) or $50,000, is consumer surplus that had gone to consumers when the market was competitive but now goes to the monopoly.

What about the consumer surplus of area *E* that consumers got under competitive market conditions? Consumers no longer get it. Monopoly doesn't get it either. This consumer surplus is lost to society because monopoly produces less; 50,000 compared to the 100,000 units produced in the competitive market. Economists refer to this loss as a *deadweight loss* because what the consumer loses is not offset by someone else's gain.

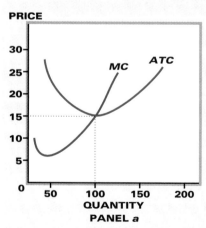

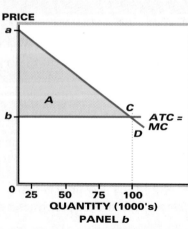

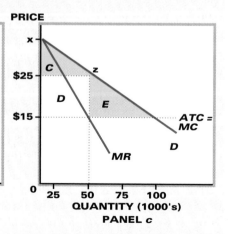

Some, But Not All, Economists Agree

Many economists share Schumpeter's view. John Kenneth Galbraith, for example, compares the likelihood of innovation among large and small firms:

> There is no more pleasant fiction than that technical change is the product of the matchless ingenuity of the small man forced by competition to employ his wits to better his neighbor. Unhappily, it is a fiction. Technical development has long since become the preserve of the scientist and the engineer. . . . Because development is costly, it follows that it can be carried on only by a firm that has the resources associated with considerable size.

Yet Schumpeter's bigness hypothesis is rejected as theoretically unsound and empirically invalid by a considerable number of other economists. They are quite reluctant to abandon a conventional wisdom that dates back to Alfred Marshall, the founding father of neoclassical economics.

It was Marshall's view that technical progress was best served in a competitive environment and that entrepreneurial inventiveness and size of enterprise were inversely related:

> It has always been recognized that large firms have a great advantage over their smaller rivals in their power of making expensive experiments. . . . But, on the whole, observation seems to show what might have been expected *a priori,* that these advantages count for little in the long run in comparison with the superior inventive force of a multitude of small undertakers.

As you see, Marshall's contention is no less assertive than Galbraith's. The debate on the validity of these conflicting theories continues inconclusively to this day. Volumes of theoretical and empirical research on the subject continue to flow, but they still offer contradictory observations. Perhaps the only thing we can conclude about innovation and firm size—and in many minds, the long-run price and output comparisons between perfect competition and monopoly—is that we can't conclude.

CHAPTER REVIEW

1. To maximize profit, the monopolist produces at an output level where $MR = MC$. This output level is less than the level associated with the monopolist's minimum ATC. It makes clear the idea that the monopolist seeks not to produce at the lowest ATC, but where economic profit—$(P - ATC)Q$—is the greatest. Barriers to entry sustain the monopolist's economic profit into and through the long run.

2. When barriers to entry are breached, the monopoly form dissolves into monopolistic competition. The many monopolistically competitive firms sell goods that are close, but not perfect, substitutes. Product differentiation shapes the firm's downward-sloping demand curve. The firm's $MR = MC$ output level creates $(P - ATC)Q$ economic profit, which attracts new firms

into the industry. The consequences of entry are as follows: (1) each firm's market share decreases; (2) the firm's demand curve shifts further to the left and becomes more elastic (reflecting the growing number of closer substitute goods in the market); (3) price falls; (4) the firm's ATC rises; and (5) economic profit decreases.

3. With more firms entering the market, the individual firm's demand curve keeps shifting to the left until ultimately—defined as the long run—it becomes tangent to the firm's ATC curve, so that $(P - ATC)Q$ is zero. The firm ends up making normal profit, which is equal to or greater than what the firm's entrepreneur could earn elsewhere.

4. Perfect competition is a market structure in which there are many firms producing perfect

substitutes, or identical goods. Because each firm's market share is insignificant relative to market demand, its demand curve is horizontal. As a result, $P = MR$, and the firm is described as a price-taker.

5. The competitive firm's $MR = MC$ output level creates $(P - ATC)Q$ economic profit, which attracts new firms into the industry. The consequences of entry are as follows: (1) market supply shifts to the right, (2) decreasing price so that (3) the firm's economic profit decreases as well. As long as economic profit exists, more firms enter, shifting market supply further to the right, which depresses price even more. As a result, the firm's horizontal demand curve falls until ultimately—defined as the long run—it becomes tangent to its ATC curve. The uniqueness about this tangency is that it occurs at the ATC's minimum level. The perfectly competitive industry ends up producing maximum output, while each of its firms, making zero economic profit, produces most efficiently.

6. Since the supply curve represents the quantities supplied at varying prices, and since competitive firms always produce where $(P =) MR = MC$, the competitive firm's supply curve is the segment of its MC curve that lies above its ATC curve.

7. The economic profit resulting from any cost-saving innovation employed by a firm in perfect competition is short-lived, because new firms are attracted into the industry by the economic profit, and firms already in imitate the innovator. As a result, the market supply curve shifts to the right, depressing price. In the long run, firms end up once again producing where $MC = MR = P = ATC$.

8. According to Joseph Schumpeter, bigness can be an advantage for an innovating firm. The economies of scale and low average costs of production available to big firms may allow them to charge prices that are actually lower than those charged by small, competitive firms. Monopoly profits permit these firms to experiment with new technologies that ultimately lead to more efficient production.

9. According to Alfred Marshall, the large number of small firms that undertake innovations will lead to the greatest efficiency in production over time. There is disagreement among economists about the exact nature of the relationship between innovation and firm size.

KEY TERMS

Price-maker
Economic profit

Normal profit

Price-taker

QUESTIONS

1. What does the statement "in monopoly, the firm *is* the industry" mean?
2. If you were an entrepreneur in a perfectly competitive market, would you attempt to innovate? Why or why not?
3. Why do firms produce where $MR = MC$? Why not at the lowest point on their ATC curves? After all, it's the most efficient level of output.
4. Why is the perfectly competitive firm's long-run supply curve identical to its marginal cost curve lying above its ATC?
5. Why are price and marginal revenue identical for the firm in perfect competition?

6. Economists refer to perfectly competitive firms as price-takers and to monopolies as price-makers. Why?
7. For perfectly competitive firms, economic profit exists only in the short run. Why?
8. Why are demand curves for perfectly competitive firms horizontal and for firms in monopolistic competition downward sloping?
9. Can you think of markets in which there is absolutely no product differentiation? If you owned a firm in such a market, what would your demand curve look like? What would the demand curve for the market look like?

10. Why does the firm's demand curve become more elastic in a monopolistically competitive market as more firms enter the market?

11. In perfect competition, imitators dampen the innovating spirit of innovators. Explain.

12. Inevitably, a firm in monopolistic competition ends up producing where its *ATC* curve is tangent to its demand curve. Explain.

13. Make the argument that consumers are better off when the economy's market structures are more competitive than monopolistic.

14. Why are economies of scale central to the argument that monopolies may end up pro-

ducing more and charging less than perfectly competitive firms?

15. Compare John K. Galbraith's and Alfred Marshall's views on innovation and plant size.

16. Perfectly competitive firms in long-run equilibrium produce at the lowest point on their *ATC* curve. They produce at maximum efficiency. Yet, producing at an output that generates maximum efficiency isn't their intent. Why, then, do they end up there?

PRACTICE PROBLEMS

1. Suppose the cost schedule for a perfectly competitive firm producing brooms is as shown in the following table:

QUANTITY	TOTAL COST
0	$ 2
1	4
2	7
3	11
4	16
5	22

If the market price for a broom is $5, how many brooms would the firm produce? Would the firm be making economic profit? How could you tell if the firm is in long-run equilibrium?

2. Suppose the firm is a monopoly and its price schedule is as follows:

PRICE	QUANTITY DEMANDED
$11.00	1
8.50	2
7.00	3
6.00	4
5.20	5

How many brooms would the firm produce? Would the firm be making an economic profit?

3. The following table shows total cost data for three firms in perfect competition:

QUANTITY	1ST FIRM'S TOTAL COST *(TC)*	2ND FIRM'S TOTAL COST *(TC)*	3RD FIRM'S TOTAL COST *(TC)*
0	1	2	3
1	3	5	6
2	4	7	8
3	6	8	11
4	9	12	15
5	13	17	20
6	18	23	26

Draw the supply curve for this perfectly competitive market.

4. Now suppose the three firms are in a monopolistically competitive market and their demand curves are as follows:

QUANTITY	1ST FIRM'S PRICE	2ND FIRM'S PRICE	3RD FIRM'S PRICE
1	$8.00	$7.00	$9.00
2	7.00	6.75	7.50
3	6.00	6.50	6.67
4	5.25	6.25	6.00
5	4.00	6.00	5.40
6	3.00	5.75	4.84

Combining their cost data in practice problem 3 with their demand curves shown here, calculate how much each firm would produce and at what price.

WHAT'S WRONG WITH THIS GRAPH?

PRICE DETERMINATION FOR A MONOPOLY

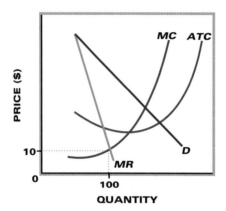

ECONOMIC CONSULTANTS

ECONOMIC RESEARCH AND ANALYSIS BY STUDENTS FOR PROFESSIONALS

Jackson Publishing, located in Toledo, Ohio, publishes a sports newsletter that focuses on the city's minor league baseball team, the Mud Hens. Until recently, Jackson Publishing enjoyed a monopoly with Mud Hens fans. A few months ago, however, Jackson Publishing encountered competition. Mud-Sports began to produce a newsletter and offer a Web site also intended for Mud Hens fans.

Phil Strang, the editor-in-chief of Jackson Publishing, has approached Economic Consultants for advice about how to increase its readership and maximize its profits. Prepare a report for Jackson Publishing that addresses the following issues:

1. In what type of competitive market does Jackson Publishing now operate?
2. What economic principles with regard to price, output, and economic profit does Jackson Publishing need to consider?

3. What strategies can Jackson Publishing implement to increase readership and maximize profit?

You may find the following resources helpful as you prepare this report for Jackson Publishing:

- **CNNSI** (http://www.sports illustrated.cnn.com/) and **ESPN** (http://espn.go.com/)—CNNSI, the partnership of CNN and Sports Illustrated, and ESPN provide national coverage of sports.
- **Kirwin Communications** (http://www.kirwin.com/)—Kirwin Communications is an advertising firm specializing in sports advertising.
- **Toledo Mud Hens** (http://www.mudhens.com/)—The Toledo Mud Hens Web site is the official site for the baseball team.

PRACTICE TEST

1. Monopolies are price-makers. That means that a monopoly
   a. knows it has no influence over price even though it faces a downward-sloping demand curve.
   b. can charge any price, and at that price maximize profit by choosing output correctly.
   c. has the ability to choose among price and output combinations.
   d. can choose its price, and consumers will be forced to buy the monopoly's output at that price because the monopoly has no competitors.
   e. can force other firms in the industry to sell at the price chosen by the monopoly.

2. Perfectly competitive firms are price-takers. That means the perfectly competitive firm
   a. knows it has no influence over price even though it faces a downward-sloping demand curve.
   b. views the market price as given and knows it cannot influence that price.
   c. accepts the market price as its own even though it can choose a different one, because it maximizes profit at the market price.
   d. cannot force other firms in the industry to sell at the price it chooses.
   e. chooses a price that maximizes profit and stays with it regardless of what other firms in the industry do.

3. When a monopoly maximizes profit, we know that it is
   a. producing in the short run.
   b. producing in the long run.
   c. producing at an output where $MR = MC$ and $P > ATC$.
   d. producing at an output where $MR = MC$ and $TC = TR$.
   e. not yet in equilibrium.

4. When a monopolistically competitive firm maximizes profit, we know that it is
   a. producing at an output where $MR > MC$.
   b. producing in the long run.
   c. producing at an output where $MR = MC$ and $P > ATC$.
   d. producing at an output where $MR = MC$ and $TC = TR$.
   e. not yet in equilibrium.

5. When a perfectly competitive firm makes economic profit, we know that it is doing all of the following except
   a. producing in the short run.
   b. producing in the long run.
   c. producing at an output where $MR = MC$.
   d. producing at an output where $P > ATC$.
   e. facing a horizontal demand curve.

6. When a perfectly competitive firm is in long-run equilibrium, we know that it is doing all of the following except
   a. facing a horizontal demand curve.
   b. producing where $MR = MC$.
   c. producing where $P > ATC$.
   d. making zero economic profit.
   e. making normal profit.

7. If a perfectly competitive firm, operating in the long run, innovates,
   a. it can raise the price of its good, because other firms in the industry will not be able to compete with it.
   b. it can make economic profit indefinitely, because other firms in the industry will shut down, not having the innovation to compete successfully.
   c. it can make economic profit but only until other firms in the industry imitate the innovation—and they will.
   d. it gains economic profit but loses its normal profit, because it isn't a normal firm any longer.
   e. it shifts out of the perfectly competitive industry to a monopolistically competitive one, because it is now differentiated.

8. A monopolistically competitive firm in long-run equilibrium
   a. makes an economic profit equal to its normal profit.
   b. has few competitors, because many firms will have shut down.
   c. produces at an output level where its demand curve is tangent to its ATC curve.
   d. produces at an output level where $P = MC$.
   e. loses its distinction of producing a differentiated product, because there are so many firms producing so many good substitutes.

9. According to economists who accept the Schumpeter hypothesis,
   a. a monopoly will produce less output than a perfectly competitive firm.
   b. a monopoly will sacrifice economic profit in the short run to produce more efficiently, thereby assuring greater economic profit in the long run.
   c. a monopoly may end up selling at a lower than perfectly competitive price if there are increasing returns to scale.
   d. one perfectly competitive firm will ultimately become a monopoly, because success will weed the inefficient ones out of the industry.
   e. in the long run, monopolistically competitive firms will ultimately become perfectly competitive, because the goods they produce become perfect substitutes.

12

PRICE AND OUTPUT DETERMINATION UNDER OLIGOPOLY

There's an old story about a slightly intoxicated fellow who was crawling around on his hands and knees searching under a streetlight for a set of keys he had lost at the other end of the block. A passerby chanced upon the scene and, hearing the sad tale, asked why he wasn't looking where he had lost it. The not-too-sober man replied that although he had lost the keys in the far, dark end of the block, it was much easier to search for them under the light.

Let's retell the story just a little differently. Suppose a professor of economics is trying to explain pricing behavior in the U.S. market system to his class. He does so by describing price determination under conditions of monopoly, monopolistic competition, and perfect competition. When asked by a student why he analyzes these market structures when, in the previous class session, he had told them that oligopoly was the dominant market structure in the economy, he replies matter-of-factly that it is much easier to explain pricing under the other market structures!

THIS CHAPTER INTRODUCES YOU TO THE ECONOMIC PRINCIPLES ASSOCIATED WITH:

- THE CONCENTRATION RATIO AND THE HERFINDAHL-HIRSCHMAN INDEX (HHI)
- BALANCED AND UNBALANCED OLIGOPOLY
- HORIZONTAL, VERTICAL, AND CONGLOMERATE MERGERS
- CARTELS
- GAME THEORY
- PRICE LEADERSHIP
- KINKED DEMAND
- BRAND MULTIPLICATION
- PRICE DISCRIMINATION

OLIGOPOLY AND CONCENTRATION RATIOS

Is the analogy appropriate? Not entirely. In fact, it's a blatant exaggeration. But like most exaggerations, it serves to emphasize a point. And the point is that for a vast number of U.S. manufacturing industries, the competition among firms within the industry is essentially *competition among the few.*

What does that mean? Let's begin our discussion with the breakfast cereal industry. If you stroll down the cereals aisle in any supermarket, you'll find various box sizes of Cap'n Crunch, Life, Quisp, Wheat Chex, Rice Chex, Raisin Bran, Rice Krispies, Corn Flakes, Special K, Froot Loops, Frosted Flakes, Honey Comb, Shredded Wheat, Cheerios, Wheaties, Lucky Charms, Trix, Kix, Kaboom, Total, and Cocoa Puffs, just to name a few. But if you check the small print on each box, you'll see that they are all the products of either Quaker Oats, Ralston Food, Kellogg, Post, or General Mills. That's competition among the few.

Another example? If you're thinking about a quick lunch before your one o'clock class, there's always a number of local eateries to choose from, but chances are you'll end up at Wendy's, McDonald's, Burger King, or Hardee's. These few dominate the multibillion-dollar fast-food industry. And if you're thinking about ketchup on your fries, it's fewness again: Hunt's, Heinz, or Del Monte.

Look at big-ticket items. American and Delta Airlines dominate the skies, with US Airways, Northwest, TWA, and United struggling along. You can count the ones that matter on one hand. Where do they get their aircraft? Don't look much past Boeing, McDonnell Douglas (which is now part of Boeing), and Lockheed Martin. There are others in the industry, but, here too, it's essentially competition among the few.

The automobile industry? You can guess, can't you? It's General Motors, Ford, and Chrysler. Even with Toyota, Honda, and Nissan nipping at their collective heels, it's still very much *competition among the few.*

Chances are, when you were in diapers, it was Procter & Gamble's Pampers or Kimberly-Clark's Huggies, and the baby food you ate was Beech-Nut, Gerber, or Heinz.

It's the fewness of firms dominating the industry that distinguishes oligopoly from other market structures. An oligopolistic industry may actually consist of many firms, but if only a few of the many dominate the industry, then it's the fewness that stamps the industry as oligopoly.

But how few are few? There's no magic number. The measure of fewness is really quite arbitrary. To identify oligopoly, economists rely on the four-firm **concentration ratio,** which is the percentage of total industry sales accounted for by the four leading firms in the industry. For example, in 1992, there were 151 firms in the aircraft industry, but the leading 4 of the 151 accounted for fully 79 percent of the industry's total sales. The concentration ratio, then, is 79, high enough to signify oligopoly in aircraft production. The remaining 21 percent of industry sales, distributed among the remaining 148 firms, ensures that each of the 148 has virtually no influence in the aircraft industry.

Tracking Concentration Ratios Through the U.S. Economy

The 1992 Census of Manufactures catalogs a series of concentration ratios for U.S. manufacturing industries. Exhibit 1 selects a sample of 15 industries from that census, showing concentration ratios at the four-firm level for each industry and the corresponding **Herfindahl-Hirschman index (HHI).**

Concentration ratio
A measure of market power. It is the ratio of total sales of the leading firms in an industry (usually four) to the industry's total sales.

Herfindahl-Hirschman index (HHI)
A measure of industry concentration, calculated as the sum of the squares of the market shares held by each of the firms in the industry.

on the net

The U.S. Census Bureau (http://www.census.gov/) maintains the Census of Manufactures (http://www.census.gov/econ/www/manumenu.html) as well as other manufacturing data.

EXHIBIT|1

CONCENTRATION RATIOS—PERCENTAGE OF TOTAL INDUSTRY SALES PRODUCED BY THE LEADING FOUR FIRMS, AND HHI

INDUSTRY	NUMBER OF FIRMS	LEADING 4 FIRMS	HHI
FOOD INDUSTRIES			
ROASTED COFFEE	134	66	1,501
COOKIES, CRACKERS	374	56	1,169
SOFT DRINKS	637	37	537
CHOCOLATE	146	75	2,188
BREAKFAST CEREAL	42	85	2,253
HOUSEHOLD INDUSTRIES			
PHOTO EQUIPMENT	832	78	2,408
REFRIGERATORS	52	82	1,891
SOAP AND DETERGENT	635	63	1,584
ELECTRONIC COMPUTERS	803	45	680
CHILDREN'S TOYS	894	44	612
HEAVY-GOODS INDUSTRIES			
FARM MACHINERY	1,578	47	993
PRIMARY ALUMINUM	30	59	1,456
AIRCRAFT	151	79	2,717
TIRES	104	70	1,743
MOTOR VEHICLES AND CAR BODIES	398	84	2,676

Source: U.S. Bureau of the Census, *1992 Concentration Ratios in Manufacturing,* 1996.

Do any of these concentration ratios surprise you? For example, would you have guessed the ratio for the cookies and crackers industry? Of the 374 firms that make up the industry, the leading 4 control 56 percent of total industry sales. Look at the ratio associated with breakfast cereals. Of the 42 firms in the industry, the leading 4 account for 85 percent of total industry sales. Look how many of the industries have ratios greater than 50 at the four-firm level.

How Oligopolistic Is the U.S. Economy?

Exhibit 2's classification of all U.S. manufacturing industries by concentration ratio provides us with a fairly reliable indicator of oligopoly's prevalence in the U.S. economy.

Using the criterion that oligopolistic behavior most likely occurs in an industry when its leading four firms account for 40 percent or more of total industry sales, it seems clear from Exhibit 2 that oligopoly is very much a fact of life in the U.S. economy. In only 86 of the 448 industries do the four leading firms fail to control as much as 20 percent of industry sales. On the other hand, in 199 of the 448 industries (that's 44.4 percent of the industries), the four leading firms control at least 40 percent of sales. There's oligopoly staring you in the face.

EXHIBIT|2

DISTRIBUTION OF MANUFACTURING INDUSTRIES BY FOUR-FIRM SALES CONCENTRATION

FOUR-FIRM CONTROL OF INDUSTRY SALES (%)	NUMBER OF INDUSTRIES	PERCENTAGE OF INDUSTRIES
0–19	86	19.2
20–39	163	36.4
40–59	120	26.8
60–79	56	12.5
80–100	23	5.1
TOTAL	**448**	**100.0**

Source: F. M. Scherer and David Ross, *Industrial Market Structure and Economic Performance,* Third Edition. Copyright © 1990 by Houghton Mifflin Company. Adapted with permission. Data refer to 1982.

Is the U.S. Economy Becoming More Oligopolistic?

If you were a betting person, would you wager that the United States is becoming more oligopolistic? Would you, for example, bet that more and more industries are becoming more concentrated in fewer and fewer firms? If your intuition tells you they are, save your money. They aren't.

APPLIED PERSPECTIVE

A CAUTIONARY NOTE ON CONCENTRATION RATIOS

However useful concentration ratios are in identifying oligopoly, they can sometimes overstate the case. How so? By ignoring three important factors: (1) cross elasticities of demand between industries producing similar goods, (2) competition from imports, and (3) the importance of secondhand markets.

Why cross elasticities? The Census of Manufactures classifies industries not on the basis of what markets they serve, but on the character of their production processes. As a result, automobiles and pickup trucks are classified as belonging to different industries even though they compete (have high cross elasticities) in the same market. In this way, their respective concentration ratios may exaggerate the market share held in both industries by each of their leading firms.

Imports also matter. For example, the 1996 automobile industry sales were reported on 7,139,884

automobiles produced and sold in the United States. These are the numbers used to calculate the concentration ratio in the automobile industry. But 1,389,240 automobiles were imported in 1996, accounting for 16.3 percent of total U.S. sales. The ratio, then, ignoring the imports, magnifies the leading firms' influence in the market.

As well, these imports and the 7,139,884 new automobiles produced in the United States in 1996 had to compete in 1996 with a robust used-car market, eroding still further the leading firms' influence in the automobile industry.

MORE ON THE NET

Review the Census of Manufactures (http://www.census.gov/econ/www/manumenu.html), published by the Census Bureau (http://www.census.gov/).

Don't feel embarrassed. Most people believe they are. Karl Marx certainly did. Over a century ago, he was convinced that the industrial giants in Western Europe and the United States would grow at the expense of small firms. This expectation was central to his economic prediction of capitalism's demise. But he was wrong.

There is no convincing evidence to support the contention that the share of industry sales controlled by the largest four firms in the U.S. manufacturing economy is growing. Exhibit 3 presents the historical record.

Can you think of other price discriminating markets that affect students? Go to the Interactive Study Center at http://gottheil.swcollege.com and click on the "Your Turn" button to submit your example. Student submissions will be posted to the Web site, and perhaps we will use some in future editions of the book!

You would be hard-pressed to make the case for increasing oligopoly with these numbers. An upward trend appears for the years 1947 to 1963. But it reverses in the succeeding period, 1963–82. The 25.2 percent for 1982 approximates the 24.4 percent for 1947, undermining any attempt to establish long-run trends.

Concentration Ratios and Market Power

Concentration ratios tell us a great deal about **market power.** In any industry where the leading four firms control 80 percent of industry sales, it's no secret that market power oozes from their corporate windows. But the distribution of that 80 percent among the leading four can vary considerably.

Market power
A firm's ability to select and control market price and output.

EXHIBIT|3

PERCENTAGE OF TOTAL INDUSTRIAL SALES PRODUCED BY INDUSTRIES WITH FOUR-FIRM SALES CONCENTRATION RATIOS OF 50 PERCENT OR MORE: 1895–1982

YEAR	PERCENTAGE
1895–1904	32.9
1947	24.4
1954	29.9
1958	30.2
1963	33.1
1972	29.0
1982	25.2

Source: F. M. Scherer and David Ross, *Industrial Market Structure and Economic Performance,* Third Edition. Copyright © 1990 by Houghton Mifflin Company. Adapted with permission.

Unbalanced oligopoly
An oligopoly in which the sales of the leading firms are distributed unevenly among them.

Balanced oligopoly
An oligopoly in which the sales of the leading firms are distributed fairly evenly among them.

In some cases, the leading firm alone may account for as much as 70 percent. Such an industry concentration is described by economists as **unbalanced oligopoly.** In other cases, the 80 percent of market sales may be dispersed fairly evenly among the four leading producers—say, 20 percent for each—giving such industries the character of **balanced oligopoly.**

Look at Exhibit 4, which compares two oligopolistic industries with identical concentration ratios.

The leading four firms in each control 80 percent of their industry's sales. But do you see how differently the 80 percent is distributed among the firms?

Look at the unbalanced oligopoly. The largest firm, by itself, controls 50 percent of the industry's sales. Its market share not only is greater than the others combined, but also is more than four times as large as the share of the next leading firm. Under these conditions, its market power may be sufficient to force its will upon the other firms in the oligopoly on matters of price and output determination.

The market power within the balanced oligopoly, on the other hand, is quite another matter. Here, the leading firm, with 23 percent of the industry's sales, is

EXHIBIT|4

BALANCED AND UNBALANCED OLIGOPOLY

Industry A is a balanced oligopoly. Sales of its leading four firms—80 percent of the industry's total sales—are distributed fairly evenly among them. For example, the leading firm's sales amount to 23 percent; the second leading firm's sales, 21 percent; the third, 19 percent; and the fourth, 17 percent. Industry B is an unbalanced oligopoly where 80 percent of the industry's sales are concentrated in the leading four firms but distributed unevenly among them. The leading firm alone accounts for 50 percent of industry sales. The second leading firm accounts for only 12 percent.

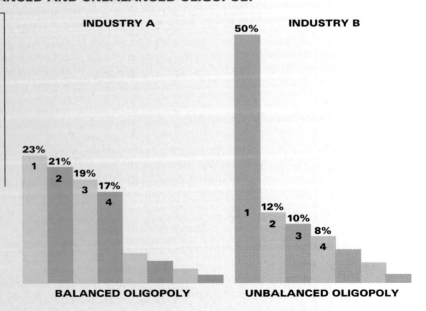

hardly more powerful than any of the other three. Under these conditions, price and output are far less likely to bear the imprint of the single largest firm.

Does the United States Have a Monopoly on Oligopoly?

Is the United States unique in the world of oligopoly? Clearly not. The concentration ratios for U.S. industries are not out of line with those in other modern industrial economies. Look at Exhibit 5.

Do these ratios look familiar? At the five-firm level, most are above 50 percent. The presence of oligopoly in Japan is unmistakable. What is more, Japanese and U.S. concentration ratios are not unusual.

The control of industry by very few firms is no less a fact of life in Western Europe and Canada than it is in the United States or Japan.

CHECK YOUR UNDERSTANDING

Why is market power most concentrated in unbalanced oligopoly?

CONCENTRATING THE CONCENTRATION

Fish feed on other fish. Oligopolies, too, have healthy appetites, which they sometimes satisfy by feeding on each other. An oligopoly can build market power by reinvesting its profit and painstakingly expanding its production capacity. But for less patient and more aggressive oligopolists, there's another route to enhancing market power. It's through the process of mergers and acquisitions. Overnight, two small firms can become one big one. Or two big ones can become even bigger. Even the biggest can become bigger.

Why do firms merge? Principally, for one of three reasons: (1) to exercise greater market control, (2) to increase their control over the suppliers of their inputs or the buyers of their goods, or (3) to expand and diversify their asset holdings. These three reasons explain horizontal mergers, vertical mergers, and conglomerate mergers.

Horizontal Mergers

The **horizontal merger** is perhaps the most easily recognized. It's a merger among firms *within the same industry, producing the same good.* When two competing airlines decide to merge, the merger is defined as horizontal. That's precisely what happened on October 1, 1986, with Northwest and Republic Airlines. Republic itself had grown out of a horizontal merger between North Central and Southern. Northwest's growth through horizontal merger was not unusual for the airline industry. TWA acquired Ozark, Piedmont merged with USAir (now US Airways), and Continental is an amalgam of People Express, New York Air, and Frontier Airlines.

Horizontal mergers are common. Many of the leading firms in leading U.S. industries are products of mergers. The

Horizontal merger
A merger between firms producing the same good in the same industry.

EXHIBIT 5

PRODUCTION CONCENTRATION RATIOS IN JAPANESE MANUFACTURING INDUSTRIES BY LEADING AND FIVE LEADING FIRMS: 1991

INDUSTRY	LEADING FIRM	FIVE LEADING FIRMS
SUGAR	12	48
BEER	50	100
NYLON	35	93
GASOLINE	17	67
GLASS	48	100
SOY SAUCE	29	50
CRUDE STEEL	26	63
COMPUTERS	55	89
TIRES, TUBES	46	98
AUTOMOBILES	34	85

Source: *Nippon, A Charted Survey of Japan, 1994/95,* Yano, I., ed., The Tsuneta Yano Memorial Society, p. 162.

THEORETICAL PERSPECTIVE

THE HERFINDAHL-HIRSCHMAN INDEX

How does the Herfindahl-Hirschman index (HHI) differ from the four-firm ratio? The concentration ratio is the *sum of each of the four leading firms'* market share in the industry, while the HHI is the *sum of the squares* of the market shares of *all the firms* in the industry. The HHI is written as

$$HHI = (S_1)^2 + (S_2)^2 + (S_3)^2 + \ldots + (S_n)^2$$

where $(S_1)^2$ is the square of the leading firm's percentage of market sales (or market share) in an industry composed of n firms. By squaring the percentages, HHI gives greater weight to firms with relatively high market power than does the four-firm concentration ratio. For example, in an industry where the leading firm has 25 percent of the industry's sales and the second-leading firm has 10 percent, the four-firm concentration ratio shows that the leading firm contributes 2½ times the contribution made by the second firm to the concentration ratio. By contrast, the leading firm in the HHI con-tributes 625/100, or 6¼, times the contribution made by the second firm to the industry's HHI.

The following table provides a comparison of HHIs for four hypothetical industries, where one is a monopoly and each of the other three is composed of 10 firms with differing market share distributions.

The most equitable market share distribution is shown in industry A. Each of its 10 firms has a 10 percent market share. Its HHI is 1,000. Market power is at its maximum in industry B. There, the only firm's market share is 100 percent. Its HHI is 10,000. Look at the market share distributions in industries C and D. The leading three firms in each command 79 percent of their industries' market sales. But the leading firm in industry C alone holds 50 percent, while the leading firm in industry D holds 30 percent. Because market share values are squared in the HHI, the HHI is 2,500 for the leader in industry C and only 900 for the leader in industry D. As a result, their HHIs are quite different: 3,204 for industry C, and 2,224 for industry D.

HERFINDAHL-HIRSCHMAN INDEXES FOR FOUR HYPOTHETICAL INDUSTRIES

INDUSTRY A		INDUSTRY B		INDUSTRY C		INDUSTRY D	
% SHARE	HHI	% SHARE	HHI	% SHARE	HHI	% SHARE	HHI
10	100	100	10,000	50	2,500	30	900
10	100	0	0	25	625	30	900
10	100	0	0	4	16	19	361
10	100	0	0	3	9	3	9
10	100	0	0	3	9	3	9
10	100	0	0	3	9	3	9
10	100	0	0	3	9	3	9
10	100	0	0	3	9	3	9
10	100	0	0	3	9	3	9
10	100	0	0	3	9	3	9
	1,000		10,000		3,204		2,224

classic example is USX (formerly U.S. Steel). As we saw in Chapter 10, J. P. Morgan bought out Andrew Carnegie's enormous steel empire and then proceeded to add 11 more steel and wire combinations—themselves collections of steel and steel-related firms—to form U.S. Steel.

Exxon also owes its primary expansion to horizontal merger activity. As Standard Oil, it was formed in 1870 by the merger of 20 Cleveland petroleum refiners. It then acquired an additional 100 competitors and ultimately controlled 90 percent of the petroleum refining industry.

The American Can Company was organized by an overnight merger of about 120 firms, giving it a 90 percent share of its industry's market. American Tobacco, too, established a 90 percent market share by merging with the industry's five leading tobacco producers. General Electric evolved out of the merger of Edison General Electric and the already-formed-by-merger Thomson-Houston.

During the first major wave of horizontal merger activity—1897 to 1904—horizontal mergers created such firms as U.S. Rubber, United Shoe Machinery, Pittsburgh Plate Glass, Eastman Kodak, U.S. Gypsum, International Harvester, and International Paper (see Exhibit 6).

A number of high-profile horizontal mergers occurred in the 1990s. Among them were Boeing and McDonnell Douglas in the aircraft industry, Exxon and Mobil in the petroleum industry, and Staples and Office Depot in the office supplies industries. A mega-media merger in 2000 linked Times-Mirror and Tribune. It brought together 11 daily newspapers (including the *Chicago Tribune,* the *Los Angeles Times,* and New York's *Newsday*) and 20 magazines. In the same year, Britain's leading drug producer, Glaxo Wellcome, merged with SmithKline Beecham, and MCI merged with Sprint to claim the major share of the communications market. The very big became bigger.

In the copper industry, Phelps Dodge bought giants Asarco and Cyprus Amax Minerals, making it the largest copper producer in the world. Cargill's acquisition of Continental Grain gave the new agri-Goliath one-third of the U.S. grain export market.

EXHIBIT | 6

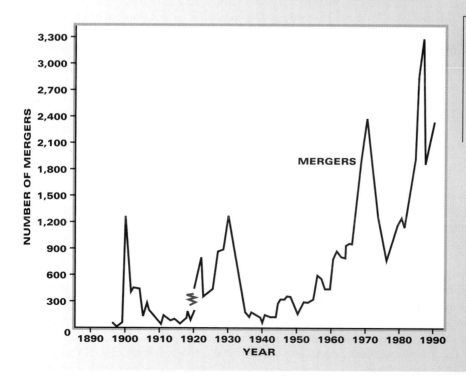

THE GROWTH OF MERGERS

During the 100-year period 1890–1990, growth of horizontal, vertical, and conglomerate mergers was erratic, but it progressively reached peaks that pushed mergers to over 1,000 per year for some years before World War II. Merger activity rose rapidly after 1950, reaching peaks of 2,500 per year in the 1970s and 3,000 per year in the 1980s.

Global or cross-national-border mergers have become commonplace. Since 1998, Daimler-Benz (Germany) and Chrysler (U.S.) merged to become the fifth-largest automaker in the world; telecom monopolies Telefonica (Spain) and KPN (Netherlands) merged to widen their European operations; and Young and Rubicam (U.S.) merged with WPP (Britain) in the largest advertising fusion in the history of the industry.

Vertical Mergers

Vertical merger
A merger between firms that have a supplier-purchaser relationship.

Vertical merger brings together firms not engaged in producing the same good. Instead, the vertical merger links firms in a supplier-purchaser relationship.

For example, USX acquires iron ore firms, coke firms, and mining firms. It owns or leases coal reserves, bulk cargo vessels, and chemical plants. Another example of vertical merging is Anheuser-Busch with its acquisitions of malt plants, yeast plants, a corn-processing plant, beer can factories, a refrigerator car firm that repairs and maintains refrigerated railroad cars used to ship beer, and a railway that ships freight by rail and truck.

If you enjoy Campbell's mushroom soup, you may be interested to know that Campbell's owns mushroom farms. Firestone, acquired by Bridgestone, not only owns tire manufacturing facilities but also has rubber plantations in Brazil, the Philippines, Ghana, and Liberia. Uniroyal, its competitor, owns rubber plantations in Indonesia, Malaysia, and Liberia. BFGoodrich owns plantations in Liberia and the Philippines, as well as synthetic tire-related chemical plants in Ireland, Holland, New Zealand, Belgium, and Costa Rica.

A number of high-profile vertical mergers occurred in the 1990s. Among them were PanEnergy and Duke Power (PanEnergy's oil and gas is used to produce Duke's electric power), Westinghouse Electric and Northrop Grumman (Westinghouse's electronic systems are used in Northrop Grumman's defense equipment), and Lockheed Martin and Loral (Loral's radar systems are used in Lockheed Martin's defense equipment).

Perhaps the glitziest vertical merger of the 1990s was that of America Online (AOL) and Time Warner. They merged to create the largest single company in cyberspace. This behemoth can place more digital content in front of more consumers than anybody or anything else in the world. Time Warner had already digested cable networks CNN, TNT, and TBS along with Tele-Communications, Inc. (TCI), the nation's largest cable distributor.

Conglomerate Mergers

Conglomerate merger
A merger between firms in unrelated industries.

CHECK YOUR UNDERSTANDING

Why do conglomerate mergers take place?

The **conglomerate merger** brings together firms that are neither in the same industry nor linked to each other in a supplier-purchaser relationship. Why conglomerates? Why would two unrelated firms decide to merge?

One reason for conglomerate mergers is the desire to diversify operations. While horizontal and vertical mergers strengthen the firm's position within the industry, the firm's fate still depends on the health of the industry. That can cause sleepless nights. By acquiring unrelated firms, the conglomerate insures itself against catastrophe if the industry itself faces severe problems.

Consider the energy business. What would you have done if you were Shell Oil, earning abnormally high profit in the late 1970s, yet having to deal with the political uncertainties of Iran, Iraq, and Saudi Arabia? Would you reinvest those windfall profits back into the Middle East? Wouldn't you have worried about competition from the nuclear and solar energy industries? Perhaps a safe strategy would be to stay in the energy business but diversify into hotels, potato chips, movies, publishing, car rentals, frozen foods, and maybe even a football franchise. If you did, you would not be alone.

Look at Borden. If you think only of milk, you don't know the company! Aside from food plants and dairy facilities, it owns chemical plants, soft drink bottling plants, petrochemical firms, and a commercial bakery in Germany.

RJR Nabisco is a recent merging of R. J. Reynolds, one of the major cigarette producers in the world, with Nabisco and Kraft Foods, two dominating firms in the food industry. R. J. Reynolds had already acquired Del Monte, Hawaiian Punch, Patio (the nation's leading frozen Mexican food), and RJR Archer, a major plastic packaging material supplier for supermarket meats.

Consider the following examples of recent high-profile conglomerate mergers. In 1996, Gillette, manufacturing toiletries, merged with Duracell, a manufacturer of alkaline batteries. Global mergers abound, among them Guiness and Metropolitan (Britain) in 1997 to form Diageo, which then in 2000 acquired Burger King (U.S.), Pillsbury Foods (U.S.), Häagen Dazs ice cream (U.S.), and a number of less virtuous items, such as Johnnie Walker whiskey, Gordon gin, and Smirnoff vodka. It has since shed Burger King.

Mergers Without Merging

JOINT VENTURES Firms don't have to really merge—or acquire each other—in order to gain the advantages associated with merging. They can remain independent and unmerged as firms yet create a **joint venture** in which they craft a merger that contains only a piece of their businesses. For example, suppose you were in the picture-framing business and joint-ventured with an interior-lighting firm. You both have experience and expertise in different aspects of interior decorating. You combine some of your resources in a joint-venture firm called *Your Home*. You're still basically an independent picture-framing firm, but you're also part of a merged venture.

Firms may be head-on competitors in one market, yet joint-venture in another. For example, AOL/Time Warner's online service competes with Microsoft's online service, but AOL/TW and Microsoft are co-investors in a high-speed cable Internet connection joint venture called Roadrunner. Sheds new light on the term "competition among firms," doesn't it?

CARTELS Cartels are another way to practice merger without having to actually buy each other's assets. Cartels simply behave as if they have merged. They get together—typically clandestinely—to establish common policy on price and market shares. By agreeing to monitor themselves and abide by joint decisions, they can behave like a monopoly, setting monopoly prices and parceling out the industry's production among themselves. In the United States, such cartel arrangements are illegal, but because it is difficult to prove **collusion,** many are operative.

DISGUISED CARTELS Just as a rose by any other name is a rose, so too is a cartel by any other name. In many states, agricultural cooperatives producing for regional and even national markets behave like cartels. They control price by voluntary agreement on production limits through quota assignments.

The citrus cooperatives in Florida and California, the dairy cooperatives in Wisconsin, the poultry cooperatives in North Carolina, the corn cooperatives in Iowa, the soybean cooperatives in Illinois, and the peach cooperatives in Georgia are just a few of the many regional and national cooperatives whose principal function is to control quantities offered on the market in order to regulate price.

GOVERNMENT-SPONSORED CARTELS Although illegal in the United States, cartels have flourished in other nations, including Western Europe. In some economies, governments have actually assisted cartel formation to replace foreign

Joint venture
A business arrangement in which two or more firms undertake a specific economic activity together.

Cartel
A group of firms that collude to limit competition in a market by negotiating and accepting agreed-upon price and market shares.

Collusion
The practice of firms to negotiate price and market share decisions that limit competition in a market.

imports with domestic production and to promote their own national exports. For example, Germany's economic development, beginning in the latter part of the nineteenth century, was essentially built with cartel production. By 1904, 385 cartels, comprising over 12,000 firms, accounted for virtually all of Germany's production of coal, iron, metals, chemicals, textiles, leather, rubber, wood, paper, and glass.

Few people have to be reminded what the Organization of Petroleum Exporting Countries, OPEC, is designed to do. It has been one of the most effective international cartels ever put together. Its membership includes the governments of Algeria, Indonesia, Iran, Iraq, Kuwait, Libya, Nigeria, Qatar, Saudi Arabia, the United Arab Emirates, and Venezuela. By setting output quotas and a common price, OPEC raised the price per barrel of crude oil from $2 in 1973 to more than $30 in 2000. The result was the greatest global redistribution of income—from the rest of the world to OPEC economies—in recorded history.

Concentration Ratios and Oligopoly Prices

Is there a relationship between oligopoly prices and concentration? If you vote yes, you're on the winning team! Many studies support the contention that price and concentration ratios move in the same direction: An increase in one is associated with an increase in the other. The relationship, however, seems to vary with the level of the ratio. Look at Exhibit 7.

The vertical axis measures oligopoly's price, ranging from relatively low (described as akin to competitive price) to relatively high (described as akin to monopoly price). The horizontal axis measures levels of the concentration ratio, from low to high. What do you see? Look at the polar ranges. Within the lower concentration ratio range, an increase in the ratio seems to have little effect on price. Increases in the ratio are accompanied by only slight increases in price. This same positive, but only modest, effect of ratio on price seems to hold as well in the upper ranges of the concentration ratio. Once a certain level of concentration has been achieved, additional increments of concentration seem unlikely to increase price at the same rate. It's in the relatively wide midrange of concentration that the influence of concentration on price appears to be strong. Here, increases in the ratio are associated with robust increases in price. The result is the S-shaped curve you see in Exhibit 7.

EXHIBIT|7

RELATIONSHIP BETWEEN THE CONCENTRATION RATIO AND PRICE

The higher the concentration ratio in an industry, the more able are firms in the industry to sell their goods at noncompetitive prices. The effect of the ratio on price is most conspicuous in the middle range of the concentration ratio.

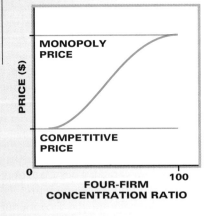

THEORIES OF OLIGOPOLY PRICING

The world of oligopoly is a highly personal one. The decision makers in an oligopolistic industry, so few in number, know each other well. They not only watch over their own business but also spend a great deal of time watching each other.

And for good reason. Any action, such as a price cut, taken by any one firm will affect very directly the market positions of every other firm in the oligopoly.

For self-protection, then, oligopolistic firms learn to react swiftly to market initiatives taken by other firms. For example, they may react to a price cut by cutting price themselves, thus denying the initiator the market advantage that was sought by the cut.

Of course, before any firm would initiate a price cut, it would take into its calculations how the others would probably react to the cut. And just anticipating their reactions may be sufficient to dissuade the firm from initiating the cut in the first place. This behavior describes mutual interdependence.

Game Theory Pricing

Does the oligopolistic game sound familiar? Firms go through the business day thinking, "If I do this, then they'll do that, then I'll do this, then they'll do that—wait—I'd better not do this!" Or, "If I do this, then they'll do that, then I'll do this, then they'll do that—wait—good, I'll do it!" The mapping out of initiation and response strategies is not unlike the game of chess.

Like chess, there is always a degree of uncertainty in the play. We really don't know, do we, what the response will be to any move we make? Thinking a strategy through is actually more like "If I do this, then they'll *probably* do that. . . ." But what are the probabilities? Each one of us would probably attach different probabilities to the same event. Some players are born risk takers. They play aggressively, forcing the game. But they don't always win.

Decision makers in oligopoly play the same way. Any strategy they adopt must include a careful study of probable reactions. They can cut price in the expectation of capturing a larger slice of the market, and sometimes they succeed. But if they calculate incorrectly, they can trigger a price war among the oligopolists, and everybody may lose.

To illustrate, let's trace some of the strategy options open to an oligopolistic firm in a two-firm personal computer industry where market power is equally shared. We suppose the price options are simple: price either high or low. Suppose the two firms are Dell and Compaq. They price independently, choosing between high and low prices. Exhibit 8 describes the severe profit consequences of this pricing game.

How would Compaq price its computers? It knows that if it selects a high price and Dell does the same, combined profit is $20. With market power equally distributed between the two, Compaq's own profit is $10. But another possibility stares Compaq in the face. If it chooses a low price while Dell chooses a high one, Compaq captures the major portion of the market. Its profit becomes $14. People still buy Dell computers but in fewer numbers, so that Dell's profit falls to $4. Their combined profit, in this scenario, is $18.

But do you think Dell would accept a pricing strategy by Compaq that undermines its market and profit share? If Dell responds by matching Compaq's lower price, they each end up with a profit of $6. That's considerably less than the $10 they each generate at high prices. How do they go about choosing a pricing strategy?

EXHIBIT 8

FIRM PROFIT, GENERATED BY HIGH AND LOW PRICING

COMPAQ'S PRICE	DELL'S PRICE	DELL'S PROFIT	COMPAQ'S PROFIT
HIGH	HIGH	$10	$10
LOW	HIGH	$ 4	$14
LOW	LOW	$ 6	$ 6
HIGH	LOW	$14	$ 4

Suppose Dell Hires *You* As Its Price Maker

Suppose you were hired by Dell to make these tough pricing decisions. You close the door to your new plush office, tell your secretary to hold all incoming calls, and get down to the serious business of "thinking price strategy."

Where do you start? Suppose you have two price options: high price or low price. Which do you choose? Be careful. As you see in Exhibit 8, there's always a risk that by reaching for more, you may end up with less. If you lower your expectations, you forgo the possibility of the "big win," but you also avoid the possibility of a "big regret."

Protecting Yourself Against the Worst-Case Scenario

Payoff matrix
A table that matches the sets of gains (or losses) for competing firms when they choose, independently, various pricing options.

It may not be a bad idea to develop a price strategy that protects you against the worst possible outcome. How do you do that? Look at Exhibit 9. It depicts the **payoff matrix** associated with different pricing strategies. The two columns—*reading down*—show the two price choices for Dell: high and low. You choose either one. The two rows—*reading across*—show the same high and low price choices for Compaq. It can choose either one. Each of the four squares composed by the choices you and Compaq make spell out the specific payoffs that each receives.

What's your worst-case scenario? It's the combination of you choosing a high price while Compaq chooses a low one (bottom left square), so that Dell ends up with the minimum $4 payoff. Compaq is delighted that you picked the high-price option. Why? Because your high price combined with its low price allows Compaq to reap a $14 payoff.

Not too smart a move on your part, is it? Can you avoid such an outcome? Absolutely—*by choosing a low-price strategy and stubbornly staying with it*. Now, regardless of what Compaq does, Dell is protected against the $4 worst-case outcome. After all, if Compaq chooses to price high while you price low (you're now in the upper right square), Dell ends up with the $14 payoff! And even if Compaq chooses to price low (bottom right square), Dell still ends up with a $6 payoff. That's considerably better than the $4 payoff.

Nash equilibrium
A set of pricing strategies adopted by firms in which none can improve its payoff outcome, given the price strategies of the other firm or firms.

In this way, pricing low guarantees you against the worst-case outcome. If the low-price strategy makes sense to you, don't you think it should make sense to Compaq as well? By pricing low, both Compaq and Dell can feel comfortable knowing that no matter what the other does, the worst-case scenario is avoided. Economists describe this matching low-price strategy as the **Nash equilibrium** (named for Princeton's Nobel laureate John Nash, who pioneered this and other contributions to game theory). The reason this pricing strategy is regarded as an equilibrium one is that once equilibrium is reached, both Dell and Compaq have no incentive to deviate from the strategy.

Pursuing an Alternative Strategy: Tit-for-Tat

Is there something bothering you about ending up in a Nash equilibrium? There should be. After all, look again at Exhibit 9 and see the

EXHIBIT 9

PAYOFF MATRIX

		DELL'S STRATEGY	
		HIGH PRICE	LOW PRICE
COMPAQ'S STRATEGY	**HIGH PRICE**	DELL = $10 COMPAQ = $10	DELL = $14 COMPAQ = $ 4
	LOW PRICE	DELL = $ 4 COMPAQ = $14	DELL = $ 6 COMPAQ = $ 6

HISTORICAL PERSPECTIVE

THE PRISONERS' DILEMMA

An illustration often used by economists to explain strategic decision making among oligopolistic firms in a game theory environment is the prisoners' dilemma. How is this game played?

Imagine a situation in which you and a partner-in-crime are caught in the dark of night breaking and entering. There has been a series of burglaries in the community during the past year, and the police believe they have finally caught the culprits. At police headquarters, they lock you up in one room and your partner-in-crime in another. A detective makes the following proposition to you: If you both confess to the series of burglaries, you both go to jail for 3 years. If neither of you confesses, and because they have no hard evidence against you on the series of burglaries, you each get 1 year for the lesser crime of breaking and entering. If you confess and your partner-in-crime doesn't, then you go to jail for six months, but your confession puts your partner-in-crime away for 12 years. On the other hand, if you don't confess, while your partner-in-crime does, he's out in six months and you languish in jail for 12 years.

FEDERAL LAW: BURGLARY IS ILLEGAL. MURPHY'S LAW: WHATEVER CAN GO WRONG WILL GO WRONG.

There it is: the prisoners' dilemma. You can't plan joint strategy with your partner-in-crime, so what do you do? Trust him? You must be kidding! The best strategy and rational decision is to confess, regardless of what your partner-in-crime does. Why? Because if your partner-in-crime confesses, you had better confess, otherwise it's 12 years! And if he doesn't confess, your confession gives you the minimum jail term.

The problem with this prisoners' dilemma analogy to oligopoly behavior is that it doesn't really replicate the situation that oligopolistic firms face. These firms are not locked up in separate rooms forced to make a once-and-for-all decision. Even if the firms don't get together, they can still signal each other and change their prices (confess/not confess) when they see what the other firms in the industry do. Nevertheless, the prisoners' dilemma does exhibit the game theory kinds of mutual interdependence and decision making that firms in oligopoly engage in.

MORE ON THE NET

Bryn Mawr's Serendip (http://serendip.brynmawr. edu/) is a multidisciplinary educational forum that induces an interactive prisoner's dilemma (http://serendip.brynmawr.edu/~ann/pd.html).

---

very real possibility of both Compaq and you each receiving a $10 payoff (upper left square) *if you both choose a high-price strategy and stay with it.* But that's asking a lot, isn't it? Can you trust Compaq to match your high price when you know—and Compaq knows—that by lowering price it walks away with a $14 payoff, leaving you with the minimum $4 payoff? Why should you take that risk?

Suppose you initiate a **tit-for-tat** price strategy that simply lets Compaq know that although you choose a high price, you will switch, if necessary, to match whatever price Compaq chooses. That's tit-for-tat. If Compaq chooses a high price, Dell stays high. If Compaq chooses a low price, Dell switches from high to low.

The risk of initiating such a tit-for-tat strategy is that if Compaq responds to your high price by choosing a low-price strategy, your immediate payoff is only $4 (bottom left square). Not what you hoped for. But that $4 payoff converts to a $6 payoff

Tit-for-tat
A pricing strategy in game theory in which a firm chooses a price and will change its price to match whatever price the competing firm chooses.

once you match—tit for-tat—Compaq's low price (bottom right square). That is to say, your initial high price is not a long-term commitment. You may suffer *at first* with a $4 payoff, but it would be only a short-run discomfort and well worth the gamble.

The advantage of going high initially is that it sends out an unmistakable signal to Compaq that you trust its intelligence to price high as well. After all, Compaq knows you're playing the tit-for-tat strategy and that if it doesn't match your high price, it will have missed the golden opportunity of enjoying a long-term $10 payoff.

Let's Not Play Games, Let's Just Collude

But why play a guessing game on price strategy when you could get together with Compaq and "negotiate" (that's polite for *collude*) an agreed-upon price. It would be a lot healthier for both of you because it eliminates the possibility of either of you misreading each other's intentions.

Suppose Compaq agrees and colludes with you on a common high-price strategy. Can you relax? Not exactly. There is always the possibility of someone cheating. Price collusion still exposes you to the worst-case outcome if Compaq agrees to the high price strategy and then cheats by pricing low. In the end, the value of a collusive agreement depends upon trust and rationality. It is really a trust in the belief that the partners to the agreement are rational enough not to violate the agreement. Sometimes it works, sometimes it doesn't.

As you see, this **game theory** explanation of pricing among the few is unlike the price-determining process under conditions of monopoly, monopolistic competition, or perfect competition. In each of those market structures, firms react only to the demand and cost structures they face. They are busy equating marginal cost to marginal revenue. They do not engage in second-guessing how the competition will respond to price decisions they make or how they, in turn, plan to respond to their competition's reaction. In monopoly, monopolistic competition, and perfect competition, prices *tend toward equilibrium.* In the game theory view of oligopoly, prices *are subject to fits of change,* reflecting firms in the act of testing each other's responses. Although oligopoly prices are typically higher than competitive ones, pricing strategies such as tit-for-tat, avoidance of worst-case scenarios, and collusion (with and without cheating) can generate for the industry alternating periods of price stability and price instability.

Godfathers and Price Leadership

Game theory is one view of how oligopolists behave. There are others. The godfather, or **price leadership,** theory explains pricing in unbalanced oligopoly, that is, when one firm in the oligopoly clearly dominates all others. These firms sometimes come to play the role of "godfather" in the industry's price-determining process.

There's a long history of price leadership. In the U.S. economy, it included at times General Motors in automobiles, Alcoa in aluminum, R. J. Reynolds in cigarettes, General Electric in refrigerators, Kellogg in breakfast cereals, USX in steel, IBM in computers, AT&T in telephones, Xerox in copying equipment, International Harvester in agricultural machinery, Standard Oil of New Jersey in petroleum, and many more. Every major industrial economy has its own set of oligopolistic price leaders, or godfathers, and in some cases, international "marriages" among them are not uncommon events.

Usually the godfather alone can set the industry's price. The other firms abide by the decision because to challenge it may provoke a price war within the industry that ends up being detrimental to the health of the weaker firms.

In most cases, however, all the firms in the oligopoly go along on the matter of price because they share a sense of common cause. The godfather accepts the responsibility of promoting peace, prosperity, and tranquility within the industry. The established price allows the weaker firms in the oligopoly to enjoy a profit that would have been unobtainable under more competitive pricing.

Exhibit 10 depicts how godfather pricing and firm output levels are determined.

Suppose 8 firms make up a chocolate oligopoly dominated by Hershey. The seven smaller chocolate firms acknowledge Hershey as godfather, allowing it alone to determine price. Each accepts the Hershey price as its own.

Suppose also that Hershey's marginal cost curve is MC_h, while MC is the sum of the marginal cost curves of all the other firms in the chocolate industry. The industry demand curve is D. Hershey's demand curve, reflecting a 25 percent market share, is D_h, and its marginal revenue curve is MR_h.

How does godfather pricing work? Hershey maximizes profit by producing 5 tons of chocolate at a price of $5 per pound. The seven other firms, pricing their chocolate at the godfather's $5 per pound, produce where $P = MC = \$5$, or at a combined output of 15 tons, that is, 75 percent of market share. In this way, they avoid conflict with the dominant and more efficient Hershey. The point of accepting price leadership is simple: prevention of honest-to-goodness price competition.

The Kinked Demand Curve

Aside from the game theory and godfather approaches to price determination in oligopoly, economists offer still another variant on oligopoly pricing that focuses on the unique character of the oligopolist's demand curve. Although downward-sloping—as all firms' demand curves are in markets other than perfect competition—the demand curve for the firm in oligopoly has a peculiar kink that results from the way firms in oligopoly view each other.

How does the kink emerge, and what significance does it play in oligopolistic pricing? The **kinked demand curve** provides another explanation of why oligopolistic firms do not lower prices to increase market share. Exhibit 11 illustrates the kinked demand curve's derivation and significance.

Kinked demand curve
The demand curve facing a firm in oligopoly; the curve is more elastic when the firm raises price than when it lowers price.

EXHIBIT | 10

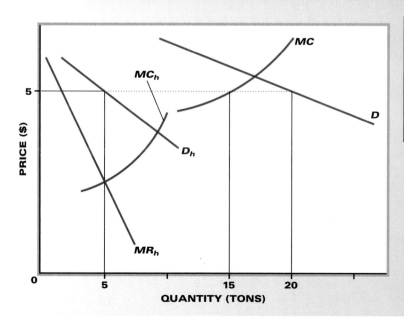

PRICE AND OUTPUT UNDER CONDITIONS OF GODFATHER OLIGOPOLY

D is the industry's demand curve. Hershey's demand curve, D_h, represents a 25 percent market share. Hershey's marginal revenue curve is MR_h. Acting as price leader, Hershey produces where its $MR = MC$, that is, at 5 tons and at a price of $5 per pound. The other seven firms in the oligopoly accept Hershey's price. The MC curve is the sum of their marginal cost curves, and they produce where $P = MC = \$5$ and at 15 tons. The industry's output is 20 tons.

Imagine Lipton engaged in price strategy. How does it view its demand curve for instant chicken soup in an industry where Libby and Campbell's are its major competitors? Suppose the prevailing price is $0.80 per box. In panel *a*, Lipton's demand curve, *YY* (*YY* stands for yes, others follow), depicts what happens to its quantity demanded when it cuts or raises price and its competitors react by doing precisely what Lipton does. That is to say, when Lipton cuts, they cut. When Lipton raises price, they raise price.

Lipton's demand curve, *NN* (*NN* stands for no, others don't follow), is considerably more elastic. It reflects what happens to quantity demanded for Lipton chicken soup when it cuts or raises price and its competitors decide *not* to follow Lipton's lead. If Lipton cuts price and others don't, quantity demanded increases considerably. On the other hand, if it raises price and others don't, Lipton becomes hard-pressed to find demanders.

Which demand curve, *YY* or *NN*, does Lipton really face? The answer is, a bit of both. If price is $0.80 and Lipton decides to raise price to $0.90, the probability is high that its competitors would stay at $0.80. That is, Lipton's demand curve at prices above $0.80 reflects *NN*. On the other hand, if Lipton decides to cut price below $0.80, others would feel compelled to cut as well. In this case, its demand curve below $0.80 reflects *YY*.

Panel *b* puts the two demand curve segments together—*NN* above $0.80 and *YY* below $0.80—to illustrate what Lipton faces when it decides to cut or raise prices. Note that the composite demand curve is kinked at $0.80.

THE MARGINAL REVENUE GAP What about Lipton's marginal revenue curve? Panel *a* in Exhibit 12 shows the marginal revenue curve associated with the kinked demand curve.

As you see, the *MR* curve in panel *a* is discontinuous. The *MR* segment above the kink traces the marginal revenue corresponding to the demand curve's *NK* segment in Exhibit 10, panel *b*. The *M'R'* segment below the kink traces marginal revenue corresponding to the demand curve's *KY* segment. Note that the kink in the

EXHIBIT|11

CONSTRUCTING AN OLIGOPOLIST'S DEMAND CURVE

The two demand curves in panel *a*—*NN* and *YY*—represent two different ways competitors respond to a price cut or price increase initiated by Lipton. If they react by doing precisely what Lipton does—cut price when Lipton cuts, increase price when Lipton increases—Lipton's demand curve is *YY*, relatively inelastic. If competitors react by *not* following Lipton's price initiative, Lipton's demand curve is *NN*, relatively elastic.

Panel *b* combines the two segments of *YY* and *NN* to reflect more realistically how competitors in oligopoly react to Lipton's price changes. When Lipton increases price, its competitors do not follow. Lipton's demand curve above $0.80, then, is *NK*. When Lipton cuts price, its competitors feel compelled to follow. Its demand curve below $0.80, then, is *KY*.

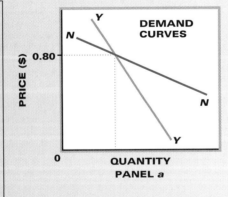

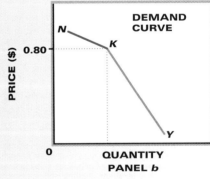

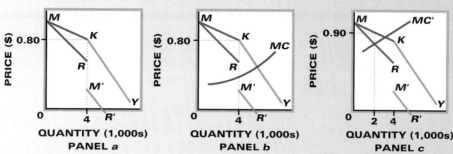

PRICE RIGIDITY IN OLIGOPOLIES WITH KINKED DEMAND CURVES

In panel *a*, the oligopoly's kinked demand curve creates a corresponding marginal revenue curve that is discontinuous at the point of the kink. The marginal revenue curve associated with the *MK* segment of the demand curve is *MR*. The marginal revenue associated with the *KY* segment of the demand curve is *M'R'*. Note the *RM'* gap created in the marginal revenue curve.

In panel *b*, the firm's marginal cost curve cuts the marginal revenue curve within the *MR* gap. Applying the *MR = MC* profit maximization rule, Lipton will produce 4,000 boxes, priced at $0.80. As long as the firm's marginal cost curve falls within the *MR* gap, price will remain at $0.80. In panel *c*, the firm's marginal cost curve *MC'* cuts the marginal revenue curve along its upper *MR* segment. Output falls to 2,000 boxes and price increases to $0.90.

demand curve at $0.80 creates a gap, *RM'*, in Lipton's marginal revenue curve. Why are we so interested in understanding the derivation of this *MR* gap? Because it explains why there can be substantial price rigidity in oligopoly despite sizable changes in the firm's costs.

PRICE RIGIDITY AND PRICE FLUCTUATIONS Look at panel *b* in Exhibit 12. Lipton's marginal cost curve can be located anywhere between *R* and *M'* and Lipton will still produce 4,000 boxes and market them at $0.80. Even if its costs—prices of raw chicken, labor, or advertising—were to increase, as long as the resultant upward shift in its *MC* curve still locates *MR = MC* within the *RM'* gap, Lipton will maximize profit by producing 4,000 units priced at $0.80.

Even when costs fall, prices may still remain rigid. Suppose a new technology is introduced by Lipton and spreads throughout the oligopoly, so that every firm's costs are cut substantially. As long as these lower costs still produce an *MC* curve that locates *MR = MC* within the *RM'* gap, price remains at $0.80.

The larger the gap, the greater is the change in costs that Lipton could tolerate without changing price. What determines the size of the gap? As you see in Exhibit 12, it depends upon the difference in slope between the two segments of the firm's kinked demand curve. This difference reflects both the price elasticity of demand for Lipton's chicken soup and the cross elasticities of demand among all the various brands produced by Lipton and its competitors. The greater the difference in the slopes of the kinked demand, the greater is the gap, and the more resistant is price to changes in cost.

But suppose that rising costs shift Lipton's MC curve upward beyond the gap, for example, to *MC'* in panel *c* of Exhibit 12. Lipton would respond by moving to a new profit-maximizing price and output. Now *MR = MC'* at 2,000 boxes. At this output level, Lipton increases price to $0.90.

CHECK YOUR UNDERSTANDING

Why don't marginal cost changes cause price to change in the kinked demand curve model?

OLIGOPOLY AND BRAND MULTIPLICATION

Have you ever wondered why there are so many brands of soaps, toothpaste, soft drinks, laundry detergents, cigarettes, and candy bars? If you read their labels carefully, you will discover that many of these brands are produced by a very few firms. The firms are typically oligopolies in industries with relatively high concentration ratios.

Brand multiplication
Variations on essentially one good that a firm produces in order to increase its market share.

Why would any firm go through the trouble of creating **brand multiplication** of the same good? The answer is market share. Each firm, reluctant to compete in price, tries to increase its profit by capturing a larger share of the market by adding more brands.

Suppose, for example, that Colgate-Palmolive and Procter & Gamble are the only two firms in the toothpaste oligopoly. Suppose, as well, that Colgate's single brand has the same market strength as Procter & Gamble's Crest. Colgate's market share can be expressed as

firm market share = number of brands × brand market share

With only one brand, Colgate-Palmolive has a 50 percent market share. Now, how would Colgate-Palmolive go about increasing its share of the toothpaste market? Suppose it introduces a second brand, Ultra-Brite, which becomes as successful as Crest and Colgate. It now has two of the three brands on the market. If each brand captures one-third of the market, Colgate-Palmolive's market share rises from 50 percent to 67 percent.

All this was done without Colgate-Palmolive having to cut price a penny. Of course, if Procter & Gamble responds by adding Gleem, its own second brand, then Colgate-Palmolive's market share falls back to 50 percent.

You can see, then, how this market share struggle can get out of hand. The game is to outbrand the competitor. An aggressive strategy would be to keep adding new brands, promoting those that succeed, replacing those that don't, and maintaining a greater number of brands on the market than the competition does.

There are limits, however, to a firm's brand multiplication. Each new brand requires physical space, independent management, and advertising expenditures. Unless a new brand can capture a good share of the market, its place in the firm's product line can be detrimental to the oligopolistic firm's profit.

As the number of brands in the industry increases, market share per brand diminishes. Given the relatively high promotional costs associated with each brand's survival, the marginal cost of adding a new brand will eventually catch up to the marginal revenue the new brand generates.

With enough time and testing, oligopolistic firms discover the optimum number of brands to produce. But the brand game is continuous; it requires an ongoing process of weeding out weak brands and strengthening the successful. That's why firms insist that their brands are "new and improved."

WHY OLIGOPOLISTS SOMETIMES PRICE DISCRIMINATE

Picture the scene. Five people in Los Angeles board United Airlines nonstop flight 224 to New York. R. J. Abrams, an executive with MCA Records, flies first class. His round-trip fare is $2,022. Alternative rock star Tanya Donelly flies coach. She bought the round-trip ticket just before boarding, paying $1,234. The trip was a last-minute decision. Her agent in New York is putting the finishing touches on a European tour and needs her input. Seated next to her, on the aisle, is Peter Soboroff, a Hollywood stuntman who is going to New York to appear on the *Late Show with David Letterman.* Buying the ticket three days in advance, he paid $622 for round-trip fare. A few rows back is Reesa Rodier. She's a fund-raiser for the Leukemia Society of America. Invited to address a New York conference only a week ago, she was able to buy a round-trip ticket, seven days in advance, for $497. Jenny Dibello sits next to Reesa. She is a professor of entomology at UCLA. She planned long in advance to see Susan Dunn in *La Bohème* at the Met. Her round-trip ticket, purchased 14 days in advance, was $318.

Five people buy the *same* good—a round-trip flight between New York and Los Angeles—and yet pay 5 very different prices. Why would United price the flight so differently? After all, if these same five people went to the same newsstand to buy the *Los Angeles Times,* they would pay the same $0.25. If they went to the same supermarket to buy Hershey almond candy bars, they would pay the same $0.55. Why, then, are their fares so different?

Segmenting the Market

Suppose Exhibit 13 records the demand schedule for the United Airlines flight.

If United Airlines does not segment its market and all costs associated with the flight are fixed—it is a scheduled flight—United would choose to price the flight at $318, earning a total revenue of $119,250.

R. J. Abrams would then enjoy an incredible consumer surplus. He would pay only $318, although he would have been willing to pay $2,022. United knows its market and looks enviously at Abrams's consumer surplus. How can they get Abrams to pay $2,022 even when others pay less? United invents first-class travel. It has several advantages. First-class passengers receive exclusive check-ins. Their seats are wider and more comfortable, their meals are more luxurious, and first-class passengers are physically separated from the common folk.

Why would anyone fly first class? Business and UN people, particularly those on expense accounts, like first class. The wealthy and privileged can afford it. Rock and movie stars enjoy a retreat from recognition. First class guarantees no professor or student in the next seat!

United also knows that some people would be willing to pay much more than $318, although not as much as $2,022. United creates a $1,234 coach fare that can be purchased and cancelled anytime prior to flight without penalty. That's the ticket Tanya Donelly bought. She would have preferred the lower fare, but she made the decision to fly on the day of the flight. She was willing to pay $1,234. By offering a no-advance-purchase fare at $1,234, United captured her ($1,234 − $318) consumer

EXHIBIT | 13

DEMAND SCHEDULE FOR A UNITED AIRLINES ROUND-TRIP FLIGHT BETWEEN LOS ANGELES AND NEW YORK

PRICE	SEATS DEMANDED	TOTAL REVENUE
$2,022	10	$ 20,220
1,500	25	37,500
1,234	40	49,360
1,000	60	60,000
800	110	88,000
622	150	93,300
497	225	111,825
318	375	119,250
200	450	90,000

EXHIBIT | 14

Price discrimination
The practice of offering a specific good or service at different prices to different segments of the market.

surplus. United also set up three different advance-purchase fares—3 days, 7 days, and 14 days with penalty on cancellation—to capture the consumer surpluses of other passengers.

By segmenting its market in this way, United's total revenue increases substantially. Compare Exhibit 14 to Exhibit 13.

As you see, United's ability to segment its market into a multiple-fare system allows it to capture $210,635 − $119,250 = $91,385 of what would have been its passengers' consumer surplus.

Is it any wonder why there are dozens of rates applied to different categories of people and conditions on international as well as domestic flights? Charter flights to Europe, Israel, Japan, Australia, and other attractive holiday locations compete with each other, and with their own rate schedules. Apex fares, purchased in advance for fixed and unchangeable departure times, and special promotional fares applied to specific periods allow the airlines to discriminate even further.

There are so many shades of **price discrimination** on these fares, each airline segmenting the market a bit finer to capture differences between obtainable prices and what people are willing to pay, that airline reservation desks sometimes can't keep up with the complicated airfare schedules.

Price Discrimination Almost Everywhere

Price discrimination on airfares is just the tip of the iceberg. The profitable strategy of segmenting markets through price discrimination is imaginatively applied to so many consumer and producer markets that it's difficult to think of any markets without some form of price discrimination.

Consider, for example, all the goods and services offered to senior citizens at discount prices. That's price discrimination. For each product, two different prices exist side by side. Why should firms introduce senior citizen prices? To capture a thought-to-be-untapped segment of the demand curve.

Children sit in the same movie theater to see the same film but pay only half the adult price. Student rates for magazines are less than regular rates. Doesn't the *Wall Street Journal* offer a student rate? Where do you think you are positioned on its demand curve? Do you see why it would expect its total revenue to increase with a price discrimination policy?

Publishers introduce best-sellers in hardcover to capture those willing and able to pay premium prices. When that market is exhausted, the same book appears in softcover at lower prices. Makes sense, doesn't it? Hotels charge regular, commercial, and convention rates for the same room. Student tickets for theater and sporting events represent another example of market segmentation.

DEMAND BY MARKET SEGMENT FOR A UNITED AIRLINES ROUND-TRIP FLIGHT BETWEEN LOS ANGELES AND NEW YORK

FLIGHT CLASS	PRICE	SEATS DEMANDED PER FLIGHT CLASS	REVENUE PER FLIGHT CLASS
FIRST CLASS	$2,022	= 10	$ 20,220
REGULAR COACH	1,234	40 – 10 = 30	37,020
3-DAY ADVANCE	622	150 – 40 = 110	68,420
7-DAY ADVANCE	497	225 – 150 = 75	37,275
14-DAY ADVANCE	318	375 – 225 = 150	47,700
TOTAL REVENUE			$210,635

Gray Area of Price Discrimination

But is it really price discrimination when box seats at the Chicago Lyric Opera are priced at $150, while you could see the same production of *La Bohème* from the fifth balcony for only $38? Some people who know opera insist that it's not the same *La Bohème* when seen from the fifth bal-

GLOBAL PERSPECTIVE

SUPPLY IS WHAT I SAY IT IS: HOW OPEC DICTATES OIL SUPPLY AND PRICE

How are oil prices determined? By forces of supply and demand in a competitive oil market? Not by a long shot! Think oil moguls in hotel rooms, privacy, and politics and power, and you've got the OPEC oil cartel.

The Organization of Petroleum Exporting Countries (OPEC) is a global cartel of 11 oil-producing countries from the Middle East (Saudi Arabia, Iran, Iraq, Qatar, Kuwait, and the United Arab Emirates); Africa (Algeria, Libya, and Nigeria); Asia (Indonesia); and Latin America (Venezuela). The cartel controls 40 percent of world crude output.

As long as OPEC members don't cheat on each other—and they often do—they can exercise substantial power over global supply and price. They decrease or increase supply at will, assigning supply quotas to each member and agreeing to abide by them. Most recently, they tailored supply to their advantage and set oil prices soaring to their highest levels—more than $30 per barrel—since the 1991 Gulf War (in which U.S.-led forces intervened militarily in 1991 to save Kuwait and Saudi Arabia from Iraqi aggression).

The cartel's quotas, renegotiated at its 11th summit meeting in Vienna, Austria, in September 2000, are, in millions of barrels per day and excluding Iraq:

SAUDI ARABIA	8.5	KUWAIT	2.1
IRAN	3.8	INDONESIA	1.4
VENEZUELA	3.0	LIBYA	1.4
UAE	2.3	ALGERIA	0.8
NIGERIA	2.2	QATAR	0.7

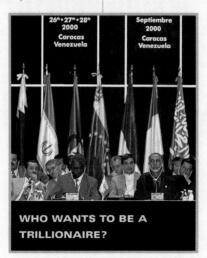

WHO WANTS TO BE A TRILLIONAIRE?

As you see, Saudi Arabia dominates the pack. There's no question about its role in determining global oil supplies and price.

At the summit meeting, Venezuelan president Hugo Chavez urged members to stand firm against the fear expressed by world leaders that the cartel's miserly output will trigger a worldwide recession. "We have relaunched OPEC united, in front of the world," Chavez triumphantly declared to the cartel's presidents, princes, and sheiks who gathered to sign onto the summit's agreements. Cartels are usually quiet about these things. Not OPEC.

cony. Does location change the good? If it does, then is it really price discrimination? Not necessarily. The question, of course, is not restricted to opera. Is watching a Montreal Canadiens hockey game at the Molson Center in Montreal from a center-ice box seat the same game you watch from an upper-balcony behind-the-goal seat? Probably not. On the other hand, if the Montreal Canadiens offer senior citizens a 10 percent discount on *any* seat, that's clearly price discrimination.

What about the thousands of quality variations that firms introduce among the goods they market? Consider oligopoly's strategy of brand multiplication. For example, how different is General Motors' Buick LeSabre from its Buick Park Avenue? The 1997 LeSabre Custom was priced at $26,170. The 1997 Park Avenue was priced at $35,660. General Motors' 1997 Cadillac Seville was priced at $46,709. Are they *really* different products?

While the Cadillac may be a superior automobile, General Motors' product line may reflect more price discrimination than product differentiation. It offers higher-priced transportation to those willing to pay the higher price. There is no deception. People who pay for Cadillacs, drive Cadillacs.

What works for General Motors works for General Electric. Consider its line of clothes dryers. It runs from the basic unit to the super deluxe model. Each move up the model range provides a more finely tuned selection of cycles and more dryer conveniences. Each model is designed to segment the demand curve as effectively as it dries clothes. Toaster ovens, personal computers, wristwatches, 35-mm cameras, furniture, tennis rackets, lawn mowers, and bicycles are a few among thousands of goods that allow for such market segmentation.

CARTEL PRICING

What about oligopolistic firms bonded together in cartels? How do they determine price? Cartel members put aside their chess-game pricing strategies. There is no need to outguess or outsmart each other. They get together to program common strategy.

Exhibit 15 depicts how the strategy works for an olive oil cartel.

The cartel takes over the price and output decision making from the firms. It behaves *as if it were* a monopoly. The cartel alone represents the industry. In panel *a*, the cartel's demand curve, *D*, is the industry's demand curve. Its marginal revenue curve is *MR*. The cartel's marginal cost curve, *MC*, is derived by adding together the firms' *MC* curves.

The cartel maximizes industry profit by producing where $MR = MC$, at an output of 14,000 barrels and at a price of $8. Each firm is committed to the cartel-derived price of olive oil. They sell at $8, producing only their agreed-upon share of the cartel's output. That output may be allocated among the cartel's firms according to geography—one firm given exclusive rights to the Southwest, another to the Midwest, another to New England—or each firm may be assigned a simple fraction of the industry's output.

EXHIBIT | 15

CARTEL PRICING AND OUTPUT ALLOCATIONS

The cartel behaves as if it were a monopoly. In panel *a,* the industry demand curve, *D,* becomes the demand curve facing the cartel. *MR* is the cartel's marginal revenue curve. The cartel's marginal cost is the sum of the firms' *MC* curves. The cartel maximizes profit for its members by producing 14,000 barrels at a price of $8.

In panel *b, MC* and *ATC* represent the marginal cost and average total cost curves of an individual firm belonging to the cartel. The firm's assigned quota is 2,000 barrels. Its profit, then, is $(P - ATC) \times Q = (\$8 - \$2) \times 2,000 = \$12,000$. But the firm knows that by raising output to 4,000 barrels, where its $MR = MC$, its profit would increase to $(\$8 - \$2.50) \times 4,000 = \$22,000$. Cheating under these circumstances is irresistible.

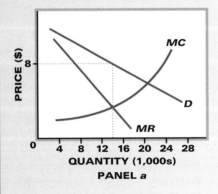

PANEL *a*

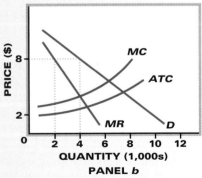

PANEL *b*

Suppose the output quota assigned to the Lynn Eckert Olive Oil Company, a member of the cartel, is 2,000 barrels. Panel *b* depicts Eckert's own demand and cost curves and the price and quantity assigned it by the cartel. If the firm abides by the cartel's rules, its profit is ($8 − $2) × 2,000 = $12,000.

But a serious problem lurks in the shadows of panel *b*. Note that Eckert's own profit-maximizing position—given the cartel price of $8—occurs not at 2,000 barrels but where its own *MR* = *MC*, that is, at 4,000 barrels. The firm, then, has a strong incentive to cheat on its quota agreement. By producing 4,000 barrels, its profit increases to ($8 − $2.50) × 4,000 = $22,000.

But how does the firm cheat without getting caught? It can produce 4,000 barrels, show 2,000 to the cartel, then launder the other 2,000 barrels through third-party marketing under different brand names or labels. It can also invade restricted markets by giving secret price concessions to the cartel's customers. Of course, what it can do, other firms in the cartel can do as well. And that's why cartels often break down.

For example, in the mid-1980s, producers of crude oil in the OPEC cartel—in particular Iraq and Iran—engaged in semisecret cheating that pushed their own outputs far beyond the agreed-upon quotas. Oil prices fell. To punish OPEC cheaters, Saudi Arabia increased its own output, forcing oil prices down dramatically. OPEC members, aware that the viability of the cartel was threatened, constructed new quotas. The OPEC members discovered, as all cartel members do, that cartels are nearly always their own victims.

CHAPTER REVIEW

1. The U.S. manufacturing economy is highly oligopolistic. Most studies of oligopoly focus on the four-firm concentration ratio. There is no convincing evidence that the degree of concentration in U.S. industry is increasing.

2. High concentration ratios suggest a great deal of market power. However, the market power in a highly concentrated industry may not be distributed evenly, as in an unbalanced oligopoly. Even distribution of market power is observed in balanced oligopoly.

3. Concentration ratios tend to overstate the degree of market power in oligopoly markets because they exclude industries producing goods that have high cross elasticities, imports, and secondhand markets. U.S. markets are no more concentrated than those found abroad in industrialized countries.

4. Concentration in an industry can increase through horizontal mergers. Vertical mergers link firms that are engaged in supplier-purchaser relationships. Conglomerate mergers link firms in totally unrelated industries. Diversification tends to reduce risk for a conglomerate.

5. Cartel formation involves firms that establish common pricing and market share policies. Cartels are able to behave as monopolists. Although cartels are illegal in the United States, some operate in disguised form. Cartels are observed in other countries and among countries, as with OPEC.

6. Price and output decisions by oligopolists tend to be interdependent. Each firm considers what the other will do if it takes a particular action. Game theory is used to describe this sort of behavior. Game theory predicts some price instability in oligopoly markets as firms attempt to undercut the prices of rivals in order to gain market share.

7. Price leadership models apply to unbalanced oligopoly. A godfather firm is a dominant firm in the industry; it can dictate price to other smaller firms. The godfather maximizes its profit by setting output where marginal revenue equals marginal cost. The other firms accept the godfather's price.

8. The oligopolist's demand curve may have a peculiar kink in it, arising from the way firms

view each other. Above the kink, the oligopolist's demand curve is relatively flat because, if the firm raises its price, rivals will not follow with price increases, so the firm loses significant sales. Below the kink, the demand curve is relatively steep, indicating that a price decrease will be matched by rivals, and the firm gains little in added sales.

9. The kinked demand curve creates two marginal revenue curves separated by a vertical gap. If $MR = MC$ anywhere in the gap, price will not change. The kinked demand curve model suggests price rigidity in oligopoly even if costs change.

10. Brand multiplication is a common oligopolistic strategy to increase market share. Market share is equal to the number of brands times the brand market share.

11. Oligopolists may also price discriminate by segmenting the market in a way that allows the oligopolist to charge consumers what they are willing to pay for the good or service. Price discrimination is readily observable in airfares.

12. Cartel pricing is intended to be cooperative. Each cartel member may be required to restrict output in order to charge the monopoly price. However, individual members may find it in their own profit-maximizing interest to exceed their quotas. When this occurs, the agreed-upon cartel price is difficult to maintain. Secret price concessions also tend to cause cartel agreements to break down.

KEY TERMS

Concentration ratio
Herfindahl-Hirschman index (HHI)
Market power
Unbalanced oligopoly
Balanced oligopoly
Horizontal merger
Vertical merger

Conglomerate merger
Joint venture
Cartel
Collusion
Payoff matrix
Nash equilibrium

Tit-for-tat
Game theory
Price leadership
Kinked demand curve
Brand multiplication
Price discrimination

QUESTIONS

1. Why would firms in oligopoly consider joining a cartel? What do firms give up by doing so? What does the cartel do that oligopolies, acting independently, cannot do?

2. Why is cheating by cartel member firms sometimes irresistible?

3. How does the behavior of an oligopolist differ from the behavior of a monopolist? From a firm in perfect competition? From a firm in monopolistic competition?

4. Why is game theory useful in describing the behavior of firms in oligopoly? According to game theorists, do oligopoly prices tend toward equilibrium? Why, or why not?

5. What are concentration ratios?

6. Is the U.S. economy becoming more oligopolistic? What evidence supports your answer?

7. What is the difference between balanced and unbalanced oligopoly?

8. How does godfathering work? Who decides price? How do other firms in the oligopoly react to the price leader? Why?

9. Explain what is meant by a kinked demand curve. Why is it kinked?

10. Why do prices in oligopolies with kinked demand curves tend to remain rigid even when the firms' costs change?

11. What are the differences among horizontal, vertical, and conglomerate mergers? Give examples of each.

12. Why do firms in oligopoly produce many brands of the same good?

13. What is price discrimination? Why would a firm want to price discriminate? Cite examples.

14. How does the Herfindahl-Hirschman index differ from the concentration ratio? Why bother with the HHI?

15. Suppose you were on a weight-controlling diet and regularly lunched on either Lean Cuisine or Healthy Choice, the only two firms in the microwave-ready, frozen diet-food industry. Why would you be happy if both firms had no qualm about cheating on each other?

16. Tit-for-tat—meaning if you raise your price, I'll match you by raising mine, and if you lower your price, I'll match you by lowering mine—seems to be a win/win strategy for both firms competing in a balanced oligopoly industry. So why does it not always end up as a win/win situation for them?

17. If the goal of both firms in a balanced oligopoly is to avoid ending up in a worst-case scenario, a Nash equilibrium results. Explain.

PRACTICE PROBLEMS

1. Suppose you were head of a nationwide hotel chain that had a supply of 10,000 rooms. And suppose that the demand schedule for these rooms per night was as follows:

PRICE	QUANTITY DEMANDED
$100	1,000
80	2,000
70	3,000
60	4,000
50	6,000
20	10,000
10	15,000

What would be the most profitable price, assuming you had a single-price policy? Now suppose you can price discriminate. How would you price your rooms and calculate the resulting total revenue? (*Hint:* think of specific rates for senior citizens, government employees, corporations, conventions, and those with advance reservations. You can add your own ideas to price discriminate.)

2. Suppose you read the 1998 Census of Manufactures in Canada and noted four-firm concentration ratios and Herfindahl-Hirschman indexes for the following oligopolistic industries:

INDUSTRY	CONCENTRATION RATIO	HHI
LUMBER	80	3,607
SHIPBUILDING	80	2,270
RAILROAD	80	1,400
SPORTS EQUIPMENT	40	337

Which one represents the most unbalanced oligopoly? Explain. Can you determine from the data which of the leading firms in sports equipment and railroads has the highest percentage of industry sales? Explain.

3. Let's play a two-firm theory of games, with high/low price options and corresponding payoffs. Imagine the game played between Nike and Reebok. Construct your own profit options for Nike in the table provided and explain what Nike would most likely do.

OPTION	NIKE'S PRICE	REEBOK'S PRICE	NIKE'S PROFIT
A			
B			
C			
D			

4. The following table provides sales data for the ten firms that make up the steel tubing industry:

FIRM	SALES
PAOLA FLYGARE STEEL	$25
D.A. STEEL	7
PIXIE STEEL	4
TIMBUCK 3 STEEL	14
J. RICHMOND STEEL	2
WAYNE COYNE STEEL	5
DESCENDANTS STEEL	18
DEAD RELATIVES STEEL	15
GEOFF MERRITT STEEL	2
THROWING MUSES STEEL	8

Calculate the industry's four-firm concentration ratio and its corresponding HHI.

5. Graph a kinked demand curve and its corresponding marginal revenue curve.

6. Lean Cuisine and Healthy Choice can charge either $4 or $2 for their microwave-ready, frozen diet foods. Using the accompanying payoff matrix, and assuming for each a pricing strategy that avoids the worst-case scenario, what price do they pick?

7. Construct a payoff matrix—by picking any two firms, any set of prices, and any payoffs associated with the pricing combinations—that shows a successful tit-for-tat pricing strategy.

PAYOFF MATRIX

HEALTHY CHOICE'S STRATEGY	LEAN CUISINE'S STRATEGY	
	PRICE = $4	PRICE = $2
PRICE = $4	LEAN CUISINE = $100 HEALTHY CHOICE = $100	LEAN CUISINE = $150 HEALTHY CHOICE = $ 20
PRICE = $2	LEAN CUISINE = $ 20 HEALTHY CHOICE = $150	LEAN CUISINE = $ 60 HEALTHY CHOICE = $ 60

WHAT'S WRONG WITH THIS GRAPH?

THE KINKED DEMAND CURVE

ECONOMIC CONSULTANTS

ECONOMIC RESEARCH AND ANALYSIS BY STUDENTS FOR PROFESSIONALS

Randy Seals heads the Yummy Cookie Company, producer of the popular Yummy brand chocolate chip cookie. While Yummy cookies enjoy national distribution, the Yummy Cookie Company is still relatively small, with revenues of about $50 million per year. Two weeks ago, Nabisco representatives approached Randy with a proposal to merge the Yummy Cookie Company with Nabisco.

Randy has hired Economic Consultants to provide him with information about mergers and for advice about whether to accept this offer to merge. Prepare a report for the Yummy Cookie Company that addresses the following issues:

1. Would this be considered a horizontal, vertical, or conglomerate merger?
2. What resources are available on guidelines for mergers?
3. What is the nature of the cookie market?
4. What economic conditions are necessary to make this merger in the Yummy Cookie Company's best interest?

You may find the following resources helpful as you prepare this report for Randy Seals:

- **Stock Smart** (http://stock smart.com/)—Stock Smart provides daily news updates on mergers and acquisitions.
- **Antitrust Policy** (http://www. antitrust.org/)—Antitrust Policy is an online journal linking economic research, policy, and cases.
- **Department of Justice, Antitrust Division** (http://www.usdoj.gov/atr/index.html)—The Antitrust Division helps enforce federal antitrust laws. Among the division's resources are federal merger guidelines (http://www.usdoj.gov/atr/index.html).
- **Federal Trade Commission (FTC)** (http://www.ftc.gov/)—The FTC enforces federal antitrust and consumer protection laws. In addition, the ftc compiles economics reports (http://www.ftc.gov/ftc/economic.htm) on the effects of its actions on business competition.

PRACTICE TEST

1. What do you call an oligopoly in which the combined market power of the four leading firms is substantial and one of those firms exercises considerably more market power than the others?
   a. Balanced oligopoly
   b. Unbalanced oligopoly
   c. Game theory oligopoly
   d. Cartel
   e. Kinked demand market power

2. What does the concentration ratio measure?
   a. The percentage of total industry sales held by the leading firms in an oligopolistic industry
   b. The percentage of total firms in the economy that are oligopolistic
   c. The number of firms in an oligopoly
   d. The percentage of total goods produced in an oligopoly that are close substitutes
   e. The number of close-substitute goods in an oligopoly

3. Suppose General Motors merges with General Electric and General Foods. Economists identify such a merger as a(n)
   a. multiple merger.
   b. vertical merger.
   c. horizontal merger.
   d. conglomerate merger.
   e. oligopolistic merger.

4. When an oligopolistic firm's price becomes the price others in the industry will accept, it is very likely that the industry is characterized by
   a. cartel behavior.
   b. a set of kinked demand curves.
   c. price leadership.
   d. mutual interdependence.
   e. collusion.

5. The kink in an oligopolistic firm's kinked demand curve occurs because
   a. competing firms will follow a price cut, but not a price increase.
   b. competing firms will follow a price increase, but not a price cut.
   c. competing firms will follow both price cuts and price increases.
   d. competing firms will not follow either a price cut or price increase.
   e. when industry demand falls, some competing firms will cut price, others will not.

6. The basic idea behind the game theory approach to oligopolistic price behavior is
   a. collusion.
   b. price leadership.
   c. mutual interdependence.
   d. price discrimination.
   e. brand multiplication.

7. How and why do oligopolistic firms practice price discrimination? They
   a. segment the market to capture consumer surplus.
   b. refuse to sell to segments of the market to keep price above equilibrium.
   c. charge different prices for different goods to different consumers to capture market share from competitors.
   d. cut price below the competition's to capture market share from competitors.
   e. segment the market to capture market share from competitors.

8. Oligopolistic industries have few firms, but many produce multiple brands. Why?
   a. To price discriminate
   b. To increase market share
   c. To stabilize a destabilizing set of prices
   d. To collude with other firms in the industry
   e. To create a cartel that generates monopoly-like profit

9. What is a cartel and what does it do? It is
   a. a group of firms that collude to limit competition to increase profit, which they divide among themselves.
   b. a legal monopoly that is subsidized by government to foster greater economic development.
   c. a group of firms that agree to set a price in accord with the price leader to increase both industry profit and their own.
   d. an illegal grouping of foreign firms that collude to raise price in other markets to increase both industry profit and their own.
   e. a cooperative organization that sets the price for the entire industry to increase industry profit and the profit of each member of the cooperative.

10. What is the Herfindahl-Hirschman index? It is
    a. the list of oligopolistic industries according to their concentration ratios, from highest to lowest.
    b. the list of mergers that occur in any year in oligopolistic industries, according to type, such as horizontal, vertical, or conglomerate.
    c. a measure of market power in an industry, summing the squares of the market shares of all the firms in the industry.
    d. a measure of market power in an industry, extending the concentration ratio from four leading firms to eight leading firms.
    e. a list of oligopolistic industries identified by geographic location, such as Southeast, Midwest, or New England.

Have you ever tried to improve upon an already impressive performance? You know how difficult that can be. Imagine, then, trying to improve upon paradise! Where do you start?

To many economists, the world of perfect competition is the closest thing on earth to economic paradise. It's simply beyond improvement. How can you improve upon $P = MC = MR = ATC$, where all market prices are at their lowest possible levels, all goods are produced at the minimum point on their average cost curves, and the quantities supplied are greater than the quantities that would be forthcoming under

ANTITRUST AND REGULATION

13

CHAPTER

any other market condition? No matter how you look at it, *it's magnificent!*

So what's the problem? The only flaw in this otherwise perfect world is the annoying fact that perfect competition does not exist. At least not in our world of high concentration ratios. The real world is essentially one of monopoly, of monopolistic competition, and of oligopoly. If there ever was a perfectly competitive paradise, then we have lost it. We now live in an economic paradise lost.

THIS CHAPTER INTRODUCES YOU TO THE ECONOMIC PRINCIPLES ASSOCIATED WITH:

- REGULATING A NATURAL MONOPOLY
- "FAIR" PRICE
- MARGINAL COST PRICING
- LAISSEZ-FAIRE
- NATIONALIZATION
- THE THEORY OF CONTESTABLE MARKETS
- THE THEORY OF COUNTERVAILING POWER
- THE THEORY OF CREATIVE DESTRUCTION
- PATENTS
- ANTITRUST LEGISLATION

LEARNING TO COPE WITHOUT PERFECT COMPETITION

How do you regain a lost paradise? Is it even possible? And if it is, do we really want to live in that economic paradise again? There is no consensus among economists on any of these basic questions.

Some believe that perfect competition, if it ever existed, is no longer obtainable. Why not? Because modern technology dictates firm size. The enormous economies of scale that modern technology generates equate bigness with efficiency and at the same time rule out the possibility of easy entry. The idea that our economy today can again be composed of many small firms competing against each other is sheer fantasy. To undo the concentration ratios we observe in modern industry involves the undoing also of the technologies that created them. Of course, that's impossible. To some economists, it's also undesirable.

If monopoly and oligopoly are simply inevitable outcomes of modern technology, what then should we do about the monopoly and oligopoly prices they generate?

Even among economists who accept the inevitability of monopoly, very different policies are prescribed concerning what we ought to do. Some insist that government ought to regulate monopoly prices. Others believe government should just take monopolies over, or at least nationalize those particular industries that are absolutely vital to our nation's economic health.

Other economists disagree with the view that monopolies are inherently undesirable. They are convinced that both monopoly and oligopoly present no danger to our economic well-being. They believe we would do better to leave these firms alone. What they advocate as policy is "do nothing," or *laissez-faire*. Finally, there are economists who believe we can recapture paradise or get considerably closer to it than we are now. How? By cutting up monopolies into several pieces and having these piecemeal firms compete against each other. These economists support an aggressive pursuit of antitrust activity.

Let's survey five competing views on what we ought to do about monopolies and oligopolies. Later, we will examine each in more detail. Look at Exhibit 1.

Regulating Monopoly

Why regulate? Because monopolies are both inevitable and bad, and regulating what they do is the least disruptive of all policy alternatives. That is, if monopoly prices are unacceptable, there's no need to do away with the monopolies. Just do

EXHIBIT | 1

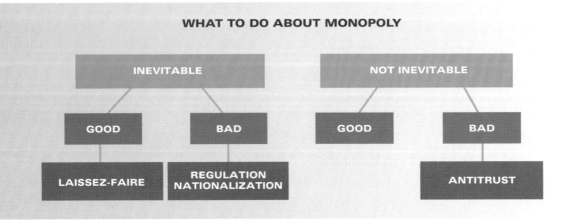

WHAT TO DO ABOUT MONOPOLY

away with their prices. For example, the government can regulate monopoly price to conform more closely to the price that would exist if the markets were competitive.

Simple solution? Not exactly. Price regulation may cause other problems and raise a new set of issues. For example, which monopolies should be regulated? Who decides? Government? An independent agency? What about the cherished idea of "freedom in the marketplace"? Are regulation and freedom really compatible? These issues can create much heated debate even among economists who appreciate the usefulness of government regulation.

Nationalizing the Industry

Other economists accept the inevitability of monopolies and agree that they are undesirable but come to different conclusions about how to deal with them. Instead of regulating monopolies, they recommend that the government simply nationalize them, that is, take them over. They believe that compared to regulation, nationalization is less complicated and much less troublesome to administer.

But which monopolies should government take over? All or only some? If only some, then which ones? Who decides what policies these nationalized industries should pursue?

Should government nationalize failing giant monopolies that, despite exercising considerable market power, would still collapse if left alone? That's precisely how Amtrak came into being. Many economists believe that if the government hadn't taken over passenger rail service, the service would have ceased to exist. Creating Amtrak, they argue, was a survival decision.

Taking a Laissez-Faire Approach

Other economists also see monopolies and oligopolies as inevitable but do not regard them as detrimental to the health of our economy. Unlike the advocates of regulation or nationalization who see a positive role for government, they recommend a **laissez-faire** policy (no government interference), believing that competition and therefore competitive prices exist in markets composed of highly concentrated industries and even monopolies.

To understand their view, think about prizefighters who compete even though there are only two in the ring. The competition is often severe enough to generate knockouts. Admittedly, some fights are fixed, but these are the exception, not the rule. Firms typically behave like prizefighters. Two alone will compete to drive prices to competitive levels.

As well, the *potential threat* of firms entering highly concentrated markets (as distinct from actual entry) is sometimes sufficient to discipline pricing policy. Even monopolies, fearing such *potential* competition, may behave as if there actually were many firms in the market. Economists refer to such markets as **contestable markets.** This potential threat of entry serves to moderate monopoly and oligopoly prices.

Other economists share the laissez-faire prescription but see competitive prices as stemming not from contestable markets but from competing economic *power blocs* that cancel out each other's enormous market strengths. Left alone, these competing economic power blocs end up moderating prices to acceptable levels.

Encouraging Concentration

Some economists put a more positive face on the presence of monopoly and oligopoly. These less-competitive markets, they argue, thrive for good reason. They are technically superior. They generate low prices because they are able to capture the economies of scale that bigness offers. Society benefits. Rather than recommend

on the net

The federal government nationalized the passenger rail service, creating Amtrak (http://www.amtrak.com/).

Laissez-faire
Government policy of non-intervention in market outcomes. Translated, it means "leave it be."

Contestable market
A market in which prices in highly concentrated industries are moderated by the potential threat of firms entering the market.

INTERDISCIPLINARY PERSPECTIVE

PATRICK HENRY AND KENNETH BOULDING ON FREEDOM AND REGULATION

It was March 1775 when Patrick Henry rode into the small town of Culpeper, Virginia. In the middle of the town square was a minister tied to a whipping post, his back laid bare and bloody with the bones of his ribs showing. He had been whipped mercilessly. Asked what the man had done to deserve such a beating, the reply was that the man refused to be licensed as a minister.

Those who tell the story believe it to be the incident that sparked Patrick Henry to write the famous words that later became the rallying cry of the revolution: "What is it that Gentlemen wish? What would they have? Is life so dear, or peace so sweet, as to be purchased at the price of chains and slavery? Forbid it, Almighty God! I know not what course others may take, but as for me, give me liberty or give me death!"

The idea that individual freedom and license (or regulation) are mutually exclusive seems to be intuitively obvious. It also seems reasonable to argue that any form or regulation must undermine the sum total of choices a person has and, ipso facto, diminishes by some extent that person's freedom.

However obvious that view of freedom and regulation may be to some, it was not so obvious and, in fact, was challenged by economics philosopher Kenneth Boulding. He argued that freedom can expand along with regulation, and, in fact, in many cases, its very expansion necessitates regulation. Why? Because as people's incomes increase, as technologies develop, and as our social conventions change, the number of choices among activities that people can do increases. The number of choices measures our degrees of freedom. But here's the rub: As our choices of activities expand, they sometimes conflict with other people's choices, and it is the resolution of this possible conflict that necessitates regulation.

Look at panel *a* of the accompanying figure. Two individuals—Alex Maxwell and Henry Frayne—are free to do any of the activities contained within their respective circles (each dot within the circles represents a possible activity). For both Alex and Henry, any activity chosen does not interfere with the other person's freedom of choice or action. For example, Alex has the income and the available technology to ride his horse to market (activity *x* within Alex's set of possible activities) without prevent Henry, who also has the income and technology, from doing the same (activity *y*).

But suppose, because their incomes expand and technology changes, that their activity choices grow, depicted by the two larger circles in panel *b*. Now there's a problem. They each have the income and technology to fly a small aircraft 5,000 feet above the Sears Tower in Chicago at precisely 10:45 A.M. Thursday (activity *z*). That is, they both have the freedom to make that one choice. But if they so choose, they jeopardize not only their own lives but also the lives of thousands in downtown Chicago. That's why regulation of our airspace came into being.

CONTROL TOWER TO TWA 234: "STAY IN YOUR PATTERN UNTIL FURTHER ADVISED."

But are they less free in panel *b* with regulation than they are in panel *a* without? That's the question Boulding raises. For example, are we less free because governments restrict our freedom of travel by regulating traffic at high-traffic intersections? Or are we less free because government limits a hamburger franchise's freedom to put any meat it chooses in its hamburgers? Are we less free because we insist on licensed physicians?

Compare the areas of nonconflicting activities available to Alex and Henry in panels *a* and *b*. Panel *b* wins. But the larger nonconflicting area comes along with an area of conflicting activities that necessitate regulation. Regulation, however distasteful to some, is as vital to our well-being—and freedom, according to Boulding—as our incomes, technology, and social conventions.

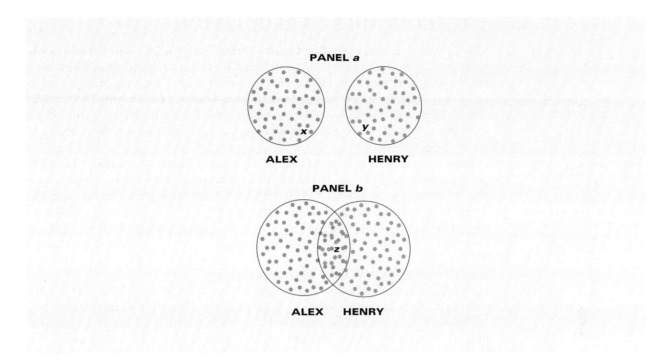

that the government curtail bigness, these economists suggest that the government should do everything possible to promote it.

Splitting Up Monopoly

A very different set of economists rejects the idea that bigness is inevitable or technically superior. Instead, they insist that the economies-of-scale argument regularly used to justify bigness has been overworked and inappropriately applied to most monopoly cases.

Like obesity, they argue, monopolies are neither inevitable nor desirable. If monopolies have no technical superiority, why then do they tend to overshadow competitive markets? *Because monopolies violate the rules of the game.* Monopolies use muscle as well as ingenuity to win their way into market control.

If market concentration is neither inevitable nor desirable, what should we do about it? Many economists believe we should shatter monopolies into fragments and establish laws that prevent their restoration. There is no need to regulate monopolies or to run them. Government simply enacts antitrust (meaning antimonopoly) legislation and allows the courts to do the rest. Monopolies who violate antitrust laws now risk becoming criminal offenders.

Hasn't government always been in the business of legislating against undesirable, antisocial behavior? Antitrust advocates believe there is no reason why the marketplace should be exempt. Antitrust legislation should identify anticompetitive market activity as criminal and root it out.

But this is easier said than done. Is the mere presence of monopoly itself sufficient evidence of anticompetitive market activity, or must the evidence show intent and *prove* criminal behavior? As you might expect, proponents of antitrust are divided into hardliners and moderates on this issue.

With this cursory outline of the alternative policies behind us, let's look in more detail at the economics of regulation, nationalization, laissez-faire, increased concentration, and antitrust policy.

The Department of Justice (http://www.usdoj.gov/) and the Federal Trade Commission (http://www.ftc.gov/) enforce federal antitrust laws.

THE ECONOMICS OF REGULATION

In the state of nature, lions and jackals eat their prey just as monopolies and oligopolies may eat up small competitive firms. We cannot change natural behavior, but there is good reason to believe that we can at least change *what* the predators eat. If you muzzle the lion, you control its diet. This tactic works with monopolies as well. Monopolies will always have a healthy appetite for monopoly profit, but if you take away their price-making function, you take away as well their ability to create monopoly profits.

Regulation
Although ownership of the regulated firm remains in private hands, pricing and production decisions of the firm are monitored by a regulatory agency directly responsible to the government.

That's what government **regulation** of monopoly is about. It separates monopoly pricing from monopolies. The price-making function is taken over by government-appointed regulatory commissions. The public utilities commission, for example, decides what rates the electric power company can charge. The price a regulatory commission picks to replace the unregulated monopoly price depends upon its assessment of the company and its market.

Regulating a City Bus Monopoly

Let's begin our analysis of the economics of regulation by supposing that you are the mayor of a fairly large city whose bus company enjoys, as most private bus companies do, a natural monopoly position. The natural monopoly is a price-maker. It picks its output at $MR = MC$, aiming of course to generate maximum profit. Wouldn't you do the same?

Exhibit 2 represents the bus company's market. It picks a price of $1.80 per fare and transports 80,000 passengers per day. Its total revenue is $1.80 \times 80,000 = $144,000. The average cost per passenger at an 80,000-passenger level is $1.20. Total cost, then, is $1.20 \times 80,000 = $96,000. The bus company ends up with a daily profit of $144,000 - $96,000 = $48,000.

EXHIBIT 2

THE CITY BUS COMPANY

The City Bus Company is a monopoly. The industry demand curve, *D*, is the demand curve the company faces. *MR*, *ATC*, and *MC* are its marginal revenue, average total cost, and marginal cost curves. Left unregulated, the firm prices its fare at $1.80, providing service to 80,000 passengers.

Deciding that the $1.80 fare is unacceptable, the community regulates the bus company. It can structure a zero-profit outcome (as in perfect competition) by picking a "fair" price of $0.90, where $P = ATC$. The number of passenger fares increases to 140,000. The community could instead choose a marginal cost pricing policy, where $P = MC = $0.30. The number of passenger fares increases to 180,000. But at 180,000, $ATC = $0.70. The community subsidizes the bus company by $0.40 per fare to cover losses emerging from its marginal cost pricing option.

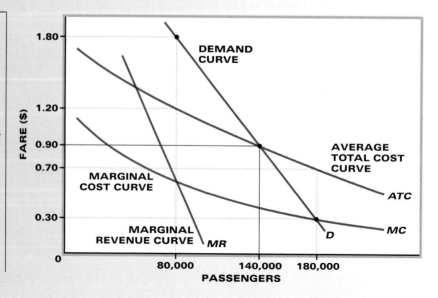

This is a troublesome situation. People without private transportation complain about the high price. A round-trip fare from home to work costs $3.60, which is prohibitive for many. Since so many retail shops and corner groceries have fallen away to the large franchises and supermarkets at shopping centers, public transportation has become an essential good in the community's life.

There's no reason, of course, to blame the bus monopoly for the $1.80 fare. It does only what every other firm in the city does. It tries to maximize profit. Competitive firms do the same. Other monopolies do the same. The city's only Triple A baseball team, for example, prices tickets the same way.

But what should you do? If you're like most mayors, you will decide to regulate the public transportation industry, but not the baseball team. Why? Because public transportation directly affects the economic well-being of the entire community, whereas baseball games are a matter of individual leisure-time choice. It's a judgment call, isn't it?

CHECK YOUR UNDERSTANDING

Why do cities regulate bus transportation?

Perhaps the first thing you would want to do is appoint a regulatory commission to decide how to regulate the industry to best serve the community's interests. The focus of the regulation would be on price and output.

If the monopoly fare of $1.80 is unacceptable, what is appropriate? The regulatory commission knows that if the firm were in perfect competition, it would end up making zero profit. Perhaps that's where to start. It decides to reproduce the competitive $P = ATC$ outcome.

Setting a "Fair" Price: $P = ATC$

Look again at Exhibit 2. Suppose the regulatory commission sets the bus fare at $0.90, where $P = ATC$. It considers $0.90 a "fair" price because the bus company, stripped of its monopoly profits, is entitled to cover its costs. Of course, the company still would enjoy normal profit, as it would under perfect competition.

What about the passengers? They appear to benefit. After all, the bus fare falls from $1.80 to $0.90. As a direct result, the volume of traffic increases from 80,000 to 140,000 passengers.

Is pricing according to the $P = ATC$ rule as uncomplicated as it appears in Exhibit 2? Not by a long shot. Once price is fixed at average total cost, the question becomes, Who regulates the regulated monopoly's average total cost?

For example, who determines whether new buses are needed? If you were the regulated monopolist and knew that the commission sets price equal to your average total cost, wouldn't you want to buy a string of new buses? The new and most heavily equipped buses might be frightfully expensive, but since the commission sets $P = ATC$ anyway, why not? What's the loss?

Who determines whether bus drivers should receive salary bonuses? Imagine what the average total cost curve of Exhibit 2 would look like if bus drivers earned the equivalent of NBA basketball salaries. Since the bus company is prohibited from profit making, why should management be concerned about keeping labor costs under control?

The ATC curve, under these conditions, could quickly shift upward, and with it, the $P = ATC$ position. After a while, the "fair" price might begin to look less and less fair.

What has happened here? In an honest effort to control the high monopoly price, the regulatory commission, through price regulation, has simply substituted one form of market inefficiency for another.

But regulatory commissions can read Exhibit 2 and spot the problem of cost drift just as well as you can. They can, and many do, monitor costs as well. Bus drivers may go on strike just because regulatory commissions are vigilant on cost containment. The firm may want new buses, but it doesn't always get them. The idea of fair price is seldom treated lightly by regulatory commissions.

Applying Marginal Cost Pricing: $P = MC$

Marginal cost pricing
A regulatory agency's policy of pricing a good or service produced by a regulated firm at the firm's marginal cost, $P = MC$.

Another option the regulatory commission might pursue is **marginal cost pricing,** setting $P = MC$. This occurs in Exhibit 2 at 180,000 passengers and at a price of $0.30.

Compare the $P = ATC$ choice of $0.90 with 140,000 passengers to the $P = MC$ choice at $0.30 with 180,000 passengers. Why the difference? Why would any commission prefer $P = MC$? Because $P = MC$ indicates society's optimal use of resources.

Look at fair price $P = ATC$. The value that people place on a service is measured by the price they are willing to pay. At 140,000 passengers, the value people place on transportation is higher than the value of the resources used to produce that transportation. The price they are willing to pay for one more trip is $0.90; the value of the resources needed to produce that trip—measured by marginal cost—is $0.40. That is, at 140,000 passengers, $P > MC$. Wouldn't society be better served if more passengers rode the buses?

$P = MC$ at 180,000. The 180,000th passenger is willing to pay $0.30, precisely the value society places on the resources used to produce the 180,000th ride. This $P = MC$ condition describes the socially optimum use of resources.

But if the regulatory commission agrees to this price, the firm's revenue is only $0.30 \times 180,000 = \$54,000$. But now $ATC = \$0.70$, so that total cost is $\$0.70 \times 180,000 = \$126,000$. You see the problem, don't you? The bus company suffers a loss. If the commission wants the regulated monopoly to produce bus service at $P = MC$, then it must provide the firm with a $72,000 subsidy.

What about the passengers? Do they really get a $0.30 bus ride? Not really. The $0.30 excludes the subsidy. Somebody has to pay it. The $72,000 subsidy comes from the taxpayers. Non–bus users now find themselves paying for services they do not use, creating a redistribution of after-tax income in the economy.

CHECK YOUR UNDERSTANDING

Why must the city subsidize bus transportation if price is regulated at $P = MC$?

Who Regulates the Regulators?

Although the intent of regulation is to correct the abuses of monopoly, the outcome can sometimes produce quite the opposite effect. Instead of regulating monopolies, regulatory commissions may end up protecting them.

Who are the regulators? Who gets appointed to commissions? Typically, they include people who can provide useful, specific expertise to the commission's deliberations. It seems reasonable to expect at least some of the commissioners to have a working knowledge of the industry and the finer points of its management problems. This kind of expertise generally comes only after years of experience inside the industry.

These commissioners certainly are not there to undermine the commission's mission, nor do they always represent management's view. But their knowledge and experience command considerable respect on the commission, and their appreciation of management's position—having been there themselves—sometimes creates the impression (if not the fact) that the regulators are the very people whose industry is being regulated.

It is not a question of industry conspiracy, but it can be a delicate matter. For example, should ex–police officers be appointed to a city's civilian police review board? After all, who better appreciates the problems that police confront daily on duty? Who can better advise on procedure? But is that the view that should prevail?

An example of regulators using regulation on behalf of the regulated is the Interstate Commerce Commission's handling of the transportation industry. Congress created the ICC in 1887 to regulate the prices railways were charging along noncompetitive routes. Over the years, the ICC established rate schedules to check the railroad's monopoly power and to protect rural communities against railroad price discrimination.

But by the end of the 1930s, the transportation industry had changed dramatically. The development of extensive highway networks matched the furious output of Detroit's automobile and truck assembly lines. Almost overnight, independent trucking firms mushroomed across the country, providing competitive freight transportation for both long and short hauling.

The railroads' monopoly on transportation was broken. But rather than allow this new trucking competition to force freight rates down, the ICC's response was to contain it. Almost instinctively, the ICC became the protector of the railroads. It expanded its regulatory range to include trucking. The ICC decided how many and which truckers could carry what goods which way on what routes. Truckers were tied to rates that served to protect the railroads. In other words, far from regulating monopoly in the interests of the consumer, the ICC now served to stifle competition.

The ICC's behavior was not unique in the world of regulation. The Federal Communications Commission, established in 1934 to regulate the telephone, telegraph, radio, and later television industries, has also played the dual role of regulator and protector. The Civil Aeronautics Board, established in 1938 to regulate commercial aviation; the Securities and Exchange Commission, established in 1934 to oversee the corporate securities market; the Federal Maritime Board, established in 1950 to regulate intercoastal and international shipping; and the Federal Energy Regulatory Commission, established in 1959 to regulate the energy industry, have all played, at some time, the protector's role.

The Economics of Deregulation

"Throwing the engines in reverse" is perhaps the best way to describe the economics of **deregulation.** It reflects a recent and widely held view among economists and government that the regulations imposed over the years for many industries, such as banking, energy, transportation, and communications, have become obsolete, and in some instances, even counterproductive. As a result, a movement toward deregulation in many parts of the economy took place in the 1980s.

Deregulation
The process of converting a regulated firm into an unregulated firm.

But the dismantling process was never seen as a miracle cure to the problems associated with regulating industry. Nor was there any intention of wiping regulation entirely out of government policy or of allowing a return to monopoly pricing. Industry concentration is still viewed by many economists as a serious economic problem, and the use of regulation to control pricing and output in concentrated industries is still regarded as legitimate and effective.

CLIPPING CAB'S WINGS   The deregulation of commercial aviation is one of President Jimmy Carter's legacies. In 1978 he lured Alfred Kahn out of Cornell University to head the Civil Aeronautics Board (CAB). That appointment was not unlike putting a hungry fox in charge of the chicken house. Kahn immediately went to work dismantling the board's regulatory powers and ended up doing away with the board altogether.

Initially, as new airline companies were established and more flights were added to already existing lines, unprofitable routes were dropped and price competition

THE MICROECONOMICS OF PRODUCT MARKETS

for the growing air traffic was encouraged. Almost instantaneously, the highly rigged airfare schedules disintegrated, resulting in bargain-basement prices. At the same time, the innovation of the hub-and-spoke system expanded service by the major airlines and by the newly formed commuter lines.

But not all economists are comfortable with deregulation. Although firm entry and firm expansion did create greater competition and lower airfares during the 1980s and 1990s, it also forced many of the new and some of the well-established airlines into bankruptcy. In the long run, some economists fear, the industry's concentration ratio may recover to its pre-deregulation levels, and airfares may even surpass their pre-deregulation highs.

FOR WHOM THE BELL TOLLS Perhaps the most dramatic deregulation event of the 1980s was the uncrowning of American Telephone and Telegraph (AT&T), which controlled every aspect of telephone service in the United States. People did not own their own phones. They had to rent them from AT&T and use AT&T's domestic and overseas lines. But the development of satellite technology paved the way for deregulation. It became technologically possible for smaller firms to compete with AT&T on price and service.

In 1978 the Federal Communications Commission ruled that AT&T must provide its competitors who produced telephone equipment with access to its lines. This allowed GTE, MCI, and others to compete with the former monopoly on telephone service. Long-distance rates began to fall almost immediately after these new firms entered the industry.

An earlier ruling by the FCC had disallowed AT&T's monopoly on the sale of telephone hardware and gave AT&T's competitors access to its lines. Consumers now had the choice of buying their phones from a variety of competing firms.

The Surface Transportation Board (http://www.stb.dot.gov/) maintains news and recent publications. The Federal Communications Commission (http://www.fcc.gov/) provides the full Telecommunications Act of 1996 (http://www.fcc.gov/telecom.html) as well as commentary on the act.

DEREGULATION MARCHES ON The Interstate Commerce Commission (ICC), seen by many as the epitome of government regulation, came to an end in 1995 when Congress replaced it with the much weaker Surface Transportation Board. Many saw this move as strong evidence of a bipartisan commitment to continuing deregulation.

Although the Federal Communications Commission has not been abolished, the Telecommunications Act of 1996 altered its scope of authority. In many areas, deregulation replaced regulation. For example, cable rates, a former domain of the FCC, were deregulated. The act also deregulated the FCC's engagement in such regulated areas as concentration of radio or television holdings. On the other hand, the FCC's scope was broadened in other areas. For example, local governments lost their power to control the locations of wireless towers. The FCC now decides many of these issues, although most often by not acting.

THE ECONOMICS OF NATIONALIZATION

Nationalization
Government ownership of a firm or industry. Price and production decisions are made by an administrative agency of the government.

The economics of **nationalization** is not at all complicated. The government simply buys the shares held by the shareholders of the targeted monopoly. In some economies, nationalizing an industry is an even less complicated procedure. Governments simply confiscate the property.

How do governments buy firms? Typically, they exchange their own bonds for the nationalized firm's shares. Assessing the firm's net worth could be a problem, but as a rule, governments in the business of nationalizing have been rather generous.

The government's main concern is hardly the measure of the firm's net worth. Instead, it is what to do with the firm once it has it.

Price Options Facing Government

Consider the city bus monopoly of Exhibit 2. Suppose the municipal government, unhappy with the $1.80 fare, decides not to regulate the company, but to buy it out. Once it owns the company, what does the city do?

Who runs the bus company? Most likely the same people who ran it before! Why should the city replace an experienced management staff? The reason for the government's takeover was the monopoly's price, not its personnel.

What about management's view of the takeover? Who owns the bus company should make little difference to managers. Their expertise is still applicable. Would the bus drivers feel uneasy? Their paychecks are now signed by the city's financial agent. But if the banks still cash the checks, should they complain? They run the same buses along the same lines to pick up the same passengers. Do you suppose the passengers, paying the same fare, care one way or the other?

Of course, somebody has to decide what the fares ought to be. If it isn't the regulatory commission, then it's some agency of government. The options available to the agency are precisely those that faced the regulatory commission. After all, they both understand Exhibit 2.

The government is unlikely to run the bus company as a profit-maximizing monopoly, charging a $1.80 fare and making $48,000 monopoly profit, although it is possible. The mayor could argue that the $1.80 fare is in the public interest, since the $48,000 profit adds to city revenue, allowing the government to reduce taxes by $48,000. And cutting taxes is always popular. The government agency can also choose either a $P = ATC$ or a $P = MC$ pricing strategy. The issues involved in each are precisely the issues faced by the regulatory commission.

Can the Government Run Industry Efficiently?

Whatever the evidence, many people strongly believe that government-run industry is inherently inefficient. One reason why government industry often appears to be struggling is that government often takes over a struggling industry! Amtrak replaced a troubled set of private railroads. Before Amtrak came into being, the railroads that became Amtrak were on the brink of bankruptcy. This situation was not unique. The coal industry in England was in terrible shape when the British government took it over in 1946.

No one, not even the government, believes that nationalizing sick industries is perfect medicine. Why, then, does the government knowingly get itself involved in losing propositions? Because it views the alternatives as worse. Allowing private railroads to go under may get the government off the hook, but it may not serve the economy well.

But not all nationalization is designed to prop up failing private industry. Many economies resort to nationalization for the same reason other economies resort to regulated industry—that is, to control prices. For example, international airlines come in all ownership forms. Some are unregulated private firms, some are government regulated, and others are government owned.

OWNERSHIP AND EFFICIENCY   It is virtually impossible to distinguish ownership on the basis of performance. How would you know that El Al Israel Airlines is owned by the government of Israel? Or that British Airways is privately owned? Have

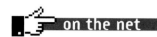

Can you tell that El Al Israel Airlines (http://www.elal.co.il/) is owned by the Israeli government and British Airways (http://www.british-airways.com) is privately owned?

You, too, can own part of the Green Bay Packers (http://www.packers.com/).

you ever visited Ireland? The Irish landscape is even greener than the beautiful green depicted in *National Geographic*! You can fly there on Aer Lingus and never know that the government of Ireland owns the controlling interest in the airline.

Do you think the average cost of flying an Aer Lingus passenger from Boston to Dublin is any higher than the average cost of flying that route on a privately owned airline? Do you suppose Aer Lingus uses more fuel? Or its aircraft depreciate faster? Or its pilots are any less experienced?

Do you have to be private and profit motivated to be efficient? Well, consider this: the Green Bay Packers, the National Football League's oldest team, is organized as a nonprofit corporation. It is publicly owned by 1,915 shareholders and governed by 45 directors and a seven-person unpaid executive committee. Its 4,634 shares do not appreciate and pay no dividends. The Packers are the only "public" team in the league, which otherwise prohibits public ownership of teams. Inefficient? Their public form of ownership doesn't seem to have stopped them from winning three Super Bowls—the latest in 1997—or from being a perennial power in the NFL.

Our state university systems are government owned. The University of North Carolina, for example, is administered by the State of North Carolina. The government determines the tuition, fees, and level of student enrollment just as Duke University, a private institution in Durham, North Carolina, decides its tuition, fees, and level of enrollment. Would you suppose professors at the state-owned university are less efficient than professors at Duke? Students at both universities probably use the same text for Economics 101!

BUT THE GOVERNMENT CAN'T GO BROKE Why, then, are so many people, including many economists, convinced that government industry naturally breeds inefficiency? The one explanation that makes the view seem so reasonable is the simple fact that governments cannot go bankrupt.

The viability of a private firm depends, ultimately, upon making a profit. The firm can absorb short-run losses and can muddle through with low-level profit in the longer run, but what it cannot do is absorb large losses over long periods of time. One day, it just runs out of money.

Not so with a government-owned firm. It can absorb continuing losses without ever having to face the prospect of closure. Why? Because it can usually rely on tax revenue to subsidize its operation. This possibility—and the certainty of the government's survival—must blunt the cutting edge of its management. By removing the possibility of failure, government managers also lose the incentive to excel. Sound reasonable?

THE ECONOMICS OF LAISSEZ-FAIRE

Other economists see the same industry concentrations very differently from those who advocate regulation or nationalization. They see no reason to follow either. Although they acknowledge the presence and inevitability of bigness, they are not at all disturbed by it. Why not?

The reason is that even with considerable industry concentration, there is still enough competition to generate acceptable price and output levels.

The Theory of Contestable Markets

Many students don't cheat on exams, not because there are so many faculty proctoring the exam but because the few who are proctoring may catch a cheater copying someone else's work. That threat alone is enough to keep other students who may think of cheating from doing so.

The theory of contestable markets is based on that kind of thinking. The primary consideration that keeps firms in highly concentrated industries from charging a high, noncompetitive price is not the number of firms actually competing in the industry, *but rather the threat of other firms entering the industry to compete.* Many oligopolistic markets are contestable in this way.

For example, the government-owned Canadian National Railways does not stop in every small town served by the privately owned Canadian Pacific Railways, but the government is nonetheless confident that the Canadian Pacific will not take advantage of its monopoly position in those one-railroad communities. What restrains the Canadian Pacific? It's fear that the Canadian National would change its routing to include those communities. After all, the Canadian National has the equipment and labor force to quickly make the shift.

NBC may be the only television network with an affiliate station in Winnemucca, Nevada, but if its advertising rates and profits there were high by industry standards, CBS, ABC, and Fox would probably rush into the market. In other words, the fact that an industry is highly concentrated does not necessarily mean the absence of moderate pricing. As long as markets are contestable, firms still end up with competitive-like pricing.

The theory of contestable markets challenges, then, the necessity of regulating or nationalizing industries that operate in highly concentrated markets. Society, according to this argument, will be better served by a policy of laissez-faire.

Critics of the contestable markets theory find the argument compelling but its applicability terribly limited. A market isn't contestable if significant barriers to entry exist. The idea that firms can easily switch resources from one line of production to another just doesn't ring true. Examples cited, such as the Canadian railroad competition, are the exception to the rule, and even in that market, switching lines involves considerable cost. Firms just don't behave that way. If firms are worried about threats of entry, shouldn't the firms who are threatening entry also worry that by actually entering the market, they will run down profits? What, then, is the significance of the threat? Proponents of regulation and nationalization do not believe that the contestable-markets logic applies to the real world.

The Theory of Countervailing Power

If competition doesn't exist among firms *within* a highly concentrated industry, then according to some economists, it may still exist *among* highly concentrated industries. This interindustry competition may be sufficient to generate acceptable prices anyway.

How does it work? Concentration creates economic power. The economy is a collection of economic power blocs competing with each other. *Power begets* **countervailing power.** The economy's markets are polarized into four competing power blocs: industrial, labor, agricultural, and retail. Their prices are determined by their relative strengths.

Countervailing power
The exercise of market power by an economic bloc is ultimately counteracted by the market power of a competing bloc, so that no bloc exercises undue market power.

Consider, for example, the relations between the industrial and retail blocs. Suppose the canned food oligopoly, composed of Lipton, Libby's, and Campbell's, faces a retail market composed of thousands of competitive grocery stores. The oligopoly's market strength *vis à vis* the grocery stores allows it to charge high wholesale prices. It ends up capturing most of the profit in the canned food market.

After all, what choices do the small grocery stores have? If they want to sell canned foods, they can sell only Lipton's, Libby's, or Campbell's. Competition among themselves drives their own retail prices down to the costs fixed by the oligopoly. At best, they end up with normal profit.

But it's precisely that kind of market power imbalance that triggers the creation of a countervailing power. In this case, the power comes not from the small retail grocers, although consumer cooperatives sometimes work, but rather from the transformation of the entire retail grocery industry. Oligopoly replaces competition within retail trade. Kroger, IGA, Jewel, Safeway, Winn-Dixie, Grand Union, and other supermarket chains develop to displace the small grocery stores.

While Lipton, Libby's, and Campbell's can dictate price to a small grocer, they can't dictate to these large chains. Market power checks market power. Wholesale prices are now negotiated between two oligopolies, producing a more equitable distribution of profits between them. *All this happens without government involvement.*

Kmart, Tru-Value, Wal-Mart, and Sears check the market power of oligopolies that produce light durable goods. Corporate agribusinesses replace family farms to restore the power balance between the industrial and agricultural blocs. Labor unions provide the countervailing power in wage rate negotiations with oligopolistic firms in the industrial bloc.

The Theory of Creative Destruction

Creative destruction
Effective competition that exists not among firms within highly concentrated industries but between the highly concentrated industries themselves. Such competition ensures competitive prices.

Another theory explaining why government intervention in the market is unnecessary—much like the theory of countervailing power—is the theory of **creative destruction.** It argues that although it may be difficult for firms to break into a monopolized industry, it has been much less difficult for them to break the monopolized industry's hold on a market.

For example, while no new steel firms can compete with a steel monopoly, an aluminum monopoly competes with it in the automobile and construction markets. Similarly, in the energy market, oil competes with coal, not new coal firms with an established coal firm.

Monopolies, then, are destroyed by this creative process. Look at railroads. In the prime of their life, their economic power was virtually unopposed. They set discriminatory freight rates that created fortunes for the robber barons. What finally trimmed railroad rates was not more railroads coming into the industry, but rather the new trucking and airline industries.

Can you think of other examples in which new industries emerge to check the monopoly or oligopoly power of an existing industry? Go to the Interactive Study Center at http://gottheil.swcollege.com and click on the "Your Turn" button to submit your example. Student submissions will be posted to the Web site, and perhaps we will use some in future editions of the book!

What brought the coal oligopoly to its knees was not more coal competition but the advent of petroleum. What checked the economic power of the bottling oligopoly was not the influx of more bottling firms but the aluminum can. Examples abound. They reflect our real competitive life. The role of government? None. Automatically, countervailing powers are created within the economy to ensure that even in an economy characterized by highly concentrated markets, acceptable prices still obtain.

THE ECONOMICS OF ENCOURAGING MONOPOLY

Some economists not only reject the view that monopoly is injurious to the economy's well-being, but actually prefer monopoly structures to competition. Why? Firm size makes a difference. As we saw in Chapter 11, monopoly can take advantage of economies of scale. Exhibit 3 restates Schumpeter's argument, developed in Chapter 11.

EXHIBIT | 3

FIRM SIZE AND ECONOMIES OF SCALE

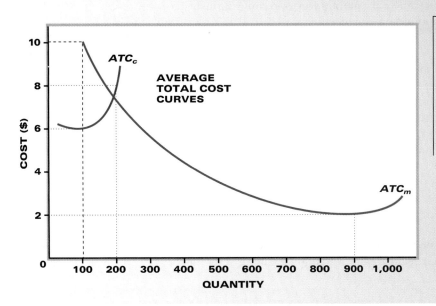

ATC_c and ATC_m are the average cost curves of two firms in an industry. The ATC_c curve describes a smaller firm with relatively limited capacity. At low levels of output, the smaller firm's ATC is less than that of the larger firm. For example, at output 100, at ATC_c's minimum, ATC_c = $6, and ATC_m = $10. Note that beyond output of 175, the ATC of the larger firm is less than the ATC of the smaller firm. At 900, the larger firm's minimum ATC_m = $2.

Even under the most efficient conditions, the competitive firm in Exhibit 3 cannot compete with the monopoly. Compare ATC_c and ATC_m. The competitive firm simply cannot produce beyond 100 units without encountering substantial increases in its ATC. Its ATC = $6 at 100 units but increases to ATC = $8 at 200 units. The monopoly's ATC reaches its minimum at 900 units. There, ATC = $2. It's no contest.

If Exhibit 3 represents our modern economy, you can see why some economists don't believe that the government serves any useful function by controlling prices. If the government is to play any role at all, it should promote bigness.

In fact, that's what government often ends up doing, even while extolling the virtues of competition. Monopolies can turn some of their profits into innovation-producing research. We benefit from newer, higher-quality, and lower-priced goods. The proof is in the legislation. The government understands the need to encourage new product development and creates a **patent** system that gives an innovating firm 20 years of legal protection from competition on newly developed technology. The competitive firm usually cannot generate new technology because it lacks the profit cushion for failed experiments.

What role can government play? According to laissez-faire advocates, it can foster an environment favorable to innovating industries. It can encourage basic research and industrial development by providing a wide assortment of tax incentives. In short, it can alter some of the costs associated with dynamic change.

Patent
An exclusive right granted by government to market a product or process for 20 years.

THE ECONOMICS OF SPLITTING UP MONOPOLY

A very different view of government's role is held by economists who reject as big-business hogwash the representation of economies of scale in Exhibit 3. To them, competition among small-scale firms is still both possible and preferred.

It is preferred because the theories of contestable markets, countervailing power, and creative destruction just don't reflect reality. Government regulation of monopoly only adds inefficiency to an already inefficient market structure. Nationalization adds even more dead weight.

How can real competition overcome industry concentration? By splitting up monopolies into smaller firms, each still able to capture the industry's economies of scale.

If competitive markets are both obtainable and socially preferred, why then are there so few? According to many economists who advocate **antitrust policy,** the answer, in a nutshell, is foul play. Natural monopoly notwithstanding, the overwhelming number of monopolies come into being and persist, they argue, by unfair market practices.

Is real competition possible? To them, there is nothing inevitable about monopoly. What is the government's role? Crime stopping. The task of government is to identify unfair market behavior, identify the market violators, curtail their activities, and restore fairness to the marketplace. *This can be done by legislation.*

This view that competition is still doable and preferable is an integral part of our democratic tradition and free enterprise philosophy. Our long and continuing history of antimonopoly legislation attests to our belief in it. Competing views about monopoly's inevitability, even with its economic advantages, have always been outside our mainstream thinking. Let's look at the history of U.S. antitrust legislation.

Antitrust policy
Laws that foster market competition by prohibiting monopolies and oligopolies from exercising excessive market power.

CHECK YOUR UNDERSTANDING

What role do proponents of antitrust assign to government?

THE HISTORY OF ANTITRUST LEGISLATION

An 1881 *Atlantic Monthly* article by Henry D. Lloyd, entitled "Story of a Great Monopoly," cited John D. Rockefeller of Standard Oil as the nation's prime trust maker. Rockefeller epitomized everything that was wrong with our economy. Standard Oil's tyrannical growth to control the nation's petroleum-refining industry destroyed any semblance of workable competition and signalled to many what our economic future would look like. Many were frightened.

Lloyd's piece found a ready audience. There was already considerable antimonopoly agitation in the country. By 1888, an election year, both Republicans and Democrats sensed the popularity of this issue and vowed to break the trusts. The Democrats even put antitrust policy into their party platform.

Learn more about Standard Oil (http://www.history.rochester.edu/fuels/tarbell/main.htm).

The Sherman Antitrust Act of 1890

In 1890, Senator John Sherman, brother of Civil War general William Sherman, reintroduced a bill he had twice before offered the Senate. The bill was designed to protect market competition from the treachery of monopoly activity. This time, it passed the Senate with only one dissenting vote and cleared the House unanimously. It was signed into law on July 2, 1890, by the Republican president, Benjamin Harrison.

The act contains eight sections, but the main thrust is found in Sections 1 and 2. Section 4 invests the Department of Justice with powers to enforce the law:

Section 1. *Every contract, combination in the form of trust or otherwise, or conspiracy, in restraint of trade or commerce among the several states, or with foreign nations, is declared to be illegal.*

Section 2. *Every person who shall monopolize, or attempt to monopolize, or combine or conspire with any other person or persons, to monopolize any part of the trade or commerce among several states, or with foreign nations, shall be deemed guilty of a felony. . . .*

Section 4. *The several circuit courts of the United States are hereby invested with jurisdiction to prevent and restrain violations of this Act; and it shall be the duty of the several*

Review the Sherman Antitrust Act (http://www.law.cornell.edu/uscode/15/1.shtml).

HISTORICAL PERSPECTIVE

CHRONOLOGY OF KEY ACTS AND COURT DECISIONS

1867: The National Grange (Granger movement) was formed, aiming to improve the social, economic, and political status of farmers. It reacted to declining farm prices, growing indebtedness of farms, discriminatory railroad freight rates, and acquisition by the railroads of public lands that farmers used as new farmland. The Grange agitated for government regulation of railroad rates and succeeded in a number of states, including Illinois, Iowa, Minnesota, Wisconsin, and California. Although most Grange-inspired laws were repealed, some were upheld by the Supreme Court and served as the basis for later legislation in the field of railroad and public-utility regulation.

1887: The first regulatory agency, the Interstate Commerce Commission, was created to regulate the railroads.

1890: The Sherman Antitrust Act outlawed restraint of trade or monopolized trade.

1895: The Supreme Court upheld a monopoly producing 98 percent of the country's sugar output on the grounds that the Sherman Act applied only to commerce and not to production.

1903: The Antitrust Division was established under the Department of Justice.

1911: American Tobacco Company and Standard Oil Company were ordered to dissolve.

1914: The Clayton Act was passed to regulate price discrimination, tying contracts, and exclusive dealings, mergers, and interlocking directorates.

1914: The Federal Trade Commission was established to prohibit unfair methods of competition not specifically prohibited by the Sherman and Clayton Acts.

1918: The Supreme Court struck down the Keating-Owen Child Labor Law of 1916, which prohibited interstate commerce of goods produced with child labor, on the grounds that the Sherman Act applied only to commerce (transport of goods), not production.

1922: Agricultural cooperatives were exempted from antitrust laws.

1934: The Securities Exchange Act was established to protect the investor by imposing stringent disclosure requirements.

1936: The Robinson-Patman Act forbade price discrimination.

1937: The Miller-Tydings Act legalized price fixing between manufacturers and dealers to protect small dealers.

1948: The Reed-Bulwinkle Act amended the Interstate Commerce Act to legalize price fixing by rail, water, or motor carrier.

1950: The Celler-Kefauver Act closed a Clayton Act loophole by prohibiting mergers through asset acquisition.

1953: The Supreme Court declared baseball exempt from antitrust laws.

1960: The Bank Merger Act directed regulatory agencies to consider the competitive effects of mergers before approving them.

1969: The Newspaper Preservation Act exempted newspapers from antitrust law.

1977: The Airlines were deregulated.

1980: Railroads (Staggers Act), trucking (Motor Carrier Act), and banking (Depository Institutions Deregulation Act) were deregulated.

1982: A 13-year antitrust suit against AT&T ended with the creation of spinoff regional Bell companies.

1996: Communications industries were deregulated.

---

district attorneys of the United States, in their respective districts, under the direction of the Attorney General, to institute proceedings in equity to prevent and restrain such violations.

It reads tough, but in practice the act seemed to be a paper dragon. At first, the problem was its vagueness. What was meant by "restraint of trade" or by "monopolizing" or by "conspiracy"? And how does the Department of Justice go about proving its case?

In the decade that followed—in spite of Justice's newly created Antitrust Division, which successfully prosecuted Standard Oil and American Tobacco—it became increasingly obvious that a better description of what constitutes illegal monopoly practice was needed. This came with the Clayton Act of 1914.

The Clayton Act of 1914

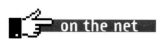

Review the Clayton Act (http://www.law.cornell.edu/uscode/15/12.shtml).

The Clayton Act gave the courts explicit direction. It described four specific anti-competitive activities: (1) price discrimination among purchasers, (2) exclusive contracts where purchasers would agree, as a condition of sale, not to buy from competitors, (3) one firm's acquisition of voting stock in another firm in the same industry, and (4) board members who served on boards of directors of competing firms.

Clayton was on target. Price discrimination was widely practiced. For example, a firm with an already large share of a national market could cut prices in regional markets where it faced competition, leaving its prices untouched in safer, less-competitive markets. This two-price system knocked out competition and made potential competitors think twice about entering.

Exclusive contracts also reduced competition. For example, if a large, nationally known sports equipment firm made sporting goods shops agree not to sell its competitors' equipment, then the large firm's competition would disappear. Market muscle creates monopoly, which pumps up more muscle. If such arrangements are standard practice, new firms hardly stand a chance.

Buying voting stock was a more direct strategy of locking up competitive markets. For example, if the same sports equipment firm bought up the voting stock of its competitors, then it could establish monopoly prices for the entire industry.

Another way of killing competition was for people to sit on boards of directors of competing firms associated with the same product. Imagine a board member of the sports equipment firm also sitting as a board member of other sporting goods firms. Convenient? Interlocking directorships of this kind could well affect business decisions. Other firms in the industry—competitors—would have reason to suspect unfair practices.

The Federal Trade Commission Act of 1914

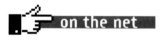

Review the Federal Trade Commission Act (http://www.law.cornell.edu/uscode/15/41.shtml).

In the same year as the Clayton Act, 1914, Congress created a second means of antitrust enforcement when it passed the Federal Trade Commission (FTC) Act. The FTC was established specifically to monitor markets. It was charged with investigating unfair and deceptive practices and could, if it believed a situation warranted it, *initiate* complaints. After calling a public hearing on a complaint, it could issue a cease-and-desist order. The cited firm could, of course, appeal the order in court.

The FTC was expected to be a major contributor to the effectiveness of antitrust legislation. Prior to the FTC, the Antitrust Division of the Justice Department handled both the investigation and the prosecution of anticompetitive activity.

Plugging the Loopholes

Review the Robinson-Patman Act (http://www.law.cornell.edu/uscode/15/13.shtml).

The Sherman, Clayton, and FTC acts are the core of modern antitrust legislation. Two additional acts extended their coverage.

The Robinson-Patman Act of 1936 amended the Clayton Act on price discrimination. It was designed to help small stores survive the blitz of growing retail chains. Until the act was passed, large firms could offer price discounts to selected buyers, often with the intent to damage their smaller competitors. The smaller firms, naturally, claimed that this practice was unfair. Under Robinson-Patman, *selective* discount deals became illegal.

The Celler-Kefauver Merger Act of 1950 closed a loophole that had been used to circumvent the Clayton Act. Clayton had made it illegal to buy a competitor's voting stock. But it said nothing about buying a competitor's patents, plant, and equipment. The result, of course, was the same as if the competition's voting stock had been bought—a disguised merger. The Celler-Kefauver Act put a lid on that activity but allowed smaller firms the privilege of merging if merging enhanced their ability to survive.

Funding Antitrust Legislation

It is sometimes easier to pass a dozen laws than to enforce one. This is particularly true when no funds are appropriated by the government for law enforcement.

Imagine, for example, a town council voting unanimously in favor of capital punishment for overnight street parking, *but appropriating zero funds for its enforcement.* How could anyone be arrested, then, if no one is hired to do the arresting? Is the punishment under these zero-funding conditions really severe?

How seriously, then, should we take antitrust legislation? That's open to question. After all, congressional allocations to the Antitrust Division of the Department of Justice and to FTC in 2000 totaled less than $250 million, or about as much as breakfast cereals companies spend on advertising. Budgets earmarked for antitrust activity were cut almost in half during the 1990s—even as antitrust and FTC caseloads grew.

The costs of investigation and litigation are extremely high. Increasing the government's caseload is futile, whatever the merit of the antitrust cases, if there are no funds to prosecute them fully. And it is foolhardy to go after the big firms when one major legal battle with a giant like IBM, Exxon, or General Motors could exhaust the better part of the FTC's and Justice's thin budgets. The FTC is simply no match for the army of highly talented and highly paid corporate lawyers that the defendant corporations can field.

But antitrust has gone to court. Its record, over the years, has been rather modest. Nevertheless, it has had its hard-earned victories and has left some mark on the behavior of monopolies.

ANTITRUST GOES TO COURT

Street bullies are typically big. But would you go about calling every big person you meet on the street a bully? That's the issue the courts faced over the years in deciding what constituted violations of antitrust laws.

The Rule of Reason

In its early decisions, the Supreme Court distinguished between acceptable and unacceptable monopolies by examining market behavior. Just being a monopoly was insufficient evidence of guilt.

For example, its 1911 ruling in the Standard Oil case was based on the evidence that Standard Oil's *behavior,* not its size or its share of the market, violated the Sherman Antitrust Act. Because Standard Oil used monopoly power to stifle competition, the Court decided against it and ordered the breakup of Standard Oil. This criterion became known as the **rule of reason.**

This same rule of reason was applied against American Tobacco, and in later decisions to find U.S. Steel, Eastman Kodak, and International Harvester innocent of antitrust violations. In the U.S. Steel case, the Court acknowledged U.S. Steel's monopoly position but did not find that the company abused its monopoly power to undermine competition.

CHECK YOUR UNDERSTANDING

Why is antitrust legislation only as good as the funding that stands behind it?

Rule of reason
A judicial standard or criterion by which a firm's size within an industry is insufficient evidence for the court to rule against it in an antitrust suit. Evidence must show that the firm actually used its size to violate antitrust laws.

GLOBAL PERSPECTIVE

INTERNATIONAL CRIME STOPPERS: ANTITRUST GOES GLOBAL

The following is an excerpt from remarks made by Joel Klein, former U.S. assistant attorney, to the American Bar Association in Washington, D.C., April 2000.

I'm pleased to report that [antitrust] enforcement is beginning to take hold globally. It used to be that the United States stood almost alone in the world in our commitment to antitrust enforcement. Until the 1990s, a not infrequent reaction of foreign governments to news that the Antitrust Division was investigating the activities of international cartels was to leap to the defense of "their" firms, accuse the U.S. of "extraterritorial" tendencies, threaten to invoke blocking statutes, and express astonishment that any country should even want to have procompetitive laws, much less enforce them. Happily, the global environment in which we work today is radically different. In the past decade, a strong interest in having free markets defended by sound antitrust laws and sound antitrust enforcement has spread throughout the world. Over 80 countries now have antitrust laws—most of them enacted during the past decade—and another 25 countries are in the process of drafting such laws.

We have been working with our counterparts abroad to assist them in strengthening their anti-cartel enforcement efforts. For example, last fall an unprecedented gathering of over 80 anti-cartel enforcers from nearly 30 countries on six conti-

DO I LOOK LIKE A CRIMINAL? NEVER MIND.

nents met in Washington for the first International Anti-Cartel Enforcement Workshop to share information about the nuts and bolts of cartel enforcement and to foster the development of cooperation on cartel issues among antitrust authorities around the world.

Finally, there is a growing appreciation among international businesses that safe harbors for international cartel activity are rapidly shrinking. This last point was dramatically made again today with the announcement that four more foreign nationals have agreed to plead guilty and serve time in a U.S. prison for their participation in the vitamin conspiracy. Together with the two Swiss Hoffmann–La Roche executives who went to jail last year, all of the high level Hoffmann–La Roche and BASF business executives responsible for the conspiracy pleaded guilty and face jail sentences. What is particularly remarkable about these cases is that all of these defendants agreed to travel here, submit to U.S. jurisdiction, and go to prison even though they resided outside of the United States.

A few years ago these results would have been unimaginable. However, these defendants came to realize that the world is changing and growing increasingly intolerant of price fixers.

Source: Remarks made to the American Bar Association, April 2000. Reprinted with permission from Joel Klein.

The Per Se Criterion

In the aftermath of World War II, Supreme Court decisions underwent substantial change. The Court's composition now reflected President Franklin D. Roosevelt's appointees. It became known, by some with anger, by others with admiration, as Roosevelt's Court. It was a precedent-changing Court in many respects. Among the issues reinterpreted by the new Court was the question of what constituted violations of antitrust laws.

In the 1945 decision against Alcoa, Judge Learned Hand wrote that firm size, **per se,** was the issue. It was his view, shared by the majority of the Court, that the Sherman Act did not mean to differentiate between good and bad monopolies. It outlawed monopolies *per se.* Size was the criterion. Alcoa's 90 percent share of the market was therefore sufficient evidence for the Court to find against the company.

The Court was not particularly impressed with the economies-of-scale argument. Acknowledging that monopolies sometimes result from success in honest competition, not by market manipulation or intimidation, it still ruled that monopoly, whatever its history or intent, was a threat to industrial democracy and therefore in violation of the antitrust laws.

In two landmark 1958 merger decisions, it disallowed Bethlehem Steel from acquiring Youngstown Steel and prevented Pabst Brewing Company and Blatz Brewing Company from merging. In both cases, the Court's message was clear. The competitive character of the industries, already threatened by high concentration, would have been further damaged by the mergers.

In 1962 the Court ruled for the government against the Brown Shoe Company's intended purchase of the G. R. Kinney Company. Here the concern was both horizontal and vertical merging. Both were retail shoe companies, but Brown was also a shoe manufacturer and would have gained access to Kinney's retail outlets.

In the 1965 Vons Grocery case, the Court decided against the merger of two Los Angeles supermarkets, the third- and sixth-largest chains in the area, because they would have enjoyed a 7.5 percent share of the Los Angeles market. That was a large enough share for the Court to concur with the government.

Rethinking the Reinterpretation

But the political character of the Supreme Court changed again in the 1970s and so too did the Court's interpretation of what the antitrust acts meant. Once again, it looked at what monopoly does in the marketplace rather than size. The rule-of-reason criterion again seemed more appropriate than the per se criterion.

The transition back to rule of reason could be seen in the government's 1969 case against IBM's control of the computer industry. Initially, the issue was size. The government charged that IBM's market share violated Section 2 of the Sherman Antitrust Act.

The case came to trial in 1975. IBM explained its superior performance record. It argued that its monopoly position was a result of its market success, not an instrument used to achieve it. As the costly case dragged on, it became clear that the old per se criterion no longer was sufficient to decide against a company. In 1982 the Reagan administration simply dropped the suit against IBM.

Conglomerates and the Court

The philosophy of antitrust legislation, from the first days of enactment, was to protect the competitiveness of industry. But a very different kind of antitrust focus has emerged in recent years, a focus on the conglomerate. What distinguishes conglomerates from horizontal and vertical mergers is that conglomerates are not industry-specific. The conglomerate merges firms from totally unrelated industries.

These mergers raise interesting questions concerning the relationship between antitrust and conglomerates. If the antitrust laws were designed strictly to protect the competitiveness of industry, then why should conglomerate mergers be a threat to competitiveness, since the industries affected by the merger are unrelated?

Did Mobil Oil's 1970 purchase of Montgomery Ward in any way affect the competitiveness of either the petroleum industry, to which the parent Mobil belongs, or

Per se
A judicial standard or criterion by which a firm's size within an industry is considered sufficient evidence for the court to rule against it in an antitrust suit.

the retail industry, which it acquired? After all, Montgomery Ward had no intentions of selling petroleum. Nor was Mobil about to go into the department store business.

What sections of the Sherman Act had the Mobil conglomerate violated? Or in what way had Mobil's purchase of Montgomery Ward violated the Clayton or Federal Trade Commission Acts? Since the industries involved were left essentially intact, is antitrust really an issue in situations involving conglomerates?

In 1979 the FTC blocked Exxon from purchasing Reliance, an electric motor company. Exxon did not pursue the issue to the courts. But the courts have since indicated that conglomerates are virtually immune under existing law, and Congress seems little inclined to challenge that interpretation.

The mood of Congress and the president on antitrust and conglomerates had unmistakably shifted in the 1980s to reflect a more accommodating view toward large corporations. The economies -of-scale argument once more became fashionable. It was widely accepted that when conglomerates pooled their financial resources, they could expand output to capture the full measure of economies of scale. Bigness promoted efficiency.

BUT FTC AND JUSTICE ARE STILL IN BUSINESS

Nobody is turning off the lights and locking the doors at the FTC and Justice offices. These agencies are still very much in business, despite limited funding and—according to some antitrust advocates—lackluster leadership. Their concern, as always, is getting the most out of every antitrust dollar. How can they monitor and act upon the flood of mergers that take place each year?

Using the Herfindahl-Hirschman Index

In 1982 the Department of Justice established new guidelines for its merger monitoring. The guidelines are based on the Herfindahl-Hirschman index, which separates contestable from noncontestable mergers. For example, any industry whose index exceeds 1,800 invites antitrust intervention. Mergers that occur in an industry whose index falls in the 1,000 to 1,800 range and result in raising the industry's index by 100 or more may be subject to challenge. Mergers that occur in industries whose values are below 1,000 will be left alone.

Going After the Precedent

Another way FTC and Justice can maximize the use of their budgets and efforts is by the selection of mergers they challenge. A merger may be highly contestable but remain uncontested by Justice. Why? Because Justice's strategy is not only to contest, but to win. If a highly contestable merger involves an extraordinarily high financial commitment, Justice may decide to bypass that case in favor of challenging a much less powerful adversary where it can set a precedent. That is, the most cost-effective way of challenging the big ones is not by direct legal assault but by setting precedents.

DO WE HAVE A POLICY ON MONOPOLY?

There seem to be nearly as many ideas on what to do about monopoly as there are economists addressing the issue. And all ideas seem to have found a place among the economists' policy prescriptions. Public utilities, for example, are highly regulated industries in the United States, and the justification for the regulation has been based primarily on the analysis of price determination under conditions of monopoly.

APPLIED PERSPECTIVE

YOU WANNA MAKE $15,000 A MONTH WORKING AT HOME?

In a wholesale crackdown on deceptive marketing in cyberspace, the Federal Trade Commission charged nine companies that market their products on the Internet with making false or unsubstantiated advertising claims.

"Cyberspace is a new frontier for advertising and marketing," said Jodie Bernstein, former director of the FTC's Bureau of Consumer Protection. "But the Internet will not achieve its commercial potential if this new frontier becomes the 'Wild West' of fraudulent schemes."

The nine cases involve online marketing for a range of phony schemes including credit repair ripoffs, bogus income opportunities, a phony grant assistance offer, and a computer equipment supply scam.

The FTC charged five of the companies with making false claims about repairing consumers' credit records. Using ads that made claims such as "Guaranteed credit repair" and "How to remove judgments, including bankruptcy, from your credit file," the companies urged consumers to send fees ranging from $19.95 to $750 to get instructions or assistance on how they could remove adverse items.

Two of the companies claimed that, for a fee, they could provide consumers with instructions to establish new credit identities and files. The statements made by the five companies were false, the FTC alleged, and the instructions for creating new credit files could violate federal criminal law.

Four defendants were charged with making unsubstantiated earnings claims for the work-at-home businesses they advertised online. Touting earnings such as "Earn up to $4,000 or more each month!" and "Our home workers' first-year income averages $38,000," they sold programs at prices ranging from $9.95 to $147. The FTC charged that by using such statements, the defendants represented that the earnings were representative of what consumers could expect to achieve and that they had a reasonable basis to substantiate them. In fact, th challenged earnings representations are false and unsubstantiated, the FTC said.

"We have seen business opportunity scams for everything from vending machines to FCC-licensed telecommunications projects," Bernstein said. "Last week, we announced cases against seven companies that marketed fraudulent schemes for 900-number programs. We intend to be just as vigilant in policing the fraud that pops up on the Internet," she said.

Another FTC complaint targeted an advertiser who claimed to match consumers with private foundations with "billions of dollars" to give away to consumers. Advertising touted "FREE CASH GRANTS BY MAIL" and offered, for a fee, to match consumers with private foundations likely to give them money for business, travel, education, or debt consolidation.

The FTC complaint alleges that through the use of statements such as "Most of our clients are approved for cash grants," the defendant represented that the majority of his clients receive a cash grant. The claim is false and unsubstantiated, the FTC alleged.

The proposed agreement to settle these charges would prohibit the defendant from making similar false and unsubstantiated claims and from misrepresenting the services or assistance he provides for obtaining grants, loans, or other financial products or services.

"We want our message to be loud and clear," Bernstein said. "The Internet opens a world of opportunities for consumers. Unfortunately, it also presents opportunities for scam artists."

HELLO. THERE MUST BE SOMETHING WRONG. I ONLY MADE $8.42 THIS MONTH.

Not all economists are convinced that regulation has been appropriately applied. Many advocate deregulation in the belief that regulation has been an over-worked policy and that in many cases technological change has changed the character of the regulated industry. The United States has shown a clear disinclination toward nationalization of industry. For example, in dealing with the chronic problem of passenger railroad transportation, Congress passed laws that regulated, deregulated, and finally resorted to Amtrak, a mild form of nationalization. Congress has not yet debated the issue of denationalizing the post office, although the suggestion is often made.

It is difficult to gauge how successful the laissez-faire doctrine has been in formulating policy on monopoly. To some economists, the lack of government aggressiveness against monopoly demonstrates the strength of laissez-faire thinking. Many economists are thoroughly convinced that, left unfettered, monopolies generate prices that are no higher, and perhaps even lower, than prices that would obtain under conditions of perfect competition.

What role has antitrust policy played in our economy? The FTC and Justice have pursued landmark cases that attempted to reduce or at least prevent an increase in an industry's concentration ratio. If the use and effectiveness of antitrust policy on prices in the U.S. economy is controversial among economists, what remains fairly uncontroversial is that no consensus exists among them concerning what we ought to do about monopoly.

CHAPTER REVIEW

1. There is no consensus among economists concerning appropriate policy in handling issues of monopoly and oligopoly pricing.

2. Some economists believe that monopoly and oligopoly are inevitable and harmful. They generally advocate regulation and, in some cases, even nationalization. Other economists agree that monopoly and oligopoly are inevitable but they argue that monopoly and oligopoly are not harmful, but actually beneficial. They generally subscribe to laissez-faire policy. Many economists hold still another view. They reject the idea that monopoly and oligopoly are inevitable. They also believe these market structures are harmful to society, and they advocate antitrust policy.

3. Advocates of regulation, recognizing the benefits associated with economies of scale, propose to separate the pricing function from the monopolist. Regulatory commissions replace the monopolist, and either a fair price ($P = ATC$) or marginal cost pricing ($P = MC$) replaces the monopoly price.

4. The problem with regulation is that it often ends up protecting the regulated industries from honest-to-goodness competition instead of the consumer from industries' market power. As well, in fair price cases where $P = ATC$, production costs have a tendency to drift upward, and along with them, the regulated price.

5. Deregulation reverses the regulatory process. Changes in technology may create possibilities of entry into what otherwise was a natural monopoly. In such cases, competition supersedes regulation.

6. Advocates of nationalization, recognizing the benefits associated with economies of scale, propose that government should own and run the monopoly and select a price equal to either ATC or MC. There is no compelling reason why a government-run monopoly should be less efficient than a regulated monopoly.

7. Laissez-faire advocates argue for no government intervention in the marketplace. They contend that in oligopoly, competition among the few is

still meaningful competition. Among the explanations offered to support laissez-faire is the theory of contestable markets, which maintains that the threat of potential entry prevents firms from taking full advantage of their market power.

8. A second explanation is the theory of countervailing power, which suggests that even though there is little, if any, competition within each industry, competition exists among the economic blocs that make up the economy's markets, checking the market power of monopoly and oligopoly to raise price.

9. A third explanation is the theory of creative destruction, which argues that competition arises less from within industries than from the new industries created by technological progress. These new industries compete with and destroy old industries.

10. The patent system is regarded as a contributor to an economy's well-being because it encour-

ages technological innovation. The patent is a government-issued monopoly right granted to firms for a specified period of time.

11. Antitrust legislation exemplifies the belief that the best way to deal with monopoly and oligopoly power is to break it up. U.S. antitrust legislation includes the Sherman Antitrust Act of 1890, the Clayton Act of 1914, the Federal Trade Commission Act of 1914, the Robinson-Patman Act of 1936, and the Celler-Kefauver Merger Act of 1950.

12. Court decisions involving antitrust have changed from the rule of reason in the early twentieth century to the per se criterion in the post–World War II period. During the 1970s, the courts shifted back again to the rule of reason. The courts accommodated conglomerate mergers in the 1980s.

KEY TERMS

Laissez-faire
Contestable market
Regulation
Marginal cost pricing

Deregulation
Nationalization
Countervailing power
Creative destruction

Patent
Antitrust policy
Rule of reason
Per se

QUESTIONS

1. Describe five different views economists hold concerning what to do about monopoly and oligopoly pricing.
2. Discuss the difference between fair pricing and marginal cost pricing in regulated industries.
3. Why do some economists favor nationalization rather than regulation of industry? What are the advantages and disadvantages of nationalization?
4. Why would economists argue in favor of allowing monopolies and oligopolies to set their own prices undisturbed by government? What assumptions do they make concerning economies of scale?
5. What is a contestable market?

6. Why do some economists argue in favor of antitrust laws? What assumptions do they make concerning economies of scale?
7. What is the difference between the courts' use of the per se criterion and the rule of reason criterion in deciding whether firms violate antitrust laws?
8. Outline the principal legislation enacted by Congress since 1890 to monitor and control monopoly in the U.S. economy.
9. "There's no way you'll get your bear if there's no bullet in your gun." How does this saying apply to the Antitrust Division of the Department of Justice?
10. Why deregulate a regulated industry?
11. Who regulates the regulators? Is it a problem?

WHAT'S WRONG WITH THIS GRAPH?

FAIR PRICE AND MARGINAL COST PRICING: NATURAL MONOPOLY

ECONOMIC CONSULTANTS

ECONOMIC RESEARCH AND ANALYSIS BY STUDENTS FOR PROFESSIONALS

Wicker, Inc., produces wicker baskets. Over the past ten years, most of Wicker's competitors have either ceased operations or changed directions to manufacture other products. As a result, Wicker now controls over 80 percent of the wicker basket market. Even though Wicker had no direct control over the actions of its competitors, Wicker is afraid that, given its disproportionate control over the wicker basket market, the firm will face sanctions from the government.

Wicker, Inc., has hired Economic Consultants to advise Wicker's owners about the basics of antitrust law. Prepare a report for Wicker that addresses the following issues:

1. What types of business practices do federal antitrust laws and regulations prohibit, and what governmental bodies enforce these laws and regulations?

2. On the surface, does Wicker need to worry about governmental intervention into its practices?

3. What conditions in Wicker's operations do the owners need to pay attention to in light of antitrust laws and regulations?

You may find the following resources helpful as you prepare this report for Wicker:

- **The Department of Justice, Antitrust Division** (http://www.usdoj.gov/atr/)—The Antitrust Division maintains antitrust guidelines for businesses.
- **Federal Trade Commission** (http://www.ftc.gov/ftc/business.htm)—The Federal Trade Commission maintains materials to help businesses comply with federal antitrust laws and regulations.
- **American Bar Association (ABA), Antitrust Section** (http://www.abanet.org/antitrust/home.html)—The ABA provides a legal forum for the analysis of policies and developments affecting competition.

PRACTICE TEST

1. Advocates of a laissez-faire policy toward monopoly's pricing practice believe that
   a. monopoly prices are not any higher than the prices that would obtain in a more competitive environment.
   b. there are no substantial barriers to entry, so that government intervention to regulate monopoly prices is unnecessary.
   c. government intervention to regulate monopoly prices is necessary because there are substantial diseconomies of scale in monopolistic industries.
   d. government intervention to regulate monopoly prices is necessary because there are substantial economies of scale in monopolistic industries.
   e. government intervention to regulate monopoly prices is necessary because there are constant returns to scale in monopolistic industries.

2. Suppose that the electric provider in a particular region is a natural monopoly, and government decides to regulate it by imposing a fair-price policy. The results will be
   a. price equal to average total cost, but output decreases.
   b. price equal to marginal cost, but output decreases.
   c. price equal to average variable cost, and output increases.
   d. price equal to average total cost, and output increases.
   e. price equal to marginal cost, and output increases.

3. The price-regulating policy that requires government to subsidize the natural monopoly is
   a. antitrust.
   b. deregulation.
   c. fair price.
   d. marginal cost pricing.
   e. average cost pricing.

4. One of the problems associated with regulating industry, as witnessed by the practices of the Interstate Commerce Commission, is that
   a. regulatory commissions often don't understand the economics of regulation.
   b. regulatory commissions often end up protecting the monopolies they were intended to regulate.
   c. regulatory commissions, managed by government bureaucracies, are typically more inefficient than unregulated monopolies.
   d. there is a substantial time lag between identifying an offending monopoly and regulating it.
   e. there is a substantial time lag between regulating an offending monopoly and obtaining the desired results.

5. What is the basic idea underlying the theory of countervailing power, and what policy does it suggest with respect to government's role in regulating prices? It assumes that
   a. the economy is composed of competing economic blocs that ensure that no one bloc acquires undesirable market power, so that laissez-faire is the appropriate policy.
   b. the economy is composed of competing economic blocs that organize to create undesirable market power, so that regulation is the appropriate policy.
   c. the economy is highly monopolized but the threat of potential entry into the markets of these monopolies by new firms keeps monopoly prices in check, so that laissez-faire is the appropriate policy.
   d. the economy is highly monopolized and the threat of potential entry into the markets of these monopolies by new firms is nonexistent, so that regulation is the appropriate policy.
   e. in time, monopoly markets become highly competitive because of changing technologies, so that laissez-faire is the appropriate policy.

6. What is the basic idea underlying the theory of contestable markets, and what policy does it suggest with respect to government's role in regulating prices? It assumes that
   a. the economy is composed of competing economic blocs that ensure that no one bloc acquires undesirable market power, so that laissez-faire is the appropriate policy.
   b. the economy is composed of competing economic blocs that organize to create undesirable market power, so that regulation is the appropriate policy.
   c. the economy is highly monopolized but the threat of potential entry into the markets of these monopolies by new firms keeps monopoly prices in check, so that laissez-faire is the appropriate policy.
   d. the economy is highly monopolized and the threat of potential entry into the markets of these monopolies by new firms is nonexistent, so that regulation is the appropriate policy.
   e. in time, monopoly markets become highly competitive because of changing technologies, so that laissez-faire is the appropriate policy.

7. Advocates of antitrust policy reason that the bigness of monopolies creates _____ and therefore recommend as appropriate policy _____.
   a. economies of scale/leaving them alone
   b. no economies of scale/splitting them up
   c. no diseconomies of scale/splitting them up
   d. no diseconomies of scale/leaving them alone
   e. unfair political and economic advantages/splitting them up

14

EXTERNALITIES, MARKET FAILURE, AND PUBLIC CHOICE

Imagine what would happen if an Iroquois, hunting for deer on Manhattan Island long before the Europeans arrived, spotted one grazing just about where Times Square would later be. Suppose he took careful aim with his bow and arrow, and missed.

Who would gain from the miss? No question about it, the deer would gain. Who would lose? Obvious again, the hunter. Now imagine that centuries later a New Yorker, spotting a low-flying pigeon in Times Square during rush hour, decides it would make an excellent meal. He aims his high-powered telescopic rifle and fires. Suppose he, too, misses. Who gains? The pigeon, of course. Who loses? The New Yorker, and perhaps an unsuspecting tourist from Milwaukee who was about to cross Broadway at 42nd Street.

The point of the story is that almost every activity in our modern world involves unsuspecting **third parties.** This

THIS CHAPTER INTRODUCES YOU TO THE ECONOMIC PRINCIPLES ASSOCIATED WITH:

- POSITIVE AND NEGATIVE EXTERNALITIES
- PROPERTY RIGHTS
- MARKET FAILURE
- POLLUTION TAXATION AND OBLIGATORY CONTROLS
- PURE PUBLIC GOODS AND NEAR-PUBLIC GOODS
- PUBLIC CHOICE
- GOVERNMENT FAILURE

point applies to economic activity as well. If people toss their own garbage onto their own front lawns, neighbors would be the losers. Not only would their property values fall, but even their health might suffer.

If people smoke in elevators, others walk away with tobacco-fumed clothing, and sometimes coughing.

If fishermen used boats with gas engines on small inland lakes, many of these lakes would become polluted, denying many vacationers the enjoyment of clean water. If farmers use chemical fertilizers and insecticides on their crops, people in the surrounding areas may develop serious health problems.

On the other hand, there is also the possibility of unsuspecting third parties *enjoying* the results of someone else's activities. For example, if your neighbor plants trees, shrubs, and flowers on her property, its beauty and the birds it would attract could add much enjoyment and increased value to your own property.

If you lived directly across the street from Wrigley Field in Chicago, you could see all the Cubs' home games free from your rooftop!

ECONOMIC EXTERNALITIES

Economists call these effects on unsuspecting third parties **externalities.** After all, the people or companies that initiate the activity—the garbage tosser, the farmer fertilizing crops, and the person planting trees—do so to *benefit themselves.* How their actions affect you and others is, in most cases, quite beside the point, which is the economist's point. The activity's effect on others is completely excluded from—that is, it is external to—the decision about whether to undertake the activity.

Identifying Negative Externalities

Some externalities are defined as negative externalities. For example, your loss of well-being caused by your neighbor tossing garbage onto his *own* property is a negative externality associated with his garbage disposal. It's negative because it diminishes your well-being, and it's an externality because your neighbor probably never considered your well-being when he disposed of his garbage. In this simple example, the cost of the negative externality may be easy to calculate. It's the cost involved in cleaning up the mess. A neighborhood teenager may charge $20 to haul it away.

But not all negative externalities are so easily measured. For example, how do you calculate the loss of well-being in your neighborhood caused by a nearby paint factory polluting the air? Suppose the factory denies any responsibility in causing anyone's loss of well-being. Or suppose it claims only partial responsibility, citing other polluters such as the airport 30 miles away, the highway traffic only 1 mile away, outdoor barbecues, and cigarette smokers. How do you prove that the factory is responsible, and how do you calculate its negative externality? In modern societies, the most important negative externalities are precisely those that are the most difficult to measure and the most difficult to track to specific offenders.

Identifying Positive Externalities

What about positive externalities? These externalities serve to increase people's well-being. For example, suppose your neighbor landscapes her property beautifully. Wouldn't you derive pleasure from that landscaping? It's positive because it adds to your well-being, and it's an externality because your neighbor probably never considered your well-being when she landscaped. Calculating positive externalities is no less difficult than calculating negative externalities. After all, you may be able to measure the enjoyment you derive from that externality, but you're probably not the only one in the neighborhood who enjoys that externality. How, then, do you calculate the total increase in well-being associated with that landscaping?

Do you suppose neighbors would come forward to announce their increased well-being? Hardly. Since their well-being never entered the landscaper's cost-benefit calculation about landscaping in the first place, they are strictly third-party beneficiaries, or **free riders.**

EXTERNALITIES AND PROPERTY RIGHTS

Why can't your neighbor lay claim to the positive externalities generated by her landscaping and enjoyed by the free-riding neighbors? Or why can't we place the cost to society that negative externalities generate onto the polluters who created the negative externalities? The reason is that the **property rights** associated with the people who either suffer the negative externalities or enjoy the positive externalities are poorly defined.

Third parties
People upon whom externalities are imposed.

Externalities
Unintended costs or benefits that are imposed on unsuspecting people and that result from economic activity initiated by others. Unintended costs are called negative externalities, and unintended benefits are called positive externalities.

Free rider
Someone who consumes a good or service without paying for it. Typically, the good or service consumed is in the form of a positive externality.

Property rights
The right to own a good or service and the right to receive the benefits that the use of the good or service provides.

APPLIED PERSPECTIVE

CELEBRITIES AND PROPERTY RIGHTS: A MATERIAL VIEW

While air rights are well defined in the American legal system, rights to unimpeded views or to picturesque views have not been similarly protected. Typically, these rights are not are not acquired with the purchase of land, but may be acquired through a covenant or the purchase of an easement.

Popular singer Madonna was involved in a recent lawsuit over an issue less sexy than those typically associated with her, but still controversial. A neighboring Malibu property owner had filed the suit in 1987, before the singer bought the house. He claimed

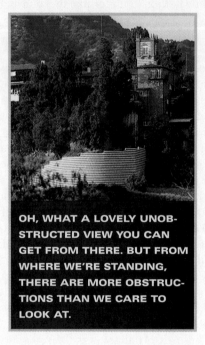

OH, WHAT A LOVELY UNOBSTRUCTED VIEW YOU CAN GET FROM THERE. BUT FROM WHERE WE'RE STANDING, THERE ARE MORE OBSTRUCTIONS THAN WE CARE TO LOOK AT.

that shrubbery, now belonging to Madonna, blocked his view of the city below and had caused the value of his formerly $3.5 million home to decline by $1 million. Madonna countersued, accusing him of trespassing and of verbal abuse. In December 1990, a California superior court rendered a decision, citing an existing covenant which ensures an unobstructed view to all lots in the neighborhood. Madonna was ordered to trim the hedges and trees surrounding her estate.

CONSIDER

If you were a member of the California superior court, how would you rule? Does Madonna have a case? Is she entitled to enjoy her property as she sees fit?

Why the confusion over property rights? If all forms of property were privately owned by individuals who had clear, legal, and recognized title to their property, there would be no problem. They would have the exclusive right to the benefits derived from its use or sue for loss if anyone damages it.

For example, if, backing out of your driveway, you hit your neighbor's car parked across the street, you would be liable to pay your neighbor for all damages. If a police officer were called on the case, she would first identify ownership by asking to see your and your neighbor's car registration. She would then cite you with a moving violation, which identifies you as the injuring party and your neighbor as the injured. The auto body shop estimates the damage, and you pay your neighbor the cost of repair. Case closed.

But not all property disputes are associated with individuals having clear and recognized title. For example, who owns the air that the paint factory pollutes? Who has legal title to it? Who owns the birds that nest in your neighbor's trees? Who can claim legal title to them?

Because some forms of property are not easily privatized and title to them is virtually impossible to claim, no one has an interest in defending or maintaining the property.

For example, you may get upset when you see a driver toss an empty beer can onto the highway, but you would hardly speed up, signal the driver over, and make a citizen's arrest. After all, it's only a beer can along a long stretch of road, and, anyway, it's not your property. But that is precisely why there are empty beer cans scattered along the highways.

Would you think of checking the exhaust emission system of your neighbor's automobile and making a complaint? Could that one automobile really affect your well-being? Anyway, is it your air that's being polluted? Do you *own* it? This is a big part of why Denver and Los Angeles are blanketed in smog.

When Exxon's supertanker *Valdez* rammed into a reef off the Alaskan coast in 1988, spilling into the sea the millions of barrels of crude oil it was transporting, it created an economic disaster not only for the Alaskan fishing and tourist industries but for Alaskan wildlife as well. In other words, Exxon's carelessness damaged the economic well-being of thousands of unsuspecting third parties. But who owns the sea? Who owns the sea life that was destroyed?

The Alaska spill, although calamitous, was only one of many that occurred in the 1980s and 1990s. For example, eight years later, in 1996, a Liberian-registered tanker, *Sea Empress,* hit rocks near the port of Milford Haven in Wales, spilling 70,000 tons of oil to create the worst ecological disaster in British history. In 1997, fishing villages in northwestern Japan were third-party victims of a 5,200-ton oil slick created by the sunken Russian tanker *Nakhodka.* Oil coated their beaches and destroyed much of their highly prized shellfish beds. Only months later, Japan suffered its worst-ever oil spill when a supertanker struck a shallow reef in Tokyo Bay, this time leaking 13,400 tons of crude oil onto the bay's famed fishing grounds.

But it isn't just oil spills that harm unsuspecting third parties. A 1985 accident—the release of deadly methyl isocyanate gas—at Union Carbide's chemical plant in Bhopal, India, killed 4,500 people in Bhopal. In 1986, a meltdown occurred at the nuclear power plant in Chernobyl, Ukraine (then part of the USSR), when a controlled experiment in the plant's fourth reactor went wrong. Two explosions blew the top off the reactor building, releasing for 10 days clouds of radioactive material into the atmosphere. People were saturated with radiation 100 times greater than that released by the Hiroshima bomb. Seventy percent of it fell on Belarus, a Russian republic located north of the Ukraine, and 10 years later babies there were still being born without arms, eyes, or limbs. Over a half million people were engaged in the cleanup of Chernobyl, many of whom are now dead or sick. An estimated 15 million people were in some way victimized by the disaster. The costs associated with their health needs have been estimated at $60 billion.

Although the Indian courts ruled that Union Carbide was legally responsible and liable for damages caused to third parties, no suit was brought against the Soviet government, the legal property owner of the Chernobyl nuclear station.

Why not? Because the property issue wasn't the Chernobyl plant. It was the atmosphere! And *who actually has legal title to the atmosphere that the Chernobyl plant contaminated?*

What incentive would lead people, companies, and governments to be careful about creating negative externalities when they know their actions affect "only" a property form that cannot be claimed? It's frightening, isn't it? How can we begin to address the problem of pollution when our concepts of property make it difficult and sometimes impossible to attach specific costs to specific properties?

Space-age technologies that allow us to walk on the moon and send satellites to Mars and Venus also allow us to create even more dangerous threats to our environment than we have yet imagined. An old love song once assured us: "The moon

Why might Exxon (http://www.exxon.com/) devote part of its corporate Web site to highlight its pro-environmental policies?

belongs to everyone, the best things in life are free." This may no longer be true. We may now be in a position to pollute the moon just as effectively as we have dirtied our own earthly environment. After all, *who owns the moon?*

WHY SHOULD ECONOMISTS BE INTERESTED IN EXTERNALITIES?

Aside from the fact that economists breathe the same foul air and drink the same contaminated water as everyone else in a polluted environment, their interest in externalities goes one step further. Externalities strike at the heart of the economists' understanding of how the market system works.

Perhaps the issue of property rights and externalities on the moon is still a bit far out, but the presence of positive and negative externalities associated with almost every economic activity undertaken in our economy calls into question the efficacy of our market system. How come?

Defining Market Failure

One of the powerful arguments in favor of allowing markets to determine what gets produced in an economy—and in what quantities—is the fact that markets generate maximum efficiency. How so? Consider the following illustration.

Suppose you took a family heirloom, an exquisite Louis XIV antique chair, and chopped it into pieces for firewood. Crazy? Perhaps so. But perhaps not. If you weren't freezing, or if there was ample firewood available, you would probably be a candidate for the loony bin. But if you were freezing to death, then chopping that chair into firewood makes perfectly good sense.

You see the point, don't you? Suppose that chair was valued at $25,000. People were willing to pay that sum of money for it. If you used the chair for firewood, that fire better be worth $25,000! If the fire was used to add atmosphere to your living room, how much could that atmosphere be worth? $25,000? Most unlikely. In such a case, you use a resource worth $25,000 to produce a good worth considerably less! That's dumb, or in the economists' language, a grossly inefficient use of a resource.

If, on the other hand, the fire was to keep you alive, then the question is, What's your life worth? $25,000? Of course! In this case you use a resource worth $25,000 to produce a good—your life—worth considerably more. That's smart, or in the economists' language, an efficient use of the resource.

Let's take that idea one step further and bring it to the marketplace. Suppose you were in the bread-making business and bought ingredients on the market—flour, eggs, milk, yeast—valued at $4. Freshly baked, the bread was sold on the market for $3. Is that an efficient use of resources? Not at all. You didn't create value, you reduced it. On the other hand, if the market had valued the bread at $5, the bread-making activity would be considered an efficient use of resources. The value of the good produced is greater than the value or cost of the resources. Now value is created.

Let's add a twist to this story. Suppose there were negative externalities in making the bread. The coal-fired ovens created minor pollution—but pollution nonetheless—that was estimated at $3 per loaf. Now the cost involved in making bread changes. Before, it was strictly private cost—your own cost—which was $4. Now, an added cost in bread making of $3 emerges, which has nothing to do with your own cost of making bread, but which nonetheless is a cost to society. The **social cost,** then, is $7. Is bread making under these conditions of negative externalities an efficient use of resources? No longer. You didn't create value, you actually reduced it.

Social cost
The cost to society of producing a good. This cost includes both the private costs associated with the good's production and the externalities cost generated by its production.

CHECK YOUR
UNDERSTANDING

How do you measure social costs?

This bread making under conditions of externalities is an illustration of **market failure.** Because the market does not incorporate externalities into its cost calculations, it *appears* to be signaling an efficient use of resources—creating value—when, in fact, it is anything but efficient.

Too Many Chickens, Too Low a Price

Let's consider a case of such market failure by looking at a more commonplace example, the packaged chickens that you see stacked on the refrigerated shelves at your neighborhood supermarket. How do these chickens get there? As you might guess, it all begins "down at the farm." But that "farm" is not what you may think it is and certainly not what it used to be. Chicken farming once involved tens of thousand of competing small farmers servicing local and regional markets. No longer. Today, the independent, small chicken producers are almost extinct. Instead, the industry is dominated by a few major producers—Perdue, Tyson, and Smithfield among them—who control every phase of poultry production, from the corn and soybean mills that feed the birds to the processing plants that slaughter, clean, dress, and package them for national and international markets. What happened to the small farmer? Many became contract farmers, servicing the major poultry producers. These producers, who own both the chicks and the feed, assign them to contract farmers who raise the chicks on the contract farmers' own land (formerly, their own chicken farms). When the chicks are mature, they are returned to their owners—the large producers—for processing. Then it's on to the market, where supply and demand determines price.

So where's the market failure? Well, consider this: A fuzzy yellow chick becomes a plump five-pound bird in its six-week march from coop to kitchen. *Along the way, it leaves more than its weight in waste (chicken manure),* which contains large amounts of phosphorus, nitrogen, and potassium as well as other chemicals added to the chicks' diet by the large chick-owning producers. In Arkansas alone, *more than 5,000 tons of chicken waste is produced daily* and dumped into the environment. The dumping grounds have become overly saturated and the waste eventually makes its way into wells, ditches, streams, rivers, and lakes. The result is staggering water pollution in Arkansas and in the nine other large chicken-producing states that together account for 80 percent of the eight billion chickens produced annually in the United States. Scientists have linked this waste pollution to the toxic fish-killing microbe pfiesteria, which destroys not only fish but also tourist industries that depend on clean water. As well, pfiesteria is a hazard to human health, creating ailments ranging from body lesions to short-term memory loss.

Panel *a* in Exhibit 1 portrays the demand and supply conditions in the market for chicken. Equilibrium price and quantity are at $4 and 8 billion chickens, point *e.*

The value consumers place on the 8 billionth chicken, $4—which is what the demand curve reflects—is precisely the value of the resources used to produce that 8 billionth chicken (its marginal cost)—which is what the supply curve reflects.

What about the 6 billionth chicken? The value consumers place on that chicken, measured on the demand curve, is $6, point *a,* while the value of the resources used to produce that chicken is only $3, point *b.* In other words, one kind of good (resources) valued at $3 is used to create another kind of good (chicken) valued at $6. Like magic, value is created!

Now look at the value comparisons for the 10 billionth chicken. Not a wise use of resources, is it? One kind of good (resources) valued at $5, point *c,* is used to create another kind of good (chicken) valued at $2, point *d.* Like magic gone awry, value is destroyed.

Market failure
The failure of the market to achieve an optimal allocation of the economy's resources. The failure results from the market's inability to take externalities into account.

CHECK YOUR UNDERSTANDING

Why is producing more than equilibrium quantity not a good idea?

THE EFFECT OF EXTERNALITIES ON THE MARKET FOR CHICKEN

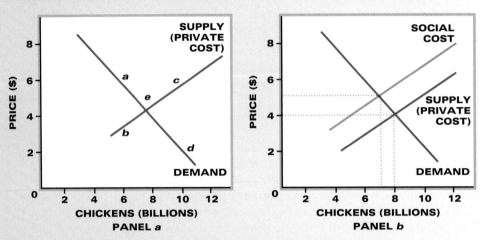

In panel *a*, the demand curve reflects the value people place on chicken. The supply curve reflects the marginal cost curves of firms producing chicken. These costs are private, representing only the firms' costs of production. The market generates an equilibrium price of $4, and the quantity demanded and supplied is 8 billion. Panel *b* incorporates into the calculation of cost the $1.60 associated with cleaning up the pollution caused by producing a chicken. It shifts the supply curve—now called the social cost curve—to the left, which raises the equilibrium price to $5 and lowers the quantity demanded to 7 billion chickens.

What conclusion can you draw? How about this: Keep producing chickens as long as the value consumers place on them is greater than the value of the resources used to produce them. Look at panel *a* of Exhibit 1 again. That production guideline gets us to the equilibrium quantity of 8 billion chickens. That equilibrium quantity represents the most efficient use of resources in the market for chickens.

What About the Pollution?

But there's a serious problem with this scenario. The market does not—it actually cannot—take into account the externalities cost to society of the chicken waste produced.

After all, the supply curve in panel *a* represents only the firms' private costs. That is to say, when a firm calculates what it costs to produce chicken, only those costs actually incurred by the firm are considered. It ignores the pollution created. But the polluting firm is certainly not alone.

Do breweries consider the cleanup costs of the beer cans littering our highways as part of their costs of production? Does the price tag on a Buick include the cleanup costs of the pollution it will create? Do farmers include the pollution costs caused by chemicals used in crop production? *These are real costs to society.* That is why the cost of producing chicken, calculated by the firms themselves, always understates the real opportunity cost of producing chicken, that is, what society gives up to acquire those chickens. The difference between the firms' private costs and the social costs—that is, the real costs to society—is shown in panel *b* of Exhibit 1.

GLOBAL PERSPECTIVE

CANADIANS KNOW THAT ACID RAIN NEEDS NO PASSPORT

WHAT CAUSES ACID RAIN?

Acid rain is rain, snow, or fog that is polluted by acid in the atmosphere and damages the environment. Two common air pollutants acidify rain: sulfur dioxide (SO_2) and nitrogen oxide (NOX). When these substances are released into the atmosphere, they can be carried over long distances by prevailing winds and return to earth as acidic rain, snow, fog, or dust. When the environment cannot neutralize the acid being deposited, damage occurs.

WHERE IS ACID RAIN A PROBLEM?

Acid rain is a problem in eastern Canada because many of the water and soil systems in this region lack natural alkalinity—such as a lime base—and therefore cannot neutralize acid naturally. Provinces that are part of the Canadian Precambrian Shield—such as Ontario, Quebec, New Brunswick, and Nova Scotia—are hardest hit because their water and soil systems cannot fight the damaging consequences of acid rain. In fact, more than half of Canada consists of susceptible hard rock (granite) areas that cannot neutralize the effects of acid rain.

WHERE HAVE ALL THE TREES GONE, LONG TIME STANDING?

FROM WHERE DO SULFUR DIOXIDE EMISSIONS COME?

Sulfur dioxide (SO_2) is generally a by-product of industrial processes and burning of fossil fuels. Ore smelting, coal-fired power generators, and natural gas processing are the main contributors. In 1995, for instance, U.S. SO_2 emissions were measured at 16.8 million tons—a full six times greater than Canada's 2.7 million total tons. But the sources of SO_2 emissions from the two countries are quite different. While 61 percent of Canada's emissions come directly from industrial sources, 66 percent of U.S. emissions are from electrical utilities.

Canada cannot win the fight against acid rain on its own. Only reducing acidic emissions in both Canada and the United States will stop acid rain. More than half of the acid deposits in eastern Canada originate from emissions in the United States. Areas such as Muskoka-Haliburton and Quebec City receive about three-quarters of their acid deposits from the United States. In 1995, the estimated transboundary flow of sulfur dioxide from the United States to Canada was between 3.5 and 4.2 million tons per year.

FROM WHERE DO NOX EMISSIONS COME?

The main source of NOX emissions is the combustion of fuels in motor vehicles, residential and commercial furnaces, industrial and electrical-utility boilers and engines, and other equipment. In 1995, Canada's largest contributor of NOX was the transportation sector, which accounted for approximately 60 percent of all emissions. Overall, NOX emissions amounted to 2.0 million tons in 1995. By comparison, U.S. NOX emissions for 1995 amounted to 21.7 million tons— 10 times more than Canada's.

The influence of transboundary flows of air pollutants from the United States into Canada is significant. Overall, about 24 percent of the regional-scale ozone episodes experienced in the United States occur simultaneously in Ontario. An analysis of ozone concentrations at four sites in extreme southwestern Ontario, taking wind factors into account, provides an estimate that 50 to 60 percent of the ozone at these locations is of U.S. origin.

CONSIDER

Draw a graph of a market for coal-fired generated electricity produced by U.S. public utilities and explain why market failure arises—that is, why price is too low and the quantity produced is too high.

Let's suppose the pollution cost associated with a chicken is $1.60. Adding this cost to the supply curve that reflects the private costs of producing chicken generates the social cost curve of panel *b*.

Now compare. If pollution costs are ignored, the market generates an equilibrium price of $4, and 8 billion chickns are demanded and supplied. Market failure, pure and simple. Why? Because if the social costs are considered, the equilibrium price is $5, and 7 billion chickens are demanded and supplied. In other words, the market is inefficient, pricing chickens too low and producing more than it should. To generate maximum efficiency, the market should be pricing chickens at $5 and producing only 7 billion.

CORRECTING MARKET FAILURE

Explaining market failure is easier than correcting it. Firms can measure their own private costs to the penny. But measuring externalities is as much a matter of imagination and conjecture as it is of accurate cost accounting. We simply know too little about environmental impact to confidently trace out social cost curves for various industries. Yet, we have to try.

After all, what are the alternatives? If we can't be exact about them, we can still be vaguely right. That is to say, if we can't correct the market failure, we can at least try to improve upon it. But how?

Government's Attempt to Correct Market Failure

CHECK YOUR UNDERSTANDING

Why rely on government to correct market failure?

Typically, we rely upon government. Why? Government may not know exactly what these social cost curves look like, but it has access to more relevant information than any private firm or individual and, moreover, is in the business of collecting that information. Compared to other interested parties, such as the polluting industries and people subject to pollution, government is probably also the most objective.

But what can it do? Government can pursue any or all of three policy options. It can (1) create new property forms to handle externalities, (2) levy a pollution compensation tax on the polluting industry, and (3) enforce an environment-protecting set of standards on the polluting industry.

Creating New Property Forms

Public beaches are sometimes overcrowded, noisy, littered with trash, and even dangerous to children. The surrounding picnic areas may be torn up by people and by automobiles and improperly parked pickups. Just as coal-fired power plants pollute our atmosphere, people can pollute beach areas. Of course, government can patrol beaches and penalize violators of public property. The patrol costs represent the externalities cost.

Another way of reducing abuse of public beaches is to convert them into private property by auctioning them off to private enterprise. If the beaches were privately owned, the owners would have a strong incentive to maintain them. After all, their beach access fees and the number of people willing to pay those fees would depend on how secure, clean, and spacious the beaches are. Having legal title to the beach would assure them that anyone damaging their property would be liable.

In this way, everyone gains. The government's auction brings in revenue, the new property owners earn profit, and the people have access to a more attractive beach.

But can government sell the atmosphere over a coal-fired power plant as easily as it transfers ownership of a beach area? Obviously not. The option of a shift to private ownership, then, has serious limitations.

THEORETICAL PERSPECTIVE

COASE THEOREM AND MARKET FAILURE

The idea of market failure is almost as devastating as the idea of no Santa Claus. Does market failure mean that we must always rely on government intervention to obtain an efficient use of our resources? Well, yes and no, but mostly no. While there may be positive or negative externalities associated with almost every market activity, in most cases the externalities are so minor that their impact on market efficiency is rather negligible. For example, boom boxes can be annoying, but they're really no reason to bring in the army. Most people just grin and bear it. And for most people, it works. In countless cases, grinning and bearing it is the most reasonable solution.

There's yet another solution to the boom box annoyance that does not involve government. This is what the *Coase theorem* is about. Economist Ronald Coase argued that in many market situations involving externalities, individuals are themselves quite capable of solving the externalities problem. How?

Coase sets the scene. Three prerequisites are necessary: (1) only a few people are involved, (2) their property rights are clearly recognized, and (3) the costs associated with negotiating an acceptable private outcome are minimal. These prerequisites seem to be met in our boom box illustration, so let's use it to explain Coase's idea.

Suppose Ray Cooper sits on his front porch every morning during the summer months and plays his boom box at full volume. Brenda Neilsen, a next-door neighbor and registered nurse, works the third shift at Barnes Hospital and sleeps mornings. At least she tries to. She approaches Ray with a proposition. She says she appreciates the fact that he is entitled to play his boom box whenever and wherever he wants. She acknowledges that she can-not legally get him to tone it down. But, she tells him, she is willing to pay him $25 a week for not using his boom box. Actually, she considers that cost quite reasonable. She would actually be willing to pay him $50, if he insists. Ray mulls over the $25 offer. It's not bad at all. He could do other things or go over to his uncle's barn to play his boom box, and he could certainly use the $25. He wouldn't do it for $10, but he would for $20. The $25 offer then is music to his ears. They agree.

Coase's point is made. You don't *always* need government to create an efficient use of resources when externalities arise. A private market—in this case, a market for peace and quiet—solves the problem of externalities. Brenda is happy with the outcome. She pays $25 for peace and quiet, which she values at $50. Ray is happy because he gets $25 for providing peace and quiet, which he values at $20. Negotiating externalities privately, they both come away ahead.

But let's not forget the prerequisites to the Coase theorem. What use is the theorem in solving problems of acid rain? Can millions of people affected by acid rain privately negotiate a mutually acceptable outcome? Or can thousands of lung cancer victims privately negotiate a mutually acceptable outcome with tobacco companies? Is clear title to property not an issue here? Are the costs of negotiation minimal? What about automobile pollution? Who negotiates with whom? Are property rights clear? Are costs negligible?

Admittedly, the use of the Coase theorem may be severely limited, but it still does show under what conditions people might solve their own problems.

MORE ON THE NET
Learn more about Ronald Coase (http://www.nobel.se/economics/laureates/1991/).

Levying a Pollution Compensation Tax

Another option available to government is to tax polluters. Look again at Exhibit 1, panel *b*. Suppose government *believes* that $1.60 is an accurate measure of the negative externalities associated with the production of chicken. It can levy a tax of $1.60 per chicken, which it can then use to clean up the environment. Simple enough? The government can either do its own environment cleaning or contract the cleaning to private firms.

The advantage of such a pollution compensation tax is that it falls squarely on the producers and consumers of chicken. Vegetarians don't pay. And people who eat very few chickens pay less tax than do those who eat more.

Creating Obligatory Controls

Instead of taxing the polluting industry, the government can impose obligatory controls. Such controls are the most common form of government intervention in environmental protection. Think about our municipal ordinances. Aren't leash laws obligatory controls designed to protect the community from the damage that unsupervised dogs can do? What about leaf-burning laws? Aren't they obligatory controls designed to protect the community from polluting its own atmosphere? Or what about sign ordinances? Aren't they obligatory controls designed to protect the beauty of our surroundings?

But why controls? Why doesn't government instead just allow people to buy the right to have their dogs roam about freely? Or buy the right to burn leaves? Or buy the right to post any size billboard or grotesque neon fixture? Or buy the right to dispose of garbage in the front yard? Isn't that essentially what a pollution compensation tax would allow industry to do?

If government were to price these rights properly, it could control pollution at *any* targeted level. For example, if it wanted to eliminate pollution completely, it could price these rights clear out of the market. But it can also set prices at *any* lower level, generating *any* degree of pollution control. In fact, by setting different prices for different industries and regions, government can produce virtually any quality control it wants, assuming it had reliable external cost data.

The Environmental Protection Agency

Government has traditionally controlled externalities by directive rather than by price. That's how the Environmental Protection Agency (EPA) works. Established in 1970 and operating within the executive branch of government, EPA has become *the* environmental regulatory agency of the nation. It administers all of Congress's environmental control acts, among them the Clean Air Act, the Water Pollution Control Act, the Safe Drinking Water Act, and the Toxic Substances Control Act.

Perhaps the most familiar obligatory EPA controls are those associated with the automobile industry. They affect your own automobile. EPA has given you no choice but to buy unleaded gasoline. It directs the automobile industry to install catalytic converters as standard equipment in your automobile. It is illegal for you to remove it, even though it's your own property.

EPA sets the maximum permissible number of hydrocarbon, carbon monoxide, and nitrous oxide pollutants for all automobile emission systems. EPA has made these emission standards tougher through the years and over the objections of the automobile industry.

Through its directives, EPA also controls the quantity and quality of pollutants that firms in other industries discharge into our water, land, and atmosphere. For example, to safeguard our water supply, EPA regulates the pollutants that industry, agriculture, and communities are allowed to discharge into ground and surface water. EPA can direct plants that dump wastes into rivers and lakes to install water purification systems that use the most economically effective technology available.

Although EPA *seems* to be rather busy, many environmentalists argue that it isn't busy enough. Others complain that it's busy doing the wrong thing, focusing far too much on environmental protection but ignoring the opportunity costs that the pro-

The U.S. Environmental Protection Agency (EPA) (http://www.epa.gov/) represents the federal government's concerns with pollution and the environment.

APPLIED PERSPECTIVE

LIVING IN AN IMAGINARY BUBBLE

Although EPA relies principally upon directives to specific firms in specific industries, it does provide a strategy allowing some flexibility to an individual firm in choosing its level of pollution. For example, in a growing number of cases, instead of setting one emission standard for all plants, EPA instead assigns one standard to a particular *set* of plants, allowing them to decide for themselves how to satisfy the standard.

This *bubble concept* of pollution control—an imaginary bubble containing all the participating plants involved in the one EPA emission standard—allows plants within the bubble to buy and sell pollution rights among themselves. For example, plants that are relatively clean can sell some of their polluting rights to the dirtier plants within the bubble who prefer to pay for the extra rights rather than cut production to meet their share of the emission standard. In this way, EPA succeeds in holding the bubble to a fixed emission standard while allowing internal buying and selling of rights to achieve the bubble's most efficient way of satisfying the standard.

MORE ON THE NET

The EPA's National Center for Environmental Economics (http://www.epa.gov/economics) conducts research on the economic costs and benefits of environmental regulations and pollution control programs.

tection imposes on particular industries and society. For example, if EPA made newer and even more expensive scrubbers mandatory for coal-fired electric production, society might end up with no pollution, but perhaps with no electricity either.

EXTERNALITIES AND PUBLIC GOODS

What about externalities that are positive? How do they affect market outcomes? Consider again your landscaping neighbor and the free riders who enjoy positive externalities associated with her landscaping.

Let's change the scenario slightly. Suppose a commercial gardener told her that the landscaping would cost $7,000, and she weighs that cost against the $6,000 value she places on the landscaping. You know what would happen, don't you? No landscaping.

Being a free rider, you lose the positive externality, which you value at, say, $300. Suppose other free riders in the neighborhood lose their positive externalities valued at $3,000. The social value of the landscaping, then, is $9,300, considerably more than its $7,000 cost. In other words, the landscaping actually represents an efficient use of society's resources. But left to the market, it won't be done.

Suppose, at a neighborhood barbecue, the issue is discussed and all but one agree to contribute to the landscaping. The holdout knows that if the landscaping gets done, he can't be denied the positive externality.

What happens? Even without his contribution, the landscaping might get done. But if he's not the only free rider—that is, if other neighbors think as he does—the probability is high that there will be no landscaping.

Positive Externalities and Market Failure

Let's extend this landscaping illustration to the community level. Everybody loves trees, but how many would be planted if decisions were left strictly to individuals? Look at the market for trees in Exhibit 2.

CHECK YOUR UNDERSTANDING

Why is the social value of the tree $120?

The equilibrium price is $100, and 500 trees are demanded and supplied. Consider the 500th tree. The value it creates to the person who bought it is $100, which is precisely its marginal cost (the value of the resources used to produce it). But this price and quantity signal market failure. Why? Because the market ignores the positive externalities other people acquire from the tree. If each tree generates positive externalities of $20, we can construct a social demand curve for trees by adding the $20 to the demand curve that reflects only the individual or private valuation of trees. The 500th tree now has a social value of $120.

A new equilibrium results, reflecting the social value of the trees. Quantity is 600 trees and price is $110. But how do we get people to buy 600 trees? After all, left on their own, nobody buys that 600th tree because the individual's value of it is only $90 (point *a* on the private demand curve), $20 below its marginal cost. The only way to get 600 trees planted is by government creating a $20 subsidy (or rebate) for each purchase of a tree. Now a person who was willing to buy that 600th tree at $90 will pay $110, knowing that $20 will be rebated.

Positive Externalities and Public Goods

The community could survive quite well with 100 fewer trees if it chooses not to have government intervene. But some goods will not be produced without government intervention, and in these cases, not producing them can be quite detrimental to the community's well-being. Typically, these are pure **public goods,** which are goods with considerable positive externalities, whose value to society is not diminished even when more people consume them, and whose value cannot be withheld from anyone.

Public good
A good whose benefits are not diminished even when additional people consume it and whose benefits cannot be withheld from anyone.

For these goods, the market simply doesn't work. That is to say, left to the market, the goods will not be produced even though they may generate considerable social value. A classic illustration of a pure public good is the harbor lighthouse. Nobody thinks of building a lighthouse for personal use, because most of the value generated by it is in the form of positive externalities. Moreover, once a lighthouse is built, anyone can use it as much as they wish without diminishing other people's use of it. For example, it doesn't shine less brightly guiding ten boats to harbor than it does guiding five. Nor can anyone be excluded from using it. When the guiding light is on, it cannot be selective. It shines for all.

How, then, does a public good, like a lighthouse, get built when everyone using it is essentially a free rider? Relying on voluntary contributions

EXHIBIT 2

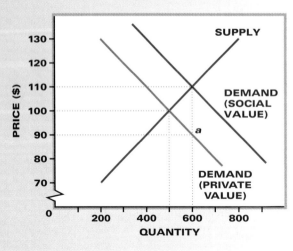

THE EFFECT OF EXTERNALITIES ON THE MARKET FOR TREES

Incapable of accounting for positive externalities, the market creates an equilibrium price of $100 and an output of 500 trees. If the $20 of externalities per tree is considered, the demand curve shifts to the right, creating an equilibrium price of $110 and an output of 600. But this requires a government subsidy of $20 per tree.

from people who derive positive externalities won't work, just as it didn't in our landscaping illustration. How, then, do we get a lighthouse? We rely on government intervention. Government builds it and taxes the community accordingly.

Public Goods and Near-Public Goods

The lighthouse is about as pure a form of public good as there is. Can you think of any other? What about national defense, or clean air, or clean water? Is it possible to exclude someone from enjoying the benefits of pollution control? Does anyone's consumption of clean air reduce other people's consumption of the air?

What about water? Not quite the same as clean air. After all, at some point, continued consumption by anyone could lead to a reduction in someone else's use. Clean water, then, is very close, but not exactly a *pure* public good.

What about national parks? The benefits, like those of the

Can you think of any other pure or near-pure public goods? Go to the Interactive Study Center at http://gottheil.swcollege.com and click on the "Your Turn" button to submit your example. Student submissions will be posted to the Web site, and perhaps we will use some in future editions of the book!

lighthouse and clean air, are exclusively external. But national parks are not pure public goods. Up to a point, people can enjoy the parks without reducing the enjoyment others derive. But if too many people visit the parks, congestion will reduce the value other people derive from the park. Moreover, unlike a pure public good, people can be excluded quite simply if the government charges a high admission fee.

There are many *near-public goods*. For example, everybody can consume nearly as much as they want of a freeway at 2 A.M. without reducing other people's consumption of the road. But not during the 5 P.M. rush hour. Also, people can be excluded from consuming the good if the government changes the road from a freeway to a tollroad.

What about public health? To the extent that government can prevent epidemics, everyone gains and no one is excluded. Even the simple hygiene that the government provides—all those shots that school nurses gave you—created considerable positive externalities in the form of preventive medicine.

What about education? Does everyone's utility increase when children go through the public school system? Education is the single most important contributor to our society's long-run economic growth. Our leadership in technology depends on a continuous investment in basic research. Our ability to use modern technology depends on the education our labor force receives. The flow of goods and services *available to everyone* at relatively low prices, then, is the positive externality that education offers. Our market system cannot exclude anybody, contributors to education or not, from enjoying the increases in societal well-being that education provides.

PUBLIC GOODS AND PUBLIC CHOICE

Most people agree that public goods and many near-public goods properly belong in the government's domain. Why? Because they think that the government, more so than the market, can best decide the quantity and quality of public goods that society should consume. Does that view make sense? Is allowing the government to make the choices about public goods the best way to overcome market failure?

Suppose everyone in the community agrees that the public library is a necessary public good and agrees as well that everyone should be taxed to pay for its use. The question then is, How much library should the community buy? And does that quantity represent an efficient use of resources?

Voting Your Demand for Public Goods

Suppose the public library in your community is accessible Monday through Friday, 9 A.M. to 5 P.M. And suppose, because you attend school during those hours, you find it rather inconvenient to use the library and you organize a political campaign to extend its hours. How many more hours, if any, will the community buy?

For convenience, let's suppose the community consists of only three people: you, Mindy Manolakes, and Brad Novicoff. Exhibit 3 describes the added value, in dollars, each derives when evenings and weekends are added to the library's hours.

Suppose the cost for each additional extension of library hours is $300. It is shared equally by the members of the community, so that each person pays a $100 tax for each extension. If the issue of the library's extended hours is brought to a vote and if everyone votes to satisfy his or her self-interest, how many units of library-hour extension will the community buy?

Will the community vote for the Sunday extension? Look at the value each derives from the Sunday extension. In every case, it is equal to or greater than the $100 tax. For example, Mindy's positive externality is $150, or $50 greater than the tax she pays. Brad's positive externality is $100, which is equal to the tax he pays. How would you vote? Your $100 tax provides you with $250 of benefit. The community will vote yes for Sunday.

What about Saturday's extension? The vote will be 2 to 1 in favor, Brad alone voting against it. But the vote will be 2 to 1 against Wednesday, you alone voting for it. The community, then, by democratic vote, buys only weekend extensions.

EXHIBIT | 3

THE DERIVATION OF GOVERNMENT FAILURE

ADDED HOURS	POSITIVE EXTERNALITIES OF ADDED HOURS			
	YOU	MINDY	BRAD	TOTAL
SUNDAY	$250	$150	$100	$500
SATURDAY	200	120	80	400
WEDNESDAY	150	90	60	300
FRIDAY	100	60	40	200
TUESDAY	50	30	20	100
THURSDAY	25	15	10	50
MONDAY	15	9	6	30

Government Failure

Just as we saw people in the community reacting to market prices and failing to buy the quantity of a public good that creates maximum efficiency, so we see the same people voting for public goods yet failing to buy the most efficient quantity. After all, that quantity is reached when the community's total positive externality equals the total marginal cost—that is, the tax. That occurs in Exhibit 3 with the third extension, Wednesday, where total positive externality equals the tax of $300. That is to say, by relying on the political process, a less than efficient quantity of library hours is purchased, generating what economists describe as **government failure.**

Government failure
The failure of the government to buy the quantity of public goods that generates maximum efficiency.

WHEN REPRESENTATIVES VOTE "ON BEHALF OF THE PEOPLE"

Government failure may be worsened when voting on specific issues is delegated to representatives who are elected to political office. Not everyone in the community has the time, the knowledge, or the interest to vote on every public goods issue. As a result, government decision making substitutes for direct voting. But how accurately do the public goods choices made by representatives of government reflect the demands of their constituents for those public goods?

Even with an honest effort, can representatives measure their constituents' specific costs and benefits to reach a yes or no decision on the purchase of a public good? There is another issue. To what extent are representatives, particularly in an off-election year, sufficiently in touch with their constituents to get the information shown in Exhibit 3, however imprecisely it may be expressed? Do they ask for it, or must representatives rely on people making themselves heard? How can representatives assess the costs and benefits to the community of any public good when, say, less than 10 percent of the people make their views known? Should representatives assume that those who didn't participate in the discussion of the issue have no interest in the political outcome?

How well can Mindy, Brad, and you be served when the government makes the decision on the library hours? Is government failure more or less likely when representatives substitute for direct voting?

However difficult it may be for individuals to measure the benefits they derive from extended library hours, it would be even more difficult for them to measure the benefits they derive from public goods more remotely felt, such as national defense. How would Mindy, Brad, or you calculate the individual benefits derived from government's purchase of another F-16 fighter plane? Would you be unable to make an educated response? Yet these are the kinds of public goods that representatives buy.

THE POLITICAL POWER OF "SPECIAL INTERESTS" The prospect of government failure becomes even more apparent when the government's choices of public goods are not intended to reflect the will of the people.

Economists hold different views about how government functions. Some believe that representatives, accepting the public trust, attempt to produce public goods that enrich the common good. There are always problems, of course, identifying the common good, just as there are problems assessing the worthiness of public goods. But the belief held is that at least an honest effort is made to represent the public choice.

Other economists, questioning this view of **public choice,** see these same representatives as people who choose to run for office, whose campaigns are financed by special interests, and who vote for or against legislation depending on how the vote affects the basic support they need to stay in office. That is to say, representatives, like most other people, are guided by self-interest. They are more likely to cater to special interests who depend on government purchases than to the vast majority of the people they were elected to serve.

For example, if a book publishers' association targets its political contributions to receptive representatives, the outcome of a government vote on library-hour extensions may well be different from the outcome associated with the Exhibit 3 data. What about the government's purchase of defense goods, where billions of dollars are at stake? It is not entirely surprising then that a **special-interest lobbying** industry plays some role in public choice.

The government's choice of public goods may sometimes reflect only the preferences for public goods expressed by very few people. In this way, government may fail to correct or even improve upon the market's failure to achieve an efficient use of resources in producing public goods.

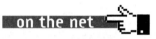
on the net

AARP (http://www.aarp.org/) and the National Parent Teacher Association (PTA) (http://www.pta.org/) are examples of special-interest groups.

Public choice
The theory of collective decision making.

Special-interest lobby
A group organized to influence people in government concerning the costs and benefits of particular public goods.

Living with Government Failure

If we can't live without public libraries or public roads or public education or national defense—to name just some of the public goods associated with the functioning of a modern economy—then we have to learn to live with some degree of government failure. How responsive representatives are to their constituents, and how willing individuals are to educate themselves on the costs and benefits of buying public goods and to make their choices known, affect the dimensions of government failure.

Economists accept the inevitability of government failure just as they accept the inevitability of market failure associated with public goods. But, as we have seen, they may look to different causes. Some economists see government failure resulting from the impossibility of achieving an efficient use of resources in producing public goods even though the government makes every effort to achieve it. Other economists—public-choice economists—see the impossibility resulting as well from the nature of the political process itself.

These two differing views about the motivation of government and the effect of that motivation on government's choices of public goods lead invariably to the striking differences of opinion that economists hold concerning what role government ought to play in our economy.

CHAPTER REVIEW

1. Costs and benefits that affect third parties are called negative and positive externalities. Pollution is an example of a negative externality. Your neighbor's landscaping, which you enjoy as a free rider, is an example of a positive externality.

2. If property rights were well defined, externalities would not exist. Polluters would have to pay for the damage they impose on others. People who generate positive externalities would be properly compensated.

3. The presence of externalities suggests market failure. Activities that generate negative externalities impose costs on people for which they are not compensated. For example, polluters don't include pollution costs as part of the marginal cost of goods whose production creates the pollution. Even though the producer sets price equal to marginal private costs, price is less than marginal social cost, indicating that too much production is occurring.

4. Correcting for negative externalities means forcing producers to face the social costs of their activities. This can be done by creating new property forms, by levying pollution taxes to match the size of the negative externality, or through obligatory controls.

5. Correcting for positive externalities means creating a mechanism to compensate those who create positive externalities. In practice, this is often very difficult, because of the free-rider problem. One solution is to have the government subsidize the goods or provide these goods itself.

6. Government may provide pure public goods and near-public goods. One person's consumption of a public good does not exclude others from consuming it, nor does it deplete the good for others to consume. The benefits from pure public goods are exclusively external.

7. The government may provide pure public goods and near-public goods in a manner that is consistent with the public interest. Public servants may make enlightened public choices. However, it is easy to envision situations where the government makes choices that are self-serving or that serve only narrow special interest groups. Under these circumstances, one might question government's wisdom in the choice of public goods, that is, public choice.

KEY TERMS

Third parties
Externalities
Free rider
Property rights

Social cost
Market failure
Public good

Government failure
Public choice
Special-interest lobby

QUESTIONS

1. Everyone knows that cigarette smoking is harmful to your health. But is it also harmful to people who live or work among smokers? Discuss this issue in terms of the third-party economic externalities created and their relationship to the market's ability to allocate resources efficiently.

2. Suppose someone next door plays her stereo so loudly that you complain. However, people living directly across the hall compliment her on her taste in music and ask her to continue playing it. What solution can you suggest?

3. People want more national security, more social welfare, and lower taxes. It just doesn't make sense, or does it?

4. Describe the following in terms of generating positive, negative, or zero externalities: (a) a foot of snowfall in mid-January; (b) living a mile away from an international airport; (c) your neighbor painting a mural on the side of his house that faces yours; (d) your neighbor's watchdog, who is known to have an unpleasant

disposition; (e) a superstudent in a class in which grades are curved; and (f) high-spirited motorcyclists.

5. Describe why externalities generate market failure.

6. What is a public good? How does it differ from a near-public good?

7. Why do economists believe government failure is inevitable?

8. Can you name your member of Congress or representative to state government? When was the last time you wrote or spoke to either of them? Or they to you? About what issue?

9. What do public-choice economists assume guides the behavior of elected people in government?

10. What is the function of a special interest or lobby?

11. Make the case that government-financed student loans benefit society. Make the case against such loans.

PRACTICE PROBLEMS

1. The market for flu shots during late fall is shown in the following table:

PRICE	QUANTITY DEMANDED	QUANTITY SUPPLIED
$50	1,000	9,000
40	3,000	7,000
30	5,000	5,000
20	7,000	3,000
10	9,000	1,000

Suppose the community derives a positive externality of $10 for every flu shot administered. What is the extent of market failure in this situation? What price and quantity does the market generate, and what price and quantity should it generate to achieve an efficient use of resources? How can this outcome be obtained?

2. The market for oil-based paint is shown in the following table:

PRICE	QUANTITY DEMANDED	QUANTITY SUPPLIED
$50	1,000	9,000
40	3,000	7,000
30	5,000	5,000
20	7,000	3,000
10	9,000	1,000

PRICE	QUANTITY DEMANDED (BOXES)	QUANTITY SUPPLIED (BOXES)
$50	1,000	9,000
40	3,000	7,000
30	5,000	5,000
20	7,000	3,000
10	9,000	1,000

Suppose the production of the paint creates a negative externality of $10 for each unit of paint, which is the cost of repairing the damage to the environment caused by the paint-generated pollution. What is the extent of market failure in this situation? What price and quantity does the market generate, and what price and quantity should it generate to achieve an efficient use of resources? How can this outcome be obtained?

3. Let's create a somewhat more complicated situation. The market for beeswax candles is shown in the following table:

Suppose the community derives a positive externality of $10 per box. The bees pollinate the flowers, which adds value to the community's appearance. But at the same time, they are a menace to the community because they are voracious stingers. The negative externality is estimated to be $10 per box. What is the extent of market failure in this situation? What price and quantity does the market generate, and what price and quantity should it generate to achieve an efficient use of resources? How can this outcome be obtained?

WHAT'S WRONG WITH THIS GRAPH?

THE EFFECT OF A NEGATIVE EXTERNALITY ON MARKET PRICE AND OUTPUT: FROM POINT *e* TO POINT *e'*

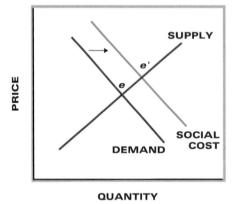

ECONOMIC CONSULTANTS

ECONOMIC RESEARCH AND ANALYSIS BY STUDENTS FOR PROFESSIONALS

Clean Air for Everyone (CAFE), an environmental action group located in Wheeling, West Virginia, was created to address the damage done by acid rain to the local environment. A number of local lakes and forests have suffered the effects of acid rain, which at times is as acidic as lemon juice.

CAFE's organizers have approached Economic Consultants for more information about what the government does to control acid rain, and what citizens can do to help stop this pollution. Prepare a report for CAFE that addresses the following issues:

1. What policy options may government pursue to lessen or stop acid rain?

2. What policies has the federal government implemented to address acid rain? Do any of these policies affect West Virginia?

3. What policies has West Virginia implemented to fight acid rain?

You may find the following resources helpful as you prepare this report for CAFE:

● **U.S. Environmental Protection Agency (EPA)** (http://www.epa. gov/)—The EPA provides detailed information about pollution policies and prevention programs. In particular, the EPA maintains a section devoted to acid rain (http:// www.epa.gov/acidrain/). Also, the regional office that includes West Virginia has materials on air pollution (http://www.epa.gov/reg3artd/).

● **Sierra Club** (http://www.sierraclub.org/ cleanair/)—The Sierra Club, a nonprofit environmental organization, maintains a section that addresses air pollution.

● **West Virginia Department of Environmental Protection (DEP)** (http://charon.osmre.gov/)— The DEP provides information on West Virginia legislation and policies concerning air pollution.

PRACTICE TEST

1. The principal reason the market fails to incorporate the costs or benefits of externalities is because
   a. externalities are consciously hidden by firms that generate them.
   b. they are government generated.
   c. there are no clear-cut, identifiable ownership rights to these externalities.
   d. externalities are costly, and neither firms nor consumers are interested in buying or selling them.
   e. externalities are typically undervalued, so that there is no market to buy or sell them at their real prices.

2. Externalities refer to
   a. the unintended costs or benefits imposed on third parties, resulting from market activity that ignores its effect on these third parties.
   b. market activity of third parties, creating costs and benefits that distort market outcomes.
   c. third-party outcomes that enhance the value of the goods produced on the market as well as their costs.
   d. the unintended effects of government regulation on the efficiency of production.
   e. the unintended effects of government regulation on price.

3. An example used in the text to illustrate a positive externality is
   a. the sounds heard by homeowners near O'Hare airport in Chicago when aircraft land and take off.
   b. the sounds made by birds nesting in trees planted by people, heard by their neighbors.
   c. the higher grades students receive by reading beyond the required text.
   d. the physical benefit people derive from doing physical exercise.
   e. students studying in groups.

4. North Carolina is a hog-processing state. Many of its processing plants use state-of-the-art technology. After the waste products are disposed of—dumped into lakes and rivers—we are able to buy pork chops on the meat market for $2.50 per pound. Not a bad price, but the problem is that
   a. price will increase in the long run because it does not include the costs of hog-waste disposal.
   b. price ignores the positive externalities associated with hog-waste disposal.
   c. price does not reflect the true cost to society of producing pork chops.
   d. people who have property rights to the lakes and rivers will sue the hog processors.
   e. because no one has property rights to the lakes and rivers, the cleaning up of these lakes and rivers will be left to environmental groups who will lobby Congress to curb pork production.

5. Because the market does not take into account the externalities associated with the production of pork, its market price
   a. is higher and output lower than an efficient use of resources would generate.
   b. is lower and output higher than an efficient use of resources would generate.
   c. is lower and output lower than an efficient use of resources would generate.
   d. is higher and output higher than an efficient use of resources would generate.
   e. generates maximum efficiency because it is higher than the equilibrium price.

6. To overcome the distorting influence on price of externalities (such as those created in hog-processing plants),
   a. government can levy a tax to cover externality costs, which will shift the supply curve to the left.
   b. government can levy a tax to cover externality costs, which will shift the supply curve to the right.
   c. government can levy a tax to cover externality costs, which will shift the demand curve to the left.
   d. government can levy a tax to cover externality costs, which will shift the demand curve to the right.
   e. pork producers can raise price to cover externality costs, which will shift the supply curve to the right.

7. *Free rider* refers to people who
   a. receive unintended benefits from positive externalities.
   b. receive intended benefits from positive externalities.
   c. pay the costs of unintended negative externalities.
   d. pay the costs of intended negative externalities.
   e. neither receive nor pay the costs of externalities.

8. *Government failure* refers to
   a. the inability of government to tax negative externalities.
   b. the inability of government to estimate how much tax is needed to cover the costs of negative externalities.
   c. the inability of government to identify which economic activities generate negative externalities.
   d. the failure of government to buy quantities of public goods that represent an efficient use of resources.
   e. the failure of government to buy public goods that serve the public need rather than special interests.

PART 4

THE MICROECONOMICS
OF FACTOR MARKETS

Tune into the conversation. It's about *your* course. Just change the names, and it's *your* campus, *your* classroom, *your* professor, *your* classmates, and *you*.

It's 10 minutes before the lecture begins. Professor Gottheil arrives a little early this time and takes up chatting with the few students who, too, came to class early. Ann Kiddo, a graduating senior in finance, asks him a question.

ANN: Professor Gottheil, I've got a silly question to ask, and I'm a little embarrassed about asking it because—

GOTTHEIL: Ann, there's no such thing as a silly question. Only silly answers. Go ahead.

ANN: Well, I've been toying with the idea of going into business. I've always loved flowers and was thinking about opening a florist shop in my hometown. My uncle left me some money that should be enough to get me started. But I don't know where to start. How many people should I hire? I mean, is there a correct number? If so, how do I find it out? I told you it's a silly question.

GOTTHEIL: Not silly at all. And there is a correct number, which you will discover for yourself. Look at any business. You see people working at very specific jobs. How many work at how many jobs depends on the nature and size of the business. Now, you're not going to start out being another Wal-Mart, are you?

ANN: *(Laughing.)* Oh no! I'm going to start out rather small, with a florist shop like Mr. Dold's. He has four people working for him. I used to work for him when I was in high school.

GOTTHEIL: Think about your own skills. Your accounting and finance courses will help you manage the financial end of the business, but it may not be the thing you want to do or can do best. A lot of your questions and problems can be answered only in the nitty-gritty process of doing. Now to your question: Let's suppose you start out with one assistant.

ANN: Is one enough?

GOTTHEIL: Well, let's see what enough is. Start with just that one. Two pairs of hands and two heads are a lot more productive than one, right? Well, you'll want to measure just how much more productive it is. Compare your shop's net revenue before you hire to the net revenue after you hire. For example, suppose you pay that assistant $300 a week, and the work he or she does in your shop adds $800 to your accounts receivable. That's a pretty good deal, isn't it? You net $500.

ANN: Well, if two heads are better than one, three heads are probably better than two!

GOTTHEIL: That's right. But how much better? You will probably find that your second assistant raises your net revenues, but not by as much as the first one did.

ANN: Why's that?

GOTTHEIL: For many reasons. Think about it. There are many ways of improving your business when you add workers, and it just makes sense that the most obvious and productive way of using workers was already done when you hired the first one. Not only that, but since you probably had a choice in the hiring, the person you hired as your first worker was probably the brightest and most energetic of the lot. Right? But listen, the second one may still be a great hire. Suppose he or she adds $500 to your sales and costs you $300. That's still adding a net revenue of $200. Not bad, is it?

ANN: I think I get the picture. There's really no magic number. I'll get to the correct number eventually. I guess that's what Mr. Dold must have done.

GOTTHEIL: That's right, Ann. Mr. Dold, AT&T, Baskin-Robbins, and Wal-Mart. And now you.

continued on next page

CHAT ECONOMICS

ANN: Professor Gottheil, close your eyes. OK? Now picture a beautiful yellow rose. Take your time. OK? Is it locked in your memory? Ok. It's my gift to you. Thanks for telling me it wasn't a silly question.

Ann may not realize it, but she derived her hypothetical firm's demand for labor, analyzed issues regarding the supply of labor, contemplated wage rate, considered factors such as education that affect earning, and calculated her firm's net revenues. Pretty heavy stuff, but all very important to Ann's future success as the owner of a florist shop.

As you read through the next few chapters, consider Ann and your own goals for the future, if you become confused. After all, as Ann discovered for herself, understanding the economic concepts in the next few chapters will directly affect your future success in business.

WAGE RATES IN COMPETITIVE LABOR MARKETS

The story is told about an old panhandler who regularly worked the corner of Wabash and Adams streets in downtown Chicago. For years, every Friday morning, a generous storekeeper who owned a shop nearby would give him a dollar. One Friday morning, however, the panhandler was refused. Shocked at the rebuff, he asked why. The storekeeper told him that business had been so bad, he couldn't afford to part with the dollar. The panhandler indignantly replied: "Because *your* business is bad, why should I have to suffer?"

Coal miners in West Virginia could ask the same question about their unhappy lot. When oil replaced coal as the primary energy source in the United States, coal prices and output fell dramatically. Mines were forced to shut down. Coal miners, still willing to give the same honest effort down at the mine, nevertheless found their jobs and their wage rate adversely affected.

You don't need to convince Nebraska farm laborers that when the price of corn is down, well-run farms fold, good John Deere equipment goes on the auc-

tion block, and their own wage rate is jeopardized. That is no news either to seasonal peach pickers in Georgia or loggers in Oregon.

Why are wage rates what they are? Why do some hardworking, honest folk who have both the capacity and inclination to work earn a decent wage rate, while others in the community, no less hardworking, honest, or willing to work, take home a fraction of what their neighbors earn?

Let's pursue these wage rate questions by looking at a simple coal-producing economy and tracing through the factors that seem to explain why coal miners earn what they do. Of course, the factors that determine coal wages are also at work in the steel, automobile, housing, newspaper, and clothing industries. They will help us understand why steelworkers, autoworkers, bricklayers, reporters, and dressmakers earn what they do.

THIS CHAPTER INTRODUCES YOU TO THE ECONOMIC PRINCIPLES ASSOCIATED WITH:

- MARGINAL PHYSICAL PRODUCT OF LABOR
- MARGINAL REVENUE PRODUCT
- THE LAW OF DIMINISHING RETURNS
- MARGINAL LABOR COST
- THE PROFIT-MAXIMIZING LEVEL OF EMPLOYMENT
- FIRM AND INDUSTRY DEMAND FOR LABOR
- THE SUPPLY OF LABOR
- THE BACKWARD-BENDING SUPPLY CURVE OF LABOR
- WAGE DIFFERENTIALS
- MINIMUM WAGE LAWS

YOU LOAD SIXTEEN TONS AND WHAT DO YOU GET?

Let's set the scene by examining the Charles Edwards Coal Mining Company, located in Harlan County, Kentucky. It is one of 1,000 coal mining firms in the region, and they all face competitive markets both in selling coal and in hiring coal miners.

To begin, suppose that everything required to mine coal—the drilling, blasting, and transport equipment, as well as the coal itself—is on the Edwards site. That is, everything but labor.

What would a typical day at the Edwards mine be like? Pretty quiet! It's obvious that without coal miners, no coal can be mined. Machines alone can't mine coal.

Hiring Miners, One at a Time

Charles Edwards will, of course, hire coal miners. It really makes no difference which one the company hires first because we assume that *all miners have equal skills.* Why make that assumption?

Because it is probably true. Although no 2 miners are alike—some are stronger, others brighter, others perhaps more energetic, and others may be more cooperative with fellow workers—the differences are overshadowed by the similarities of effort and performance.

Let's get the mine operating. Perhaps it is silly to imagine a mining firm functioning with only 1 miner, but let's do it anyway. The firm can then add a second, a third, a fourth, and so on, while we observe each time what happens to the output of coal as miners are added to the payroll.

The table in Exhibit 1 records output performance.

Look first at column 2. With no miners employed, no coal is produced. When 1 miner is put to work, coal output increases to 16 tons. When 2 are employed, output increases to 34 tons. Read down column 2. It records output produced with varying numbers of miners.

Picture the scene at the mine. With only 1 miner working, that miner is a very busy person. First comes the task of dynamiting and drilling loose tons of coal. The miner then operates the loading machine that transfers the coal to rail cars. The miner switches function again to ferry the coal out of the mine shaft. Then back to the dynamite. The result is 16 tons.

With 2 miners employed, some division of labor occurs. The miners cooperate. One handles the blasting and drilling, the other takes care of loading and transporting. The result is much higher productivity in the mine. By doubling employment from one to two miners, output more than doubles, increasing from 16 to 34 tons.

When Edwards increases employment to 3 miners, the new division of labor affords even greater productivity. Each miner becomes more specialized and more efficient, and the time lost in switching off and starting up different tasks is reduced. Output increases to 54 tons.

Marginal physical product
The change in output that results from adding one more unit of a resource, such as labor, to production. *MPP* is expressed in physical units, such as tons of coal, bushels of wheat, or number of automobiles.

MARGINAL PHYSICAL PRODUCT Another way of reading the information in column 2 is by tracking the **marginal physical product** of labor—that is, the change in output, ΔQ, resulting from a change in the number of miners employed, ΔL. The marginal physical product, *MPP*, is written as:

$$MPP = \frac{\Delta Q}{\Delta L}$$

EXHIBIT | 1

OUTPUT AND MARGINAL PHYSICAL PRODUCT CURVES

EFFECT OF ADDITIONAL MINERS ON OUTPUT AND REVENUE

(1) MINERS	(2) OUTPUT	(3) MARGINAL PHYSICAL PRODUCT *(MPP)*	(4) TOTAL REVENUE *(P = $2)*	(5) MARGINAL REVENUE PRODUCT *(MRP)*
0	0	0	—	—
1	16	16	$ 32	$32
2	34	18	68	36
3	54	20	108	40
4	72	18	144	36
5	88	16	176	32
6	102	14	204	28
7	114	12	228	24
8	124	10	248	20
9	132	8	264	16
10	138	6	276	12
11	142	4	284	8
12	144	2	288	4

In panel *a*, the output curve is upward sloping, increasing by large amounts until 3 miners are employed, then increasing by smaller and smaller amounts when more than 3 miners are employed.

In panel *b*, the marginal physical product (*MPP*) curve maps the increases noted in the output curve. The *MPP* increases for the first 3 miners—the second miner's *MPP* = 18, the third miner's *MPP* = 20—then falls steadily as more miners are added to production. The *MPP* of the twelfth miner is 2 tons.

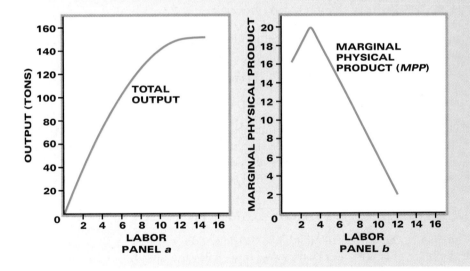

PANEL *a*

PANEL *b*

Column 3 records the *MPP* for Charles Edwards. The same data are shown in the graphs in Exhibit 1.

The *MPP* of the first miner is 16 tons. Why 16 tons? Because output increases from 0 to 16 tons when employment increases from 0 to 1 miner. When the company employs a second miner, output increases from 16 to 34 tons. The *MPP* of the second miner, then, is $34 - 16 = 18$ tons. Because everything else at the mine remains unchanged except for the addition of this second miner, *the 18-ton increase in output is attributed to the hiring of this second miner.*

The *MPP* of the third miner is $54 - 34 = 20$ tons. The *MPP* of the fourth is $72 - 54 = 18$ tons.

MPP AND THE LAW OF DIMINISHING RETURNS Note that beyond the third miner, *MPP* declines. As miners are added, one at a time, the additions to output become smaller and smaller. *Total output, of course, continues to increase,* but by diminishing numbers of tons. This is shown by the eventual flattening of the curve in Exhibit 1, panel *a,* and by the negative slope of the *MPP* curve in panel *b.*

Why this **law of diminishing returns?** Digging deeper into the mine takes more time. Extended mineshafts require more supports, more rail tracks, and more extensive ventilation and communication systems. Adding miners to a given stock of coal-producing machinery must eventually create a less-than-efficient match of labor to capital. Perhaps the most obviously inefficient match of labor to capital in a mine would be two miners working with one pick.

What happens to coal production when more than 12 miners are employed? The *MPP* of the twelfth miner is 2 tons. Could the thirteenth miner's *MPP* fall to 0? Or below 0? Can you imagine so many miners down in the mineshaft getting in each other's way that adding the thirteenth miner *reduces* output? It can happen.

Converting Tons into Revenue

The Charles Edwards Coal Mining Company, although visibly in the business of mining coal, is also in the business of mining money. In the last analysis, it wants dollars, not coal. Suppose that Edwards sells its coal in a perfectly competitive output market. If the price of coal is $2 per ton, the firm sees the fourth miner adding not just 18 tons to its output, but $36 to its total revenue. We can convert each miner's *MPP* in Exhibit 1 into **marginal revenue product,** *MRP,* by applying the formula

$$MRP = MPP \times P,$$

that is, the miner's marginal physical product multiplied by the price of coal. MRP can also be written as

$$MRP = \frac{\text{change in } TR}{\text{change in } L},$$

the addition to the firm's total revenue when an additional miner is hired.

Look again at Exhibit 1, this time at column 5. *Since MRP is simply a revenue reflection of MPP,* it, too, starts declining after the third miner. The twelfth miner, for example, adds only $4 to Edwards's total revenue.

DERIVING THE FIRM'S DEMAND FOR LABOR

The quantity of labor demanded, like the demand for any good, depends on price. If the price of labor—that is, the **wage rate**—falls, the quantity demanded of labor increases. In this respect, the law of demand applies to miners just as it applies to microwaves, microchips, and mayonnaise.

Deriving Marginal Labor Cost

The table in Exhibit 2 records Edwards's labor costs when it hires different quantities of miners.

If the wage rate is $20, the **total labor cost,** *TLC,* of hiring one miner is $20. *TLC* increases to $40 when 2 miners are hired, to $60 when 3 are hired, and so on. Because the labor market is perfectly competitive, the Charles Edwards Coal Mining Company is assured that no matter how many miners it hires, it cannot influence the wage rate. Total labor cost, *TLC,* for Edwards, then, is simply the number of miners, *L,* multiplied by the wage rate, *w:*

Law of diminishing returns
As more and more units of one factor of production are added to the production process while other factors remain unchanged, output will increase, but by smaller and smaller increments.

Marginal revenue product
The change in total revenue that results from adding one more unit of a resource, such as labor, to production. *MRP,* which is expressed in dollars, is equal to *MPP* multiplied by the price of the good.

Wage rate
The price of labor. Typically, the wage rate is calculated in dollars per hour.

Total labor cost
Quantity of labor employed multiplied by the wage rate.

$$TLC = wL$$

What about **marginal labor cost,** *MLC*? The *MLC* allows the firm to read its *TLC* information in a slightly different way. *MLC measures how much the company's total labor cost increases when each additional miner is hired:*

$$MLC = \frac{\text{change in } TLC}{\text{change in } L}$$

Marginal labor cost
The change in a firm's total cost that results from adding one more worker to production.

Now look at the graphs in Exhibit 2.

When Edwards increases its mining crew from 8 to 9 miners, *TLC* increases from $160 to $180, or by $20. For the ninth miner, *MLC* = $20.

Look at column 4 in the table and then at panel *b*. *MLC* = $20 for *every miner*. That is, for every miner Edwards hires at the $20 wage rate, that hire raises Edwards's total labor cost by $20.

DERIVING THE MARGINAL LABOR COST CURVE

LABOR COSTS FOR COAL MINERS ($ PER HOUR)

(1) MINERS (L)	(2) WAGE RATE (w)	(3) TOTAL LABOR COST (TLC)	(4) MARGINAL LABOR COST (MLC)
0	$20	$ —	$ —
1	20	20	20
2	20	40	20
3	20	60	20
4	20	80	20
5	20	100	20
6	20	120	20
7	20	140	20
8	20	160	20
9	20	180	20
10	20	200	20
11	20	220	20
12	20	240	20

Marginal labor cost (*MLC*), panel *b*, is the additional cost of hiring an additional worker. In a perfectly competitive labor market where the firm can hire as many workers as it wishes at the prevailing wage rate, the *MLC* curve is horizontal and equal to the wage rate. In the case of Edwards, *w* = *MLC* = $20 per hour for any number of workers.

The total labor cost (*TLC*) curve, panel *a*, shows the number of workers multiplied by the wage rate they receive. When one worker is hired at $20 per hour, the total labor cost is $20. When 5 workers are hired, the *TLC* is 5 × $20 = $100.

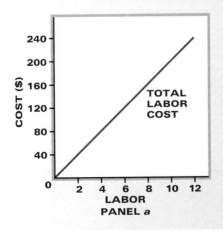

PANEL a

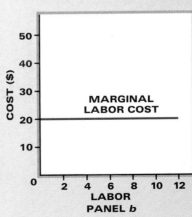

PANEL b

EXHIBIT|2

Demanding Miners Until $MRP = w$

Given the *MRP* data of Exhibit 1 and the wage rate data of the table in Exhibit 2, how many miners will the Charles Edwards Coal Mining Company hire at the $20 wage rate? Let's again consider one miner at a time, starting with the first.

It makes sense for Edwards to hire the first miner. After all, the miner adds $32 to the firm's revenue and only $20 to cost, thereby increasing the firm's revenue by

$$\$32 - \$20 = \$12.$$

What about hiring the second? Again, it makes sense. Why? Because the second miner's *MRP* = $36. The second miner adds to revenue

$$\$36 - \$20 = \$16.$$

CHECK YOUR UNDERSTANDING

How does a firm determine how many workers to hire?

Why stop there? What about the third, fourth, fifth, and so on? In each case, Edwards compares the *MRP* of each additional miner to the wage rate. The hiring rule is simple. If the miner's *MRP* > *w*, hire. If the miner's *MRP* < *w*, don't hire. If this rule is adhered to, Edwards will continue to hire miners until the *MRP* of the last miner hired equals the miner's wage rate,

$$MRP = w.$$

At a wage rate of $20, *MRP* = *w* at the eighth miner. The Charles Edwards Coal Mining Company, then, hires 8 miners.

If the wage rate falls to $8, Edwards hires 11 miners since now *MRP* = *w* at the eleventh miner. If the wage rate triples from $8 to $24, will Edwards still hire that eleventh miner? No, because that eleventh miner adds only $8 to Edwards's revenue but costs Edwards $24. Edwards will cut the number of miners it hires to 7.

Exhibit 3 sums up these *MRP* = *w* hiring decisions to represent Edwards's demand schedule and demand curve for labor.

What we see is that *the demand curve for labor is precisely the laborers' MRP curve.* When *w* = $40, the quantity demanded is 3 miners because *MRP* = *w* = $40 at the

EXHIBIT 3

THE DEMAND FOR LABOR

The firm hires workers as long as the worker's *MRP* is greater than or equal to the worker's *MLC,* or wage rate. When the wage rate *w* = $28, Edwards hires 6 miners; the sixth miner's *MRP* = $28. When *w* = $16, Edward hires 9 miners; the ninth miner's *MRP* = $16. When *w* = $4, Edwards hires 12 miners. That is why the demand curve for labor is precisely the firm's *MRP* curve.

DEMAND SCHEDULE FOR LABOR

WAGE RATE	MINERS DEMANDED
$40	3
36	4
32	5
28	6
24	7
20	8
16	9
12	10
8	11
4	12

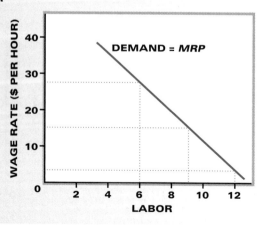

third miner. When the wage rate falls to \$4, the quantity demanded increases to 12 because now $MRP = w = \$4$ at the twelfth miner. Each point on the demand curve reflects an $MRP = w$ position.

What Shifts the Demand for Labor?

A CHANGE IN THE PRICE OF THE GOOD Imagine a winter with long stretches of below-zero weather. Factory and home furnaces work overtime. The demand curve for coal shifts to the right, creating a new and higher short-run equilibrium price for coal. Let's suppose the price of coal increases to \$3 a ton.

Suppose nothing else changes. The miners at Edwards work the same hours with the same equipment, producing the same physical quantities. In other words, the miners' *MPP* curve remains unchanged.

What happens to the firm's demand curve for miners under these conditions? Look at the table in Exhibit 4.

Although the miners' *MPP* remains unchanged, their *MRP* is affected by the change in the price of coal. For example, at the old price of \$2, the *MRP* of the first miner employed was \$32—that is, the 16 tons produced fetched \$2 per ton on the coal market. Because of the cold weather, the same 16 tons produced by that same first miner now add \$48 to the firm's revenue.

As you see, for each miner added to employment, the same *MPP* now contributes a higher *MRP*. The graph in Exhibit 4 portrays this *MRP* shift.

The *MRP* curve—the firm's demand curve for miners—shifts to the right. At each wage rate, more miners are hired. If the price of coal were to jump to \$10, the demand curve would shift even further to the right. *That's why miners like cold weather!*

SHIFT IN THE DEMAND CURVE FOR LABOR CAUSED BY AN INCREASE IN THE PRICE OF THE GOOD

THE DERIVATION OF *MRP* USING OLD AND NEW PRICES

COAL MINERS	MPP	OLD MRP = MPP x \$2	NEW MRP = MPP x \$3
0	0	\$ 0	\$ 0
1	16	32	48
2	18	36	54
3	20	40	60
4	18	36	54
5	16	32	48
6	14	28	42
7	12	24	36
8	10	20	30
9	8	16	24
10	6	12	18
11	4	8	12
12	2	4	6

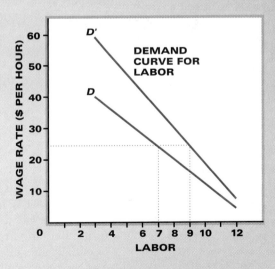

An increase in the price of coal from \$2 to \$3 causes the demand curve for labor to shift to the right, from *D* to *D'*. At every wage rate, the number of miners demanded by Edwards increases. When the price of coal is \$2 and when $w = \$24$, Edwards hires seven miners. After the price increases to \$3, at $w = \$24$, Edwards hires nine miners.

IMPROVEMENTS IN TECHNOLOGY Imagine what would happen down at the mine if the Charles Edwards Coal Mining Company decided to replace its old coal mining machinery with the most advanced mining technology. Look at Exhibit 5.

Compare the *MPP*s. Before the new technology was put in place, the first miner produced 16 tons. After the new technology replaced the old, that same miner produced 32 tons, twice as much.

What about the second miner? Twice as productive, from 18 to 36 tons. What about the third, fourth, and so on? Working with new technology, labor is twice as productive. The *MRP* curve shifts to the right. In other words, *either rising coal prices or employment of more advanced technology will shift the demand curve for miners to the right.*

No surprise, is it, that the *MRP* of West Virginia miners is considerably higher than the *MRP* of Chinese miners working in the Shensi Province of northern China? Why? Principally because more and better coal mining technology is used in the United States than in China. The workers' productivity does not necessarily reflect personal effort. Our technology in the hands of Chinese miners would probably produce equivalent results.

EXHIBIT 5

THE DERIVATION OF *MRP* USING OLD AND NEW TECHNOLOGY (PRICE OF COAL = $2)

COAL MINERS	OLD TECH MPP	NEW TECH MPP	OLD TECH MRP	NEW TECH MRP
0	0	0	$ 0	$ 0
1	16	32	32	64
2	18	36	36	72
3	20	40	40	80
4	18	36	36	72
5	16	32	32	64
6	14	28	28	56
7	12	24	24	48
8	10	20	20	40
9	8	16	16	32
10	6	12	12	24
11	4	8	8	16
12	2	4	4	8

INDUSTRY DEMAND FOR LABOR

So far, our analysis has focused only on the Charles Edwards Coal Mining Company's demand for labor. But suppose the company is only one of a thousand mining firms operating in Harlan County. And suppose, too, that the mining firms have essentially the same quality coal deposits, use the same technology in mining coal, and compete for the same miners in the same labor market.

If all coal mining firms are identical to Edwards, then the miners' *MRP* curve in *any* of the industry's 1,000 coal mining firms would be the same as any other. The industry demand curve for labor, then, is Edwards's, magnified 1,000 times. That's what we see in Exhibit 6.

EXHIBIT | 6

INDUSTRY DEMAND FOR LABOR

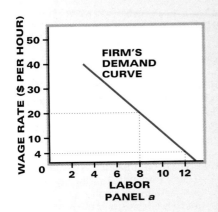

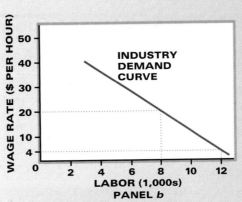

In panel *a*, Edwards's *D* = *MRP* curve indicates that it hires 8 workers at a wage of $20 per hour. With 1,000 firms identical to Edwards, the industry demand curve for labor is the horizontal sum of the firms' *MRP* curves. In panel *b*, we see that 8 × 1,000 = 8,000 miners will be hired at a wage of $20 per hour.

In panel *a*, at *w* = $20, the quantity of labor demanded by Edwards is 8 miners. For the coal mining industry, shown in panel *b*, quantity demanded of labor is 8,000 miners. At *w* = $4, the quantity of labor demanded by Edwards is 12 miners, and the quantity demanded by the coal mining industry is 12,000.

But suppose not all the 1,000 mining firms in the industry are identical. For example, some firms may have access to rich coal deposits, while others mine low-quality coal. Or some firms may be using old mining technology, while others use the most advanced technology. As a result, the number of tons mined by miners—the first, second, third, and so on—in each firm would differ. Each firm's demand curve for labor, then, would be different. For example, while Edwards demands 8 miners at *w* = $20, the Erin Doyle Coal Mining Company, located seven miles down the road, demands 14 (assuming the fourteenth miner's *MRP* at Doyle is $20). Each firm will continue to demand miners as long as the *MRP* of the miner is greater than or equal to the wage rate.

THE SUPPLY OF LABOR

Let's now consider how much labor the people of Harlan County are willing to supply to coal mining firms at different wage rates.

Miners have choices. They can choose to work or not to work, and those who choose to work typically face more than one work option. But not all miners have the same work options or share the same preferences for work and leisure. For example, some miners may be workaholics and actually prefer mining to doing anything else with their time. To them, the opportunity cost of mining (the value they place on their next best alternative to mining) is zero. But they are unusual folks. Most people place *some* value on what they can otherwise do with their time. The opportunity cost of working, different for different people, determines how many people in Harlan County would be willing to work at differing wage rates.

Consider, for example, miner Steve Carosello. His next best alternative to mining is the $5.50 per hour he can earn as a school bus driver. A $6 offer at the coal

C H E C K   Y O U R
U N D E R S T A N D I N G

What determines how many people are willing to work at different wage rates?

INTERDISCIPLINARY PERSPECTIVE

BRUCE SPRINGSTEEN ON WORK

Charlie Rose (interviewing Bruce Springsteen): Have the songs gotten more political over time, you think?

Bruce Springsteen: My music? I don't know. I think my music . . . what I wrote about, always had political implications. And I suppose it came up out of . . . originally . . . my home life, you know, and my experience growing up, and my relationship with my father, and trying to understand the concept of work, and how work plays a central role in your life. And I had two real very different examples. My mother's relations with work was very joyous and very happy and provided the entire family with stability and it . . . what she gained from it was an entire mode of behavior. You get up in the morning, at a certain time, you prepare yourself. You get yourself ready to go to your job. You walk down the street. You're there at a particular time of the day, and you interact with your co-workers. That's a big part of your social life, and your work life, and your place in the world. You know, you're doing something that has a purpose. The reason you're there . . . besides just feeding your family. You're part of the social fabric. You're what's holding the world together; you're what's holding your town together. You're what's holding your family together. And I always remember she walked with tremendous pride. And strength . . . enormous strength. And it gave great

BORN IN THE USA.

comfort . . . great, great comfort to the child. That makes sense, you know. I understand. My dad had a different experience. His work was involved with pain. He lost his hearing when he worked in a plastics factory. He lost a lot of hearing. He struggled to find work and to go to work. It led to . . . the regulation of behavior that work provides . . . wasn't a big part of his life, and that was painful, you know, for everybody involved. That's essential, that's essential. That's essential for the way we live and think about ourselves, and who we are, and the place we live in. And so I saw both sides of it. I saw what happens when that's not present. There is pain, and there is anger, and deep, deep . . . it's a destructive force. You wither away, you waste away. You don't know where you're going or who you are, and you take it out on people you care about, which is something you don't want to do, you know. But it happens. So that's what I wrote about. That's what I wrote about. That was really, really important. It's the single thing I've written about. My entire life. That fundamental idea, the importance of that idea in society. The cost of not providing that . . . so that people can take care of their families, to have productive jobs. The debasement of ourselves in not having a society . . . that provides for all our citizens. It grew up from there, It grew up from my experience.

Source: From an interview on the *Charlie Rose* TV show. Reprinted with permission courtesy of charlierose.com, inc.

mine, then, exceeds Steve's $5.50 opportunity cost. He is one of the 1,000 people in the table in Exhibit 7 willing to mine at $6. If, on the other hand, the wage rate offered at the mine is $5 per hour, Steve would not be willing to work there because the $5.50 he can earn driving the bus is higher. In other words, the $5 wage rate at the mine is below his opportunity cost.

The table in Exhibit 7 records the number of workers willing to work at different wage rates. Nobody goes down into the pits for $5 per hour. At $w = $6, 1,000 miners show up. An $8 wage rate meets the opportunity cost of 2,000 miners.

THE SUPPLY CURVE OF LABOR

THE SUPPLY SCHEDULE OF COAL MINERS

WAGE RATE ($ PER HOUR)	QUANTITY OF LABOR SUPPLIED
$ 0	0
6	1,000
8	2,000
10	3,000
12	4,000
14	5,000
16	6,000
18	7,000
20	8,000
22	9,000
24	10,000

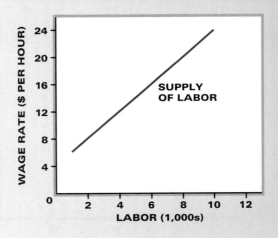

The supply curve of labor is upward sloping. The higher the wage rate, the more willing are workers to supply greater quantities of labor. At $w = \$6$, 1,000 workers are willing to supply their labor. At $w = \$20$, 8,000 workers offer their labor. At $w = \$24$, 10,000 workers are willing to work.

Now look at the graph in Exhibit 7. The supply curve for labor is upward sloping because the higher the wage rate, the more people's opportunity costs are met.

What Shifts the Supply Curve for Labor?

Note that at a $10 wage rate, 3,000 people are willing to work the mines. That number could increase or decrease depending on changes in the miners' alternative employment opportunities, changes in the population size of the coal mining region, and changes in people's wealth.

CHANGES IN ALTERNATIVE EMPLOYMENT OPPORTUNITIES If new industries, willing to pay wage rates higher than $10, came to Harlan County, many people who were previously willing to work the mines at $10 would be drawn away from mining to these new employment opportunities. Edwards and other mining firms would soon discover fewer than 3,000 miners available at $10 (and fewer than the numbers shown in the table in Exhibit 7 at each wage rate). The miners' supply curve in the coal industry of Exhibit 7 would shift to the left, from S to S_1, in Exhibit 8.

On the other hand, if firms were to leave Harlan County, some people who had been working for those firms would now find the $10 wage rate at the mines their best work opportunity. As a result, more than 3,000 would be willing to work at that wage. With fewer work alternatives for everyone in Harlan County, more miners than those shown in the table in Exhibit 7 would show up for work at each wage rate. The supply curve of Exhibit 8 would shift to the right.

CHANGES IN POPULATION SIZE Changes in the region's population would also shift the miners' supply curve of labor. For example, if the mining companies

CHECK YOUR UNDERSTANDING

Why does the labor supply curve slope up?

EXHIBIT | 8

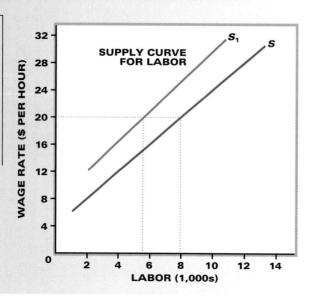

CHANGES IN THE SUPPLY CURVE OF LABOR

Changes in alternative employment opportunities, population size, and wealth affect the number of people willing to work the mines at different wage rates. An increase in alternative employment, a fall in population, and an increase in wealth shifts the supply curve of labor to the left, for example, from S to S_1.

continually violate mine safety codes, so that a sizable number of miners decide to leave Harlan County, the coal mining firms would soon discover fewer miners than those shown in the table in Exhibit 7 willing to supply their labor at any wage rate. As a result, the supply curve of labor would shift to the left.

On the other hand, what happens to the supply curve of labor in Harlan County if busloads of Canadian miners from the depressed mining towns of Nova Scotia migrate in? It shifts to the right, doesn't it?

CHANGES IN WEALTH

Consider as well how changes in people's wealth influence their willingness to supply labor. If you suddenly became a millionaire, how much time would you be willing to spend down in the mine? What wage rate would lure you away from leisure? Let's be more down-to-earth. If an unexpected inheritance tripled your wealth, would the mining firm's time-and-a-half wage rate persuade you to give up weekends? Unlikely. Most people are like you. When people have more wealth, they choose more leisure and less work. The result: The supply curve of labor shifts to the left. On the other hand, if fortune fades and wealth falls, the supply curve of labor shifts to the right.

The Backward-Bending Supply Curve

Are all supply curves of labor *endlessly* upward sloping? Not at all. Suppose you were offered a job paying $10 million, but the job required you to work or to be on call 24 hours a day with no vacations, weekends, or holidays until retirement at age 70. Would you take it?

Not many would. The wage rate is excellent, but the opportunity cost is simply too high. Most people can be enticed by higher wage rates to increase the quantity of labor they supply, but only up to a point. Beyond that, increases in the wage rate may actually result in *less*, not more, labor supplied.

For example, Ray Cooper, a miner at Edwards, figures that $100,000 would be more than sufficient to satisfy his needs. Of course, more income is preferred, but not if obtaining more would cut into his leisure time. How would Cooper respond to changes in the wage rate? Look at Exhibit 9.

If the wage rate was $40 per hour and Cooper worked a 50-hour week for 50 weeks a year, he would earn $100,000. If the wage rate increased to $65 per hour, Cooper's income—assuming he worked the same 50 hours per week—would be $162,500. Is he happy about the wage rate increase? Wouldn't you be? But how does he respond? He could either take the $162,500 or reduce the hours of work, earn somewhat less, but enjoy more leisure. Exhibit 9 shows what he does.

At a wage rate of $65, Cooper cuts back to 40 hours per week and ends up with $130,000. As a result, he gains 500 more hours of leisure. To Cooper, the value of that extra leisure is worth much more than $162,500 − $130,000 = $32,500.

As Exhibit 9 depicts, at wage rates above $65, Cooper cuts back on the number of hours he supplies even more. That is, Cooper's supply curve of labor at wage rates above $40 is backward bending.

Conceptually, the backward-bending supply curve makes sense. But we seldom experience it. Typically, workers are willing to supply more labor when wage rates increase.

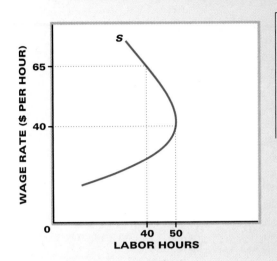

THE BACKWARD-BENDING SUPPLY CURVE OF LABOR

Typically, an increase in the rate induces workers to increase the quantity of labor they supply. But once the wage rate reaches a certain level, which may vary for each worker— $w = 40 in the case of Ray Cooper's supply curve, S—further increases in the wage rate only encourage workers to cut back on the quantity of labor they are willing to supply.

EXHIBIT | 9

DERIVING EQUILIBRIUM WAGE RATES

Exhibit 10 combines the industry demand curve for labor of Exhibit 6 with the industry supply curve for labor of Exhibit 7 to create a complete picture of the labor market for miners.

Look at panel *a*. The industry demand for labor, *D*, is the sum of the 1,000 firms' *MRP* curves. The miners' supply curve of labor, *S*, reflects their willingness to supply varying quantities of labor at varying wage rates. The equilibrium wage rate is $20, and the quantity of labor supplied and employed by the 1,000 coal mining firms is 8,000. At wage rates higher than $20 per hour, an excess supply of miners emerges, driving the wage rate down. At wage rates below $20, an excess demand for labor emerges, driving the wage rate up.

Picture the scene at the Charles Edwards Coal Mining Company. As far as the firm is concerned, it knows that it is only 1 of 1,000 firms competing for workers in the miners' labor market. By itself, Edwards has no influence on the miners' wage rate. Hiring one or even five more miners makes no noticeable difference in a labor market of thousands of miners.

That's why Edwards, in panel *b* of Exhibit 10, faces a horizontal supply curve of labor at $w = 20. It can hire one miner at $20 per hour, two miners at $20 per hour each, or as many miners as it wants at $20 per hour. Edwards ends up hiring eight miners because at the eighth miner, $w = MRP = 20.

CHECK YOUR UNDERSTANDING

Why is the firm's supply curve for labor horizontal?

EXPLAINING WAGE RATE DIFFERENTIALS

Understanding how technology and the price of the goods produced by labor affect *MRP*, and understanding as well how the supply curve of labor is affected by the laborer's opportunity cost, gives us some insight into why different wage rates exist in different labor markets.

EXHIBIT | 10

THE LABOR MARKET

In panel *a*, the supply curve, *S*, shows the number of hours that workers are willing to work at various wage rates. The demand curve, *D*, represents the quantity of labor that firms in the labor market demand at these wage rates. The equilibrium wage rate in the labor market is $w = \$20$, and the quantity of labor demanded and supplied is 8,000.

In panel *b*, Edwards accepts the $w = \$20$ as given. At that wage rate, and with the *MRP* shown as its demand curve for labor, Edwards hires eight workers, which is where its $MRP = w$.

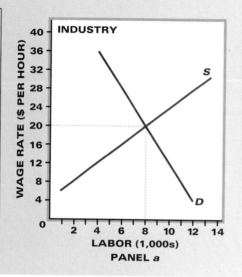

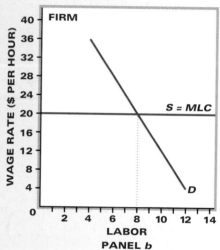

Narrowing Wage Rate Differences

THE CALL OF THE NORTH If, in the 1960s, you had to guess which of two people's wage rates was the higher, without knowing anything more than that one was working in the South and the other was working in the North, you would have been right more times than not to pick the northerner's wage rate.

After all, the manufacturing industries in the North had more capital and advanced technology than those in the South. (Picture their *MPP*s.) Moreover, northern industries were typically less competitive than those in the South— oligopoly in the manufacturing North compared to highly competitive agriculture in the South—so that the prices of northern goods were generally higher than those produced in the South. This combination of higher prices and more capital-using technology produced higher *MRP*s for northern workers.

The supply side, too, seems to have worked in the northern workers' favor. They had more attractive job opportunities and, consequently, were much less willing to accept the low wage rates that southern workers accepted coming off low-paying southern farms.

It isn't entirely surprising, then, that southerners would eventually make their way north. Throughout the 1940s, 1950s, and 1960s, millions of people migrated from the small towns of Louisiana, Mississippi, South Carolina, Alabama, and Georgia to the major cities in New York, New Jersey, Ohio, Michigan, and Illinois.

But during these same decades, while people migrated north, industries relocated south to take advantage of the lower southern wage rate. The result is depicted in the shifts in the labor demand and supply curves in both regions, as shown in Exhibit 11.

In panel *a*, depicting the North's labor market, the supply curve of labor shifted to the right, from S_{n1} to S_{n2}. At the same time, northern industries relocating in the South shifted the demand curve for labor from MRP_{n1} to MRP_{n2}. Combined, these shifts depressed the North's wage rate from $45 to $35.

on the net

The Current Population Survey (CPS) (http://www. bls.census.gov/cps/cpsmain. htm), conducted by the Bureau of the Census, is the primary source of information on the labor force characteristics of the U.S. population. The CPS provides estimates for employment, unemployment, earnings, hours of work, and other indicators.

EXHIBIT | 11

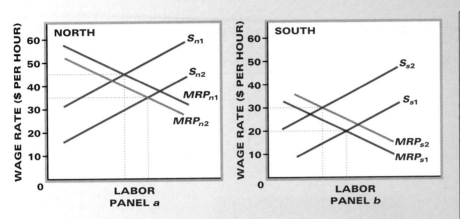

NORTH-SOUTH WAGE RATE DIFFERENTIALS

In panel *a,* the equilibrium wage rate in the North in the pre-immigration period of labor and relocation of factories is $45. Immigration from the South shifts the labor supply curve from S_{n1} to S_{n2}, and the relocation of northern factories to the South shifts the demand curve for labor from MRP_{n1} to MRP_{n2}. As a result, the equilibrium wage rate in the North falls from $45 to $35. In panel *b,* the equilibrium wage rate in the pre-emigration period of labor and before the influx of northern factories to the South is $20. The emigration of labor to the North shifts the labor supply curve from S_{s1} to S_{s2}, and the relocation of northern factories to the South shifts the demand curve for labor from MRP_{s1} to MRP_{s2}. As a result, the equilibrium wage rate in the South increases to $30. The North-South wage rate differential narrows.

Meanwhile, the same labor migration and industry relocations had the opposite effect in the South. There, in panel *b,* the migration of labor shifted its supply curve to the left, from S_{s1} to S_{s2}, while the addition of newly transplanted industries raised the demand curve for labor from MRP_{s1} to MRP_{s2}. Combined, these shifts raised the South's wage rate from $20 to $30. As a result, the wage rate differential between the North and South narrowed. Before it was $45 − $20 = $25. After the migration, the wage differential was $35 − $30 = $5.

But the regional labor markets took on a very different face from the 1970s onward when industrialization in the South and Southwest created a population magnet. Atlanta, Charlotte, Miami, Dallas, Houston, and Phoenix were just a few among scores of large and small southern and southwestern cities drawing populations from other regions in the United States as well as from abroad. Just look at the numbers in Exhibit 12.

EXHIBIT | 12

NET DOMESTIC MIGRATION AND IMMIGRATION FOR THE NORTHEAST, MIDWEST, SOUTH, AND WEST: 1985–94 (1,000s OF POPULATION)

	NORTHEAST	MIDWEST	SOUTH	WEST
NET DOMESTIC MIGRATION	–3,005	–116	2,377	873
IMMIGRATION FROM ABROAD	2,254	1,549	3,606	4,350
NET TOTAL MIGRATION	–752	1,433	5,983	5,222

Source: Bureau of the Census, *Statistical Abstract of the United States, 1996* (Washington, D.C.: U.S. Department of Commerce, 1996), p. 32.

GLOBAL PERSPECTIVE

IMMIGRANT LABOR SUPPLY: AN AMERICAN TRADITION

Give me your tired, your poor,
Your huddled masses yearning to breathe free,
The wretched refuse of your teeming shore.
Send these, the homeless, tempest-tost to me.
I lift my lamp beside the golden door!

Powerful words, aren't they? You'll find these words carved on the base of the Statue of Liberty and on the lips and minds of many, many Americans whose families came to the United States as penniless immigrants, seeking work and a better life. That tradition continues to this day.

Of the 12.7 million new jobs created in the United States since 1990, immigrants have filled 38 percent. To some Americans, that's good news. To others, it's bad news. It's bad, Mark Krikorian, executive director of the Center for Immigration Studies, argues, because "we are importing people whose skills are not conducive to this 21st century, high-tech economy of ours." He worries that we are importing "instant poverty" and that this will only contribute to our welfare spending obligations.

WELCOME.

The good-news argument, subscribed to by most economists, is that even the unskilled, impoverished immigrant is a national blessing. The growth of our economy depends on the availability of a labor supply willing and able to work productively at all kinds of jobs, and there are simply insufficient numbers of Americans to do that. Moreover, our colleges and universities are graduating many immigrants to the United States in all disciplines so that, just like the American-born, many unskilled immigrants become skilled and even more highly productive.

But the truth of the matter is that we are opening our gates to more than *"your tired, your poor, your huddled masses."* We are importing as well highly qualified, high-tech foreigners whose talents and abilities are sorely needed in our economy.

Case in point: There is a great demand in the United States for specialists in the field of information technology. During the past decade, computer software companies in India have been providing software developers to companies in the United States. In fact, more than 25 percent of our Fortune 500 companies have looked to India's high-tech labor supply to meet some of their software requirements. Among them were IBM, Microsoft, Novell, Oracle, AT&T, Hewlett-Packard, General Motors, Sears, Citibank, Boeing, Coca-Cola, and United Airlines.

What is true for the information technology industry and immigrants from India is true for other U.S. industries and immigrants from everywhere. Our economy could not have grown at the rate it did without the ready access to an immigrant labor supply. For many Americans, then, whose own jobs were created by the robustness of the growing economy, the availability of an immigrant labor supply accounts, in part, for their own economic well-being.

CROSSING THE RIO GRANDE As if this domestic migration wasn't enough of a headache for workers in the Southwest and West, they were further upset by the difficult-to-stem migration coming across the border from Mexico. How would you feel if you were a worker in Arizona having to compete with newly arrived northeastern, midwestern, and Mexican workers?

It's easy to understand why Mexican workers want to come north. When they compare their situation in Mexico to the employment opportunities north of the border—even for very low-paying U.S. jobs—they have more than enough incentive to cross the Rio Grande.

HISTORICAL PERSPECTIVE

THE IRON LAW OF WAGES: A 19TH-CENTURY VIEW OF OUR FUTURE

The 19th-century essayist and historian Thomas Carlyle called economics a "dismal science" not because he believed the science of economics was shoddy but because the predictions made by classical economists of the early 19th century concerning the workers' future were so downright depressing. What were these predictions?

Thomas Malthus and David Ricardo, two celebrated economists at the time, reasoned that wages must eventually fall to a level that sustains only the workers' minimal physical existence. Why? Because if demand and supply in the labor market generate any wage above subsistence, the first thing workers will do is have more children! The increased population will shift the supply curve to the right and the wage will fall. How far downward? Until it reaches the lowest possible level of subsistence. If, for some reason, wages rise above this level, people will quickly celebrate by having

THIRTY MEALS A DAY DOESN'T LEAVE MUCH ROOM FOR SURPLUS INCOME.

more children, causing wages to return to the subsistence level. Economists referred to this tendency for wages to cling to subsistence as "the iron law of wages." Not a very pretty picture of our future, is it?

This "iron law" was so powerful an idea that it transferred over into the literary world of Europe. For example, in Emile Zola's *Germinal*, a novel whose story is set in the coal towns of France, Souvarine discusses the plight of the worker: "Raise wages—how can you? They're fixed by an iron law to the smallest possible sum, just the sum necessary to allow the workers to eat dry bread and get children. If they fall too low the workers die, and the demand for new men makes them rise. If they rise too high more men come, and they fall. It is the balance of empty bellies, a sentence to a perpetual prison of hunger."

The idea of an "iron law" based on population growth may seem alien to us now, but it was more than compelling then. And in some part of our own 21st century—in some of the lesser-developed countries in Asia, Africa, and Latin America—such a 19th-century mindset may still hold considerable sway.

It's also easy to understand why U.S. industries want to locate south of the Rio Grande. Low wage rates attract industry as much as high wage rates attract workers.

THE MAPLE LEAF FOREVER? Wage rate differentials also help to explain the migratory traffic on our northern border. Over the years, hundreds of thousands of Canadians have moved south to take advantage of the wage rate differential between Canada and the United States, and at the same time American-owned industry has moved north to take advantage of lower Canadian wage rates.

How do Canadians feel about this? Many in Canada are unhappy about losing so many productive citizens to the United States and see the American "industry invasion" of Canada as undermining Canadian independence. Yet most working Canadians, setting aside national pride, understand the connection between the

GLOBAL PERSPECTIVE

THE MARKET IS MIGHTIER THAN THE SWORD

A half century ago, German troops marched triumphantly into Eastern Europe to trigger World War II. German-focused economic activity there soon followed. The idea was to use East European resources, mainly its labor, to bolster German industrial output. Germany's ambitions were thwarted, and its economy was destroyed.

Fifty years later, the German economic recovery from that war is regarded by many economists as nothing short of remarkable. Some refer to it as an economic miracle. Its standard of living ranks among the highest in Europe, and Germany's industrial capacity makes it one of the most powerful nations on the continent.

Here's the irony: Germany's economic success has created the climate for a new invasion of Eastern Europe! Admittedly, the causes and circumstances are entirely different, and, unlike the old, the new invasion is welcomed in Eastern Europe. At the same time, it is causing a growing uneasiness at home. Why? What has happened?

If you combine Germany's robust economic growth rates with its strong labor unions and the government's willingness to tax, the resulting high wage rates and taxes make producing elsewhere—where wage rates and taxes are lower—look awfully attractive. The average German wage level of $30 an hour (nearly twice that of the United States and Britain) plus six weeks' vacation and an extra month's salary as a Christmas bonus may explain the large emigration of Ger-

THINK THESE ROPES WILL WORK? THERE'S NO WAY THESE PROTESTING GERMAN WORKERS CAN PREVENT FACTORIES FROM MOVING TO MORE ATTRACTIVE PLACES.

many's leading industrial firms. This exodus of German capital—including Volkswagen, Mannesmann, Audi, and Henkel—employs several million East European workers.

The consequence of this extraordinary exodus on employment at home has been troubling, creating more than 12 percent unemployment. German workers are wondering whether they will be able to hold on to the dwindling number of jobs and to the wage rates and fringe benefits they have become so accustomed to.

A survey by Germany's Chamber of Commerce and Industry showed that 28 percent of its 6,000 leading industrial firms plan to move their production out of the country over the next three years. Nearly two-thirds of these companies cited high labor costs as the principal reason. Germany's central bank, the Bundesbank, records that investments abroad by German companies nearly doubled in 1995 and rose another 40 percent in 1996, and it predicts the trend will accelerate unless measures are taken to stem wage costs.

MORE ON THE NET

In addition to its German facilities, Audi (http://www.audi.com/) has production facilities in Brazil, China, Hungary, Indonesia, Malaysia, the Philippines, and South Africa. German investment is also strong in the United States. Organizations such as the German American Business Association (http://www.gaba.org/) have arisen to help foster German investment in the United States.

massive industrial inflow from the United States and the upward shift in their *MRP* and wage rate.

EUROPE'S *GASTARBEITERS* *Gastarbeiter* translates into "guest worker." It has become a common expression in Europe, largely because so many of these people migrated north and east during the 1960s, 1970s, and 1980s to seek higher wages. By 1990, over 5 million *gastarbeiters* were working in northern Europe. Most came from southern Europe and North Africa, the largest numbers from Italy, Turkey, and the former Yugoslavia.

West Germany and France were the principal destinations, and even tiny Switzerland absorbed enough migration to make up fully one-third of its labor force. These *gastarbeiters,* lured away from friends and family by wage rate differentials between their own and the host economies, shifted the labor supply curves in both economies. They were willing to work at jobs others would not touch and at wage rates others would not accept. As wretched as their conditions may have been in the host economy, *gastarbeiters* clearly improved their living standards.

HOW UNIVERSAL IS EXHIBIT 11? It really isn't surprising to discover that people everywhere and seemingly from time immemorial have responded in much the same way when confronted with regional wage rate disparities. The attraction of higher wage rates elsewhere has always been sufficient to spark even long-distance mobility. The lure of higher wage rates in the United States and Canada enticed millions of European men and women to cross the Atlantic in the 19th century. For the same reason, millions of people in Asia, Africa, and Latin America today leave their villages, friends, and family for the chance to work in the higher-paying, overcrowded cities.

THE EFFECT OF IMMIGRATION LAWS The U.S. Constitution guarantees citizens the right to move freely within and between all 50 states. An economics graduate from Purdue University can gather her belongings in West Lafayette and head for the Phoenix labor market, where wage rates are thought to be higher, without having to consider passports, visas, or immigration quotas.

But a graduate of McGill University in Montreal, Canada, with Phoenix on his mind, may get only as far as the international border at Plattsburg, New York. Without a work permit issued by the U.S. Immigration and Naturalization Service, the McGill graduate stays in Canada.

Are the U.S. immigration laws extraordinarily restrictive? Not really. All governments tend to be selective in admitting immigrants, designing laws to meet domestic concerns.

The supply curve of labor, then, depends not only on the supply conditions in the labor market but also on government's immigration policy. A move to a less-restrictive immigration policy, for example, could shift the supply curve of labor in the receiving economy to the right, creating downward pressure on the wage rate.

on the net

The U.S. Department of Immigration and Naturalization (INS) (http://www.ins.usdoj.gov/) enforces the immigration laws of the United States.

PERSISTING WAGE DIFFERENTIALS

If top-seeded tennis players can earn over $250,000 for a few hours' play, why aren't more people playing that brand of tennis? The answer, of course, is that very few people are capable of playing championship tennis.

Although people may be more alike than not, they may still be different in temperament, talent, and intelligence. These differences separate many people into **noncompeting labor markets.** Wimbledon champion Pete Sampras, for example, would be no one's first choice to perform neurosurgery.

Specific talents, limited to small numbers of people, create unique labor markets that not only allow for relatively high wage rates but also protect the wage rate against erosion. To see this, think about the labor markets for surgeons and butchers.

Suppose that surgeons earn $100 per hour, while butchers earn $20. Wouldn't most butchers prefer the $100 wage rate? But can they perform brain surgery? As attractive as the surgeon's wage rate is, the scarcity of people capable of performing surgery keeps the supply curve from shifting to the right.

Noncompeting labor markets
Markets whose requirement for specific skills necessarily excludes workers who do not have the required skills.

That is also why NBA basketball players' wage rates are considerably higher than those of even surgeons. Don't you think most surgeons would abandon their operating rooms if they could dunk basketballs like Shaquille O'Neal?

THE ECONOMICS OF MINIMUM WAGE RATES

The problem with persisting wage differentials is not that some people earn millions. It is instead the inability of many people to compete successfully in any occupation that provides an adequate living standard.

Whatever the reasons, individuals become trapped in labor markets where the *MRP* is extraordinarily low and the supply of labor plentiful. The resulting wage rate is insufficient to provide a decent living. Once in, how do these people break out of the low-wage-rate trap?

Many solutions have been proposed and tried. Perhaps the simplest and most direct way of raising low wage rates is simply to outlaw them! That is, the government can legislate minimum wage laws that prohibit employers from hiring people at wage rates below a specific level.

It is not as peculiar a solution as it may appear. After all, almost every economic interest group in our economy has pleaded with government to get into the business of legislating prices. Farmers, for example, have successfully lobbied government to set minimum farm prices. Producers of industrial goods have persuaded government to protect their prices by legislating tariffs on imports. The result was to shift income from nonfarmers to farmers in the one case, and from consumers to producers in the other.

But are low-wage-rate-earning people really better off with minimum wage laws? Look at Exhibit 13, which shows the market for low-skilled labor.

on the net

The Department of Labor provides information on the minimum wage (http://www.dol.gov/dol/esa/public/minwage/main.htm).

THE EFFECTS OF MINIMUM WAGE RATES

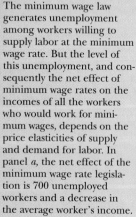

EXHIBIT | 13

The minimum wage law generates unemployment among workers willing to supply labor at the minimum wage rate. But the level of this unemployment, and consequently the net effect of minimum wage rates on the incomes of all the workers who would work for minimum wages, depends on the price elasticities of supply and demand for labor. In panel *a*, the net effect of the minimum wage rate legislation is 700 unemployed workers and a decrease in the average worker's income.

But in panel *b*, which assumes different price elasticities of demand and supply, only 100 workers lose their jobs after the minimum wage rate legislation, and the resulting workers' income at the minimum wage rate increases.

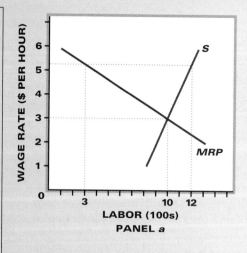
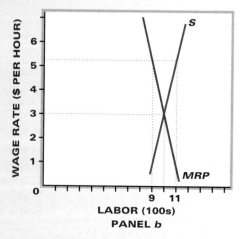

PANEL *a*

PANEL *b*

GLOBAL PERSPECTIVE

IS MINIMUM WAGE REALLY AN EMPLOYMENT PROBLEM?

Many economists believe that the minimum wage is instrumental in pushing firms out of countries with high minimum wages to countries with low or no minimum wages. So the warning goes out: Minimum wages can be detrimental not only to firms but to workers as well.

Other economists, Professor Ephraim Kleiman at Israel's Hebrew University among them, just aren't convinced that a minimum wage is the uprooting culprit. Using his native country as the example, he writes: "Many minimum wage earners in Israel are employed in sectors that are unable to pass along added labor costs to the consumer because these sectors are in competition with foreign bodies. Isn't there a fear that the higher minimum wage could induce those sectors to either shut down or move their operations to

"WHAT ARE YOU GOING TO DO WITH THAT EXTRA $1 AN HOUR?" "BUY A MERCEDES."

countries with cheap labor, such as Jordan or Egypt? In fact, many firms are enticed by the possibility of setting up operations in areas where they would not be subject to [trade union] constraints and where the minimum wage is half of that of Gaza [a region adjacent to Israel]. These companies would move their operations to these countries even if the minimum wage in Israel were half of the current wage. As compared to these considerations, the factor of raising the minimum wage seems downright negligible."

Kleiman acknowledges that U.S. studies on this issue have yielded no definitive results. Why then, he asks, do some economists insist that minimum wage is an employment problem? He concludes that at best, they are merely expressing a scholarly "gut feeling," and at worst, they are somewhat less than forthright.

Source: Reprinted with permission from Prof. Ephraim Kleiman, The Hebrew University of Jerusalem.

In panel *a*, the $3.00 equilibrium wage rate is inadequate to provide anyone working a 40-hour week with an acceptable living standard. Can you picture yourself trying to make it through the week on $120?

Suppose government legislated a $5.15 minimum wage rate. Every working member of Exhibit 13 now takes home $210 weekly. It still creates a formidable challenge to make ends meet, but it beats $120 hands down.

But now a new, perhaps no less severe problem for low-wage-rate earners emerges. *Employers cannot be expected to hire workers whose* MRP *is below the $5.15 legislated minimum wage rate.* Look at panel *a*. Employers hire only 300 workers at *w* = $5.15. They are forced to dismiss 700 of the previously hired 1,000 workers. Why? Because the *MRP*s of the 301st to the 1,000th worker now fall below the minimum wage rate. (Since 1,200 low-wage-rate-earning people are now willing to supply their services at $5.15, the unemployment created by the minimum wage is actually 1,200 − 300 = 900 workers.)

That's not what the government had in mind when it legislated the minimum wage. Not only has the $5.15 wage rate knocked 700 people out of work, but the total income of low-wage-rate-earning people as a group actually falls.

Figure it out. Prior to the minimum wage legislation, total hourly income earned by these people was $3.00 × 1,000 = $3,000. After the minimum wage rate was imposed, total hourly income was $5.15 × 300 = $1,545.

But suppose panel *b*, not panel *a*, describes the labor market for these low-wage-rate-earning people. A very different outcome emerges. The $5.15 minimum still creates unemployment among those willing to work at minimum wages, but now it's only 100 workers. The total hourly income received by the low-wage-rate-earning people of panel *b* is $5.15 × 900 = $4,635. (Even if the $4,635 were distributed among all 1,100 willing to work at the minimum wage rate, the average wage rate would increase to $4,635/1,100 = $4.21, considerably better than the previous minimum wage of $3.00.)

As you see, the impact of minimum-wage-rate legislation on low-wage-rate-earning people depends ultimately on the price elasticities of demand and supply of labor. In other words, it depends on whether panel *a* or panel *b* is a more accurate reflection of real-world labor demands and supplies. Although economists hold strong views on this critical issue, there is no real consensus.

THE ETHICS OF $w = MRP$

Many working people believe that they should be paid more than they currently earn. This is not surprising. Most people have a well-developed sense of self-worth. But is there any evidence supporting their belief? Should miners, for example, earn more? Should peach pickers in Georgia? Economists typically have shied away from addressing *should* questions. Yet most economists accept market-determined wage rates as ethically defensible, even if wage rates in some labor markets are exceptionally low, because market-determined wage rates are based on individual merit—that is, they reflect workers' *MRP*s.

Are there any jobs you can think of that would fall outside the w = MRP *ethic? Go to the Interactive Study Center at http://gottheil.swcollege.com and click on the "Your Turn" button to submit your example. Student submissions will be posted to the Web site, and perhaps we will use some in future editions of the book!*

Consider the labor market for miners in Harlan County, Kentucky. Miners there receive a wage rate equal to their *MRP*, which is the equivalent of what they produce. The ethic underlying this wage rate is expressed as *From each according to his or her contribution, to each according to his or her contribution.*

A tennis star's $250,000 earnings at Wimbledon are considerably higher than the wage rate earned by a Kentucky miner, yet each individual is paid exactly what that individual contributes. If people with skills not highly demanded in the economy end up earning low wage rates, they are not necessarily underpaid. Underpayment, according to this ethic, occurs only when people receive less than the full measure of their *MRP*.

Why then minimum wage rate legislation? The answer may have little to do with the issue of merit. Many economists are driven by compassion to support minimum wage laws. Others accept minimum wage legislation as the lesser of two evils, believing that the intolerable living conditions of low-wage-rate-earning people may lead to social unrest and other societal ills that are far less desirable than minimum wage rates.

On the other hand, there are economists, also driven by compassion, who oppose minimum wage laws. To them, such laws serve only to undermine the personal incentives needed to coax people out of low-paying labor markets. Others oppose minimum wage laws because they believe that each individual ought to receive the value of his or her productive contribution.

Yet, both the economists who favor minimum wage rates and those who do not agree on this: Any wage rate differential between two people producing the same *MRP* signals a gross violation of the $w = MRP$ ethic. This kind of wage rate differential has long hurt women and minorities in many labor markets. Many routinely confront racial, religious, or sexual discrimination that, upon examination, shows up as the primary source of their wage rate differentials.

THE EFFICIENCY WAGES THEORY

Even though firms in competitive labor markets can hire as many workers as they wish at the equilibrium wage rate, many firms still end up paying their workers a wage rate in excess of the equilibrium rate, a rate that economists define as **efficiency wages.** Are these firms less interested in profit making than are firms that pay the equilibrium rate? Or are they just foolish, or perhaps simply unaware of what's going on in their labor market? In most cases, it's none of the above. What, then, is going on? Why would a firm choose to pay a wage rate higher than the market signals?

Often, it's for good reason. First, it allows the firm to select the more qualified workers. Not all workers are alike, and if differences in energy, skill, and experience matter, then the firm paying above-market rates will get the cream of the crop. Second, the firm counts on the higher rate to increase workers' morale and motivation on the job, which should raise labor's *MPP*—shifting the *MRP* curve to the right—so that the higher rate may actually pay for itself. Third, workers earning above-market rates are less likely to leave, so that labor turnover is relatively low, saving the firm the costs of hiring and training new recruits. Fourth, it may deter workers from joining unions, which may end up costing the firm less in the long run. And finally, many firms believe that fairness has its own rewards. If the firm is making profit, it should share some of it with its workforce, even if the market suggests it's unnecessary.

Efficiency wages
A wage higher than the market's equilibrium rate; a firm will pay this wage in the expectation that the higher wage will reduce the firm's labor turnover and increase labor productivity.

CHAPTER REVIEW

1. A competitive labor market consists of a considerable number of workers and a considerable number of firms supplying labor and demanding labor in a market where no worker or firm has sufficient market power to influence the price of labor, which is the wage rate.

2. The marginal physical product of labor describes the quantity of goods an additional worker adds to production while the other factors of production—capital and land—remain unchanged. The total physical product increases initially at an increasing rate, but after a certain point in production, the increases become smaller and smaller as more

workers are added, reflecting what economists describe as the law of diminishing returns.

3. Marginal revenue product is marginal physical product multiplied by the price of the good. It is the value of the marginal physical product expressed in dollars.

4. Just as each worker, when employed, adds marginal revenue product to the firm, each worker also adds to the firm's labor cost. Because the labor market is competitive, both workers and firms accept the market-derived wage rate as given. The wage rate (or marginal labor cost) is the firm's cost of adding a worker to production. To hire the profit-maximizing number of

workers, the firm will hire workers until the worker's marginal revenue product equals the wage rate.

5. The marginal revenue product curve is the firm's demand curve for labor. Increases in either the price or the marginal physical product will shift the demand curve for labor to the right. As a result, the firm hires more workers.

6. The market demand curve for labor is the sum of individual firms' demand for labor. The market supply of labor reflects the opportunity costs of each worker. If the wage rate increases, more workers are willing to offer their labor on the market, because the higher wage rate now meets their opportunity costs. Changes in workers' employment opportunities, in workers' wealth, and in population size affect the supply of labor.

7. The equilibrium wage rate is determined by the interaction of the market demand for and the supply of labor. Each firm then hires workers whose marginal revenue product exceeds or equals that rate.

8. Where wage differentials exist in two different labor markets, the mobility of labor from low-wage markets to higher-wage markets and the mobility of firms from high-wage markets to lower-wage markets tend to reduce the differentials. When mobility is absent, as in the case of noncompeting labor markets, the wage differentials persist.

9. Minimum wage laws set a price floor above the market-determined wage rate in markets that generate low equilibrium wage rates. There is little consensus among economists concerning the effect minimum wage laws have on employment.

10. Efficiency wages are above the equilibrium wage the market generates. Firms offer these higher wages in the expectation of luring better-qualified workers, enhancing labor productivity, and reducing labor turnover.

11. Market wage rates express the underlying ethic that people are paid for the value of what they produce.

KEY TERMS

Marginal physical product
Law of diminishing returns
Marginal revenue product

Wage rate
Total labor cost
Marginal labor cost

Noncompeting labor markets
Efficiency wages

QUESTIONS

1. In explaining how the marginal physical product of labor is derived, economists assume that other factors of production, such as capital and land, are held fixed. Why is this assumption necessary?

2. What is the relationship between the law of diminishing returns and the downward slope of the marginal physical product curve?

3. What is the relationship between the marginal physical product of labor and the marginal revenue product of labor?

4. Suppose the Chris Corpora Coal Mining Company currently employs 17 workers at $14.50 per hour, which is the prevailing wage rate in the perfectly competitive market for miners. Suppose also that the marginal revenue product of the seventeenth worker is $12.50.

What should the firm do? Why? What hiring rule should it follow?

5. Farm workers' *MRP* in Canada keeps falling even though they keep producing more output. Explain.

6. Why might a farm worker in Zambia earn less than a farm worker in Canada?

7. Suppose Eastern European economies, following the collapse of Soviet power in Europe, begin to demand more farm goods from Canada. What impact, if any, would you expect this new demand to have on farm wage rates in Canada?

8. Suppose Zambian farmers begin to use more insecticides and chemical fertilizers. What impact would such uses, if successfully adopted, have on Zambian farm wage rates?

9. Recall the analysis of pollution costs in the previous chapter. How would pollution considerations—cleanup costs resulting from increased use of insecticides and chemical fertilizers in Zambia—affect Zambian farm wage rates? *Hint:* Consider price changes resulting from shifts in the supply curve in the farm-goods market.

10. Why is the marginal labor cost identical to the wage rate in perfectly competitive labor markets?

11. What is the relationship between a firm's marginal labor cost and the industry's supply curve of labor?

12. How does the opportunity cost of work influence the character of the supply curve of labor?

13. Suppose yesterday was your lucky day. You won $7 million in the Kentucky State Lottery, and the Charles Edwards Coal Mining Company (where you work) raised the wage rate from $12.50 to $17.50 per hour. How would you respond to these pieces of news? What would happen to the quantity of labor you would be willing to supply at the mine? Why? What about your good friend, Adam Schmidt, who works the same shift as you? He didn't win the lottery. What do you suppose would happen to the number of hours he would be willing to work?

14. Two good friends, Mo Jo Nixon and Natalie Merchant, grew up together, went to the same schools, ranked identically in IQ testing, excelled in every subject, and went on to earn Ph.D.'s. Natalie became a professor of finance; Mo Jo became a professor of English. Both teach at the same college. Natalie earns $55,000, while Mo Jo earns $37,000. Is there economic injustice in this story? Perhaps discrimination? How can you explain the income differential?

15. How could one government's immigration policy affect wage rates in other economies?

PRACTICE PROBLEMS

1. Suppose the price of leather gloves is $12. Graph a demand curve for leather-glove laborers from the following data concerning their total physical product:

QUANTITY OF LABOR	TOTAL PHYSICAL PRODUCT
0	0
1	35
2	65
3	90
4	110
5	125
6	135
7	140

2. Show what happens to the demand curve for labor when the price of gloves falls to $6. What happens when the price increases to $20?

3. Consider the following perfectly competitive labor market.

QUANTITY OF LABOR	MARGINAL REVENUE PRODUCT	TOTAL LABOR COST
5	$2.00	$ 5.00
10	1.50	10.00
15	1.25	15.00
20	1.00	20.00
25	0.85	25.00
30	0.75	30.00
35	0.70	35.00

How many laborers would be hired? At what wage rate?

4. The following tables show the demand and supply schedules in U.S. and Canadian labor markets:

CANADA

PRICE	QUANTITY DEMANDED (MILLIONS)	QUANTITY SUPPLIED (MILLIONS)
$30	2	10
25	4	8
20	6	6
15	8	4
10	10	2

UNITED STATES

PRICE	QUANTITY DEMANDED (MILLIONS)	QUANTITY SUPPLIED (MILLIONS)
$50	10	50
40	20	40
30	30	30
20	40	20
10	50	10

What is the wage differential between Canada and the United States? What kinds of changes (directional) would you expect to occur in both the supply of and demand for labor in both countries?

WHAT'S WRONG WITH THIS GRAPH?

THE EFFECT OF A MINIMUM WAGE ON WAGE RATES AND EMPLOYMENT

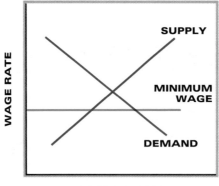

ECONOMIC CONSULTANTS

ECONOMIC RESEARCH AND ANALYSIS BY STUDENTS FOR PROFESSIONALS

Jeff Kaufman works as an electrician in Boston. Jeff, originally from Detroit, recently married his wife, Elizabeth, who until the marriage lived in Montreal, Canada. Jeff and Elizabeth have decided to leave Boston and move to Detroit.

Jeff and Elizabeth have hired Economic Consultants to inform them about the labor market for electricians in Detroit, the value of Jeff's labor in Detroit as compared to in Boston, and any immigration issues with Elizabeth that may arise. Prepare a report for Jeff that addresses the following issues:

1. What are the conditions of the labor market for electricians in Detroit?
2. Jeff earns $60,000 per year as an electrician in Boston. How much money will he need to earn in Detroit to have a comparable standard of living?
3. Do Jeff and Elizabeth need to worry about immigration issues? If so, which issues?

You may find the following resources helpful as you prepare this report for Jeff:

- **U.S. Department of Labor** (http://www.dol.gov/)—The Department of Labor supports a number of initiatives, such as America's Career InfoNet (http://www.acinet.org/) and America's Job Bank (http://www.ajb.dni.us/), that provide a wealth of information about occupations.
- ***The Detroit News*** (http://www.detnews.com/)—The *Detroit News* provides job listings for the Detroit area.
- **The Salary Calculator** (http://www.homefair.com/homefair/cmr/salcalc.html)—The Salary Calculator enables you to compare the cost of living in hundreds of U.S. and international cities.
- **America's Labor Market Information System (ALMIS)** (http://almis.dws.state.ut.us/)—ALMIS, sponsored by the Department of Labor, offers national and state-specific labor market information.
- **U.S. Department of Immigration and Naturalization (INS)** (http://www.ins.usdoj.gov/)—The INS provides information of the laws and regulations that affect immigration.

PRACTICE TEST

1.

NUMBER OF WORKERS	QUANTITY OF BASKETS PER HOUR
0	0
1	10
2	28
3	40
4	48
5	53

The table shows for a perfectly competitive labor market and a perfectly competitive market for baskets the number of baskets that various quantities of workers can produce per hour. The marginal physical product of the fifth worker is
a. 53.
b. 53 × 5 = 265.
c. 53/5 = 10.6.
d. 53 − 48 = 5.
e. 10 + 28 + 40 + 48 + 53 = 179.

2. If the price of baskets is $3, then the marginal revenue product of the fourth basket is
a. $48.
b. $572.
c. $12.
d. $24.
e. $378.

3. If the wage rate for basket makers is $24 per hour, the basket firm will hire
a. two workers.
b. three workers.
c. four workers.
d. five workers.
e. no workers.

4. The supply curve of labor in the basket-making industry
a. is downward sloping, reflecting the law of diminishing returns.
b. is downward sloping, reflecting the marginal revenue product of labor.
c. is upward sloping, reflecting the marginal revenue product of labor.
d. is upward sloping, reflecting the workers' opportunity costs.
e. is horizontal because the market for labor is perfectly competitive.

5. The three factors that determine the industry's wage rate are
a. MPP of labor, MRP of labor, MFC of labor.
b. MRP of labor, price of the good, supply of the good.
c. MPP of labor, price of the good, supply curve of labor.
d. MRP of labor, price of the good, MPP of labor.
e. MRP of labor, price of labor, supply curve of labor.

6. An improvement in basket-making technology will shift the demand curve for labor to the
a. left, because each worker now produces less additional revenue than before.
b. left, because fewer workers are required to produce the same quantity of baskets.
c. right, because the new technology raises the price of baskets.
d. right, because the demand curve for labor is downward sloping.
e. right, because improved technology shifts the marginal physical product of labor curve to the right.

7. What shifts the supply curve of labor? A change in
a. technology.
b. the price of the good.
c. the marginal revenue product of labor.
d. alternative employment opportunities.
e. the price of other goods.

8. Suppose English workers earn twice the wage rate earned by Irish workers. Comparing their labor markets graphically, how can you explain that wage rate differential?
a. The MPP curve for Irish workers lies below (closer to the origin) the MPP curve for English workers.
b. The supply curve of labor in England lies below the supply curve of labor in Ireland.
c. The demand curve for labor in Ireland lies above (out to the right of) the demand curve for labor in England.
d. Prices of all goods are higher in Ireland than they are in England.
e. There is greater use of technology in Ireland than in England.

9. The imposition of minimum wage rates would tend to have the greatest effect on employment in which of the following instances?
a. Demand for labor is elastic, supply of labor is elastic
b. Demand for labor is inelastic, supply of labor is elastic
c. Demand for labor is elastic, supply of labor is inelastic
d. Demand for labor is inelastic, supply of labor is perfectly inelastic
e. Demand for labor is perfectly inelastic, supply of labor is elastic

APPENDIX

WHO EARNS WHAT?

Engineers and farm workers earn more today than engineers and farm workers earned 50 years ago. In fact, farm workers earn more today than engineers did 50 years ago. What counts in determining people's earnings?

PRODUCTIVITY COUNTS

Productivity counts. During the past 50 years, there's been a marked long-run upward movement in almost everyone's real output per hour worked. People's *MRP* curves have been shifting outward to the right decade after decade, creating both greater employment and higher wage rates. Look at the dramatic picture in Exhibit A1, which shows changes in labor productivity and real hourly compensation.

Focus first on the growth path of labor productivity. From 1960 to 1973, labor productivity grew at an annual rate of 2.8 percent. That rate slowed to 1.1 percent from 1973 to 1995. It increased by 2.9 percent from 1995 to 1999.

Is labor productivity linked to wage rates? Judge for yourself. Look at the growth path of real hourly compensation and compare it to labor productivity. The two curves are almost indistinguishable.

LABOR PRODUCTIVITY AND REAL HOURLY COMPENSATION: 1960–95

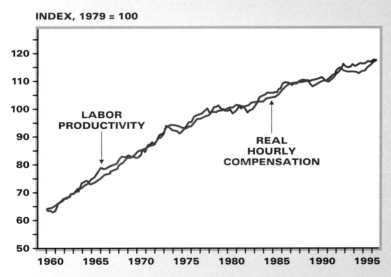

INDEX, 1979 = 100

Labor productivity grew 2.8 percent annually during the 1960–93 period and by 1.1 percent annually from 1973 to 1995. Real hourly compensation growth closely followed labor productivity's growth path.

Source: *Economic Report of the President, 1997,* Washington, D.C., 1997, p. 151 and *Economic Report of the President, 2000,* Washington D.C., 2000, p. 79.

EDUCATION COUNTS

What about the role of education? No high school dropout ends up being chief orthopedic surgeon at the Mayo Clinic. Look at Exhibit A2.

It isn't by chance that only 1.7 percent of managerial and professional people have not completed high school, or that 63.2 percent of them have college degrees. A similar polarization appears among the technical, sales, and administrative support jobs. Only 4.4 percent of them do not have a high school diploma, while 60 percent have gone to college. The education input reverses for blue-collar workers. Almost one-quarter of the operators, laborers, and fabricators are high school dropouts, while only 4.9 percent have college degrees.

Does education matter? You'd better believe it! Exhibit A3 matches occupations to earnings.

Managers and professionals in 1996 made almost twice the weekly earnings—$718 versus $391—that people made as operators, laborers, and fabricators. They earned more than double the earnings of farm laborers and people working in service-related occupations.

OCCUPATION OF EMPLOYED CIVILIANS BY EDUCATIONAL ATTAINMENT: 1995 (PERCENTAGE)

	MANAGERIAL/ PROFESSIONAL	TECHNICAL/ SALES/ ADMINISTRATIVE SUPPORT	SERVICE	PRECISION PRODUCTION	OPERATORS/ LABORERS/ FABRICATORS	FARMING
LESS THAN 4 YEARS OF HIGH SCHOOL	1.7	4.4	20.2	16.3	24.7	30.9
4 YEARS OF HIGH SCHOOL ONLY	13.0	35.3	42.5	46.6	50.2	37.6
1 TO 3 YEARS OF COLLEGE	22.1	36.7	28.2	29.5	20.1	20.0
4 YEARS OF COLLEGE OR MORE	63.2	23.6	9.1	7.5	4.9	11.5

Source: Bureau of the Census, *Statistical Abstract of the United States, 1999* (Washington, D.C.: Department of Commerce, 1999), p. 428.

MEDIAN WEEKLY EARNINGS OF FULL-TIME WAGE AND SALARY WORKERS BY OCCUPATION: 1996

OCCUPATION	MEDIAN WEEKLY EARNINGS
MANAGERIAL AND PROFESSIONAL	$718
TECHNICAL, SALES, AND ADMINISTRATIVE SUPPORT	441
SERVICE	305
PRECISION PRODUCTION	540
OPERATORS, FABRICATORS, LABORERS	391
FARMING	294

Source: Bureau of Labor Statistics, *Employment and Earnings* (Washington, D.C.: Department of Labor, January 1997), p. 214.

MINORITY STATUS COUNTS

Regardless of whether you're a manager or laborer, you would probably fare better if you also happen to be a white male.

Disparities According to Race

Race counts. Earnings disparities according to race, in many instances, reflect a combination of discrimination still practiced today and the powerful consequences of discrimination practiced generations before. Exhibit A4 shows what you proba-bly know or could guess. Black and Hispanic workers receive lower weekly wages than do white workers.

In 1998, Hispanics aver-aged 68.4 percent of white weekly earnings, while blacks fared somewhat better, averag-ing 77 percent. The race dis-parities were greater among men than among women.

Disparities According to Sex

Chances are, if you're a work-ing woman, you're earning less than a man at the same job. Exhibit A5 tells the story.

Women's weekly earnings in 1995 were 75.5 percent of what men earned. Once off the farm, the earnings gap ratios fall well below 75 percent. Such disparities raise the issue of **comparable worth,** which advocates that people who bring to the workplace comparable skills should receive compa-rable wages.

EXHIBIT|A4

MEDIAN WEEKLY EARNINGS OF FULL-TIME WAGE AND SALARY WORKERS BY RACE AND HISPANIC ORIGIN: 1998

	WEEKLY EARNINGS
WHITE	$545
MEN	615
WOMEN	468
BLACK	426
MEN	468
WOMEN	400
HISPANIC	370
MEN	390
WOMEN	337

Source: Bureau of Labor Statistics, *Employment and Earnings* (Washington, D.C.: Department of Labor, September 1997), Table D19, p. 148.

Comparable worth
The idea that jobs that are comparable—having the same characteristics—should be paid the same wage rate.

EXHIBIT|A5

WOMEN'S AND MEN'S MEDIAN WEEKLY EARNINGS BY OCCUPATION: 1998

	MEN	WOMEN	WOMEN/ MEN
ALL OCCUPATIONS	$598	$456	75.5
MANAGERIAL AND PROFESSIONAL	905	655	73.0
TECHNICAL, SALES, AND ADMINISTRATIVE SUPPORT	606	419	68.9
SERVICE	389	296	74.0
PRECISION PRODUCTION	587	408	69.5
OPERATORS, FABRICATORS, LABORERS	456	377	71.9
FARMING	307	272	84.7

Source: Bureau of the Census, *Statistical Abstract of the United States, 1999* (Washington, D.C.: U.S. Department of Commerce, 1999), p. 445.

HOW IMPORTANT ARE MINIMUM WAGES?

For many people, what they earn depends more on what government legislates than on what they are able to derive from labor markets. Exhibit A6 shows the increases in the minimum wage since 1975 and traces the value of the minimum wage—measured in constant dollars—from 1938 to 1997. As you see, the past 30 years have been unkind to those on minimum wages. The real purchasing power of the minimum wage fell rather dramatically from a high of $7.49 in 1968 to a low of $4.40 in 1989. Only in the last few years of the 1990s did it rise above $5.00. While the rest of the economy was enjoying the economic boom of the 1990s, those on minimum wages were struggling with a $5.00-per-hour wage rate.

MINIMUM HOURLY WAGE RATES, 1975–2000, AND THE VALUE OF THE MINIMUM WAGE, 1938–97

YEAR	MINIMUM WAGE
1975	$2.10
1977	2.30
1979	2.90
1981	3.25
1990	3.80
1991	4.25
2000	5.15

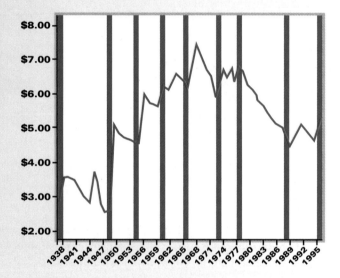

The shaded blocks on the graph represent years in which the Fair Labor Standards Act was amended to raise the minimum wage.

If you listen to workers who've been on the job for a whole lot of years talk about their experiences, chances are they will tell you about the time—maybe more than one time—that they were ready to tell their boss to "take this job and shove it." Many actually did! It's quite natural that work-related antagonisms build during stressful work periods, sometimes stretching disagreements to a breaking point. Resentments store up. You may have long been unhappy with your wage rate, your wage increase, your working conditions, or the demands made on you for overtime work. Here's the point: If you happen to work for a small firm in a large city, your boss's power to control your work life is limited. If you don't like your situation, you can walk out into the sunlight, confident of finding another job among the countless firms in the big, sprawling city. But it's quite

WAGES AND EMPLOYMENT: MONOPSONY AND LABOR UNIONS

another matter if you happen to be working for a very large firm in a very small town. You may be out of luck. In this situation, your boss's power to control your work life may be greater than you like. Whatever your grievances, you know that if you walk out on your job, sunlight may be all you get.

Let's keep this fact in mind as we pick up the story of the Charles Edwards Coal Mining Company.

Suppose that the firm, in a series of acquisition moves, buys out every other coal mining firm operating in Harlan County. That's a dramatic change. What had been a region with a thousand competitive, thriving coal mining firms becomes through these acquisitions a one-company county.

MONOPSONY: WHEN THERE'S ONLY ONE BUYER OF LABOR

Can you picture the scene? In the beginning, Edwards merely replaces the signs at the mine entrances. The Greg Mechtly Coal Company, for example, is now part of Edwards. No mining operation actually shuts down. Total coal production in the county remains unchanged.

What about the miners? As far as they are concerned, little has changed. They still work at the same mines with the same machinery and are paid the same wage rate. They mine the same tonnage. The only change, at least at the beginning of Edwards's consolidation, is in the name. They are now all part of Edwards.

But real change is imminent. Not only do the miners soon realize that their only source of employment in the county is Edwards, *but the firm too realizes that it has become the only firm hiring miners in the county.* Economists define its new labor market position, the only buyer of labor, as **monopsony.**

Monopsony
A labor market with only one buyer.

The Supply Curve of Labor as Seen by the Monopsony

Edwards, as a monopsonist, no longer thinks about hiring nine or ten miners. It now thinks in terms of thousands. It also knows that because it is the only firm buying labor in the region, the supply schedule of miners is precisely the market labor supply schedule we saw in the last chapter. That schedule is reproduced here in Exhibit 1.

 *your turn*

Can you think of another example in which one firm dominates a labor market? Go to the Interactive Study Center at http://gottheil.swcollege.com and click on the "Your Turn" button to submit your example. Student submissions will be posted to the Web site, and perhaps we will use some in future editions of the book!

When Edwards announces that it is willing to hire at a $10 wage rate, 3,000 miners show up to work, *as they had before.* Miners' willingness to supply labor does not depend on the number of firms buying labor. Why should it?

EXHIBIT 1

SUPPLY CURVE OF LABOR FACING A MONOPSONIST

The monopsonist, as the only buyer of labor in the market, faces the market labor supply curve. It has no competitors for that labor. Since the labor market reflects the willingness of workers to supply varying quantities of labor at varying wage rates, the monopsonist is free to choose among the various combinations of wage rates and labor supply. What's available in this case? At $w = \$6$, the quantity of labor supplied is 1,000 workers. At $w = \$8$, the quantity of labor supplied is 2,000. At $w = \$20$, the quantity of labor supplied is 8,000. The supply curve of labor is upward sloping.

THE SUPPLY SCHEDULE OF COAL MINERS

WAGE RATE ($ PER HOUR)	NUMBER OF MINERS
$ 0	0
6	1,000
8	2,000
10	3,000
12	4,000
14	5,000
16	6,000
18	7,000
20	8,000
22	9,000
24	10,000

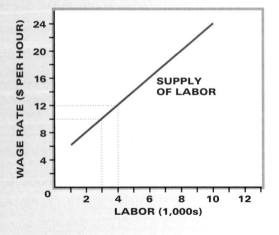

If Edwards wants more than 3,000 miners, it will have to raise the wage rate offered to meet the higher opportunity costs associated with the additional miners. For example, if it needs 4,000 miners, it will have to raise the wage rate to $w = \$12$.

The labor supply curve of Exhibit 1 changes the way Edwards thinks about hiring. In the old days, when it was just one of a thousand mining firms competing for labor, it took the wage rate given by the market. It had no choice. If it offered less than that market rate, it could hire nobody. Now, Edwards is the market.

Edwards can pick the wage rate it wants. But whatever rate it picks, it gets only those miners willing to work at that wage rate. It can't choose $w = \$6$, for example, and hope to get more than 1,000 miners.

What wage rate, then, should it choose? Look at the labor cost options Edwards now faces as a monopsonist. They are shown in Exhibit 2.

EXHIBIT | 2

RELATIONSHIP BETWEEN THE *MLC* CURVE AND THE SUPPLY CURVE OF LABOR

LABOR COST DATA

WAGE RATE	NUMBER OF MINERS	TOTAL LABOR COST *(TLC)*	ADDITIONAL LABOR COST PER 1,000 MINERS	MARGINAL LABOR COST *(MLC)*
$ 0	0	—	—	—
6	1,000	$ 6,000	$ 6,000	$ 6
8	2,000	16,000	10,000	10
10	3,000	30,000	14,000	14
12	4,000	48,000	18,000	18
14	5,000	70,000	22,000	22
16	6,000	96,000	26,000	26
18	7,000	126,000	30,000	30
20	8,000	160,000	34,000	34
22	9,000	198,000	38,000	38
24	10,000	240,000	42,000	42
26	11,000	286,000	46,000	46

Both the *MLC* curve and the supply curve of labor, *S*, are upward sloping. The *MLC* curve lies above the supply curve because when the monopsonist increases employment, it must not only offer a higher wage rate to attract more workers but also raise the wage rates of those already working. When the firm increases employment from 3,000 to 4,000, it raises the wage rate from $10 to $12 per hour. Its total labor cost increases from $30,000 to $48,000, or by $18,000 per hour. That is, the 4,000 − 3,000 = 1,000 additional workers cost the firm $18,000, or $18,000/1,000 = $18 per hour per worker. Even though each of these added workers receives only a $12 wage rate, they each add $18 to the firm's labor cost.

Reading the Table in Exhibit 2

How does Edwards read the table in Exhibit 2? The wage rate it has to pay to get additional miners and the costs those additional miners add to the firm are not the same. Compare wage rates and marginal labor cost in the table.

If w = $6, Edwards can hire 1,000 miners. The firm's total labor cost (*TLC*) then is $6,000, that is, $6 × 1,000. The *MLC* of each of those first 1,000 miners is $6. In this one case, w = *MLC*.

But note what happens thereafter. If Edwards wants to hire more labor, it has to raise the wage rate. Suppose it raises it to w = $8. The quantity of labor supplied increases to 2,000. *TLC* increases to $8 × 2,000 = $16,000, while *MLC* increases to ($16,000 − $6,000)/1,000 = $10.

Do you see what happened? The second group of 1,000 miners hired gets a wage rate of $8, yet each costs the firm $10. Why? Because Edwards is obliged not only to pay those new 1,000 miners $8, but to raise the wage rate of the 1,000 hired earlier at $6 to $8.

When the firm figures the cost of the second 1,000 miners, *both their wages and the cost of bumping up the wage rates of the first 1,000 miners are calculated.* Edwards adds the $2 × 1,000 = $2,000—that represents the bump—to the $8 × 1,000 = $8,000 that is the cost of hiring the new miners. The total is $10,000. Each of those 1,000 new miners, then, costs the firm $10,000/1,000 = $10.

The graph in Exhibit 2 traces the relationship between the wage rates and the *MLC* associated with hiring miners.

Notice how the supply curve and *MLC* curve diverge as more miners are hired. That's because the need to bump up the wage rates of miners already hired gets to be increasingly expensive as the firm hires more miners.

CHECK YOUR UNDERSTANDING

When a firm hires a worker, why does that worker cost the firm more than the wage rate paid to the worker?

CHOOSING THE EMPLOYMENT/WAGE RATE COMBINATION UNDER MONOPSONY

How many miners does the Charles Edwards Coal Mining Company actually hire? Edwards follows the revenue-maximizing rule practiced in the previous chapter. It continues to hire miners as long as *MRP* > *MLC*. It stops hiring when the miners' *MRP* = *MLC*.

The table in Exhibit 3 combines the cost data of Exhibit 2 with the firm's demand for miners. This demand, as we know, reflects the miners' *MRP*, which, for simplicity's sake, we assume takes the form shown in column 4.

Note that *MRP* = *MLC* at $26 and at 6,000 miners. Edwards hires 6,000 miners, paying them each a wage of $16, which is $10 below their *MRP*.

The Return to Monopsony Power

You can imagine the resentment growing in Harlan County. Remember that during the competitive days of the previous chapter, miners received their *MRP*. But Edwards defends itself, insisting that its behavior hasn't changed. It uses the same hiring guidelines it used in the last chapter, employing up to the miner whose *MRP* = *MLC*.

After all, isn't it unreasonable to expect the firm to hire miners who cannot produce sufficient revenue to cover the additional labor cost the hiring imposes on the firm? But that's precisely what happens beyond the 6,000th miner. Look at that 7,000th miner. That miner adds $24 to revenue but $30 to the firm's labor cost.

CHECK YOUR UNDERSTANDING

Why don't the miners receive a wage rate equivalent to their *MRP*?

EXHIBIT | 3

DETERMINING THE WAGE RATE, EMPLOYMENT, AND RETURN TO MONOPSONY POWER

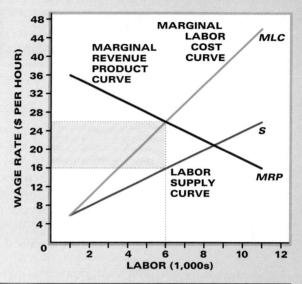

LABOR	WAGE RATE	MARGINAL LABOR COST (MLC)	MARGINAL REVENUE PRODUCT (MRP)
0	$ 0	—	—
1,000	6	$ 6	$36
2,000	8	10	34
3,000	10	14	32
4,000	12	18	30
5,000	14	22	28
6,000	16	26	26
7,000	18	30	24
8,000	20	34	22
9,000	22	38	20
10,000	24	42	18
11,000	26	46	16

The firm will hire as long as the *MRP* generated by the hired worker is greater than or equal to the worker's *MLC*. The firm stops hiring at 6,000 miners. The *MRP* of the 6,000th worker is $26, but that's not what the firm pays the worker. That 6,000th worker is willing to work for $16, which is what that worker and all the other employed workers receive. The difference between the workers' *MRP* of $26 and their $16 wage rate generates for the firm a return to monopsony power of ($26 − $16) × 6,000 = $60,000, the shaded rectangle.

The miners complain that their *MRP* = $26, yet they receive a wage rate of only $16. Aren't they entitled to their *MRP*? In the competitive labor market of the last chapter, $w = MRP$. But not any more!

Edwards can pay the 6,000 miners a wage rate of $16 because 6,000 miners have indicated—look at the supply curve of labor—that they are willing to work at $16.

The difference between the wage rate that the 6,000th miner is willing to take and the *MRP* of that miner, multiplied by total employment, is the **return to monopsony power.** Edwards's return to monopsony power is shown in the graph in Exhibit 3.

The monopsony returns that Edwards is able to capture from its 6,000 miners is $(MRP - w) \times L = (\$26 - \$16) \times 6,000 = \$60,000$, indicated by the shaded rectangle in Exhibit 3. The miners argue that the $60,000 would belong to them *if the labor market were competitive*. But it isn't competitive.

Return to monopsony power
The difference between the *MRP* and the wage rate of the last worker hired, multiplied by the number of workers hired.

ENTER THE UNITED MINE WORKERS' UNION

What can the miners do? The monopsony condition of Exhibit 3 is ripe for the United Mine Workers' Union (UMW). Let's suppose the **labor union** sends Michael Kulikowski, an experienced organizer, down to Harlan County, Kentucky, to talk to the mine workers.

Labor union
An association of workers, each of whom transfers the right to negotiate wage rates, work hours, and working conditions to the association. In this way, the union presents itself as a single seller of labor on the labor market.

His message would be simple: Miners must no longer be willing to offer their labor services at the wage rates shown in Exhibit 1. *They must confront Edwards with a very different supply curve of labor.*

Miners should hold out for $26. Not one miner should agree to work for less. By holding tight at $26, they will get $26. But how do they do that? That's where the union comes in. The miners vote to give the UMW union authority to represent them in negotiations with Edwards. They will work or stay out of work at the union's direction. In effect, the UMW becomes the supplier of labor in Harlan County.

Edwards now sees a completely different labor market. What it confronts is the union's offer of labor services shown in the table in Exhibit 4.

Employment and Wages in a Unionized Labor Market

The union is quite willing to allow the monopsonist to choose however many miners it wants to hire. Michael Kulikowski, the union organizer, knows what Edwards will do. The firm will hire the same 6,000 miners, but this time at $w = \$26$ instead of $w = \$16$. The miners will now end up with the $60,000 that had formerly been the return to monopsony power. Why is Michael so sure? Look at the graph in Exhibit 4.

The horizontal supply curve of labor at $w = \$26$ is what the union offers. Edwards can hire 1 or 10,000 at that wage rate. But not one miner for a penny less! The new, union-designed $MLC = w$ is $26. Edwards, resigned to this new labor market, will hire, as it always does, where $MRP = MLC$. That, Michael Kulikowski points out, is precisely at the old level of 6,000 miners.

But a problem arises. Look again at the table in Exhibit 2. At $w = \$26$, 11,000 miners are willing to work. That creates an excess supply of $11,000 - 6,000 =$

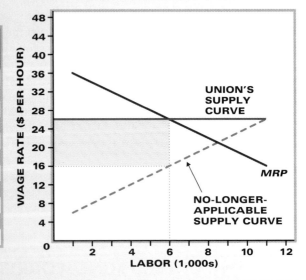

THE UNIONIZED LABOR MARKET

THE SUPPLY OF MINERS OFFERED BY THE UNION

UNION'S SUPPLY SCHEDULE		COST TO EDWARDS OF UNION-ORGANIZED LABOR	
MINERS	WAGE RATE	TLC	MLC
0	—	—	—
1,000	$26	$ 26,000	$26
2,000	26	52,000	26
3,000	26	78,000	26
4,000	26	104,000	26
5,000	26	130,000	26
6,000	26	156,000	26
7,000	26	182,000	26
8,000	26	208,000	26
9,000	26	234,000	26
10,000	26	260,000	26

The union changes the supply curve of labor from the preunion, upward-sloping curve (shown dashed) to the unionized, horizontal supply curve of labor, at $26. The first curve is no longer available to the monopsony. At $w = \$26$, the monopsony can choose to hire as many workers as it wishes. It hires workers as long as the *MRP* generated by each new worker is greater than or equal to the worker's *MLC*. The firm ends up hiring 6,000 workers, because at 6,000, $MRP = MLC$. Now the workers receive $26, the full value of their *MRP*.

APPLIED PERSPECTIVE

THE 1990s HAVE BEEN TOUGH GOING FOR UNIONS: A CASE IN POINT

Melrose Club is a luxurious private resort situated on South Carolina's Daufuskie Island in Beaufort County, which sits out on the Atlantic just north of Savannah, Georgia. Memberships sell for $75,000, plus $2,300 annual dues. Its neighboring island is South Carolina's famed Hilton Head.

If you had spent any time at the Melrose Club before October 1994, the last thing that would have come to mind is labor unions. But not after. In that October, Melrose Club employees—waiters, cooks, housekeepers, and drivers—voted 98 to 45 to join Local 465 of the International Union of Operating Engineers. It was a historic happening not only for the Melrose Club, but for Beaufort County—its first union ever—and not an insignificant event in South Carolina itself, considering that only 2.3 percent of its private-sector workers are unionized.

The vote did not guarantee union success. It just gave the union license to negotiate. It took the union 2 years to finally win a contract, winning wage raises—averaging 13 percent over 2 years—and benefits.

But less than 5 months after their union contract was ratified, most workers found themselves out of work and their union struggling to survive. Why? What happened?

Simply put: The Melrose Club owners quit the game. They quietly sold the resort to Club Corporation of America, based in Dallas, and before the club changed hands, the retiring owners fired all its employees. Few of them have been rehired by the new owners. Why not hire back? The Dallas group insists it needed a fresh start to reverse the financial mess it inherited. Its labor policy? A completely free hand to hire the best-qualified people for every position. The union sees that as nothing more than old-fashioned union busting. In January 1997, union representative David Miller went to the National Labor Relations Board (NLRB), accusing the new owners of unfair labor practices.

If the board rules in favor of the union, the owners may be forced to rehire the workers and pay them lost wages. If the union loses, it will have to either give up the fight or start all over again, trying to organize the new workers. But this time, it will be an even tougher battle because the new workers are acutely aware of what can happen to your job when you vote to unionize.

MORE ON THE NET

The National Labor Relations Board Web site (http://nlrb.gov/) provides press releases, weekly summaries, and much more about labor disputes in the United States.

5,000 miners. Edwards, understandably, will hire no more than 6,000 because the 6,001st miner's *MRP* is less than $w = \$26$. The union, then, must control its labor supply; otherwise the excess supply will undo its collective strength. That's not always easy to accomplish.

The Dynamics of Collective Bargaining

Suppose Edwards decides not to accept the union demand for $w = \$26$. Instead, it offers to increase the wage rate from $16 to $20. The union can ask for $w = \$26$, but asking is not the same as getting.

Edwards simply says it won't hire at $w = \$26$. The union now has 2 choices. Michael can recommend that miners accept the $20 offer, which is still $4 more per hour than they had earned in the nonunion, unorganized labor market, or he can recommend that miners reject the firm's offer and go out on **strike.**

CHECK YOUR UNDERSTANDING

What happens to the quantity of labor supplied if the union successfully raises the wage rate to equal *MRP*?

Strike
The withholding of labor by a union when the collective bargaining process fails to produce a contract that is acceptable to the union.

Collective bargaining
Negotiation between a labor union and a firm employing unionized labor, to create a contract concerning wage rates, hours worked, and working conditions.

Suppose the miners vote to accept the $20 offer. Edwards and the miners now share the disputed $60,000 return to monopsony power. As you can well appreciate, the miners' decision to accept or reject the firm's offer ultimately depends upon their assessment of their own **collective bargaining** power relative to the firm's.

If they sense that they can get more, they reject the firm's offer and go on strike. No coal is mined, Edwards earns no revenue, and miners, of course, earn no income.

Miners cannot stay out on strike forever. Nor can mining firms survive without mining. It is only by reassessing each other's ability to tolerate the damaging effects of the strike that the impasse can be broken.

Does the union have the financial resources to continue the strike? Can the firm stay closed without losing its own customers? Does the firm have enough financial resources to wait out the strike? Playing chicken is a nerve-racking business. Strikes are not pleasant for the miners or for the mining firms. But both sides realize that a great deal is at stake.

Unions realize that it takes a long time to make up the revenue lost through a strike. In some cases, they never make it up. But unions also know, as baseball managers do, that you keep arguing with the umpire for the benefit of the *next* call. A long, protracted strike is a signal to the firm to reassess the workers' determination. Of course, workers have to make the same reassessments about the firm.

In other words, both firms and unions are involved in a very risky business of signaling, stating intentions, and concealing agendas. They continually reassess all the factors and push for the best wage agreement they can possibly make. The prize is the return to monopsony power.

HIGHER WAGE RATES VERSUS MORE EMPLOYMENT

Suppose the union is successful in getting that $26 wage rate and successful in holding the labor force to 6,000. Success, however, may invite the disquieting feeling that perhaps the union miscalculated and should have asked for more.

At the next negotiation round, suppose the union raises its demand to $w = \$30$. But this time, it confronts two circumstances it may not have anticipated.

First, because the supply curve is upward sloping, at $w = \$30$ more people are willing to work the mines. As a result, the union's ability to control the labor supply weakens. Second, because the *MRP* curve is downward sloping, at $w = \$30$ (look at Exhibit 4) the firm *cuts* the number of miners employed to 4,000. That is, at $w = \$30$, more people want to work and fewer people are hired.

What does the union do with 2,000 cut from the 6,000 previously working miners? What does it do with the increasing pressure of others wanting to join the labor market?

The union can't just wish them away. But how can it control the labor supply? It can discourage replacements for workers who are retiring. It can create unreasonably long apprenticeship periods. It can impose exceptionally high initiation fees. It can create programs that retrain and relocate miners already in the market. It can simply turn a deaf ear to the unemployed. But whatever the strategy, it is clear to the union, as it is to surgeons in the AMA and basketball players in the NBA, that fewer numbers allow for greater freedom to pursue higher wage rates.

CHECK YOUR UNDERSTANDING

How can unions limit the supply of unionized workers?

INTERDISCIPLINARY PERSPECTIVE

FROM THE UNION SHOP TO THE BROADWAY STAGE

The 1950s seemed to have been a decade of unbounded union vitality. Twenty-five percent of the labor force had already been unionized. From the heavy industries of steel, construction, coal, and automobiles to the lighter industries of clothing, foods, and elementary education, workers proudly carried their union cards and engaged actively in the union experience. Unions were part of Americana.

What unions did and why they did what they did ended up as the subject matter of a long-running musical comedy hit on Broadway: *The Pajama Game* (music and lyrics by Richard Adler and Jerry Ross).

The story line was simple: Can love survive a battle between labor (the female lead) and management (the male lead)? The issue was a union demand for a 7½-cent raise. It may seem like a pitifully small sum to argue about, let alone to strike for, but in a delightful show-stopping song, the female lead explains to her co-workers why the 7½ cents means a heck of a lot:

SEVEN AND A HALF CENTS DOESN'T BUY A HELLUVA LOT.

I figured it out. I figured it out
With a pencil and a pad I figured it out
7½ cents doesn't buy a helluva lot
7½ cents doesn't mean a thing
But give it to me every hour, 40 hours every week
That's enough for me to be living like a king

Looking ahead 5 years, she continues:

Only five years from today, only five years from today
Five years . . . that's 260 weeks . . . times 40 hours
every week . . .
at roughly 2¼ hours overtime . . . at time and a half
for overtime . . . comes to exactly $852.74!

Is it worth it?

That's enough for me to get
an automatic washing
machine
A year's supply of gasoline
Carpeting for the living room
A vacuum instead of a
blasted broom
Not to mention a 40-inch
television set

In the end, boy-gets-girl (girl-gets-boy) and the union gets the raise. As much fun and entertainment as *The Pajama Game* was on the 1950s stage (and through many revivals), workers don't really have to go to Broadway to learn that the fight for a few pennies is serious business and often worth the agony of a strike.

Monopsonist Demands More, Union Reluctant to Supply

Suppose Edwards shifts to a new, more productive form of technology or benefits from a sudden increase in the price of its coal. Either event would shift its miners' *MRP* curve to the right, as illustrated in Exhibit 5.

Under these new conditions, what would Edwards do? It would want to hire 7,000 miners and would be willing to pay a wage rate of $30. That creates a sizable increase in the number of miners employed and *in the number of tons of coal produced.*

The union is also delighted with the shift in the *MRP* curve, but it may have other designs. It sees that the *MRP* of its 6,000th miner has increased from $26 to

EXHIBIT|5

UNIONIZED LABOR MARKET: NEW TECHNOLOGY APPLIED

When new technology shifts the workers' *MRP* to the right, from *MRP* to *MRP'*, the firm and the union may react differently. The firm is prepared to increase employment to 7,000, where *MRP'* = *MLC* = $30. But the union, instead of providing 7,000 miners at a $30 wage rate, may prefer to raise the wage rate from $26 to $32, keeping employment at 6,000 miners.

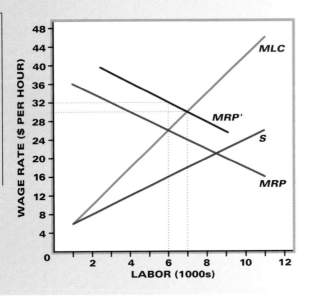

$32. What a great opportunity! If it can hold the quantity of miners it supplies to the firm at 6,000, it can push for a $w = \$32$ contract. Edwards will pay the $w = \$32$ because $MRP' = MLC$ at $32.

But an aggressive Edwards may challenge such union control over its labor supply. It could appeal directly to nonunion miners and offer them $w = \$26$. Why wouldn't they accept? You can see, then, that the inherent conflict is not only between the hiring firm and labor, but *between nonunion labor and union labor over the issue of employment versus wage rates.*

THE CLOSED SHOP Perhaps the most effective way of controlling the labor market is for the union to insist that the firm hire only unionized miners. In this way, the union decides whether to satisfy the firm's labor demands. Economists call such an arrangement a **closed shop.**

Although firms relinquish control of their labor supply to the union, the closed shop can sometimes be quite a convenient arrangement for the firm. Relations between the firm and the union aren't always antagonistic. The closed shop can serve as a useful labor filter, providing the firm with a reliable supply of workers.

THE UNION SHOP But the closed shop, however convenient, still denies the firm the right to choose its own labor. It is one thing to agree on a wage rate contract, but quite another to give up the right to decide on the quantity and quality of labor hired.

The union sees the firm's right to hire anyone, whether union or nonunion, as a potential threat to its ability to raise the wage rate. The firm sees the union's monopoly on the hiring and firing of labor as a barrier to its economic growth.

The **union shop** is a form of compromise. It safeguards the firm's right to employ as many miners as it wants, but it insists that all miners hired must join the union.

How does it work? Suppose Edwards wants to hire more than the union can supply. Under the union shop rules, the firm can recruit anyone from anywhere as long as those recruited join the union. In this way, the union can still decide what wage rate to accept, and the firm decides, after negotiating the rate, how many miners to employ.

Closed shop
An arrangement in which a firm may hire only union labor.

Union shop
An arrangement in which a firm may hire nonunion labor, but every nonunion worker hired must join the union within a specified period of time.

UNIONS IN THE UNITED STATES: A BRIEF HISTORY

It is difficult to identify the beginnings of union activity in the United States because informal arrangements among workers and employers have always existed.

Still, the first attempt by workers to organize on some sort of permanent basis seems to have occurred in 1792 when the Philadelphia shoemakers created the Federal Society of Journeymen Cordwainers.

Why did they organize? The shoemakers saw their wage rates and status in the craft threatened by competition from low-paid, unskilled workers that employers were hiring in increasing numbers. In 1799, the union went on strike to counter a wage cut. The employers responded by taking the organized workers to court.

On what charges? On conspiring to interfere with employers' rights to operate freely in the labor market. The court obliged, finding the shoemakers guilty of criminal conspiracy. It ruled that union organizing to promote a collective interest was a criminal act. This criminal conspiracy doctrine dictated court decisions until 1842, when the *Commonwealth* v. *Hunt* decision ruled that unions were not illegal. It did not, however, bestow legality upon them. For almost a century thereafter, unions fell into a twilight zone, somewhere between legality and illegality.

The Knights of Labor

If solidarity is in the workers' own interest, why not organize all workers into one giant union? That's precisely what the Knights of Labor tried to do. In 1869 it became the first union to organize across all skills, all industries, and all regions.

It was interested not only in pursuing higher wage rates for its members, but also in bringing about structural change in the economy and society. It campaigned vigorously against the use and abuse of child labor and promoted worker-owned cooperatives.

But the Knights had difficulty convincing workers to look beyond their own paycheck. Most workers were more interested in their wage rate than in changing society. Yet the Knights had its moment of glory. While other unions in the 1880s couldn't deliver, the Knights struck the railroads and won. Nothing succeeds like success. By 1886 it had 700,000 members.

But it was an inglorious slide into oblivion thereafter. The Knights suffered ill-advised and costly strikes, lost money by financing poorly organized cooperatives, and felt the heavy hand of the Pinkerton detective agents hired by employers to infiltrate and disrupt its organizing activity.

But perhaps the major factor in its demise was its inability to convince its own members of the importance of its wider goals. Most weren't interested in social and economic change. They seemed quite prepared to accept the existing economic system, provided the system was generous.

The American Federation of Labor

Although it was difficult for workers to organize during those early antiunion years, many still did. By the end of the 19th century, workers had organized mainly along craft lines, such as unions of welders, painters, or plumbers. Painters and welders working for the same shipbuilding firm, for example, belonged to two separate unions and negotiated two separate contracts.

Samuel Gompers, an official of the Cigar Maker's Union, understood what workers wanted and understood also what it took to get what they wanted. He once remarked that a worker's worst enemy was an employer who didn't make a profit. He knew that a union's ability to win higher wages depended on the firm's ability to pay. And that's all he wanted.

Disenchanted with the Knights of Labor, to which his cigar makers' union belonged, Gompers and some other unionists broke from the Knights in 1881 and five years later formed the American Federation of Labor (AFL).

Visit Union Web (http://www. unionweb.org/) and review *A Short History of American Labor.*

Learn more about Samuel Gompers (http://www. uniononline.com/html/ leaders/gompers.htm).

From its inception, the AFL was designed to promote strictly economic goals, such as higher wage rates, shorter hours, and better working conditions. Its motto was simple and direct: "More More, Now Now!"

Structurally, the AFL was set up as a loose-knit umbrella organization of highly autonomous **craft unions.** The AFL's primary function was to establish general objectives and guidelines and to settle jurisdictional disputes among its craft union members.

For example, when two unions disagreed on which had the right to organize a targeted set of workers, the AFL came in to mediate. With technology constantly changing the character of labor activity, craft identity became highly contested. But AFL mediation didn't always settle jurisdictional disputes.

Because the AFL was craft related, most of the nation's unskilled workers were left unorganized. Fruit pickers, janitors, farm workers, garbage collectors, and night watch people, for example, hardly involved in craftlike activity, had nowhere to go. Although the focus on crafts meant the AFL lost potential members, it also meant that unskilled, noncraft workers, whose *MRP* was relatively low, would not act as deadweight on the craft unions' efforts to raise wage rates. The AFL showed little sympathy for the growing number of economically powerless workers.

The Congress of Industrial Organizations

The more technology changed, the more craft distinctions blurred. By the 1930s, new manufacturing industries created even more jurisdictional problems as assembly-line production stamped uniformity of skills across craft lines. Many in the AFL saw that its craft orientation was increasingly becoming an impediment to further union growth. But the more successful craft unions felt threatened by industrial growth and stubbornly resisted restructuring.

What would restructuring mean? The creation of **industrial unions.** That is, unions would be organized along industrial rather than craft lines. For example, all workers in the textile industry would organize as a textile union. Its members would include everyone from fabric cutters, sewing machine operators, finishers, and pattern makers to shipping clerks and janitors at the textile plant. These were people with very different skills, working in different crafts, but belonging to a common industry. The AFL's concern was that incorporating all skills in a single organization would weaken the power of the more skilled workers to negotiate a wage contract.

In 1935, a number of industrial unionists, soured by the AFL's refusal to restructure, organized their own association. The Congress of Industrial Organizations (CIO) came into being by first bringing together the mine workers, garment workers, textile workers, and a few others. National industrial unions were founded to reorganize workers. By 1938, the CIO became a competing national labor federation.

The AFL-CIO Merger: 1955

The competitive struggle between the AFL and CIO continued throughout and beyond the Depression of the 1930s, the World War II years of the 1940s, and into the postwar period of the 1950s. By 1955, both the AFL and the CIO could see beyond their own limited horizons. The future of American unionism depended on union cooperation, not confrontation.

The strengths of these two federations, secured by their own longevity, allowed them to merge in 1955 to form the AFL-CIO. It brought both craft and industrial

---

Craft union
A union representing workers of a single occupation, regardless of the industry in which the workers are employed.

Industrial union
A union representing all workers in a single industry, regardless of each worker's skill or craft.

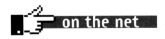

The AFL-CIO (http://www.afl cio.org/) provides news and publications about the union.

unions under one roof. The idea was to project one voice for labor and to settle, in a less public arena, the inevitable jurisdictional disputes among specific unions.

Labor, Congress, and the Courts

Throughout the 19th century and well into the third decade of the 20th century, Congress, the courts, the media, the general population, and even many workers were overwhelmingly antiunion. Exhibit 6 traces the growth of union membership.

As you see, the growth of union membership was lackluster in its early years but quite robust during the mid-1930s to mid-1940s. It continued strongly, with some backsliding, from the mid-1950s to the mid-1970s but declined steadily to 16.3 million in 1996. As a percentage of the civilian labor force, union membership grew until the mid-1950s, but after that it declined rather steadily from 26 percent in 1955 to 14.5 percent in 1996.

The unions' success in attracting membership varied with the economic climate of the times and with the attitude of Congress, the courts, and the media. Between 1900 and 1930, union membership was somewhat erratic, rising and falling with the swings of economic fortune and with political events. It soared to 5 million during World War I when the high demand for labor overcame businesses' dislike for bargaining with unions. But in the war's aftermath, antiunion business activity combined with an antiunion Congress and the courts to undo whatever gains unions had made earlier. Bitter jurisdictional disputes among the craft unions in the 1920s also compounded the problem, and union membership fell by almost a third.

By 1932, the Depression created over 13 million unemployed, accounting for 25 percent of the labor force. Confidence in business was shaken. Considerably more sympathetic to labor's plight, the Roosevelt administration and Congress enacted a series of prolabor laws that shaped a new future for unions. The courts eventually concurred.

THE NORRIS–LA GUARDIA ACT OF 1932 The first major piece of prolabor legislation was the Norris–La Guardia Act of 1932. It outlawed yellow-dog contracts. These were contracts that firms made workers sign as a condition of employment. Typically, the stated condition was that joining a union automatically nullified the worker's employment contract.

CHECK YOUR UNDERSTANDING

Why did labor unions grow so rapidly during World War I?

 **on the net**

The Legal Information Institute (http://www.law.cornell.edu/), a research activity of the Cornell Law School, maintains statutes, court cases, and other materials relevant to labor (http://www.law.cornell.edu/topics/labor.html).

UNION MEMBERSHIP SINCE 1900

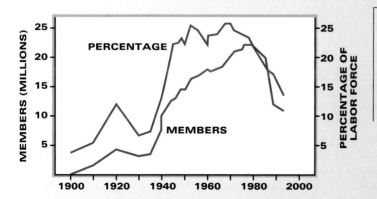

The graph depicts the dramatic increase in union membership from the mid-1930s to the early 1980s. The downward slide in membership is even more dramatic in the succeeding short period of the mid-1980s to the 1990s. Note also the percentage of the labor force unionized. The percentage increased rapidly from the 1930s through the 1950s, remained fairly stable at approximately 25 percent until the 1980s, and then dropped dramatically to 11 percent by 1993.

EXHIBIT | 6

GLOBAL PERSPECTIVE

UNIONIZATION ELSEWHERE

While union member-ship as a percent of the labor force in the United States fell rather dramatically over the past five decades—from approximately 25 percent in the 1950s to 14 percent today—union strength in most other democratic, mar-ket economies remains relatively high. Look at the accompanying exhibit.

The range is considerable, with union representation everywhere—except for France—substantially higher than in the United States. Can you describe Sweden and Denmark as

anything other than "union economies"? For most other European Union countries, the percentages double those in the United States.

The histories of unionization in these countries are different from ours, and the social and cultural roles that unions play in their societies differ as well. In many European countries, unions are an integral part of the political process and are directly linked to specific political parties.

Source: *Country Commerce* (New York: The Economist Intelligence Unit, 2000); and Ebbinghaus, Bernhard, and Jelle Visser, *The Societies of Europe: Trade Unions in Wester Europe Since 1945,* eds. Peter Flora, Frantz Kraus, and Franz Rothenbauer, (New York: Grove's Dictionaries, 2000).

UNION MEMBERSHIP AS PERCENT OF LABOR FORCE			
SWEDEN	95.3%	GREECE	35.0%
DENMARK	81.2%	CANADA	33.0%
IRELAND	65.0%	BRITAIN	32.2%
NORWAY	55.0%	GERMANY	30.7%
BELGIUM	50.7%	NETHERLANDS	25.1%
AUSTRIA	40.7%	JAPAN	22.0%
ITALY	38.5%	FRANCE	8.7%

THE WAGNER ACT OF 1935 The single most important piece of labor leg-islation was the National Labor Relations Act of 1935, called the Wagner Act. For the first time, Congress, with the courts concurring, legislated that firms must bargain in good faith with unions. The act was regarded by unions as their Magna Carta. Businesses were forced to accept unions as legitimate institutions in collec-tive bargaining. The act also created the National Labor Relations Board (NLRB) to oversee compliance.

The NLRB guaranteed the unions' right to conduct elections freely among work-ers and to represent the workers if the majority voted for unionization. The NLRB also conducted investigations of unfair labor practices. It cited firms for interfering

GLOBAL PERSPECTIVE

IMF INTERVENES IN THE KENYA TEACHER'S STRIKE

Teachers in Kenya, who returned to work after a 15-day strike, discovered that they were fighting a force bigger than their own government.

The IMF (International Monetary Fund), an international loaning agency that had made substantial loans to Kenya over an extended period of time, made it known that they would not approve an urgently needed new loan to Kenya if the Kenyan government acceded to the teachers' demands.

The background: Teachers in Kenya receive an average basic salary of US $150 per month. The largest teachers union, KNUT, arguing that for most teachers this was not enough to live on, successfully negotiated an agreement with the Kenyan government for a 200 percent increase over a five-year period. That's when the IMF stepped in. It put pressure on the Kenyan government to renege on its union contract obligations or face an IMF refusal on a new loan. The threat worked. The government refused to implement the second phase of the agreed-upon increase. Teachers, frustrated by their

WE TEACH YOUR CHILDREN. DON'T WE MATTER?

own economic plight and angered by the government's unwillingness to stand up to the IMF, went on strike. Their short-lived strike was supported by 70 percent of the Kenyan population.

Why did the IMF exercise its clout in this way? Kenya is heavily indebted, and pays 25 percent of government revenue to service the debt. More than half the debt is owed to multilateral institutions, including the World Bank and IMF.

To the IMF, it's a matter of misplaced priorities. Kenya cannot commit to such extensive social spending—regardless of its merit—without having the resources to do so. Curbing the government's appetite is an unpleasant but necessary role that the IMF plays in the hope of helping Kenya assume a more responsible budgetary policy.

The unions see the issue quite differently. To them, it's a matter of the powerful versus the powerless. Unions simply don't have the leverage to force the government to live up to its commitment. As well, there's the matter of education. Kenya's teachers ended the strike, KNUT leader Ambrose Adongo said, "because of our love for parents and children."

with unions' efforts to organize, for refusing to bargain with recognized unions, and for discriminating against prounion workers in their employ.

Unionism appealed now to the Depression-conscious workers. With the creation of the CIO in 1935, total union membership increased to almost 9 million by 1940. The high demand for labor during World War II gave unions even more power. By 1950, membership reached 15 million.

THE TAFT-HARTLEY ACT OF 1947 The years following World War II were a period of digestion and maturity. Now regarded as an accepted institution in American economic life, unions had to cope with their own success. Congress took a second look at union activity and responded in 1947 with the Labor Management Relations Act, called the Taft-Hartley Act. Although the act was regarded by unions as an antilabor piece of legislation, Congress was responding principally to the unions' abuse of power. The act outlawed the closed shop, replacing it with the union shop.

The act also prohibited unions' unfair labor practices and made unions bargain in good faith as well. It prevented unions from pressuring workers during union elections. It prohibited unions from striking in support of other unions' strikes.

LABOR MANAGEMENT REPORTING AND THE LANDRUM-GRIFFIN ACT In 1959, Congress enacted the Labor Management Reporting and Disclosure Act, called the Landrum-Griffin Act, in response to growing concerns about criminal activity by unions. In a real sense, Landrum-Griffin was designed to protect the worker *from the union*. The act specified rules of conduct between the union and its own members. For example, it required full financial disclosure of union revenues and expenditures. It sought to protect workers from rigged elections. It specified penalties for union leaders guilty of misusing union funds and required full disclosure of the salaries of union officials.

THE CIVIL RIGHTS ACT OF 1964 Another major piece of legislation affecting union activity directly was the Civil Rights Act of 1964. Again, the legislative purpose was to protect workers from institutionalized union power. The principal issue now was racial and sexual discrimination. Women and minorities, over the years, had been held back by the unions' seniority rules and by union manipulation of the labor markets to protect the status of white men, who dominated unions. The act required unions to adopt affirmative action policies within their own ranks.

CHAPTER REVIEW

1. A monopsony is the only buyer of labor. It faces the market supply curve of labor.

2. In a monopsonist market, the marginal labor cost curve lies above the supply curve of labor because it includes the increase in wages of workers already hired at lower wage rates.

3. The monopsonist maximizes profit by hiring workers whose *MRP* is greater than or equal to their *MLC*, so that the profit-maximizing level of employment occurs where *MRP* = *MLC*.

4. At the profit-maximizing level of employment, the difference between that *MRP* = *MLC* level and the wage rate multiplied by the level of employment generates for the monopsonist the return to monopsony power.

5. The wages-maximizing supply curve of union labor presented to the monopsonist is horizontal at the *MRP* = *MLC* level.

6. Because the supply curve of union labor is horizontal, it is identical to the marginal labor cost curve.

7. The union and the monopsonist engage in collective bargaining.

8. If the union succeeds in negotiating a wage rate equal to the worker's *MRP* = *MLC*, workers end up with what monopsonists captured as return to monopsony power.

9. If the union negotiates a wage rate higher than the *MRP* = *MLC* level, an excess supply of labor emerges to weaken the union's control of the labor supply.

10. An adoption of new technology shifts the demand curve for labor to the right, providing the union with the option of either negotiating for higher wage rates at the existing level of employment or negotiating for higher employment at the existing wage rate.

11. A closed shop gives the union complete control over the labor supply, while a union shop allows the firm to hire as many workers as it wishes, but the workers hired must join the union.

12. Union activity in the 18th and 19th centuries was thwarted by court decisions holding that such activity constituted criminal conspiracy. The Knights of Labor represented the union movement's first sustained success.

13. The American Federation of Labor (AFL), founded in 1886, was the organization of craft unions. The Congress of Industrial Organizations (CIO), founded in 1935, was the organization of industrial unions. They merged in 1955 into the AFL-CIO.

14. Union membership peaked at more than 20 million members in the 1970s, falling dramatically in the 1990s to below 15 million. The 1932 Norris–La Guardia Act and the 1935 Wagner Act guaranteed the unions' right to collective bargaining. The 1947 Taft-Hartley Act outlawed the closed shop, while the 1959 Landrum-Griffin Act, dealing with the issue of unions' financial and electoral abuses, protected the workers' interests vis-à-vis the unions. The 1964 Civil Rights Act guaranteed the right to union representation for minorities.

KEY TERMS

Monopsony
Return to monopsony power
Labor union

Strike
Collective bargaining
Closed shop

Union shop
Craft union
Industrial union

QUESTIONS

1. How does monopsony differ from monopoly?

2. Explain the return to monopsony power.

3. Consider two labor markets. Both have identical *MRP* curves, but the first has an elastic supply curve of labor while the second has an inelastic supply curve of labor. Compare their returns to monopsony power.

4. If you were a union organizer, how would you go about persuading workers to join the union? You can assume they are familiar with the economic concepts discussed in this chapter.

5. How do unions change the supply curve of labor, and what effect does it have on the quantity of labor supplied and on the wage rate?

6. Why do unions strike? Do strikes always benefit workers?

7. Discuss the trade-offs unions face negotiating for higher wage rates and levels of employment.

8. Compare closed and union shops. If you were an employed union member, which type of shop would you prefer? Why? If you were a job-seeking nonunion worker, which type of shop would you prefer? Why?

9. Compare craft and industrial unions. If you were a night security guard employed at Ford Motor Company during the 1920s, would it be likely that you would be a union member? Why or why not?

10. What acts are regarded as the most significant pieces of prolabor legislation?

11. Why would union members support legislation limiting immigration?

12. Discuss union membership since the 1970s.

PRACTICE PROBLEMS

1. The following table represents the David Narcizo Drum Company's supply curve of labor:

WORKERS	WAGE RATE	MLC
1	$ 7.50	
2	8.75	
3	10.00	
4	11.25	
5	12.50	
6	13.75	
7	15.00	

Calculate the marginal labor cost corresponding to each wage rate and graph the *MLC* curve it forms.

2. Calculate (from problem 1) the return to monopsony power when employment is six workers.

3. The following table represents the David Narcizo Drum Company's *MRP:*

WORKERS	MRP
1	$50.00
2	35.00
3	25.00
4	20.00
5	17.50
6	15.00
7	13.50

Calculate the number of workers the firm will hire. What wage rate will workers receive?

4. Calculate the highest wage rate the union can negotiate that is consistent with the level of employment already established by the firm.

5. Fill in the table and answer the following questions.

QUANTITY LABOR	TOTAL PRODUCT	PRICE OF THE GOOD	TR	MRP	WAGE RATE	TLC	MLC
0							
1	10	$10			$10		
2	18	9			15		
3	24	8			20		
4	30	7			25		
5	32	6			30		

a. How many workers will the firm hire?
b. What wage rate will workers receive?
c. What is the firm's return to monopsony power?
d. Draw a graph that depicts the monopsony labor market of the table.

WHAT'S WRONG WITH THIS GRAPH?

MONOPSONY LABOR MARKET

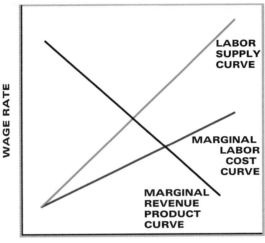

ECONOMIC CONSULTANTS

ECONOMIC RESEARCH AND ANALYSIS BY STUDENTS FOR PROFESSIONALS

The Speed Shoe Company produces high-quality running shoes for track athletes. Speed currently has a manufacturing plant in Birmingham, Alabama, in which employees are not unionized. About one-half of Speed's sales occur in the United Kingdom, and Speed's owners wish to build a manufacturing plant in England. However, the owners are worried that the cost of labor will be much higher than at its Birmingham plant, given union activities in England.

Speed has hired Economic Consultants to analyze the reach and influence of unions in England. Prepare a report for Speed that addresses the following issues:

1. What is the state of organized labor in England?
2. In your opinion, will Speed encounter stiffer or weaker union opposition in England (as compared to in Birmingham) if it pursues nonunion labor for its manufacturing plant?

You may find the following resources helpful as you prepare this report for Speed:

● **The Trades Union Congress (TUC)** (http://www.tuc.org.uk/)—The TUC has 74 member unions representing 6.7 million workers in Great Britain.
● **Labour Research Department** (http://www.1rd.org.uk/)—The Labour Research Department is an independent research organization focusing on trade unions in Great Britain.
● **infoBASE EUROPE** (http://www.ibeurope.com/)—infoBASE EUROPE provides information on unions throughout Europe.
● **International Labour Organization** (http://www.ilo.org/)—The International Labour Organization, part of the United Nations, provides information on organized labor activities around the world.

PRACTICE TEST

1. A monopsony is
   a. a market in which only a single firm hires labor.
   b. a firm that produces goods without employing labor.
   c. a market in which there are many firms attempting to hire labor, but only a few laborers offering their services on the labor market.
   d. a market in which laborers are hired by a monopoly.
   e. a market in which there are many buyers and sellers of labor, so that no buyer or seller can influence the wage rate.

2. The supply curve of labor as seen by a monopsonist is
   a. downward sloping, because the law of diminishing returns applies to all markets, including labor.
   b. downward sloping, because the monopsonist can reduce the wage rate if more laborers are willing to work.
   c. horizontal, because the monopsonist can hire as many laborers as it wishes without affecting the wage rate.
   d. upward sloping, because in order to hire more laborers, the monopsonist must meet the laborers' increasing opportunity cost.
   e. upward sloping, because the monopsonist will raise the wage rate to deter unions from entering the labor market.

3. The marginal labor cost
   a. curve is identical to the monopsonist's supply curve of labor.
   b. represents what the monopsonist pays each laborer, which is typically lower than the wage rate on the labor market.
   c. represents what the monopsonist pays each laborer, which is typically higher than the wage rate on the labor market.
   d. is the cost to the monopsonist of hiring an additional laborer.
   e. is the total wage bill that the monopsonist pays hiring its laborers.

4. The return to monopsony power is
   a. the difference between the *MRP* and the wage rate of the last laborer hired multiplied by the number of laborers hired.
   b. the difference between the *MRP* and the *MLC* of the last laborer hired multiplied by the number of laborers hired.
   c. the difference between the *MLC* and the wage rate of the last laborer hired multiplied by the number of laborers hired.
   d. the difference between the *MRP* and the wage rate of the last laborer hired divided by the number of laborers hired.
   e. the difference between the *MRP* and *MLC* of the last laborer hired divided by the number of laborers hired.

5. When laborers agree to have a union represent them,
   a. the firm that does the hiring first negotiates with the individual laborer, then has the wage rate agreement with the laborer ratified by the union.
   b. the firm that does the hiring first negotiates with the union, then has the wage rate agreement with the union ratified by the individual laborer.
   c. the firm faces a horizontal supply curve of labor fixed by the union.
   d. the firm faces an upward-sloping supply curve of labor as it did before, but the union, not the firm, chooses the point on the curve.
   e. the demand curve for labor becomes the union's demand.

6. Unions, when successful in negotiating with firms, sometimes must trade off one goal for another, such as
   a. accepting the terms of the agreement or striking.
   b. accepting higher wage rates or higher employment.
   c. accepting short-run wage increases or long-run wage increases.
   d. increasing union dues (laborers' payment to the union) or being more efficient managing union activity.
   e. being more resistant to firm pressure or negotiating on more accommodating terms.

7. When unions first appeared on U.S. labor markets,
   a. they were supported by Congress, and the court system ruled consistently in their favor, which encouraged unionization.
   b. they were supported by Congress, but the court system ruled consistently against them, which discouraged workers from joining unions.
   c. they confronted a hostile Congress, although the court system ruled in their favor.
   d. they confronted a hostile Congress and a court system that ruled consistently against them.
   e. they had little difficulty signing members, particularly those in the unskilled trades earning low wage rates.

8. By the end of the 19th century, labor unions had succeeded in organizing their members along _____ lines, and together, in 1886, these unions formed the _____.
   a. industrial/Congress of Industrial Organizations (CIO)
   b. industrial/International Ladies Garment Workers Union (ILGWU)
   c. industrial/American Federation of Labor (AFL)
   d. industrial/Knights of Labor (KOL)
   e. craft/American Federation of Labor (AFL)

Have you ever seen money work? Think about it. Have you ever seen a dollar bill go to work the way people do? For example, can you imagine a dollar bill getting up in the morning and going to work at the Charles Edwards Coal Mining Company? Can you imagine a dollar bill producing tons of coal? Can you visualize a marginal physical product curve for dollar bills? This may sound absurd, but don't be too sure.

Economists believe that money, in the form of capital, is productive in precisely the same way that people are. In the chapter on wage rates and employment under perfect competition, we saw that as more miners were hired by the Charles Edwards Coal Mining Company, total tonnage increased. Remember how we derived labor's productivity. We assumed that everything required to mine coal—the drilling, blasting, and

INTEREST, RENT, AND PROFIT

17

THIS CHAPTER INTRODUCES YOU TO THE ECONOMIC PRINCIPLES ASSOCIATED WITH:

- MARGINAL PHYSICAL PRODUCT OF CAPITAL AND MARGINAL REVENUE PRODUCT OF CAPITAL
- LOANABLE FUNDS AND EQUIPMENT CAPITAL
- INTEREST RATE DETERMINATION
- THE ETHICS OF EARNING INTEREST-BASED INCOME
- THE PRESENT VALUE OF A PROPERTY
- PURE RENT, DIFFERENTIAL RENT, AND LOCATION RENT
- WAGE-RELATED RENTS
- PROFIT-RELATED INCOME

transport equipment, as well as the coal itself—was already on the Edwards site. Everything but labor.

We then added workers. We saw that without a single miner, no coal could be produced. All the mining equipment in the world couldn't produce a solitary nugget without someone actually working the equipment. And when miners were added, one by one, total output increased. The more miners, the higher the tonnage.

What makes sense for labor makes sense as well for capital. We calculate the productivity of capital the same way. But this time, we assume that Edwards starts with a fixed supply of miners and coal resources. The company has everything required to produce coal except capital.

Can you picture the scene at the mine? How can miners be expected to mine coal without so much as a pick and shovel? What can they possibly do? They cannot scratch their way into the pits with bare hands. The combination of an ample quantity of miners, an ample quantity of coal resources, and no capital equipment produces no coal. We see this in Exhibit 1.

Does the table in Exhibit 1 look familiar? It should. It shows what happens to output when a resource, in this case, capital, is added to production. You may want to compare the table in Exhibit 1 here to the table in Exhibit 1 in the preceding chapter on wage rates and employment. Do you see the similarity?

Marginal revenue product of capital
The change in total revenue that results from adding one more dollar of loanable funds to production.

Look at capital's total physical product, *TPP.* Working with one unit of capital—$1,000 worth of capital equipment—miners are able to produce a total physical product of 250 tons. If the price per ton of coal is $2, then the **marginal revenue product of capital** is $2 \times 250 = $500.

EDWARDS'S DEMAND FOR LOANABLE FUNDS

The downward-sloping demand curve for loanable funds is identical to the firm's *MRP* of capital curve. If the rate of interest, *r,* which is the price the firm has to pay for loanable funds, is 15 percent, the quantity of loanable funds demanded by the firm is $8,000. Every one of the first $7,999 produces for the firm a revenue greater than $0.15. The $8,000th produces exactly $0.15. That is why the firm will borrow as much as $8,000 of loanable funds at *r* = .15. If *r* = .20, the quantity of loanable funds demanded by the firm falls to $7,000, because every dollar it buys over the $7,000th produces an *MRP* that is less than $0.20.

LOANABLE FUNDS	TOTAL PHYSICAL PRODUCT (TONS)	MARGINAL PHYSICAL PRODUCT (TONS)	MARGINAL REVENUE PRODUCT (MRP)	MRP/DOLLAR (%)
$ 0	0	—	—	—
1,000	250	250	$500	50
2,000	475	225	450	45
3,000	675	200	400	40
4,000	850	175	350	35
5,000	1,000	150	300	30
6,000	1,125	125	250	25
7,000	1,225	100	200	20
8,000	1,300	75	150	15
9,000	1,350	50	100	10
10,000	1,375	25	50	5

MARGINAL REVENUE PRODUCT OF CAPITAL

INTEREST RATE (%)

LOANABLE FUNDS ($1,000s)

This is a very impressive revenue generated by the first $1,000 employed. Calculating the *MRP per dollar*, each of the first thousand dollars earns $500/$1,000 = $0.50, or 50 percent.

If Edwards decides to use $2,000, then *TPP* = 475 tons. The *MPP* of the second unit of $1,000 **loanable funds** is 475 − 250 = 225 tons. The *MRP per dollar* for each of the second thousand dollars is $0.45, or 45 percent.

Loanable funds
Money that a firm employs to purchase the physical plant, equipment, and raw materials used in production.

FROM LOANABLE FUNDS TO EQUIPMENT CAPITAL

But how does Edwards add a second unit of $1,000 loanable funds to the already employed first $1,000? It isn't quite the same as adding a second miner to one miner already employed. The first miner is the same miner with or without the second employed. But in the case of loanable funds, the doubling of loanable funds used in production *may require changing the physical character of the first $1,000 worth of loanable funds employed.*

For example, if the first unit of $1,000 was used to purchase 20 picks and shovels, and an additional $1,000 was later added to buy another 20 picks and shovels, there is no problem. But suppose the most productive use of $2,000 is not 40 picks and shovels, but one pneumatic drill. Here's the problem. How can Edwards purchase the $2,000 drill when it already has the first $1,000 worth of capital in the form of 20 picks and shovels?

Edwards has no such problem when it considers hiring more workers. It can hire, lay off, and rehire miners without affecting their individual physical characteristics. A mining crew of 10 miners can be reduced to a mining crew of 9 miners without changing any individual miner. But Edwards cannot add to or withdraw loanable funds from production without changing the total stock of equipment that the loanable funds buy. Once any quantity of loanable funds is employed in production, it takes the definite physical form of **capital equipment** and is unalterable in the short run. It is impossible to add $1,000 of loanable funds to $1,000 worth of capital equipment already fixed in the form of picks and shovels and end up with a $2,000 pneumatic drill.

Capital equipment
The machinery a firm uses in production.

In reading the table in Exhibit 1, then, we assume that the calculations Edwards makes in adding or subtracting units of capital are made while capital is still in its money form.

EDWARDS'S DEMAND FOR LOANABLE FUNDS

How much in loanable funds will Edwards demand? The quantity demanded depends on the amount of money per dollar borrowed, that is, the **interest rate**, firms are obliged to pay to obtain them. After all, nobody lends money for free. The higher the interest rate, the less loanable funds will the firm demand.

Interest rate
The price of loanable funds, expressed as an annual percentage return on a dollar of loanable funds.

Let's suppose the interest rate, r, is 15 percent. That is, Edwards can get as much in loanable funds as it desires at r = .15.

Look again at Exhibit 1. Would you advise Edwards to borrow? How much? Consider the first $1,000. For each of the first $1,000, *MRP* = $0.50. Since it costs Edwards only $0.15 per dollar to borrow that money, that's a net gain of $0.50 − $0.15 = $0.35 per dollar used in production.

What about the second $1,000? Each of these dollars adds $0.45 − $0.15 = $0.30 to Edwards's revenue. Each of the third $1,000 adds $0.40 − $0.15 = $0.25

to revenue. Although the *MRP* of capital falls as the quantity of capital employed increases—the law of diminishing returns applies—it is not until the 8,000th dollar that *MRP* = $0.15.

The *MRP* = *MFC* Rule

Marginal factor cost
The change in a firm's total cost that results from adding one more unit of a factor (labor, capital, or land) to production.

The *MRP* = *MFC* maximization rule—that is, marginal revenue product equals **marginal factor cost**—applies to capital just as the *MRP* = *MLC* rule applies to labor. Edwards will continue adding loanable funds to production as long as its *MRP* is greater than or equal to the marginal cost of employing loanable funds, *MFC*. Edwards's demand curve for loanable funds, then, is its *MRP* curve. This is shown in the graph in Exhibit 1.

If *r* = .15, Edwards demands $8,000 of loanable funds. If *r* = .20, Edwards demands $7,000. And so on.

LOANABLE FUNDS IN THE ECONOMY: DEMAND AND SUPPLY

The Charles Edwards Coal Mining Company is only one of many thousands of firms operating in the economy. As you can imagine, each of these firms has its own Exhibit 1, with its own *MRP* curve. The economy's demand for loanable funds, then, at *r* = .15, is the sum of each firm's demand for loanable funds at *r* = .15. This is shown in Exhibit 2. At *r* = .15, $12 million is demanded.

Where do the loanable funds come from? People supply the loanable funds. They are willing to supply the capital *for a price*. The price, offered by the firms using the capital, is the rate of interest. The higher the rate of interest, the greater the quantity of loanable funds supplied.

Loanable funds market
The market in which the demand for and supply of loanable funds determines the rate of interest.

People can do two things with their income. They can spend it or save it. There is, of course, good reason to do some of both. People spend at least some of their income on household necessities. But they also spend part of their income on items whose consumption could be postponed without inflicting permanent damage to body and soul.

Why would anyone be willing to postpone consumption? One good reason is that the money saved and supplied to the **loanable funds market** earns a rate of interest. Most people would get excited about the prospect of earning 15 percent on their savings.

Of course, not everybody gets equally excited about interest. You would expect people with different incomes to behave differently. And they do. Low-income people, for example, generally spend most of their waking hours figuring out how to make ends meet. Their ability to save is limited. In some cases,

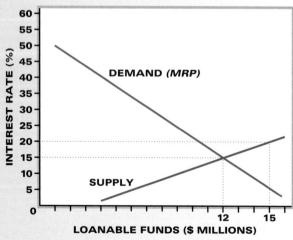

EXHIBIT 2

THE ECONOMY'S DEMAND FOR AND SUPPLY OF LOANABLE FUNDS

The downward-sloping demand curve for loanable funds reflects the sum, at every interest rate, of the quantity of loanable funds demanded by each firm.

The upward-sloping supply curve reflects the willingness of people to supply quantities of loanable funds at varying interest rates.

DEMAND (MRP)

SUPPLY

INTEREST RATE (%)

LOANABLE FUNDS ($ MILLIONS)

it is flat zero. The prospect of earning interest by offering their savings to the loanable funds market is, therefore, probably the furthest thing from their minds.

But not for other people. Earning interest is a sufficient inducement for people who can supply savings to the loanable funds market. Look again at Exhibit 2.

The supply curve of loanable funds is upward sloping. At low rates of interest, the quantity of loanable funds offered to the market is relatively low. But as the rate increases, the quantity supplied increases as well.

THE EQUILIBRIUM RATE OF INTEREST

What determines the equilibrium rate of interest? Supply and demand. As you see, the equilibrium rate of interest is 15 percent. If the rate were higher, say, $r = .20$, an excess supply would emerge on the market. Competition among suppliers of loanable funds would drive the rate down. If the rate were lower, say, $r = .10$, the excess demand for loanable funds among borrowers would drive the rate up.

The rate of interest remains unchanged as long as the demand and supply conditions in the loanable funds market of Exhibit 2 are themselves unchanging. But if conditions change, affecting either demand or supply, then the equilibrium rate will change as well. Look at Exhibit 3.

Let's imagine a situation in which the housing industry is entering a boom period, but at the same time consumers are spending more on housing by taking the money out of savings. The demand curve for loanable funds would shift outward to the right from D to D', while the supply curve would shift inward to the left from S to S'. The combined effect of these shifts drives the equilibrium rate to $r = .25$.

What else could explain an outward shift in the demand curve for loanable funds? Anything that increases capital's *MRP*, such as a change in the marginal physical product of capital, or a change in the price of the product produced by that capital, or new firms entering the market, each adding to the market its own demand for loanable funds.

What about supply? The shift from S to S' usually reflects a change in people's preferences for more present and less deferred consumption. For example, if you expect future prices to increase, you may withdraw your savings from the loanable funds market and take that vacation to Hawaii now.

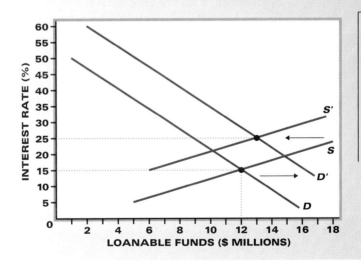

CHANGES IN THE RATE OF INTEREST

When the demand curve for loanable funds increases from D to D' at the same time that the supply curve of loanable funds decreases from S to S', the equilibrium rate of interest increases from $r = .15$ to $r = .25$.

EXHIBIT|3

THE ETHICS OF INCOME FROM INTEREST

At $r = .15$, suppliers of loanable funds receive as interest payments $0.15 for every dollar supplied. Suppose Diane Pecknold supplies $400,000 to the loanable funds market. At $r = .15$, she receives interest of $60,000 per year.

Let's suppose also that she lives in the coal mining region of Harlan County. But unlike her coal mining neighbors, she does not get up at 6 o'clock every morning to make her way to the coal pits. Instead, she rises at 10, takes her morning coffee in the sunroom, and spends the rest of the late morning hours leisurely scanning the financial section of the local newspaper. She frequently lunches with the local banker and typically spends her afternoons fishing in a private lake for smallmouth bass. In other words, life for money supplier Diane Pecknold is not entirely unpleasant.

She is also the topic of conversation among her coal mining neighbors. Down at the pits, they refer to her as "unproductive." Some see her as a parasite, "living off the sweat of the working class." But is Diane Pecknold really unproductive? Is she really a parasite?

While Diane sleeps comfortably during the early morning hours of the workweek, *her capital is busy working for her.* It earns its *MRP,* just as miners earn theirs. If Pecknold is not entitled to the fruits of her property, who is? After all, the $400,000 loanable funds advanced by Diane Pecknold is her property, just as the miners' muscle power is theirs.

Somebody Did the Saving

How did Diane Pecknold come by $400,000? Suppose she accumulated the $400,000 of loanable funds over a long period of time. It could represent years of saving. While others were busy spending their income on consumption items, Diane Pecknold saved.

As a result, she managed to put aside $10,000 from her first year's salary, and she supplied it to the loanable funds market at $r = .15$. If she kept it there untouched for 20 years, it would have grown from $10,000 to $166,664. It is not difficult, then, to understand how, with a determined effort to save, a $400,000 stock of loanable funds can be accumulated.

But suppose Diane Pecknold didn't save at all. Suppose, instead, she inherited the $400,000 from her parents. Is she no less entitled to the interest it bears? After all, *somebody did the saving.* How did her parents come by the $400,000? Are they not entitled to bequeath their savings to their children?

Property and Property Rights

The ethical question underscoring Diane Pecknold's claim to interest payments raises the broader issue of property and property rights. What is property? And who has claim to its productivity?

Let's look beyond Diane Pecknold's claim to interest. Is a student who scored a perfect exam not entitled to an A simply because she hadn't studied for the exam? Is it fair to other students that, because she has an exceptional mind, she can exert minimal effort and yet top the class? Her superior performance reflects her high IQ. But what did she do to warrant having one? If she inherited her intelligence from her parents, is she, then, really entitled to the rewards it creates?

Or what about the musical genius of violinist Gil Shaham? Is that not a marketable property? Should he not be entitled to the rewards it affords him? What about Shaquille O'Neal? He's one of the highest-paid basketball players in the NBA. Is it fair that he is rewarded for a natural ability he did little to acquire?

Everyone, it appears, possesses some particular set of physical or mental properties that works for her or him. The A student, blessed with a high IQ, earns a high grade without having to exert much effort. Gil Shaham's genius works the classical concert circuit. Shaquille O'Neal's innate ability works in the NBA.

HISTORICAL PERSPECTIVE

USING MONEY TO MAKE MONEY WAS NOT ALWAYS AN ACCEPTED PRACTICE

Among the oldest known references to usury are those found in ancient Indian religious manuscripts. The earliest such record derives from the Vedic texts of ancient India (2000–1400 B.C.), in which the "usurer" (*kusidin*) is mentioned several times and interpreted as any lender of interest. More frequent and detailed references to interest payment are to be found in the later Sutra texts (700–100 B.C.), as well as the Buddhist Jatakas (600–400 B.C.). It is during this latter period that the first sentiments of contempt for usury are expressed. For example, Vasishtha, a well-known Hindu lawmaker of that time, made a special law that forbade the higher castes of Brahmanas (priests) and Kshatriyas (warriors) from being usurers or lenders at interest. Also, in the Jatakas, usury is referred to in a demeaning manner: "hypocritical ascetics are accused of practicing it."

By the second century A.D., however, usury had become a more relative term, as is implied in the Laws of Manu of that time: "Stipulated interest beyond the legal rate being against [the law], cannot be recovered: They call that a usurious way [of lending]." This dilution of the concept of usury seems to have continued through the remaining course of Indian history so that today, while it is still condemned in principle, usury refers only to interest charged above the prevailing socially accepted range and is no longer prohibited or controlled in any significant way.

Usury is criticized in other world religions and philosophies as well. Plato, Aristotle, Cicero, Seneca, and Plutarch all condemned the practice, and these sentiments were manifested in the civil law of the time. In Judaism, the practice of usury is at times forbidden, discouraged, or scorned in such texts as Exodus, Leviticus, and Deuteronomy. The Christian Church fervently took up the debate for well over a thousand years, with the Roman Catholic Church in the eighth century declaring usury a criminal offense, and in the fourteenth century declaring secular pro-usury legislation null and void. Disapproval of usury in Islam was well established during Muhammad's life and reinforced by various teachings in the Holy Qur'an dating back to around 600 A.D.

THE HOLY KORAN (CIRCA 600 AD): TAKE NO USURY.

Should Diane Pecknold's loanable funds be treated differently? It is a property, like intelligence or physical ability acquired through inheritance. It works the loanable funds market. Is not every property holder with legitimate rights to the property entitled to receive the *MRP* the property generates?

The Marxist View of Interest-Derived Income

Not all economists are willing to justify interest-derived claims to income on the basis of capital's productivity or as a reward for saving. Marxists, for example, are quick to dismiss these arguments as simplistic, self-serving apologies.

While Marxists have no trouble understanding that supply and demand for loanable funds determine the interest rate, they do question how the supply of loanable funds got into the hands of the suppliers in the first place. Their own explanation is radically different. To them, the answer is theft. All private property, Karl Marx asserted, originates in theft.

In this interpretation of history there are no ethical foundations to property claims whatsoever. Diane Pecknold's claim to her $400,000 loanable funds property and to the $60,000 interest it generates annually has about as much validity to a Marxist as an eagle's claim to a bunny rabbit. It's strictly predatory.

PRESENT VALUE

Let's stay, for a moment, with Diane Pecknold's good fortune. Suppose she receives a letter from a law firm in Raleigh, North Carolina, telling her that she has inherited a 40-acre tobacco farm from a distant uncle. The farm, she discovers, generates an annual net income of $28,000. Although nobody, including Diane Pecknold, looks a gift horse in the mouth, she is still curious to know just how much the farm is worth. How would she go about calculating the value of the property?

Her first thought is on the mark. She knows that her $400,000 in loanable funds earns her $60,000 annually in interest. She figures, therefore, that if the farm earns annually a little less than one-half of $60,000, it should be worth a little less than one-half the value of her $400,000 loanable funds.

Once the idea is understood, the calculations become rather simple. She figures her annual interest as follows:

$$R = rPV,$$

Present value
The value today of the stream of expected future annual income a property generates. The method of computing present value is to divide the annual income generated, R, by the rate of interest, r. That is, $PV = R/r$.

where R represents the annual return on the property, PV represents the property's **present value,** and r represents the rate of interest.

In the case of her newly acquired farm, Diane Pecknold knows that $r = .15$ and the annual return on the property is $28,000. Rewriting our simple equation, the present value of the property—that is, the farm—is simply

$$PV = R/r$$

or $28,000/.15 = $186,666.67. As she originally thought, the value of the farm is just a little under $200,000.

Effect of Changing Interest Rates on Property Values
Suppose the rate of interest dropped to 10 percent. What would happen to the value of Pecknold's farm? The arithmetic is simple enough.

$$\$28,000/.10 = \$280,000$$

CHECK YOUR UNDERSTANDING

Why does a decrease in the interest rate increase the present value of a property?

At $r = .10$, the value of the farm shoots up to $280,000. The farm's value, then, increases as interest rates fall. Does this inverse relationship between interest rates and property value make sense?

Suppose you wanted to create a bank account that provides steady annual interest of $28,000. If the interest rate is 15 percent, how much would you need to put into the account? The answer is $186,666.67. But if the interest rate is 10 percent, wouldn't more money be needed in the account to generate the same $28,000 annual return? How much would be needed now to generate $28,000 annually? $280,000.

Since the farm generates $28,000 year after year, shouldn't its value at $r = .15$ be equivalent to the value of a $186,666.67 bank account, and at $r = .10$ be equivalent to the value of a $280,000 account?

Property Values and Price Floors

Suppose Diane Pecknold develops a strong interest in this North Carolina tobacco farm. She learns that the farm produces 10,000 pounds of Bright Leaf tobacco each season, which is sold at $2.80 per pound. But she soon discovers that the price of tobacco has a long and troubled history. The $2.80 it fetches on the market is a politically determined floor price, set by government to protect tobacco producers. The equilibrium price that would prevail in a free market—if the government didn't interfere—would be $2. Exhibit 4 depicts the price circumstance she and other tobacco farmers face.

Diane Pecknold knows that as long as the government keeps supporting the price of tobacco at $2.80, the profit from her annual tobacco crop will stay at $2.80 × 10,000 = $28,000. The value of the farm property at $r = .15$, then, remains at $186,666.67.

But suppose the government abandons its price support of tobacco, allowing price to adjust downward to its $2 market value. The value of her crop falls from $28,000 to $2 × 10,000 = $20,000.

What happens to the value of the farm? The present value of a property generating $20,000 annually is $20,000/.15 = $133,333.33. In other words, Diane Pecknold's tobacco farm is valued at $186,666.67 only because tobacco prices have been artificially inflated by the government to $2.80, well above the $2 price that the market would generate.

You can see, then, why tens of thousands of farmers today might be uncomfortable. Many bought farms at inflated values. If price supports are withdrawn, property values could come crashing down, destroying much of the value of the loanable funds farmers have tied up in their farms.

Almost Anything Is Marketable Property

A North Carolina tobacco farm fits well into our image of what a property is. It is tangible. A brick house is about as tangible a property as any you could describe. But property, in the world of economics, need not be physical.

Imagine having a bubbling brook surface on your property with water all year round tasting as delightful as Perrier. If you can sell access to the brook for $10 per year and 1,000 people buy into the deal, the present value of the brook would be $10,000/.15 = $66,666.67.

Or imagine owning a popcorn company that nets $500,000 annually. And suppose Bonnie Blair, the U.S. Olympic speedskater who won six gold medals in the 1988, 1992, and 1994 Winter Games, allows you to use her name and face on your popcorn box. Your new designer

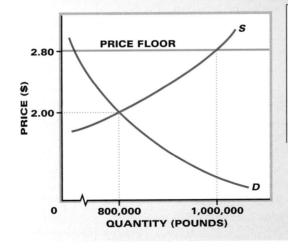

PRICE AND OUTPUT IN THE TOBACCO MARKET

The market demand and supply curves intersect at $P = $2 and $Q = 800,000$. The market-determined value of the tobacco crop is $2 × 800,000 = $1,600,000. The government-imposed price floor is fixed at $2.80. At that price, tobacco farmers supply 1,000,000 pounds. The value of tobacco farms increases with a price floor.

EXHIBIT | 4

popcorn now nets an income of $1.5 million annually. The capitalized value of Bonnie Blair's name, then, becomes ($1,500,000 − $500,000)/.15 = $6,666,666.67. That is to say, a name can also be valuable property.

You can see, can't you, why winning at Wimbledon is so financially important to the players? Their names become valuable properties that enhance the market value of the rackets they promote and, as a result, the market value of the firms producing the rackets.

INCOME FROM RENT

If you were playing a word-association game and someone said "rent," what would you say? Most people would say "apartment" or "house." But economists wouldn't. To economists, rent describes a payment for the use of a resource in production. The resource generating the rent can be labor or capital or land. That is, rent is paid to laborers for the use of their labor in precisely the same way that rent is paid to landowners for the use of their land.

Economists define **rent** as *the difference between what the resource receives as payment for its use in production and the payment that was necessary to bring the supply of the resource into being.* Let's see how this works.

The Derivation of Land Rent

Consider rent derived from the use of land. Even without improvements, land is a productive resource. It is the wellspring of our raw materials, our foodstuffs, and our fuels. Perhaps the most remarkable feature about land is its supply price, or cost. We don't have to use any labor or capital to bring land in its natural state into existence. It is simply there, part of our natural heritage. Economists, therefore, consider the supply price of land to be zero.

How does land rent arise? Consider the island economy depicted in panel *a* of Exhibit 5, where its 120,000 acres are privately owned and used to produce the island's food. The island's supply curve of land, *S*, is vertical, reflecting the fact that the 120,000 acres are always available for cultivation, whatever the price per acre. The three demand curves for land—the *MRP* curves of land—are each downward sloping, reflecting the law of diminishing returns.

Why three demand curves for land? Each describes a different size of population on the island. To illustrate how these different populations affect rent determination, let's start with demand curve *D*, which represents a low-level population. The demand curve *D* falls to 0 at the 40,000th acre because relatively little food is needed to support the island's scant population. Eighty thousand acres are left unused. The price of land is $0. That is to say, land on the island is a free good. How could any landowner get a penny of **land rent** under these conditions?

But let's suppose that population growth increases the demand for food. As a result, the price of food rises. Because *MRP* of land = *MPP* of land × price of food, the *MRP* curve increases, which is shown in panel *a* of Exhibit 5 as an upward shift in the demand curve for land, from *D* to D_1. All 120,000 acres are cultivated. The price of land, determined by the intersection of demand and supply, is now $50 per acre. But note: Although food producers using the 120,000 acres pay the $50 per acre market price of land, the supply price of land—the cost to the landowners of bringing land into being—remains $0. After all, the 120,000 acres were always there! Nobody had to do anything to bring them into being. The land rent, then, which is the difference between the payment the resource receives ($50 per acre) and its supply price ($0), is the $50. In other words, in the D_1 and *S* market for land,

Rent
The difference between what a productive resource receives as payment for its use in production and the cost of bringing that resource into production.

CHECK YOUR UNDERSTANDING

Why is the supply price for land zero?

Land rent
A payment to landowners for the use of land.

landowners, who have done absolutely nothing to bring their land into being, end up with a rent of $50 per acre. Adam Smith, in his celebrated 1776 *The Wealth of Nations,* described this rent-emerging outcome in the following way: "Landlords reap where they have never sowed." Perceptive, wasn't he?

Suppose population continues to increase, driving up food prices and, consequently, the *MRP* of land. This is shown as a shift in the demand curve for land from D_1 to D_2. As you see, the price of land, determined by the new intersection of demand and supply in the land market, increases from $50 to $75 per acre. Because it still costs $0 to bring those 120,000 acres into being, land rent increases from $50 to $75 per acre.

Differential Rent

Let's now add a new dimension to rent determination by examining an economy in which the supply of land is not entirely costless. For example, consider the Netherlands, where the energetic Dutch, having run out of usable land to feed their population, resorted to wresting land from the sea by building a system of dikes. The supply price of those captured-from-the-sea acres—that is, the maintenance cost of the dike system—is greater than $0.

Panel *b* in Exhibit 5 depicts the Dutch land market. The supply curve of land, *S,* is upward sloping in a steplike fashion. The first 40,000 acres are above sea level and require no cost to bring into being. But that's not the case for the remaining 80,000 acres. For example, the second 40,000 acres require a $50 maintenance cost per acre, while the third 40,000 acres—further out to sea—require a $75 cost per acre.

DERIVING LAND RENT AND DIFFERENTIAL LAND RENT

In panel *a*, the supply curve for land is fixed at 120,000 acres. The supply price for these acres is $0. When the demand curve for land is D, the price per acre is $0, creating no land rent. When population increases to shift demand for land to D_1, the price per acre increases to $50, creating a $50-per-acre land rent. When demand for land increases to D_2, the price per acre increases to $75, creating a $75-per-acre land rent. In panel *b,* the supply curve for land is upward sloping, creating different supply prices for the 120,000 acres. The supply price is $0 for the first 40,000 acres, $50 for the second 40,000, and $75 for the third 40,000. When demand is D, there's $0 rent. When it increases to D_1, the first 40,000 acres receive $50 per acre rent, while the second 40,000 under cultivation is $0-rent land. When demand increases to D_2, the first 40,000 receives $75 per acre, the second 40,000 receives $25 per acre, and the last 40,000 becomes $0-rent land.

INTERDISCIPLINARY PERSPECTIVE

THE FATHER OF FISH

Traveler: Once in a while, if you travel far inland, you will chance upon an old man sitting by a river. This man has a big knife, but he does not intend it for you. Rather, he just sits there and whittles away at pieces of wood. All day and all night he whittles. The chips and splinters fly off and drop into the water, where they become alive. And by the time they reach the sea, they've turned into salmon, char, cod, capelin, lumpsuckers, and

IN THE BEGINNING . . .

halibut. This man is the father of all fish. Do not kill him.

CONSIDER

A beautiful story of creation, isn't it? It is an Eskimo tale that appears in a collection of stories gathered and retold by Lawrence Millman in a volume titled *A Kayak Full of Ghosts.* To an economist, it tells not only how the Eskimo people describe Genesis, but also provides information on the supply price of fish, land, and other natural resources. Resources are magical gifts of nature. Cost to society? Zero.

Differential land rent
Rent arising from differences in the cost of providing land.

Let's use the three demand curves to illustrate how **differential land rent** emerges in the Netherlands. With scant Dutch population, the demand curve for land is D, downward sloping to 0 at 40,000 acres. There is no need for more acreage, so that the price of land and land rent are $0. But suppose that a population increase shifts the demand curve for land from D to D_1. Instead of accepting the fixity of land supply at 40,000 acres, the Dutch build a dike system that increases land supply from 40,000 to 80,000 acres. But the second 40,000 acres comes into being only at a $50 cost per acre.

The market price per acre—determined by the intersection of demand and supply—is $50 per acre, just as it was in panel *a*. But look at land-rent derivation in this case. The supply price of land for the first 40,000 acres—the cost to the landowners of bringing those acres into being—remains $0. The land rent per acre, then, which is the difference between the market price those acres command ($50) and their supply price ($0), is $50. Total land rent is $50 × 40,000 acres, or $2,000,000 (the gold-shaded area A). What about land rent on the 40,000 acres captured from the sea? It's not $50, but $0. Why? Because the supply price of those acres—the cost of bringing them into being—is $50, which equals the $50 market price of land. In other words, the last 40,000 acres are $0-rent-yielding acres.

If the demand curve for land shifts to D_2, adding another 40,000 acres to supply at a supply price of $75, then the market price of land rises to $75 per acre. Note what it does to land rent. On the first 40,000 acres, land rent increases from $50 to $75 per acre. On the second 40,000 acres, it increases from $0 to $25, and land rent on the last 40,000 acres is $0. Total land rent, then, increases to $4,000,000—$75 × 40,000 acres = $3,000,000 on the first 40,000 acres (the gold- and green-shaded areas A and B), and $25 × 40,000 acres = $1,000,000 on the second 40,000 acres (the green-shaded area C).

HISTORICAL PERSPECTIVE

THE CORN LAWS CONTROVERSY IN 19TH-CENTURY ENGLAND

The rent analysis of Exhibit 5 has historical roots. During the 1790s, the price of corn (which we call grain) in England more than doubled, and it continued to increase during the early decades of the 19th century. This extraordinary upward thrust in corn prices triggered a bitter controversy among English capitalists and landowners over the relationship between the price of corn and rent, and the impact this relationship had on the distribution of income.

The conventional wisdom among economists of the 19th century was that landowners—then the most powerful class in England—were the sole benefactors of an unavoidable circumstance: The growth of population made cultivable land more scarce, and this increasing land scarcity drove up rent. Since rent was regarded as a cost of production, higher rent meant higher food costs and higher food prices. In other words, high rent *explains* high food prices.

David Ricardo, one of the most brilliant economists of the period (and perhaps since) joined in the discussion on rent and food prices but reversed the order of causation. In his celebrated book *On the Principles of Political Economy and Taxation* (1817), he developed the theory of differential rent. Ricardo argued that land has nothing to do with the cost of producing food. Labor and capital are the only real costs.

How then do land and rent come into the picture? Since population growth forces farmers to bring more land under cultivation, and since the new lands are typically less fertile than lands already in cultivation (requiring more labor time to produce the same quantity of food), and since price is determined by the costs of producing on the least-favorable land, the farmers working the more favorable lands reap the differential between their own costs of producing food and the increasing price of food. That differential is rent. In other words, price is rent-determining; rent is not price-determining. That is to say, high food prices *explain* high rent.

How, then, to keep rent in check? Ricardo's answer was international trade. Importing cheaper corn from Europe would reduce the need to cultivate poor English land, reduce the cost of producing food, and reduce corn prices in England; this, in turn, would reduce rent. The English land-owning class understood the argument only too well and, to protect its rent, voted in Parliament—which it controlled—for corn laws that fixed high tariffs on imported corn. Keeping imported corn out meant keeping English rents in.

While the corn laws were good news for English landowners, they were bad news for English capitalists. After all, restricting corn imports kept corn prices high at home. The money wages that capitalists paid to workers, then, had to be raised to keep pace with the rising corn prices. Higher money wages meant lower profit. The trade-off was clear and politically loaded: High rents for landowners or high profits for capitalists.

The struggle between the landowning and capitalist classes over the corn laws raged on until mid-century. In the end, the growing economic and political power of the English capitalist class prevailed, and in 1846 the corn laws were repealed.

MORE ON THE NET

Learn more about the ideas of David Ricardo (http://www.systemics.com/docs/ricardo/david.html) and review *On the Principles of Political Economy and Taxation* (http://socserv2.socsci.mcmaster.ca/~econ/ugcm/3ll3/ricardo/index.html).

Location Rent

The analysis used to explain differential rent explains **location rent** as well. Location rent arises from differences in the cost of transporting goods from the location of the producing acre to the market. Exhibit 6 depicts the circumstances that give rise to location rents. Again, suppose three different demand curves for food reflect three different-sized populations. Suppose the low-level population's demand for food can be satisfied by cultivating acres adjacent to the market, shown in the center of the circle. Acre *a* is one such acre. These are no-rent-yielding acres as long as

Location rent
Rent arising from differences in land distances from the marketplace.

CHECK YOUR UNDERSTANDING

Which acres receive no rent?

the supply price of land, including transportation costs in getting goods produced on these acres to market, is $0. But suppose population growth increases the demand for food, causing producers to cultivate acres some distance away from the market. After all, there are just so many acres adjacent to the market, and no more! Suppose acre *b*, 25 miles from the market, is cultivated, and its goods are transported to market at a cost of $10. The supply price (including cost of transportation) of acre *b* is $10, and the acre becomes the new no-rent land. On the other hand, acre *a*, having no transportation cost associated with it, enjoys a newly found $10 location rent.

If the demand for food increases to bring acre *c*, 50 miles from the market, into cultivation, the supply price increases to account for a higher transportation cost, say, $20. Now acre *c* becomes the no-rent land, acre *b* enjoys a $10 location rent, and acre *a*'s location rent increases to $20. You see the similarity to differential land-rent derivation, don't you? In both cases, it's the difference between the market price of the acre and its supply price. With respect to location rent, landowners whose acres are close to the market are fortunate; those whose acres are just beyond the acres needed to satisfy the market might just as well own an acre on the moon.

RELOCATING THE MARKETPLACE CHANGES LANDOWNERS' FORTUNES Which landowner gets what location rent depends, as we see, on where the marketplace is located. For example, if the marketplace of Exhibit 6 were replaced by a marketplace located at acre *c*, a very different set of landowners would end up with rent. Acre *a* would become no-rent land.

EXHIBIT | 6

A NEW SET OF RENT-YIELDING ACRES

The market is located at the center of the concentric circles. The supply price of all acres under cultivation reflects only the cost of transporting the goods from the acres to market. When the demand for land is limited to those acres at the market, there is no location rent. When demand increases to bring acre *b* into cultivation, the supply price per acre increases to $10, creating a $10 location rent on all acres adjacent to the market. When demand increases to bring acre *c* under cultivation, the supply per acre increases to $20, creating a $20 location rent for acre *a* and a $10 location rent for acre *b*. Acre *c* becomes the new $0-rent acre.

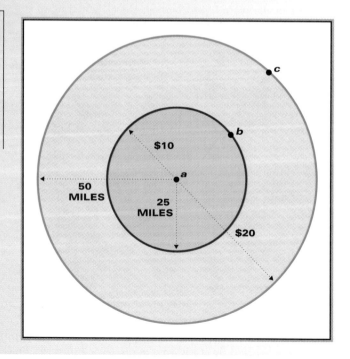

SHOPPING MALLS REARRANGE RENTS It isn't difficult to understand, then, how a new shopping mall, built on the outskirts of town, will create absolute havoc among landowners of downtown property. If Sears, J.C. Penney, and other department stores decide to relocate to shopping malls, rents accruing to downtown properties are virtually destroyed.

What once had been high-rent downtown property becomes potential urban blight overnight. What once had been a source of substantial location rent becomes virtually worthless overnight. On the other hand, there are people who by chance own property close to the new shopping mall, and overnight they become high-location-rent receivers. In the fast-changing modern world of marketplaces, location rents come and go.

Wage-Related Rents

Rent emerges as a component of wage-related income as well. Consider baseball players' incomes. How many times have you seen a superstar interviewed on television after signing a $2 million contract tell the interviewer that although the money is all right, he really loves the game and, gosh, would have played for nothing?

Is he believable? Of course not! But if he really would play for nothing, his $2 million income would be entirely **wage-related rent.** After all, rent is the difference between what a resource receives and what it takes to bring the supply of that resource to the market. His professed willingness to play for nothing sets his supply price at $0. The difference, then, between his income and his supply price is the full $2 million.

He probably would have signed the contract for something less than $2 million. How much less? Suppose his next-best job opportunity would be selling insurance, which would provide him with an income of $30,000. In this circumstance, he would play baseball for anything above $30,000. The rent component of his $2 million baseball contract then is $1,970,000.

Can you imagine how much of quarterback Jeff George's income is rent? But what about opera singers, fashion designers, lawyers, university deans, and corporate presidents? For many, a good part of their incomes are well above their supply price. In fact, almost everyone's income has some element of rent built into it. What examples can you offer?

Consider the incomes earned by the coal miners in Exhibit 7.

The equilibrium wage rate is $13. But as you see in the supply curve of labor, only the 125th miner has a $13 supply price. Every one of the 124 other miners employed would have worked for less. For example, even at a $4 wage rate, 10 miners would work, although they certainly prefer the $13 wage rate they receive to the $4 they would be willing to accept. The $13 − $4 = $9 difference is the rent component in their $13 wage rate.

What about the other coal miners? The total rent generated in the labor market of Exhibit 7 is the sum of the differences between the $13

on the net

Consider what may happen to landowner rents as shopping malls, like ShowNow.com (http://www.stores.shopnow.com/) form in cyberspace.

Wage-related rent
The difference between what a resource receives and what it takes to bring the supply of that resource to market.

EXHIBIT | 7

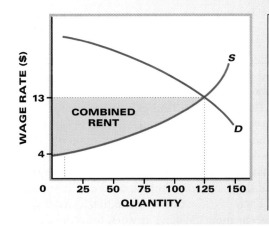

THE RENT COMPONENT IN COAL MINERS' WAGES

The supply curve of labor, *S*, reflects the miners' willingness to supply labor at varying wage rates. The equilibrium wage rate is $13 and the quantity of labor demanded and supplied is 125. At a wage rate of $4, the quantity of labor supplied is 10. For these 10 coal miners, the wage they receive is $13 − $4 = $9 more than their supply price—that is, the price they would have been willing to work for. This $9 difference defines the rent component of their wage. Of the $13 × 125 = $1,625 wage income earned by the 125 coal miners, the shaded area represents their combined rent.

equilibrium wage rate and the specific supply prices of each miner. Of the $13 ×
125 = $1,625 wage income earned by the miners, the shaded area in Exhibit 7 rep-
resents their combined rents.

your turn

*What examples of wage-related rent can you
offer? Go to the Interactive Study Center at
http://gottheil.swcollege.com and click on the
"Your Turn" button to submit your example. Student submissions will be posted to the Web site,
and perhaps we will use some in future editions
of the book!*

Think about the work you have
done, the wage rate you received,
and the minimum rate you would
have accepted. Like quarterback
Jeff George and the coal miners
of Exhibit 7, wouldn't some part
of your wage-related income be
pure rent?

INCOME FROM PROFITS

Laborers, loanable funds suppliers, and landowners receive wages, interest, and
rent because they provide the resources used in production. What do entrepreneurs provide that explains their source of income?

Profit Income earned by entrepreneurs.

   Profit is the reward for undertaking the uncertainties of enterprise. Many people
have great ideas about products and production and some of them actually transform their ideas into successful realities, but if the willingness to take a chance at
enterprise is lacking, great ideas remain just great ideas.

We Are a Nation of Thomas Edisons

Everybody knows the story of Thomas Edison. He not only invented the electric
light but converted the invention into a massive fortune by creating the General
Electric Company. He is *the* classic example of the entrepreneur. But let's play
lightly with history and make up another version of the popular Thomas Edison
story. Let's imagine he invented the electric light and stopped right there.

   Suppose Edison felt uneasy about committing himself to the financial obligation
involved in setting up the General Electric Company. Suppose he was quite willing
and able to contribute all his creative and organizational energies to mass-producing
the electric light, but he was unwilling to bear the financial uncertainties of enterprise. If that were the Thomas Edison story, we might still be reading by candlelight.

   Or, consider still another version of the tale. Thomas Edison's electric light could
not long remain a secret. Some energetic entrepreneur heard about Edison's invention, bought the rights to his patent, and even put him on salary as production manager. We still end up with General Electric and the electric light. Thomas Edison, in
this version, ends up a millionaire. But no matter how much salary he receives, he
never earns one penny of profit. Profit is the reward for entrepreneurship.

   While large industrial conglomerates cast giant shadows over the thousands of
small firms that make up our economy, these small firms are still very much alive
and flourishing. Their successes are forever invitations for others to try. And others
always do.

   Chef Ra's Pizza House, Julia Johnstone's Shoe Repair, Frances Reedy's Computer
Service, Jenny McMahon's Beauty Shop, P. Gregory Springer's Record Swap, Eric
Schor's Dry Cleaners, Paul Chastain's Electrical Appliances, Garret Jakobsson's
Bookstore, Karen Turk's Plumbing, Jon Ginoli's Construction, and Geoff Merritt's
That's Rentertainment video store are products of entrepreneurship. These firms
and thousands of others flood the yellow pages of every city's telephone directory.

   Each of these firms, at one time, was just a good idea in the mind of a would-be
entrepreneur. Making it work took physical and psychological stamina, business

acumen, a twist of good luck, and a willingness to accept the inevitable fortunes or misfortunes of enterprise.

Geoff Merritt, for example, founded That's Rentertainment with $200,000, four years' experience as a Blockbuster manager, and some new ideas. In less than three years, his firm showed a net return of $125,000. But Merritt knew that this $125,000 was not all a return on entrepreneurship.

After all, he could have stayed at Blockbuster and earned a salary of $50,000. Although he never considered the time spent at his own firm as salaried labor, the labor time he put into the company does nonetheless represent a $50,000 opportunity cost.

But the $50,000 isn't the only opportunity cost incurred. The $200,000 invested in setting up the video store could have been invested instead in the loanable funds market at 15 percent. That would have yielded $30,000. In other words, Geoff Merritt could have earned $80,000 annually in salary and interest if he had chosen not to become an entrepreneur.

What, then, is Merritt's profit? It is his income adjusted for the implicit costs of his labor and money capital. In other words, $125,000 − $80,000 = $45,000 of income is real profit, representing the return on entrepreneurial ability.

Geoff Merritt, owner of That's Rentertainment (http://www.rentertainment.com/), left his job with Blockbuster video to become an entrepreneur. Geoff also owns Parasol Records (http://www.parasol.com/), an independent record label located in Urbana, Illinois.

The Invisible Entrepreneurs at General Motors

What about the profit earned by large corporations like General Motors? Is any part of their corporate profit a return on entrepreneurial ability? Where would you find entrepreneurs at General Motors? Who, for example, are its visionaries? Who designs the automobiles, gets the auto plants in motion, unravels the knots, acquires financial obligations, and risks everything on the uncertainties of consumer choice?

There are people at General Motors who do the same things Merritt does. Although decision making there is not combined in one person, the necessary talent to make decisions on what to produce and how to produce it is there. Decision-making talent is found in the planning and research departments, in engineering and design, and even in the departments of finance and marketing.

But the people working in these departments are not risking their money. It is the stockholders who venture their money. Stockholders own the company and hire corporate managers to run the business. The managers' incomes are strictly salary. In theory, GM's stockholders have the decision-making powers to hire or fire anyone, to produce what they want, and to decide how they want it produced. That is, the ultimate power of entrepreneurial decision making rests with them. GM's corporate profit is their income. They alone assume all the uncertainties of the business. Even though stockholders may be silent and perhaps even invisible, they are nonetheless General Motors's entrepreneurs.

Visit General Motors (http://www.gm.com/). What information about stockholders is available?

CHAPTER REVIEW

1. The productivity of capital can be measured in much the same way as we measure the productivity of labor. Adding dollar increments of capital to a production process increases total physical product but by smaller and smaller amounts, which generates the downward-sloping marginal physical product of capital curve.

2. The marginal revenue product of capital per dollar is the marginal physical product of capital per dollar multiplied by the price of the good the capital produces.

3. A firm's demand for loanable funds (which it transforms into capital equipment) is the *MRP* of capital per dollar employed. A firm will employ the quantity of loanable funds up to the dollar where $MRP = MFC$.

4. The market demand curve for loanable funds is the sum of the MRP of the capital curves of the individual firms.

5. The supply curve of loanable funds is upward sloping. It reflects the willingness of people to make these funds available, the quantity depending on the interest rate.

6. The argument used to justify interest-bearing income is based on the idea that capital is a person's property just as labor power is the property of the worker and that the owner of capital is entitled to the MRP produced by the capital just as a worker is entitled to the MRP produced by his or her labor.

7. The present value of a property is equal to the annual revenue generated by the property divided by the interest rate. The revenue-yielding property can be tangible, as in a farm, or intangible, as in a name.

8. Land rent is the difference between what an acre receives as payment for its use—the market price of land—and the cost of bringing that acre into being—its supply price.

9. Differential land rent arises from differences in the supply price of the acres brought into production.

10. Location rent arises from differences in the transportation costs of bringing an acre's production to market.

11. Wage-related rent arises from differences in the opportunity cost of bringing labor into production. It reflects the difference between what a worker receives (the wage rate) and what the worker would have been willing to work for (the supply price).

12. Profit is what entrepreneurs earn for undertaking the risks and uncertainties of enterprise. It is distinct from the wages or salaries entrepreneurs may receive for providing managerial skills. The entrepreneurs associated with modern corporations are its many stockholders, who assume all corporate risk and uncertainty, which generate for the stockholders their profit (or losses). Corporate managers earn salaries.

KEY TERMS

Marginal revenue product of capital
Loanable funds
Capital equipment
Interest rate

Marginal factor cost
Loanable funds market
Present value
Rent
Land rent

Differential land rent
Location rent
Wage-related rent
Profit

QUESTIONS

1. Economists use precisely the same tools to analyze rates of interest as they do to analyze wage rates. Discuss.

2. How does a firm decide what quantity of loanable funds it should demand from the loanable funds market when the interest rate is 10 percent?

3. Why would anyone be willing to supply loanable funds on the loanable funds market?

4. Distinguish between loanable funds and capital equipment.

5. What factors change the rate of interest?

6. What arguments can you make to justify people living off interest-derived income?

7. What arguments can you make against people living off interest-derived income?

8. You don't have to work to be productive. Explain.

9. Suppose you were interested in buying the New York Yankees. If the Yankees generated an annual income of $30 million and if the rate of interest was 10 percent, what would be

the present value of the New York Yankees? If the rate of interest fell to 5 percent, would you have to pay more, less, or the same for the team? Explain.

10. Government's support of farm prices has affected the value of farm property. Why?

11. A little strip of land by Fenway Park in Boston, which is the home of the Boston Red Sox, is a choice location for a sandwich shop. There, a hot dog sells for $3. Two blocks away, the same hot dog sells for $1. The rent paid by the Fenway Park sandwich-shop owner is much higher than the rent paid by the owner of the shop two blocks away. Is the $3 hot dog price high because rent is high at the Fenway Park location, or is rent there high because hot dogs sell for $3?

12. If the coal mining firms were able to get together and cut miners' wage rates in half, many coal miners would quit the mines. On the other hand, if major-league owners were able to get together and cut baseball salaries in half, very few of the ballplayers would quit baseball. Why?

13. When Sears decides to move from its downtown location to a shopping mall on the outskirts of town, some people suffer loss of rent, while others end up getting more rent. Why?

14. The market for loanable funds is described in the following demand and supply schedule.

INTEREST RATE (%)	QUANTITY DEMANDED	QUANTITY SUPPLIED
14	$1,000	$5,000
12	2,000	4,000
10	3,000	3,000
8	4,000	2,000
6	5,000	1,000

Suppliers of loanable funds would prefer 14 percent to any other interest rate in the table. But 14 percent is not what they will receive. Why not? Explain fully.

15. Graph the loanable funds market of question 14. Suppose the government imposes an interest rate ceiling of 12 percent. What consequences would that ceiling have on the loanable funds market?

PRACTICE PROBLEMS

1. Calculate, using the following table, the marginal revenue product of capital for each of the five quantities of capital when the price of eggs is $0.10 per egg.

LOANABLE FUNDS	TOTAL PRODUCT (EGGS)	SUPPLY PRICE (PER $)
$10	25	.05
20	45	.10
30	60	.15
40	70	.20
50	75	.25

2. Calculate the equilibrium rate of interest in the egg-producing economy of practice problem 1.

3. Calculate, using the following table, the missing rates of interest, annual revenues, and present values.

INTEREST RATE	ANNUAL REVENUE	PRESENT VALUE
.10		$2,000
.05	$50	
	$20	$1,000

4. Calculate, using the following table, the total value of differential rent generated in the economy when the market price per acre is $30.

ACRES	SUPPLY PRICE
1	$ 0
2	10
3	20
4	30
5	40

5. Calculate, using the following table, the total value of location rent generated in the economy when it costs $2 per mile to transport an acre's goods to market, when the supply price per acre is the acre's transportation cost, and the market price per acre is $40.

ACRES	DISTANCE FROM MARKET (MILES)
1	0
2	5
3	10
4	15
5	20

6. How much wage-related rent is generated in each of the following cases?

PROFESSION	SALARY	NEXT BEST ALTERNATIVE	SALARY AT NEXT BEST ALTERNATIVE	WAGE-RELATED RENT
PROFESSOR OF MUSIC	$ 55,000	PROFESSOR OF HISTORY	$ 55,000	
WELDER	$ 48,000	PLUMBER	$ 42,000	
SCHOOLTEACHER	$ 35,000	SOCIAL WORKER	$ 30,000	
COLLEGE BASKETBALL COACH	$750,000	SCHOOLTEACHER	$ 35,000	
RADIOLOGIST	$350,000	PROFESSOR OF MEDICINE	$120,000	
STAND-UP COMIC	$ 80,000	ACCOUNTANT	$ 65,000	

7. How much wage-related rent is generated in the labor market when the equilibrium wage rate is $20?

QUANTITY SUPPLIED OF LABOR	WAGE RATE
1	$10
2	$12
3	$14
4	$16
5	$18
6	$20
7	$22
8	$24

WHAT'S WRONG WITH THIS GRAPH?

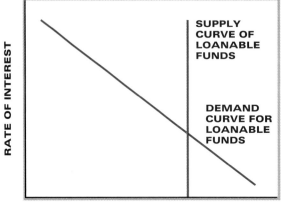

MARKET FOR LOANABLE FUNDS

ECONOMIC CONSULTANTS

ECONOMIC RESEARCH AND ANALYSIS BY STUDENTS FOR PROFESSIONALS

Kirsten Gentry is an engineer with a computer manufacturer in San Francisco, California. Kirsten has lived in an apartment for the past three years, and she now wishes to buy a home. Kirsten earns $60,000 per year, and she has a take-home salary (after taxes and deductions) of $3,000 per month. Kirsten wishes to devote no more than 40 percent of her take-home salary to a monthly mortgage payment, and she is able to contribute $15,000 as a down payment.

Kirsten has hired Economic Consultants to help her figure out what type of home she can afford. Prepare a report for Kirsten that addresses the following issues:

1. What is the maximum amount Kirsten wishes to spend on monthly mortgage payments?
2. Assume that Kirsten wants a simple 30-year, fixed-interest-rate mortgage, and that the lowest interest rate available to her is 8 percent. What is the most expensive home Kirsten can afford? (Assume there are no other fees associated with the mortgage.) What types of homes are avail-

able to Kirsten in this price range?
3. Kirsten has the option to move to her firm's offices in Omaha, Nebraska, at the same salary. Is her opportunity to purchase a larger home better in Omaha? What are the opportunity costs of moving to Omaha? Kirsten, for example, loves fresh seafood.

You may find the following resources helpful as you prepare this report for Kirsten:

- **Hugh's Simple Loan Payment Calculator** (http://www.interest.com/hugh/calc/simple.cgi)—Hugh's Simple Loan Payment Calculator enables simple, fixed-rate mortgage calculations.
- **RE/MAX Realtors of San Francisco** (http://www.sanfrancisco-homes.com/)—RE/MAX provides home listings for the San Francisco area.
- **Metropolitan Omaha Builders Association (MOBA)** (http://www.moba.com/) MOBA provides home listings for the Omaha area.

PRACTICE TEST

1. The marginal revenue product of capital is
   a. the marginal physical product of capital divided by the interest rate.
   b. the change in the marginal physical product divided by the change in the quantity of capital.
   c. the change in total revenue resulting from adding a dollar of loanable funds to production.
   d. the total revenue derived from the last dollar of loanable funds multiplied by the interest rate.
   e. the rate of interest.

2. The rate of interest is
   a. the marginal revenue product of capital.
   b. the price of loanable funds, expressed as an annual percentage return on a dollar of loanable funds.
   c. the difference between the cost of borrowing and the cost of lending a dollar of loanable funds.
   d. the difference between the marginal revenue product of capital and the marginal physical product of capital.
   e. the charge or penalty firms pay to banks for having failed to meet their loan obligations to the bank.

3. The marginal revenue product of capital is to the interest rate what
   a. the marginal revenue product of labor is to the wage rate.
   b. the marginal factor cost of capital is to the marginal physical product of capital.
   c. the interest rate is to present value.
   d. present value is to property value.
   e. rent is to the marginal factor cost of land.

4. The $MRP = MFC$ rule is used to
   a. calculate how much profit a firm makes hiring a factor of production.
   b. determine how much of a good a firm should produce to maximize profit.
   c. equate the interest rate to the rate of profit.
   d. determine the quantity of a factor of production the firm should employ.
   e. equate marginal revenue product to marginal factor cost.

5. The supply curve of loanable funds
   a. is downward sloping, reflecting how the law of diminishing returns is applied to the loanable funds market.
   b. is downward sloping, relating the quantity of saving supplied on the loanable funds market to the interest rate.
   c. is upward sloping, relating the quantity of saving supplied on the loanable funds market to the interest rate.
   d. is horizontal, relating the quantity of saving supplied on the loanable funds market to the interest rate.
   e. is horizontal, relating the firm's willingness to use loanable funds at different interest rates.

6. The present value of a property depends on the stream of future revenues from that property and the interest rate. The relationship between these revenues, the rate, and present value is that
   a. present value is equal to the annual return on a property divided by the interest rate.
   b. present value is equal to the annual return on a property multiplied by the interest rate.
   c. present value is equal to the interest rate divided by the annual return on a property.
   d. present value is equal to the difference between the annual return on a property and the annual rate of interest payments.
   e. the interest rate multiplied by present value equals the annual return on a property.

7. Rent is defined as
   a. the payment a landlord receives for the leasing of property.
   b. the difference between the marginal physical product of a resource and the marginal physical product of the resource's next best alternative.
   c. the difference between what a resource receives as payment for its use in production and the cost of bringing that resource into production.
   d. the marginal physical product of land.
   e. the marginal revenue product of land.

8. Once upon a time Little Red Riding Hood was on her way to Granny's when a big bad wolf leaped out of the woods. He was just about to eat her up when Superboy came by and slew the wolf. Granny, ever so thankful, offered Superboy her granddaughter in marriage or land that generated revenues of $100 every year, forever. Knowing that the interest rate was 10 percent, Superboy chose the land. Disappointed, Little Red Riding Hood asked why he chose the land, and he replied: "Because you aren't worth

   _____.
   a. 10 percent a year."
   b. $100."
   c. $1,000."
   d. $100,000."
   e. $1 million."

18

INCOME DISTRIBUTION AND POVERTY

Why are some people rich and others poor? Why are there so many more poor? Can anything be done about the distribution of income among people? *Should* anything be done about it? Would it really matter what we do?

Questions about the rich and the poor are, of course, not the monopoly of economists. They arise from the political, ethical, and even religious foundations of our society. The Bible, for example, tells us very little about how people come to acquire income, but it is very explicit about what we should do with it once we get it. The one thing we cannot do—and expect redemption—is ignore the poor:

> When you reap the harvest in your field, and overlook a sheaf in the field, do not turn your back to get it. . . . when you beat down the fruit of the olive trees, do not go over them

THIS CHAPTER INTRODUCES YOU TO THE ECONOMIC PRINCIPLES ASSOCIATED WITH:

- THE LORENZ CURVE
- THE GINI COEFFICIENT
- RAWLS'S THEORY OF JUSTICE
- LIFE CYCLE WEALTH
- THE CASE FOR INCOME EQUALITY
- THE CASE FOR INCOME INEQUALITY
- POVERTY THRESHOLDS
- NEGATIVE INCOME TAX

again; that shall go over to the stranger, the fatherless, and the widow.

These caring directives are matched by concerns over differences between rich and poor. The biblical text tells us that it is unacceptable not only to ignore the needs of the poor, but also to condone the wasteful extravagance of the rich.

The Greek philosophers wrestled with the same issues. Plato and Aristotle, no less concerned about the distribution of income among rich and poor, tied their arguments not to sin and salvation but to political instability. Plato, writing in the aftermath of the Peloponnesian wars, saw a functional relationship between income inequality and political discontent.

He argued for policy that would limit the extremes among rich and poor. In his *Laws,* he suggested that the income of the richest citizen should be no greater than five times the income of the poorest. Plato's concerns were shared by Aristotle. He, too, considered poverty the parent of revolution and crime. Unlike Plato, however, he relied on individual benevolence, believing it more important to equalize desires than property.

The questions concerning income distribution haven't really changed that much in 2,500 years. We still ask why some people are rich and others poor, and why there still seem to be so many more poor than rich. Many still ask whether anything can be done about the situation. And there are many who, no less compassionate than others, are uncertain whether anything should be done—assuming that anything could be done.

But there is one difference. Although we still wrestle with the same questions concerning income distribution, we are also wrestling with questions concerning income determination. Moreover, the one seems to have direct bearing on the other. A person's income seems to be connected to that person's productive contribution in the market. The rich are rich, then, because they are relatively productive. The poor are poor because they are not.

NOT TOO MANY COAL MINERS ARE MILLIONAIRES

You can generally make a fair guess about a person's economic status merely by knowing the principal source of the person's income. Coal miners are typically 100 percent wage earners. It is unlikely, no matter how successful the United Mine Workers Union may be in raising wages, that a coal miner would be found among the top 500 richest people in the country.

Other people earn income by other means. For example, for some individuals, the only source of income is the interest they receive. Landowners' income is derived from rent. Some individuals do nothing but cash the dividend checks they receive as corporate stockholders.

These different forms of income—wages, interest, rent, and profit—are not mutually exclusive. An individual's income may be some combination of these four forms of income. Most coal miners' incomes are wage derived, yet some miners may invest some loanable funds and generate modest sums of interest. Some may be shareholders in corporations that yield dividends. Some may even own real estate that provides rental income. But no matter how many of these income forms contribute to their total income, most coal miners would still think of themselves as wage earners and not see themselves as particularly rich.

Who are the very rich? They too probably have multiple sources of income, but it is highly unlikely that wages would count as their primary source. What makes them rich, and separates them from coal miners, are their interest, rent, and profit.

When there is a shift in either the supply curves or *MRP* curves of labor, capital, or land, the equilibrium wage rates, interest rates, and rents also change. As a result, people's incomes increase or decrease. A fall in the interest rate or an increase in the wage rate makes some people richer and others less so. Income disparities among people widen or narrow. But such price changes seldom make poor people rich, or rich people poor. You are more likely to identify the rich and poor by their primary form of income than by the ebbs and flows in their income. Rich people become poor—and the poor, rich—most often by changing their occupation or their source of income.

MEASURING INCOME DISTRIBUTION

Every society has its own rich and poor. In some the rich are considerably richer than the poor. In others the income disparities between rich and poor are less extreme. Would you suppose that income is more equal in Russia than in Sweden? How about Sweden compared to the United States? How would you measure the differences in income distribution? Has income inequality among rich and poor in the United States changed much since 1950? How would you go about measuring the change?

There are two principal techniques used by economists to measure an economy's income distribution. These are the Lorenz curve, developed by American statistician Max Lorenz, and the Gini coefficient, developed by Italian statistician Corrado Gini.

The Lorenz Curve

The **Lorenz curve** provides a quick visual expression of income distribution. It shows what percentage of an economy's total income each part of the population receives. Typically, the population is divided into deciles—10 groups, each with 10 percent of the population—or into quintiles—5 groups, each with 20 percent of the population—arranged in sequence from poorest to richest.

THE LORENZ CURVE: A HYPOTHETICAL CASE Perhaps the best way to illustrate Lorenz's technique is to imagine three economies with identical population sizes and total incomes, but with very different patterns of income distribution.

Suppose Washtenau, Springfield, and Holmes each have 1,000 people and $200,000 total income. The per capita income in each economy is $200, but that does not mean that everyone receives $200. Some receive much more, others much less. The table in Exhibit 1 records how the $200,000 is distributed among the 1,000 people in each economy.

The first quintile contains the economy's poorest 200 (of its 1,000 people), the second quintile contains its next 200 poorest, and so on to the fifth quintile, containing its richest 200 people.

Washtenau's distribution portrays *perfect income equality.* Look at the percentage of total income received by each quintile of population. Each 20 percent of the population, each quintile, receives precisely 20 percent of the economy's total income. No one quintile receives more than any other. As you can imagine, there's no distribution equivalent to Washtenau's in the real world, although some economies are closer to perfect income equality than others.

Income distribution in Springfield represents *perfect income inequality.* Look at the percentage of total income received by each quintile of population. Suppose 999 people receive nothing, and one person receives the entire $200,000. That is, four quintiles of the population receive 0 percent of total income, and they are joined by everyone but one of the remaining quintile, who also receive 0 percent of total income. One person—the richest in the economy—ends up with 100 percent of total income. Needless to say, there's no distribution equivalent to Springfield's in our real world, although some economies are much closer to perfect income inequality than others.

What about Holmes? Its poorest quintile receives just four percent of the economy's $200,000 income. The next poorest quintile fares slightly better. It receives seven percent. The richest quintile receives 44 percent of the economy's total income.

If you lived in Holmes, you would probably have little difficulty distinguishing the rich from the poor. They live in different neighborhoods, drive different auto-

Lorenz curve
A curve depicting an economy's income distribution. It records the percentage of total income that a specific part of the population—typically represented by quintiles, ranging from the poorest to richest—receives.

EXHIBIT|1

LORENZ CURVES FOR THE COMMUNITIES OF WASHTENAU, SPRINGFIELD, AND HOLMES

The percentage of population is measured along the horizontal axis, and the percentage of total income the population receives is measured along the vertical axis. Because everyone in Washtenau receives the same income, the Lorenz curve for Washtenau lies along the diagonal. In the Springfield economy, everyone but the richest person receives no income. The Lorenz curve for Springfield falls along the horizontal axis, up to the 100 percent point of population, then rises vertically to 100 percent of income. The Lorenz curve for Holmes shows that the poorest 20 percent of its population receives 4 percent of its income, the poorest 40 percent receives 4 + 7 = 11 percent, and so on, cumulatively, until 100 percent of the population receives 100 percent of the income.

PERCENTAGE OF THE ECONOMY'S TOTAL INCOME HELD BY EACH POPULATION QUINTILE

QUINTILE	WASHTENAU	SPRINGFIELD	HOLMES
POOREST	20	0	4
SECOND	20	0	7
THIRD	20	0	15
FOURTH	20	0	30
RICHEST	20	100	44
TOTAL $	$200,000	$200,000	$200,000

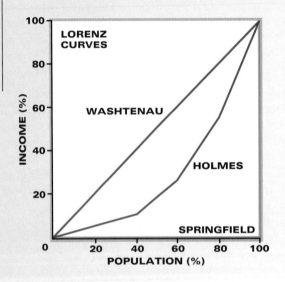

mobiles, go to different schools, eat different foods, take different vacations, work at different occupations, and have different expectations of their children. That is to say, the rich don't just have more money. They have different lifestyles and go through life with much higher levels of self-confidence and self-esteem. These are consciously and subconsciously transmitted to their children, who, in turn, are more able than others to eventually place themselves in the higher quintiles of the economy's income distribution.

The graph in Exhibit 1 translates the table into a Lorenz curve.

How do we graph Washtenau's income distribution? Its Lorenz curve lies along the diagonal of the graph. *Any* 20 percent of the population, which is measured on the horizontal axis, receives 20 percent of total income, which is measured on the vertical axis. *Any* 40 percent of the population receives 40 percent of total income, and so on, cumulatively, to 100 percent of the population receiving 100 percent of total income. *On the diagonal the Lorenz curve represents perfect income equality.*

What about the Lorenz curve for Springfield? It lies along the horizontal axis, from the origin to 100 percent of population, then runs perfectly vertical at that point up to 100 percent of total income. That is, the *Lorenz curve for Springfield is formed by the two sides of a right angle.* Everyone, except the one rich person, receives

CHECK YOUR UNDERSTANDING

Why does a Lorenz curve closer to the diagonal represent a more equal distribution of income?

a total of 0 percent of the economy's income, tracing out the horizontal segment of the Lorenz curve. That one rich person, receiving all the income, traces out the vertical segment of the curve.

Look at Holmes's Lorenz curve. It lies in the area below the diagonal—its distribution is not as equal as Washtenau's—and above the two sides of the right angle—it's also not as unequal as Springfield's. As indicated in the table in Exhibit 1, the poorest quintile receives only 4 percent of the economy's income. Eighty percent of the population—all but the richest quintile—receives 56 percent of total income. The richest quintile alone receives 44 percent.

LORENZ CURVES FOR SWEDEN, BRAZIL, FRANCE, AND THE UNITED STATES Most of the world's distributions are similar to the Lorenz curve for Holmes, positioned somewhere in the area between perfect equality and perfect inequality. But some are closer to the diagonal than others. Look at Exhibit 2. Do the Lorenz curves surprise you?

For example, are you surprised to discover that Sweden's Lorenz curve lies closest to the diagonal, reflecting the most equal income distribution among the four economies shown here? The Lorenz curve for Brazil reflects the most unequal income distribution. The U.S. distribution, slightly more equal than France's, occupies middle ground.

Many of the Lorenz curves drawn for economies are, at best, only rough estimates of the underlying reality. Income data, particularly for less-developed economies like Brazil's, are typically incomplete and, in some cases, nonexistent. Even for economies such as those of Sweden, France, and the United States, Lorenz curve comparisons can be somewhat hazardous.

Some economies have more government-provided goods, such as national security, transportation systems, national parks, health care, education, housing, and food, than others. The distribution of these services among individuals is sometimes impossible to trace. For example, do the rich and poor place the same value on the national security provided them? How much of the national parks or education do the poor receive compared to the rich? Should we simply divide total government spending by total population and *assume* that each person receives the same value? In some economies, these government-provided services make up a larger percentage of total income than in others. How, then, can we compare different Lorenz curves with confidence? We can't.

Gini coefficient
A numerical measure of the degree of income inequality in an economy. It ranges from zero, depicting perfect equality, to one, depicting perfect inequality.

Gini Coefficients of Inequality

Another way to measure an economy's income distribution is by calculating its **Gini coefficient.** The coefficient transforms the Lorenz curve into a numerical value. How is that done? Look at the Lorenz curve of Exhibit 3.

EXHIBIT|2

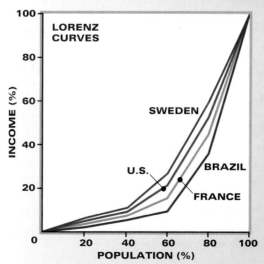

LORENZ CURVES FOR SWEDEN, FRANCE, BRAZIL, AND THE UNITED STATES

The poorest quintile in Sweden receives 7 percent of Sweden's income; its richest quintile receives 40 percent. The poorest quintile in Brazil receives 2 percent; its richest quintile, 66 percent of Brazil's income. These two sets of data trace out the Lorenz curves for Sweden and Brazil. The U.S. curve lies below the Swedish, and the French curve lies slightly below the U.S. curve, but above the Brazilian curve.

EXHIBIT | 3

The Gini coefficient is simply a ratio of the two areas produced by the Lorenz curve. The first is area A, lying between the diagonal and the economy's Lorenz curve. The second is area B, lying below the curve. The Gini coefficient, G, is calculated as

$$G = A/(A + B).$$

If an economy's income distribution is perfect equality, as we saw in the hypothetical example of Washtenau, the Lorenz curve lies on the diagonal, so that A, the area between the curve and the diagonal, compresses to 0. If area $A = 0$, then $G = A/(A + B)$ is also 0. In other words, *the Gini coefficient expressing perfect equality is 0.*

THE GINI COEFFICIENT

The Gini coefficient is the ratio of the two areas produced by the Lorenz curve, $G = A/(A + B)$. Area A lies between the diagonal and the Lorenz curve. Area B lies below the Lorenz curve. In the case of perfect equality, the Lorenz curve lies on the diagonal, so that area A collapses to 0. The Gini coefficient, then, is 0. In the case of perfect inequality, the Lorenz curve lies on the horizontal and vertical axes so that area B collapses to 0. The Gini coefficient, then, is 1. In all real-world economies, the Gini coefficient is greater than 0 but less than 1.

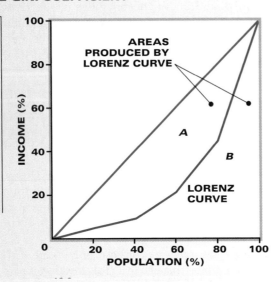

If an economy's income distribution is perfect inequality, as we saw in the hypothetical example of Springfield, the Lorenz curve would lie along the two sides of the right angle in Exhibit 3, so that B, the area below the curve, compresses to 0. If area $B = 0$, then $G = A/(A + B) = 1$. That is, *the Gini coefficient expressing perfect inequality is 1.*

Although the Gini coefficient is a convenient way to discuss and compare income equality across various economies, remember that it is no more accurate than the data on which it is based.

The U.S. Department of Commerce, Bureau of the Census (http://www.census.gov/), provides current and historical data on income and poverty.

HOW UNEQUAL IS OUR INCOME DISTRIBUTION?

What about income distribution in the United States? How does it compare to that in other countries? Is it constantly changing, or does it remain relatively fixed? What strikes you about Exhibit 4? Is it its rigidity? For the first decade—1970 to 1980—of the quarter-century data, there seems to be very little change in the quintiles' share of aggregate income. But this changes in the last 19 years—1980 to 1999—particularly in the lowest and highest quintiles. Look as well at the rather percepti-

EXHIBIT | 4

SHARE OF AGGREGATE INCOME RECEIVED BY HOUSEHOLDS, BY QUINTILE AND TOP 5 PERCENT, AND GINI COEFFICIENT: 1970–99

	Q1	Q2	Q3	Q4	Q5	TOP 5%	GINI
1999	3.6	8.9	14.9	23.2	49.4	—	0.457
1995	3.7	9.1	15.2	23.3	48.7	21.0	0.450
1990	3.9	9.6	15.9	24.0	46.7	18.6	0.428
1985	4.0	9.7	16.3	24.6	45.3	17.0	0.419
1980	4.3	10.3	16.9	24.9	43.7	15.8	0.403
1975	4.4	10.5	17.1	24.8	43.2	15.9	0.397
1970	4.1	10.8	17.4	24.5	43.3	16.6	0.394

Source: U.S. Bureau of the Census, *Money Income in the United States: 1995,* Current Population Reports, P60-193 (Washington, D.C.: U.S. Government Printing Office, 1996); and U.S. Bureau of the Census, *Money Income in the United States: 1999,* Current Population Reports, P60-220 (Washington, D.C.: U.S. Government Printing Office, 1999).

EXHIBIT|5

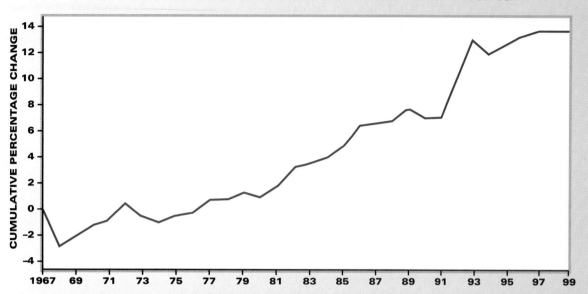

PERCENTAGE CHANGE IN HOUSEHOLD GINI COEFFICIENT: 1967–99

Source: U.S. Bureau of the Census, *Current Population Survey,* March 1999.

The cumulative effects of annual changes in the Gini coefficient became rather pronounced over the years 1967 to 1995. The coefficient in 1989 was 8 percent higher than in 1967; in 1993, it was 13 percent higher.

ble jump during the 1980–95 period in the share going to the top 5 percent of households, from 15.8 to 21.0 percent. That's a whopping 33 percent increase! Marvelous if you're one of the top 5 percent; something less than marvelous if you're not. In fact, if you're one of the bottom 60 percent of the distribution (where most families are), you've taken an 11 percent cut in income share.

This overall upward drift toward greater income inequality shows up in the moderate, but fairly persistent, rise in the Gini coefficient, from .394 in 1970 to .457 in 1999. Exhibit 5 shows the percentage change in the Gini coefficient over this period. The upward-sloping character of the curve reflects the cumulative percentage change since 1967. For example, the Gini coefficient for 1993 is 13 percent higher than the Gini coefficient for 1967. Note the very few times the curve actually dips to show a year-to-year decrease in inequality.

Is Income More Unequal in the United States Than in Other Countries?

How does our economy's income distribution compare to that of other economies? For example, how does it compare to the economies of Western Europe, Canada, and Japan? Would you expect disparities between rich and poor in the United States to be greater? Look at Exhibit 6. Note how similar the quintile shares in Canada, the United Kingdom, and France are to those in United States, and how they differ from those in Japan, Sweden, and the Netherlands, whose distributions are considerably more egalitarian.

EXHIBIT|6

INCOME DISTRIBUTION IN THE MID-1980s, SELECTED COUNTRIES, BY QUINTILE

	Q1	Q2	Q3	Q4	Q5
JAPAN	8.7	13.2	17.5	23.1	37.5
THE NETHERLANDS	8.2	13.1	18.1	23.7	36.9
SWEDEN	8.0	13.2	17.4	24.5	36.9
WEST GERMANY	6.8	12.7	17.8	24.1	38.7
ITALY	6.8	12.0	16.7	23.5	41.0
FRANCE	6.3	12.1	17.2	23.5	40.8
UNITED KINGDOM	5.8	11.5	18.2	25.0	41.0
CANADA	5.7	11.8	17.7	24.6	40.2

Source: *European Economy: 1996 Broad Economic Policy Guidelines,* no. 62 (Brussels, 1996), and *World Development Report,* 1996 (Washington, D.C.: World Bank, 1996).

Yet the differences among the income distribution patterns in Exhibit 6 and for the United States seem particularly insignificant when compared to the distributions for the less-developed countries shown in Exhibit 7.

Through the eyes of the Brazilian poor, the rich in Brazil must be incredibly rich. Look at the percentage of income Brazil's richest and poorest quintiles receive. The rich receive over 30 times the income of the poor. Similar inequalities characterize Chile, Kenya, and Zimbabwe.

Economists attribute the greater inequalities among many less-developed economies to the character of their economies. Most are predominantly agricultural. Their relatively strong dependence on agriculture restricts the range of employment opportunities and increases dependence on world commodity markets.

The prospect for breaking out depends on the creation of nonagricultural employment. A new Motorola plant in Malawi creates manufacturing jobs in regions where none had existed before. An oil refinery in Algeria opens up a host of construction, clerical, and engineering jobs. A Volkswagen assembly plant in Brazil creates a mini-Detroit. A modern shirt factory in Egypt demands and pays for skilled labor.

The more diverse the manufacturing activity, the greater the numbers and varieties of skilled, semiskilled, administrative, managerial, and professional jobs created. The industrialization process in less-developed economies draws the agricultural poor from the countryside to the cities, broadening the base of their middle class. The greater income inequalities there reflect the stage of their development process.

Wealth
The accumulated assets owned by individuals.

EXHIBIT|7

INCOME DISTRIBUTION IN LESS-DEVELOPED ECONOMIES, BY QUINTILE

	YEAR	Q1	Q2	Q3	Q4	Q5	GINI
BRAZIL	1989	2.1	4.9	8.9	16.8	67.5	63.4
CHILE	1994	3.5	6.6	10.9	18.1	61.0	56.5
VENEZUELA	1990	3.6	7.1	11.7	19.3	58.4	53.8
MEXICO	1992	4.1	7.8	12.5	20.2	55.3	50.3
KENYA	1992	3.4	6.7	10.7	17.0	62.1	57.5
JORDAN	1991	5.9	9.8	13.9	20.3	50.1	43.4
THAILAND	1992	5.6	8.7	13.0	20.0	52.7	46.2
ZIMBABWE	1990	4.0	6.3	10.0	17.4	62.3	56.8

Source: *World Development Report,* 1996 (Washington, D.C.: World Bank, 1996). The footnote to the table in the report reads: "These estimates should be treated with caution."

Distribution of Net Wealth

Net wealth among population deciles tends to be far more unevenly distributed than income. A person's **wealth** reflects not only this year's income but the accumulated assets of a lifetime. People also inherit assets—other people's wealth—so that individual wealth sometimes reflects asset accumulation over several lifetimes. No surprise then, is it, to discover that the difference between people's wealth is even greater than the difference between their incomes?

Almost everybody, including most of the poor, owns some **life-cycle wealth.** Most people own their refrigerators, automobiles, and clothing. Many own their own homes. Many have bank accounts. But fewer people own substantial holdings of bonds, corporate stock, commercial real estate, and rental property.

These kinds of wealth holdings tend to be much more unequally held. For example, in 1995, the richest half of 1 percent of households owned 27.5 percent of the country's household net worth. The top 1 percent owned 42.2 percent of all stock. Most of us have some savings, but did you know that the richest 5 percent of the population in the United States holds 50 percent of the personal savings?

Life-cycle wealth
Wealth in the form of nonmonetary assets, such as a house, automobiles, and clothing.

How unequal is unequal wealth? Exhibit 8 measures the distribution of wealth holdings in the United States.

Even back in colonial days—two years before our political independence—wealth holdings of the colonists were highly unequal. Look at the .730 Gini coefficient for 1774. Did wealth distribution change much in two centuries of accumulation? The Gini coefficient for 1973 was .810, and the wealthiest decile held 69.8 percent of the nation's net wealth. The least wealthy 50 percent of the population held only 1 percent of net wealth!

DISTRIBUTION OF NET WEALTH OF U.S. FAMILIES (1774 AND 1973)

DECILE	1774	1973
POOREST	-2.0	—
SECOND	—	—
THIRD	1.0	—
FOURTH	2.0	0.1
FIFTH	3.0	0.9
SIXTH	5.0	2.6
SEVENTH	7.0	4.5
EIGHTH	11.0	7.3
NINTH	18.0	13.8
RICHEST	55.0	69.8
GINI COEFFICIENT	.730	.810

Sources: Jones, A. H., *Wealth of a Nation to Be—The American Colonies on the Eve of Revolution* (New York: Columbia University Press, 1980); and Greenwood, D., "An Estimation of U.S. Family Wealth and Its Distribution from Macro Data, 1973," *The Review of Income and Wealth*, Series 29, I, March 1983, pp. 23–44.

EXHIBIT|8

IS THERE AN OPTIMAL INCOME DISTRIBUTION?

What an economy's wealth or income distribution *should* be is not really an economic issue. It concerns personal and societal ethics and values. There are, however, economic arguments that people, including economists, make to explain why one kind of distribution might be preferable to another.

The Case for Equality

THE RANDOMNESS OF PERSONAL MISFORTUNE IS A MISFORTUNE One of the most powerful arguments offered in support of income equality is the belief that good fortune is distributed randomly. Those who have it become rich, those who don't become poor. Income inequality, then, has no more justification than a lottery result.

Some people, no more deserving than others, *chance* into jobs that allow for quick advancement and excellent income. Many, *by chance,* make the right moves

THEORETICAL PERSPECTIVE

INEQUALITY AND THE WINNER-TAKE-ALL SOCIETY

One provocative hypothesis offered to explain part of the increase in within-group inequality is the expansion of winner-take-all markets, where top performers reap far greater rewards than do others whose ability is only slightly inferior. For example, it is not uncommon to see a star professional athlete make millions of dollars a year while another, slightly less talented athlete earns far less. It has been argued that markets such as these have become more pervasive in the American economy, with the results that ours is increasingly a winner-take-all society.

Huge wage premiums for small differences in performance may now be observed in law, medicine, investment banking, academics, and other professions. Windfalls to the top producers in these

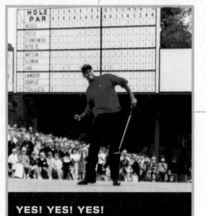

YES! YES! YES!

fields have become increasingly common as computing and telecommunications technology have advanced, facilitating the flow of information, and as transportation costs have been reduced, increasing mobility. These factors increase competition to hire the best performers, increasing their wages. How large a share of the observed increase in earnings inequality may be attributed to the expansion of winner-take-all markets remains unknown.

MORE ON THE WEB

To investigate this hypothesis in further detail, review Chapter 5, "Inequality and Economic Rewards," of the 1997 Economic Report of the President (http://www.umsl.edu/services/govdocs/erp/1997/).

Source: Adapted from *Economic Report of the President, 1997* (Washington, D.C.: U.S. Government Printing Office, 1997), p. 172.

---

horizontally and vertically through the maze of labor markets, layering one success upon another. Others, no less bright and capable, seem to be at the wrong place at the wrong time.

Some people, at least for a while, seem to have that magic business touch. They time their investments just right. They know when to expand production and, while others are expanding, when to cut back. They raise prices at just the right time and lower them at other times to stay ahead of the competition.

To many all this appears to be the result of business acumen. But to others, it is just a matter of luck. Good fortune, ignoring talent and effort, smiles upon some and frowns upon others. Who gains and who loses, then, is randomly determined.

Even more unsettling than the randomness of good fortune is the random distribution of disaster. A stroke or heart attack can undo years of career building and drive a secure household into instant bankruptcy. Chronic diseases bleed household incomes. There is simply no way to protect a household from accidental misfortune. Can anyone at any time really feel secure? What protection is there against involuntary unemployment? How do you protect yourself against a new technology that makes your particular skill obsolete? Is there *any* level of savings that can guarantee financial security?

These are rather depressing thoughts, aren't they? Shakespeare's Hamlet, facing choice and contemplating his alternatives, forsook chance for the certainty of an anguished future:

> For who would bear the whips and scorns of time
> Th' oppressor's wrong, the proud man's contumely,
> The pangs of dispriz'd love, the law's delay
> The insolence of office, and the spurns
> That patient merit of th' unworthy takes,
> When he himself might his quietus make
> With bare bodkin?

Hamlet knew, as so many do, the reason why:

> The undiscover'd country, from whose bourn
> No traveller returns, puzzles the will,
> And makes us rather bear those ills we have
> Than fly to others that we know not of.

Many of us, comparing the whims of fortune with the present value of our expected future income, would rather trade fortune for the certainty of moderate income. In this sense, income equality becomes the preferred distribution.

RAWLS'S THEORY OF JUSTICE Harvard philosopher John Rawls comes to the same conclusion. The tyranny of random events and the fear of losing badly in the game of random selection is the reason, he suggests, why people who look objectively at distribution alternatives would choose income equality.

But how can anyone be expected to look objectively at such alternatives? The rich will always prefer inequality, and the poor, with little to lose, will always choose income equality.

To overcome this self-interested bias, Rawls imagines a society "in the making." It is in the process of adopting a set of production and distribution rules that will be binding on all members. Since nobody yet knows what the agreed-upon rules will be or what position he or she will occupy in the society, the likelihood of ending up a septic tank cleaner is as great as ending up a film critic.

What pattern of distribution will this society choose? The fear of being in the lowest-paying job will outweigh any other consideration. To prevent such a disaster, people will opt for income equality. If forced, they would accept moderate levels of inequality, as long as the worst-case outcome is still tolerable.

THERE'S NOTHING RANDOM ABOUT INEQUALITY Many socialists, Marxists in particular, make the case for equality not because inequality is founded in randomness but because inequality has been rigged from the start. To them, everyone is capable of acquiring the skills to do almost anything. Given proper training, anyone can master carpentry, walk on the moon, design hydroelectric dams, run General Motors, or teach classics. People are created equal.

What, then, causes income inequality? Why do some people live off their stocks, bonds, and rents while others live by the sweat of their brow? The socialist answer is property. Unequal distribution of property creates unequal distribution of income. How do people come to have property? The socialist answer is theft. Their idea is eloquently expressed by poet Carl Sandburg:

> "Get off this estate."
> "What for?"
> "Because it's mine."

Learn more about John Rawls and his ideas (http://www.stack.nl/~cas/fil/philos/rawls.html).

CHECK YOUR UNDERSTANDING

According to Rawls, why would people choose income equality over inequality?

"Where did you get it?"
"From my father."
"Where did he get it?"
"From his father."
"And where did he get it?"
"He fought for it."
"Well, I'll fight you for it."[1]

To undo these rigged income inequalities, then, requires the undoing of private property. Marxists are prepared to undo both. Other socialists, while acknowledging the connection between property and unequal income, are not prepared to go that far.

How do you achieve income equality while still adhering to a private property economy? The socialist prescription is to knock down the barriers to equal opportunity. In this way, the excesses of income inequality are reduced.

But undoing these barriers or the entire property system is merely the *means* to achieve an end. The end is what really counts. And that is income equality. Ultimately, the socialist argument reduces to a simple proposition: People should share equally in the bounty of the earth.

EQUALITY AND MAXIMUM UTILITY Economist A. P. Lerner makes a case for equality based on the presumption that equality produces the greatest welfare for the greatest number of people. In making the case, he shows that for any two people, equal income distribution maximizes their combined utility of money. Look at Exhibit 9.

Let's assume that Gen Clark's downward-sloping marginal utility curve of money, *a*, reflecting the marginal utility of the goods and services that money can buy, is drawn from left to right. Ben Cohen's marginal utility curve, *b*, is drawn from right to left. Suppose their combined income is $20. Let's start with income inequality, assuming that Cohen has $12 and Clark only $8. Although Cohen is no doubt pleased with this unequal distribution, the combined utility they derive from their incomes is less than maximum.

Why? Because Gen Clark has fewer dollars, the marginal utility of her last dollar, the 8th, is 60 utils, point *x*, considerably higher than the 40 utils of Ben Cohen's 12th dollar, point *y*. If we take Lerner's advice and give Clark $1 of Cohen's income, the utility she gains from this extra $1—the marginal utility of her 9th—is 55 utils, point *z*. But Cohen's income is now $1 less. The utility he loses by giving up the $1 is 40 utils. *And that's Lerner's point.* By transferring $1 from Ben Cohen to Gen Clark, their combined utility increases by $55 - 40 = 15$ utils.

Income inequality, although reduced, still persists. Gen Clark's income at $9 is still $2 less than Ben Cohen's at $11. There is still room to expand total utility. How? The marginal utility of Clark's 9th dollar is 55 utils, 10 utils greater than the 45 utils of Cohen's 11th dollar. If yet another $1 is transferred from Cohen to Clark, Clark's utility gain is 50 utils—the marginal utility of her 9th dollar—while Cohen loses the 45 utils of his 11th dollar. This second transfer of $1, then, added another $50 - 45 = 5$ utils to their combined utility.

But that does it. Total utility is maximized when each has $10 income. Look at their marginal utility at $10 income. It is 50 utils. If another $1 were transferred to Gen Clark, Ben Cohen would lose 50 utils while Gen Clark gained 45 utils. This last transfer would reduce their combined utility by 5 utils.

---

1. Excerpt from THE PEOPLE, YES by Carl Sandburg, copyright © 1936 by Harcourt, Inc., and renewed 1964 by Carl Sandburg, reprinted by permission of the publisher.

EXHIBIT | 9

EQUALITY AND MAXIMUM UTILITY

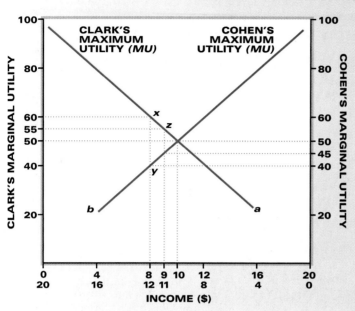

Gen Clark's marginal utility curve for money is drawn from left to right. Ben Cohen's marginal utility curve for money is drawn from right to left. The marginal utility of their 10th dollar is 50 utils. At any distribution of the $20 total income other than equality—$10 each—the marginal utilities of their dollars would be unequal. A shift of $1, from the one whose marginal utility for money is lower to the other whose marginal utility for money is higher, would raise their combined total utility. At equality, then, combined total utility is maximized.

But Lerner's proof of maximum utility rests on the assumption that everyone's utility functions are alike. For example, he would have to assume that Gen Clark's and Ben Cohen's marginal utility curves were identical to get his results. But why assume that?

Why would Lerner make such an assumption when he knows, as you do, that no two people derive identical satisfaction when it comes to spending money? If you were in his shoes, what assumption would you make? Realizing it's impossible to know for certain whose utility curve is really higher, would you guess Cohen's curve to be higher than Clark's? Why? What if his were really lower? That would be the worst possible guess. Assuming Clark's is higher creates the same problem. Why not, then, just assume that they are equal? Wouldn't it be safer? In this way, we minimize the damage of making a mistake. That's precisely why Lerner assumed that they were identical.

HOW THE CHINESE ARRIVED AT LERNER'S CONCLUSIONS
An old Chinese rule on property distribution preceded Lerner's conclusions. How do you bequeath property so that everyone involved acknowledges equality? So that everyone feels he or she has a fair share? Suppose the task is to divide an estate between two children. Neither can be trusted to make a fair division.

Assuming identical utility functions, maximum total utility is achieved by allowing one child to do the dividing and the other to choose first from among the two sections. The divider will be forced to create two equal shares. After all, it would be foolish to divide them unevenly knowing that the other has first choice. The chooser can't complain. After all, if the properties are unevenly divided, having first choice guarantees a higher-valued share.

GLOBAL PERSPECTIVE

CLIMBING OUT OF POVERTY IS BECOMING MORE DIFFICULT

The United States has been a country of opportunity since its inception. During the 1787 drafting of the U.S. Constitution, Gouverneur Morris of Pennsylvania argued that those whose livelihood relied on an employer weren't independent enough to be free citizens and shouldn't vote. Thomas Jefferson later responded that Morris's point may have been valid for Europe's dirt-poor wage earners. But Americans, he said, could always find another job or earn a decent living on the abundant farmland here.

As long as this country's working poor had a chance to work their way out of the bottom, Americans have tolerated wide gaps between rich and poor. After all, the United States, unlike more rigid economies in Europe, has always been dynamic enough to provide steady upward mobility for workers.

Or has it? Or is it now? A spate of new research on U.S. income mobility seems to weaken the optimism of Jefferson's appraisal. A dozen or so academic studies have examined data that follow the same individual for many years. This allows them to go beyond research showing rising income inequality to reveal a more unsettling trend: As the economy stratified in the 1980s, workers at the bottom became less likely to move up in their lifetimes.

Even more astonishing, American mobility now looks worse

IT'S NICE TO KNOW I'M NOT ALONE. . . . THAT'S HOW I USED TO FEEL.

EUROPE: GREATER UPWARD MOBILITY THAN THE UNITED STATES

SHARE OF POOR WHO LEFT POVERTY WITHIN A YEAR†

THE NETHERLANDS	44%
SWEDEN	37%
FRANCE	28%
GERMANY*	26%
IRELAND	25%
U.S. WHITE	17%
U.S. BLACK	8%

†Average of all years in the 1980s.
*Excluding the former East Germany

Source: Adapted from February 26, 1996, issue of *Business Week* by special permission, copyright © 1996 by The McGraw-Hill Companies, Inc.

than Europe's (see the exhibit). In 1993, Northwestern University economist Greg J. Duncan and several European economists found that throughout the 1980s, only 17 percent of poor American families moved at least 20 percent above the poverty line within a year, versus 25 percent to 44 percent of the European poor. Overall, more than 56 percent of the bottom-fifth American families remained there for at least 5 years, versus 52 percent in Germany, according to Syracuse economist Douglas Holtz-Eakin. "Most economists simply can't believe that the U.S. has the same mobility as Germany," says Richard Burkhauser, a Syracuse economist who also has studied the 1980s data.

Nor do the 1990s seem to be turning out much differently. Census data to 1994 show the same inequality patterns of the '80s.

Economic opportunity has been shrinking for long enough now that families trapped at the bottom are beginning to show the attributes of a permanent lower class. Thomas Jefferson would be worried.

MORE ON THE NET
Visit EconDebate Online (http://www.swcollege.com/bef/econ_debate.html) for the latest perspectives addressing why income inequality has increased in the United States.

The Case for Inequality

EQUALITY VERSUS EFFICIENCY Many economists, acknowledging some merit in the equality arguments, still opt for tolerable levels of inequality. They do so by drawing upon the connection between productive contribution and economic reward. People should receive their *MRP*. And since the *MRP*s generated in competitive markets are everywhere different, income inequality is totally justified. The distribution ethic is simple: Contribution merits reward.

But there is more to their case for inequality than its ethic. Many argue that without the reward linkage, productive people would lack the incentive to contribute as much as they do. After all, most productive contributions are not effortless. Denying people the full measure of their contribution, then, will ensure less than the full measure of their energies. In other words, the economy's output would be less than its productive potential.

Look at Exhibit 10. Suppose the economy's national income is $900 billion, and its income inequality, measured by the Gini coefficient, is .45. Let's now suppose that society decides to generate greater income equality. It transfers income from rich to poor, to push the Gini coefficient to .35. However, with $G = .35$, the level of national income falls to $700 billion. The income transfers discouraged maximum production. The national income curve maps the relationship between levels of inequality and levels of national income.

What may be bad for the economy, however, may still be good for people occupying the lower quintiles of income distribution. Their incomes may increase even though national income decreases as a result of greater equality. Look at the income curve for the poorest 60 percent. It records their income at different levels of inequality. As you see, when $G = .35$, these people receive—because of greater

CHECK YOUR UNDERSTANDING

If income is distributed more equally, what happens to the level of national income?

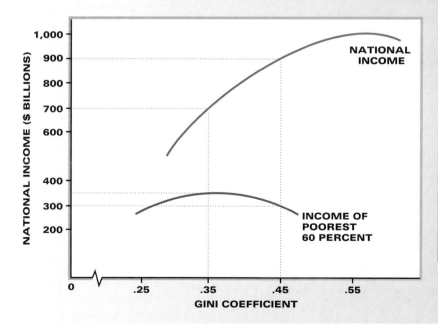

EFFECT OF INEQUALITY ON NATIONAL INCOME

The vertical axis measures levels of national income, and the horizontal axis measures the degree of inequality, expressed in terms of the Gini coefficient. At the origin, $G = 0$, reflecting perfect income equality. The hill-shaped national income curve maps the trade-off between maximum output and income equality. At $G = .45$, income is $900 billion. If government policy of redistributing income forces G to .35, production disincentives and inefficiencies emerge that reduce national income to $700 billion. The hill-shaped income curve of the poorest 60 percent maps the income received by the poor at varying levels of inequality. At $G = .45$, the poor receive $300 billion of the $900 billion national income. At $G = .35$, the poor receive $350 billion of the $700 billion national income.

income equality—$350 billion of the $700 billion, which is more than the $300 billion they receive when national income is $900 billion.

But there is a limit to the gains the poor can receive by such methods of income transfer. If a Gini coefficient of .30 was imposed, the decline in national income would become so pronounced that everyone would be worse off, including the poor. Even though the poor's share of national income would increase, the absolute amount of income they received would fall.

EQUALITY VERSUS ECONOMIC GROWTH Because the rich can afford to save a higher percentage of their income than can the poor, they tend to do the economy's investing. In this way, the economy's growth rate and investment are linked to income inequality. The richer the rich, the greater the investment and the higher the rate of growth.

Paradoxically, the poor are supposed to benefit from income inequality as well. How? Even though with $G = .45$ their share of national income is relatively small, the investments made by the rich increase the rate of growth of national income, so that eventually the absolute size of the poor's small share becomes larger than before. The rising tide of national prosperity raises all ships, both large and small. This concept is shown in Exhibit 11.

Again, let's suppose the economy's national income is $900 billion. The curves trace two different income paths for the poorest 60 percent of the population. The high-growth path reflects high income inequality, $G = .45$. In year 0, the poor's income is only $300 billion. The lower-growth path reflects a state of less income inequality, $G = .35$. Here, in year 0, the poor's income is $500 billion.

What do you see? After 15 years, the income earned by the poorest 60 percent of the population surpasses the income that would be generated by the growth rate associated with greater income equality.

EXHIBIT | 11

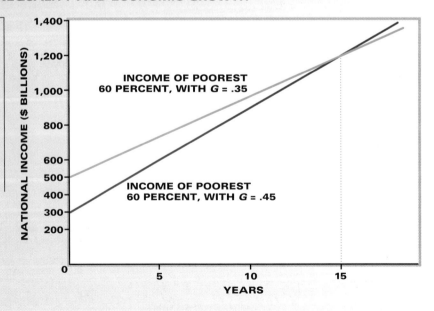

INEQUALITY AND ECONOMIC GROWTH

The vertical axis measures levels of national income and the income received by the poor. The horizontal axis measures time. At the origin, national income is $900 billion. The curves trace two different income paths for the poorest 60 percent. The high-growth curve reflects $G = .45$. The less-rapid income growth curve reflects $G = .35$. In 15 years, the absolute level of income received by the poor with $G = .45$ catches up to the income they would have received with $G = .35$. Beyond 15 years, the poor's income with $G = .45$ is actually higher.

DO WE HAVE TO LIVE WITH POVERTY?

It is unlikely that any society, with the possible exception of an Israeli kibbutz, prefers and lives with perfect equality. Most people, including economic planners in the People's Republic of China, accept the fact that there will *always* be people in every society who are poorer than others.

But it is one thing to be in the poorest quintile of a population, and quite another to be *actually* poor. They are not always the same. Many living in the poorest quintile in the United States, for example, have a standard of living considerably higher than the standard enjoyed by 75 percent of the Bangladesh population. Who, then, is poor?

Many in the lowest quintile can afford to put together a reasonably nutritious diet, a change of clothes, some kind of automobile, electricity in their homes, some access to hospitalization, and basic education—all of which add up to considerably more than the food, shelter, health, transportation, and education that 75 percent of the U.S. population had in the mid-19th century. Does this mean that there are now considerably fewer poor people in the country?

Defining Poverty

When is someone living in poverty? Perhaps the best way to answer this question is by first asking what it is we want to know. But that's the problem. We aren't entirely clear what kind of information we seek.

AS A PERCENTAGE OF MEDIAN INCOME To many people, and many economists, poverty is a relative concept. People are only poor relative to others. One way, then, of defining poverty is to arbitrarily select some percentage of the population's **median income** as the **poverty threshold.** Those with incomes below that threshold level are considered to be living in poverty. For example, if the threshold level selected is 50 percent of median income and if median income is $10,000, then those earning less than $5,000 would be below the poverty line. If the government selects a threshold level of 40 percent, fewer people would be classified as living in poverty. If, over time, median income increases more rapidly than the incomes of the poor, the poverty ranks swell. How many live in poverty, then, depends not on a person's particular income, but upon the relationship between that income and the income of others.

Median income
The midpoint of a society's income distribution, above and below which an equal number of individuals (or families) belong.

Poverty threshold
The level of income below which families are considered to be poor.

MEETING BASIC NEEDS Another way of identifying poverty is by describing some *minimal acceptable physical standard of living* that people ought to have. Those whose incomes are insufficient to afford that standard are considered poor. As you can imagine, such a definition of poverty can produce as many poverty threshold levels as there are opinions on what constitutes minimal standards of living. In fact, various government agencies have identified as many as 124 different poverty levels.

Since 1920, the Bureau of Labor Statistics has constructed an annual subsistence standard-of-living budget for U.S. families. Such a budget, you would think, would not change if subsistence is regarded simply in terms of basic needs. After all, a quart of milk contributes as much nutritional value to a poor family in 1990 as it did to a poor family in 1920. But our perceptions of basic needs change. A heated house may have been a luxury in 1920, but it is perceived as a basic need today. High school education may have been a luxury in 1920, but it is obligatory today. Because retail stores were typically interspersed among houses and apartment

The U.S. Bureau of Labor Statistics (http://www.bls.gov/) compiles data on unemployment, prices, living conditions, and compensation, among other topics.

Can you think of goods or services that were considered luxuries while you were in elementary school that are now commonplace or may even be regarded as basic to our needs? Go to the Interactive Study Center at http://gottheil. swcollege.com *and click on the "Your Turn" button to submit your example. Student submissions will be posted to the Web site, and perhaps we will use some in future editions of the book!*

EXHIBIT | 12

PERCENTAGE OF PERSONS BELOW THE POVERTY LEVEL, BY RACE, 1960–97

	1960	1970	1980	1997
ALL PERSONS	22.2	12.6	13.0	13.3
WHITE	17.8	9.9	10.2	11.0
BLACK	55.1*	33.3	32.5	26.5
HISPANIC	NA	NA	25.7	27.1

NA = not available
*Refers to data for 1959
Source: Bureau of the Census, *Statistical Abstract of the United States, 1999* (Washington, D.C.: Department of Commerce, 1999), p. 483.

EXHIBIT | 13

FAMILIES IN POVERTY, BY SELECTED CHARACTERISTICS: 1997

	PERCENTAGE BELOW POVERTY
FAMILIES	
TOTAL	10.3
WHITE	8.4
BLACK	23.6
HISPANIC	24.7
EDUCATION OF HOUSEHOLDER	
NO HIGH SCHOOL DIPLOMA	24.1*
SINGLE MOTHERS	49.7*

*Refers to 1992
†Refers to 1994
Source: *Statistical Abstract of the United States, 1999* (Washington, D.C.: Department of Commerce, 1999), p. 484.

buildings, people years ago could shop by foot. Today, with residential neighborhoods separated from shopping centers and downtown malls, the automobile has become a basic need. In other words, our concepts of basic needs are always changing.

The most commonly used poverty threshold that reflects basic needs was developed by the Social Security Administration in 1964 and revised in 1981 by the Federal Interagency Committee. It is based on the Department of Agriculture's 1961 Economy Food Plan. Let's see what kind of picture it paints.

Who and How Many Are in Poverty?

The percentage of people who fall below the poverty threshold, as calculated by the Social Security Administration, is shown in Exhibit 12.

Are we making headway? Look at the decade of the 1960s. Between 1960 and 1970, the percentage of people in poverty fell from 22.2 percent to 12.6 percent. The decline among blacks in poverty was even more dramatic. But that substantial progress came to an abrupt halt, and since then the percentage of people in poverty has remained almost unchanged.

Who are the poor? Look at the family characteristics shown in Exhibit 13.

Not surprising, is it? As you see, poor families make up a little more than 10 percent of the U.S. population, yet 49.7 percent of all single mothers fall below the poverty line.

FIGHTING THE WAR ON POVERTY

Do we care? Michael Harrington's *The Other America: Poverty in the United States,* published in 1962, addressed the issue of America's neglected poor. Its message was unmistakable. Life in the United States was not nearly as comfortable as the comfortable would like us to believe. His message was not original. Many had written on poverty before. What was unique about Harrington's book was its reception. The timing was right.

Lyndon Johnson's War on Poverty

In 1964, President Lyndon B. Johnson put the issue of our nation's poor on the national agenda. He called for a war on poverty. Reaction was mixed. Some people regarded it as unnecessary and even self-defeating. Eliminating poverty, they argued, depended more on the benefits the poor derive from being part of a strong and growing market economy than on government-sponsored income transfers.

Others applauded the president's recognition of the problem but viewed his commitment as entirely too weak. More funding was needed for more programs for a longer period of time. It appeared more a measured skirmish than an all-out war.

Whatever the intent of the Johnson war on poverty, it marked the beginning of a broad-based set of programs funded by federal, state, and local governments to address specific poverty issues. The benefits were in the form of **cash assistance** and **in-kind assistance.**

Cash assistance
Government assistance in the form of cash.

In-kind assistance
Government assistance in the form of direct goods and services, such as Medicaid or food stamps.

Making an Honest Effort?

How much funding? Since 1964 the number of people eligible for assistance, as well as the funding of the poverty program, has expanded significantly. Exhibit 14 shows the 1996 expenditures on various poverty programs. Far and away the biggest item in the government's poverty program—including federal, state, and local expenditures—is medical care, and the biggest item within the medical care category is the $159.4 billion spent on Medicaid, which pays for inpatient hospital care, physician's services, skilled nursing facilities, medication, and dental care.

The cash aid big-ticket items are Supplemental Security Income (SSI) and Aid to Families with Dependent Children (AFDC). The $30.4 billion in SSI payments are made to the elderly, blind, and disabled who are unable to work. The $23.7 billion AFDC payments supplement food, shelter, and clothing for the dependent children of the poor.

Of the $39.0 billion in food benefits, $27.3 billion is in the form of food stamps. The food stamp program is the government's primary way of helping the poor maintain nutritious diets. Those eligible receive monthly stamp allotments, the value of the individual allotment depending on income and size of household.

CASH AND NONCASH BENEFITS FOR PERSONS WITH LIMITED INCOME: 1996

ITEM	AMOUNT ($ BILLIONS)
MEDICAL CARE	177.6
CASH AID	91.7
FOOD BENEFITS	39.0
HOUSING BENEFITS	27.2
EDUCATION AID	16.3
SERVICES	10.1
JOBS AND TRAINING	4.6
ENERGY ASSISTANCE	1.2

Source: *Statistical Abstract of the United States, 1999* (Washington, D.C.: Department of Commerce, 1999), p. 389.

EXHIBIT 14

HISTORICAL PERSPECTIVE

DOES WELFARE CONDEMN THE POOR TO POVERTY?

Helping the poor has always been a subject of much controversy. The issue of remedying economic need with welfare squares off against its possible consequences, promoting personal irresponsibility and creating an addiction to dependence.

People of good will line up on both sides of this issue. David Ricardo, a founding father of the 19th-century classical school of economics, was adamant about the evils of welfare. Writing on the subject of the poor laws in England, legislated to help the poor, Ricardo had this to say:

> The clear and direct tendency of the poor laws is not, as the legislature benevolently intended, to amend the condition of the poor, but to deteriorate the condition of both poor and rich. . . .
>
> It is a truth which admits not a doubt, that the comforts and well being of the poor cannot be permanently secured without some regard on their part, or some effort of the legislature, to regulate the increase of their numbers, and to render less frequent among them early and improvident marriages. The operation of the system of poor laws has been directly contrary to this. They have rendered restraint superfluous, and have invited imprudence, by offering it a portion of the wages of prudence and industry.

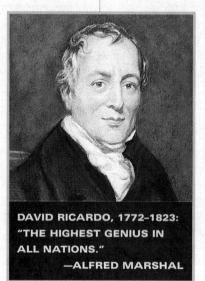

DAVID RICARDO, 1772–1823: "THE HIGHEST GENIUS IN ALL NATIONS." —ALFRED MARSHAL

The nature of the evil points out the remedy. By gradually contracting the sphere of the poor laws; by impressing on the poor the value of independence, by teaching them that they must look not to systematic or casual charity, but to their own exertions for support, that prudence and forethought are neither unnecessary nor unprofitable virtues, we shall by degrees approach a sounder and more healthful state.

Sound familiar? These thoughts seem to be no less current among many economists of the 21st century than they were to David Ricardo. Although fully appreciating why the poor laws were legislated, Ricardo still believed that the cure was worse than the disease. Welfare blunts the passion to improve oneself. Welfare creates an unwholesome reliance on others. Welfare allows marriages and family when both are personally unaffordable. In essence, welfare takes away from individuals the idea that they are responsible for their own well-being.

Is Ricardo stonehearted about this? Are the poor really made irresponsible and addicted to dependence by accepting welfare? These are not easy questions to answer, and those who have tried have not met with universal acceptance. But they are at the heart of positions economists have taken and continue to take on the issue of welfare.

Source: Ricardo, David, *On the Principles of Political Economy,* London, 1817.

The two major items in the $27.2 billion housing assistance category are the $19.7 billion in rent subsidies and low-income housing assistance. Education aid is primarily in the form of Pell grants and the Head Start program. Since its beginning, Head Start has served more than 11 million economically disadvantaged preschool children. It provides an array of educational and social services designed to compensate for the absence of an intellectually stimulating home environment—

the kind of home life that more affluent preschoolers typically enjoy. Head Start represents an important weapon in the government's attempt to break the transfer of poverty from one generation to the next.

Is the war on poverty effective? Exhibit 15 seems to show, at least compared to the wars waged on other fronts in other countries, that the successes are rather minimal. The reduction in the percentage of the population below 50 percent of median income after taxes and transfers are accounted for is hardly per-

POPULATION BELOW 50 PERCENT OF MEDIAN INCOME (LATEST OECD DATA)

	BEFORE TAXES AND TRANSFERS	AFTER TAXES AND TRANSFERS
CANADA	19.0	15.4
FRANCE	20.6	8.9
WEST GERMANY	12.4	8.5
THE NETHERLANDS	18.9	4.7
SWEDEN	18.4	12.1
UNITED KINGDOM	24.0	12.4
UNITED STATES	19.4	18.7

Source: *OECD Economic Surveys, Germany, 1996* (Paris: OECD, 1996), p. 90.

ceptible, falling from 19.4 to 18.7 percent. On the other hand, the tax and transfer weaponry—keeping with the war metaphor—has made rather notable changes in the extent of poverty in many other countries. It halved poverty in the United Kingdom, from 24.0 to 12.4 percent, and in the Netherlands it shrunk the poverty population from 18.9 to 4.7 percent.

THE NEGATIVE INCOME TAX ALTERNATIVE

One way to reduce poverty as well as the costs of administering poverty programs is to devise a system that *automatically* provides those in poverty with enough money to maintain a minimum standard of living and, at the same time, allows the poor to earn as much as possible without penalty.

Many economists regard the **negative income tax** as such a scheme. They see it as the most attractive alternative to an overburdened and underfunded poverty program. Economists are particularly impressed with its political cleanliness and simplicity. It can be administered routinely by the Internal Revenue Service. It actually creates an incentive to work. It avoids the stigma of handouts.

How does it work? Suppose the government sets the minimum income level for a family of four at $10,000 and taxes all income at 50 percent. Corresponding incomes, taxes, and after-tax incomes are shown in Exhibit 16.

If the household earns no income, it *receives* a negative tax of $10,000 from the government—just as you would receive a tax refund from the IRS—which, added to the household's $0 independent income, represents total after-tax income.

If the household earns $5,000, it pays a 50 percent tax

Negative income tax
Government cash payments to the poor—an income tax in reverse—that is linked to the income levels of the poor. The cash payments decrease as income levels increase. The payments are designed to provide a minimum level of income to the poor.

EXHIBIT | 16

THE NEGATIVE INCOME TAX APPLIED (TAX = 50%)

INDEPENDENT INCOME	NET NEGATIVE (–) OR POSITIVE (+) TAX	AFTER-TAX INCOME
$ 0	$–10,000	$10,000
5,000	–7,500	12,500
10,000	–5,000	15,000
20,000	0	20,000
25,000	+2,500	22,500
30,000	+5,000	25,000

APPLIED PERSPECTIVE

A TALE OF TWO CITIES, 2000

One city is in the midwest and villagelike; the other is an eastern seaboard metropolis. The midwestern city—Urbana, Illinois—is surrounded by corn and soybean. The other—Washington, D.C.—is the capital of the United States. Urbana's landscape is flat, its horizons unmarked by hill or valley; Washington is surrounded by a rich variety of geography. In almost every respect, these two American cities are as different as any two cities can be. Yet in 2000, they were drawn together by one marvelous feature: The head coaches of their football teams—the University of Illinois's Fighting Illini in Urbana and the Washington Redskins of the NFL—are brothers.

What has the tale of these two brothers in these two cities to do with the issues of income distribution and poverty? Much. Growing up in a single-parent family household in Martinez, California, the Turner brothers, Ron and Norv, knew firsthand the meaning of economic insecurity. Having a reliable store of family savings or a steady flow of family income was a luxury they seldom experienced.

But they muddled through their early years. Their caring mother worked tirelessly. Ron and Norv helped when they could. With a strong dose of perseverance, a solid sense of family responsibility, and a dash of good luck, both chose professional

I'LL GET BY WITH SOME HELP FROM MY FRIENDS.

sports as their careers, and ended up as head coaches in these two football-proud cities.

While both Ron and Norv appreciate that tenacity, hard work, family cohesion, and luck had much to do with their ultimate success, they also know that they could never have achieved their accomplishments if California's welfare system hadn't been there to help them through those early hard years.

Receiving welfare didn't make the Turner family dependent on welfare; it helped them win the fight against depending on welfare. Receiving welfare didn't destroy Ron and Norv's competitive edge; it allowed them to sharpen that edge to their advantage (and to the advantage of collegiate and professional football). Receiving welfare gave them a chance to be productive citizens, as it does for millions of other people struggling through hard times.

When the 21st century came into being, Ron was in Urbana, having coached the Fighting Illini to a college bowl victory. His brother Norv was in Washington, having taken his Redskins to the NFL playoffs. But every large American metropolis or small city or town or village has Ron and Norv stories of their own. Our welfare systems, however fraught with abuses (real and imagined), have been life support systems for countless people who have gone on to lead productive lives. They may not all be head coaches or CEOs or brain surgeons, but they count no less in the larger scheme of things.

on that income, like everyone else. On April 15, the household calculates the $5,000 \times 50\% = \$2,500$ tax due. This leaves the household with an after-tax *independently derived* income of $2,500. But it still receives the $10,000 negative income tax, so that total after-tax income is $12,500. As far as the IRS is concerned, its net payment to the household is $7,500, representing the $10,000 paid out as negative tax and the $2,500 it receives in taxes.

Suppose the household's independent income is $20,000. Its tax obligation [$20,000 \times 50\%$] now equals the $10,000 negative income tax. The household and the IRS break even. The household's after-tax income is its independent income. The IRS pays nothing to the household.

If the household's independent income increases to $30,000, it pays $30,000 × 50% = $15,000 to the IRS, but receives $10,000, so that its after-tax income is $25,000. The IRS clears $5,000.

As you see, there is beauty in simplicity. All households, including the poorest, have a strong incentive to work. The more income earned, the higher the household's after-tax income. Moreover, the poor are ensured a minimum after-tax income of $10,000—it can vary, of course—and the entire operation avoids government meddling in the lives of the people.

To some economists, the attractive features of the negative income tax are precisely the source of its weakness! From a macroeconomic perspective, the real problem of the poor is not that they have less income than others, but that they *produce* less income than others. The negative income tax ignores this crucial distinction. Anthropologists Ruth and Oscar Lewis in their life study of poverty recognized that a "culture of poverty" sets the poor apart from others and keeps the poor locked in poverty.

To undo such a cultural stranglehold requires more than adding to household income. It requires a radical change in the poor's perception of themselves, of their future, and of the society they live in. To bring about such change requires large investments in the economic and social environments of the poor. Higher private incomes alone cannot address these needs.

CHAPTER REVIEW

1. People's incomes are derived from wages, interest, rent, or profit, or from combinations of them.
2. The Lorenz curve is a graphic view of income distribution. Population is divided into five groups of 20 percent—quintiles—from the poorest to the richest, and the Lorenz curve traces out the shares of total income each of these quintiles receives.
3. The Gini coefficient translates the Lorenz curve into a single number. It is the area lying between the diagonal and the curve divided by the total area under the diagonal. A Gini coefficient of 0 represents perfect equality, while a coefficient of 1 is perfect inequality. Gini coefficients associated with industrial market economies typically range between 0.25 and 0.45.
4. Income inequality tends to be higher in less-developed economies than in industrially advanced ones, reflecting the predominance of agricultural production and the narrow range of employment opportunities.
5. The distribution of net wealth is less equal than the distribution of income. In 1973, the bottom 50 percent of U.S. families held only 1 percent of total net wealth.
6. A case for income equality can be made on several grounds, among them the randomness of personal misfortune, the preference to avoid the possibility of being poor over any other possible distribution outcome, and the idea that equality generates maximum total utility for society.
7. A case for income inequality can be made on several grounds, among them the idea that effort and reward are inexorably linked, and the direct relationship between inequality, economic growth, and, ultimately, the economic well-being of low-income people.
8. Poverty can be described in relative terms, such as a percentage of median income, or in absolute terms, such as a minimally acceptable standard of living.
9. The percentage of people below the poverty threshold fell dramatically in the 1960s and

has risen moderately since. A disproportionate number of those who are poor belong to
minority and single-female-headed households.

10. The artillery used to fight the war on poverty
includes cash and in-kind assistance, such as
Medicaid, food stamps, Head Start, housing
assistance, and Aid to Families with Dependent Children.

11. The negative income tax is an alternative to
government assistance. It transfers income
to people whose pre-tax income is below a
specific level, without creating the disincen-
tives to work normally associated with government assistance.

KEY TERMS

Lorenz curve
Gini coefficient
Wealth

Life-cycle wealth
Median income
Poverty threshold

Cash assistance
In-kind assistance
Negative income tax

QUESTIONS

1. What is a Lorenz curve? How does it illustrate
income inequality?

2. What is the relationship between a Gini coefficient and a Lorenz curve?

3. How does U.S. income distribution in the
1990s compare to U.S. distribution from the
1950s through the 1970s?

4. Discuss the two different ways economists
define poverty.

5. What is the basic idea John Rawls offers to
support the argument for income equality?

6. The case for inequality can be made on the
grounds that equality stymies economic
growth. Explain.

7. The case for equality can be made on the
grounds that it generates the greatest total
utility for society. Explain.

8. "If you insist on equality, you must accept the
consequent inefficient allocation of the economy's resources." Explain.

9. What are the notable characteristics of families who live below the poverty threshold?

10. How does a negative income tax system work?
Why do some economists prefer it to government assistance as a means of redistributing
income?

11. Distinguish between income and wealth.
Which has greater inequality?

PRACTICE PROBLEMS

1. Suppose an economy consists of 5 people
whose combined income is $100,000. Their
individual incomes are Leslie, $4,000; Lynn
$8,000; Kristen, $18,000; Paul, $25,000; and
Carol, $45,000. If the government creates a
negative income tax system with a minimum
income of $10,000 and a tax rate of 50 per-
cent, how much income tax does each
person pay?

2. Use appropriate percentages to fill in the
blank cells of the table that represents a set
of data for a Lorenz curve.

PERCENT OF POPULATION	PERCENT OF INCOME
20	2
20	
20	20
20	
20	50

WHAT'S WRONG WITH THIS GRAPH?

LORENZ CURVE

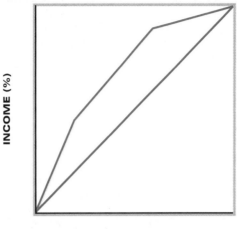

INCOME (%)

POPULATION (%)

ECONOMIC CONSULTANTS

ECONOMIC RESEARCH AND ANALYSIS BY STUDENTS FOR PROFESSIONALS

Alice Gorman will soon begin a counseling service in New York City for families below the poverty level. Alice, working with a group of volunteers, intends to teach individuals and families what government benefits are available and how to receive these benefits. Also, Alice's service will help these families find new or better jobs.

Alice has asked Economic Consultants to show her how federal poverty programs operate. She also would like to better understand the economics behind why some people are poor and others are rich. Prepare a report for Alice that addresses the following issues:

1. What are the current poverty conditions in the United States?
2. What are the major federal poverty programs? Who is eligible for these programs? What benefits are available?
3. Briefly explain the economic positives and negatives in making a case for income equality and for income inequality.

You may find the following resources helpful as you prepare this report for Alice:

- **The Bureau of the Census** (http://www.census.gov/)—The Census Bureau provides current and historical data on income and poverty.
- **Economic Statistics Briefing Room (ESBR)** (http://www.whitehouse.gov/fsbr/esbr.html)—The White House maintains the ESBR to provide easy access to current federal economic indicators, including income and earnings statistics.
- **Health Care Finance Administration (HCFA)** (http://www.hcfa.gov/)—The HCFA administers federal health benefits, such as Medicaid.
- **Administration for Children and Families** (http://www.acf.dhhs.gov/)—The Administration for Children and Families manages Aid to Families with Dependent Children (AFDC) benefits.
- **Social Security Administration (SSA)** (http://www.ssa.gov/)—The SSA manages Supplemental Security Income (SSI) benefits.
- **National Center for Policy Analysis (NCPA)** (http://www.ncpa.org/)—The NCPA provides links to commentary on the economy and income inequality.

PRACTICE TEST

1. Questions about the rich and poor have always been part of our intellectual and ethical heritage. The chapter begins with a brief commentary on philosophers who considered these important questions. If you recall, they were
   a. Hobbes and Locke.
   b. Marx and Engels.
   c. Plato and Aristotle.
   d. Hegel and Descartes.
   e. Mill and Bentham.

2. If the Lorenz curve for a country, let's say, Costa Rica, falls along the diagonal, then we know that for Costa Rica,
   a. income equals wealth.
   b. 100 percent of Costa Rican financial assets are in the form of income.
   c. there is 100 percent poverty in Costa Rica.
   d. there is perfect income equality.
   e. there is perfect income inequality.

3. If you read that the Gini coefficient in Costa Rica was 0.45 and in Peru 0.23, then you know that
   a. 45 percent of the Costa Ricans and 23 percent of Peruvians lived in poverty.
   b. 55 percent of the Costa Ricans and 77 percent of Peruvians lived in poverty.
   c. income inequality was higher in Costa Rica than in Peru.
   d. income inequality was higher in Peru than in Costa Rica.
   e. 68 percent of the combined Costa Rican and Peruvian population had the same income.

4. The one thing we can say, comparing the U.S. Gini coefficient to those in developing countries like Kenya, Ivory Coast, and Brazil, is that there is
   a. greater income equality in the United States.
   b. a greater number of people in poverty in the United States.
   c. a greater percentage of people living in poverty in developing countries.
   d. greater income inequality in the United States.
   e. a greater percentage of people living in poverty in the United States.

5. The distribution of wealth in the United States is
   a. more unequal than its distribution of income.
   b. more equal than its distribution of income.
   c. about the same as its distribution of income.
   d. compared to other countries, the most equal in the world.
   e. compared to other countries, the most unequal in the world.

6. John Rawls's theory of justice
   a. argues that if people were to look objectively at the issue of income distribution, they would choose to allow for inequality.

   b. argues that if people were to look objectively at the issue of income distribution, they would choose equality.
   c. argues against private property, which is the root of economic inequality and political discontent.
   d. argues for private property, even though it creates some degree of income inequality because private property is the root of economic growth.
   e. argues that the idea that "there will always be the poor among us" is wrong.

7. The proof of the theory—proposed by A. P. Lerner—that income equality ends up creating the highest total utility for a society rests on the assumption that
   a. no one in the society opposes the income equality outcome.
   b. everyone has the same marginal utility curve for money.
   c. property is evenly distributed within the society.
   d. there are no recipients of privately held income, such as wages, interest, profit, and rent.
   e. everyone has the same skills and job opportunities.

8. Advocates for income inequality argue that equality
   a. is unnatural.
   b. undermines efficiency.
   c. denies private property.
   d. undermines consumption.
   e. creates excess saving.

9. Economists define poverty in 2 different ways. They are
   a. as a percentage of median income and as a percentage of average income.
   b. as meeting basic needs and as earning a critical minimum income.
   c. as a percentage of median income and as meeting basic needs.
   d. as a percentage of median income and as earning a critical minimum income.
   e. as earning a critical minimum income and as a percentage of average income.

10. The negative income tax
   a. is an across-the-board tax cut designed to reduce income inequality.
   b. applies to poor people only if they are not earning income.
   c. applies to everyone not earning income.
   d. is a cash payment of government designed to provide a minimum level of income for the poor.
   e. is government in-kind (as opposed to cash) assistance to the poor to provide a minimum standard of living for the poor.

PART 5

THE WORLD ECONOMY

Tune into the conversation. It's about *your* course. Just change the names, and it's *your* campus, *your* classroom, *your* professor, *your* classmates, and *you*.

Professor Gottheil and his student, Chris Stefan, a senior majoring in international economics, meet up with each other walking across campus. Gottheil had just assigned the chapters on international trade and exchange rates for next week's discussion. Chris opens the conversation.

CHRIS: Professor Gottheil, I don't know if you recognize me, but I'm in your 10 o'clock class.

GOTTHEIL: You're Chris Stefan, and you sit in the second row.

CHRIS: That's right! If it's not too much of an imposition, could I chat with you while we're walking?

GOTTHEIL: No imposition at all. What's on your mind?

CHRIS: I've already read the chapters on international trade and exchange rates, and I'm really confused. I mean . . . really confused. Mainly about exchange rates. But I'm also sort of puzzled about the way you arranged the chapters in the text.

GOTTHEIL: You mean the chapter organization? What's wrong?

CHRIS: Well, throughout the semester you kept mentioning that we live in a global economy. You kept stressing the term *global*, and how important international trade is in our lives. Many of the examples you use in the text are international, yet we don't really get to international trade and exchange rates until now, toward the end of the course! Why did we wait so long? I mean, don't these chapters belong up front in the textbook because they're so important?

GOTTHEIL: OK, I see your point. You're right about how important these chapters are. But what we really have to understand before we can appreciate the value of international economics are the basic principles of economics, which are what you've been reading about up to now. Once you know the principles, you can apply them everywhere and to all things. Look, we buy bananas from Honduras, and that's called international trade. But is there something special about this trade? Not really. In terms of understanding how economics works, buying bananas from Honduras is no different than buying oranges from California. If you understand how supply and demand for oranges determines the prices of oranges, you really understand all there is to know about international trade and international prices. It's the

exact same economics, just carried across international borders. That's why we can leave international trade and exchange rates until now.

CHRIS: You say understanding the market for oranges is the same as understanding the market for bananas, but is it? It doesn't seem that simple to me. Where do exchange rates fit in? I can understand buying oranges for dollars, but what baffles me is the market for other people's money, like buying so many pesos for a dollar or so many dollars for a peso. That's a different kind of thing, isn't it?

GOTTHEIL: Not really. Let me try to unconfuse you by explaining exchange rates in a very different context. Just forget all about oranges, bananas, dollars, and pesos for now.

CHRIS: OK.

GOTTHEIL: Suppose there are two night spots on campus featuring live entertainment. Let's call them Mabel's and the Blind Pig. And suppose both Mabel's and the Blind Pig sell sets of tickets—say, 10 tickets to a set. Students buy these packets of tickets—let's pick an easy number, say, 100 Mabel's sets and 100 Blind Pig. Are you with me so far?

CHRIS: Sure. There are 200 sets of tickets sold to students and these tickets—2,000 of them—buy admission to live entertainment events. Right?

GOTTHEIL: Right. You can't get in without a ticket. Well, suppose the Breeders are booked to play at Mabel's, and a lot of people holding tickets to the Blind Pig want to see the Breeders. And suppose the Flaming Lips are booked to play at the Blind Pig, and a lot of other students holding Mabel's tickets want to see the Flaming Lips. What do you think would happen?

CHRIS: Well, if I had a Blind Pig ticket but wanted to go to the Breeders concert at Mabel's, I would try to trade my Blind Pig ticket to someone who had Mabel's

continued on next page

CHAT ECONOMICS

tickets but wanted to see the Flaming Lips concert at the Blind Pig.

GOTTHEIL: That makes good sense. And suppose there were 10 like you who wanted to trade Blind Pig tickets for Mabel's tickets, and 10 others who had Mabel's tickets looking for Blind Pig tickets. You would be able to exchange 1 for 1 and satisfy all 20 students. Right?

CHRIS: That's right.

GOTTHEIL: But let's suppose there were 10 like you looking for Mabel's tickets, but only 5 like the other students looking for Blind Pig tickets. Then what? How would you get a Mabel's ticket?

CHRIS: If I really wanted to see the Breeders at Mabel's, I would offer 2, maybe even 3 of my Blind Pig tickets for a single Mabel's.

GOTTHEIL: What if others like you offered 3 Blind Pig tickets, too. You may still not get 1.

CHRIS: That's right. But if I offered 4, maybe someone who had a Mabel's ticket would say, "Hey, I could get to see 4 Blind Pig concerts if I give up the Breeders concert at Mabel's. That's a good deal—I'll do it."

GOTTHEIL: Well that's right, Chris. And that's all there is to exchange rates. Nothing more complicated, and you already understand how it works. Just substitute the United States and Mexico for the two night spots, and substitute U.S. dollars and Mexican pesos for the two kinds of tickets. If you're in the United States and you want to buy something from Mexico, you have to first get Mexican "tickets." We call their tickets Mexico's currency, which is the peso. What we have to give up to get those pesos depends on how many of our own "tickets"—called dollars—Mexicans want, and that depends on how much they want to buy from us. If we want to buy more from Mexicans than they want to buy from us, just like you had to give up more Blind Pig tickets for the Mabel's ticket, we will have to give up more dollars for pesos. These dollars for pesos determine the exchange rate, and the reason why there's a market for other people's money is because we want things from each other.

CHRIS: You know, I think I actually have a better feel for international trade and exchange rates now. I'll try to keep Mabel's and the Blind Pig in mind when I read the chapters again.

To understand how the world economy works, keep in mind the principles you have learned so far. You can apply these principles everywhere and to all things, including the next few chapters.

INTERNATIONAL TRADE

19

Imagine yourself driving in late August along Trans-Canada Highway 401 through the Canadian farmlands of southern Ontario. Suppose you cross the border at Port Huron, Michigan, and continue south along Interstate 69 to Interstate 74, then turn west through central Indiana and Illinois. If you're interested in corn farms, you'll be impressed by the changing heights of the corn stalks you see along the route. They stand under 5 feet in Ontario but reach well over 8 feet in Illinois. That's why so many farmers grow corn in Illinois.

If you later connect with Interstate 57 and drive south to St. Louis, you will see, just off the highway, a profusion of oil wells scattered among the corn fields. Their pumps keep churning away, but the wells don't really produce much oil. At least not nearly the barrels that oil wells in Oklahoma produce.

THIS CHAPTER INTRODUCES YOU TO THE ECONOMIC PRINCIPLES ASSOCIATED WITH:

- ABSOLUTE ADVANTAGE
- COMPARATIVE ADVANTAGE
- FREE TRADE
- TARIFFS
- QUOTAS
- CUSTOMS UNIONS
- FREE TRADE AREAS

If you think about it for a while, you may come to the conclusion that folks in Illinois would be much better off if they just produced corn and left the oil producing to folks in Oklahoma. And you'd be right. Not only would they be better off, but so would folks in Oklahoma. Economic specialization always creates a win-win outcome.

To explain why it's win-win, let's analyze the Illinois economy and compare what people there end up producing and consuming before and after economic specialization. We'll also show that what works for Illinois works as well for Oklahoma, for Mexico, and for the rest of the world.

INTRASTATE TRADE

Illinois Corn for Illinois Oil

Imagine the Illinois economy sealed off from the rest of the world. And suppose that working people in Illinois are either corn farmers or oil producers. In other words, Illinois is a two-goods economy. Let's also suppose that labor is the only resource used to produce goods and that it takes 1 hour of labor to produce either a bushel of corn or a barrel of oil. And to round out the supposes, let's suppose that there are 200 labor hours.

Exhibit 1 portrays Illinois's production possibilities. If the straight-line curve looks unfamiliar to you—a production possibilities curve typically balloons out from the origin—it is because we assume away the law of increasing costs.

How many barrels and bushels does Illinois produce? Look at point *a*. It shows that if Illinois devotes all of its 200 hours of labor to corn production, it produces 200 bushels of corn and 0 barrels of oil. On the other hand, if it puts its 200 hours to oil production, it produces 200 barrels of oil and 0 bushels of corn, point *b*. It can also choose any combination of corn and oil, such as 100 bushels of corn and 100 barrels of oil, point *c*. Let's suppose the choice is point *c*.

If corn farmers want to trade corn for oil, or oil producers want to trade oil for corn, how do they do it? How do they arrive at mutually acceptable prices? For example, how many bushels of corn would an Illinois oil producer expect to get trading a barrel of oil? What about the corn farmer? How many barrels of oil would he get for his bushel? If they produce and sell in competitive markets, the relative prices of oil and corn reflect the relative costs of producing oil and corn.

Given their cost equivalents, a bushel trades for a barrel. That is, if a corn farmer is willing to trade 10 bushels of corn, she can expect to get 10 barrels of oil for them.

EXHIBIT | 1

ILLINOIS PRODUCTION POSSIBILITIES CURVE

The production possibilities curve is drawn as a straight line, reflecting the fact that the opportunity cost is one barrel per bushel regardless of the number of bushels or barrels produced. The economy can use its 200 hours of labor to produce any combination of oil and corn, such as 100 bushels of corn and 100 barrels of oil, shown at point *c*.

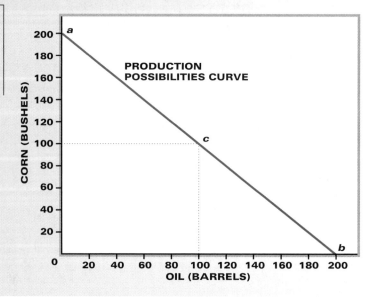

EXHIBIT | 2

Oklahoma Corn for Oklahoma Oil

Let's now look at Oklahoma and suppose, as we did for Illinois, that the Oklahoma economy has 200 hours of labor and is sealed off from the rest of the world. Let's also suppose that Oklahomans, like the folks in Illinois, produce corn and oil, but the labor costs involved in producing corn and oil are different. It takes not 1, but 4 hours of Oklahoma labor to produce a bushel of corn. Their oil fields, however, are another matter. They are gushers. It takes only 20 minutes of labor to fill up a barrel.

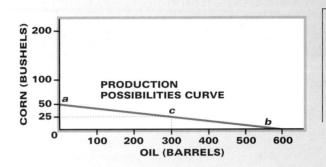

OKLAHOMA PRODUCTION POSSIBILITIES CURVE

The opportunity cost of producing a bushel of corn is 12 barrels of oil. The economy can use its 200 hours of labor to produce any combination of the two, such as 300 barrels of oil and 25 bushels of corn, shown at point *c.*

Exhibit 2 represents Oklahoma's production possibilities. Look at point *a.* If Oklahoma devotes its 200 labor hours to corn, it gets 50 bushels of corn and 0 barrels of oil. If it devotes the 200 labor hours to oil, it gets 600 barrels of oil and 0 bushels of corn, point *b.* Suppose it chooses point *c,* 100 labor-hours producing 25 bushels of corn and 100 labor-hours producing 300 barrels of oil. Since corn and oil exchange according to their relative costs, 1 bushel of corn trades for 12 barrels of oil.

INTERSTATE TRADE

Let's now relax the assumption of sealed-off economies and suppose that people in Illinois can trade with people in Oklahoma, and vice-versa. Imagine yourself as an Illinois corn farmer looking for oil. Here are your options. You can stay in Illinois and trade—at Illinois prices—your bushel of corn for a barrel of oil, or you can take your bushel of corn to Oklahoma and there—at Oklahoma prices—get 12 barrels of oil. No difficulty deciding what to do, right?

For the same reason, an Oklahoma oil producer prefers to buy corn in Illinois. Instead of getting ¹⁄₁₂ of a bushel of corn for his barrel in Oklahoma, he gets an entire bushel of corn trading in Illinois.

It's no secret what would happen if Illinois and Oklahoma engage in **free trade.** Oklahoma oil producers would quickly drive Illinois oilers out of business. Think about it. How can any Illinois oiler who has to pay 1 hour of labor for each barrel compete against a producer who can fill a barrel in 20 minutes?

Free trade
International trade that is not encumbered by protectionist government policies such as tariffs and quotas.

What about corn producers? Here, the tables are turned. Oklahoma farmers wouldn't stand a chance. By the time they could put a bushel of corn together, the Illinois farmer would have 4 in the bin.

The Case for Geographic Specialization

The case for geographic specialization, producing corn in Illinois and oil in Oklahoma, is simple enough: Everybody benefits. We all end up with more corn *and* more oil.

EXHIBIT | 3

PRODUCTION OF CORN AND OIL IN ILLINOIS AND OKLAHOMA, BEFORE AND AFTER FREE TRADE (BUSHELS AND BARRELS)

	NO TRADE		FREE TRADE	
	CORN	OIL	CORN	OIL
ILLINOIS	100	100	200	0
OKLAHOMA	25	300	0	600
TOTAL	125	400	200	600

How can we show the benefits? Suppose people in Illinois use their 200 labor-hours to produce corn exclusively, and people in Oklahoma use their 200 labor-hours to produce oil exclusively. How much better off would they be with this kind of geographic specialization? Exhibit 3 compares their combined productions before and after specialization and free trade.

The results of specialization are dramatic. Illinois workers now produce 200 bushels of corn, or 60 percent more than the amount that two states, with the same number of labor-hours expended, had produced before free trade.

The oil yields are also impressive. The 200 hours of labor expended in Oklahoma produce 600 barrels, or 50 percent more than the amount the two states, with the same number of labor-hours expended, had produced before free trade.

What set of relative prices—barrels in terms of bushels—would they end up with? The price should fall somewhere between 1 barrel per bushel prevailing in Illinois and 12 barrels per bushel prevailing in Oklahoma.

Let's suppose the price is 3 barrels per bushel. Exhibit 4 shows the gains that trade offers to both Illinois and Oklahoma.

Look at Oklahoma's consumption. People there produce 600 barrels of oil, keep 300 barrels for themselves, and sell the remaining 300 barrels to Illinois for 100 bushels of corn. They now have four times their pre-trade corn consumption.

What about people in Illinois? Having bought 300 barrels of oil from Oklahoma with 100 of their 200 bushels of corn, they have 100 bushels of corn left. Look at their improved condition. They have 200 more barrels than their pre-trade consumption. In other words, everybody gains!

Impressive? That's why we consume Oklahoma oil, Illinois corn, Washington apples, Michigan automobiles, Georgia peaches, Idaho potatoes, Florida grapefruit, Hawaii pineapples, Ohio steel, Pennsylvania coal, Oregon lumber, New York banking, North Carolina furniture, Iowa hogs, Louisiana sugar, Wyoming cattle, Vermont maple syrup, and California wine.

CHECK YOUR UNDERSTANDING

Why would an Oklahoma oil producer buy Illinois corn?

EXHIBIT | 4

CORN AND OIL CONSUMPTION IN ILLINOIS AND OKLAHOMA, BEFORE AND AFTER FREE TRADE (BUSHELS AND BARRELS)

	NO TRADE (PRODUCTION = CONSUMPTION)		FREE TRADE (PRODUCTION)		FREE TRADE (CONSUMPTION)	
	CORN	OIL	CORN	OIL	CORN	OIL
ILLINOIS	100	100	200	0	100	300
OKLAHOMA	25	300	0	600	100	300

Nobody Loses?

Are we all always winners? Does nobody lose? Why, then, do we find some people objecting vigorously to free trade? Well, imagine how you would feel if, as an Illinois oil producer, you suddenly discovered an Oklahoma oil producer selling oil in your backyard.

You wouldn't be overjoyed, would you? In fact, you probably couldn't survive the competition. Of course, there's always a place for you farming corn. Still, it isn't entirely painless to give up doing what you know best, oil rigs, and turn to corn farming.

You can count on some oilers trying to prevent Oklahoma oil from coming into Illinois. How could they do that? By exercising political muscle on their Illinois legislators. Nothing really new, is it? That's the primary reason we have protective tariffs.

Of course, if everything else fails, you could always get on a Greyhound bus bound for Tulsa. That's assuming Oklahoma places no restrictions on interstate immigration.

INTERNATIONAL TRADE

The same economic argument that promotes interstate free trade should promote international free trade. After all, why should national boundaries have any bearing on the economic benefits that people derive from free trade?

Suppose, for example, that it takes only 10 minutes to produce a barrel of oil in Mexico. That's half the labor cost of an Oklahoma barrel. Suppose also that it takes Mexican farmers one hour to produce a bushel of corn.

The conditions are ripe, now, for exploiting the full benefits of **international specialization** and trade. United States corn for Mexican oil. Why not? *Everybody ends up with more corn and more oil.*

Let's pursue the argument. Exhibit 5 details the before-and-after conditions of international free trade. Before free trade, the United States split its 400 labor-hours evenly, with 200 hours devoted to oil and 200 to corn production. Mexico did the same with its 400 labor-hours.

U.S. oilers now face the same problem Illinois oilers did before interstate trade. How can U.S. oilers survive against a more efficient Mexican competitor?

Look at the relative prices of corn and oil in the United States and Mexico. U.S. farmers could get 3 barrels of oil for their bushel of corn. However, if they sold their bushel of corn on the Mexican market at Mexican prices, they could take home 6 barrels of oil!

Mexican oilers will immediately discover the advantages of international free trade as well. Why should they sell their oil for Mexican corn? The relative prices in Mexico—6 barrels to 1 bushel—will give the Mexican oiler only ⅙ bushel of corn for his barrel. By selling the Mexican barrel north of the border at U.S. prices, the Mexican takes home ⅓ bushel of corn. That's twice the quantity of corn that could be obtained in Mexico.

International specialization
The use of a country's resources to produce specific goods and services, allowing other countries to focus on the production of other goods and services.

PRODUCTION OF CORN AND OIL IN THE UNITED STATES AND MEXICO, BEFORE AND AFTER FREE TRADE (BUSHELS AND BARRELS)

	NO TRADE		FREE TRADE	
	CORN	OIL	CORN	OIL
UNITED STATES	200	600	400	0
MEXICO	200	1,200	0	2,400
TOTAL	400	1,800	400	2,400

EXHIBIT 5

International competition will drive both the United States and Mexico to specialize. The United States becomes the corn producer; Mexico becomes the oil producer.

As we see in Exhibit 5, total production increases from 400 bushels of corn and 1,800 barrels of oil to 400 bushels of corn and 2,400 barrels of oil. That's a net gain of 600 barrels of oil.

What set of prices—barrels in terms of bushels—would prevail on the international market? Clearly, it has to be at least 3 barrels per bushel, otherwise U.S. farmers would do better buying oil at home. It also has to be no more than 6 barrels per bushel, because Mexican oilers can purchase a bushel of corn in Mexico for 6 barrels.

Exhibit 6 shows what happens to the consumption of corn and oil in the United States and Mexico before and after free trade when price is 4 barrels per bushel.

The United States produces 400 bushels of corn, keeps half, and exports the remaining 200 bushels to Mexico in exchange for 800 barrels of oil. Free trade has increased U.S. oil consumption by $800 - 600 = 200$ barrels.

What about Mexico? Having bought 200 bushels of corn from the United States with 800 barrels of oil, it is left with $2,400 - 800 = 1,600$ barrels, which is 400 barrels more than it had before. Both the United States and Mexico have gained.

ABSOLUTE AND COMPARATIVE ADVANTAGE

Some trading economies are considered perfect trading partners because each can produce one of the goods with fewer resources than the other, that is, using less labor.

Absolute advantage
A country's ability to produce a good using fewer resources than the country it trades with.

Economists describe each economy engaged in such trade as having an **absolute advantage.** In our illustration of interstate trade, Illinois has an absolute advantage in growing corn, and Oklahoma has an absolute advantage in producing oil. It's easy to think of real-world absolute advantage cases. What about trade of Japan's automobiles for Egypt's cotton? Do you suppose each country has an absolute advantage? Or Colombian coffee for U.S. steel? Or Czech glass for Russian caviar? Or Israeli oranges for Icelandic fish? Or Dutch tulips for Danish furniture?

Comparative Advantage

Absolute advantage, however, is not always the condition under which nations trade. In fact, absolute advantage is not present when the United States trades corn for Mexican oil (see Exhibit 5 again).

EXHIBIT | 6

CORN AND OIL CONSUMPTION IN THE UNITED STATES AND MEXICO, BEFORE AND AFTER FREE TRADE (BUSHELS AND BARRELS)

	NO TRADE (PRODUCTION = CONSUMPTION)		FREE TRADE (PRODUCTION)		FREE TRADE (CONSUMPTION)	
	CORN	OIL	CORN	OIL	CORN	OIL
UNITED STATES	200	600	400	0	200	800
MEXICO	200	1,200	0	2,400	200	1,600

There, Mexico uses fewer resources than the United States to produce oil—10 minutes per barrel versus 20 minutes per barrel—but the same quantity of resources as the United States to produce corn—both one hour per bushel. The United States had no absolute advantage in trading with Mexico. Yet Mexico still gains by specializing in oil.

Why? Why should Mexico bother importing corn from the United States when it can grow its own corn at home using the same quantity of labor that Americans use? The reason is that even though the absolute cost of producing corn in Mexico is the same as it is in the United States, the *opportunity cost of producing corn in Mexico is higher.* Consider this: The one hour of labor used to produce corn in Mexico could be used to produce 12 barrels of oil. That is, Mexico gives up 12 barrels of oil to get that 1 bushel of corn. In the United States, Americans give up only 3 barrels of oil to produce a bushel of corn. In other words, the opportunity cost of producing corn in the United States is considerably lower. This lower opportunity cost is defined by economists as a **comparative advantage** for the United States.

The United States has a comparative advantage—a lower opportunity cost—in producing corn, and Mexico has a comparative advantage—a lower opportunity cost—in producing oil. Both countries gain if each specializes in producing the good that affords it a comparative advantage. Even if Mexico had an absolute advantage over the United States in both corn and oil production, it would still benefit Mexico to abandon producing the good that has the higher opportunity cost.

How Much Is Gained from Free Trade Depends on Price

Look at Exhibit 7. Suppose price is 4 barrels per bushel. Look at Mexico's consumption of oil and corn before and after trade. Mexico, specializing in oil, keeps 1,600 of the 2,400 barrels it produces and trades the remaining 800 barrels to the United States for corn. It ends up, then, with 200 bushels of corn. This 1,600 barrels and 200 bushels compares favorably to the 1,200 barrels and 200 bushels Mexico would have consumed if it did not trade with the United States.

Suppose, however, that the price is set at 5 barrels per bushel instead of 4. The gains from trade are now distributed somewhat differently. At 5 barrels per bushel, the United States, still producing 400 bushels of corn, keeps half and exports the remaining 200 bushels to Mexico for 1,000 barrels of oil. That's $1,000 - 800 = 200$ barrels more than it got from Mexico when the price was 4 barrels per bushel.

CHECK YOUR UNDERSTANDING

Why would Mexico import U.S. corn when it can produce the corn using the same labor-hours?

Comparative advantage
A country's ability to produce a good at a lower opportunity cost than the country with which it trades.

EXHIBIT|7

CORN AND OIL CONSUMPTION IN THE UNITED STATES AND MEXICO, UNDER CONDITIONS OF NO TRADE AND FREE TRADE

	NO TRADE		FREE TRADE			
			4 BARRELS/BUSHEL		5 BARRELS/BUSHEL	
	CORN	OIL	CORN	OIL	CORN	OIL
UNITED STATES	200	600	200	800	200	1,000
MEXICO	200	1,200	200	1,600	200	1,400

What about Mexico? Having bought 200 bushels of corn from the United States with 1,000 barrels of oil, it is left with 1,400 barrels, which is still more oil than it consumed before free trade. That is, the shift in price from 4 to 5 barrels per bushel shifts the gains from free trade to the United States. If the price increases to 6 barrels per bushel, the gains from trade would shift *completely* to the United States.

Political power sometimes influences international prices and therefore the distribution of gains among the trading nations. During the era of European colonialism in the 17th through 19th centuries, lopsided gains were commonplace. Trade between the colonies and the European colonial powers was often politically engineered, giving the Europeans exclusive rights to markets and at prices designed to shift most of the gains to them.

Today, it's not so much political power as the market power of supply and demand that determines international prices. An increase in world demand for corn, for example, will have more influence in shifting prices from $2 to $3 per bushel than all the speeches in the Mexican Assembly or the U.S. Congress.

CALCULATING TERMS OF TRADE

Many of the less-developed countries (LDCs) of Asia, Africa, and Latin America are behind the proverbial eight ball when it comes to international prices and gains from trade. Why? LDC exports, which are typically agricultural, trade on highly competitive markets. Their principal **imports** from the industrially advanced economies, on the other hand, are manufactured goods traded in markets that tend to be far less competitive. As a result, new technologies in agriculture and shifts in demand for agricultural exports over the years have depressed the LDCs' **export** prices, while new technologies in manufacturing and changing demands for manufacturing imports have raised the LDCs' import prices.

Imports
Goods and services bought by people in one country that are produced in other countries.

Exports
Goods and services produced by people in one country that are sold in other countries.

The Dilemma of the Less-Developed Countries

Exhibit 8 illustrates the problem facing the less-developed economies. It shows what happens to the prices of Japanese motorcycles and Bolivian tin when demands and supplies for these goods change over time. Let's look at 1995 and 2001.

In panel *a,* a strong increase in demand combines with a moderate increase in supply to raise the price of motorcycles from $6,000 to $7,500. (These are hypothetical numbers, of course.) In panel *b,* a moderate increase in demand combines with a strong increase in supply to decrease the price of tin from $6,000 to $5,000 a ton. Back in 1995, Bolivians bought a motorcycle with a ton of tin. Not so in 2001. Now, it takes 1½ tons of tin to buy that same motorcycle.

Economists express Bolivia's deteriorating international trade position with Japan in the **terms of trade** equation:

Terms of trade
The amount of a good or service (export) that must be given up to buy a unit of another good or service (import). A country's terms of trade are measured by the ratio of the country's export prices to its import prices.

$$\frac{\text{index of export prices}}{\text{index of import prices}} \times 100$$

Using Bolivia's tin export prices to represent the index of its export prices in general, and using Japan's motorcycle prices to represent the index of the price of goods Bolivia imports, then the terms of trade for Bolivia in 1995 was

$$\frac{\$6,000}{\$6,000} \times 100 = 100.$$

JAPANESE MOTORCYCLE AND BOLIVIAN TIN EXPORTS

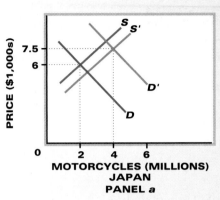

MOTORCYCLES (MILLIONS)
JAPAN
PANEL *a*

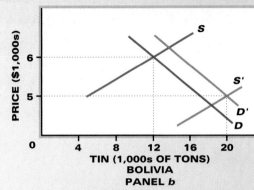

TIN (1,000s OF TONS)
BOLIVIA
PANEL *b*

Panel *a* depicts the shifts in the demand for and supply of Japanese motorcycles. The robust demand shift, from *D* to *D'*, combines with the moderate supply shift, from *S* to *S'*, to raise the price of motorcycles from $6,000 to $7,500. Panel *b* depicts the shifts in the demand for and supply of Bolivian tin. The moderate demand shift, from *D* to *D'*, combines with the robust supply shift, from *S* to *S'*, to reduce price from $6,000 to $5,000 per ton.

Look what happens in 2001. Bolivia's terms of trade deteriorates to

$$\frac{\$5,000}{\$7,500} \times 100 = 66.7.$$

Bolivia's exports end up with only 67 percent of their former purchasing power. Of course, the Japanese are delighted. The gains from international trade move in their favor. And there isn't much Bolivia can do about it. It simply obeys the dictates of the markets. Should Bolivia give up trading with Japan? Certainly not! Bolivia is still better off trading than not trading. After all, the opportunity cost of producing a motorcycle in Bolivia is, more likely than not, greater than the 1½ tons of tin it must now pay for the Japanese motorcycle.

**C H E C K   Y O U R
U N D E R S T A N D I N G**

Why shouldn't Bolivia stop trading when its terms of trade worsens?

Looking at Real-World Numbers

What do real-world LDC terms of trade look like? Two features seem to dominate: year-to-year volatility and for many LDCs, steadily worsening terms of trade. The data in Exhibit 9 show a worsening condition for ten LDCs over the period 1995–98. In the Central African Republic, for example, a unit of exports in 1998 buys less than two-thirds of the imports it was able to buy in 1995. For Pakistan, a unit of its exports in 1998 buys a little less than 90 percent of what that unit bought in 1995.

As you see in Exhibit 10, most of the data for the six LDCs show evidence of high

LDC TERMS OF TRADE FOR 1998 (1995 = 100)

PAKISTAN	88.9	COLOMBIA	84.6
NIGERIA	86.8	REPUBLIC OF CONGO	82.3
UGANDA	78.2	ETHIOPIA	89.1
ZAMBIA	83.7	JAMAICA	77.3
CENTRAL AFRICAN REP.	64.3	BURUNDI	76.2

Source: *World Development Indicators, 2000,* The World Bank.

EXHIBIT|10

TERMS OF TRADE VOLATILITY FOR LDCS: 1990–98 (1995 = 100)

	1990	1992	1994	1996	1998
BURUNDI	74.6	56.7	102.8	74.1	76.2
ETHIOPIA	89.6	139.0	83.7	89.0	89.0
GUATEMALA	83.4	91.9	97.3	89.2	100.0
NIGERIA	161.0	117.0	102.2	163.2	86.8
UGANDA	74.1	61.5	66.9	80.1	78.2
BANGLADESH	92.9	82.9	93.6	102.5	98.8

Source: *World Development Indicators, 2000,* The World Bank.

volatility during the 1990–98 period. Burundi's terms of trade, for example, bounced from 56.7 in 1992 to 102.8 in 1994 to 74.1 in 1996.

WHO TRADES WITH WHOM? TRACKING INTERNATIONAL TRADE

on the net

The World Trade Organization (WTO) (http://www.wto.org/), an international body addressing trade among nations, provides data and analysis on international trade.

Small wonder that the world's economies are engaged in massive exchanges of almost every kind of familiar and exotic good. We find food processors from France, television sets from Japan, wool sweaters from Scotland, processed meat from Australia, microchips from Israel, cheese from Switzerland, coffee from Brazil, tin from Bolivia, anchovies from Portugal, shirts from China, and shoes from Italy in almost every one of our metropolitan and small-town markets.

They are found as well in markets all over the world. No surprise also that the United States is a major world trading partner. Our imports provide vital markets to many exporting countries. Our exports rank among the highly competitive goods and services sold on international markets.

More and more, the world's economies are becoming linked into one unified market network. In 1999, more than 15 percent of the world's GDP made its way onto the international market in the form of exports. That compares to less than 3 percent of the world's GDP in 1970. As communications and transportation technologies become even more advanced and accessible, we should expect that exports and imports in the 21st century will account for even higher percentages of the world's production.

The one striking observation we can draw from international trade statistics is that the big ones play with the big ones and even the little ones want to play with the big ones. Look at Exhibit 11.

EXHIBIT|11

PERCENTAGE DISTRIBUTION OF EXPORTS TO DEVELOPED, LDCs, AND OTHER ECONOMIES: 1999

EXPORTER	EXPORTS TO	
	DEVELOPED	LDCs
DEVELOPED	72.9	26.4
LDCs	58.4	34.7
WORLD	68.0	30.9

Source: *Direction of Trade Statistics, Yearbook 2000* (Washington, D.C.: International Monetary Fund, 2000).

1999 EXPORTS AND IMPORTS OF THE MAJOR DEVELOPED ECONOMIES ($ BILLIONS)

	EXPORTS	IMPORTS		EXPORTS	IMPORTS
UNITED STATES	$702.1	$1,059.4	CANADA	$238.5	$214.8
GERMANY	541.1	472.2	ITALY	230.2	216.6
JAPAN	419.4	311.3	THE NETHERLANDS	200.3	187.5
FRANCE	300.9	291.3	BELGIUM	178.9	163.9
BRITAIN	268.2	317.9	KOREA	144.8	119.8

Source: *Direction of Trade Statistics, Yearbook 2000* (Washington, D.C.: International Monetary Fund, 2000).

Approximately two-thirds of world exports in 1999 were exported to the industrially developed countries. The less-developed countries accounted for the remaining one-third. The major markets for the exports of the developed economies were themselves. They absorbed 72.9 percent of their own exports. They also absorbed 58.4 percent of LDC exports.

The Major Leagues

There's no doubt which of the developed economies play in the major leagues. Exhibit 12 lists them in order of their 1999 trade volumes.

The United States dominates the list. Its $1,761.5 billion trade volume is followed by Germany's $1,013.3 billion. But, as you see, all 10 countries have annual trade volumes in excess of $250 billion. That puts them in a league by themselves.

WHO DOES THE UNITED STATES TRADE WITH?

There is so much heated discussion over our trade relations with Japan that sometimes we tend to forget that Japan comes in third to our primary trading partners, Canada and Mexico.

Proximity is important. Look at Exhibit 13. Trade between Canada and the United States represents the largest trade flow between any two countries in the

1999 U.S. TRADE WITH ITS MAJOR TRADING PARTNERS ($ BILLIONS)

	U.S. EXPORTS TO	U.S. IMPORTS FROM		U.S. EXPORTS TO	U.S. IMPORTS FROM
CANADA	$162.9	$198.8	CHINA	$25.6	$97.4
MEXICO	86.4	109.5	KOREA	22.2	31.8
JAPAN	57.7	134.0	THE NETHERLANDS	19.3	8.9
BRITAIN	38.5	39.9	FRANCE	18.8	26.7
GERMANY	27.0	55.8	ITALY	10.1	23.2

Source: *Direction of Trade Statistics, Yearbook 2000* (Washington, D.C.: International Monetary Fund, 2000).

INTERDISCIPLINARY PERSPECTIVE

TRADE AND CULTURE

Disneyland Paris is the number one tourist destination in Europe! Does that surprise you? The United States's own Disneyland and Disney World are tourist magnets attracting millions of Americans and foreign visitors year after year. But that's understandable. Disney is as American as apple pie and has come to symbolize, both here and abroad, what American culture is, circa 2000.

But *Europe?* While the changing of the guards at Buckingham Palace makes a lovely Kodak moment and strolling the Champs-Elysées or climbing the Eiffel Tower are activities that European tourists—and the French, in particular—love to do on vacation, none of them can exert the pull on European hearts and wallets that Mickey Mouse can.

And wouldn't you think that would annoy the French? In fact, they're almost schizophrenic about it! On the one hand, the French are frightfully proud of their culture—their food and drink, their music, their cinema, their fine arts and entertainment—but on the other hand, they seem to be more and more willing to trade in their baguette for the Big Mac, their wine for Coke, and their cinema for Hollywood.

What had been uniquely French about the French is becoming less and less so and what is American about the French is becoming more and more so. And it's not because U.S. marines are imposing an unwanted American culture on the defenseless French. It is, instead, the French going into the marketplace with their hard-earned francs and with much eagerness to buy that American culture. The lesson is learned everywhere: In an open and free market economy, consumer sovereignty dictates.

What annoys the French annoys others as well. The Canadians, sharing a 3,000-mile open border with the United States, are particularly anxious about the Canadian infatuation with American culture. They fear that in the free exchange of goods,

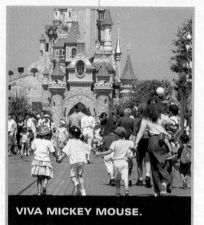

VIVA MICKEY MOUSE.

services, ideas, and culture, the cherished differences—real and imagined—between Canadian and American life will all but disappear.

Whether there's any legitimacy to the French or Canadian or any other national concern about erosion of culture, the question arises about trade and culture in the 21st century: Can *any* national culture survive the global market?

That's what was at the heart of the matter when in June 1998, culture ministers from 23 countries met in Canada at the invitation of the Canadian government to discuss their shared fear that the United States routinely and aggressively sacrifices culture for free trade.

The immediate provocation for the Canadians was their loss to the United States at the World Trade Organization (WTO) of a vital cultural matter. The WTO struck down Canada's 80 percent excise tax on split-run editions of foreign (mainly U.S.) magazines. The WTO insisted that America's *Newsweek, Time, U.S. News & World Report,* and others should be able to compete on equal terms with Canadian magazines, such as *Maclean's.* The Canadian fear is that in an open and competitive marketplace, Canadian-owned and Canadian-focused *Maclean's* would not survive. That is, Canadian readers would prefer the American choices just as many Canadian television viewers prefer America's CNN to its Canadian equivalents.

Another incendiary issue to Canadians is the fate of hockey in Canada. To many sports-minded Canadians, Canadian culture is hockey. But that, too, is changing. In the mid-1990s, two of the seven Canadian teams in the National Hockey League (NHL) left Canada for the green pastures (read: money) to the south: the Winnipeg Jets to Phoenix and the Quebec Nordiques to Colorado. No less upsetting to Canadian hockey fans was the sale of the Montreal Canadiens in 2001 to an American multimillionaire, the Canadiens' only non-Canadian owner in its 91-year history. While the nationality of buyers and sellers is of little consequence in the U.S. marketplace, it is a matter of much concern in Canada.

But what are the Canadian—and French, and Spanish, and British, *and American*—alternatives to the global marketplace? Is national culture destined to be a casualty of modern technology, as were the stagecoach, the steam locomotive, and first-class mail? The marketplace, it appears, takes no prisoners.

MORE ON THE NET

Visit the International Network on Cultural Policy (http://www.pch.gc.ca/network-reseau/eng.htm), which grew out of the cultural meeting that took place in Ottawa in 1998. What is the goal of this network? How does it intend to achieve this goal?

world. Mexico ranks as our second largest trading partner. U.S. exports to Canada and Mexico were greater than the combined U.S. exports to all the other countries shown in Exhibit 13.

No wonder many Canadians are upset about our benign neglect of them. Important as they are to us, however, we are much more important to them. The United States alone bought 83.2 percent of Canada's 1999 exports to the world. U.S. markets also bought as much as 89.6 percent of Mexico's exports.

Their import packages, too, carry a clear U.S. stamp. U.S. exports to Canada added up to 87.2 percent of their total 1999 imports, and U.S. exports to Mexico accounted for 88.1 percent of its 1999 total imports. For both neighboring economies, that's an enormous one-country dependence.

The singular importance of the United States to Canada and Mexico is striking when compared to their next-best markets. For example, Canada's 208 billion in exports to the United States was followed by its $5.3 billion exports to Japan. Mexico's $120.4 billion exports to the United States towered over its $1.2 billion exports to Canada.

DO WE NEED PROTECTION AGAINST FREE TRADE?

No one, not even those who lobby Congress for protection against free trade, deny the economic benefits that free trade offers. The evidence is overwhelming. The arguments against free trade, then, are made strictly as *exceptions to the rule*. They address particular circumstances.

Ask U.S. oil producers how much they benefit when we allow Mexican oil into U.S. markets. The economic pain *they* suffer is, unquestionably, real. Although in general the nation gains from free trade—tens of millions of U.S. oil consumers now pay less for oil—some individuals do get hurt.

How do we weigh the widespread general gains against the particular losses? Should we simply ignore the downside of free trade, or is that pushing a good thing too far? For example, should we sacrifice gains to protect injured parties? *All* injured parties?

A number of classic arguments have been made against *indiscriminate* free trade. These have had considerable effect not only in persuading Congress to limit trade in specific industries of our economy, but also in persuading other governments to do precisely the same in their economies, and for the same reasons.

The National Security Argument

Suppose France's Mirage is a less costly, more effective fighter aircraft than our own F-16. Should we close down our F-16 factories and import Mirages? Although this move might create gains from trade for both the United States and France, we do not want to rely on France for our national survival. Most of the major industrial economies of the world produce their own security systems, even though most understand that they forfeit the gains that would result from international specialization. Production of weapons, munitions, missiles, tanks, submarines, aircraft carriers, cannons, and radar equipment are obvious candidates for protection against free trade on national security grounds.

Some goods, however, are less obvious, and that's when abuse begins. It's not terribly difficult, particularly for industry lobbyists, to draw some connection between any industry and national security.

The national security argument against free trade has a long and active history. As early as 1815, the British Parliament enacted a series of corn laws that established tariffs on grain imports from Europe. Although corn law advocates insisted that England must never be beholden to Europeans for their food supply, their main objective was to protect the English landlord class (and their rents) from the cheaper European grain.

What worked then, works today. Our agricultural industries, too, have invoked the national security argument to protect markets from cheaper imports.

In fact, almost everything can be brought under the umbrella of the national security argument. In times of national crisis, can we really rely on foreign supplies of sheet metal? What about photographic equipment, surveying instruments, lumber, pharmaceuticals, steel fabrication, optical equipment, orthopedic equipment, radio communication systems, and petrochemicals? Shouldn't they, too, qualify for protection on national security grounds?

If you had to make the case in Congress for widening protection on grounds of national security, what other industries would you suggest protecting? Go to the Interactive Study Center at http://gottheil.swcollege.com and click on the "Your Turn" button to submit your example. Student submissions will be posted to the Web site, and perhaps we will use some in future editions of the book!

The Infant Industries Argument

Learning curves—time required to gain expertise—apply to new industries just as they do to people. Because of that, it's sometimes unfair to expect a fledgling industry at home to survive free trade competition from its older, more-experienced foreign competitors. It needs more time.

Protecting infant industries from foreign competition, then, has some validity, because without such protection, many promising industries just wouldn't get started. It's perhaps worthwhile for a country to suffer the higher prices of its own less-efficient new industries in the short run because it expects to gain from greater efficiency and lower prices in the long run.

But how long is the long run? When is an industry's infancy period over? There's the problem. The comforts of protection, once experienced by the infant industry, are difficult to forgo. Many, having run the learning curve many times over, are still as inefficient as they were the day protection was granted. Others remain protected under new guises. Our steel industry, for example, was protected as an infant industry over a century ago and is still protected today. It's an argument that can too easily be abused.

The Cheap Foreign Labor Argument

Perhaps the most frequently invoked battle cry against indiscriminate free trade is the injustice of having to compete in markets against foreign firms that employ cheap labor. How can the U.S. textile industry, for example, employing highly paid unionized labor, compete against textiles imported from Jamaica, China, Brazil, Mexico, the Philippines, and Malaysia? Those countries, even if unions exist at all, still pay wage rates considerably below U.S. levels. Some argue that the U.S. textile industry can't compete, and the consequences are declining wages rates, real incomes, employment, and standards of living at home.

You may wonder if that is really so. The cheap foreign labor argument ignores the fact that higher levels of productivity (output per hour) typically accompany the higher wage rates in the United States, so that the wage cost per unit of U.S. manufactured goods is not necessarily higher than the wage cost associated with the foreign good.

If raincoats produced in China are less costly because of cheap labor than the raincoats produced in New York, shouldn't we take advantage of the lower price? After all, isn't that precisely why we engage in specialization? Rather than lowering our standard of living, trade with low-wage economies increases the real goods we are able to purchase, so that our living standards should actually improve.

Of course, the widespread gains consumers enjoy from such trade are not universally shared. Some people end up losing. Some firms, for example, cannot survive the competition. People lose jobs and don't always find new ones. Entrepreneurs fail, and many never recover. Stockholders lose their investment, and many never invest again.

CHECK YOUR UNDERSTANDING

What is the major flaw in the cheap foreign labor argument supporting protection?

The Diversity-of-Industry Argument

Some economies have become so highly specialized in one or two production activities that these alone account for a major share of national product and, typically, an even greater share of exports. Think, for example, of Saudi Arabia and oil, or Honduras and bananas. When the prices of their few specialized exports are relatively high, their economies perform well. When prices fall, however, their economies suffer.

Since these prices reflect the swings of demand and supply in the international market, in many cases the fate of highly specialized economies is out of their hands. Moreover, if the swings are erratic, these economies also tend to become unpredictable and unstable.

No one wants to live in an unstable world. Good enough reason to diversify industrial production, isn't it? That's where protection comes in.

Many less-developed countries argue for such protection. They understand the costs involved in abandoning specialization but still prefer the greater economic stability that the protection affords. In their case, it may make sense. However, it is hardly the argument that industries in the United States can make for protection. The United States and Western European economies are already sufficiently diversified.

The Antidumping Argument

Some industries seeking protection insist that it is not lack of absolute or comparative advantage on the international market that does them in, but rather the sinister strategies of their foreign competition. Why sinister? Because their foreign competitors dump goods on the market, *priced below cost,* to knock them out of the game. Once the competition is eliminated, these sinister producers—now monopolists—

will use their monopoly power to raise prices to levels even higher than they were before. That's pretty cheeky, isn't it?

Dumping
Exporting a good or service at a price below its cost of production.

Our Congress thought so, and made **dumping** on our markets illegal. The problem is, how do we go about proving that low-cost foreign goods are priced below cost? One way is to compare the export prices of the foreign producer to the prices it charges in its own domestic market. That's not always easy to do, and sometimes the comparisons are rigged to support inefficient producers in the United States.

The Retaliation Argument

Should we allow other countries free access to our markets if they restrict our exports in theirs? That's rather unfair, isn't it? Yet that's precisely the trading conditions we confront with many of our trading partners. Perhaps the most glaring case of such lopsided access is our trading experience with Japan. Our complaints to them about their restrictive practices seem to fall on deaf ears.

Many U.S. producers, frustrated by Japanese protection of their own domestic markets, call for retaliation. If the Japanese won't allow us free entry into their markets, they argue, we should simply deny them free entry into ours. Since we are a major market for their exports, the retaliation may "encourage" them to rethink their protection strategies.

It may in fact work. With greater access to their markets, our own export and even import volumes would most likely increase, benefiting both us and the Japanese. It may make sense, then, to threaten retaliation—and even in some cases to carry out the threat.

But suppose retaliation doesn't work. If it leaves us with less, not greater trade, it makes no sense at all. After all, even with restricted access to their markets, we still benefit by importing Japanese goods. Otherwise, we wouldn't import them.

THE ECONOMICS OF TRADE PROTECTION

How do we restrict imports? Basically, with tariffs and quotas. What are they, and how do they work?

Tariffs

Tariff
A tax on an imported good.

A **tariff** is a government-imposed tax on imports. It can be levied as a percentage of the import's value or as a specific tax per unit of import. Like any other tax, it becomes government revenue. Although U.S. importers pay the tariff to U.S. customs when importing foreign goods, they typically shift at least part of it onto the consumer by raising prices. To the consumer, the tariff is invisible. After all, do you really know what percentage of the price you pay for an Italian bike is the tariff on the bike and what percentage represents the price the Italian bike producer actually receives?

The U.S. International Trade Commission (http://www.usitc.gov/), the Office of the U.S. Trade Representative (http://www.ustr.gov/), and the U.S. Department of State (http://www.state.gov/www/issues/economic/trade_reports/) issue reports on foreign trade barriers and unfair practices.

How can a U.S. tariff on bikes protect U.S. producers? Let's suppose that bike manufacturers in the United States cannot produce a bike as inexpensively as manufacturers in Italy. Suppose the Italians price their bikes in U.S. markets at $200, which is $250 less than the $450 price for U.S. bikes on the U.S. market.

Without a tariff, the U.S. manufacturers are in serious trouble. How can they compete with the cheaper Italian bike? But suppose Congress, persuaded by any one of the protectionist arguments, imposes a 100 percent tariff, that is, a $200 add-on to the price of Italian bikes. Exhibit 14 shows what happens to the price and quantity of bikes bought and sold under conditions of no foreign trade, unrestricted foreign trade, and tariff-restricted foreign trade.

TARIFF-RESTRICTED TRADE

EXHIBIT | 14

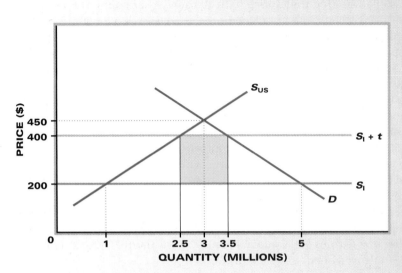

The supply curve, S_{US}, records the quantity of bikes U.S. producers are willing to supply at varying prices. The demand curve records the quantity of bikes Americans are willing to buy at varying prices. With no foreign suppliers, 3 million would be bought and sold at an equilibrium price of $450.

S_I records the willingness of Italian bike producers to supply any quantity at $200. When Italian suppliers are allowed to enter the U.S. market, equilibrium price and the quantities of bikes demanded and supplied in the United States change dramatically. Price falls from $450 to $200 and the quantity demanded increases to 5 million; 1 million supplied by U.S. producers and 4 million imported from Italy.

If the U.S. government imposes a 100 percent tariff on bikes, the Italian supply curve in the United States becomes $S_I + t$. At a price of $400, 3.5 million bikes are demanded: 2.5 million supplied by U.S. producers and 1 million imported from Italy. The shaded area shows the U.S. government's tariff revenue.

The supply curve, S_{US}, represents the quantities of bikes that U.S. producers are willing to supply at various prices. The demand curve represents U.S. demand for bikes. If the market were completely insulated from foreign competition, U.S. manufacturers would be busy producing 3 million bikes and selling them at a price of $450.

Let's now introduce free trade. Suppose Italian producers are willing to supply any quantity of bikes at a $200 price. The Italian supply curve on the U.S. market is shown as S_I. How does that supply affect U.S. manufacturers?

At a $200 price, U.S. consumers increase their quantity demanded from 3 to 5 million bikes. Only 1 million of the 5 million, however, would be supplied by U.S. manufacturers. That is, the U.S. firms lose 2 million of their former sales to Italian competitors and now have only 20 percent of this new, flourishing market. We now import 4 million Italian bikes. You can imagine how the U.S. bike manufacturers would react.

Suppose a 100 percent tariff, t, is applied to bikes. The Italian supply curve shifts to $S_I + t$, and the price of Italian bikes in the U.S. market increases to $400. At this higher price, the quantity demanded by U.S. consumers falls from 5 to 3.5 million. U.S. firms produce 2.5 million, and importers of Italian bikes provide the other million.

In other words, the tariff gives the U.S. bike industry a new lease on life, but only at the expense of the U.S. consumer. What about government? It ends up with a revenue of $200 × 1 million = $200 million, the shaded rectangle in Exhibit 14.

Quotas

Sometimes governments prefer to restrict imports by imposing a **quota** instead of a tariff. What's the difference? Tariffs are import taxes added to prices; quotas limit the amount of a good that is allowed into the country at any price.

Quota
A limit on the quantity of a specific good that can be imported.

The outcomes are different. Let's suppose that instead of placing a 100 percent tariff on Italian bike imports, the government limits the number of imports to 500,000 units. Picture the scene. U.S. importers would be busy making long-distance calls to Rome to buy up the 500,000 Italian bikes. These are brought into the U.S. market at the free trade price of $200 each. What happens now? Look at Exhibit 15.

The supply curve is horizontal until we reach 1.5 million bikes, reflecting 500,000 supplied by Italian producers and 1 million that U.S. producers are willing to supply at $200. At higher prices, the supply curve becomes S', the horizontal sum of the U.S. supply curve, S, and the 500,000 quota.

There we have it. The U.S. producers suffer a slight fall from the quantities they would sell if there were no Italian competitors in the market, from 3 million to 2.75 million. Quota protection raises the price from $200 to $420, although it is still less than the $450 that would prevail without competition from Italy.

What about the Italian bike producers? They sell their 500,000 quota to importers at $200 per bike. The importers, then, end up with a $420 − $200 = $220 windfall on each bike.

The protection options with the quota are almost countless. Each specific quota yields a unique U.S. production and market price. As with the tariff, there's no magic number that defines every quota. It could be any number, depending on the objectives of the government and U.S. producers.

Other Nontariff Barriers

Tariffs and quotas are not the only mechanisms that can be used by domestic producers and by government to reduce imports. The government can also pass a law that specifies highly restrictive health and safety standards that imports must meet. For example, the government can insist that all Italian bikes be dismantled and reassembled by U.S. bike inspectors—at a cost, say, of $75 per bike—to guarantee safety.

EXHIBIT | 15

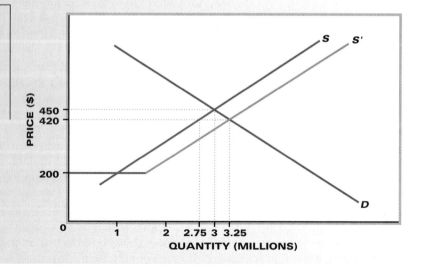

QUOTA-RESTRICTED TRADE

With no free trade, 3 million bikes are bought and sold in the United States at an equilibrium price of $450. If the U.S. government sets an import quota of 500,000 bikes, the relevant supply curve becomes S' (which is S + 500,000). The equilibrium price falls to $420, and 3.25 million bikes are bought and sold, of which 2.75 million are produced by U.S. suppliers.

That's not a particularly creative idea. The Japanese once prohibited ski imports because, they maintained, only Japanese skis were suitable for Japanese snow. The Germans disallowed foreign-brewed beer on grounds of health and safety. U.S. beef imports were shut out of European markets because U.S. cattle were fed with government-approved hormones.

In some cases, import barriers are self-imposed by foreign exporters who agree to "voluntarily" limit the quantity of their exports. For example, Japanese automakers voluntarily agreed to limit auto exports to the United States. They understood the alternatives: Volunteer or face higher tariffs or lower quotas.

NEGOTIATING TARIFF STRUCTURES

Whatever tariff structure a nation chooses, it would seem only fair that the structure, once established between two trading partners, should apply to all other countries as well. For example, if the United States and France agree to a mutual reduction, from 40 to 25 percent, in their tariffs on imported wine, then a third country, say Portugal, should be allowed to sell its wine in the United States and France at the same 25 percent tariff rate. Otherwise, international trade would be marked by country-to-country discrimination.

This idea of tariff **reciprocity** became the guiding principle industrial nations adopted after World War II in establishing rules of international trade. The aim was to increase the free movement of goods across national boundaries, and to do so nondiscriminately.

GATT

The **General Agreement on Tariffs and Trade (GATT)** served as the framework for this multilateral trade objective. Nations came together under GATT rules to negotiate trade policies. Organized in the aftermath of World War II with 22 nations participating, GATT has grown to 97 member nations plus 9 observer nations. It includes all industrial market economies, several from Eastern Europe, and more than 50 economies from the less-developed countries. Together, these GATT members represent over 80 percent of all international trade.

GATT's principal objective is to reduce the level of all tariffs. The nondiscriminating provision of GATT is called the *most-favored nation clause.* The clause applies to all member nations. What is offered to one member as a tariff concession is offered to all.

As you might expect, the United States's role in GATT, which is critical to GATT's functioning, reflects Congress's own interest in promoting free trade. In 1962, Congress legislated the Trade Expansion Act, which led to the Kennedy rounds of tariff cuts. Later, the Tokyo round, which cut tariffs further, was negotiated under the authority of the 1974 Trade Reform Act. The most recent GATT round of negotiations—the Uruguay round—tackled the issue of reducing nontariff protective barriers to trade.

GATT Concessions to Less-Developed Countries

The less-developed countries were never really happy with GATT. In fact, they were downright annoyed. With good reason. They saw it as strictly a rich nation's club. How could they be excited about lowering their own tariffs when their principal concern was economic development? After all, if the infant-industry argument against free trade had meaning anywhere, didn't it make most sense for them?

Reciprocity
An agreement between countries in which trading privileges granted by one to the others are the same as those granted to it by the others.

GATT (General Agreement on Tariffs and Trade)
A trade agreement to negotiate reductions in tariffs and other trade barriers and to provide equal and nondiscriminating treatment among members of the agreement. Around 100 countries are members of GATT.

Review GATT (http://
trading.wmw.com/gatt/)
in its entirety.

GLOBAL PERSPECTIVE

HOW MUCH DO BARRIERS TO IMPORTS COST JAPANESE CONSUMERS?

Mention Japan's trade barriers to its trading partners, and they will leave you in no doubt about their effects. They will point to firms in their countries that cannot price their way into Japanese markets, and lament the profits and jobs that are lost to protectionism.

Such moans are understandable. And yet a hefty chunk of the cost of Japanese protection is paid not by foreigners, but by the Japanese themselves. Trade barriers, which raise the price of foreign goods or keep them out altogether, force consumers to buy more costly domestic alternatives. They also distort firms' inputs, pushing them toward expensive local sources and raising the prices of goods made at home. Indeed, the most persuasive argument for scrapping trade barriers, in Japan or anywhere else, ought to be that they damage protected economies.

DID YOU SEE THE MANIFEST? THIS IS ALL GOING TO JAPAN. MOST UNUSUAL. THEY TYPICALLY DON'T IMPORT MUCH.

So much for the theory. But how much does Japan really pay for its own protection? In a new book (*Measuring the Costs of Protection in Japan*, Institute for International Economics, 1995), three Japanese economists, Yoko Sazanami, Shujiro Urata, and Hiroki Kawai, provide an answer. They compare the price of imports on the dockside (i.e., before tariffs and wholesalers' markups have been added) with the price of Japanese goods at the factory gate. They use the difference to estimate the cost of trade barriers to Japanese consumers.

They conclude that Japanese protection is limited to agricultural products and a few manufacturing industries. Where protection exists, though, it is heavy (see table). They estimate that in 1989 the prices of some foods were several hundred percent higher than import prices. Japanese-made radios and televisions were over 600 percent more expensive than imports. Clothing was marked up by nearly 300 percent; petrol by more than 200 percent.

DIFFERENCE BETWEEN PRICE OF DOMESTIC GOODS AND IMPORTS: 1989 (AS A PERCENTAGE OF IMPORT PRICE)

	PRICE DIFFERENCE	TARIFF RATE	IMPLIED NONTARIFF BARRIER RATE
MILLED RICE	737.1	0.0	737.1
TEA AND COFFEE	718.4	11.9	706.5
COSMETICS	661.6	2.0	659.6
RADIOS AND TVs	607.0	0.0	607.0
WHEAT	477.8	0.0	477.8
SOYBEANS	423.6	0.0	423.6
CLOTHING	292.6	10.4	282.2
PETROL	229.0	5.5	223.5

Source: Y. Sazanami, S. Urata, and H. Kawai, Datastream.

The cost to Japanese consumers totals around 15 trillion yen a year ($110 billion at 1989 exchange rates), or 3.8 percent of GDP. The cost to the Japanese economy as a whole is a good deal smaller, because protection earns profits for domestic producers and tariff revenues for the government. But the estimated damage is still hefty, at about 0.6 percent of Japanese national income. Moreover, say the three economists, these numbers may understate the costs of protection. More foreign competition would force Japanese industry to become more efficient: costs and prices would fall.

In addition, the prices of imports are affected by trade restraints. By making imports scarcer, they create monopoly power for foreign suppliers (as long as imports and domestic goods are not perfect substitutes). This enables them to charge higher prices for their wares in countries that protect local producers.

The conclusion for Japanese consumers (and policy makers) is a sobering one: Trade barriers not only push up the price of Japanese goods, they probably make imports dearer as well.

MORE ON THE NET

The Japanese Ministry of Economy, Trade and Industry (http://www.meti.go.jp/english/index.html), the Japan External Trade Organization (http://www.jetro.go.jp/top/index.html), and the Japan Economic Foundation (http://www.jef.or.jp/) provide news and information on Japanese trade.

Source: "Japan's Protection Racket," *The Economist,* January 7, 1995. © 1995 The Economist Newspaper Group, Inc. Reprinted with permission. Further reproduction prohibited. http://www.economist.com

GATT got the message. The less-developed countries are exceptions to the GATT rules. Although enjoying most-favored nation status, their exports typically face lower tariffs than industrial nations grant to each other. Moreover, reciprocity rights do not apply to the less-developed countries. They can enjoy the industrial economies' tariff concessions without having to reciprocate.

Customs Unions

In 1958, the six West European economies of France, Germany, Italy, Holland, Belgium, and Luxembourg established a **customs union**—the **European Economic Community (EEC)**—whose special trade arrangements allowed for complete free trade within the union and a common tariff schedule against the rest of the world. That's precisely the economic arrangement that exists between Vermont and California, isn't it? In the 1970s, Denmark, England, and Ireland joined the community. In the 1980s the EEC expanded again to include Greece, Spain, and Portugal. In the 1990s, Iceland, Finland, Sweden, and Austria joined. Hungary, Poland, the Czech Republic, Estonia, and Slovenia are next in line.

The objectives of the EEC raise fundamental questions that concern the reciprocity principle underlying the GATT agreements. For example, if the United States lowers its tariff against French wine, according to GATT instruction it must also lower its tariff against wine imported from other countries.

The United States is disadvantaged, however, when it comes to competing with French wine in Britain. While French wine comes into Britain tariff-free, California wine faces a common EEC tariff. That's not fair, say California wineries. The French respond that California wine comes in tariff-free to Vermont; French wine doesn't. It's the same, *n'est-ce pas?* Not exactly. California trade with Vermont is strictly domestic; trade between France and England is still international. *GATT's rules apply only to international trade.*

Customs union
A set of countries that agree to free trade among themselves and a common trade policy with all other countries.

European Economic Community (EEC)
A customs union consisting of France, Italy, Belgium, Holland, Luxembourg, Germany, Britain, Ireland, Denmark, Greece, Spain, Portugal, Iceland, Finland, Sweden, and Austria.

Free Trade Areas

Free trade area
A set of countries that agree to free trade among themselves but are free to pursue independent trade policies with other countries.

A variant of the customs union is the **free trade area.** The single difference between it and the customs union, such as the EEC, is that the free trade area permits free trade among members, but each is allowed to establish its own tariff policy with respect to nonmembers. In other words, the free trade area permits each member greater independence in trade policy making.

The North American Free Trade Agreement

North American Free Trade Agreement (NAFTA)
A free trade area consisting of Canada, the United States, and Mexico.

By far the most significant trade agreement concluded by the United States is with Canada and Mexico. In 1989 both the U.S. Congress and the Canadian House of Commons enacted the **North American Free Trade Agreement (NAFTA).** Mexico joined NAFTA in 1993, making it the largest free trade area in the world, matching the total production of goods and services of the EEC.

NAFTA calls for the elimination of all tariffs, quotas, and other trade barriers within 10 years. Although over 75 percent of Canadian-U.S. trade was tariff-free even before NAFTA, the expansions in both U.S. and Canadian markets that NAFTA is expected to create makes the agreement a very significant economic event for both countries. Canadians gain a considerable advantage vis-à-vis other exporting countries in a market ten times the size of its own. On the other hand, the United States, having faced tariff rates in Canada higher than those Canadians faced in the United States prior to NAFTA, gains more when both cut their rates to zero.

Still, NAFTA was not engineered without some political controversy. Although some debate concerning its merits took place in the United States, NAFTA was a major political issue in Canada. The U.S. economy has always been regarded by Canadians as a potentially threatening colossus. Some Canadians feared that free access to each other's markets would result in U.S. production overwhelming their own. But their voices were muted by the logic of comparative advantage. It proved too much for Canadians to ignore.

Mexico's entry into NAFTA generated a somewhat more unsettling promise for the future. Although the expansion of all three markets—Canada, Mexico, and the United States—is seen by all three as an outcome of Mexico's membership in NAFTA, a disquieting note is voiced in the United States and Canada. The issue is low-wage Mexican labor. With tariffs completely eliminated, many worry that low-wage Mexican labor will lure firms, particularly labor-intensive ones, out of Canada and the United States to Mexico. Polluting firms that are forced to adhere to tough Canadian and U.S. environmental regulations will also be attracted to Mexico, where pollution regulations are fewer and poorly enforced.

Advocates of NAFTA respond with compelling arguments of their own. The economic development of Mexico, which NAFTA will assist, provides not only markets for Canadians and Americans, but employment opportunities for Mexicans. In other words, NAFTA can help reduce the illegal immigration flow across the Rio Grande. And the low-wage jobs that Americans and Canadians will lose are precisely the jobs that should be lost in the United States and Canada. The greater production in Canada and the United States that Mexico-included NAFTA generates should be able to reemploy those Canadian and American job-losers in higher-paying jobs.

TRACKING TARIFFS SINCE 1860

Some people see a half glass of water as being half empty, while others view the same glass as half filled. It's just a matter of how you look at things. The same idea applies when we assess tariffs and trade performance. Look at Exhibit 16.

EXHIBIT | 16

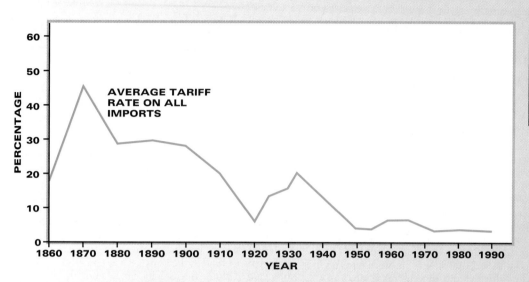

AVERAGE U.S. TARIFF RATES ON IMPORTS

The dramatic increase in the rates during the 1920s and early 1930s evaporated by 1950. Thereafter, the rates steadily declined and by 1970 were less than 10 percent.

Source: *Economic Report of the President,* January 1989 (Washington, D.C.: U.S. Government Printing Office, 1989), p. 152.

Just a cursory glance shows that whatever our view about whether tariffs are too high or too low, they have clearly dropped dramatically during the past 50 years.

As you can see, our tariff history shows some erratic behavior. In earlier years, our international trade policy was clearly protectionist. During the period 1870 to 1900, the average tariff rate on imports was over 25 percent. But note how the average tariff rate on all imports steadily declined during the next two decades.

The skyrocketing of rates during the 1920s and early 1930s appears as an exception, the direct result of the highly protectionist Fordney-McCumber Tariff Act of 1922 and the Smoot-Hawley Tariff Act of 1930. The Reciprocal Trade Agreement Act of 1934 reversed the upward movement in rates, and by 1950, rates were back to pre-1920 levels. Since 1970, the rates have fallen below 10 percent and continue to decline.

Are our tariff rates still too high? The average U.S. tariff, 1990–93, was 5.9 percent, which compares to Canada's 10.5 percent, Australia's 9.8 percent, Japan's 6.3 percent, and the EEC's 6.7 percent.

APPLIED PERSPECTIVE

IS NAFTA WORKER FRIENDLY?

The heated discussion in the United States that preceded the passage in 1993 of the North American Free Trade Agreement (NAFTA) continues unabated almost a decade later. The mountains of research on NAFTA's impact on real GDP, trade, and employment in the United States have resolved very little. Economists, typically in agreement on matters of free trade, line up on both sides of the NAFTA issue. Their central concern—although by no means the only one—is jobs: job creation and job losses.

Jobs, it appears, was also the principal reason some members of Congress voted in favor of NAFTA. They believed that NAFTA would promote economic growth and that the growth would increase jobs and wages in their districts. Others in Congress voted against the legislation because they feared NAFTA would result in fewer jobs and lower wages in their districts. Many of them saw the logic in 1992 presidential candidate Ross Perot's argument that "If you're paying $12, $13, $14 an hour for factory workers and you can move your factory south of the border, pay a dollar an hour for labor, have no health care . . . have no environmental controls, and no retirement and you don't care about anything but making money, there will be a giant sucking sound going south . . . ."

But has there really been a sucking sound? Among the many studies that estimate the impact of NAFTA on job creation or job losses are Robert Scott's (1999) and Mary Bolle's (2000). Scott focused on documenting state-by-state job losses. According to him, NAFTA was responsible for destroying 440,172 U.S. jobs over the period 1994–98. The big losers were California with approximately 45,000 job losses, Michigan, with over 30,000, and New York, with over 25,000. Others that registered losses greater than 15,000 were Georgia, Illinois, North Carolina, Ohio, Pennsylvania, Tennessee, and Texas. What Scott didn't estimate, however, were NAFTA-created jobs.

Mary Bolle's research, on the other hand, addressed both state-by-state job creations and losses for the same period, 1994–98. In her account,

Texas led with a net job creation (job creation minus job loss) of 116,816. California followed with a net gain of 101,406 jobs. Michigan gained 79,304, Illinois gained 37,389, and New York gained 28,387. Only Vermont and New Mexico ended up with negative numbers, but their combined losses were less than 2,000 jobs.

What's the significance of Scott's NAFTA-induced loss-only estimates when Bolle's research included both state losses and gains? Aside from the methodological differences associated with their acquiring and applying relevant data, Bolle's net gain estimates tend to paint a rosier picture of NAFTA's job impact than they perhaps deserve.

If 100 jobs are lost and at the same time another 100 jobs are created, the benefits associated with the jobs gained don't necessarily cancel out the negatives associated with the losses. After all, the 100 workers who lost their jobs may have been relatively well paid, experienced, and older. Finding new and comparable jobs for them may be difficult. On the other hand, the majority of the 100 jobs gained may have gone to less experienced, younger, and perhaps lower-wage workers. That is to say, even though the job numbers net to zero, the impact on workers may not be zero. For this reason, Scott's job-loss data is significant and points to a probable source of real NAFTA-generated problems in the U.S. economy. It may also explain why some economists and members of Congress continue to be less excited about the net gains in jobs than others.

The importance of the job loss data imports as well on the peripheral issue of workers' wage bargaining ability when jobs are threatened by the potential exodus of U.S. companies to Mexico and Canada. Professor Kate Bronfenbrenner, NAFTA's Labor Secretariat, reported that U.S. companies often exercise the threat option when confronted with union efforts to organize U.S. workers.

The argument isn't that NAFTA's impact on U.S. jobs is "worker unfriendly." It is instead that the job creations NAFTA induced—as valuable as they are to U.S. workers and to the U.S. economy in general—still must be measured against the not inconsiderable job losses and economic distress that fall disproportionately on some U.S. workers.

CHAPTER REVIEW

1. The prices of goods in competitive markets reflect their costs of production. Any differences in the costs of producing a specific good in any two countries—or within regions of a country—present opportunities for geographic specialization that, when taken, result in more total goods produced.

2. If the United States can produce a good using fewer resources than, say, Canada, then the United States is said to have an absolute advantage over Canada in producing that good.

3. If the United States can produce a good whose opportunity cost is lower than the opportunity cost of producing the good in, say, Canada, then the United States is said to have a comparative advantage over Canada in producing that good.

4. In a two-country, two-goods world, specialization will create absolute, comparative, or both types of advantages for both countries, and goods will exchange at prices that fall within the relative price range—or relative labor costs—in each of the countries. The gains each country derives from international trade depend upon the prices at which the two goods trade for each other.

5. While both countries gain from specialization and free trade, people in each country who produce goods that have been displaced by the more efficient producer in the other country end up losing, at least in the short run.

6. The quantity of Canadian goods the United States gets trading a unit of its own goods with Canada depends on the prices of the goods it exports and imports. The terms of trade for the United States measures the ratio of its export prices to its import prices and reflects the purchasing power of a U.S. unit of goods.

7. Because the less-developed economies specialize and trade in agricultural goods while industrially advanced economies specialize and trade in manufactured goods, and because changes in relative prices tend to favor manufactured goods, changes in terms of trade typically work to the disadvantage of less-developed economies.

8. The industrially advanced economies do most of the world's trading, and their trading is mostly with each other.

9. The United States's major trading partners are Canada, Japan, and Mexico, and the United States is even more important to them as a trading partner than they are to us.

10. Advocates of limitations to free trade cite the following reasons for exceptions to free trade: national security, infant industries, cheap foreign labor, diversity of industry, antidumping, and retaliation against countries limiting our exports to them.

11. Tariffs and quotas are used to limit free trade. A tariff is a tax on imported goods that, by raising its price, makes domestic goods more competitive. A quota, by limiting the quantity of imported goods, creates a larger market share for domestic goods than tariffs do.

12. The General Agreement on Tariffs and Trade (GATT) seeks to lower tariffs. A tariff concession offered to one member of GATT must be offered to all. GATT members offer LDCs lower tariffs than are granted to industrial countries, without demanding reciprocity.

13. A customs union, such as the European Economic Community, allows free trade among member countries and a common trade policy with all other countries. A free trade area allows free trade among member countries but grants each member country the right to pursue independent trade policies with other countries.

KEY TERMS

Free trade
International specialization
Absolute advantage
Comparative advantage
Imports
Exports
Terms of trade

Dumping
Tariff
Quota
Reciprocity
GATT (General Agreement on Tariffs and Trade)

Customs union
European Economic Community (EEC)
Free trade area
North American Free Trade Agreement (NAFTA)

QUESTIONS

1. Why do nations trade?
2. Georgia exports its peaches to Maine, and Maine exports its lobsters to Georgia. Considering this trade alone, do you suppose Georgia and Maine are trading under conditions of absolute or comparative advantage? Make an educated guess about resource use and opportunity cost in producing those goods in Georgia and Maine.
3. Suppose Canadians can produce a bushel of wheat for half the cost it takes to produce a bushel in Belgium. And they can produce a ton of fish for only one-quarter the Belgium cost. Should Canadians bother trading with Belgium? If not, why not? If they do trade, what should each end up producing?
4. Suppose the cost of producing a bushel of wheat in Canada is $2 and the cost of producing a ton of fish is $20. If Canada and Belgium do decide to trade, what range of international prices—bushels of wheat per ton of fish—would be acceptable to both?
5. Lower tariffs create greater international specialization. Explain.
6. Many Detroit autoworkers do not buy the argument that everybody gains in international trade. What's their point?
7. Suppose Iraq can produce surface-to-surface missiles more efficiently than we can, while we are able to produce artichokes more efficiently than they can. Should we specialize in artichokes, trading them for Iraqi missiles? Make the pro and con arguments.
8. The Irish complain that they never got a chance to make automobiles because the English, their major trading partner, are more experienced and therefore more efficient at it. Would-be Irish automakers ask their government to impose a tariff on foreign automobiles to help them get started. Can you make the case supporting their complaint and request?
9. American sport-fishing equipment producers argue that Japanese manufacturers are selling rods, reels, and tackle below Japanese cost in American markets to drive out American competitors. The American producers ask for quotas on such imports. They argue that, without government-imposed quotas on the Japanese sport-fishing equipment, American sportfishermen will ultimately pay more. Can you make the case supporting the American producers' complaint and request?
10. What is reciprocity?
11. What economic arguments can be made to support the idea of the European Economic Community?
12. Canada, Mexico, and the United States have negotiated a free trade agreement. Many Canadians, Mexicans, and Americans opposed the agreement, but even more supported it. Why would anyone oppose it? Or support it?

PRACTICE PROBLEMS

1. The U.S. demand for, U.S. supply of, and Japanese supply of VCRs are shown in the following schedule.

| | UNITED STATES | | JAPAN |
PRICE	QUANTITY DEMANDED	QUANTITY SUPPLIED	QUANTITY SUPPLIED
$100	500	100	100
200	400	200	200
300	300	300	300
400	200	400	400
500	100	500	500

If Japanese VCRs are prohibited from entering the United States, what will be the equilibrium price and quantity bought and sold by Americans in the VCR market in the United States?

2. Suppose the United States allowed Japan free trade privileges in the U.S. market. What would happen to the equilibrium price and total quantity of VCRs bought and sold in the U.S. market?

3. Suppose the United States imposed a $100 tariff on each Japanese VCR imported. What would happen to the equilibrium price and total quantity bought and sold in the United States?

4. Graph the situations described in practice problems 1 to 3.

5. England and France can produce both wine and cloth. The English use 80 labor-hours to produce a unit of cloth and 40 labor-hours to produce a unit of wine. The French use 100 labor-hours to produce a unit of cloth.

	CLOTH	WINE
ENGLAND	80	40
FRANCE	100	

Fill in the blank cell—labor-hours to produce a unit of French wine—to show France's absolute advantage in producing wine. Explain.

6. Fill in the blank cell—labor-hours to produce a unit of French wine—to show France's comparative advantage in producing cloth. Explain.

7. Fill in the blank cell—labor-hours to produce a unit of French wine—to show no advantage to either France or England in trading with each other. Explain.

WHAT'S WRONG WITH THIS GRAPH?

TARIFF-RESTRICTED TRADE

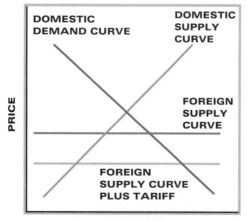

ECONOMIC CONSULTANTS

ECONOMIC RESEARCH AND ANALYSIS BY STUDENTS FOR PROFESSIONALS

Viva, a U.S. bicycle firm, designs and manufactures racing bicycles, favorites of world-class riders in the United States. Given the increased success of bicycle racing in the United States, many European riders have expressed interest in buying Viva bikes. However, Viva bikes currently are sold only in the United States, although Viva's owners want to expand their distribution into Europe, particularly into France, Italy, and Germany.

Viva's owners have hired Economic Consultants to examine what barriers exist to selling Viva bikes in France, Italy, and Germany. Prepare a report for Viva that addresses the following issues:

1. What barriers, if any, exist to exporting bikes into France, Italy, and Germany?
2. What government agencies exist to assist firms in exporting their products?

You may find the following resources helpful as you prepare this report for Viva:

- **The World Factbook** (http://www.cia.gov/cia/publications/factbook/)—*The World Factbook* provides information on trade with France, Italy, and Germany.
- **U.S. International Trade Commission (ITC)** (http://www.usitc.gov/)—The ITC issues reports on foreign trade barriers and unfair practices.
- **U.S. Department of State** (http://www.state.gov/www/issues/economic/trade_reports/)—The U.S. State Department publishes *Country Reports on Economic Policy and Trade Practices,* which is based on information supplied by U.S. embassies and analyzed and reviewed by the Department of State in consultation with other U.S. government agencies.
- **Bureau of Export Administration** (http://www.bxa.doc.gov/)—The Bureau of Export Administration administers export control policies, issues export licenses, and prosecutes violators.
- **International Trade Administration (ITA)** (http://www.ita.doc.gov/) The ITA provides export assistance and information by country and by industry. Of note is the Trade Information Center (http://www.ita.doc.gov/tic/).
- **Export-Import Bank of the United States (Ex-Im Bank)** (http://www.exim.gov/)—The Ex-Im Bank is an independent U.S. government agency that helps finance the overseas sales of U.S. goods and services.

PRACTICE TEST

1. If Canada has an absolute advantage over Cuba in the production of wheat, it means that
   a. Canada can produce more wheat than Cuba.
   b. the price of wheat is higher in Canada than it is in Cuba.
   c. the price of wheat is higher in Cuba than it is in Canada.
   d. fewer resources are used to produce wheat in Canada than in Cuba.
   e. the opportunity cost of producing wheat in Canada is lower than in Cuba.

2. If Cuba has a comparative advantage over Canada in the production of sugar, it means that
   a. Cuba can produce more sugar than Canada.
   b. the price of sugar is higher in Cuba than it is in Canada.
   c. the price of sugar is higher in Canada than it is in Cuba.
   d. fewer resources are used to produce sugar in Cuba than in Canada.
   e. the opportunity cost of producing sugar is lower in Cuba than in Canada.

	WHEAT (BUSHELS)	SUGAR (SACKS)
CANADA	200	600
CUBA	200	1,200

3. The table shows the production and consumption of wheat and sugar in Canada and Cuba under conditions of no trade. When free trade occurs, the entire gains from such trade shift completely to Canada when the price of sacks per bushel is
   a. 3 sacks per bushel.
   b. 4 sacks per bushel.
   c. 5 sacks per bushel.
   d. 6 sacks per bushel.
   e. 7 sacks per bushel.

4. The terms of trade is said to worsen for Cuba when
   a. its volume of exports increases more than its volume of imports.
   b. its volume of imports increases more than its volume of exports.
   c. its export prices increase more than its import prices.
   d. its import prices increase more than its export prices.
   e. it minimizes its gains from trade.

5. The United States's most important trading partner is
   a. Germany.
   b. United Kingdom.
   c. Japan.
   d. Mexico.
   e. Canada.

6. Which of the following arguments against free trade is based on the idea that industries should be protected through their learning-curve stage of development?
   a. Cheap foreign labor
   b. Diversity of industry
   c. Infant industry
   d. Antidumping
   e. Retaliation

7. When the United States imposes a tariff against Canadian leather goods, it
   a. limits its imports of Canadian leather goods to a specific quantity.
   b. fixes a percentage rate on the price of the imported goods, which creates a revenue that becomes a subsidy for domestic leather producers.
   c. fixes a percentage rate on the price of the imported goods, which creates a revenue for the U.S. government.
   d. disallows the importation of Canadian leather goods unless Canadians allow an equal value of U.S. leather goods into Canada.
   e. disallows the importation of Canadian leather goods.

8. The nondiscriminatory provision of GATT is called the
   a. most-favored nation clause.
   b. free trade clause.
   c. limited reciprocity clause.
   d. affirmative-action-in-trade clause.
   e. nontariff barrier clause.

9. The members of the North American Free Trade Agreement (NAFTA) are
   a. Canada and the United States.
   b. Canada, Mexico, and the United States.
   c. Japan and the United States.
   d. the European Community, Canada, Mexico, and the United States.
   e. Canada, Mexico, North West Territories (NWT), Greenland, and the United States.

10. A customs union is several countries that agree to free trade
    a. among themselves and a common trade policy with other countries.
    b. among themselves and allow each to determine its own policy with other countries.
    c. among themselves and with every other country.
    d. with other countries, fixing common tariffs among themselves.
    e. with other countries, fixing common quotas among themselves.

CHAPTER

20

EXCHANGE RATES, BALANCE OF PAYMENTS, AND INTERNATIONAL DEBT

Suppose you were on vacation on an exotic South Pacific island and chanced upon a native craftsman finishing off a beautiful teakwood carving of a swordfish. Just the thing you were hoping to find. Suppose you offered to buy it for $10, but the craftsman insisted on 4 yaps. After all, it's the only money he knows. He can buy anything he wants with it. The U.S. dollar? It's as unfamiliar to him as the yap is to you. It's not accepted on the island. You raise the offer to $20, but he won't budge. It's yaps or nothing.

Frustrating, isn't it? But, really, if the craftsman can't use the dollar in his everyday business of life, what good is it to him?

Let's change the scene. Suppose the craftsman was on vacation in Boston and noticed streams of cars heading toward Fenway Park. Upon inquiring, he discovers that they are all going to a Red Sox baseball game. Suppose he joins the crowd just to see how U.S. natives play.

He offers 4 yaps, but the ticket vendor insists on $10. He raises the offer to 6 yaps, but nobody at Fenway Park will take the yaps. They politely explain to him that Bostonians haven't heard of the yap and that it simply won't pass as currency in Boston. He goes away disappointed, never to see Nomar Garciaparra belt one out of the park.

THIS CHAPTER INTRODUCES YOU TO THE ECONOMIC PRINCIPLES ASSOCIATED WITH:

- EXCHANGE RATES
- FOREIGN EXCHANGE MARKETS
- APPRECIATION AND DEPRECIATION OF CURRENCIES
- FLOATING AND FIXED EXCHANGE RATES
- ARBITRAGE
- DEVALUATION
- BALANCE OF PAYMENTS
- INTERNATIONAL DEBT AND DEBT SERVICE

THE MONEY TOWER OF BABEL

It would be convenient if everyone in the world used one currency, but, alas, we don't. The French use French francs. The Swiss use their own francs, the British use the pound, Italians use the lira, Jordanians use the dinar, Israelis use the shekel, Mexicans use the peso, Brazilians use the cruzado, Japanese use the yen, Chinese use the yuan, Spaniards use the peseta, Canadians use the Canadian dollar, and we, of course, use the U.S. dollar. And there are many more economies, each with its own specific currency.

How then do we trade? How do we buy each other's goods? We know why some French fishermen may want to buy Greek boats, but how do they actually go about paying for them? With French francs? Why would Greeks take the francs? Nobody uses francs in Athens. How do the Japanese buy Brazilian coffee? What would a Brazilian want with yen? What would the South Pacific island craftsman do with U.S. dollars?

THE FOREIGN EXCHANGE MARKET:
THE BUYING AND SELLING OF CURRENCIES

Perhaps the only way we could persuade the South Pacific craftsman to accept U.S. dollars is to find someone on his island who wants U.S. goods and needs U.S. dollars to buy them. Then we could just swap dollars for yaps. It would work. But finding each other—that is, people with dollars looking for yaps meeting people with yaps looking for dollars—is too accidental. Yet if there were enough such people looking for each other's currencies, we could establish a currency market, or **foreign exchange market,** where people could easily buy dollars with yaps and yaps with dollars.

That's what the foreign exchange market is all about. Suppose we still want to buy that teakwood swordfish. The islander wants 4 yaps for it. We can now exchange our dollars for yaps on the foreign exchange market. With the purchased yaps, we buy the teakwood carving. But is 4 yaps a reasonable price for the carving? How can we measure its worth in dollars? It would depend on how many dollars it takes to buy a yap.

The price of the yap in terms of dollars depends, like other prices, on market demand and supply. Look at Exhibit 1.

The foreign exchange market determines how many dollars it takes to buy a yap just as the umbrella market determines how many dollars it takes to buy an umbrella. The equilibrium price of a yap, shown in Exhibit 1, is $3. If the islander asks 4 yaps for the teakwood swordfish, its price in dollars is $12. Economists define the price of one country's currency, such as the dollar, in terms of another country's currency, such as the yap, as the **exchange rate.**

The Demand Curve for Yaps

If the exchange rate was not $3 but, say, only $1 per yap, then the 4 yap teakwood carving would be considerably less expensive *in terms of dollars.* And because it's cheaper, we would buy more carvings. That's simply the law of demand, isn't it? But to buy more carvings, we would need more yaps. In Exhibit 1, the quantity demanded of yaps increases from 30,000 to 50,000 when the exchange rate drops from $3 to $1 per yap. That's why the demand curve for yaps is downward sloping.

What about the craftsman? Whether the exchange rate is $3 or $1 per yap, that is, whether we end up paying $12 or $4 for the carving, he still ends up with 4 yaps.

Foreign exchange market
A market in which currencies of different nations are bought and sold.

Exchange rate
The number of units of foreign currency that can be purchased with one unit of domestic currency.

CHECK YOUR UNDERSTANDING

Why do we buy more foreign goods when the exchange rate—dollars for yaps—decreases?

EXHIBIT | 1

FOREIGN EXCHANGE MARKET

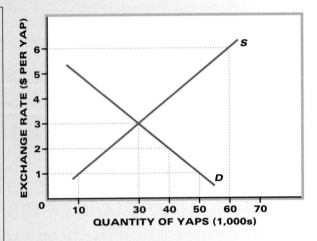

Keep this in mind when you think about exchange rates: Americans demand yaps to buy South Pacific goods, and South Pacific islanders supply yaps to buy U.S. goods.

The demand curve for yaps, *D*, depicts the demand for yaps at varying rates of exchange, that is, number of dollars required to buy a yap. At $2 per yap, the quantity of yaps demanded is 40,000. At $3 per yap—the yap is now more expensive, that is, people have to give more dollars to buy a yap—the quantity of yaps demanded falls to 30,000.

The supply curve of yaps, *S*, depicts the supply of yaps at varying rates of exchange, dollars for yaps. At $6 per yap—1 yap buys a $6 U.S. good—the quantity of yaps supplied by people holding yaps and wanting to buy dollars is 60,000. At $1 per yap—1 yap now buys only a $1 U.S. good—the quantity of yaps supplied by people holding yaps and wanting to buy dollars is 10,000.

At $1 per yap, a 50,000 − 10,000 = 40,000 excess demand for yaps emerges, driving up the exchange rate. The market reaches equilibrium at $3 per yap, where the quantity of yaps demanded and supplied is 30,000.

How does he feel about the exchange rate? If he had any say in the matter, he would probably prefer the $1 per yap. Why? Because at $1 per yap, we buy more of his carvings.

The Supply Curve of Yaps

What about the supply curve of yaps in Exhibit 1? The South Pacific islanders supply yaps—exchange them for dollars—to buy our goods. Suppose a South Pacific islander on vacation in New York spots a graphite fishing rod in a window at Macy's. It sells for $60. He immediately translates the price into yaps. After all, that's the currency he's familiar with. At $3 per yap, that rod costs him 20 yaps. Not a bad buy. But at $1 per yap, the rod's price jumps to 60 yaps. It makes a difference.

That's why the supply curve of yaps is upward sloping. At $3 per yap, South Pacific island people find U.S. goods relatively inexpensive *in terms of yaps* and end up buying more goods. To buy more, they supply yaps for dollars. That's what we see in Exhibit 1. The quantity supplied of yaps increases from 30,000 to 60,000 as the exchange rate increases from $3 to $6 per yap.

CHECK YOUR UNDERSTANDING

Why is the supply curve of a foreign currency upward sloping?

Shifts in the Demand Curve for Yaps

Changes in the dollars-for-yaps exchange rate cause people demanding yaps to change the quantity of yaps demanded, which is shown as a movement along the demand curve for yaps in the foreign exchange market. But what causes the demand curve itself to shift?

CHANGES IN INCOME Imagine what would happen to our demand for yaps if our incomes increased by, say, 20 percent. With more dollars in our pockets, we end up buying more goods. Suppose among the more goods we buy are teakwood carvings from the South Pacific islands. To buy more teakwood imports, we need more yaps. Look at Exhibit 2.

Our demand curve for yaps shifts to the right. As a result, the equilibrium exchange rate increases from $3 to $5 per yap, and the quantity of yaps demanded and supplied on the foreign exchange market increases from 30,000 to 50,000.

CHANGES IN TASTE

What about changes in taste? If teakwood carvings catch on, the increased demand for the carvings creates an increase in the demand for yaps as well.

On the other hand, suppose our tastes change from wood carvings to Irish cut glass. What happens to our demand for yaps? The fall in demand for teakwood carvings shifts our demand for yaps to the left, depressing the exchange rate to below $3 per yap.

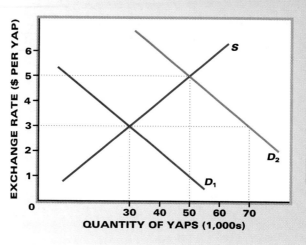

EFFECT OF AN INCREASE IN THE DEMAND FOR YAPS ON THE DOLLARS-FOR-YAPS RATE OF EXCHANGE

The demand curve for yaps shifts from D_1 to D_2, reflecting an increase in demand for yap-priced imports. At the old equilibrium exchange rate of $3 per yap, a new 70,000 − 30,000 = 40,000 excess demand for yaps emerges, driving the equilibrium exchange rate from $3 to $5 per yap, where the quantity of yaps demanded and supplied is 50,000.

EXHIBIT | 2

CHANGES IN INTEREST RATES

A fall in the interest rate in the United States or a rise in the interest rate in the South Pacific island will affect the demand for yaps as well. For example, suppose you were looking through the pages of the *Wall Street Journal* and came upon an announcement that the Teakwood Carvings Company, a South Pacific island firm, wants to expand its plant capacity and expects to finance the expansion by offering bonds, in denominations of 10,000 and 20,000 yaps, at a 10 percent rate of interest. If the rate of interest offered by U.S. companies on their corporate bonds is 6 percent, the 4 percent rate spread makes the South Pacific bond rather attractive. Wouldn't you be tempted to buy a 10,000-yap bond?

But how do you go about buying the bond? You first must exchange your dollars for 10,000 yaps and with the purchased yaps, buy the 10,000-yap bond. That shifts the demand curve for yaps to the right, as in Exhibit 2.

Shifts in the Supply Curve of Yaps

Just as changes in U.S. incomes, tastes, and interest rates shift the demand curve for yaps, changes in South Pacific incomes, tastes, and interest rates shift the supply curve of yaps. After all, South Pacific islanders are very much like us.

If their incomes increase, wouldn't you expect that they, too, would buy more goods, which might include imports from the United States? Their increase in demand for U.S. goods results in an increase in their demand for U.S. dollars. They buy dollars by supplying yaps; that is, the supply curve for yaps shifts to the right. The effect of this supply shift on the dollars-for-yaps rate of exchange is depicted in Exhibit 3.

The equilibrium exchange rate decreases from $3 to $2 per yap, and the quantity of yaps demanded and supplied on the foreign exchange market increases from 30,000 to 40,000. And if the interest rate on the island falls, wouldn't that fall

EXHIBIT | 3

EFFECT OF AN INCREASE IN THE SUPPLY OF YAPS ON THE DOLLARS-FOR-YAPS RATE OF EXCHANGE

The supply curve of yaps shifts from S_1 to S_2, reflecting an increase in demand for dollar-priced imports. At the old equilibrium exchange rate of $3 per yap, a new $50,000 - 30,000 = 20,000$ excess supply of yaps emerges, driving the equilibrium exchange rate from $3 to $2 per yap, where the quantity of yaps demanded and supplied is 40,000.

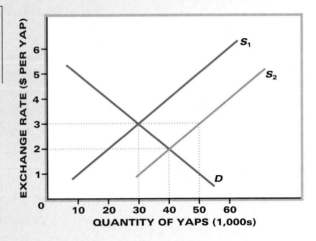

encourage islanders to look elsewhere for possible investments? They may end up buying U.S. bonds, which creates a demand for U.S. dollars and a supply of yaps.

FLOATING EXCHANGE RATES

Imagine a world of economies, all importing and exporting goods from each other, investing in each other's capital markets, and demanding and supplying each other's currencies to carry out these many international transactions. That would create a multiplicity of exchange rates, each one reflecting the specific demand and supply condition for its own national currency.

Floating exchange rate
An exchange rate determined strictly by the demands and supplies for a nation's currency.

Such an array of exchange rates would be **floating,** that is, in a continuous state of flux, adjusting always to the changing demand and supply conditions in the international market for goods and capital.

Depreciation and Appreciation

The market forces that determine floating exchange rates are really no different from the market forces that determine the prices of goods such as umbrellas, microwave popcorn, and houses. Yet, curiously, many people seem to be more than just a little confused about the significance of a change in exchange rates.

Appreciation
A rise in the price of a nation's currency relative to foreign currencies.

CBS Evening News's Dan Rather and his media friends report regularly on how the U.S. dollar has fared against other currencies during the week. For example, in reporting the dollar's **appreciation,** meaning we pay fewer dollars for a yap, or the dollar's **depreciation,** meaning we pay more dollars for a yap, they typically go one step further by referring to the appreciation as a *strengthening* of the dollar and to the depreciation as a *weakening* of the dollar.

Depreciation
A fall in the price of a nation's currency relative to foreign currencies.

In other contexts, the words *strength* and *weakness* convey moral attributes. Do they convey the same in foreign exchange markets? Is a weak dollar bad? Not if we're interested in exporting U.S. goods. After all, Italians, who are getting more

APPLIED PERSPECTIVE

TOURISTS AT THE MALL

Imagine having a cousin George from Calgary in Alberta, Canada, who came to visit you in the summer of 2001, bringing with him 302 Canadian dollars that his mother gave him to buy gifts for the Calgary family. Suppose he shopped in your neighborhood mall and the gift shops there were willing to exchange his Canadian dollars for U.S. dollars at the 2001 exchange rate. He would end up buying gifts worth 200 U.S. dollars. Not knowing much about free-floating exchange rates, he would be a little disappointed. Why? Because his mother told him that when she visited your folks back in 1960, she was able to use her 302 Canadian dollars to buy as much as 302 U.S. dollars' worth of gifts. What could possibly explain the difference?

Suppose also that at the mall, George and you met a Japanese tourist from Tokyo who also was gift

FANTASTIC BUY! I WOULD SPEND TWICE AS MANY YEN IN JAPAN TO BUY SOMETHING NOT HALF AS NICE.

shopping for family back home. You notice that she exchanges 2,350 Japanese yen for 200 U.S. dollars and makes the same purchases your cousin does. While you are all waiting for gift wrapping, she tells you a surprising story. Her mother was here back in 1960 and she, too, bought 200 U.S. dollars' worth of gifts. But her mother had to exchange 7,160 Japanese yen for those gifts! What could possibly explain the difference?

If tourists from Italy, Britain, and Germany were at the mall, what stories would they tell about buying U.S. gifts with lire, pounds, and marks in 1960 and 2001?

MORE ON THE NET

The Board of Governors of the Federal Reserve Board publishes current and historical exchange rates (http://www.federal reserve.gov/releases/H10/).

Source: End-of-year exchange rates from International Monetary Fund, *International Financial Statistics* (Washington, D.C.: IMF, 1997).

EXCHANGE RATES OF SELECTED COUNTRIES (CURRENCY UNITS PER U.S. DOLLAR)

YEAR	CANADIAN DOLLAR	JAPANESE YEN	FRENCH FRANC	GERMAN MARK	ITALIAN LIRA	BRITISH POUND
1960	1.00	358	4.90	4.17	621	.36
1970	1.01	358	5.52	3.65	623	.42
1980	1.19	203	4.52	1.96	931	.42
1990	1.16	134	5.13	1.49	1,130	.52
2001	1.51	117.5	7.10	2.11	2,094	.69

dollars for their lire, buy more U.S. goods. That makes our exporters happy. It also contributes to employment in the United States.

On the other hand, if we're interested in consuming imports, then a strong dollar isn't bad. Why? We can buy Italian imports more cheaply.

Arbitrage Creates Mutually Consistent Exchange Rates

Suppose you pick up a copy of *USA Today* and read the following set of exchange rates: (1) 2 U.S. dollars per British pound, (2) 2,000 Italian lire per British pound, and (3) 1,500 lire per U.S. dollar. You go over it again to make sure you have read it correctly. No mistake. What would you do?

Wouldn't it be profitable for you to take $100 to the foreign exchange market and buy 150,000 lire? With those 150,000 lire, you could then buy 75 British pounds. You take the 75 British pounds and buy 150 U.S. dollars. Look what you've done. You started with $100 and ended up with $150. That's **arbitrage.**

Can you do this forever? Not really. Because others, too, will probably have noticed the chance for arbitrage; together the total buying and selling of currencies will change the demand and supply curves in the foreign exchange market, making all exchange rates mutually consistent with each other.

Problems with Floating Exchange Rates

Sometimes free-floating exchange rates are not desirable. Suppose we are importers of wood carvings and strike a deal with a South Pacific island producer to buy 1,000 pieces at 4 yaps each, with the exchange rate at $3 per yap. We expect, then, to pay $12,000. Six months later when the 1,000 wood carvings are delivered, we send a check for $12,000 only to be told that it is now insufficient. Why? Because in the six months between the contract agreement and the delivery, the exchange rate changed from $3 to $5 per yap. The 4,000 yaps we promised to pay, expecting that they would cost $12,000, now cost $20,000. There goes our profit and more.

Of course, the exchange rate could have gone the other way. For example, it could have fallen to $2 per yap. We would then end up with a windfall. Instead of paying $12,000 for the 1,000 carvings, we would have to pay only $8,000.

But our business is importing, not gambling. Floating exchange rates add an element of uncertainty to international trade, making it a less reliable venture than simple domestic trade.

Fixing Exchange Rates

Can we avoid that kind of uncertainty? After all, shifts in demand and supply curves that change equilibrium levels of exchange rates simply reflect our changing preferences. Do we really want to interfere with these preferences?

Perhaps the way out of the dilemma is to *fix* exchange rates—to no longer allow them to float—in such a way that uncertainty is reduced to zero, but at the same time allow demand and supply conditions on the market to dictate the quantities of imports and exports.

How can this be done? Look at Exhibit 4. Panel *a* depicts what happens to the exchange rate over three years of changing demands for island goods when the rate is allowed to float. Look at the first year. Demand, *D*, and supply, *S*, generate an exchange rate of $3 per yap. The quantity demanded and supplied is 30,000 yaps.

Suppose in the second year an increase in demand for South Pacific island goods shifts the demand for yaps to the right, to D_1. The exchange rate increases to $4 per yap, and the quantity demanded and supplied increases to 40,000 yaps.

Now suppose in the third year the demand for island goods decreases. This time, the demand curve for yaps shifts to the left, to D_2. The exchange rate falls to $2 per yap, and the quantity demanded and supplied decreases to 20,000 yaps.

These roller-coaster exchange rates are precisely what we want to avoid. If the rate can drop from $4 to $2 per yap in one year, what's in store for us next year?

Arbitrage
The practice of buying a foreign currency in one market at a low price and selling it in another at a higher price.

CHECK YOUR UNDERSTANDING

What disadvantage can a free-floating exchange rate create?

Not a very comfortable world if you're an importer or exporter calculating profits and losses on constantly fluctuating exchange rates. But what can we do?

Let's bring government into the market. The government announces that it is replacing the floating exchange rate system with a **fixed exchange rate.** All trade will take place at the government's fixed rate of exchange. Follow the effects of government intervention in Exhibit 4, panel *b*. Suppose the government fixes the exchange rate at $3 per yap. How can it keep it fixed when our demand for imports from the South Pacific island changes?

The first year is no problem. The economy's exports and imports themselves create a set of demand and supply conditions on the exchange rate market that, by chance, drives the rate precisely to the government's fixed rate. The quantity demanded and supplied is 30,000 yaps, and the market clears.

In the second year, demand for South Pacific island goods increases, raising our demand for yaps to D_1. Look what happens. At that rate, the quantity demanded becomes 50,000 yaps. However, only 30,000 are supplied. The market now generates an excess demand of 20,000.

How can the government handle the 20,000-yap excess demand pressure on the foreign exchange market? It does so *by coming up with its own supply of yaps*. It goes into the foreign exchange market to exchange its own 20,000 yaps for $60,000. It absorbs the entire excess demand for yaps, relieving pressure on the exchange rate. Of course, to play such a role, the government must have sufficient **foreign exchange reserves.**

Look at panel *b*'s third year. A fall in demand for South Pacific island goods shifts the demand curve for yaps to the left, to D_2. At $3 per yap, only 10,000 yaps are demanded but 30,000 are supplied, creating now an excess supply of 20,000 yaps. This time, the government intervenes by supplying $60,000 of its own dollar reserves to buy up the 20,000 excess supply of yaps. We're back where we started. The government has replenished its foreign exchange reserves.

TRADE UNDER FREE AND FIXED EXCHANGE RATES

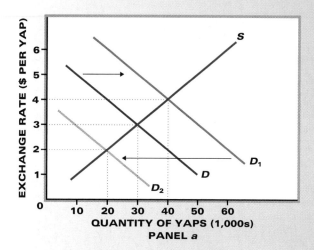

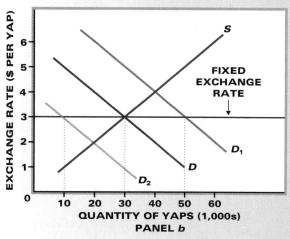

Panel *a* depicts changes in the equilibrium exchange rate—dollars per yap—caused by shifts in the demand curve. In panel *b*, the U.S. government fixes the exchange rate at $3 per yap and supports that rate regardless of changes in the U.S. demand for yaps.

Fixed exchange rate
A rate determined by government and then maintained through the process of buying and selling quantities of its own currency on the foreign exchange market.

Foreign exchange reserves
The stock of foreign currencies a government holds.

GLOBAL PERSPECTIVE

BRAZIL AND THE IMF

What happens to the price of imports when a country devalues its currency? Well, imagine Brazil devaluing its currency, the real, by, say, 50 percent—from two reals per U.S. dollar to 3 reals per dollar. If you lived and worked in Brazil, earning 500 reals per week you might be justifiably upset. Why? Because the Maytag dishwasher you were planning to buy at the appliance store down the street has just increased in price from 2,000 reals to 3,000 reals. That's a smack in your pocketbook! The appliance store is not at fault. After all, the dishwasher, produced in New Jersey, is priced at $1,000. To import it, the store must buy the $1,000, and at the devalued real, that's 3,000 reals. Even prices of locally produced goods will inflate with devaluation, at least those made with imported materials. Devaluation creates inflation.

Is devaluation, then, such a great idea? It may be if Brazil is experiencing chronic unfavorable balances of trade and wants to bring exports and imports more in balance—which is what the International Monetary Fund (IMF) advises Brazil to do—but be careful! The inflationary consequences can be so destabilizing and demoralizing that the cure may be worse than the disease.

That's what worried Brazil's president, Fernando Henrique Cardoso, who faced such a problem and much pressure from the IMF. As a defender of Brazil's poor, he knows that in spite of the fact that IMF economists called the 1994 Mexican peso devaluation—which it helped engineer—a success, the devaluation created an inflationary whirlwind that

THE SCENE: A RIO DE JANEIRO MARKETPLACE TEEMING WITH GOODS. BUT THERE ARE FEWER AND FEWER AMERICAN IMPORTS. THEY'VE BECOME TOO EXPENSIVE.

pushed as many as 20 million Mexicans below the poverty line. He also knows about the IMF's "success" in getting Thailand to float its exchange rate for the baht, which many believe sparked an Asian monetary crisis.

What's wrong with the IMF? It's not that the IMF misdiagnoses the economic problems plaguing many of the less-developed economies or prescribes inappropriate medicine. It's just that, at times, the doses prescribed are so strong—according to some economists—that they end up killing the patient. The IMF, of course, dismisses this view as the apologetics of those who refuse to bite the bullet. It sees itself as trustworthy and straightforward: If there's an economic problem, such as undisciplined fiscal policies or persistent trade imbalances, the country should take corrective action. To the IMF, the aggressive manipulation of exchange rates is both appropriate and effective.

Some economists believe that instead of the IMF coaxing Brazil into a devaluation, it should have used its power to support currency stability. This would have entailed letting the government and the economy adapt to a sound currency rather than having Brazil adapt the currency to the vagaries of its budgetary policy.

MORE ON THE NET

For current information on the Brazilian economy, visit the Brazilian embassy in London (http://www.brazil.org.uk/) or review *Gazeta Mercantil,* a Brazilian newspaper covering economics, business, political, and financial news. Also review current news at the IMF (http://www.imf.org/external/news.htm).

What If the Government Runs Out of Foreign Exchange Reserves?

Exhibit 4, panel *b*, is carefully drawn to allow the third year's excess supply of yaps to replenish the shortage created by the excess demand for yaps in the second year. Unfortunately, life isn't always that convenient. The economy's foreign exchange reserves can build up far beyond sufficient levels or can be drawn down to dangerously low levels.

Suppose the excess demand for yaps, shown for only panel *b*'s second year, persists year after year. How long can the government keep digging into its foreign exchange reserves before it comes up empty? And what can it do if it confronts that predicament?

ADJUSTING THE EXCHANGE RATE Perhaps the simplest remedy is **devaluation** to adjust the fixed exchange rate at a higher level. For example, if the government fixed the exchange rate at $5 instead of $3 per yap, our exports would rise, our imports would fall, and excess demand for yaps would disappear. The drain on the government's foreign exchange reserves would cease.

IMPOSING IMPORT CONTROLS A second option is to impose **import controls** by tariff and quota adjustments. By either raising tariffs or lowering quotas, the government can limit imports. Either way, it can shift the economy's demand curve for yaps as far to the left as it needs to bring the quantity of yaps demanded and supplied into line at $3 per yap.

IMPOSING EXCHANGE CONTROLS Another way of accomplishing the same goal is for the government to introduce **exchange controls.** It can require exporters earning yaps to turn them over to the government in exchange for dollars at the $3 per yap rate. In this way, government ends up with all the yaps in the economy. It then rations them out among importers, keeping the quantity of yaps demanded and supplied in balance.

BORROWING FOREIGN CURRENCIES Finally, the government can go to the **International Monetary Fund (IMF)** or into the foreign exchange market and borrow yaps to cover the country's excess demand for yaps. Sometimes borrowing is the most reasonable option. In periods of crisis, such as wars or famines, the government cannot afford to cut basic imports, nor can it easily increase exports. To stabilize the economy, its best option may be borrowing. The IMF was created in 1944 to provide temporary loans of foreign currencies to countries that borrow to stabilize their own currency. The loan is actually a purchase-and-resale agreement in which the borrowing country sells its own currency to the IMF for the foreign currencies, agreeing to reverse the transaction at a later date.

But if not held in check, borrowing can lead to problems. Just as doctors who prescribe narcotics to overcome postoperative pain always worry about addiction, so must governments who borrow foreign currencies to overcome economic crises worry about becoming addicted to the habit. Borrowing, and the interest payments that accompany it, can too quickly lock an economy into unmanageable international debt.

BALANCE OF PAYMENTS

An economy's **balance of payments** account provides a statement of the economy's financial transactions with the rest of the world. For example, the U.S. balance of payments account for 1999, shown in Exhibit 5, records the dollars that flowed into

---

Devaluation
Government policy that lowers the nation's exchange rate; its currency instantly is worth less in the foreign exchange market.

Import controls
Tariffs and quotas used by government to limit a nation's imports.

Exchange controls
A system in which government, as the sole depository of foreign currencies, exercises complete control over how these currencies can be used.

CHECK YOUR UNDERSTANDING
What does the IMF do?

International Monetary Fund (IMF)
An international organization formed to make loans of foreign currencies to countries facing balance of payments problems.

on the net

Visit the International Monetary Fund (http://www.imf.org/).

Balance of payments
An itemized account of a nation's foreign economic transactions.

EXHIBIT | 5

THE U.S. BALANCE OF PAYMENTS ACCOUNT: 1999 ($ BILLIONS)

CURRENT ACCOUNT	
1. MERCHANDISE EXPORTS	684.4
2. MERCHANDISE IMPORTS	–1,030
3. BALANCE OF TRADE	–345.6
4. EXPORT OF SERVICES	271.9
5. IMPORT OF SERVICES	–191.3
6. INCOME RECEIPTS ON INVESTMENTS	276.2
7. INCOME PAYMENTS ON INVESTMENTS	–294.7
8. UNILATERAL TRANSFERS	– 48.0
9. BALANCE ON CURRENT ACCOUNT	–331.5
CAPITAL ACCOUNT	
10. CHANGE IN U.S. ASSETS ABROAD	–430.2
11. CHANGE IN FOREIGN ASSETS IN U.S.	753.6
12. STATISTICAL DISCREPANCY	8.1
13. BALANCE ON CAPITAL ACCOUNT	331.5

Source: *Survey of Current Business* (Washington, D.C.: U.S. Department of Commerce, January 2001), p. 56.

the U.S. economy in 1999 from the rest of the world and the dollars that flowed out of the United States to the rest of the world. These flows influence the demand and supply for foreign exchange.

Balance on Current Account

The **balance on current account** summarizes U.S. trade in goods and services, net investment income, and unilateral transfers that occur during the current year. Exports of goods and services and income receipts on investments abroad represent dollar inflows ($+$) from the rest of the world. Imports of goods and services and income payments to the rest of the world represent dollar outflows ($-$).

Balance on current account
A category that itemizes a nation's imports and exports of goods and services, income receipts and payments on investment, and unilateral transfers.

The Bureau of Economic Analysis publishes U.S. balance of payments data (http://www.bea.doc.gov/bea/bpatbl-d.html).

Balance of trade
The difference between the value of a nation's merchandise exports and its merchandise imports.

MERCHANDISE EXPORTS Look at line 1. The single most important source of dollar inflow was the $612.1 billion that foreigners paid for our merchandise exports. How do exports contribute to the dollar inflow?

Suppose Dennis Wiziecki, a British engineer from Liverpool, wants to buy a $30,000 Buick LeSabre manufactured in Detroit. He first needs to get his hands on $30,000. After all, that's the currency General Motors wants. How does he get the dollars? By trading his own British pounds for U.S. dollars in the foreign exchange market. That is, the Buick export from the United States creates the demand for U.S. dollars. Dennis buys the $30,000 with his British pounds, then transfers the $30,000 to General Motors in Detroit. That's a $30,000 inflow into the U.S. balance of current account.

MERCHANDISE IMPORTS Line 2 records the $1,030 billion outflow from the United States to the rest of the world. That's a lot of dollars going out. Of course, it represents a lot of imports coming in.

How do imports translate into dollar outflow? Well, suppose Carolyn Hatch, a New York tea importer, decides to buy 500 pounds of Darjeeling tea from India. She learns that the Indian tea exporter wants 50 rupees per pound. That adds up to 25,000 rupees. Carolyn obtains 25,000 rupees by going into the foreign exchange market. There, she supplies U.S. dollars in exchange for Indian rupees. This simple transaction represents a U.S. dollar outflow.

BALANCE OF TRADE The focus of much discussion and debate on the balance of payments is fixed on the **balance of trade** account, that is, the value of exports minus the value of imports, shown in line 3. The terms we use to describe the balance reveal how we view it. For example, when exports are greater than imports, we describe the balance as *favorable*. When imports are greater than exports, the balance is described as *unfavorable*.

In 1999, the value of the goods we exported was $345.6 billion less than the value of the imports of foreign goods we bought. As Exhibit 6 shows, the United States has been running negative balances of trade since 1975.

Negative balances are seen by American industrial workers as a factor that undermines their economic well-being. If the bumper-to-bumper traffic in Cleveland is a stream of imported Toyotas and Hondas, Detroit becomes a wasteland.

How do you switch from an unfavorable to a favorable balance of trade? Depreciate the exchange rate? Impose import quotas? Increase tariffs? Considerable pressure from American exporters and labor unions is continually being brought to bear on the Congress and the administration.

EXPORT OF SERVICES   Another source of U.S. dollar inflow into the current account was the $271.9 billion export of services, shown in line 4 of Exhibit 5. When Mary Constantine, an account executive in one of Italy's leading advertising agencies, flew from Rome to New York on TWA, she had to purchase the $900 ticket with U.S. dollars. After all, that's the currency TWA demands. To make life more convenient for its passengers, TWA may accept her Italian lire and itself go into the foreign exchange market, exchanging lire for $900.

What about exports carried out of the United States by foreigners? For example, when Ryan Walter, a Dubliner, spends his vacation in Cincinnati, that vacation is equivalent to our exporting goods and services to Ireland. If he stays at the Cincinnati Hyatt Hotel, isn't that equivalent to an export of our services? He supplies Irish pounds and demands U.S. dollars for the hotel service.

The *United States Foreign Trade Data* (http://www.ita.doc.gov/industry/otea/usftd/), published by the International Trade Administration, includes monthly analysis of U.S. trade balances.

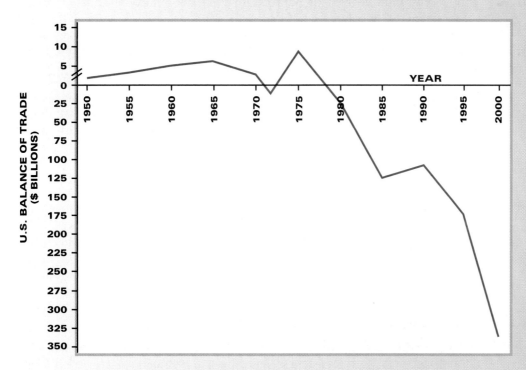

U.S. BALANCE OF TRADE: 1950–2000

The year 1975 marks a watershed in the U.S. balance of trade accounts. It turned from moderate surpluses for most years prior to 1975 to deficits. Note the sharp plunge in the U.S. balance of trade (increases in the annual deficit) from 1983 to 1987, with a slight improvement (more moderate deficits, but deficits nonetheless) thereafter.

EXHIBIT|6

IMPORT OF SERVICES What about the $191.3 billion of imported services, shown in line 5? Remember Mary Constantine's flight to New York on TWA? Now suppose, at the same time, Jonathan Richman, a welder from Kenosha, Wisconsin, decides to visit Canada. He buys a deluxe package tour that includes round-trip fares, hotels, and sightseeing trips to Montreal. Just as TWA demanded U.S. currency, Air Canada and Canadian hotels demand Canadian dollars. The travel agent handling the tour takes Jonathan's U.S. dollars to the foreign exchange market and there trades them for the needed Canadian dollars. Jonathan's trip, then, represents an outflow of U.S. dollars.

INCOME RECEIPTS ON INVESTMENTS Many U.S. companies have investments abroad that earn income. For example, United Fruit, a U.S. food conglomerate with investments in Honduran banana plantations, earns income each year selling bananas to the rest of the world. Part of the income earned remains in Honduras as additional investment, and part ends up in the United States as income receipts. The $276.2 billion, shown in line 6, is the sum of the income receipts of U.S. investments in the rest of the world.

INCOME PAYMENTS ON INVESTMENTS In the same way that U.S. investments abroad create annual income that flows into the United States, so do foreign investments in the United States generate income that flows out of our economy. The Japanese investment in an Ohio Honda plant, for example, generates income that is repatriated to Japan. In 1999, such income payments, or outflows, amounted to $294.7 billion.

Unilateral transfers
Transfers of currency made by individuals, businesses, or government of one nation to individuals, businesses, or governments in other nations, with no designated return.

UNILATERAL TRANSFERS The final item in the current account is **unilateral transfers.** These are both private and government income transfers that we make to governments or to people abroad—typically family members living there—or receive from people living abroad. In 1999, net outflow of unilateral transfers amounted to $48 billion.

What are private transfers? Suppose you decide to study at Oxford, England, and your parents send you $100 monthly. That represents a unilateral transfer of dollars. It's described as unilateral because it flows in only one direction—in this case, out of the United States. What do you do with $100? March right down to an Oxford bank to exchange it for British pounds. After all, the local restaurant takes British pounds, not U.S. dollars.

Can you think of other activities that involve unilateral transfers? Go to the Interactive Study Center at http://gottheil.swcollege.com and click on the "Your Turn" button to submit your example. Student submissions will be posted to the Web site, and perhaps we will use some in future editions of the book!

Foreign students studying in the United States create private unilateral dollar transfers that flow in the opposite direction, that is, into the United States. There are thousands of students from the rest of the world on U.S. campuses who exchange their own currencies for U.S. dollars.

The economic and military aid that the U.S. government provides other governments is an example of a government unilateral transfer. Although such aid represents a dollar outflow, the recipient countries typically use the aid to purchase U.S. goods (adding to our exports).

BALANCE ON CURRENT ACCOUNT Line 9 sums up the inflows (+) and outflows (−) on the U.S. current account, which in 1999 amounted to −$331.5 billion.

Balance on Capital Account

What about capital account entries? These entries refer to the flow of capital into and out of the United States that takes place when people buy and sell real and financial assets across borders.

CHANGES IN U.S. ASSETS ABROAD When a U.S. natural-fiber broom company decides to take advantage of the low labor costs in Mexico to build a factory on the outskirts of Mexico City, it needs pesos to construct the plant, buy and install the machinery, and hire workers. How does the company get the pesos? By supplying dollars on the foreign exchange market (an outflow of dollars). In the end, U.S. assets abroad, in the form of a new broom factory in Mexico, increase.

You don't have to be a broom company to own assets abroad. Individuals can buy assets abroad as well. For example, suppose Gary Adelman, a university professor, chanced upon a prospectus at his broker's office describing a new stock issue by an Israeli medical equipment company and bought 50,000 shekels worth of the stock. His assets now include a piece of the Israeli company. But to get that asset, he created an outflow of dollars.

In 1999 the outflow of dollars from the United States that ended up as changes in U.S. assets abroad amounted to $430.2 billion, shown in line 10 of Exhibit 5.

CHANGES IN FOREIGN ASSETS IN THE UNITED STATES Just as Gary Adelman can buy assets abroad, so can foreigners buy U.S. assets. Imagine a Saudi sheik, sitting in his living room in Mecca reading *The Wall Street Journal.* He reads that the U.S. government has put a new issue of its bonds on the market at a 6 percent rate of interest. He decides to buy $10 million of them. But how? He needs U.S. dollars to make the purchase. His broker goes into the foreign exchange market, supplying the sheik's Saudi riyals and demanding 10 million U.S. dollars. The bond is a U.S. asset.

Foreigners buying any U.S. asset—such as Japanese automakers building an Ohio automobile factory—provide an inflow of dollars. In 1999 changes in foreign assets in the United States amounted to $753.6 billion (line 11). As you see, changes in foreign assets in the United States in 1999 were higher than changes in U.S. assets abroad.

BALANCE ON CAPITAL ACCOUNT Subtracting capital inflows from capital outflows and introducing an 8.1 billion statistical discrepancy produces a $331.5 billion **balance on capital account,** shown in line 12. As you see, it equals the negative $331.5 billion in the current account.

Balance on capital account
A category that itemizes changes in the foreign asset holdings of a nation and that nation's asset holdings abroad.

WHAT IS A BALANCE OF PAYMENTS PROBLEM?

Do U.S. dollar inflows and outflows always cancel each other out? Is it by chance or is there some kind of magic at work bringing these dollar flows into balance? And if current and capital accounts always balance, how can we possibly end up with a balance of payments problem?

The problem associated with the balance of payments is how the balance is obtained. Consider, for example, what happens when the outflow of dollars to pay for our imports exceeds the inflow of dollars earned by our exports. Some source of financing has to be found to cover the difference. Foreigners don't export for the love of it. And currencies don't just materialize out of thin air.

How, then, do we cover? There are three alternatives. First, we can dip into our foreign currency reserves. For example, if we import more from Japan than we

GLOBAL PERSPECTIVE

THE EURO

Look at the exchange rates listed in *The Wall Street Journal*. One U.S. dollar buys 2094 Italian lire. One U.S. dollar buys 0.69 British pound sterling. One U.S. dollar buys 2.11 German marks. These exchange rates—U.S. dollars for specific European currencies—will all but disappear in July 2002 when 11 of the 15 countries of the European Union discard their national currencies in favor of a common currency, the euro.

Making the shift to the euro are Austria, Belgium, Finland, France, Germany, Ireland, Italy, Luxembourg, the Netherlands, Portugal, and Spain. Not participating in the first round of this monetary union—but likely to join anyway—are the United Kingdom, Greece, Denmark, and Sweden.

Why the shift? The euro represents a major commitment to the idea of a "State of Europe." It virtually undermines the ability of any one country within the European Union to pursue independently its own national economic interests. By giving up the French franc, for example, France cannot control the money supply in France. Nor is it able to control its exchange rate—to devalue or appreciate—to promote French trade. While the French no doubt will continue to celebrate Bastille Day, its adoption of the euro necessarily alters for the French the meaning of French political independence.

Replacing the central bank of France, the central bank of Italy, the central bank of the Netherlands, and so on is a new European central bank. The

A NEW GIANT IN THE WORLD OF CURRENCY.

advantage: People, trade, and investment will be able to move throughout the European Union as easily as people, trade, and investment move through the 50 states of the United States. And just as the economic strength of the United States is greater than the sum of its parts, so it is expected that the economic strength of Europe will be greater than the sum of its parts. The euro is indispensable in putting the European parts together. Global economic power—vis-à-vis other national or regional economies, and the United States in particular—is the sought-after European Union goal.

Will the euro successfully challenge the U.S. dollar as *the* international currency? Not likely, at least not in the foreseeable future. Even though the combined countries of the European Union rival the United States in population, GDP, volume of trade, and banking, most of the people and institutions involved in global economic activity—importers, exporters, international lenders, international borrowers, commercial and central banks—rely on and use the currency that other global participants are using. That currency is the U.S. dollar and is likely to remain the dollar for a long time. Like the English language, people use the dollar internationally because, at this time and in this world, everyone else is using it.

MORE ON THE NET

Find out more about the euro, including what the banknotes and coins will look like, at http://www.euro.ecb.int/.

export to Japan, we can use our yen reserves to cover the difference. Second, the Japanese may decide to buy some of our assets, such as the Sears Tower in Chicago. Their supply of yen to buy the dollars needed for the Sears Tower purchase may be just the yen we need to cover the difference between our imports from and exports to them. Third, we can go into the foreign exchange market or to the IMF to borrow the needed yen. Each alternative serves to bring dollar inflows and outflows into balance.

But that's also how we get into trouble! How deep are our currency reserves? How many assets do we really want to sell off? How many foreign currency loans can we take out before foreigners close the door?

Do Trade Imbalances Always Create Problems?

Governments are not always concerned about trade imbalances even when their economies import considerably more than they export. Why not? Because if an economy's principal imports are in the form of industrial and agricultural machinery, the government may expect that by building up the economy with these imports, the economy will *eventually* expand its export markets. That is, the government believes that imports, properly selected, can contribute to future exports and, therefore, *future* dollar inflows.

Foolhardy? Not really. No one would call a farmer foolhardy for scattering seed during spring sowing. The late summer harvest is expected to more than make up for the cost of seed. If imports modernize the economy's productive capacity and improve its competitiveness in world markets, then greater export sales would make the earlier balance of payments problem a gamble well worth taking.

The problem with such a strategy is that it doesn't always work. There is simply no way of guaranteeing that imports intended to develop the productive base of the economy today translate into exports tomorrow. Too often, governments are too optimistic about their export prospects. They view the future through rose-colored glasses. In the end, what was thought to be a calculated risk becomes a real problem.

In many cases, an economy's deficit on current account may not reflect any government strategy at all, not even a failed one. It may simply record the economy's lackluster export performance, at least compared to its import appetites. But why lackluster, and why the appetite?

HOW DEFICITS ON CURRENT ACCOUNT DEVELOP

The Trouble with Being Popular

It's sometimes hard to stay out of trouble when you're too popular. That may be precisely why the United States sometimes gets into balance of payment difficulties. Paradoxically, it is the strength and stability of the U.S. economy compared to other economies that creates the problem. That's the way many economists explain the sharp reversal from favorable balances on current account to deficit ones during the mid-1980s.

Foreigners shopping around the world for attractive investment opportunities found them right here in the United States. In very few other economies did they find such inviting combinations of investment security and reasonable rates of return. Not surprisingly, then, foreigners invested in the U.S. economy, supplying their own currencies on the foreign exchange market and demanding U.S. dollars.

But consider what this popular demand for U.S. dollars does to the U.S. exchange rate. It drives it up. *We now find foreign goods relatively inexpensive in terms of dollars, while foreigners find our goods increasingly expensive in terms of their currencies.* As a result, we import more and export less. If foreigners persist in viewing our economy as a popular domicile for their investments, we may end up with chronic deficits on current account.

The High Cost of High Interest Rates

We can arrive at the same deficit on current account when our interest rates climb above those prevailing in other economies. Canadians, for example, compare interest rates offered at home and abroad and choose those yielding the highest rates. Many individuals, regardless of nationality, invest in securities offering the highest rates. The rising U.S. interest rates in the 1980s shifted the demand curve for the U.S. dollar to the right, driving up the exchange rate on the U.S. dollar. As a result, it made imports more attractive, our exports less attractive.

In this same way, domestically driven monetary policy can inadvertently affect the balance on current account. If the Fed, fighting inflation in the economy, raises its discount rate, it may trigger an increase in interest rates. If the interest rates in the United States climb above foreign rates, the demand for U.S. dollars will increase, appreciating the U.S. dollar, and in this way contributing to the deficit on current account.

The High Cost of Budgetary Deficits

Keeping in mind this link between exchange rates and interest rates, imagine what happens to the deficit on current account when the government, pursuing a purely domestic fiscal policy, finances its deficit budget by selling government securities. If it offers a relatively high interest rate to attract buyers, wouldn't foreigners be just as receptive to the securities offer as Americans?

Budgetary deficits can affect exchange rates and, consequently, balances on current account.

The High Cost of Low Productivity

There's little that the government can do—even correcting for troublemaking monetary and fiscal policies—if the economy's level of productivity, compared to the levels of productivity in other economies, is low and falling. Maintaining export markets becomes increasingly difficult for industries that cannot compete with foreign prices and quality. In fact, when confronted by stiff foreign competition, domestic producers have difficulty holding on to their own domestic markets.

In an economy characterized by low productivity, there are no quick-fix solutions. Unless its industries make the effort to match foreign competition by adopting successful technologies or by creating a more productive culture within its management and labor force, the economy's balance on current account position will steadily worsen.

How serious can a trade imbalance become? How much can an economy borrow or how much of its assets can it sell to finance chronic deficits on current account before pressure builds up to force changes in its exchange rate? Ultimately, depreciation of its rate must occur, making its exports cheaper and its imports more expensive. But unless a low-productivity economy confronts the problem of its low-level productivity, even exchange rate adjustments won't work in the long run.

INTERNATIONAL DEBT

International debt
The total amount of outstanding IOUs a nation is obligated to repay other nations and international organizations.

It isn't only the very low-income, low-productivity, less-developed economies that make their way to lending institutions. In many cases, it is economies with higher incomes, among them relatively high performers that still find themselves strapped to substantial **international debt.** It doesn't matter whether an economy is borrowing to survive or borrowing to sustain high-gear development—both are still borrowing. If the high-gear economy jams, it can create international debt havoc.

A large volume of international debt in economies, such as Argentina's $144 billion, is not the only, or even the best, measure of the debt's burden on an economy. A small or moderate amount of international debt can become a very heavy burden on a developing economy if the interest payments on the debt account for a large percentage of the economy's export revenues.

Exhibit 7 records the **debt service** (the ratio of interest payments on the debt to the economy's exports) for 10 less-developed debtor economies.

Once debt accumulates, it is sometimes difficult to pay off, or even keep under control. Imagine yourself in debt to a credit agency, with the interest payments you make each month on the debt eating up as much as 30 percent of your monthly take-home pay. Not much room to maneuver, is there? Look at Argentina's debt service in 1998. It represents 58.2 percent of Argentina's 1998 exports. Unless Argentina changes the character of its balance of payments, that debt service may become increasingly unmanageable.

Debt service
Interest payments on international debt as a percentage of a nation's merchandise exports.

WILL IT ALL WORK OUT RIGHT IN THE LONG RUN?

David Hume, an 18th-century political philosopher, explained why Spain's demise as an economic superpower was inevitable. Hume argued that Spain lost its ability to compete successfully in world markets because it was so successful in amassing great quantities of gold, then the international currency, from the New World. The more gold Spain acquired, the less able it was to maintain its export markets.

Hume understood why. He saw the relationship between money, prices, exchange rates, and exports. As money, in the form of gold, flowed into Spain, it drove up Spanish prices, making foreign imports less expensive in Spain and Spanish exports more expensive abroad. As a result, Spain's balance on current account became negative, with gold now flowing out of the country. It was as unavoidable as the common cold.

We can apply that same logic to our modern economies. In spite of what they try to do, economies with negative balances on current account will find their exchange rates falling. And unless these rates are propped up by government intervention, they will fall to stem the currency outflows. As long as a negative balance

on the net

The World Bank (http://www. worldbank.org/) maintains data on international debt.

DEBT SERVICE OF SELECTED COUNTRIES, AS A PERCENTAGE OF EXPORTS: 1998

ZIMBABWE	38.2	BRAZIL	74.1
BANGLADESH	91.1	ARGENTINA	58.2
HAITI	81.6	SUDAN	97.9
EGYPT	94.9	MYANMAR	53.3
GHANA	28.4	PARAGUAY	52.5

Source: The World Bank, *World Development Indicators, 2000* (Washington, D.C.: World Bank, 2000).

EXHIBIT 7

APPLIED PERSPECTIVE

FORGIVING THE INTERNATIONAL DEBT OF LDCs

Some people with limited incomes and unlimited appetites borrow to satisfy their insatiable appetites. Too often, the borrowing becomes habitual. And that can be very dangerous business. The borrowing, of course, is not interest-free; very quickly, the interest payments the borrowers are obliged to make get to be as burdensome as, if not more burdensome than, the debt repayment itself. So they borrow again to cover their interest and debt obligations and the debt numbers spiral upward. How long does it take before their debt situation becomes utterly hopeless?

What would you do if you were one of these people? Work harder to increase your income? Curb your appetite? How about going to your creditors on bended knees to ask for debt forgiveness. After all, they may know, as you do, that forgiveness or not, you're not going to repay the debt *ever* because you simply can't.

Many developing (or not so developing) countries are in precisely that situation. With limited GDPs and unlimited appetites, they plunge into international borrowing that eventually puts them in that hopeless situation. What can they do about it? What can their creditors—commercial banks, Western governments, the World Bank, and the International Monetary Fund (IMF)—do about it?

Can these developing countries really "work harder" to increase their GDPs? Not if, as it is for many, their resources and energies are diverted to war activity or to curbing internal conflicts. And even if they were to "work harder" on their economies, most are agriculturally based and because agricultural prices are typically weak on world markets, their GDP growth performance can't be anything but unimpressive. Adding to their woes is the fact that industrial world economies, receptive to special interests at home, are reluctant to open their markets to LDC agricultural exports.

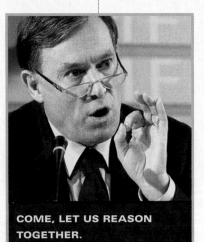

COME, LET US REASON TOGETHER.

What about curbing their appetites? Theoretically, LDC borrowing was designed to develop productive capacity. But in fact, too much of their debt was siphoned off by corrupt government leaders—in many cases, nonelected, military dictatorships (Suharto, Marcos, Samoza, Noriega, and Banzer, to name a few)—and stored away in Swiss, Bahamian, and Cyprus banks. Debt that did find its way into development projects was often mismanaged or used to support politically showcased, grandiose development schemes that had minimal if any impact on the economies of these nations. The development success stories were simply too few.

The result was that for most of the debtor nations, the debt created more problems than it solved.

Most of the $2 trillion of LDC debt is owed by 33 countries, 90 percent of them African. None of them are able to repay. What's left to do?

The issue of forgiveness is on the table. Creditor nations and institutions, such as the United States and the IMF, are disposed to forgive many for much of their debt, *but with strings attached*. The IMF wants assurances that the debtor nations "get their houses in order." By that it means cutting spending to stabilize their currencies; slashing social spending on education, health, and social services; cutting government employment and payrolls; converting inefficient small-scale farming to large-scale export crop farming; and privatizing public industries. The IMF formula is traumatic: Living standards must get worse for many in the indebted world—particularly the middle class and poor—before they can bet better.

The IMF positions has been challenged not only by the indebted countries, but also by the World Bank and creditor governments such as the United States. The United States favors debt relief only if the debtor countries apply the savings toward primary health and education. Non-governmental organizations (NGOs) such as Oxfam America support that position and emphasize poverty reduction as well.

There appears to be little disagreement among the debtor and creditor nations concerning the basic problem and solution: The major percentage of the debt is beyond repayment, and creditor forgiveness of the debt is the only viable policy option.

MORE ON THE NET

Find out about the International Monetary Fund at http://www.imf.org/. The World Bank Group's home page is at http://www.worldbank.org/, and Oxfam America is at http://www.oxfamamerica.org/.

exists, the exchange rate will keep on falling. Eventually, the rate will reach the level appropriate to a zero balance on current account. It takes only time.

This automatic correction mechanism, however, may also push the economy into lower living standards. Some people may be pleased when the economy's exchange rate generates a zero trade balance, but it is somewhat less pleasing if the economy cannot afford to provide the majority of its population with the necessities of life.

In many cases, that is indeed what results. If the Zambian kwacha, for example, is driven so low relative to the U.S. dollar that its people lose the ability to import needed food, then whatever the equilibrium level of its exchange rate, Zambia's standard of living falls. Equilibrium levels of exchange rates, perhaps inevitable, do not guarantee a desirable outcome.

But what's to be done? Is there anything the less-developed economies like Zambia can do to correct their international trade and debt problems? Perhaps the starting point is first to understand why their economies look the way they do. That's the task we set for ourselves in the next chapter.

CHAPTER REVIEW

1. The U.S. demand curve for French francs is downward sloping. When the price of the franc—dollars for francs—is relatively high, a 10-franc bottle of French wine for an American is relatively expensive in terms of the dollars needed to pay for the wine. When the dollars-for-francs exchange rate falls, that same 10-franc bottle of wine for the American is now less expensive in terms of dollars. Because wine now costs fewer dollars, the quantity demanded by the American increases. This increase in quantity demanded of wine creates the increase in quantity demanded of francs.

2. The French supply curve of francs is upward sloping. When the price of the franc—dollars for francs—is relatively high, a $10 CD for the French is relatively inexpensive in terms of the

francs needed to pay for the CD. When the dollars-for-francs exchange rate falls, that same $10 CD for the French is now more expensive in terms of francs. Because the CD now costs more francs, the quantity demanded by the French decreases. This fall in quantity demanded of CDs creates the decrease in quantity supplied of francs.

3. The demand curve for French francs—reflecting U.S. demand for French goods—and the supply curve of French francs—reflecting French demand for U.S. goods—create on the foreign exchange market the equilibrium exchange rate of dollars for francs (or francs for dollars).

4. Shifts in the demand and supply curves for francs—occasioned by changes in income,

tastes, and interest rates—change the equilibrium exchange rate. Appreciation of the dollar means we pay fewer dollars for francs, while depreciation of the dollar means we pay more dollars for francs.

5. To decrease the volatility of its exchange rate, a government may impose a fixed exchange rate. This may require the government to intervene in the foreign exchange market, using its foreign exchange reserves to buy and sell foreign currencies in sufficient quantities to eliminate any excess demand or supply generated on the foreign exchange market.

6. When the fixed exchange rate becomes difficult to maintain, the government can resort to policies such as devaluation, import controls, exchange controls, or borrowing foreign currencies.

7. An economy's balance of payments account describes its financial transactions with the rest of the world. The current account adds up exports and imports of merchandise and services, income payments and receipts on investments, and unilateral transfers. The capital account shows the sum of changes in the value of overseas assets and the value of foreign assets in the economy. The difference between merchandise exports and merchandise imports is the balance of trade. When imports exceed exports, there is an unfavorable balance of trade.

8. Exports of services occur when foreigners purchase U.S. services. When Americans travel overseas they create service imports. When we earn income on our investments overseas, an inflow of dollars from the rest of the world is created. Similarly, when foreign companies operating in the United States earn profits, dollars flow abroad. Unilateral transfers are payments by individuals that are sent abroad and exchanged for a foreign currency.

9. The capital account line for changes in U.S. assets abroad shows the extent to which firms in the United States have invested overseas. These investments create an outflow of dollars. Foreign firms' investments in the United States show up as changes in foreign assets in the United States. Such investments create an inflow of dollars.

10. If the outflow of dollars to pay for imports exceeds the inflow of dollars to pay for exports, then the difference must be financed. Four financing options exist. Reserves of foreign currency can be drawn down. Domestic assets can be sold. Government securities can be sold. Or a country can go into foreign exchange markets and borrow the difference.

11. It may make sense for a country to import more than it exports if the kinds of goods being imported contribute to future gains in productivity.

12. International debt can become a problem for a developing country if interest payments on the debt take a large percentage of export revenues. The debt service is the percentage of a country's exports that interest payments on the debt represent.

KEY TERMS

Foreign exchange market
Exchange rate
Floating exchange rate
Appreciation
Depreciation
Arbitrage
Fixed exchange rate

Foreign exchange reserves
Devaluation
Import controls
Exchange controls
International Monetary Fund (IMF)
Balance of payments

Balance on current account
Balance of trade
Unilateral transfers
Balance on capital account
International debt
Debt service

QUESTIONS

1. Why would anyone in Butte, Montana, or Lyons, France, want yaps?
2. How could people get the yaps they want?
3. Suppose the equilibrium exchange rate is $3 per yap. Explain what that rate signifies in terms of quantities of goods imported and exported.
4. What does *arbitrage* mean, and how does it work?
5. How can the government fix an exchange rate? Can the government fix it at any level, for any length of time? Discuss the limitations that a government faces in maintaining a fixed rate.
6. What control mechanisms can a government introduce to support its exchange rate policy?
7. What are the major categories and items in a balance of payments account?
8. How would each of the following affect the U.S. balance of payments account?
   a. Every month, a Bangladeshi professor at the University of Utah sends $200 to his family living in Bangladesh.
   b. A Japanese businessperson in Nagasaki buys 100 shares of General Motors stock.
   c. The U.S. government sells 20 Patriot missiles to the Israeli government.
   d. The U.S. government gives the Russian government 50 million tons of wheat, priced at $3 per ton, in the form of a unilateral transfer.
9. In some cases, a balance of payments problem really isn't a problem at all. Yet in other cases, it could signal a fundamental problem in the economy. Explain.
10. Some economists argue that our budgetary deficits contribute to our balance of payments problems. How do they make their case?
11. Balance of payments problems and long-term international debt plague the less-developed economies. The two issues are related. Explain.

PRACTICE PROBLEMS

1. The only information given for the following table is that the equilibrium exchange rate is 4 Israeli shekels per U.S. dollar.

SHEKELS PER U.S. DOLLAR	QUANTITY DEMANDED (SHEKELS)	QUANTITY SUPPLIED (SHEKELS)
6		
5		
4		
3		
2		

Fill in the blank cells, constructing quantity demanded and quantity supplied schedules so that the equilibrium exchange rate occurs at 4 shekels per dollar.

2. Change the numbers in the table in practice problem 1 so that the equilibrium exchange rate is 5 shekels per U.S. dollar. What explanation can you offer for such changes?

3. Suppose the following data represent Israel's international transactions (in shekels). What is Israel's balance of trade? What is its balance on current account? What is its balance on capital account?

ITEM	SHEKELS
MERCHANDISE EXPORTS	10
CHANGE IN FOREIGN ASSETS IN ISRAEL	2
EXPORTS OF SERVICES	5
INCOME RECEIPTS ON INVESTMENT	3

ITEM	SHEKELS
MERCHANDISE IMPORTS	−8
CHANGE IN ASSETS ABROAD	−5
IMPORT OF SERVICES	−4
INCOME PAYMENTS ON INVESTMENT	−2
UNILATERAL TRANSFERS	−1

4. How would each of the following events affect the quantity demanded and quantity supplied

schedules in practice problem 1? Indicate whether the numbers in the schedules would increase or decrease and the resulting increase or decrease in the equilibrium exchange rate. Then show how each event would affect the numbers in each of the categories in practice problem 3.

a. A U.S. manufacturer moves a factory from New Jersey to Israel.

b. Hilton builds a new 150-room hotel in Jerusalem.

c. The United States removes its tariff on oranges from Israel.

d. Israeli citizens working in the United States send part of their income back to Israel.

WHAT'S WRONG WITH THIS GRAPH?

FOREIGN EXCHANGE MARKET

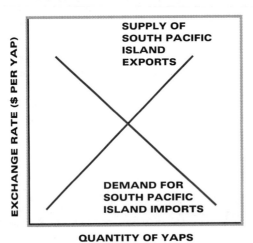

QUANTITY OF YAPS

ECONOMIC CONSULTANTS

ECONOMIC RESEARCH AND ANALYSIS BY STUDENTS FOR PROFESSIONALS

David Tietlebaum recently opened Excursions Around the World, a travel agency that conducts tours in over 50 countries. Before opening Excursions Around the World, David worked as a tour guide in Europe and, in this role, had experience with different currencies and exchange rates. However, as owner of Excursions Around the World, David must be able to explain to customers how exchange rates work and, in particular, what the value of their own currency is in relation to the currency of the country, or countries, these customers want to visit.

David has hired Economic Consultants to prepare a brochure that customers may read to familiarize themselves with foreign currencies and the dynamics of exchange rates. Prepare a brochure for Excursions Around the World that addresses the following issues:

1. What information is available about foreign currencies?

2. In basic terms, how do exchange rates work? What do customers traveling in foreign countries need to consider about exchanging currencies?

3. Where can customers find current information about exchange rates?

You may find the following resources helpful as you prepare this brochure for Excursions Around the World:

- **Currency News** (http://biz.yahoo.com/reports/currency.html)—Yahoo! Finance provides the latest news, taken from Reuters, concerning currencies.
- **The Interactive Currency Table** (http://www.xe.com/ict/) and **Universal Currency Converter** (http://www.xe.com/ucc/)—The Interactive Currency Table and the Universal Currency Converter, maintained by Xenon Laboratories, automatically provide exchange rate values and foreign exchange rate conversions.
- **Pacific Exchange Rate Service** (http://pacific.commerce.ubc.ca/xr/)—This service provides access to current and historic daily exchange rates. Also provided is a list of all the currencies of the world and the countries' exchange rate arrangements.
- **Federal Reserve Statistical Release, Foreign Exchange Rates** (http://www.federalreserve.gov/releases/H10/)—The Federal Reserve releases, every Monday, official foreign exchange rates.

PRACTICE TEST

1. Which of the following would cause the demand curve for the French franc to shift to the right?
   a. A decrease in the exchange rate of francs for dollars
   b. An increase in the exchange rate of francs for dollars
   c. A decrease in foreigners' tastes for French goods and services
   d. A decrease in French interest rates
   e. A decrease in foreigners' incomes

2. If the supply curve for German marks shifts to the left, then
   a. the demand curve for German marks will shift to the right.
   b. the equilibrium exchange rate of German marks for other currencies will rise.
   c. there will be more marks in equilibrium held in world markets.
   d. the equilibrium exchange rate of German marks for other currencies will fall.
   e. the demand curve for German marks will shift to the left.

3. If the United States fixes its exchange rates, such as four Belgian francs per dollar, then to keep it fixed at the four-francs-per-dollar rate,
   a. Belgian and American exporters and importers must agree to keep their mutual trade in balance.
   b. Belgian and American exporters and importers must agree not to trade at any other exchange rate.
   c. The U.S. government must do the exporting and importing for the United States.
   d. both the U.S. and Belgian governments must do the exporting and importing for their respective countries.
   e. the U.S. government must buy and sell U.S. dollars on the foreign exchange market.

4. If there is an appreciation in the dollar relative to the Japanese yen, then
   a. more dollars are needed for Americans to buy Japanese goods.
   b. Americans get fewer yen per dollar on the foreign exchange market.
   c. American goods become cheaper for the Japanese to buy than before.
   d. American goods become more expensive for the Japanese to buy than before.
   e. the supply curve of the yen will shift to the right.

5. Which of the following groups would benefit from a depreciation in the German mark relative to the Canadian dollar?
   a. Exporters of Canadian goods

   b. Exporters of German goods
   c. Consumers of Canadian goods in Germany
   d. Consumers of German goods in Germany
   e. Importers of Canadian goods

6. One problem with floating exchange rates is that they
   a. do not take into account shifts in the demand for a nation's currency.
   b. do not take into account shifts in the supply of a nation's currency.
   c. add uncertainty to international trade.
   d. decrease price variability in world markets.
   e. eliminate the possibility of arbitrage in foreign exchange markets.

7. If Costa Rica uses import controls to maintain its foreign exchange reserves, it means that the Costa Rican government
   a. uses international borrowing to finance its imports.
   b. sells foreign exchange reserves to finance its imports.
   c. imposes tariffs and quotas to limit its imports.
   d. devalues the Costa Rican peso to limit its imports.
   e. appreciates the Costa Rican peso to limit its imports.

8. All of the following except one are included in a nation's balance on current account. Which one?
   a. Foreign exchange reserves
   b. Unilateral transfers
   c. Export of services
   d. Income receipts on investments
   e. Income payments on investments

9. Which of the following is an example of a unilateral transfer?
   a. The United States borrows dollars from Italy in the foreign exchange market.
   b. Spain purchases oil from Venezuela.
   c. Norway pays dividends on bonds issued to Chinese citizens.
   d. A French citizen working in the United States sends money home to her family.
   e. Colombia imports shoes from Italy.

10. Interest payments on a country's international debt are referred to as
    a. debt service.
    b. loan payments.
    c. currency devaluation.
    d. trade imbalances.
    e. income payments on investments.

21

THE ECONOMIC PROBLEMS OF LESS-DEVELOPED ECONOMIES

Imagine two infants born at the same instant, one in the delivery room of the maternity ward at Barnes Hospital in St. Louis, Missouri, the other in a one-room, earthen-floored, mud brick home in El Fashn, a small village along the Nile river in Egypt, about 150 miles south of Cairo.

Like all newborns, these are two beautiful human beings. But, tragically, they face very different futures. The Missouri baby will probably survive her early years and just as probably live to the ripe old age of 85. The El Fashn baby, on the other hand, will have a much less certain chance of surviving to her first birthday and, according to life tables for Egypt, has a life expectancy at birth of only 62 years.

The Missouri baby, like most in the United States, can expect to attend a day-care center and then at age five join

the neighborhood kids in kindergarten. Her education is compulsory; she will attend elementary and high school. Moreover, the probability is quite high that she will graduate from some college or university with a degree that prepares her for an intellectually and financially rewarding, productive life.

What about her counterpart in Egypt? The El Fashn infant may learn how to read and write, but the chances of her acquiring an advanced degree are rather remote. She will probably marry at an early age, have more than seven children, and work long, hard hours on a few nonirrigated cultivated acres surrounding the village.

THIS CHAPTER INTRODUCES YOU TO THE ECONOMIC PRINCIPLES ASSOCIATED WITH:

- POVERTY IN THE LESS-DEVELOPED COUNTRIES (LDCs)
- ECONOMIC DUALISM
- THE BIG-PUSH STRATEGY FOR ECONOMIC DEVELOPMENT
- THE UNBALANCED GROWTH STRATEGY FOR ECONOMIC DEVELOPMENT
- FOREIGN INVESTMENT IN THE LDCs
- ECONOMIC AID TO THE LDCs

Perhaps the most disheartening part of this tale of two cities, at least for the Egyptian baby, is that the story repeats. Her children will probably face similar prospects. The unfairness—isn't it unfair?—continues.

CONFRONTING NATIONAL POVERTY

Being poor is certainly no crime. But *accepting* poverty and allowing it to continue unchecked seem to be, perhaps, crimes not only against the population's impoverished victims, but against those generations of impoverished yet to come. Who's to blame? Obviously, people whose standards of living are not much above physical subsistence don't *choose* to remain poor. The world they inhabit affords them little choice. Is their national poverty, then, inevitable? Is there nothing anyone can do?

Economists, at least since the early 1950s, focused some attention on the issue of persisting national poverty in the economies of Asia, Africa, and Latin America. It was clear in 1950, and even clearer now, that the kinds of problems confronting these economies in their attempt to achieve higher standards of living differ fundamentally from those faced by the industrial economies of the West.

The Language of National Poverty

The language used by economists to describe these economies has changed over time. In the 1950s, economists began to take a hard, close look at the economies of Asia, Africa, and Latin America. For the first time they were seen as something more than trading posts for our raw materials. During that period, economists were quick to identify their national poverty as endemic, the consequence of economic *backwardness* or *underdevelopment.*

The terms seemed appropriate. The differences between Canada and Egypt, for example, cannot be measured in terms of higher or lower GDP. The real differences are not quantitative, but qualitative. Egypt's inability to raise its standard of living has more to do with its social, political, and economic institutions and with its perceptions of past, present, and future than with any lack of effort or personal talents.

Economies that have yet to invest in basic energy, housing, education, or transportation systems or that have yet to develop legal, financial, and communication systems to support modern ways of producing goods and services simply cannot compete in the same economic world as the industrial economies of the West. In this sense, the terms *backwardness* and *underdevelopment* conveyed that idea.

Less-developed countries (LDCs)
The economies of Asia, Africa, and Latin America.

But in the 1960s, economists dropped the terms *backwardness* and *underdevelopment* in favor of *newly developing countries,* or **less-developed countries (LDCs).** The change reflected the view that the terms *backwardness* and *underdevelopment* were much too prejudicial. After all, many Asian, African, and Latin American societies, although poor and lacking the prerequisites of development, were in other respects the equals of their counterparts in the West. The United Nations, with expanding memberships from the newly independent former colonies, had much to do with promoting this language change.

There Are Important Differences Among the Less-Developed Economies

Sometimes, labels can be misleading. Many of the less-developed economies have, indeed, made considerable progress. For example, in the past 25 years, Brazil, Korea, Singapore, Hong Kong, Israel, Taiwan, and Iran have made spectacular leaps in modernizing and developing their economies, achieving for their people substantially higher levels of per capita income. And many other developing economies have made moderate progress.

But many others haven't. Some LDCs still seem to be stalled in a mode that keeps yielding, decade after decade, the same kinds of subsistence-level incomes and the same employment opportunities and investment patterns that inhibit them from making even very modest transitions to modernization.

LDC PER CAPITA INCOMES

While there is no consensus among economists concerning just what specific level of per capita income or what specific rate of output growth would allow us to identify LDCs, *some* levels and *some* rates are so obviously troublesome that economists have little difficulty making the identification.

Exhibit 1 compares the income performance records of 15 LDCs of the world.

The data in Exhibit 1 are about as striking and painfully clear as any set of income numbers can possibly be. Even though you have to be on guard against translating these incomes into the purchasing power they would represent in our own economy, still, would you question the economic impoverishment they suggest?

Look at Ethiopia's $100 and Kenya's $350 per capita income for 1998. Consider the per capita income growth rates for these economies over the 1990–98 period. How can their average annual growth rates suggest anything but economic sluggishness?

Even though a dollar does not provide you with as much purchasing power in the United States as it would a person earning its equivalent in an LDC, still, the low-level per capita income data in Exhibit 1 paints a fairly accurate picture of national poverty in the LDCs. The $390 annual per capita income in Ghana, for example, is pitifully low no matter what purchasing power measure you choose to use. According to data in the 2000 *World Bank Atlas,* people in more than 40 LDCs, including India's 930 million people, have per capita incomes less than $500 a year.

Nor does the future look particularly bright for some of the LDCs of Exhibit 1. The 1990–98 per capita income growth for several was actually negative—the people became poorer. Algeria's per capita income, for example, fell 1.0 percent each year during the years of Exhibit 1.

How successful or unsuccessful an economy is in raising its per capita income depends not only on how well it generates economic growth, but also on how well it contains population growth. If

on the net

The World Bank (http://www.world bank.org/) maintains economic data (http://www.worldbank.org/data/) on the regions and countries of the world. *The World Factbook* (http://www.cia.gov/cia/publications/factbook/) maintains region- and country-specific economic, political, and cultural profiles.

EXHIBIT 1

PER CAPITA INCOME, PER CAPITA INCOME GROWTH RATE, AND POPULATION GROWTH RATE IN SELECTED LDCs: 1990–98

	PER CAPITA INCOME $	PER CAPITA INCOME GROWTH RATE	POPULATON GROWTH RATE
LOW-INCOME LDCs			
ETHIOPIA	100	2.6	2.6
DEM. REP. CONGO	110	–8.5	3.6
KENYA	350	0.0	3.1
MONGOLIA	380	–1.5	2.2
GHANA	390	1.4	3.1
LOW-MIDDLE-INCOME LDCs			
ZIMBABWE	620	–0.2	2.1
CAMEROON	610	–2.3	3.2
IVORY COAST	700	1.4	3.1
SRI LANKA	810	3.9	1.4
SYRIA	1,020	1.3	3.3
UPPER-MIDDLE-INCOME LDCs			
ALGERIA	1,550	–1.0	2.5
VENEZUELA	3,530	–0.1	2.5
BOTSWANA	3,070	0.9	2.9
SOUTH AFRICA	3,310	–0.1	2.3
BRAZIL	4,630	1.7	1.6

Source: The World Bank, *World Bank Atlas, 2000* (Washington, D.C.: World Bank, 2000).

EXHIBIT|2

PERCENTAGE OF POPULATION UNDER 15 YEARS OF AGE FOR SELECTED COUNTRIES: 1997

	PERCENTAGE UNDER 15		PERCENTAGE UNDER 15
ETHIOPIA	46.3	UNITED STATES	21.4
GHANA	41.7	UNITED KINGDOM	19.1
PAKISTAN	40.9	FRANCE	18.5
NIGERIA	44.4	GERMANY	15.2
KENYA	42.1	THE NETHERLANDS	18.2
PHILIPPINES	37.0	AUSTRALIA	20.8

Source: *Statistical Abstract of the United States, 1999* (Washington, D.C.: U.S. Department of Commerce, 1999), p. 835.

CHECK YOUR UNDERSTANDING

What does per capita income depend on?

population grows faster than income, per capita income falls. It's simple but devastating arithmetic:

$$\text{per capita income growth} = \frac{\text{income growth}}{\text{population growth}}$$

Therein lies an LDC's double-whammy problem. While income growth has been less than impressive in some LDCs, population growth has been *too* impressive. Look at the population data in column 4 of Exhibit 1. Some of the LDCs have population growth rates greater than 2.5 percent per year. This means that their economic growth rates must be at least 2.5 percent per year just to sustain their already low-level per capita incomes.

High population growth rates also create an age distribution profile that loads the population in the under-15-years-old group. The consequences for national poverty are dire. Look at the contrast between the age distributions in the LDCs and those of the industrially advanced economies shown in Exhibit 2.

Almost half the population of Ethiopia is under 15 years old. Most of them—particularly those under 10 years of age—although consuming meagerly, still consume more than they are able to produce. Because they represent so large a proportion of Ethiopia's population, these many-mouths-to-feed Ethiopians undercut Ethiopia's ability to shift resources from the production of consumption goods to the production of capital goods. Economists refer to this condition as the vicious circle of poverty: People are poor because they can't invest in capital goods, and they can't invest in capital goods because they are poor. The problem is illustrated in the production possibilities curve of Exhibit 3.

CHECK YOUR UNDERSTANDING

What is meant by the vicious circle of poverty?

Point *a* signals the predicament. The demands of Ethiopia's growing population force it to devote its meager resources almost exclusively to the production of consumption goods, impeding the development of its capital goods production. Point *b* is where it prefers to be. But how do you get there with a fast-growing population? Is Ethiopia, or any of the other economically troubled LDCs, willing to adopt a population policy similar to the one initiated in China in the 1970s, which limits

EXHIBIT | 3

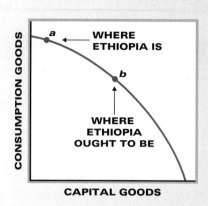

THE VICIOUS CIRCLE OF POVERTY

WHERE ETHIOPIA IS

WHERE ETHIOPIA OUGHT TO BE

CONSUMPTION GOODS

CAPITAL GOODS

If Ethiopia is going to get onto an economic growth path, it will have to move down along its production possibilities curve from point *a* to a production possibilities position that affords it greater capital goods production, such as point *b*. That may be difficult with population growth at 2.6 percent per year.

families to one child? Unlikely. But it was effective. China's 1985–95 population growth rate was down to 1.3 percent.

OTHER INDICATORS OF THE LDCs' LACK OF ECONOMIC WELL-BEING

When you think of investments in capital goods production, you are more likely to think about building machinery and the factories that house the machinery than anything else. These investments are very tangible and very productive. But the capital investments that yield the highest payoffs in an economy are not necessarily those made in machinery and factories. Investments in **human capital**—in the form of education and health care—rank among the most important of the capital goods contributing to national economic growth. The problem is that although their payoffs are relatively high, they require considerable time to generate. Better health and education improve a person's working efficiency, but the improvement occurs gradually and the gains in productivity resulting from it are spread over a person's lifetime.

For these and other reasons, many LDCs, anxious for quick, visible investment payoffs, are disinclined to put their very limited resources in human capital development. Exhibit 4 records the consequences.

The direct link between LDCs' poverty and life expectancy is unmistakable: Life expectancy among the poorest of the LDCs peaks at 50 years, while it reaches 80 among the industrial economies of the world. Moreover, life expectancy is predicted to increase even further in the richer countries and to actually decline in some of the poorest countries of Africa.

Almost half of the world's people suffer from diseases related to contaminated or insufficient water. While considerable progress has been made in providing safe water in many LDCs, as many as two-thirds of them still lack adequate sanitation or safe water. Africa is especially far from reaching acceptable standards. Look at Exhibit 4, column 6. More than 30 percent of the population of half the LDCs have no access to safe water.

Human capital
The investment in workers' health and knowledge, acquired through education, training, and/or experience that enhances their productivity.

EXHIBIT|4

LIFE EXPECTANCY, INFANT MORTALITY, PEOPLE PER PHYSICIAN, PERCENTAGE OF CHILDREN IN SCHOOL, AND PERCENTAGE OF PEOPLE WITH SAFE WATER FOR SELECTED COUNTRIES: 1998 OR LATEST YEAR AVAILABLE

	LIFE EXPECTANCY (YEARS)	INFANT MORTALITY (PER 1,000)	PEOPLE PER PHYSICIAN	PERCENTAGE OF CHILDREN IN SCHOOL	PERCENTAGE OF PEOPLE WITH SAFE WATER
LOW-INCOME LDCs					
ETHIOPIA	43	107	37,811	18	27
DEM. REP. CONGO	48	90	15,442	49	27
KENYA	51	76	7,751	73	53
MONGOLIA	66	50	414	67	66
GHANA	60	65	13,705	60	56
LOW-MIDDLE-INCOME LDCs					
ZIMBABWE	43	115	7,671	91	77
CAMEROON	54	77	11,594	64	41
IVORY COAST	46	88	19,023	49	72
SYRIA	69	28	1,161	79	85
SRI LANKA	73	16	2,507	55	46
UPPER-MIDDLE-INCOME LDCs					
ALGERIA	71	35	1,137	81	79
VENEZUELA	73	21	634	81	79
BOTSWANA	46	62	5,189	91	70
SOUTH AFRICA	63	51	1,875	97	70
BRAZIL	67	33	749	85	72

Source: Ruth Leger Sivard, *World Military and Social Expenditures, 1966* (Washington, D.C.: World Priorities, 1966), pp. 30–52, and The World Bank, *World Bank Atlas, 2000* (Washington, D.C.: World Bank, 2000).

What about education? Between 1960 and 1995, the proportion of LDC children attending primary school increased from less than 50 to 75 percent. Yet, lack of education remains one of the chief obstacles to social progress. In the South Asian and African countries ravaged by war and civil unrest, enrollment in the primary levels is critically low. The school-aged population in Africa, for example, is growing almost twice as fast as elsewhere, but a quarter of those of primary school age are not enrolled. Look at Ethiopia, Ivory Coast, and the Democratic Republic of the Congo in Exhibit 4, column 5.

ECONOMIC DUALISM

Of course, not everybody in the LDCs suffers these basic deprivations. Some live as well as your neighbors. Many LDC doctors, lawyers, merchants, accountants, exporters and importers, manufacturers, hotel owners, bank managers, cosmetics salespeople, customs officials, and government clerks have access to safe water, hospitals, education, decent housing, telephones, automobiles, and a variety of imported durables that make their lives relatively comfortable.

APPLIED PERSPECTIVE

CHINA'S POPULATION POLICY: ONE COUPLE, ONE CHILD

What do you know about China? Probably that it has the largest population in the world. And you're right. China's 1.26 billion people account for as much as 21 percent of the world's total. That's very many people! In fact, to China's economic and social planners, that's simply too many! It interferes, they believe, with China's ability to create the instrumentalities for rapid economic development. China has been at war with underdevelopment since its 1949 revolution. Its fight to increase standards of living—per capita income—is waged on two fronts: the need to increase GDP and the need to curb population growth.

To deal with its critical demographic concern, the Chinese government in the 1970s introduced an uncompromising family planning policy that confronted China's reality. The policy advocates the practice of "one couple, one child," allowing "a second child only with proper spacing and in accordance with the laws and regulations."

What are these "laws and regulations?" They're excessively harsh by anyone's standards. For example, all pregnancies must be authorized by the government. Menstrual cycles are publicly monitored and pelvic examinations are performed on women suspected of being pregnant. Unauthorized pregnancies are terminated by abortion when detected regardless of the stage of pregnancy. Mandatory IUDs are inserted in women with one child. Removal is difficult and x-ray detection is capriciously applied. There is mandatory sterilization of couples with 2 or more unauthorized children. Women are required to obtain a birth coupon before conceiving a child, the coupon serving as a food rationing device. Without it, family food allotment remains unchanged so that per capita food consumption within the family falls when family size increases without authorization.

THE MESSAGE IS CLEAR IN ANY LANGUAGE.

These stringent procedures and practices have resulted in a high rate of infanticide and, in particular, the abandonment of female infants. But the cold facts are that China's population growth, since the initiation of the "one couple, one child" policy, has been brought under effective control. From 1970 to 1999, China's birth rate decreased from 3.34% to 1.53%. The total fertility rate of Chinese women fell below replacement levels.

The impact of the falling birth rates on family size is notable. Average family size fell from 4.54 members in 1980 to 3.36 members in 1999. Families with 4 or more members fell from 46.3 percent of total families to 23.3 percent. Compared to the developed countries of Europe and North America, China has accomplished these changes in a relatively short period of time.

Chinese planners translate these achievements into movements along and shifts in China's production possibilities curve. By averting the births of an estimated 250 million people and basing the per-child rearing costs from birth to 16 years at 19,000 yuan, China was able to shift resources valued at approximately 4.75 trillion yuan from consumption goods production to investment. That shift contributed to China's "second front" effort to raise standards of living: GDP growth. China's GDP quadrupled since 1980.

Have the high costs been too high? You be the judge.

MORE ON THE NET

Visit the China Population Information and Research Center at http://www.cpirc.org.cn/eindex.htm to find articles and updates on China's population strategy.

The problem is that such a lifestyle is reserved for the few. Most people in LDCs live in remote villages, in overpopulated cities, or on their outskirts, in crowded, squalid shelters. Their employment, if they are employed, is typically in low-productivity agriculture or marginal service-related jobs.

These two very different worlds exist side by side without affecting each other. Exhibit 5 illustrates this **economic dualism.**

The demand curve for workers, *D*, in the traditional sector of panel *a* is relatively low, reflecting traditional technology and weak prices. The supply curve of labor, *S*, reflects the availability of large numbers of unskilled workers with low opportunity costs willing and even eager to work at minimum wage rates.

In comparison, the modern sector of panel *b* yields substantially higher wage rates. The demand curve, *D'*, reflects industrial technology applied to the export market, where productivity is higher and prices firmer. Its labor supply curve, *S'*, is relatively steep, reflecting the scarcity of technical skills in the LDCs.

This economic dualism tends to persist because the skills of those in the traditional sector are completely inadequate for the modern sector. They lack the education, the technological culture, and the specific talents, as well as the knowledge needed to obtain them. Although sharing the same geography, they are as far removed from that modern world as they are from the moon. The vast majority of these people are trapped in poverty conditions.

Economic dualism
The coexistence of two separate and distinct economies within an LDC; one modern, primarily urban, and export-driven, the other traditional, agricultural, and self-sustaining.

C H E C K   Y O U R   U N D E R S T A N D I N G ▶

Why does economic dualism tend to persist?

E X H I B I T | 5

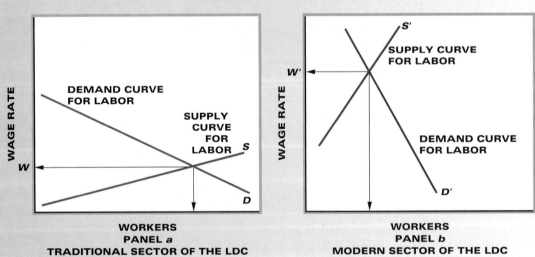

ECONOMIC DUALISM

WAGE RATE

DEMAND CURVE FOR LABOR

SUPPLY CURVE FOR LABOR *S*

W

D

WORKERS
PANEL *a*
TRADITIONAL SECTOR OF THE LDC

WAGE RATE

S'

SUPPLY CURVE FOR LABOR

W'

DEMAND CURVE FOR LABOR

D'

WORKERS
PANEL *b*
MODERN SECTOR OF THE LDC

In the traditional sector of the LDC, depicted in panel *a*, the demand curve for labor, *D*, is relatively low and flat. The relatively low opportunity costs associated with traditional labor produce the relatively flat supply curve of labor at relatively low wage rates, *S*. The traditional market, then, generates the relatively low equilibrium wage rate, *W*.

The modern sector of the LDC, depicted in panel *b*, contrasts sharply with the traditional sector of panel *a*. The demand curve for labor, *D'*, is higher. The higher opportunity costs associated with the skilled workers in this sector generate a steeper supply curve of labor, *S'*. The equilibrium wage rate is *W'*, considerably higher than *W*.

THE ABSENCE OF BASIC PREREQUISITES

Some things are so basic to the proper functioning of an economy and to economic progress in general, and so commonplace in our own economy, that we are sometimes inclined to overlook their importance.

Political Instability

For example, can you imagine how difficult it would be to plan our economic future if we thought not only that our government could be overthrown overnight, but that the character of our political system would change radically with the overthrow?

Laws become meaningless when governments that displace each other too frequently and by force are inclined to set aside past government commitments and, at times, even basic property rights. Such political discontinuities must interfere with routine economic decision making, increasing people's uncertainty everywhere in the economy.

For example, how can anyone rely on a military junta or on a revolutionary party government whose political support among the people is always questionable and whose legitimacy can be contested only in disruptive ways? How can such a regime provide confidence in anyone's economic future when its own time horizon is, by past experience, short?

In many LDC economies, juntas, single-party regimes, and puppet-like monarchies are precisely the kinds of governments that hold power. Generals in government are soon deposed by their colonels, and one revolutionary party is undone by another, with each new regime always claiming power on behalf of the people. For many, secret police and political prisoners are commonplace.

While some changes in regime may represent new faces in old uniforms or new revolutionary parties replacing old ones, many incoming regimes actually do go about undoing much in the economy.

Nonscientific Perceptions

A no-less-fundamental factor inhibiting economic development is the perceptions LDC citizens have concerning their economic status, the societal goals they consider most desirable, and the accepted ways they go about pursuing them. These perceptions reflect the psychological, religious, and cultural character of LDC economies.

THE POWER OF TRADITIONALISM Consider Exhibit 1 once more. The high population growth rates are no accident. Large numbers of children are highly desired, particularly sons. The opportunity cost, measured in terms of sacrificed material goods and services, of having large families is clearly understood. *These are choices people make.* They just reflect a different set of accepted values.

Just as people in some LDCs are reluctant to exchange large families for more goods, so also are they reluctant to part with known and accepted ways of producing goods for new and more productive ways. Their reliance on custom and tradition is a powerful inhibitor of development. In this respect, too, they differ substantially from the way people in industrial economies view technology. We are quick to discard the familiar when new goods or ways of producing them are offered.

That same healthy respect for custom and tradition works against willingness to apply scientific methodology to the everyday business of life. Peasants are slow to adopt modern chemistry or even mechanization, and they are disinclined to change the kinds of crops they cultivate. Even if LDC governments are eager to help the peasants increase productivity, the governments often meet resistance.

How do you overcome traditionalist perceptions of life, or how do you modify the behavior of the ruling regimes? Without applying value judgments to either, we can consider them deadweights to economic development. Unless some modification takes place, it is highly unlikely that tradition-bound LDC economies can make the transition to economic modernization.

The Absence of Infrastructure

While overcoming noneconomic barriers is critical to any effort at development, several economic barriers pose equally insurmountable obstacles. Among them is the conspicuous absence of economic **infrastructure.**

What is infrastructure? When we think about how our own economy works, we tend to take for granted the money and banking system that provides the major investment loans to our nation's businesses; the educational system that turns out the incredible varieties of skills and basic research that actually run our nation's production lines; the extensive transportation and communications system—interstate roads, railroads, airports, canals, telephones, Internet sites, postal systems, television stations—that links almost every piece of our geography into one market; the energy system that powers our factories; and, of course, the market system itself, which brings our nation's goods and services into our households.

Although the basic systems that make up our economic infrastructure were either completely absent or underdeveloped when the United States became a republic, they are now so common to us that we tend to overlook the fact that without them our national productive capacity would suddenly and dramatically collapse.

Imagine transplanting a modern Detroit automobile plant to Chad, an African country southwest of Egypt. Even if U.S. technicians were sent along to put it in place, this major piece of private direct investment would probably do the Chadians little good.

Why? Because physical plants themselves cannot create output. The manufacture of automobiles requires, at the least, a variety of skilled workers, engineers, accountants, salespeople, plant managers, and maintenance crews. Just who in Chad would be qualified? But that's just the beginning.

Who would do the financing? Chadians have always financed the purchase of seed for their few acres or a new milk cow with funds drawn from their own savings or from a moneylender, but neither the moneylender nor the saver is capable of financing an automobile plant. The Chadian banking system is still embryonic.

The plant, of course, requires some energy source. What good is the plant and its state-of-the-art machinery if there is no electricity to power it? Chad simply doesn't have the megawatts. But suppose it did—what's the point of the plant if there are no decent roads in the country?

Obviously, we've only scratched the surface of the problem. Even with a road system, the plant would still require an accessible service station industry, with ready stocks of fuel, spare parts, repair equipment, and, most important, people with completely different sets of skills, to make it work. It gets rather complicated, doesn't it?

Infrastructure
The basic institutions and public facilities upon which an economy's development depends.

Review *The World Factbook* profile of Chad (http://www.cia.gov/cia/publications/factbook/geos/cd.html).

Can you think of any other components of an infrastructure that would be needed in order to transplant an automobile plant to Chad besides the ones mentioned in the text? Go to the Interactive Study Center at http://gottheil.swcollege.com and click on the "Your Turn" button to submit your example. Student submissions will be posted to the Web site, and perhaps we will use some in future editions of the book!

GLOBAL PERSPECTIVE

INTERNET AND INFRASTRUCTURE

The unusually high rates of labor productivity growth in the United States and in many of the OECD countries during the last decade of the 20th century can be largely attributed to the coming of age of computer technology. Just as the copper age, iron age, bronze age, and petroleum age linked new and improved labor productivity with new and improved technology, this computer age is associated with an impressive productivity lift in the 21st century.

Already, we have experienced the effects of this incredible technology. During the last few decades of the 20th century, the Internet boosted efficiency and enhanced global market integration dramatically. It raised labor productivity by increasing procurement efficiency, strengthening inventory control, lowering retail transaction costs, and eliminating layers of production intermediaries. The prices of most goods and services have fallen as a result while product quality has improved. And that's only the beginning. Our economic future looks even brighter than our recent high-performance past. The only question is: Which economies belong to the "our" of "our economic future"? Where do developing countries fit in?

The Internet represents basic infrastructure. It is as indispensable a prerequisite to economic development as are roads, electric power, housing, education, and health. The Internet provides a platform for firms in the developing world to leapfrog from the traditional to the most advanced technologies, allowing them to compete successfully with the industrial economies in producing high-value-added goods and services. It can do this by lowering costs of transportation and communication, making previously inaccessible markets of the industrial world accessible to them. It may even reverse the chronic worsening of terms of trade for the developing economies.

www.sina.com.cn

CAN'T WAIT FOR THAT TECH JOB.

As attractive as these prospects may seem, they remain for many countries in the developing world only tantalizing potential and for some no more than fantasies. The reality they face is an extraordinary Internet gap between themselves and the rest of the world. This gap is shown in the accompanying table.

Narrowing the Internet access gap may be exceedingly difficult for many of the developing economies. It requires considerable capital outlay and the availability of highly skilled labor, both typically in short supply. In 1966, the average cost of Internet access in Africa was over $60 per month, more than most Africans' total monthly income. That is why it may seem more reasonable for developing countries to stay focused on the lesser skill-demanding, labor-intensive technologies. But such a short-sighted view will only keep the Internet gap shown in the table wide open. A new version of the vicious circle of poverty results: the developing country can't access the Internet because it is poor, and it is poor because it cannot access the Internet.

Still, prospects may not be as bleak as they appear to be. After all, the costs of accessing the Internet continue to fall—thanks to incredible and continuing technological changes in the computer industry—and these costs may soon make access affordable for many in the developing countries. Note that the Internet access shown in the table for the developing countries, while considerably less than access for the developed countries, is still not zero. In Kenya, telecommunication microwave towers are beginning to dot the landscape. Some access is even filtering down to the education process, where it must take root: A senior school in Kampala, Uganda, has a virtual exchange program, via the Internet, with a comparable high school in Jackson Hole, Wyoming. All roads have beginnings.

continued on next page

INTERNET HOSTS PER 10,000 POPULATION AND PERSONAL COMPUTERS PER 1,000 POPULATION FOR SELECTED COUNTRIES

	INTERNET HOSTS	PERSONAL COMPUTERS
ALGERIA	0.0	4.2
ARGENTINA	27.8	44.3
BOLIVIA	0.5	7.5
BRAZIL	18.5	30.1
EGYPT	0.3	9.1
INDIA	0.2	2.7
INDONESIA	0.7	8.2
KENYA	0.2	2.5
MOROCCO	0.3	2.5
NICARAGUA	2.2	7.8
PAKISTAN	0.2	3.9
PERU	3.1	18.1
ZIMBABWE	0.9	3.0
UNITED STATES	1,122.6	458.6
CANADA	365.7	330.0
ISRAEL	160.4	217.2
FRANCE	82.6	207.8

Source: The World Bank Group, 2000. "Internet hosts" refers to the number of computers with active Internet protocol (IP) addresses connected to the Internet.

Where do all these skilled people come from? Without a modern educational system, the answer is nowhere. Too few colleges in Chad graduate engineers, accountants, and doctors. Its literacy rate is critically low. Peasants farming in traditional ways rely upon experience, not education.

To educate people involves not only the monumental task of acquiring compliance—a population willing to send its children to school—but the funds needed to build the schools and to staff them. Where do these funds come from?

As you can see, the automobile plant would quickly rust unless it were accompanied by an expansive set of direct and indirect investments. That's all but impossible. Chadians have neither the material nor the human resources to undertake such a tremendous development departure. Chad's poverty trap seems rather formidable, doesn't it?

PURSUING STRATEGIES OF DEVELOPMENT

If you were asked to map out a grand strategy for economic development in Chad, just where would you begin? Economists have struggled with this vexing challenge and have come up with essentially two competing strategies. Both focus on the task of breaking the vicious circle of underdevelopment that traps the LDCs into national poverty.

The vicious circle of underdevelopment refers to LDCs that are poor because of the underdeveloped state of their economies, a state of underdevelopment that persists because they are poor. It's both logical and frustrating. The only way to cut into that self-sustaining trap is by massive doses of infrastructure and accompanying investments. But how? Is there a particular order or sequence of investing that works? Who does what investing? What role does government play? Should the private sector do it alone?

The Big Push

One idea that has found a receptive audience among development economists is the **big-push** strategy. It argues that because each potential investment's success depends upon there being a market for its output, none of the potential projects ever get realized because none have ready markets.

How do you create ready markets for, say, 1,000 potential investment projects when none exist? By investing in the 1,000 projects *all at once*. That's the idea behind the big push.

For example, a new rubber tire plant would have no chance of succeeding unless it had an automobile plant to serve. Investing in both tire and automobile plants provides the ready market for the tire plant. Investing in road construction provides the beginnings of a market for automobiles and trucks. After all, the tire plant needs trucks to move its raw materials in and its tires out to market—impossible without a road system, possible with one. The road construction project itself needs trucks to move its equipment and materials. That, too, becomes a market for the auto plant.

Investments in steel and concrete production now become feasible because each can see a new, ready market. Steel is the primary raw material in automobile production. It is also needed in the construction of the physical plants. Concrete's major market emerges with road construction. Both steel and concrete works, of course, need trucks and automobiles. The automobile market expands.

You can see the connections to investments in the mining industries, can't you? Iron ore, if available, is used in the production of steel. If ore is produced, it finds a ready market in steel, which in turn becomes a market for automobiles and trucks. Of course, none of this could happen without the infrastructure investment in roads.

HOW BIG MUST A BIG PUSH BE? The bigger the total all-at-once investment commitment, the easier it is to generate ready, attractive markets for each project. And that's the trick. But it's just the first phase. Once the big push is introduced, creating ready markets for the interlocking projects, the growing markets in the economy make many other investment projects attractive.

In other words, the big-push strategy triggers a dynamic swelling of investments in the economy that serves to break through the vicious circle of underdevelopment. There is a critical minimum level required for a big push to set the strategy in motion. The initial projects must be carefully chosen to take advantage of the economy's human and material resources and synchronized to form interlocking markets. And each of the selected projects must be large enough to absorb the other outputs.

Is there an upper bound to a big push? Is bigger always better? The problem with grandiose big-push schemes is not only their cost, but the inevitability of confronting bottlenecks that can stall an otherwise well-planned strategy. Among the first of the serious bottlenecks confronted is the shortage of technical expertise and skilled production-line workers. There are always many in the economy eager

Big push
The development strategy that relies on an integrated network of government-sponsored and -financed investments introduced into the economy all at once.

to work, but almost as many lacking the simplest of skills required to operate modern technology.

Breakdowns in production lines are common to all economies, but if the skills and materials needed to maintain the lines are too few and spread too thinly across too many big-push projects, the big push becomes distorting and itself distorted. Like a picture puzzle, the pieces must be formed to fit and put together to make the fit; otherwise, the picture is lost.

It sometimes pays to think in more modest and reasonable terms rather than pursue a big-push strategy, and to curb an ambitious development appetite to guarantee proper digestion.

WHO DOES THE PUSHING?   Big-push economists argue that such an interlocking, balanced set of infrastructure and development investments can be initiated, financed, and managed only by government. Why government? Because such a scheme requires long-term planning, and its rewards are forthcoming only in the long run. Who else but government has a time horizon big enough to make such investments and wait upon their results?

Entrepreneurs in the private sector cannot be expected to invest long term in an economy with limited investment promise. After all, it is unreasonable to expect them to think that by the time their output is ready for market, there will be a market. What assurances do they have? How are they supposed to know that others are thinking the same thoughts? And if they wait upon others to start, nothing starts.

But once the government-sponsored big push gets underway, the private sector is indeed expected to participate. Entrepreneurs do so not because they want to develop the economy, but because they now discover a stream of new, profitable opportunities that the big-push strategy has created.

WHO FINANCES THE BIG PUSH?   Big-push strategies, depending on their aggressiveness, require enormous national commitments that can sometimes tax an economy beyond its capabilities. Government funds the push because no one else can.

How? Primarily through taxes. But levying even more taxes on an already impoverished people not only is painful but can be destabilizing. Because government's ability to tax incomes is restricted by its lack of effective tax collecting at the source, LDC governments typically rely on sales taxes on consumer goods and on customs duties. The results tend to be regressive. Egypt's attempt in the 1970s to cut government subsidies on food led to riots in Cairo that almost brought the government down.

Less painful to LDCs in the short run, but perhaps more costly in the long run, is government's attempt to finance the big push by external borrowing from foreign private and government lending agencies. Ultimately, LDCs pay for the development they undertake.

The Unbalanced Development Strategy

The competing strategy to the big push relies essentially upon entrepreneurs themselves doing the major part of investing and funding development once projects become potentially profitable.

How do investments, unprofitable before the strategy, suddenly become profitable? Like the big-push strategy, the profitability of private investment projects depends upon the initial undertaking of infrastructure projects. In this respect, the unbalanced development strategy still counts on government initiative. But unlike

CHECK YOUR UNDERSTANDING

Why is government the logical choice to execute the big push?

the big push, these initial government undertakings are tailored in size and scope. How does it work?

The strategy is based on the idea that every investment, however small, has its own set of **forward and backward linkages** into the economy. Once undertaken, the investment creates new demands and new supplies in the economy. That's the trick. Production projects emerge to satisfy these new demands, and their outputs make other previously unfeasible projects feasible. These new projects, now undertaken, create a succeeding round of entirely new demands and new outputs. And so on.

LINKAGES IN SRI LANKA Imagine the Sri Lankan government thinking about a strategy to get its development process started. Suppose Sri Lanka, a world supplier of raw tea, does not have its own tea processing plants. Its tea is shipped in bulk to the industrial economies and there gets treated.

But no longer. The Sri Lankan government decides that tea is the trigger industry in its development process. It invests in a large, modern processing plant that prepares the raw tea for the consumer market. While the plant goes into construction, a number of Sri Lankans take note.

It becomes quite clear that when the government-owned tea processing plant gets underway, it will need packaging material. A sharp Sri Lankan entrepreneur seizes the opportunity. He can now get into the container business with a ready market. Government doesn't have to worry about packaging. It created the backward linkage.

But the container factory can produce more packaging than the government-owned processing plant can absorb. Once in operation, it can diversify its packaging product to satisfy almost every packaging demand. In other words, the development process, triggered by the processing plant, created an imbalance between packaging supply capacity and the government's demand for packaging.

Such an imbalanced development process is preferred by some economists to the balanced development strategy of the big push. Why? Because not only is there a new supply source where one hadn't existed before, but the imbalance will spark new forward and backward linkages throughout the economy. How does it work?

Since it is no longer necessary for Sri Lankan businesses to import expensive packaging into the economy—domestic supply, employing Sri Lankan labor, is typically less expensive and more accessible—the availability of this domestic supply can make the difference between a profit and a loss to businesses for which packaging is a major input.

Other businesses, now confident about getting access to this new supply, expand their operations. But their expansions create new imbalances between their new supplies and the demands for their goods.

The mutually reinforcing imbalances caused by new supplies creating new demands— forward linkages—and these new demands creating new and different supplies—backward linkages—play off against each other, forming a dynamic chain reaction of economic development.

The attraction of such a development strategy is that it places minimal stress on government. It requires neither a grandiose design nor a grandiose taxing scheme. Again like a picture puzzle, the individual linkage pieces make up the development picture, but the actual picture isn't known beforehand.

WHO DOES THE INVESTING? The key to success in the unbalanced strategy is the role played by entrepreneurs. The idea is that in all societies, in whatever stage of economic development, there are always creative, energetic people who,

Forward linkages
Investments in one industry that create opportunities for profitable investments in other industries, using the goods produced in the first as inputs.

Backward linkages
Investments in one industry that create demands for inputs, inducing investment in other industries to produce those inputs.

APPLIED PERSPECTIVE

THE ROAD TO BETTER FARMING

On present trends, Africa's population will double in the next 20 years, pushing its people on to ever more marginal land. Over-grazed pastures will turn to desert. Topsoil on newly cultivated hillsides will be washed away. Exhausted soil will support fewer crops. And ever more Africans will go hungry.

Or so environmental doomsters claim. Not so, argues a new study by researchers from Britain's Overseas Development Institute and the University of Nairobi. Using colonial records, satellite images, and field research, they have looked at farming in the Machakos district of Kenya, a region of low rainfall and occasional drought, over the period 1930–90. Sixty years ago most farmers kept cattle—for milk, meat, and as a bride price—and grew some grain and pulses. The region faced periodic food shortages: during the 1940s and 1950s it needed regular famine relief. Soil erosion had deeply scarred the landscape.

By 1990 the population had swelled fivefold, to 1.4 million. Result: disaster? No. Total output had risen fifteenfold: more land was under cultivation (by 1979 there was no unclaimed land left) and yields per square kilometer were up tenfold. The "badlands" of the past had been transformed into a landscape of neatly terraced hills and fenced fields.

How did it happen? Most important, Machakos became integrated fairly early—during the 1960s—into the market economy. Farmers diversified from subsistence crops into ones they could trade: coffee, bananas, peas, pawpaws. Under British rule the region's Kamba people had not been allowed to grow coffee in competition with white farmers, or to sell grains outside the area without a permit. After independence in 1963, land reform and the lifting of some state controls encouraged smallholders to invest in higher-value crops—and to conserve soil and water so the land could support them.

Capital for investment came from new opportunities to earn money outside farming. By 1990 most farm families in Machakos had at least one son or daughter earning money from nonfarm work, such as weaving baskets or making carvings for tourists. This helped families buy better tools, fertilizer, drought-resistant strains of maize, and seed for second crops to plant among first ones to take advantage of Kenya's second seasonal rains.

Decent road links to Nairobi, dating from the 1950s, made a huge difference. It became profitable to grow fruit and vegetables as Asian traders began to travel to Machakos to buy crops—and later other goods—for city markets.

Better communications also helped government advisers spread news about new farming methods. Yet expert advice was not the key. Productivity grew fastest between 1960 and 1980, when the government, busy with more promising farming areas, was making no special effort for Machakos. Yet farmers there invested hard in better land and crops: advised or not, they had the incentives, and the means, to gain from doing it.

WHERE THERE WAS ONCE LITTLE, THERE IS NOW PLENTY. PEOPLE EAT, BUT PEOPLE ALSO PRODUCE.

MORE ON THE NET

The Bureau of African Affairs (http://www.state.gov/www/regions/africa/index.html), part of the State Department, provides data and information about Africa. Africa Online (http://www.africaonline.com/) also offers news, information, and resources about Africa.

presented with a chance at enterprise, will take it. Personal commitment is stronger and more reliable than government commitment and reliability.

WHO DOES THE FUNDING? While government triggers the process by funding and putting into place some of the economy's key infrastructure investments, the primary source of development finance is the private sector. Entrepreneurs themselves are expected either to invest their own savings in their own businesses or to find the funding in the banking system.

Although for most LDCs the banking system is limited or nonexistent, it is precisely the demands for private business loans that create the *rationale* for commercial banking. If domestic banks aren't available, foreign banks, lured by the new prospects, will come in. It's just a matter of time before Sri Lankan entrepreneurs get into the banking business.

FOREIGN DIRECT INVESTMENT

You might think that LDC governments would jump at the chance of having foreign direct investment join in their development programs. After all, foreign direct investment is about the only way an LDC economy can get into development at zero opportunity cost. Exhibit 6 illustrates its appeal.

Without foreign direct investment, the LDC economy must sacrifice $120 - 90 = 30$ consumption goods to expand capital goods from 10 to 15. There is no other way. But suppose it now decides to invite foreign investment. If it attracts 5 units of foreign capital goods, it can stay at 120 consumption and still get 15 capital goods into its development process. Point C in Exhibit 6 is impossible without foreign investment.

Foreign direct investment typically brings in not only new capital goods but new expertise. As well, it provides the LDCs with markets in the industrial economies that otherwise would be unavailable.

As a contributor to LDC development, foreign investment just seems too good to be true. Yet almost universally, LDC governments have had serious reservations about designing their development programs with a foreign direct investment imprint. Why their reluctance?

Images from the Colonial Past

The arguments for and against foreign investments are based as much upon emotion as upon economic logic. Many development economists argue that it was the uninvited foreign direct investment of the colonial

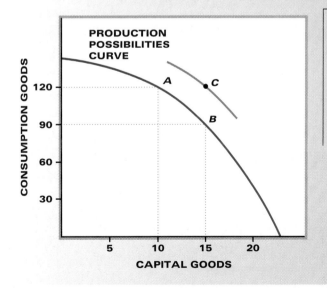

PRODUCTION POSSIBILITIES CURVE WITH FOREIGN INVESTMENT

Without foreign investment, the production possibilities for the LDC economy are restricted to combinations of capital goods and consumption goods along the *AB* curve. Position *C* is an impossible choice. With the added capital resources provided by foreign investments, *C* is attainable.

EXHIBIT|6

19th century that left LDC economies underdeveloped in the first place. The LDCs' inability to pursue domestic industry, they insist, was not a result of failing to provide the human and material resources required, but rather the result of coercive interference by colonial regimes in the LDCs.

By colonial design, LDC economies became economic caricatures, restructured into raw material supply bases for the West. Their entrepreneurs had no freedom to operate, except perhaps in small-scale retail trade or in traditional artisan production. The promising industries were reserved for the colonial power. Managerial skills remained underdeveloped because those employment opportunities, too, were available only to the colonial power.

To some economists, then, it would be the height of irony if after finally gaining independence—in some cases at great human sacrifice—the LDCs were to turn right around and invite back into their economies the colonial powers, even if the economic gains from foreign investments were undeniable.

Yet the contribution that foreign direct investment can make to an LDC development process is just too important to overlook, even for the most reluctant LDCs. Although worried about the consequences of inviting in foreign investment, the LDC governments worry as well about the consequences of not inviting in foreign investment!

What do they do? Most end up with a "yes, but" policy. Yes, foreign investment is wanted, but not without serving LDC designs. Typically, foreign investment in the LDCs is well harnessed. It is subject to more-stringent regulation than is domestic investment. Foreign investors are sometimes excluded from particular fields of activity. In some economies, they are obliged to hire nationals in managerial positions or are required to meet employment quotas. In most cases foreign investors must also accept profit-repatriation ceilings. That is, foreign investment is carefully monitored to suit the development objectives of the host economy.

On the other hand, foreign direct investment in some LDCs, typically the more successful ones, is as welcome as Santa Claus at Christmas. Some LDCs provide tax holidays—as long as five years free of all domestic taxes—and some have investment subsidies to encourage foreign investment. Many offer duty-free imports of capital goods as added inducements.

Visit the U.S. Agency for International Development (http://www.usaid.gov/), part of the Department of State (http://www.state.gov/).

FOREIGN ECONOMIC AID

While foreign direct investment is essentially a private sector activity, foreign economic aid—loans and grants—is government to government. Our own aid program is housed in the Department of State and is administered by the Agency for International Development (USAID).

Exhibit 7 records the growth of our economic aid program. Aid is offered in the form of loans and grants, and the distinction is important. Loans are repayable with interest, although interest charges have typically been below market rates. In some cases, the loans

U.S. FOREIGN ECONOMIC AID: 1970–99 ($ MILLIONS)

	TOTAL	LOANS	GRANTS
1970	$ 3,676	$1,389	$ 2,288
1980	7,573	1,993	5,580
1990	10,834	756	10,078
1997	9,170	218	8,952

Source: *Statistical Abstract of the United States, 1999* (Washington, D.C.: U.S. Department of Commerce, 1999), p. 800.

GLOBAL PERSPECTIVE

FOOD FOR PEACE

There's a lot wrong with foreign aid, and critics of foreign aid are not at all shy about telling you. Much of our foreign aid goes to governments, not to people, and the recipient governments are about as corrupt as governments can be. Many are one-party governments (no real choice) or military juntas. In too many cases, the spoils of our foreign aid end up in their Swiss bank accounts. There is little, if any, accountability given or, perhaps more distressing, even demanded. In a real sense, the foreign aid we offer results in a twisted international welfare scheme: Dollars are taken from average income-earning Americans and given to not-so-average wealthy foreigners.

A National Bureau of Economic Research (NBER) paper by Professors Alberto Alesina and Beatrice Weder found that countries receiving more aid tend to have higher levels of corruption. They found no evidence that foreign aid reduces corruption levels in recipient countries. That's not what foreign aid was supposed to do.

Adding insult to injury, many of these non-democratic governments are anything but the United States' allies in international diplomacy. Their voting records at the United Nations are exemplary anti-United States.

Proponents of foreign aid emphasize the positive, and there are strong positives. Among the aid programs that work and have made a difference in the lives of destitute people is the food aid program PL 480 Food for Peace.

Food for Peace was formalized in the Agricultural Trade Development and Assistance Act of 1954. Modified many times, it establishes the policy of using the United States' abundant agricultural resources and food processing capabilities to enhance food security in the developing world through the provision of culturally acceptable nutritious food. More than 800 million people today are chronically undernourished, and more than 180 million children are significantly underweight. The strategic goal of Food for Peace is to reduce those numbers. The program gives food resources to help those in need and in crisis and seeks to eliminate the food insecurity that fuels political instability and environmental degradation.

Food for Peace's FY2000 budget was $787 million. It was used to respond to both protracted emergency food aid requirements as well as the sudden emergencies caused by natural disasters and political and economic instability. Although beneficiaries include victims of natural disasters, such as droughts, typhoons, and cyclones, the majority of programs addressed complex humanitarian situations frequently caused or complicated by civil strife. Emergency food aid targets refugees or internally displaced people, particularly malnourished or unaccompanied children, women, orphans, and the elderly.

In Kenya, for example, emergency food aid reached drought-affected groups, including 452,016 school children and 443,702 food-insecure families. The provision of food to school children maintained attendance of children at the pre-primary and primary school level in the drought-affected areas.

In Angola, emergency food aid programs responded to changing situations as the country attempted to draw away from years of war but still struggled with socioeconomic problems and instability. Food-for-work activities rehabilitated rural infrastructure and revitalized agricultural production and farming systems. By 1998, 56,393 internally displaced persons were resettled.

Activities in Peru illustrate how well-designed food aid programs can contribute to improving food security of targeted groups and thus stabilize vulnerable populations during crisis periods. In the 1980s, during the height of the civil unrest and resulting economic depression in Peru, direct food distribution activities were the primary method of reaching those without food. As civil disturbances declined and economic stability has returned, aid has gradually shifted to poverty reduction and income-generating efforts.

have been forgiven. Grants, on the other hand, are outright gifts. As you can see, for 1997 almost all of the U.S. aid flow to the LDCs was in the form of grants.

How is the aid used? It depends on the LDC's priorities at the time. In the best of times, it is used for infrastructure development. In the worst of times, but for good reason, it is used to supplement the LDC's food stocks. In either case, it tends to nudge the LDC off its low-level production possibilities curve in the same way that foreign direct investment does.

How generous have we been? It depends on the measuring rod. In terms of absolute dollars, we have been, for most years, the largest aid contributor to the LDCs. But we are also the richest contributor. Measured in terms of an aid-to-GDP ratio or an aid-to-population ratio, we rank below such donors as Canada, Norway, Sweden, Japan, the Netherlands, and France.

CHAPTER REVIEW

1. Economists have been concerned with the problem of persistent national poverty in the LDCs since the 1950s. Per capita income for most of the LDCs is not only low—under $500—but, in some cases, falling even further. Low-level economic growth combines with high-level rates of population growth to threaten already meager standards of living.

2. Many of the LDCs are caught in the vicious circle of poverty: They are poor because they don't invest in capital goods production, and the reason they don't is that they are poor. The consequences are high infant mortality rates, low life expectancy, a small percentage of people using safe water, and a small percentage of school-aged children in school. These consequences end up causing further poverty. Contributing to this poverty is the lack of political stability and a development infrastructure, and a reluctance to accept change.

3. Economic dualism refers to the condition in which a minority of the LDC population is engaged in modern technology production, earning incomes similar to those earned in industrial economies, while the rest of the population is engaged in low-level technology production earning substantially less, so that income disparity between these dual sectors of the economy is severe.

4. There are many competing development strategies for the LDCs. The big-push strategy emphasizes investment in many projects all at once to create both productive capacity and markets for the production. Government plays a dominant role as coordinator, planner, and financier of the strategy.

5. An alternative approach to development is the unbalanced strategy, which relies less heavily on government. Here, initial private sector development in key areas of the economy creates backward and forward linkages to new projects that had been unthinkable before these key investments. These linkages provide opportunities and incentives for private firms to invest, creating even more opportunities and incentives.

6. Foreign direct investment allows an LDC to create capital goods production without having to sacrifice consumption goods production. Foreign economic aid can do the same. The United States gives more economic aid, in the form of loans and grants, than any other industrial country, although it is not a relatively large donor if the aid is measured as a percentage of GDP.

KEY TERMS

Less-developed countries (LDCs)   Infrastructure   Forward linkages
Human capital   Big push   Backward linkages
Economic dualism

QUESTIONS

1. The historical data of falling birth rates and falling death rates in LDCs helps explain the difficulty they face in raising per capita incomes. Explain.

2. What is meant by the LDC poverty trap?

3. What is economic dualism, and why does it create a formidable obstacle to national economic development for LDCs?

4. Why is political stability vital to the economic development process?

5. What is economic traditionalism? Compare its characteristics to the modern sector of an economy.

6. Describe the components of an economy's infrastructure. What aspects are lacking in LDCs?

7. Describe the economic logic associated with the big-push development strategy. What are its pitfalls?

8. Describe the economic logic associated with the unbalanced development strategy. What are its pitfalls?

9. Why are some LDC governments reluctant to invite in foreign direct investment? What are the pros and cons of such investment?

10. Show the effect of foreign direct investment on an economy's production possibilities curve.

11. Professor Miguel Ramirez asks his students at Trinity College to respond to the following problem: Economists, notably those in the World Bank and the IMF, argue that free trade and open markets are important factors contributing to LDC economic growth. On the other hand, American policy makers in the early 19th century—when the United States was beginning to industrialize—pursued a highly protective strategy vis-à-vis England, the premier industrial power of the world. Should LDCs follow the advice of World Bank and IMF economists or take their cue from U.S. economic history?

Make your case using economic analyses offered in the chapters on international trade; exchange rates, balance of payments, and international debt; and the economic problems of less-developed economies.

WHAT'S WRONG WITH THIS GRAPH?

ECONOMIC DUALISM

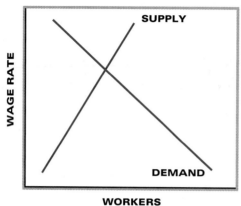

WAGE RATE

SUPPLY

DEMAND

WORKERS

TRADITIONAL SECTOR

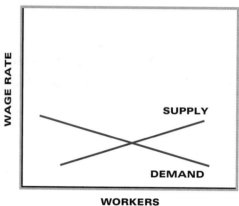

WAGE RATE

SUPPLY

DEMAND

WORKERS

MODERN SECTOR

ECONOMIC CONSULTANTS

ECONOMIC RESEARCH AND ANALYSIS BY STUDENTS FOR PROFESSIONALS

South African businesspeople and government officials have formed an organization, Economic Development in South Africa (EDSA), to map a strategy for economic development in post-apartheid South Africa. EDSA understands the need for direct foreign investment and foreign aid, but individuals within EDSA are worried that such strategies may make South Africa overdependent on foreign powers. EDSA also understands the need for controlled growth and investment, but the group is unsure about the best strategy to pursue to ensure stable growth.

EDSA has hired Economic Consultants to present to its members the pros and cons of different economic development strategies. Prepare a report for EDSA that addresses the following issues:

1. What basic strategies should South Africa pursue for economic development, particularly in terms of foreign investment?

2. What problems arise with different economic development strategies? How can South Africa avoid uncontrolled growth and investment?

3. What groups and organizations specialize in direct foreign investment and foreign aid?

You may find the following resources helpful as you prepare this report for EDSA:

- **PRAXIS: Resources for Social and Economic Development** (http://caster.ssw.upenn.edu/~restes/praxis.html)—PRAXIS provides a library of links to resources on international and comparative social development.
- **World Bank** (http://www.worldbank.org/)—The World Bank provides news, publications, and country and regional economic reports.
- **World Bank Institute** (http://www.worldbank.org/wbi/home.html)—The World Bank Institute promotes awareness of development strategies through publications and educational initiatives.
- *Finance and Development* (http://www.imf.org/fandd/)—*Finance and Development* is a joint quarterly publication of the International Monetary Fund and the World Bank.

PRACTICE TEST

1. The principal factors contributing to low per capita incomes in LCDs are
   a. high population growth and low literacy rates.
   b. traditional development and lack of infrastructure.
   c. low economic growth rates and high population growth rates.
   d. lack of foreign investment and low levels of economic aid.
   e. political instability and lack of social cohesion.

2. The vicious circle of poverty associated with LCDs refers to
   a. their ability to borrow but inability to pay their debts.
   b. their traditional sector becoming modern only to revert back to traditionalism.
   c. their misuse of capital goods over and over again.
   d. their being poor because they choose population growth over economic growth.
   e. their being poor because they cannot devote resources to capital goods production because they are poor.

3. LCDs typically end up investing relatively little in human capital because
   a. human capital is typically less productive than LCD investments in factory and equipment.
   b. human capital has a considerably longer time horizon than other types of investment.
   c. human capital has a considerably shorter time horizon than other types of investment.
   d. the investment is wasted when LCD people migrate out of the country.
   e. human capital is generally restricted to the modern sector, which does not need the capital as much as the traditional sector.

4. Economic dualism refers to
   a. the lack of integration between an LCD's traditional and modern sectors.
   b. the enormous gap between an LCD's rich and poor.
   c. the disparity between investments in consumption goods and capital goods production.
   d. the disparity between consumption and investment.
   e. the dominance of government over private citizens in an LCD's economy.

5. Among the basic prerequisites for development that are absent in LCDs are
   a. foreign investment and entrepreneurs.
   b. honest government and development strategies.
   c. human capital and market incentives.
   d. political stability and infrastructure.
   e. productive resources and technically skilled labor.

6. The big-push strategy proposes all-at-one-time multiple investments because
   a. they provide markets for each other.
   b. they create forward, rather than backward, linkages.
   c. they involve a smaller initial investment than do alternative strategies.
   d. unsuccessful projects would be canceled by successful ones.
   e. foreign governments are more inclined to finance this strategy.

7. The unbalanced development strategy
   a. relies on government to finance each stage of the strategy.
   b. creates forward, but not backward, linkages, which trigger top-down development.
   c. creates backward, but not forward, linkages, which trigger bottom-up development.
   d. creates forward and backward linkages, which play off each other to create the development.
   e. involves an imbalance between the roles played by LCD and foreign entrepreneurs.

8. Forward linkages are investments in industries that create
   a. investment opportunities for other industries using the goods produced in the first as inputs.
   b. demands for inputs, inducing investments in other industries to produce those inputs.
   c. future demands for investments in the same industries.
   d. future supplies of investment in the same industries.
   e. top-down development.

9. Some LCDs are reluctant to accept foreign investment because
   a. the LCDs fear a repeat of their colonial past.
   b. foreign firms repatriate most of the profit they earn in the LCD to the home country.
   c. foreign firms use LCD managers but pay them minimal salaries.
   d. foreign firms refuse to accept LCD government regulation.
   e. foreign firms insist on infrastructure development rather than investing in plant and equipment.

10. Economic aid from the United States to the LCDs
    a. is mainly given as loans, not grants.
    b. represents a higher percentage of its GDP compared to other donor countries.
    c. is greater than the economic aid given annually by other donor countries.
    d. is mainly for military purchases of U.S. weaponry by LCDs.
    e. is mainly allocated to sub-Saharan Africa.

PHOTO CREDITS

PRACTICE TESTS
ANSWER KEY

CHAPTER 1

1. e
2. d
3. e
4. b
5. c
6. a
7. acd
8. cd
9. da
10. ab

CHAPTER 2

1. a
2. c
3. a
4. c
5. b
6. b
7. b
8. bce
9. e

CHAPTER 3

1. b
2. ada
3. ada
4. a
5. a
6. b
7. bed
8. ede
9. ede
10. e

CHAPTER 4

1. e
2. b
3. aca
4. c
5. a
6. b
7. bb
8. bac
9. acb
10. b

CHAPTER 5

1. b
2. c
3. e
4. a
5. e
6. c
7. b

CHAPTER 6

1. c
2. c
3. ec
4. ec
5. a
6. a
7. acb
8. cb
9. bb
10. c

CHAPTER 7

1. a
2. ac
3. a
4. e
5. c
6. c
7. cc
8. cac
9. cc
10. c

CHAPTER 8

1. e
2. b
3. c
4. d
5. d
6. e
7. eaa
8. eaab
9. aba
10. a

CHAPTER 9

1. a
2. e
3. b
4. c
5. c
6. a
7. aac
8. acce
9. cce
10. e

CHAPTER 10

1. a
2. ac
3. cab
4. b
5. c
6. d
7. db
8. bb
9. bb
10. a

CHAPTER 11

1. c
2. b
3. c
4. cc
5. b
6. c
7. cc
8. cc
9. c

CHAPTER 12

1. b
2. a
3. d
4. c
5. a
6. c
7. cab
8. ab
9. ac
10. c

CHAPTER 13

1. a
2. dd
3. dd
4. b
5. a
6. cb
7. b

CHAPTER 14

1. c
2. cab
3. b
4. c
5. b
6. aad
7. aad
8. d

CHAPTER 15

1. d
2. dd
3. dc
4. cd
5. c
6. e
7. edaa
8. daa
9. a

PRACTICE TESTS

CHAPTER 16

1. a
2. d
3. d
4. a
5. c
6. b
7. d
8. e

CHAPTER 17

1. c
2. b
3. a
4. d
5. c
6. a
7. c
8. c

CHAPTER 18

1. c
2. d
3. c
4. a
5. a
6. b
7. b
8. b
9. c
10. d

CHAPTER 19

1. d
2. e
3. d
4. d
5. e
6. c
7. c
8. a
9. b
10. a

CHAPTER 20

1. b
2. b
3. e
4. d
5. b
6. c
7. c
8. a
9. a
10. a

CHAPTER 21

1. c
2. e
3. b
4. a
5. d
6. a
7. d
8. a
9. a
10. c

GLOSSARY

A

Absolute advantage A country's ability to produce a good using fewer resources than the country it trades with. (Chapters 2 and 19)

Antitrust policy Laws that foster market competition by prohibiting monopolies and oligopolies from exercising excessive market power. (Chapter 13)

Appreciation A rise in the price of a nation's currency relative to foreign currencies. (Chapter 20)

Arbitrage The practice of buying a foreign currency in one market at a low price and selling it in another at a higher price. (Chapter 20)

Average fixed cost (AFC) Total fixed cost divided by the quantity of goods produced. *AFC* steadily declines as more of a good is produced. (Chapter 8)

Average revenue (AR) Total revenue divided by the quantity of goods or services sold. (Chapter 9)

Average total cost (ATC) Total cost divided by the quantity of goods produced. ATC declines, reaches a minimum, then increases as more of a good is produced. (Chapter 8)

Average variable cost (AVC) Total variable cost divided by the quantity of goods produced. Hdeclines, reaches a minimum, then increases as more of a good is produced. (Chapter 8)

B

Backward linkages Investments in one industry that create demands for inputs, inducing investment in other industries to produce those inputs. (Chapter 21)

Balance of payments An itemized account of a nation's foreign economic transactions. (Chapter 20)

Balance of trade The difference between the value of a nation's merchandise exports and its merchandise imports. (Chapter 20)

Balance on capital account A category that itemizes changes in the foreign asset holdings of a nation and that nation's asset holdings abroad. (Chapter 20)

Balance on current account A category that itemizes a nation's imports and exports of goods and services, income receipts and payments on investment, and unilateral transfers. (Chapter 20)

Balanced oligopoly An oligopoly in which the sales of the leading firms are distributed fairly evenly among them. (Chapter 12)

Big push The development strategy that relies on an integrated network of government-sponsored and -financed investments introduced into the economy all at once. (Chapter 21)

Brand loyalty The willingness of consumers to continue buying a good at a price higher than the price of its close substitutes. (Chapter 10)

Brand multiplication Variations on essentially one good that a firm produces in order to increase its market share. (Chapter 12)

C

Capital Manufactured goods used to make and market other goods and services. (Chapter 2)

Capital equipment The machinery a firm uses in production. (Chapter 17)

Cartel A group of firms that collude to limit competition in a market by negotiating and accepting agreed-upon price and market shares. (Chapter 12)

Cash assistance Government assistance in the form of cash. (Chapter 18)

Ceteris paribus The Latin phrase meaning "everything else being equal." (Chapter 1)

Change in demand A change in quantity demanded of a good that is caused by factors other than a change in the price of that good. (Chapter 3)

Change in quantity demanded A change in the quantity demanded of a good that is caused solely by a change in the price of that good. (Chapter 3)

Change in supply A change in quantity supplied of a good that is caused by factors other than a change in the price of that good. (Chapter 3)

Circular flow model A model of how the economy's resources, money, goods, and services flow between households and firms through resource and product markets. (Chapter 1)

Closed shop An arrangement in which a firm may hire only union labor. (Chapter 16)

Collective bargaining Negotiation between a labor union and a firm employing unionized labor, to create a contract concerning wage rates, hours worked, and working conditions. (Chapter 16)

Collusion The practice of firms to negotiate price and market share decisions that limit competition in a market. (Chapter 12)

Comparative advantage A country's ability to produce a good at a lower opportunity cost than the country with which it trades. (Chapters 2 and 19)

Complementary goods Goods that are generally used together. When the price of one increases, the demand for the other decreases. (Chapter 3)

Concentration ratio A measure of market power. It is the ratio of total sales of the leading firms in an industry (usually four) to the industry's total sales. (Chapter 12)

Conglomerate merger A merger between firms in unrelated industries. (Chapter 12)

Constant returns to scale Costs per unit of production are the same for any level of production. Changes in plant size do not affect the firm's average total cost. (Chapter 8)

Consumer sovereignty The ability of consumers to exercise complete control over what goods and services the economy produces (or doesn't produce) by choosing what goods and services to buy (or not buy). (Chapter 1)

Consumer surplus The difference between the maximum amount a person would be willing to pay for a good or service and the amount the person actually pays. (Chapter 5)

Contestable market A market in which prices in highly concentrated industries are moderated by the potential threat of firms entering the market. (Chapter 13)

Corporate bond A corporate IOU. The corporation borrows capital for a specified period of time in exchange for this promise to repay the loan along with an agreed-upon rate of interest. (Chapter 7)

Corporate governance Corporate governance is concerned with the rules governing the structure of the corporation and the exercise of power and control of the corporation by shareholders, directors, and management. (Chapter 7)

Corporation A firm whose legal identity is separate from the people who own shares of its stock. The liability of each stockowner is limited only to what he or she has invested in the firm. (Chapter 7)

Countervailing power The exercise of market power by an economic bloc is ultimately counteracted by the market power of a competing bloc, so that no bloc exercises undue market power. (Chapter 13)

Craft union A union representing workers of a single occupation, regardless of the industry in which the workers are employed. (Chapter 16)

Creative destruction Effective competition that exists not among firms within highly concentrated industries but between the highly concentrated industries themselves. Such competition ensures competitive prices. (Chapter 13)

Cross elasticity of demand The ratio of a percentage change in quantity demanded of one good to a percentage change in the price of another good. (Chapter 4)

Customs union A set of countries that agree to free trade among themselves and a common trade policy with all other countries. (Chapter 19)

D

Debt service Interest payments on international debt as a percentage of a nation's merchandise exports. (Chapter 20)

Deficiency payment Government payment to farmers based on the difference between the target price set by government and the market price. (Chapter 6)

Demand curve A curve that depicts the relationship between price and quantity demanded. (Chapter 3)

Demand schedule A schedule showing the specific quantity of a good or service that people are willing and able to buy at different prices. (Chapter 3)

Depreciation A fall in the price of a nation's currency relative to foreign currencies. (Chapter 20)

Deregulation The process of converting a regulated firm into an unregulated firm. (Chapter 13)

Devaluation Government policy that lowers the nation's exchange rate; its currency instantly is worth less in the foreign exchange market. (Chapter 20)

Differential land rent Rent arising from differences in the cost of providing land. (Chapter 17)

Diseconomies of scale Increases in the firm's average total cost brought about by the disadvantages associated with bureaucracy and the inefficiencies that eventually emerge with increases in the firm's operations. (Chapter 8)

Dividend That part of a corporation's net income that is paid out to its stockholders. (Chapter 7)

Downsizing Implementing a firm's decision to decrease its plant size to produce in the most efficient manner its current volume of output. (Chapter 8)

Dumping Exporting a good or service at a price below its cost of production. (Chapter 19)

E

Econometrics The use of statistics to quantify and test economic models. (Chapter 1)

Economic dualism The coexistence of two separate and distinct economies within an LDC; one modern, primarily urban, and export-driven, the other traditional, agricultural, and self-sustaining. (Chapter 21)

Economic efficiency The maximum possible production of goods and services generated by the fullest employment of the economy's resources. (Chapter 2)

Economic model An abstraction of an economic reality. It can be expressed pictorially, graphically, algebraically, or in words. (Chapter 1)

Economic profit A firm's total revenue minus its total explicit and implicit costs. (Chapter 11)

Economics The study of how people work together to transform resources into goods and services to satisfy their most pressing wants, and how they distribute these goods and services among themselves. (Chapter 1)

Economies of scale Decreases in the firm's average total cost brought about by increased specialization and efficiencies in production realized through increases in the scale of the firm's operations. (Chapter 8)

Efficiency wages A wage higher than the market's equilibrium rate; a firm will pay this wage in the expectation that the higher wage will reduce the firm's labor turnover and increase labor productivity. (Chapter 15)

Elasticity A term economists use to describe sensitivity. (Chapter 4)

Engel's law The observation that income elasticities of demand for food are less than 1.0. (Chapter 4)

Entrepreneur A person who alone assumes the risks and uncertainties of a business. (Chapter 2)

Equilibrium price The price that equates quantity demanded to quantity supplied. If any disturbance from that price occurs, excess demand or excess supply emerges to drive price back to equilibrium. (Chapter 3)

European Economic Community (EEC) A customs union consisting of France, Italy, Belgium, Holland, Luxembourg, Germany, Britain, Ireland, Denmark, Greece, Spain, Portugal, Iceland, Finland, Sweden, and Austria. (Chapter 19)

Excess demand The difference, at a particular price, between quantity demanded and quantity supplied, quantity demanded being the greater. (Chapter 3)

Excess supply The difference, at a particular price, between quantity supplied and quantity demanded, quantity supplied being the greater. (Chapter 3)

Exchange controls A system in which government, as the sole depository of foreign currencies, exercises complete control over how these currencies can be used. (Chapter 20)

Exchange rate The number of units of foreign currency that can be purchased with one unit of domestic currency. (Chapter 20)

Exports Goods and services produced by people in one country that are sold in other countries. (Chapter 19)

Externalities Unintended costs or benefits that are imposed on unsuspecting people and that result from economic activity initiated by others. Unintended costs are called negative externalities, and unintended benefits are called positive externalities. (Chapter 14)

F

Factor of production Any resource used in a production process. Resources are grouped into labor, land, capital, and entrepreneurship. (Chapter 2)

Firm An economic unit that produces goods and services in the expectation of selling them to households, other firms, or government. (Chapter 1)

Fixed cost Cost to the firm that does not vary with the quantity of goods produced. The cost is incurred even when the firm does not produce. (Chapter 8)

Fixed exchange rate A rate determined by government and then maintained through the process of buying and selling quantities of its own currency on the foreign exchange market. (Chapter 20)

Floating exchange rate An exchange rate determined strictly by the demands and supplies for a nation's currency. (Chapter 20)

Foreign exchange market A market in which currencies of different nations are bought and sold. (Chapter 20)

Foreign exchange reserves The stock of foreign currencies a government holds. (Chapter 20)

Forward linkages Investments in one industry that create opportunities for profitable investments in other industries, using the goods produced in the first as inputs. (Chapter 21)

Free rider Someone who consumes a good or service without paying for it. Typically, the good or service consumed is in the form of a positive externality. (Chapter 14)

Free trade area A set of countries that agree to free trade among themselves but are free to pursue independent trade policies with other countries. (Chapter 19)

Free trade International trade that is not encumbered by protectionist government policies such as tariffs and quotas. (Chapter 19)

Freedom to Farm Act of 1996 Legislation enacted by Congress that phases in, over a seven-year transitional period, the complete dismantling of the government's farm price support and crop restriction systems. (Chapter 6)

G

Game theory A theory of strategy ascribed to firms' behavior in oligopoly. The firms' behavior is mutually interdependent. (Chapter 12)

GATT (General Agreement on Tariffs and Trade) A trade agreement to negotiate reductions in tariffs and other trade barriers and to provide equal and nondiscriminating treatment among members of the agreement. Around 100 countries are members of GATT. (Chapter 19)

Gini coefficient A numerical measure of the degree of income inequality in an economy. It ranges from zero, depicting perfect equality, to one, depicting perfect inequality. (Chapter 18)

Government failure The failure of the government to buy the quantity of public goods that generates maximum efficiency. (Chapter 14)

H

Herfindahl-Hirschman index (HHI) A measure of industry concentration, calculated as the sum of the squares of the market shares held by each of the firms in the industry. (Chapter 12)

Horizontal merger A merger between firms producing the same good in the same industry. (Chapter 12)

Household An economic unit of one or more persons, living under one roof, that has a source of income and uses it in whatever way it deems fit. (Chapter 1)

Human capital The investment in workers' health and knowledge, acquired through education, training, and/or experience that enhances their productivity. (Chapters 2 and 21)

I

Import controls Tariffs and quotas used by government to limit a nation's imports. (Chapter 20)

Imports Goods and services bought by people in one country that are produced in other countries. (Chapter 19)

Income elastic A 1 percent change in income generates a greater than 1 percent change in quantity demanded. (Chapter 4)

Income elasticity The ratio of the percentage change in quantity demanded to the percentage change in income. (Chapter 4)

Income inelastic A 1 percent change in income generates a less than 1 percent change in quantity demanded. (Chapter 4)

Industrial union A union representing all workers in a single industry, regardless of each worker's skill or craft. (Chapter 16)

Industry A collection of firms producing the same good. (Chapter 10)

Inferior goods Goods for which demand decreases when people's incomes increase. (Chapter 4)

Infrastructure The basic institutions and public facilities upon which an economy's development depends. (Chapter 21)

In-kind assistance Government assistance in the form of direct goods and services, such as Medicaid or food stamps. (Chapter 18)

Innovation An idea that eventually takes the form of new, applied technology. (Chapter 2)

Interest rate The price of loanable funds, expressed as an annual percentage return on a dollar of loanable funds. (Chapter 17)

International debt The total amount of outstanding ious a nation is obligated to repay other nations and international organizations. (Chapter 20)

International Monetary Fund (IMF) An international organization formed to make loans of foreign currencies to countries facing balance of payments problems. (Chapter 20)

International specialization The use of a country's resources to produce specific goods and services, allowing other countries to focus on the production of other goods and services. (Chapter 19)

Interpersonal comparison of utility A comparison of the marginal utilities that different people derive from a good or a dollar. (Chapter 5)

Invisible hand Adam Smith's concept of the market, which, as if it were a hand, guides firms that seek only to satisfy their own self-interest to produce precisely those goods and services that consumers want. (Chapter 1)

J

Joint venture A business arrangement in which two or more firms undertake a specific economic activity together. (Chapter 12)

K

Kinked demand curve The demand curve facing a firm in oligopoly; the curve is more elastic when the firm raises price than when it lowers price. (Chapter 12)

L

Labor The physical and intellectual effort of people engaged in producing goods and services. (Chapter 2)

Labor productivity The output per laborer per hour. (Chapter 8)

Labor specialization The division of labor into specialized activities that allow individuals to be more productive. (Chapter 2)

Labor union An association of workers, each of whom transfers the right to negotiate wage rates, work hours, and working conditions to the association. In this way, the union presents itself as a single seller of labor on the labor market. (Chapter 16)

Laissez-faire Government policy of nonintervention in market outcomes. Translated, it means "leave it be."

Land rent A payment to landowners for the use of land. (Chapter 17)

Land A natural-state resource such as real estate, grasses and forests, and metals and minerals. (Chapter 2)

Law of demand The inverse relationship between price and quantity demanded of a good or service, ceteris paribus. (Chapter 3)

Law of diminishing marginal utility As more of a good is consumed, the utility a person derives from each additional unit diminishes. (Chapter 5)

Law of diminishing returns As more and more units of one factor of production are added to the production process while other factors remain unchanged, output will increase, but by smaller and smaller increments. (Chapter 15)

Law of increasing costs The opportunity cost of producing a good increases as more of the good is produced. The law is based on the fact that not all resources are suited to the production of all goods and that the order of use of a resource in producing a good goes from the most productive resource unit to the least. (Chapter 2)

Less-developed countries (LDCS) The economies of Asia, Africa, and Latin America. (Chapter 21)

Life-cycle wealth Wealth in the form of nonmonetary assets, such as a house, automobiles, and clothing. (Chapter 18)

Loanable funds market The market in which the demand for and supply of loanable funds determines the rate of interest. (Chapter 17)

Loanable funds Money that a firm employs to purchase the physical plant, equipment, and raw materials used in production. (Chapter 17)

Location rent Rent arising from differences in land distances from the marketplace. (Chapter 17)

Long run The time interval during which producers are able to change the quantity of all the resources they use to produce goods and services. In the long run, all costs are variable. (Chapters 3 and 8)

Lorenz curve A curve depicting an economy's income distribution. It records the percentage of total income that a specific part of the population-typically represented by quintiles, ranging from the poorest to richest-receives. (Chapter 18)

Loss minimization Faced with the certainty of incurring losses, the firm's goal is to incur the lowest loss possible from its production and sale of goods and services. (Chapter 9)

M

Macroeconomics A subarea of economics that analyzes the behavior of the economy as a whole. (Chapter 1)

Marginal cost (MC) The change in total cost generated by a change in the quantity of a good produced. Typically, MC is used to measure the additional cost incurred by adding one more unit of output to production. (Chapter 8)

Marginal cost pricing A regulatory agency's policy of pricing a good or service produced by a regulated firm at the firm's marginal cost, $P = MC$. (Chapter 13)

Marginal factor cost The change in a firm's total cost that results from adding one more unit of a factor (labor, capital, or land) to production. (Chapter 17)

Marginal labor cost The change in a firm's total cost that results from adding one more worker to production. (Chapter 15)

Marginal physical product The change in output that results from adding one more unit of a resource, such as labor, to production. *MPP* is expressed in physical units, such as tons of coal, bushels of wheat, or number of automobiles. (Chapter 15)

Marginal revenue (MR) The change in total revenue generated by the sale of one additional unit of goods or services. (Chapter 9)

Marginal revenue product of capital The change in total revenue that results from adding one more dollar of loanable funds to production. (Chapter 17)

Marginal revenue product The change in total revenue that results from adding one more unit of a resource, such as labor, to production. *MRP,* which is expressed in dollars, is equal to *MPP* multiplied by the price of the good. (Chapter 15)

Marginal utility The change in total utility a person derives from consuming an additional unit of a good. (Chapter 5)

Market demand The sum of all individual demands in a market. (Chapter 3)

Market failure The failure of the market to achieve an optimal allocation of the economy's resources. The failure results from the market's inability to take externalities into account. (Chapter 14)

Market power A firm's ability to select and control market price and output. (Chapter 12)

Market share The percentage of total market sales produced by a particular firm in a market. (Chapter 10)

Market structure A set of market characteristics such as number of firms, ease of firm entry, and substitutability of goods. (Chapter 10)

Market-day supply A market situation in which the quantity of a good supplied is fixed, regardless of price. (Chapter 3)

Median income The midpoint of a society's income distribution, above and below which an equal number of individuals (or families) belong. (Chapter 18)

Microeconomics A subarea of economics that analyzes individuals as consumers and producers, and specific firms and industries. It focuses especially on the market behavior of firms and households. (Chapter 1)

Monopolistic competition A market structure consisting of many firms producing goods that are close substitutes. Firm entry is possible but is less open and easy than in perfect competition. (Chapter 10)

Monopoly A market structure consisting of one firm producing a good that has no close substitutes. Firm entry is impossible. (Chapter 10)

Monopsony A labor market with only one buyer. (Chapter 16)

MR = MC rule The guideline used by a firm to achieve profit maximization. (Chapter 9)

MU/P equalization principle The idea that a person's total utility is maximized when the ratios of marginal utility to price for each of the goods consumed are equal. (Chapter 5)

Multinational corporation A corporation whose production facilities are located in two or more countries. Typically, multinational corporate sales are also international. (Chapter 7)

Mutual interdependence Any price change made by one firm in the oligopoly affects the pricing behavior of all other firms in the oligopoly. (Chapter 10)

N

Nash equilibrium A set of pricing strategies adopted by firms in which none can improve its payoff outcome, given the price strategies of the other firm or firms. (Chapter 12)

Nationalization Government ownership of a firm or industry. Price and production decisions are made by an administrative agency of the government. (Chapter 13)

Natural monopoly The result of a combination of market demand and firm's costs such that only one firm is able to produce profitably in a market. (Chapter 10)

Natural resources The lands, water, metals, minerals, animals, and other gifts of nature that are available for producing goods and services. (Chapter 1)

Negative income tax Government cash payments to the poor-an income tax in reverse-that is linked to the income levels of the poor. The cash payments decrease as income levels increase. The payments are designed to provide a minimum level of income to the poor. (Chapter 18)

Noncompeting labor markets Markets whose requirement for specific skills necessarily excludes workers who do not have the required skills. (Chapter 15)

Normal good A good whose demand increases or decreases when people's incomes increase or decrease. (Chapter 3)

Normal profit The entrepreneur's opportunity cost. It is equal to or greater than the income an entrepreneur could receive employing his or her resources elsewhere. Normal profit is included in the firm's costs. (Chapter 11)

Normative economics A subset of economics founded on value judgments and leading to assertions of what ought to be. (Chapter 1)

North American Free Trade Agreement (NAFTA) A free trade area consisting of Canada, the United States, and Mexico. (Chapter 19)

O

Oligopoly A market structure consisting of only a few firms producing goods that are close substitutes. (Chapter 10)

Opportunity cost The quantity of other goods that must be given up to obtain a good. (Chapter 2)

P

Parity price ratio The relationship between prices received by farmers and prices paid by farmers. (Chapter 6)

Partnership A firm owned by two or more people who each bear the responsibilities and unlimited liabilities of the firm. (Chapter 7)

Patent A monopoly right on the use of a specific new technology or on the production of a new good. The monopoly right is awarded to and safeguarded by the government to the firm who introduces the new technology or good. (Chapters 10 and 13)

Payoff matrix A table that matches the sets of gains (or losses) for competing firms when they choose, independently, various pricing options. (Chapter 12)

Per se A judicial standard or criterion by which a firm's size within an industry is considered sufficient evidence for the court to rule against it in an antitrust suit. (Chapter 13)

Perfect competition A market structure consisting of a large number of firms producing goods that are perfect substitutes. Firm entry is open and easy. (Chapter 10)

Positive economics A subset of economics that analyzes the way the economy actually operates. (Chapter 1)

Poverty threshold The level of income below which families are considered to be poor. (Chapter 18)

Present value The value today of the stream of expected future annual income a property generates. The method of computing present value is to divide the annual income generated, R, by the rate of interest, r. That is, $PV = R/r$. (Chapter 17)

Price ceiling A maximum price set by government below the market-generated equilibrium price. (Chapter 6)

Price discrimination The practice of offering a specific good or service at different prices to different segments of the market. (Chapter 12)

Price elastic Quality of the range of a demand curve where elasticities of demand are greater than 1.0. (Chapter 4)

Price elasticity of demand The ratio of the percentage change in quantity demanded to a percentage change in price. Its numerical value expresses the percentage change in quantity demanded generated by a 1 percent change in price. (Chapter 4)

Price elasticity of supply The ratio of the percentage change in quantity supplied to the percentage change in price. (Chapter 4)

Price floor A minimum price set by government above the market-generated equilibrium price. (Chapter 6)

Price inelastic Quality of the range of a demand curve where elasticities of demand are less than 1.0. (Chapter 4)

Price leadership A firm whose price decisions are tacitly accepted and followed by other firms in the industry. (Chapter 12)

Price-maker A firm conscious of the fact that its own activity in the market affects price. The firm has the ability to choose among combinations of price and output. (Chapter 11)

Price-taker A firm that views market price as a given and considers any activity on its own part as having no influence on that price. (Chapter 11)

Product differentiation The physical or perceived differences among goods in a market that make them close, but not perfect, substitutes for each other. (Chapter 10)

Production possibilities The various combinations of goods that can be produced in an economy when it uses its available resources and technology efficiently. (Chapter 2)

Profit maximization The primary goal of a firm: To achieve the most profit possible from its production and sale of goods or services. (Chapter 9)

Profit Income earned by entrepreneurs. (Chapters 9 and 17)

Property rights The right to own a good or service and the right to receive the benefits that the use of the good or service provides. (Chapter 14)

Public choice The theory of collective decision making. (Chapter 14)

Public good A good whose benefits are not diminished even when additional people consume it and whose benefits cannot be withheld from anyone. (Chapter 14)

Q

Quota A limit on the quantity of a specific good that can be imported. (Chapter 19)

R

Ration coupon A coupon issued by the government, entitling the holder to purchase a specific quantity of a good at or below the price ceiling. (Chapter 6)

Reciprocity An agreement between countries in which trading privileges granted by one to the others are the same as those granted to it by the others. (Chapter 19)

Regulation Although ownership of the regulated firm remains in private hands, pricing and production decisions of the firm are monitored by a regulatory agency directly responsible to the government. (Chapter 13)

Relevant market The set of goods whose cross elasticities with others in the set are relatively high and whose cross elasticities with goods outside the set are relatively low. (Chapter 10)

Rent The difference between what a productive resource receives as payment for its use in production and the cost of bringing that resource into production. (Chapter 17)

Rent control Government-set price ceilings on rent. (Chapter 6)

Return to monopsony power The difference between the *MRP* and the wage rate of the last worker hired, multiplied by the number of workers hired. (Chapter 16)

Rightsizing Implementing a firm's decision to adjust its plant size to produce in the most efficient manner its current volume of output. (Chapter 8)

Rule of reason A judicial standard or criterion by which a firm's size within an industry is insufficient evidence for the court to rule against it in an antitrust suit. Evidence must show that the firm actually used its size to violate antitrust laws. (Chapter 13)

S

Scarcity The perpetual state of insufficiency of resources to satisfy people's unlimited wants. (Chapter 1)

Short run The time interval during which producers are able to change the quantity of some but not all the resources they use to produce goods and services. (Chapters 3 and 8)

Shutdown The cessation of the firm's activity. The firm's loss minimization occurs at zero output. (Chapter 9)

Social cost The cost to society of producing a good. This cost includes both the private costs associated with the good's production and the externalities cost generated by its production. (Chapter 14)

Sole proprietorship A firm owned by one person who alone bears the responsibilities and unlimited liabilities of the firm. (Chapter 7)

Special-interest lobby A group organized to influence people in government concerning the costs and benefits of particular public goods. (Chapter 14)

Stakeholder Someone who has a personal and consequential interest in the viability of the firm. (Chapter 9)

Stock Ownership in a corporation, represented by shares that are claims on the firm's assets and earnings. (Chapter 7)

Stockholder (shareholder) A person owning stock in a corporation, that is, a share of a corporation. (Chapter 7)

Strike The withholding of labor by a union when the collective bargaining process fails to produce a contract that is acceptable to the union. (Chapter 16)

Substitute goods Goods that can replace each other. When the price of one increases, the demand for the other increases. (Chapter 3)

Supply curve A curve that depicts the relationship between price and quantity supplied. (Chapter 3)

Supply schedule A schedule showing the specific quantity of a good or service that suppliers are willing and able to provide at different prices. (Chapter 3)

T

Target price A minimum price level for specific farm goods that the government sets and guarantees. (Chapter 6)

Tariff A tax on an imported good. (Chapter 19)

Terms of trade The amount of a good or service (export) that must be given up to buy a unit of another good or service (import). A country's terms of trade are measured by the ratio of the country's export prices to its import prices. (Chapter 19)

Third parties People upon whom externalities are imposed. (Chapter 14)

Tit-for-tat A pricing strategy in game theory in which a firm chooses a price and will change its price to match whatever price the competing firm chooses. (Chapter 12)

Total cost (TC) Cost to the firm that includes both fixed and variable costs. (Chapter 8)

Total labor cost Quantity of labor employed multiplied by the wage rate. (Chapter 15)

Total revenue (TR) The price of a good multiplied by the number of units sold. (Chapters 4 and 9)

Total utility The total number of utils a person derives from consuming a specific quantity of a good. (Chapter 5)

U

Unbalanced oligopoly An oligopoly in which the sales of the leading firms are distributed unevenly among them. (Chapter 12)

Underemployed resources The less than full utilization of a resource's productive capabilities. (Chapter 2)

Unilateral transfers Transfers of currency made by individuals, businesses, or government of one nation to individuals, businesses, or governments in other nations, with no designated return. (Chapter 20)

Union shop An arrangement in which a firm may hire nonunion labor, but every nonunion worker hired must join the union within a specified period of time. (Chapter 16)

Unit elastic Price elasticity is equal to 1.0. In this range, price cuts or increases do not change total revenue. (Chapter 4)

Unlimited liability Personal responsibility of the owners for all debts incurred by sole proprietorships or partnerships. The owners' personal wealth is subject to appropriation to pay off the firm's debt. (Chapter 7)

Util A hypothetical unit used to measure how much utility a person obtains from consuming a good. (Chapter 5)

Utility The satisfaction or enjoyment a person obtains from consuming a good. (Chapter 5)

V

Variable cost Cost that varies with the quantity of goods produced. Variable costs include such items as wages and raw materials. (Chapter 8)

Vertical merger A merger between firms that have a supplier-purchaser relationship. (Chapter 12)

W

Wage rate The price of labor. Typically, the wage rate is calculated in dollars per hour. (Chapter 15)

Wage-related rent The difference between what a resource receives and what it takes to bring the supply of that resource to market. (Chapter 17)

Wealth The accumulated assets owned by individuals. (Chapter 18)

INDEX